English
Français
Deutsche
Italiano
Español
Português

www.forgottenbooks.com

Mythology Photography **Fiction**
Fishing Christianity **Art** Cooking
Essays Buddhism Freemasonry
Medicine **Biology** Music **Ancient
Egypt** Evolution Carpentry Physics
Dance Geology **Mathematics** Fitness
Shakespeare **Folklore** Yoga Marketing
Confidence Immortality Biographies
Poetry **Psychology** Witchcraft
Electronics Chemistry History **Law**
Accounting **Philosophy** Anthropology
Alchemy Drama Quantum Mechanics
Atheism Sexual Health **Ancient History**
Entrepreneurship Languages Sport
Paleontology Needlework Islam
Metaphysics Investment Archaeology
Parenting Statistics Criminology
Motivational

INDIAN
DEPREDATIONS IN TEXAS.

RELIABLE ACCOUNTS

OF

BATTLES, WARS, ADVENTURES, FORAYS, MURDERS,
MASSACRES, ETC., ETC., TOGETHER WITH BIO-
GRAPHICAL SKETCHES OF MANY OF THE
MOST NOTED INDIAN FIGHTERS AND
FRONTIERSMEN OF TEXAS.

BY

J. W. WILBARGER.

SOLD BY SUBSCRIPTION ONLY.

SECOND EDITION.

AUSTIN, TEXAS:
HUTCHINGS PRINTING HOUSE,
1890.

Dedicated

TO THE MEMORY OF THE HEROIC
FRONTIERSMEN WHO BY THEIR SACRIFICES PREPARED THE
WAY FOR THE PROSPERITY WHICH TEXAS NOW
ENJOYS, I DEDICATE THIS BOOK.

THE AUTHOR.

Entered according to act of Congress in the year eighteen hundred and eighty-eight,
BY J. W. WILBARGER,
In the office of the Librarian of Congress at Washington, D. C.

Illustrated by OWEN ENGRAVING Co., Austin.

yours Truly

S. W. Wilbarger

PREFACE.

I FEEL that for those who will read the description of the conflicts and Indian cruelty contained in this volume some preface which will introduce the author to his readers and which will explain the motives which inspired him to write this book is needed. I came to Texas over half a century ago, and am now an old man, the only survivor of three brothers who served Texas in her early struggles. Josiah Wilbarger, who was scalped by the Indians a few miles east of where the capitol of Texas now is, was my brother. He survived, as this book relates, the massacre of his companions, but afterwards died from a disease of the skull caused by injuries. Having spent the prime of my life among the pioneers of Texas, and therefore knowing personally about many of the fights and massacres described in this volume, the idea occurred to me many years ago that when the early settlers were all dead their posterity would only know from tradition the perils and hardships encountered in the early settlement of Texas. When I found that no one else seemed inclined to preserve in history the story of massacres and conflicts with Indians, I undertook the work myself. During some twenty years I have carefully obtained from the lips of those who knew most of the facts stated in this volume. For their general correctness I can vouch, for I knew personally most of the early settlers of Texas, and have relied on those only whom I believed to be trustworthy. Many of the articles contained in this book were written by others, who were either cognizant of the facts themselves or had obtained their data from reliable sources. To those who have so kindly aided me in my arduous work I return my most grateful thanks. Through the courtesy of the publishing house of J. W. Burke & Co., of Macon, Georgia, who own the copyright of the book entitled "The Life and Adventures of Big Foot Wallace," I have been permitted to make some extracts from the same which I believed would be of interest to the reader. The present generation can at best have but a faint idea of the hardships, exposures and perils to which the pioneers of Texas were subjected. For ten years they contended with the Mexican nation on the west and roving bands of fierce savages on the north, when invasion of the frontier might be expected at any time. After annexation, the United States government afforded but poor protection against the Indians, and murders continued until quite recently. As one of the pioneers, I felt impelled to prepare and publish for the benefit of another generation this volume, which shows something of the dangers and difficulties under which the peace that our people now enjoy has been secured.

THE AUTHOR.

ILLUSTRATIONS.

Big foot Wallace 112

INDEX.

INDIAN DEPREDATIONS IN TEXAS.

Matilda Lockhart—The Putnam Children.

THE Comanche Indians were to Texas what the Pequot Indians were to New England and what the Sioux were to the traders and trappers of the west. Their incursions were for many years a terror to the border settlers of Texas, for they were a warlike, cruel and treacherous tribe, and as they always traveled on horseback they could swoop down unexpectedly from their distant
1838 stronghold upon the settlements, commit murders and depredations, and retreat before any effective pursuit could be made. It was a party of this tribe of Indians who captured the young lady whose sad story we are about to relate. Her father, Andrew Lockhart, emigrated from the State of Illinois in the year 1828 and settled on the Guadalupe river, in what is now DeWitt county—then DeWitt's colony. It was in the fall or winter of 1838 that Matilda Lockhart, Rhoda Putnam, Elizabeth Putnam, Juda Putnam and James Putnam left the houses of their parents one day and went to the woods to gather pecans. While they were thus engaged a party of Indians suddenly rushed upon them. They discovered the Indians too late to escape and were all captured. When the Indians first came in sight Miss Lockhart fled for the house, and possibly might have escaped had not the youngest Miss Putnam implored her not to leave her. The noble girl, pitying her youthful companion, turned to aid her and both were captured. The Indians fastened these unfortunate captives

on horses with rawhide thongs and hurried off with them into the Guadalupe mountains. Captain John Tumlinson, who was out on a surveying expedition, encountered these Indians, but as he had but six men with him and the Indians numbered at least fifty he was compelled to beat a hasty retreat. He did not know at that time that they had prisoners with them. The Indians followed Captain Tumlinson and his men about twenty-four hours, and probably would have killed them all if they had not accidentally discovered they were still in pursuit of them, long after they supposed the chase had been abandoned. The party, as they were traveling along leisurely, saw a black stump ahead of them, and, supposing it was a bear, the men halted for the purpose of killing it. Captain Tumlinson rode forward to shoot the supposed bear, and as he did so, one of the men behind happened to look back, and discovered the Indians still following their trail. The alarm was given, and the Captain and his men hastily continued their retreat. After running about half a mile through the prairie, they came to some timber, where they fell in with a large drove of mustang horses. The frightened animals divided into squads and ran off in various directions. Captain Tumlinson and his men wisely followed one of these squads, thereby making it difficult for their pursuers to find their trail, and escaped.

This raid of the Indians so terrified the settlers on the west side of the Guadalupe river that they abandoned their homes and forted together on the east side. When Captain Tumlinson arrived at the west side of the river, he found that all the houses in the settlement were deserted. He knew nothing of the capture of Miss Lockhart and the young Putnams until he crossed the river and reached the house of Mr. William Taylor, where he first heard the sad story. A company of men was immediately raised, who went in pursuit of the Indians, but all to no purpose. They had got too far ahead to be overtaken. The poor captives were carried far into the Indian country, where they suffered terribly from hunger, hardships and exposure to the inclemencies of the weather.

During her captivity Miss Lockhart said that sometimes she had to travel from fifty to seventy-five miles a day on a bare back horse, and that seldom a day passed that she was not severely flogged. In the winter of 1839 a party of these same Indians took up their quarters on the San Saba river, about one hundred miles above where the city of Austin now stands. Information of this rendezvous was given to Colonel John H. Moore, of Fayette county, who raised a party of about sixty men, and, accompanied by a party of Lipan Indians, he went to their encampment and attacked them, when a desperate fight ensued.

Miss Lockhart was in the Indian camp when this attack was made, and knowing it was made by white men, she screamed as loud as she could, hoping they would hear her and come to her rescue. The Indians, suspecting the cause of her screaming, drowned her cries with their still louder yells, and when she persisted one of them near by became so exasperated that he seized her by the hair of her head and tore out a large part of it. The father of the unfortunate girl was with the attacking party under Colonel Moore, and it was with a heavy heart that he returned to the settlement without his daughter, who had been a prisoner for over a year, and whom he felt quite sure was in the Indian village.

Upon one occasion a party of Indians who had Miss Lockhart in possession came within one or two days travel of San Antonio and pitched their camp. As they knew she was aware of their proximity to the white settlements, and fearing she might attempt to escape, they severely burned the soles of her feet to keep her from running away.

Not a great while after this a treaty was made with the Comanche Indians, under which Miss Lockhart was delivered up to the Texas Commissioners at San Antonio and subsequently sent back to her family. But the once sprightly, joyous young girl, whose presence had been everywhere like a gleam of sunshine penetrating the gloom of the wilderness, was a mere wreck of her former self. Her health was almost utterly ruined by the privations and hardships she had undergone and the brutal treatment to which she had been subjected by her savage captors.

When captured by the Indians, Miss Lockhart was only about thirteen or fourteen years of age. She was given over to the squaws, whom she served in the capacity of a slave.

Their treatment of her was much more cruel than that of the bucks. The numerous scars upon her body and limbs bore silent testimony of savage cruelty. The ladies who examined her wounds after her reclamation (some of whom are yet alive) stated that there was not a place on her body as large as the palm of the hand which had not been burned with hot irons. After lingering some two or three years, she died. Her father was a brother of Bird Lockhart, for whom the town of Lockhart, in Caldwell county, was named. As to the Putnam children, the son was reclaimed many years afterwards. He had acquired many of the habits of the Indians and spoke their language. We have been informed that Rhoda became the wife of a chief and refused to return home. Elizabeth was finally reclaimed, but Juda Putnam remained a captive among the Indians for about fourteen years. She was several times sold, and once was purchased by a party of Missouri traders, who, after retaining her for some time, sold her to a man by the name of Chinault, who subsequently moved to Texas and settled in Gonzales county, the same section in which Miss Putnam had been captured by the Indians. With this man she had lived seven years. The citizens of Gonzales county, knowing she had been an Indian captive, and seeing the strong resemblance she bore to the Putnam family, came to the conclusion that possibly she might be the long lost Juda Putnam. After a time the Putnam family began to look into the matter, and questioned her in regard to her parentage and former life. She had forgotten her own name, and could tell nothing of her life prior to the time the Indians captured her; and of that event she had but a dim and uncertain recollection, as she was only about seven years of age when captured. A sister of hers said on one occasion, when speaking of the matter, that if this lady was really her long lost sister she could be identified by a most singular mark on her person. An examination was made by this sister and some other ladies, and the mark was found precisely as it had been described. This, together with her striking likeness to the family, left no doubt in the mind of any one that she was the identical Juda Putnam who had been captured by the Indians in Gonzales county twenty-one years before.

Thus, after fourteen years captivity among the Indians and seven years with Mr. Chinault, was this young lady by a train of circumstances brought back to the very spot from whence she had been stolen, and by the merest chance was recognized and restored to her relatives. Verily, truth is often stranger than fiction.

There is a certain class of maudlin, sentimental writers who are forever bewailing the rapid disappearance of the Indian tribes from the American continent. We must confess we don't fraternize with our brother scribblers on this point. They have evidently taken their ideas of the Indian character from Cooper's novels and similar productions, which give about as correct delineation of it as are the grotesque figures a school boy draws on his slate of the animals or objects he intends to represent. There may have been, and no doubt there have been, some individuals among the Indians like those described by Cooper, *et id omne genus*, but they have been like angels' visits, few and far between. His general character may be summarily stated in Byron's words, when speaking of his hero, the Corsair: "He had one virtue linked to a thousand crimes." This solitary virtue may have been physical courage, hospitality or something else, but among his unquestionable vices may be reckoned cruelty, treachery, vindictiveness, brutality, indolence (except when spurred to action by his thirst for rapine and blood) and his utter inability to advance beyond the condition in which nature had originally placed him. There is, however, one notable exception to this general rule, which is most singular and difficult to account for. We mean the Pueblo Indians of New Mexico, who physically are similar to all the other North American tribes, but differ from them as widely in all other respects as any of the Caucasian races.

It is true there are a few remnants of tribes, as the Cherokees and Choctaws in the Indian Territory, who have made some advances towards civilization, but this is largely, if not wholly, owing to the fact that their blood has been mingled to a great extent with that of the whites. In our opinion, the aborigines of the American continent, pure and simple, were all naturally incapable of progress, and that their existence was only intended to be a temporary one, and that it should cease as soon as their places could be filled by a progressive people, such as the Anglo-Saxon race. The very fact of their rapid disappearance, that they are fast fading away under the action of that inexorable law, the "survival of the fittest," is the best proof of this.

The "old Texans" have not unfrequently been censured by some of the maudlin, sentimental writers before referred to for having treated poor Lo in a few isolated cases in a barbarous manner. Such writers probably never saw a wild Indian in their lives—never had their fathers, mothers, brothers or sisters butchered by them in cold blood; never had their little sons and daughters carried away by them into captivity, to be brought up as savages, and taught to believe that robbery was meritorious, and cold blooded murder a praiseworthy act, and certainly they never themselves had their own limbs beaten, bruised, burnt and tortured with fiendish ingenuity by "ye gentle salvages," nor their scalps ruthlessly torn from their bleeding heads, for if the latter experience had been theirs, and they had survived the pleasant operation (as some have done in Texas) we are inclined to think the exposure of their naked skulls to the influences of wind and weather might have so softened them as to permit the entrance of a little common sense.

To all such we have only to say, read over the long list of cold blooded, cowardly, inhuman murders perpetrated on innocent children and defenseless women chronicled in this book, and when you get through, our "basnet to a prentice cap," your only wonder will be that the old Texans did not always pay them back in their own coin whenever the opportunity offered, instead of doing so only in a few isolated cases.

But, now that Mr. Lo has "left his country for his country's good," we sincerely hope that in the spirit land he has found those happy hunting grounds so often referred to by his sensational chroniclers, but which were seldom alluded to by Mr. Lo himself, where he may still amuse himself with his innocent pastimes of braining phantom infants and tearing the scalps from the heads of phantom enemies—where his congeners, the bison and the elk exist in countless shadowy herds, and where he may feast himself upon intangible juicy humps and unsubstantial marrow

bones until even his Indian stomach shall cry out enough!
Nevertheless, we are glad he is gone, and that there are no
Indians now in Texas except "good ones," who are as dead
as Julius Cæsar.

> Lo! the poor Indian whose untutored mind
> Sees God in clouds and hears him in the wind,

Sounds well enough in poetry but don't "pan out" worth a
cent in prose. The Indian never saw anything in clouds
but clouds, but when it came to seeing a white man when
he was anxious for scalps, or a horse he wanted to steal, his
eyes were as keen as a hawk's.

Josiah Wilbarger.

IN the spring of 1830, Stephen F. Austin came to his new
colony, located on the upper Colorado, with two surveyors and the advance guard of emigrants for the purpose
of establishing the surveys of those who had made their
selections. Josiah Wilbarger and Reuben Hornsby were
among those who had previously been over the ground and
picked out locations for their headright leagues. Wil-
1833 barger had come to Texas from the State of Missouri
as early as 1828 and first settled in Matagorda county,
where he remained about one year and then moved up the
Colorado. It was in about the month of March, 1830, that he
selected for his headright survey a beautiful tract of land situated at the mouth of what is now known as Wilbarger creek,
about ten miles above where the San Antonio and Naco-
doches road crosses the river where the town of Bastrop
now is. After making his selection he immediately moved
on his headright league with his family and two or three
transient young men and built his occupation house, his
nearest neighbor being about seventy-five miles down the
river. In the month of April, Austin, with his surveying

party, accompanied by Reuben Hornsby, Webber, Duty and others, who had also previously made their selections, arrived, and commenced work on the Colorado at the crossing of the San Antonio and Nacogdoches road. The river was meandered to the upper corner of the Jesse Tannehill league, when the party stopped work in the month of May. Wilbarger was the first and outside settler in Austin's new colony until July, 1832, when Reuben Hornsby came up from Bastrop (where he had stopped for a year or two) and occupied his league on the east bank of the Colorado river, some nine miles below the site of Austin.

Hornsby's house was always noted for hospitality, and he, like his neighbor Wilbarger, was remarkable for those virtues and that personal courage which made them both marked men among the early settlers. Young men who from time to time came up to the frontier to look at the country made Hornsby's house a stopping place, and were always gladly welcomed, for it was chiefly through such visits that news from the States was obtained. A more beautiful tract of land, even now, can nowhere be found than the league of land granted to Reuben Hornsby. Washed on the west by the Colorado, it stretches over a level valley about three miles wide to the east, and was, at the time of which we write, covered with wild rye, and looking like one vast green wheat field. Such was the valley in its virgin state which tempted Hornsby to build and risk his family outside of the settlements. Until a few years ago not an acre of that league of land had ever been sold, but it was all occupied by the children and grand children of the old pioneer, who lived out his four score years and died without a blemish on his character.

In the month of August, 1833, a man named Christian and his wife were living with Hornsby. Several young unmarried men were also stopping there. This was customary in those days, and the settlers were glad to have them for protection. Two young men, Standifer and Haynie, had just come to the settlement from Missouri to look at the country. Early in August, Josiah Wilbarger came up to Hornsby's, and in company with Christian, Strother, Standifer and Haynie, rode out in a northwest direction to look at the country. When riding up Walnut creek, some five

SCALPING OF JOSIAH WILBARGER.

or six miles northwest of where the city of Austin stands, they discovered an Indian. He was hailed, but refused to parley with them, and made off in the direction of the mountains covered with cedar to the west of them. They gave chase and pursued him until he escaped to cover in the mountains near the head of Walnut creek, about where James Rogers afterwards settled.

Returning from the chase, they stopped to noon and refresh themselves, about one-half a mile up the branch above Pecan spring, and four miles east of where Austin afterwards was established, in sight of the road now leading from Austin to Manor. Wilbarger, Christian and Strother unsaddled and hoppled their horses, but Haynie and Standdifer left their horses saddled and staked them to graze. While the men were eating they were suddenly fired on by Indians. The trees near them were not large and offered poor cover. Each man sprang to a tree and promptly returned the fire of the savages, who had stolen up afoot under cover of the brush and timber, having left their horses out of sight. Wilbarger's party had fired a couple of rounds when a ball struck Christian, breaking his thigh bone. Strother had already been mortally wounded. Wilbarger sprang to the side of Christian and set him up against his tree. Christian's gun was loaded but not primed. A ball from an Indian had bursted Christian's powder horn. Wilbarger primed his gun and then jumped again behind his own tree. At this time Wilbarger had an arrow through the calf of his leg and had received a flesh wound in the hip. Scarcely had Wilbarger regained the cover of the small tree, from which he fought, until his other leg was pierced with an arrow. Until this time Haynie and Standifer had helped sustain the fight, but when they saw Strother mortally wounded and Christian disabled, they made for their horses, which were yet saddled, and mounted them. Wilbarger finding himself deserted, hailed the fugitives and asked to be permitted to mount behind one of them if they would not stop and help fight. He ran to overtake them, wounded, as he was, for some little distance, when he was struck from behind by a ball which penetrated about the center of his neck and came out on the left side of his chin. He fell apparently dead, but though unable to move or speak, did not lose consciousness. He knew when the Indians came around him—when they stripped him naked and tore the scalp from his head. He says that though paralyzed and unable to move, he knew what was being done, and that when his scalp was torn from his skull it created no pain from which he could flinch, but sounded like distant thunder. The Indians cut the throats of Strother and Christian, but the character of Wilbarger's wound, no doubt, made them believe his neck was broken, and that he was surely dead. This saved his life.

When Wilbarger recovered consciousness the evening was far advanced. He had lost much blood, and the blood was still slowly ebbing from his wounds. He was alone in the wilderness, desperately wounded, naked and still bleeding. Consumed by an intolerable thirst, he dragged himself to a pool of water and lay down in it for an hour, when he became so chilled and numb that with difficulty he crawled out to dry land. Being warmed by the sun and exhausted by loss of blood, he fell into a profound sleep. When awakened, the blood had ceased to flow from the wound in his neck, but he was again consumed with thirst and hunger.

After going back to the pool and drinking, he crawled over the grass and devoured such snails as he could find, which appeased his hunger. The green flies had blown his wounds while he slept, and the maggots were at work, which pained and gave him fresh alarm. As night approached he determined to go as far as he could toward Reuben Hornsby's, about six miles distant. He had gone about six hundred yards when he sank to the ground exhausted, under a large post oak tree, and well nigh despairing of life. Those who have ever spent a summer in Austin know that in that climate the nights in summer are always cool, and before daybreak some covering is needed for comfort. Wilbarger, naked, wounded and feeble, suffered after midnight intensely from cold. No sound fell on his ear but the hooting of owls and the bark of the cayote wolf, while above him the bright silent stars seemed to mock his agony. We are now about to relate two incidents so mysterious that they would excite our incredulity were it not for the high character of those who to their dying day vouched for their truth.

As Wilbarger lay under the old oak tree, prone on the ground he distinctly saw, standing near him, the spirit of his sister Margaret Clifton, who had died the day before in Florisant, St. Louis county, Missouri. She said to him: "Brother Josiah, you are too weak to go by yourself. Remain here, and friends will come to take care of you before the setting of the sun." When she had said this she moved away in the direction of Hornsby's house. In vain he besought her to remain with him until help would come.

Haynie and Standifer, on reaching Hornsby's, had reported the death of their three companions, stating that they saw Wilbarger fall and about fifty Indians around him, and knew that he was dead. That night Mrs. Hornsby started from her sleep and waked her husband. She told him confidently that Wilbarger was alive; that she had seen him vividly in a dream, naked, scalped and wounded, but that she knew he lived. Soon she fell asleep and again Wilbarger appeared to her alive, but wounded, naked and scalped, so vividly that she again woke Mr. Hornsby and told him of her dream, saying: "I know that Wilbarger is not dead." So confident was she that she would not permit the men to sleep longer, but had their coffee and breakfast ready by day break and urged the men at the house to start to Wilbarger's relief.

The relief party consisted of Joseph Rogers, Reuben Hornsby, Webber, John Walters and others. As they approached the tree under which Wilbarger had passed the night, Rogers, who was in advance, saw Wilbarger, who was sitting at the root of a tree. He presented a ghastly sight, for his body was almost red with blood. Rogers, mistaking him for an Indian, said: "Here they are, boys." Then Wilbarger rose up and spoke, saying: "Don't shoot, it is Wilbarger." When the relief party started Mrs. Hornsby gave her husband three sheets, two of them were left over the bodies of Christian and Strother until the next day, when the men returned and buried them, and one was wrapped around Wilbarger, who was placed on Roger's horse. Hornsby being lighter than the rest mounted behind Wilbarger, and with his arms around him, sustained him in the saddle. The next day Wm. Hornsby (who is still living),

Joseph Rogers, Walters and one or two others returned and buried Christian and Strother.

When Wilbarger was found the only particle of his clothing left by the savages was one sock. He had torn that from his foot, which was much swollen from an arrow wound in his leg, and had placed it on his naked skull from which the scalp had been taken. He was tenderly nursed at Hornby's for some days. His scalp wound was dressed with bear's oil, and when recovered sufficiently to move, he was placed in a sled, made by Billy Hornsby and Leman Barker (the father-in-law of Wilbarger) because he could not endure the motion of a wagon, and was thus conveyed several miles down the river to his own cabin. Josiah Wilbarger recovered and lived for eleven years. The scalp never grew entirely over the bone. A small spot in the middle of the wound remained bare, over which he always wore a covering. The bone became diseased and exfoliated, finally exposing the brain. His death was hastened, as Doctor Anderson, his physician, thought, by accidentally striking his head against the upper portion of a low door frame of his gin house many years after he was scalped. We have stated the facts as received from the lips of Josiah Wilbarger, who was the brother of the author of this book, and confirmed by Wm. Hornsby, who still lives, and others who are now dead.

The vision which so impressed Mrs. Hornsby was spoken of far and wide through the colony fifty years ago; for her earnest manner and perfect confidence that Wilbarger was alive, made, in connection with her vision and its realization, a profound impression on the men present, who spoke of it everywhere. There were no telegraphs in those days, and no means of knowing that Margaret, the sister, had died seven hundred miles away only the day before her brother was wounded. The story of her apparition, related before he knew that she was dead—her going in the direction of Hornsby's, and Mrs. Hornsby's strange vision, recurring after slumber, present a mystery that made then a deep impression and created a feeling of awe which, after the lapse of half a century, it still inspires. No man who knew them ever questioned the veracity of either Wilbarger

or the Hornsbys, and Mrs. Hornsby was loved and rever-
enced by all who knew her.

We leave to those more learned the task of explaining the
strange coincidence of the visions of Wilbarger and Mrs.
Hornsby. It must remain a marvel and a mystery. Such
things are not accidents; they tell us of a spirit world and
of a God who "moves in a mysterious way his wonders to
perform." Josiah Wilbarger left a wife and five children.
His widow, who afterwards married Talbert Chambers, was
the second time left a widow, and resided, in 1888, in Bastrop county, about thirty-five miles below the city of Austin.

The eldest son, John, was killed many years after the
death of his father by the Indians in west Texas, as related
elsewhere in this book. Harvey, another son of Josiah,
lived to raise a large family, when he died. His widow and
only son live in Bastrop county. One married daughter
lives at Georgetown and another at Belton, Texas. Of
the brothers and sisters of Josiah Wilbarger who came to
Texas in 1837, the author, and Sallie Wilbarger (who resides
in Georgetown), are the only survivors. Matthias Wilbarger, a brother, and a sister, Mrs. W. C. Dalrymple, died
many years ago. Mrs. Lewis Jones, another sister, died on
the way to Texas.

So far as our knowledge extends, this was the first blood
shed in Travis county at the hands of the implacable savages. It was but the beginning, however, of a bloody era
which was soon to dawn upon the people of the Colorado.

Owing to the sparsely settled condition of the country,
the Indians could slip in, commit murders, then slip out and
return to their mountain homes with impunity. However,
when the rich valleys of the Colorado became known, immigrants began to flock into Austin's new colony, and it
was not long until the settlers grew sufficiently strong to
organize for protection into minute companies which were
placed under the command of Colonel Edward Burleson.
These companies afforded great protection to the families,
and no doubt saved many women and children from being
murdered or carried off into a captivity worse than death.
The settlers over on the Brazos, the Guadalupe and Lavaca
had likewise formed similar organizations, but notwithstanding the vigilance and untiring efforts of these com-

panies in trying to protect the advance guard of civiliza
tion from the tomakawk and scalping knife of the hostile
savages, the bloody traces of these demons could be seen
here to-day, several miles distant to-morrow; and before
they could be overtaken they would be far into the cedar
brakes of the mountains, where they could not well be pursued.

Such was the unsettled condition of affairs in Travis
county even as late as 1846, when with annexation came
peace and happiness to a people who had been harrassed
upon one hand by the Mexican government and warlike
tribes on the other, until their means had well nigh been
spent and their patience exhausted.

To-day we enjoy the blessings of prosperity, purchased
with the blood and heroism of a sturdy class of pioneers
whom any nation would delight to honor. There are but
few of them left, but they stand like the giant oaks of the
forest, storm beaten but living evidences of the distant
past.

[NOTE.—The tree under which Wilbarger was sitting when
found by the relief party stood just at the foot of the hill,
on the east side of Pecan spring branch, about one hundred
and fifty yards above where Pecan spring school house now
stands, and about where the road leading from Austin to
Manor leads up the hill beyond the crossing on the branch.
Reuben Hornsby and his wife, Mrs. Sarah Hornsby, were
the grand parents of M. M. Hornsby, whose term of office
as sheriff of Travis county expired in 1888. When Mrs.
Sarah Hibbins's son was captured from the Indians in 1836,
near Austin, the barrel of the gun which Wilbarger had
when he was scalped was also recovered. The stock had
been broken.]

James Goacher.

THIS venerable pioneer was a native of the State of Alabama. He emigrated to Texas in the year 1835. He it was who opened the first traveled trace to Austin's new colony. He had several persons with him to assist in marking out this trail, which is to this day known as Goacher's Trace. In the performance of this work he encountered many difficulties and dangers. He after-
1837 wards settled in what is now Bastrop county. Being an enterprising man of industrious habits, it was not 'ong until he had built comfortable log cabins for the protection and safety of his family and had opened a good farm for cultivation. The new county in which he had settled was an excellent one for raising stock, and he soon had a large stock of cattle and horses around him. Fortune seemed to smile on all his efforts. Others soon moved in and settled in his vicinity, and the country where a short time before nothing was heard but the war whoop of the savage, the tramp of the buffalo and the howling of wolves, resounded with the hum of a busy and prosperous people, pursuing in peace their various avocations.

Alas! how soon were they to be rudely awakened from their dream of peaceful security by the war whoop of a merciless foe.

In 1837, while Mr. Goacher, his son-in-law and one of his sons were away from the house, cutting and hauling fire wood, a large party of Indians surrounded it, approaching it from two directions. One of these parties came across two of Mr. Goacher's eldest children who were playing near the house, and fearing they might give the alarm the brutal wretches thrust a long steel spear through the little boy's body, killing him instantly. After scalping the little fellow they seized the other child, the little girl, and made her a prisoner. After this both parties united and made a furious onslaught on the house. The inmates at the time were Mrs.

Nancy Goacher, her daughter Jane, and one or two small children. The Indians seeing there was no man on the premises made a vigorous assault, expecting, of course, an easy victory, but Mrs. Goacher was a lady of great courage and determination, and as there were several loaded guns in the house she resolved to sell the lives of herself and children as dearly as possible. She seized one gun after another and emptied their contents among her assailants. This made the Indians more furious than ever, as they had expected no resistence to their diabolical work. They shot Mrs. Goacher until she was almost literally covered with arrows. Still this brave and heroic woman stood at the door and defended her helpless children to the last. At length one of the savages who was armed with a gun fired upon her and she fell dead upon the floor. Brave, noble woman! A monument should be raised to her memory, on which should be inscribed, "A mother's deathless valor and devotion."

Mr. Goacher and his party heard the firing of the guns and hastened with all possible speed to the assistance of his family. In the hurry and anxiety of the moment they forgot to bring the arms they had with them in the woods, and when they reached the scene of disaster they were unable to render any assitance to the family or even to defend themselves. Their only chance was to make a bold rush for the house, get possession of the guns inside and then defend themselves as best they could. This they attempted to do, but alas! the Indians were too strong for them. Mr. Goacher and his son-in-law were shot down and killed. His little son endeavored to make his escape by flight, but as he turned a corner of the house he was met by an Indian who seized him and gave him a terrible shaking. This little fellow caught one of the Indian's thumbs in his mouth and bit it severely. The Indian endeavored to extricate his thumb from the boy's mouth, but failing to do so, he drew his ramrod from his gun and beat him terribly before the little fellow would let go his hold. Another son of Mr. Goacher, after he had been mortally wounded, crawled away unperceived by the Indians, to some trees, where he laid his head upon a stone and breathed his last.

This was indeed one of the bloodiest tragedies that had

MRS. CRAWFORD, WIDOWED DAUGHTER OF MR. GOACHER,
RESCUES HER CHILD FROM A WATERY GRAVE.

ever occurred up to that time in the settlement. A father, wife, son and son-in-law and two children lay cold in death, and mingled together their kindred blood, where but a few hours previously they had assembled in fancied security, within the walls of their once happy home.

But, gentle reader, the sad story stops not here. Mrs. Crawford, the now widowed daughter of Mr. Goacher—the wife of his son-in-law who had just been murdered—her two children, and the little girl who was captured by the Indians before they attacked the house, as previously stated, were all carried off captives. They suffered, as the prisoners of Indians usually do, all the insults and indignities their barbarous captors could heap upon them. One of this lady's children was a little daughter about two months old, and as the Indians were tired of hearing it cry, they determined to kill it. Accordingly one day when the famished little creature was fretting and crying for something to eat, an Indian snatched it from the arms of its mother and threw it in a deep pool of water with the intention of drowning the poor little innocent. The heroic mother, caring more for her tender offspring than her own safety, dashed boldly into the stream to save it from a watery grave. The Indians were amused by her frantic efforts to save her child from drowning, and as soon as she reached the bank with it they threw it in again, and continued the sport until the child was nearly drowned and the poor woman was almost exhausted. At last one of them seized the child, drew back its head and told another to cut its throat. The frantic mother seeing the dreadful order was about to be executed, caught up a heavy billet of wood, and with the strength born of desperation, with one blow she laid the Indian who held the knife in his hand prostrate upon the ground. The poor woman expected that instant death would be her fate, but on the contrary the Indians seemed to be favorably impressed by her heroic defense of her child. They laughed loudly at their fallen comrade, and one of them stepped forward, picked up the child and gave it to her, saying: "Squaw too much brave. Damn you, take your papoose and carry it yourself—we will not do it." They never attempted to injure the child afterwards. Thus by her heroic bravery the lady preserved the life of her infant. No doubt the Indians would have killed both mother and child had it not been that they hoped to get a good ransom for them when they reached the trading house.

After having been a prisoner among the Indians for nearly two years, and treated by them in a manner too shameful to relate, she and her little children were taken to Coffee's trading house, on Red river, and bartered off for four hundred yards of calico, a large number of blankets, a quantity of beads and some other articles.

These goods were all furnished by Mr. Coffee, the trading agent. Having released the unfortunate lady from her brutal captors, and also her two children, Mr. Coffee furnished them an escort under the control of a Mr. Spaulding, who conducted them safely to Texas. On the journey to Texas, Mr. Spaulding became much attached to the lady and eventually married her.

This brave and heroic woman has long since passed "beyond the river," but her memory still lives fresh and green in the hearts of all who knew her. Mr. Spaulding also has been dead for many years. Her children, born to her after her marriage to Mr. Spaulding, are still living in Bastrop county on or near the old Goacher Trace.

Reader, think of it! What indignities, hardships, privations and sufferings this poor woman, tenderly raised as she had been, had to endure. Her hands were tied fast behind her every night and in that condition she was fastened to a tree to prevent her from escaping. Her children also had their little hands and feet tied together every night, and were left upon the ground without any covering to protect them from the inclemencies of the weather, and scarcely received sufficient food to keep them alive. But He who notes the sufferings of all His creatures, preserved her and her children and restored them to their friends and relatives. This lady has two sons now living on the identical place where she was captured. They are worthy descendants of a heroic mother.

The writer recently visited the locality where this terrible tragedy occurred. What a change has come over it! As he looked around on that Sabbath morn, and saw in every direction comfortable homes and cultivated fields and people everywhere wending their way to "meeting," in perfect security to the sound of the "church going bells," he could but contrast the present peaceful scene with the one presented in those stormy days when the rude log huts of the pioneers were the only evidences of civilization, when on these same smiling fields, the war whoop of the savage, the scream of the panther and the howling of wolves were the only sounds to greet the ears of the terror stricken settler in his lonely home.

James Webster.

MR. WEBSTER was a native of the state of Virginia, and came to Texas at an early day. The writer became acquainted with him in Travis county in the year 1838. He was an enterprising, adventurous man, and could not remain idle while there was so much rich and unoccupied country to be settled. Accordingly, in the latter part of the summer of 1838 he loaded up his 1838 wagons, and with his family and several transient men, he made his way to the forks of the San Gabriel river with the intention of settling on his headright league.

They had reached what is known as the dividing ridge between south and north San Gabriel, when they discovered a body of Comanche Indians making their way in the direction of the settlements. This caused Mr. Webster to turn his own course back to the settlements, and, as he thought, undiscovered by the Indians. But in this he was mistaken. The keen sighted savages had seen his company, and after following them all night, about sunrise of the next morning made an attack upon them.

The whites arranged their wagons in a hollow square to protect themselves, and from within they fought desperately, even until the last man had fallen. The conflict continued from sunrise in the morning until ten or eleven o'clock. The men, thirteen in number, were all killed The Indians robbed the wagons, rolled them together and set

them on fire. Satisfied with the booty they had obtained
from this unfortunate party, they retreated to the mountains, taking Mrs. Webster and her little daughter prisoners.

Mrs. Webster's account of her two years captivity among
these Indians is very interesting. She was often compelled
to ride sixty or seventy-five miles a day, without any food
or water—sometimes for two or three days in succession.
They begged her frequently to teach them the art of making gunpowder, insisting that she knew how to make it, or
if she did not, that she could explain the process by which
the white people manufactured it.

To get rid of their importunities, she told the Indians that
the white people made it of fire coals and sand. They soon
had a large number of kettles on the fire filled with char-
coal and sand, which they boiled a long time, after which
they dried it and carefully pulverized it at a safe distance
from their fires. The mixture had somewhat the appearance of gunpowder, but unfortunately it would not explode
when a burning firebrand was applied to it. Finding the
experiment was a failure, they at length came to the conclusion that the manufacture of gunpowder was kept a
secret from the squaws of the white people.

The Indians would frequently bring paper money to her
and ask her what it was. To prevent them from trading it
for guns and munitions of war to white scoundrels who
would not hesitate to sell them a butcher knife to scalp their
own people, she told them it was of no value, and by so
doing she caused them to destroy thousands of dollars.

In her narrative Mrs. Webster gives an account of many
rich gold and silver mines she had seen, and she says that
she saw in certain localities stones that resembled diamonds
of great brilliancy, but that the Indians would not permit
her to touch one of them.

[NOTE.—These stones that Mrs. Webster supposed to be
diamonds were probably crystals of quartz or the white
topaz, as diamonds, except in a few sporadic instances, have
never been found on the continent of North America.]

Mrs. Webster and her little daughter were held prisoners
by the Indians for nearly two years. In the spring of 1840
there was an agreement entered into between the Republic

of Texas and the Comanche nation for an exchange of prisoners. The place for this exchange was at San Antonio. Accordingly at the appointed time and place the parties met to carry out the terms of this agreement. The gallant Colonel Fisher, with his battalion, together with the Commissioners, Colonel Wm. G. Cooke and General H. D. McLeod, represented the Texas government, and a number of their principal chiefs, the Comanche nation. The agreement between these parties was to the effect that both were to deliver up all the prisoners then living in their possession. The Indians, however, only brought in Miss Matilda Lockhart, when it was well known that they had several others, especially, Mrs. Webster. The chiefs were then informed that they were acting in bad faith, and would be held as hostages until all the white prisoners had been brought in. This information enraged the chiefs, who at once brought on the engagement known as the "Council House Fight," an account of which will be given later on. The Indians, when on their way to San Antonio, had left their families back about sixty miles in charge of a few warriors and Mrs. Webster and her children were with them.

The night after the chiefs left camp for San Antonio, Mrs. Webster learned from some of the squaws that they did not intend to give her up. She therefore determined, if possible, to make her escape from them. The following night she took her daughter, and watching a favorable opportunity, she stole off under cover of darkness. She found the trail the Indians had made going to San Antonio, and as it was quite plain, she had no difficulty in following it until the next morning, when, fearing pursuit, she hid herself and remained in her place of concealment all day.

It was well that she did so; for the Indians in the camp came out in pursuit of her. She saw them from the hill where she had concealed herself, following the trail, and late in the evening she saw them returning completely baffled. When night came on she resumed her journey, although from being barefooted her feet were terribly bruised and lacerated by thorny shrubs. Thus she continued her perilous journey, concealing herself in the brush during the day time and traveling by night, until she finally reached San Antonio, a few days after the Council House Fight, in a perfectly nude condition. She lay concealed in the outskirts of town until dark, when she ventured up to a Mexican hut. Poor woman. There she stood, half starved, her limbs bleeding from being lacerated by thorns and briars. She must have been a horrible sight to gaze upon. She was now among friends again, however, who supplied her with clothing, and she was soon rejoicing over her escape from a captivity worse than death.

Council House Fight in San Antonio.

WE have compiled the history of this desperate hand to hand conflict chiefly from Yoakum and Thrall's histories of Texas and from the official report of General H. D. McLeod to President Lamar, March 20, 1840. Some minor incidents, however, have been obtained from old veteran pioneers, familiar with the fight. In the early part of February, 1840, some Comanche chiefs sent

1840 word to Colonel H. W. Karnes, who was then at San Antonio, that they wished to come into town and make a treaty with the whites. This was not the first time the Comanches had feigned friendship and expressed a desire to cease hostilities towards the whites in order to throw the settlers off their guard so that they might more effectually raid the country, commit murders and then suddenly return to their mountain homes, carrying into captivity women and children and driving off all the horses they could conveniently carry with them. Our people along the border settlements had suffered so much at the hands of the red devils for the last four or five years previous that the government was disposed to give the Comanches another trial and thus test their pretended desire for peace; but, as will be seen further on, all necessary precautions were taken before the appointed time for the treaty to take place. The Indians who had been deputized to convey this message to Colonel Karnes were informed by him that if they would bring in the white captives they had—some thirteen in all—peace would be granted. The Indians promised that at the next full moon they would do so. This information having been communicated to the government, Colonel William S. Fisher was ordered to San Antonio with a force sufficiently strong to meet any emergency which might arise during the progress of the treaty. In due time Colonel William G. Cooke and General H. D. McLeod were sent forward as commissioners to treat with the Indians. According to previous appointment, on the nineteenth of March, 1840, sixty-five Comanches, including warriors, women and children, came into San Antonio to treat for peace. As stated above, they had agreed to bring in all the white prisoners whom they held as hostages. They, however, brought in but one, Miss Matilda Lockhart, whose sad history has already been recorded in the first part of this work. They were known to have several others, especially Mrs. Jane Webster, whose captivity and marvelous escape we have just narrated. Twelve chiefs, leaders of the deputation, were met by our commissioners, Colonel Cooke and General McLeod, with an interpreter in the old court house, when the question was at once asked by our commissioners: "Where are the prisoners you were to bring?" Mukwarrah, the chief who had made the promise at the former interview, replied: "We have brought the only one we had, the others are with other tribes." This was known to be a deliberate falsehood, for Miss Lockhart said she had seen several prisoners at the camp a few days before, and that they intended to bring in only one or two at a time in order to extort a greater ransom. A pause ensued, after which the chief asked in a defiant tone: "How do you like the answer?" No reply was made, but a messenger was sent to Captain Howard with orders to bring his company of soldiers into the council room. The soldiers having filed in the interpreter was then directed to inform the chief that they would be held as hostages until the other prisoners were brought in. The interpreter at first refused to tell them, saying that if he did so they would instantly fight; but the commissioners insisted, and placing himself near the door he told them and left. As he had predicted, the chiefs immediately prepared for action. Some strung their bows and drew their arrows while others drew their scalping knives. As the commissioners were retiring from the room one of the chiefs attempted to escape by leaping past the sentinel, who, in attempting to prevent him, was stabbed by the Indian. Captain Howard was also wounded in a similar manner. The fight by this t.me had become general, and it was not until the last chief in the council house was slain that the conflict ended. The Indians, who were on the outside, upon hearing the report of fire arms in the council rooms, immediately attacked the soldiers, who were stationed around the house, and fought with savage fierceness. Captain Mathew (Old Paint) Caldwell was attacked by a powerful Indian, and being unarmed, was forced to defend himself with rocks until a bullet from the rifle of one of the soldiers laid the Indian low. In an adjoining room Mr. Morgan was attacked by two Indians, but he succeeded in killing both of them. Lieutenant Dun ington was killed by a squaw, who shot an arrow entirely through his body. Judge Thompson was in the yard amusing himself setting up pieces of money for the little Indians to knock out. While thus engaged he was killed by an arrow before he even suspected danger. Judge Hood was killed inside the council house. Colonel Lysander Wells rode into the plaza just as the fight commenced when a powerful savage vaulted on behind him and first attempted to unhorse him, but failing in this he tried to guide the horse out of the plaza. The colonel attempted to draw his pistol, but owing to the fast hold the Indian had upon him was unable to do so. Finally, after circling around the plaza two or three times, one of the soldiers shot the Indian, who tumbled off upon the ground, very much to the satisfaction of Colonel Wells, who, no doubt, did not very much relish being hugged by a savage warrior. The Indians, after fighting with a desperation which evinced great courage, were finally forced by a company of soldiers under Captain Redd to take shelter in a stone house near by, where all were cut down except one warrior, who secreted himself within the walls of the building. Every inducement was offered him if he would come out. He was assured if he would surrender that he would not be hurt, but all to no purpose. Finally in order to make him leave the house, the

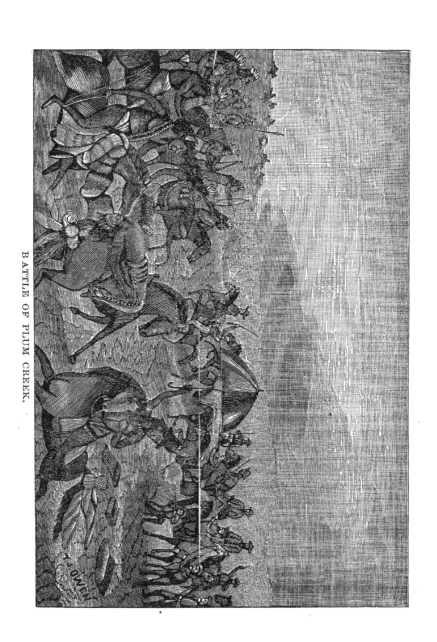

BATTLE OF PLUM CREEK.

whites made a large ball of cotton rags and saturated it thoroughly with turpentine. They then made an opening in the roof, set the ball on fire and threw it down on the Indian's head. This routed him from his lair, and as he came out he was shot dead. During the engagement a party of the savages made their way across the San Antonio river, but they were pursued and all killed except a renegade Mexican, who made his escape. All the warriors, thirty-two in number, together with three women and two children, were killed. Twenty-seven women and children were made prisoners. The Texans had seven killed and eight wounded. After the fight one of the squaws dispatched to inform the Comanches that if they would bring in all of their prisoners an exchange would be made. Several days elapsed when finally all the white prisoners were brought in and the exchange was made. Thus ended the attempt upon this occasion to patch up friendly relations with the powerful and warlike tribe of Comanches, and for some time afterwards they waged a ceaseless and bloody warfare upon the frontier settlers of Texas. Returning to their mountain homes they began planning a regular invasion upon the settlements, and it was not many months before an army of several hundred strong were on the march to avenge the death of their fallen chiefs.

Great Comanche Invasion—Attack on Victoria— Sacking of Linnville.

NOT until the summer of 1840 had the unfriendly Indians ever made a regular invasion of the white settlements in Texas. The settlers had been constantly harrassed by small bands of marauding Indians, who stole horses, killed cattle, and frequently killed and scalped such settlers as were caught out from home and were unprepared for resistance. At this time there were but few settlements 1840 between Gaudalupe and the Colorado river, and in fact, the entire country west of the Colorado river, extending to the Rio Grande. and on down to the coast.

with the exception of San Antonio, Gonzales, and a few
other small towns, was one vast expanse of uninhabited
country, and offered an easy ingress to the settlements for
the savages in this well prepared and equipped invasion.
Early in August, 1840, in the light of the moon, an army
variously estimated at from five hundred to one thousand
Indian warriors, mostly Comanches, besides a few squaws
and old men, passed southward over the territory, to the settlements near the coast, committing occasional murders on
their route.

It was on the afternoon of the sixth of August that this entire body of fiendish savages, thirsting to avenge the sad fate
of their fallen chiefs who fell in the fight at San Antonio,
known as the "Council House Fight," suddenly came upon
the town of Victoria, dealing death and destruction upon
every hand. The attack was totally unexpected—the citizens
wholly unprepared to resist such a formidable force, and the
consternation and confusion which prevailed, can better be
imagined than described. Several persons were killed and
wounded. Among those who lost their lives in defense of
the terror stricken inhabitants of the little town of Victoria,
was Doctor Gray; the names of the balance who fell at the
hands of the savages we do not remember. Those who were
not killed were only saved by barricading themselves in such
houses as offered shelter or protection. After having driven
the citizens into their forted houses the Indians withdrew
from the town, carrying with them all the horses and mules
which they could find in and around town, numbering between two and three thousand head, and camped that night
within a few miles of Victoria. No doubt gloating over
their successful raid upon the town, and rejoicing over the
large amount of property captured, they conceived the bold
idea of surprising and sacking the town of Linnville, after
murdering its inhabitants. Flushed with victory, and several thousand dollars worth of horses and mules, they at
once proceeded on their way to the little seaport town of
Linnville, situated some fifty miles from Victoria. In their
line of march they came upon Mrs. Crosby and child, both
of whom were captured and taken prisoners. Early in the
morning of August 8, some few of the inhabitants of Linnville observed in the distance a perfect cloud of dust, caused,

as they supposed, by a vast *caballada* of horses, being brought in from Mexico for trading purposes. By throwing themselves on the sides of their horses, and riding in this way, the Indians had completely concealed themselves from the vision of the unsuspecting denizens of the village. Imagine their consternation and utter dismay, when one thousand red savages, suddenly rising in their saddles, dashed upon the defenseless town, when many of the inhabitants were fast asleep. The alarm was given as soon as the discovery was made. Resistence was not thought of, and panic stricken, men, women and children, young and old, rushed for the boats which were anchored near by in the shallow water. The scene amid the confusion which prevailed was one never to be forgotten by the survivors of that terror stricken people. The war whoop of the wild Comanche commingled with the screaming of the women, the crying of the children, and the groans of the dying and wounded almost beggars description. The blood thirsty savages pursued the inhabitants into the water and captured and killed several of the fleeing and terrified populace. Among the number who met his death between the shore and the boats, was young Captain H. O. Watts, collector of customs, his young bride was captured in the water, dragged back to the shore and made a captive. Several negroes were captured and killed. Most of the inhabitants reached the boats and pulling out to sea escaped the tomahawk and scalping knife. All who failed to reach the boats were either carried away captive or ruthlessly killed by the Indians. The little town was unusually well supplied with merchandise, and the Indians sacked all the stores and private houses, taking away every imaginable kind of merchandise. They packed several hundred mules and horses with their plunder, and gathering many loose horses, they had now an immense herd, which they gaily caparisoned and bedecked with red streamers torn from the bales of merchadise, and also with ribbons, which streamed from their heads and the heads of their horses in gay profusion. Having taken every thing they could carry away, they set fire to the town and burnt it.

The Battle of Plum Creek.

THE Indians had now between three and four thousand horses and mules, several hundred of them being heavily laden with merchandise which had been pillaged from the stores before the burning of the town of Linnville. During the following night, this savage army of red skins moved off with all their booty in the direction from whence they had come. Expressmen were at once despatched 1840 to notify the citizens of the Guadalupe, Gonzales, Lavaca and Colorado settlements, and it was not long before the Texans were rallying in companies from every direction. Of course an invasion upon such a large scale could not be made by the Indians without their sign attracting the attention of the whites, who might perchance be passing through the country from one settlement to another.

The Rev. Z. N. Morrel, a noted Baptist minister of that day, whose courage upon the field of battle was ever equal to that exhibited from the pulpit stand, happened to be returning to the town of Bastrop in an ox wagon from the Guadalupe, where he had purchased a tract of land and was improving it. While passing over the divide between the Guadalupe and Lavaca rivers, at 12 o'clock on or about the tenth of August, he crossed the trail made by the Indians on their way down to Victoria and Linnville. Although driving an ox team, he made thirty miles in twelve hours, so eager was he to communicate this intelligence to Colonel Ed. Burleson and the citizens of Colorado valley. By sunrise, the morning after crossing the trail, he was in the town of LaGrange, beside the gallant old Indian fighter, Colonel Ed. Burleson. The story was quickly told, and in a few moments Burleson was mounted on his favorite war horse, ready to set out at once to organize a force to meet the enemy.

Says the Rev. Mr. Morrel (Flowers and Fruit, p. 128): "By

the time we were mounted, a man was in sight, his horse running rapidly, a paper in his hand fluttering in the breeze. The expressman presented the paper, which read about as follows:"

"General: The Indians have sacked and burned the town of Linnville; carried off several prisoners. We made a draw fight with them at Casa Blanca. Could not stop them. We want to fight them before they get to the mountains. We have sent expresssman up the Guadalupe.

(Signed) "BEN McCULLOCH."

It seems that a few companies had hastily rallied from the Gonzales, Guadalupe and Lavaca settlements and had engaged the Indians on their retreat, but the superior number of the latter caused the Texans to withdraw. Ben McCulloch, however, was not one, as will be seen later on, to permit the wily savages to swoop down upon our people with the tomahawk and scalping knife, and then stand by and see them quietly retreat to their mountain homes without giving them battle. He immediately set out for Gonzales, whipped around the enemy and joined Captain Mathew (Old Paint) Caldwell, who was in charge of a company of thirty-seven men, while Captains Ward and Bird each commanded a small company—the entire force numbering some eighty or ninety all told. These three companies camped at Plum creek on the night of the eleventh, that being the place of rendezvous agreed upon by the leaders of the respective settlements, to intercept the enemy.

The Rev. Mr. Morrell, in speaking of the movements of himself and Colonel Burleson after receiving the dispatch from McCulloch, says: "We made our way up the Colorado valley as rapidly as we could to Bastrop, notifying every one as we went. Here Colonel Burleson called a council and it was agreed that the Indians should be intercepted on their retreat at Good's, on Plum creek, twenty-seven miles below Austin." As stated above, on the night of the eleventh the three companies had gone into camp on Plum creek and were keeping a sharp lookout for the enemy. Early on the morning of the twelfth Caldwell was informed by his spies that the Indians were approaching within sight. Up to this time Colonel Burleson, with his one hundred Texans and thirteen Tonkawa Indians, under

their gallant old chief, Placido, had not yet arrived on the
ground, but "Old Paint" was there, and wherever he was
found in close proximity to Indians there was sure to be a
fight, it mattered not how much the latter outnumbered him.
Old Texans, when assembled together, living over the events
of the early history of Texas, not unfrequently ask each
other the question: "Do you remember 'Old Paint's'
speech at the battle of Plum creek?" In order that the few,
but impressive and inspiring words of the grand old warrior
may not be forgotten, we reproduce them here as nearly as
we can. Said he: "Boys, the Indians number about one
thousand. They have our women and children captives.
We are only eighty-seven strong, but I believe we can whip
h—ll out of 'em. What shall we do boys; shall we fight?"
It is useless to say that the answer all along the line was "Yes!
yes! fight!" On the previous evening, however, Felix Houston, general of the militia, had arrived upon the ground, and
being senior officer, was given the command. While the
plan of attack was being arranged Colonel Ed Burleson
came up with his forces and the men were soon thrown into
line. The Indians were now marching across the prairie
within full view. It must have been a novel sight to see one
thousand red warriors with their vast *caballado* of horses and
mules gorgeously arrayed in the goods pillaged from Linnville as they passed within full review of the Texans. There
were too many of the old Indian fighters, however, upon
the ground for this imposing band of savage warriors to
create terror in the ranks of the little Texan army of two
hundred. No sooner had Burleson arrived with his forces
from the Colorado, supplemented by Placido and his Tonkawa Indians, than he was ordered to command the right
wing, Captain Mathew Caldwell the left, while Monroe Hardeman (brother of the venerable General William P., "Old
Gotch" Hardeman) was to bring up the rear. The Indians were
at once thrown into line of battle by their gallant chief, who
led the invading host. "The enemy," says, the Rev. Z. N.
Morrell, from whom we again quote, "was disposed to keep
at a distance and delay the fight in order that the packed
mules might be driven ahead with the spoils. During this
delay several of their chiefs performed some daring feats.
According to a previous understanding, our men waited for

the Indians, in the retreat, to get beyond the timber before the general charge was made. One of these daring chiefs attracted my attention especially. He was riding a very fine horse, held in by a fine American bridle, with a red ribbon eight or ten feet long, tied to the tail of the horse. He was dressed in elegant style, from the goods stolen at Linnville, with a high top silk hat, fine pair of boots and leather gloves, an elegant broadcloth coat, hind part before, with brass buttons shining brightly up and down his back. When he first made his appearance he was carrying a large umbrella stretched. This Indian and others would charge towards us and shoot their arrows, then wheel and run away, doing no damage. This was done several times in range of some of our guns. Soon the discovery was made that he wore a shield, and although our men took good aim, the balls glanced. An old Texan living on the Lavaca asked me to hold his horse, and getting as near the place where they wheeled as was safe, waited patiently till they came; and as the Indian checked his horse and the shield flew up, he fired and brought him to the ground. Several had fallen before, but without checking their demonstrations.

"Now, although some of them had lost their lives in carrying him away, yet they did not cease their efforts till he was carried to the rear."

General Houston, who had caused the delay in making the attack, and whose men were now suffering under the constant fire of the enemy, whilst the chiefs were performing their wonderful feats, was admonished by the gallant Ben McCulloch that "that was not the way to fight Indians;" whereupon Houston ordered an immediate charge. The heroic little band of two hundred, fired with the zeal of their cause, and burning within to avenge the sad fate of those who had fallen beneath the tomahawk and scalping knife at Victoria and Linnville, now dashed forward under their respective leaders with a wild yell which fairly made the welkin ring. In the midst of the hottest part of the conflict could be seen brave old Placido (the ever faithful friend of the whites), dealing death upon every hand, while the arrows and balls of the enemy were flying thick and fast around him. Before going into the fight he had taken the precaution to tie a white rag around his arm in order that, in the heat of battle, he might not be mistaken for the enemy.

The Indians could not long withstand the furious attack of the determined Texans, and the rout soon became general. It was a running fight for twelve or fifteen miles. The pack animals and loose horses were in part abandoned, and in the flight that ensued each Indian only looked after taking care of his own scalp. Ben and Henry McCulloch, Alsey Miller and C. C. DeWitt pursued a squad of five Indians, killing all of them before they abandoned the chase. John Henry Brown (now our Colonel John Henry Brown, of Dallas, Texas), crowned himself with the honor of slaying, in a hand-to-hand engagement, the second chief in command, who wore a buffalo head with polished horns for a cap.

General Houston estimated that they killed from fifty to eighty Indians during the engagement, and captured several hundred horses and mules, with packs and baggage; while the Texans had none killed and only a few wounded. Among the latter were Doctor Sweitzer and —— Reid. Doctor Sweitzer had his right arm pinned to his body with an arrow, and was being hotly pursued by several Indians, when he was rescued from death by the gallant Henry McCulloch. Reid, who was riding a very spirited animal and was one of the last to abandon the chase, seeing an Indian about to let fly an arrow at him, threw himself flat on his horse's neck, but too late to avoid the missile. The arrow penetrated his body and was with great difficulty withdrawn. Reid, however, recovered from the wound.

Before the retreat, the Indians killed Mrs. Crosby, who, it will be remembered, was captured by them between Victoria and Linnville. Her body was found near that of a dead negro. Mrs. Watts was shot in the breast with an arrow, and was found soon afterwards, by the Rev. Mr. Morrel, whose language we quote:

"Just as the retreat commenced I heard the scream of a female voice in a bunch of bushes close by. Approaching the spot I discovered a lady endeavoring to pull an arrow out that was lodged firmly in her breast. This proved to be Mrs. Watts, whose husband was killed at Linnville. Doctor Brown, of Gonzales, was at once summoned to the spot.

GENERAL EDWARD BURLESON.

Near by we soon discovered a white woman and a negro 'roman, both dead. These were all shot with arrows when the howl was raised and the retreat commenced. While the doctor was approaching I succeeded in loosening her hands from the arrow. The dress and flesh on each side of the arrow were cut, and an effort was made to extract it. The poor sufferer seized the doctor's hand and screamed so violently that he desisted. A second effort was made with success. My blanket was spread upon the ground, and as she rested on this, with my saddle for a pillow, she was soon composed and rejoicing at her escape. Death would have been preferable to crossing the mountains with the savages. She had ridden a pack mule all the way from the coast, and when they stopped she was required to read the stolen books for their amusement. I received many letters from Mrs. Watts in after years, but never saw her again."

[Note. Mrs. Watts died in 1878, while keeping the San Antonio House in Port Lavaca. See Thrall's History of Texas, p. 466.]

Thus ended the battle of Plum Creek, fought on the twelfth day of August, 1840. After the battle the Tonkawa Indians who had fought so nobly under their trusted Chief Placido, as was their custom, busied themselves in fleecing the flesh and cutting off the feet and hands of their inveterate enemies—the Comanches. These trophies they carried home with which to celebrate the war dance.

Sketch of the Life of General Edward Burleson.

I T would seem to be almost superfluous to give in such a book as this, even a sketch of the life of one whose career is a portion of the history of our State, and of course known to all. And yet a sketch of the life of one so noted as an Indian fighter and frontiersman, certainly comes within the legitimate scope and purpose of this book. We therefore give the following outlines as briefly as possible, which have been taken chiefly from a biographical sketch of General Burleson published in 1859, to which have been added extracts from an eulogy pronounced at his funeral by the Hon. Edward Tarver.

General Burleson was born in Buncombe county, North Carolina, in 1798. When but a lad he served in a company commanded by his father under General Jackson, in what is known as the Creek War. In March, 1831, he emigrated to Texas and settled upon a place eleven miles below the town of Bastrop, where he soon rendered himself conspicuous by his readiness when called on to repel the inroads of savages, then of frequent occurrence. His unflinching courage and perseverance on such occasions brought him into favorable notice, and in 1832 he was elected lieutenant colonel of the principality of Austin.

No portion of Texas suffered more from Indian outrages than that part now known as Bastrop county, and on no part of her long suffering frontier were their forays repelled with more constant valor and firmness. Burleson, by his activity, promptness and courage, soon rose to be an acknowledged leader, while his plain and unpretending deportment and natural dignity won friends as fast as he made acquaintances.

In the battle with the Mexicans under General Cos at San Antonio he was conspicuous for his gallantry and rendered important services.

As colonel of a regiment he participated in the final battle at San Jacinto, which secured the independence of Texas. We quote here from one of his biographers: "On that bloody field Burleson added new honors to his fame as a brave soldier and tried officer. His regiment stormed the breastwork and captured the artillery and contributed its honorable share to the victory. The morning of the day on which the battle was fought General Houston ordered Burleson to detail one hundred men from his regiment to build a bridge across the bayou in case a retreat should be necessary. Burleson replied 'that he could make the detail but he had no idea the bridge would be built; that they had no axes or tools of any description, or teams to haul the timber.' Houston asked him if he intended to disobey orders. Burleson replied 'that he was not disposed to disobey orders, but that his men had much rather fight than to work.' 'Then,' said Houston, 'if you are so anxious to fight you shall have your fill before night,' and immediately made out his plan of battle. After the battle of San Jacinto, General Burleson returned to his home and was elected to the Senate of the first Congress of the Republic.

In what is known as the Cherokee war Burleson moved against the Indians at the head of five hundred men, defeated them in a hard fought battle, killing many (among them their head chief, Bowles) and drove the remainder beyond the limits of the Republic.

In the great Indian raid in 1840 General Burleson was second in command of the forces that met the Indians on Plum Creek, which defeated them with great slaughter, and recaptured a vast amount of plunder. The full details of this battle and the conspicuous part taken by Colonel Burleson we have already given to the reader.

He was in a number of hotly contested fights with the Indians, a full account of which will appear later on. It was in one of these stuborn contests—the battle of Brushy—that he lost his brother, Jacob Burleson, who had engaged the enemy before the General arrived.

Upon one occasion a party of forty-five or fifty Indians came into the settlements below the town of Bastrop, and stole a lot of horses while the people were at church. A man who had remained at home discovered them, ran to church and gave the alarm. General Burleson, with only ten men, started in immediate pursuit, and followed the trail that evening to Piney creek, near town. Next morning he was reinforced by eight men, the pursuit was continued and the enemy overtaken near the Yegua, a small sluggish stream now in Lee county. When within about two hundred yards of them, Burleson called out to the Indians in Spanish to halt; they immediately did so, and forming themselves in regular order, like disciplined troops, commenced firing by squads or platoons. When within sixty yards, the battle was opened on the part of the Texans by the discharge of Burleson's double barrel shot gun. The conflict was but of short duration. Six Indians were killed and the balance fled into a deep ravine, enveloped in thickets, and made their escape.

In 1841, General Burleson was elected vice president of the Republic by a considerable majority over General Memucan Hunt. At Monterey he was appointed by Governor Henderson—then in personal command of the Texas division, one of his aids-de-camp, and in that capacity bore a distinguished and honored part in the fierce conflicts before that city.

He died on the twenty-sixth of December, 1851, at the capital of the State, while a member of the senate then in session, and his death produced a profound sensation throughout the country, where his name had become as familiar as a household word. Eloquent eulogies were pronounced in both houses of the Legislature at his death. Says the writer of his biographical sketch. "A purer character than that of General Burleson is not to be found delineated in the annals of any country. His reputation as a soldier, not won in a single victory or single enterprise, but built up by years of service and success, was left behind him without a stain, while the purity of his conduct as a legislator escaped even the breath of suspicion. No unhallowed ambition prompted him to brave the dangers of the battle field. No petty jealousy at the laurels won by others ever found lodgement for a single moment in his noble and generous bosom. Brave, yet unambitious—modest, yet firm of purpose; simple in his manner, yet dignified—he won the friendship of the worthiest of the land, and never lost it. In him were happily blended the attributes of a successful warrior, with the republican and patriarchal simplicity of a quiet and unassuming country gentlemen, whose bravery was unsurpassed by his open and cordial hospitality. In his personal intercourse with society, whether in the camp among his comrades in arms or among his countrymen in the walks of private life, perhaps the most prominent trait of character, which was every where developed, was an inflexible love of justice, in its most extensive and significant sense. He seemed to be scarcely aware of the honors which crowded upon him as he passed through life." We will close this sketch with an extract from an eulogy pronounced by the Hon. Edward Tarver, of Washington county, at the funeral of General Burleson, which shows the high estimate placed upon him by his fellow countrymen.

"These are the departing days of the present day; this is the time when most reflecting minds are disposed to take a general retrospect of the events of the outgoing year; and I imagine that the latter days of this will be remembered as the most gloomy which have fallen upon the land for many years. To-day, Nature herself seems shrouded in mourning. All is blackness, darkness and desolation, as though she herself participated in our national sorrow and sympathized with us in our bereavement."

There is a tear for all who die,
A mourner o'er the humblest grave,
But nations swell the funeral cry.
And triumph weeps above the brave.

"The deceased has filled for many years a prominent place among the citizens of Texas, and Western Texas in particlar. In relation to her history and its soul stirring events, he might truly say, *cujus pars magnafui.* He discharged the duties of the many important stations which he was chosen to fill in the councils of his country with a single-ness of heart and purity of purpose that did honor alike to him and his country. Sir, I know his history from the be-ginning. His life has been one continued scene of peril, of suffering, and of the most trying vicissitudes. Yet, he has passed through all with a stainless and blameless reputa-tion, unsullied by the imputation of wrong, either in his public or private capacity."

H. C. Love's Hand to Hand Fight.

DURING the year 1879 Major H. D. Prendergast (now deceased) contributed to the American Sketch Book the following interesting account of a fight in Robert-son county. We reproduce the same here, in the Ma-jor's own language: In the year 1840 there occurred, near

the center of Robertson county, and not far from where the
town of Englewood now stands, one of the most des-
1840 perate personal conflicts that ever took place between
heroes of opposing clans. Since the Scottish bard celebrated the hand to hand fight between Fitz James and
Roderick Dhu, at Coilan Kogle's ford, perhaps no real combat has ever so nearly resembled the imaginary battle of the
poet's heroes in all essential particulars. It was the general
practice of the Indians to make their raids about the full
moon. On one occasion they had made a raid and stolen
several horses. The thefts were quickly discovered, and a
party made up to pursue them from Franklin, the then
county seat of Robertson county. The pursuers numbered
some six or seven. Among them were G. H. Love, now
living at Whelock, in this county, and Judge S. B. Killough,
who died about two years ago, at Whelock; Harvey Mathews, now living in Navarro county, and A. C. Love, and D.
Hill, two medical students. The pursuing party overtook
the Indians in the early morning, between and at the junction of two deep ravines. A charge was immediately made,
and the savages, abandoning their horses and camp, scattered into the adjacent thickets, excepting one warrior, who
could not find it in his heart to give up the splendid horse
he had captured the night before, but prepared to run the
gauntlet. So, mounting his horse, rifle in hand, and with
his faithful squaw mounted behind him, he made a dash to
pass between his enemies.

The first shot from A. C. Love's gun brought down the
hindmost Indian, which proved to be the squaw. Almost at
the same instant a shot from Hill's rifle disabled the horse
of the Indian, who now abandoned the idea of escape in
that way, and, leaping down from his wounded horse, ran
by Hill and fired the gun, almost touching the face of Hill,
who fell to the ground, his jaw bone shattered by the ball.
The savage now turned to flight, and being cut off from
the ravine he started across the open woods, pursued by A.
C. Love, each carrying his empty rifle. Love was a man
about twenty years old, six feet high, weighing about one
hundred and sixty pounds, and active as a panther. The
Indian, a giant of his race, was about the same height
and something heavier. The distance between them

gradually closed, until at the end of about two hundred yards the savage stopped short, turned around, and gazing fiercely a moment, sprang back to meet his foe. As they met, each clubbed his gun and aimed a murderous blow at the head of the other. The ring of their gun barrels as they clashed together could be heard for hundreds of yards. Love's collar bone was broken and one finger on his left hand crushed. After a few blows the combatants mutually threw down their guns and closed in a real Indian hug, Love's object being to make a prisoner of his brave foe. But in this contest he met with an unexpected difficulty. The Indian's arms and shoulders were entirely naked, and as Love has told the writer, he would slip through his arms like an eel. Suddenly a chill of horror ran through Love's frame as he felt the Indian's finger grappling for his (Love's) bowie-knife at his side and which he had entirely forgotten. Now came, in one terrible moment, the issue of life or death. Quick as thought Love's right hand was on the handle of his knife, when the savage changed his tactics, and throwing his arms entirely around Love, endeavored to prevent his drawing the knife.

> Now, gallant Saxon, hold thine own,
> No maiden arm around thee thrown.

In this last death struggle Love finally disengaged his left hand, and seizing the long hair of the savage, so confused him by this unexpected mode of attack that he secured a momentary advantage, and then one quick flash of the glittering steel, and the soul of the brave Indian had taken its flight to his happy hunting grounds. Just then Love's brother and other comrades returned from the pursuit of the other Indians, to find him standing erect, but exhausted, over his fallen foe.

Colonel Eldridge's Hazardous Expedition to the Wild Tribes.

D
URING the administration of General Sam Houston in the spring of 1843 he dispatched Colonel J. C. Eldridge, Commissioner of Indian Affairs, and Thomas Torrey, Indian agent, to visit all the wild tribes on the frontier for the purpose of getting them to enter into a treaty of peace with the Republic of Texas, and to accomplish this object, instructions were given the commissioners 1843 to use their utmost skill in inducing the chiefs of the different tribes to meet the commissioners representing the Republic of Texas, at Bird's Fort, on the Trinity river, on the tenth of August. General Ham P. Bee, who was then quite a young man, accompanied the expedition at the instance of his old friend, Colonel Eldridge. The three principal chiefs of the Delawares, to wit, Jim Shaw, John Connor and Jim Second Eye, were selected by President Houston to accompany the commissioners on this hazardous expedition to aid them in their undertaking. Many of the Delawares could not only speak English, but the language of all, or nearly all, of the different wild tribes. The party was finally made up, consisting of the commissioners, the three chiefs above named and several other Indians, who accompanied the party in the capacity of guides, hunters, etc., and set out from the old town of Washington, then the seat of government, in the month of March, 1843, on their perilous journey. We should have stated that Acequosh, a Waco chief, also accompanied the party. The principal village of the Comanches was situated further out on the plains than were the villages of any of the other tribes, and as will be seen later on, this fact very much delayed the progress of the expedition. The commissioners took along two Comanche children who had been captured by our people during the year 1840. These were to be returned to their people. One of them was a boy fourteen years old, named Bill Hockley, in honor of Colonel Hockley,

who had taken care of him. The other was a girl eleven years of age, named Maria. The parting of this girl, who had now become civilized and accustomed to the habits of our people, from the commissioners, was one of the most heartrending scenes ever witnessed, and will appear in this volume further on under the head of "A Comanche Princess."

The expedition was fraught with many difficulties, dangers, privations and hardships. On their way Jim Shaw became exasperated when he found that he and the two Delaware chiefs were not the commissioners, but had been sent along simply to aid Colonel Eldridge, who was the duly authorized commissioner. He and the other two chiefs threatened to abandon the party and Colonel Eldridge was just on the eve of returning home when the chiefs reconsidered the matter and agreed to go on. The journey was then continued until the head village of the Wacos had been reached, and while delayed here the wife of Chief Acequosh was taken very sick. At the instance of the old chief the commissioners rendered her such medical aid as lay within their power, and she finally recovered—a most fortunate circumstance, as the sequel will show. Several tribes were visited and many promised to attend the council at Bird's Fort. But the Comanche village, as before stated, lay far out on the plains, and being especially desirous to visit this tribe the march was continued. General H. P. Bee kept a journal of their wanderings in the wilderness in search of the head chief of the nation, and some years ago, at the request of the writer, he furnished him with an extract from his journal, with permission to make such use of it as he might see proper. The writer still has in his possession this manuscript in General Bee's own hand writing, and prefers giving the extract without alteration. It is to be regretted that the entire journal can not be published, for it is all interesting. The foregoing remarks have been made by way of preface that the reader might better understand the nature and object of the expedition. It is well known to the historian that General Houston always favored a pacific course towards the Indians, and it was for the purpose of carrying out this policy that commissioners were sent out.

Treaty Expedition to the Wild Tribes.

Extract from Journal of General H. P. Bee.

LONG before this we had exhausted the supplies we brought from the settlements. Our rice was the last to give out, and for some time we had been living upon buffalo and deer meat alone, without bread of any description, and some times without salt. Yet the diet seemed to be nourishing, owing to the fact, perhaps, that we made up in quantity what was lacking in variety and quality. Two or three pounds of buffalo meat at a meal was our usual allowance. The tallow of the buffalo is not as greasy as that of beeves. A piece of dried buffalo meat in the one hand and a good size lump of the tallow in the other are tolerably fair substitutes for bread and butter. We always carried a piece of dried buffalo meat tied to our saddles on which at any time, we could make a "hasty snack" as we rode along.

1843

After wandering for many days over the vast prairies of Northwest Texas, in search of the head chief of the Comanche nation, but without success, we halted one morning in an immense plum patch to regale ourselves upon the delicious fruit with which the bushes were covered. Whilst busily engaged in this pleasant occupation, our attention was drawn to fresh plum skins on the ground, evidently quite recently pulled, and telling us that others besides ourselves were some where in the vicinity, who were as fond of plums as we were. This incident, like Crusoe's discovery of the foot prints in the sand by the sea shore, alarmed us a good deal and destroyed our appetite for plums, for we knew very well that any band of Indians we might encounter would be much more likely to prove enemies than friends.

Before we had come to any conclusion as to what was best to be done, an object approaching us was discovered. It proved to be a Comanche Indian, with a boy seven or eight years old, riding in front of him upon a magnificent horse. He came in right amongst us, and at first we were at a loss to understand why such a large, powerful man, as he evidently was, should be riding *behind* a little boy, but he informed us that he was totally blind, and that the little boy was his guide. He told us also of our near proximity to a large village of the Comanches (of which he was one of the chiefs), and to our great joy he told us it was also the village of Pa-ha-yu-co, the head chief of the Comanche Nation, the one we had been vainly looking for during the last three months. After the little boy (who was really quite handsome, dressed in his buck skin hunting shirt and leggins ornamented with beads) had gathered as many plums as he wanted, the blind chief started back to the village, accompanied by our Delaware Indian interpreters.

Towards evening we were waited upon by a delegation from the village, who invited us to visit the place. Of course it did not take us long to saddle up, and after a couple of hours ride, escorted by fully two hundred Comanche warriors, we came to the village, where we were received with much rude but impressive ceremony. We were then conducted to the tent of the chief, Pa-ha-yu-co, who was absent, but the honors were done by Mrs. Pa-ha-yu-co No. 1, who turned out all the other Mrs. Pa-ha-yu-cos, together with their numerous children, from the tent, and placed it at our disposal. Our expressions of regret at disturbing the ladies were evidently not appreciated because not understood.

As soon as we were settled in our spacious apartments, every apperture in the lodge to admit light and air, was darkened by the copper colored visages of the crowds that thronged around to get a peep at the "pale faces"—the first that the most of them had ever seen. The thermometer was ranging probably at about one hundred and ten degrees (it was in August) and fearing suffocation, we suggested that our own tent should be stretched, which was done, and as it was open at both ends we had plenty of air, and the crowd could stare at us to their satisfaction.

As I have stated, Pa-ha-yu-co, the head chief, was absent, and we were informed that he was not expected back for a week. So we had to be patient, and settled down to our surroundings as best we could. We were a never failing source of curiosity to the Indians, who thronged our camp

day and night. The women would turn back the sleeves of
our shirts to show the white skin to' their children, for it
may readily be supposed that those parts of our persons exposed to the sun were by this time bronzed almost to the
color of the Indians themselves.

As the Comanches lived entirely upon meat, we moved
camp twice during the week we were with them, and the
system and regularity which marked the striking of the
tent (all made of buffalo skins) and the precision with
which each family took up the line of march, the tent poles
attached to the pommels of their saddles trees, and dragging behind, whilst the pack mules carried the women and
children and dogs—and the coming into position in the new
camp—the magic, as it were, by which at a signal, all the
tents on all the streets went up in their proper places, would
not have disgraced the tactics of Scott or Hardee.

On one occasion I accompanied some of the braves on a
buffalo hunt, and noticed the skill and dexterity with which
they sent the quivering arrow into the sides of the ponder-
ous animals. Their aim was very accurate—rarely failing
with the first arrow—and they always pursued a wounded
buffalo until he was dispatched; for their tradition is, "that
when the buffalo are exterminated the Comanche nation
will cease to exist also," in which probably there is much
truth, for when the supply of meat fails them, on the prairie, the Indian must live by tilling the soil, and the Comanches are so entirely nomadic in their mode of life, it is
not likely they will ever be able to subsist by agriculture,
hence, they are economical in the use of their "live stock."
They follow the immense herds of buffalo north in summer
and south in winter, as the instinct of the animal teaches it
to change its pastureage. The women always accompany
the warriors on their hunts, and as the buffolos are dispatched, they follow on behind to butcher the slaughtered
animals, cutting the meat up into long strings, which they
hang up on the bushes to dry in the wind and sun. The
women also dress the skins, some of which they ornament
on the inside with figures and devices in paint. Indian
women perform all the drudgery. They saddle and unsaddle
the horses of their lords—do not have much cooking, washing or darning to do, but they are always busy dressing

buck skins, of which their clothing is made, or in orna-menting their robes. Every warrior has more or less cap-tives, generally Mexicans, to wait upon him, and his squaws also generally have one or more captives (girls or women) to aid them in their work. I saw Mexican prisoners in their camp of all ages, from sucking babes, to grown men and women. They were of the lower or "Peon" class and their color was very similar to that of the Indians, to whom they were but little, if any, superior as far as civilization was concered, yet all I talked to wanted to return home to their own people.

The Comanches owned immense herds of horses, requir-ing a strong guard constantly with them, as they graze them frequently miles from their camp, and this, with the neces-sity of obtaining meat, is the reason why they move camp so often. When buffalos are scarce, they sometimes live upon horse meat, which I have eaten myself on several oc-casions. It is really very good, both dried and fresh, if you will only ignore the fact that *it is horse meat.* Mule meat is not so good—too much like the living animal—tough, and hard to manage.

We had now passed a week with the Comanches, and al-though the chief had neither smoked nor eaten with us, we felt no uneasiness, as we knew that such was their custom until peace was made, and, of course, no "treaty" could be entered into until the head chief was present to ratify pro-ceedings. Besides, we had been so long amongst the wild tribes, we had lost any little apprehension we might have had when we first started out for the safety our scalps.

At this time the Comanche Nation was divided into ten tribes, each with their own chief and government, and once a year delegates from all the tribes met in a general coun-cil, when one of the ten chiefs was selected as head chief of the nation until the next general assembly. Pa-ha-yu-co was the last chosen—hence the necessity of meeting him before any thing definite could be done in the way of a "treaty."

On the ninth of August, about sun set, he arrived at camp, and occupied the tent adjoining our own. We were soon after presented to him, and received with courtesy. The in-terview was informal and short, and no clue as to the feelings entertained by the chief towards us could be had from it, but the impression made was favorable. At sun rise the next morning the council met in a large circular tent, made of buffalo skins. I suppose there were one hundred warriors in the council. They were seated on the ground in a circle, diminishing in circumference as they neared the center in which was the old chief.

After taking a look at them, for we were neither invited nor expected at the meeting, we returned to our tent, leaving our Delaware interpreters to do our talking, as they had been invited, and occupied seats on the ground.

About ten o'clock a sort of committee waited upon us, informing us that couriers from the Waco village, some two hundred miles distant, where we had staid nearly a month, had arrived, saying "that since we had left their village a great many of their people had died; that we doubtless had given them poison, were bad men, and that the Comanches must kill us," and that the council wished to know what we had to say about it. Without being much disturbed by this statement, for it was too preposterous for belief, we referred them to Acequosh, a Waco chief, who had accompanied us from Texas, and eat with us at every meal, even when we were in his own village (for our rations were better than his), that his wife had been sick and we had cured her, and that we were willing to abide by the testimony he might give (Memorandum. Now suppose the squaw had died, no doubt the harmless dose of rhubarb we had administered to her with the humane intention of relieving her sufferings would have been regarded as a poison, and as the cause of her death, hence, I make a note never to give physic to ignorant and superstitious people.) I have no idea that any courier really had been sent from the Waco village, and believe the statement was a mere trick to create feeling against us.

About an hour later a runaway negro from the Choctaw Nation who had escaped and found shelter among the Comanches, and who had been with us a great deal while in their camp, came into our camp and said: "I don't understand much Comanche, but I tink dem Injuns out yonder talk 'bout killin' you fellers, maybe so dey will skin you heads." (Alluding to the scalping operation.) Of course this somewhat startled us, and we sent for our Delaware interpreters, who were at the council, and when they came we told them what the negro had said, but they ridiculed the idea; said the negro did not understand Comanche; there was nothing wrong; that the Indians were talking about making peace, etc. This satisfied us and they returned to the council. Half an hour or so afterwards one of our Delaware hunters, and one we were much attached to, came into our tent, and in that cool, unexcited, stoical manner that marks the Indian character, told us the Comanches were going to kill us. In great alarm we again sent for our Delaware interpreters, and telling them that we were men and not children, demanded to know the truth. Jim Shaw, the chief, replied that they had been desirous to conceal the peril of our situation from us as long as possible, but that what we had heard was true; that all the chiefs who had a right to speak had spoken and that they were unanimous and clamorous for our death; that they, the Delaware interpreters, had made every appeal possible in our behalf; that Acequosh, the Waco chief, had done so likewise; that they had told the council they would die with us; if the Comanches killed us they must kill them too, for that they had promised the Great White Father to take us safely back to Texas; that Texas was their home and they could not return without us. They added that the head chief had not yet spoken; that they did not know how he would go, but even should he be in our favor that his influence would not suffice to save us. We asked them when they thought we would be slaughtered, but they could give us no information on this, and they returned to the council to watch and to give us notice of what might be their final determination.

Soon afterwards our old friend, Acequosh (Old Squash we called him for short) came into the tent where we three lone white men were sitting awaiting our doom, with the big tears rolling down his dear old face, and told us we would shortly be on our way to the happy hunting grounds of the white man; that he had said all he could in our favor; that he had reminded them that his father was once a great chief, the head of a nation who were lords of the prairies, but always the friends of the Comanches; that they used to listen to the counsel of his father, for it was always good, and that they should listen to him even as their fathers had listened to his; that he had told them we were messengers of peace, bore the white flag which all good Indians held to be sacred; that the face of the Great Spirit would be turned away from them and his vengeance follow them should they kill us; but that it was all in vain, we would have to die; that he loved us as his own children and would die with us. God bless the poor old Indian, my heart yearns towards him even after this lapse of time.

It is impossible to describe my feelings and those of my companions. For a moment I was unmanned, weak with a weight on my heart that crushed me. The shock to the nervous system, now that excitement was over, and we were left alone to realize our situation, paralyzed our senses. But with me this did not last long, and I soon rallied, and with the reaction came strength and will, which prepared me to meet the horrible fate awaiting me. The thought, however, was dreadful to die in that lone prairie in the bloom of youth, for I was scarcely twenty-two, and so far from those I loved.

Then came the terrible reflection that I would be tortured to death, and all the stories I had read of the devilish ingenuity of the savage in inflicting tortures upon his victim came fresh to mind, and it was horrible. After some time we began to talk to each other, and found that each had experienced similar feelings. We then calmly discussed our situation; thought of escape—but our horses were miles away, grazing on the prairie; and if saddled before us, how could we hope to escape from a thousand warriors, when we were five hundred miles from the nearest white settlements? Flight was simply impossible. What was left to us? To die like men of our race; and such was our determination. We still had our belt pistols, and we determined to fire one into the advancing crowd that should come to take us—the other into our own brains. Such was our resolve, and I for one would most assuredly have carried it into effect. My pulse beat calmly; the bitterness of death was over, and the man, strong in the attributes of his nature, was ready.

The hours passed slowly. From twelve till four o'clock not a word was spoken in that council; but still they sat, silent and fixed in their determination to execute their helpless visitors, and waiting for the head chief to talk. At last he began. His stentorian voice reached our lonely tent, but no one came to tell us what he said, and of course we could not understand him. Soon other voices were heard, and now and then the voices of our Delaware friends. Then all was confusion—sounds of many voices together. And you may readily imagine how intently we listened to these sounds, not as bringing even for one moment a hope of escape—that was gone—but every nerve was strung to its highest pitch, anticipating the rush and fearful yells that would precede our deaths. I turned to Eldridge and said: "See the setting sun, old fellow—the last we shall see on earth."

Just then steps were heard rapidly approaching. In an instant I was on my feet, a pistol in each hand. Nearer, still nearer, they came. Suspense was overpowering. Ace-quosh burst into the tent and threw himself into the arms of Eldridge. I stood by, feeling sure that the old warrior had come to redeem his promise to die with us. He spoke to us in his native language, of which we did not understand a word. But in a moment I saw that it was joyful, not sorrowful, news he had come to tell us. The next instant our Delawares came in and told us we were saved! Can I ever forget that moment? The news was like the announce-ment of a reprieve to the criminal around whose neck the halter has been fixed. The scene that ensued might be por-trayed, but no language can describe it.

Prostrate upon the earth were the red and white men—creatures of a common brotherhood, typified and made evi-dent that day in that tent in the wilderness. Not a word was spoken—each bowed to the earth; brothers in danger, brothers by that holy electric spark which caused each in that moment, in his own way, to thank the God of his fathers for this great deliverance. Our Delawares told us that the head chief had spoken in our favor; his influence had brought over those of importance, and at the proper time the vote was taken and we were saved.

Henry Earthman.

A MONG those who settled in Fayette county at an early
date, was Henry Earthman, the father of the young
man who bears the same name, and whose sad death
we are about to relate. The early traveler well remembers the old log house which stood some eight miles
north of the town of LaGrange, near the public road, leading out from that place in a northerly direction to the
1840 settlements on the Brazos, and now the direct road
from the town of Lagrange to Ledbetter. We say he
well remembers this old structure, for the reason that it was
well known in those times, that it was here that the weary
traveler could find food and shelter for the night for himself and horse, and enjoy in good old country style the hospitality of a generous pioneer. It was under this hospitable roof that Henry Earthman—the father of the subject of
this sketch—lived. The family consisted of husband and
wife and several children. It was, we think, during the
spring or summer of 1840, that Henry and his brother, Field
Earthman, went out on the range horse hunting. It seems
that some, if not all of the horses, were hoppled, but had
strayed several miles from home, and being seen by some of
the neighbors, they notified the Earthman boys where they
would likely find them. Among the horses which had
strayed off, there was an old gray mare with a bell on.

The animal being hoppled, made it an easy matter for the
Indians to catch her. When Henry and Fields had gotten
some six or eight miles from home on Long Prairie, and in
the neighborhood of where Ashen's store now stands, they
heard the rattling of the old gray mare's bell, and looking
across the prairie in the direction from whence the sound
came, they discovered "old gray" lying down in the tall sedge
grass, as they supposed, to take a rest. One of the boys remarked: "Yonder is old gray," and immediately turned

their course in that direction. When they had approached within a few yards of the animal, imagine their surprise when up sprang a lot of Indians with bows and arrows, which they wielded with telling effect. Henry was killed, whereupon Fields wheeled his horse and ran for life. No one understands the habits and customs of frontier people better than the wily red man. They had discovered that the horses were hoppled, and that they had strayed off from home; and knowing full well that when the owners should ascertain this fact, they would soon be out to hunt them, they conceived the idea of killing the old mare, taking off the bell, and when they discovered the owners hunting them on the prairie, they would rattle the bell to attract their attention. The plan worked well, for the Indians, who, after killing the animal, concealed themselves near by in the tall sedge grass and patiently awaited the approach of the "pale faces." Poor Henry, as we have stated, fell a victim to their well laid trap, but Fields made good his escape. Parties went out in pursuit upon being notified by the brother who made his escape, but the Indians by this time had gotten too much the start to be overtaken. Many of the Earthman family still reside in Fayette county, honored and respected citizens. Isaac Earthman now resides in the little town of Winchester, Fayette county; William, at Hookerville, and Mrs. Gus Kennedy, sister of Isaac, William, Henry and Fields Earthman, resides in Rabbs Pinery, Fayette county.

Colonel Snively's Expedition

IN the spring of 1843, Colonel Jacob Snively obtained permission from the government to raise a force for the purpose of intercepting Armijo, the Governor of New Mexico, who was on his way from Independence, Missouri, to Santa Fe, with a large train loaded with valuable

merchandise. This Armijo was the same villain who had
captured the "Santa Fe expedition" in 1841, and who
1843   had treated with such inhuman barbarity the Texan
prisoners taken on that occasion. The object of the
expedition was to seize him and his train by way of retaliation, for the cruelties and indignities he had heaped upon
the Texans when he had them in his power.

Colonel Snively left Austin with fifty-six men, and proceeded to Georgetown on Red River, where his force was
increased to one hundred and eighty-five. From there he
marched to where the road leading from Independence,
Missouri, to Santa Fe crosses the Red river, and from
thence to the crossing of the Arkansas river, where he
halted and sent out scouts to keep him advised of Armijo's
approach.

While at this place Colonel Snively obtained information
to the effect that a large Mexican force was above, intended
as an escort for Armijo, after the caravan should cross the
river.   Snively at once sent out scouts to ascertain the locality and strength of this force. His scouts found the encampment of the Mexicans, and on their return reported
their number to be between five and six hundred. Sometime afterwards a part of Snively's command encountered a
detachment from this force, killing seventeen or eighteen,
and capturing seventy or eighty prisoners, besides a number of horses, saddles, arms, etc.

As time passed on and nothing was heard from the scouts
sent out by Colonel Snively to notify him of Armijo's approach, the men became discontented, and when they finally
came and reported they had made no discovery, about
seventy of Colonel Snively's men, under command of Captain Eli Chandler, left for home. Colonel Snively then liberated all the Mexican prisoners he had taken at the fight
before mentioned, and furnished their wounded with horses.
He then moved his camp some distance above, on the river,
where he determined to await the arrival of Armijo's caravan and capture it, if possible, after it should cross the river
into Texas. About the thirtieth of June, the scouts he had
sent out to notify him of its approach, came into camp and
reported that Armijo's train was near at hand, escorted by
about two hundred United States dragoons with two pieces

of artillery, under the command of Captain Philip St. George Cooke. The same day Captain Cooke and his command crossed the river (although he had been instructed by the United States government to escort Armijo to the Arkansas river and no further) and planted his artillery in such a position as to sweep the camp occupied by Colonel Snively and his men. He demanded their unconditional surrender in spite of Colonel Snively's protestation that they were upon Texas soil, and as he was anxious to avoid any conflict with United States troops, even if there had been any chance of defending himself, he complied with the demand. Captain Cooke then ordered them to deliver up their arms, but graciously allowed them to retain ten or fifteen guns for their defense in a country filled with hostile Indians and several hundred miles from home. Fortunately, however, before the arms were given up, some of Snively's men were smart enough to conceal their rifles and turn in a number of old scopels and muskets in place of them, taken from the Mexicans in the fight heretofore mentioned. After this gallant achievement Captain Cooke recrossed the river and encamped. Subsequently, however, no doubt realizing the fact, that he had acted in a manner that was not only harsh but unwarranted by the orders of his government, he sent a message to Colonel Snively to the effect that he would escort his men to Independence, Missouri, should they desire to go there. About forty of Colonel Snively's men accepted this gracious invitation and left. A courier was immediately dispatched by Snively to Captain Chandler, requesting him to wait for them. He did so, and a day or so afterwards the two parties were reunited. At that point they encamped and sent out scouts to watch the movements of Armijo's caravan. Three or four days afterwards these scouts returned to camp and stated that the caravan had crossed the river. Some of the men were in favor of pursuing the caravan, while others thought it best to abandon the enterprise altogether and return home. Colonel Snively and about sixty-five others determined to continue the pursuit. They followed the caravan for some days, but when they came up with it they found the escort was too strong to be attacked with any hopes of success by their small force, badly armed as it was, and they turned their course homeward. On their way

home Colonel Snively and his men encamped on a little
stream called Owl creek. He had sixty-three men with him,
but only about one-half of them were armed, and while encamped at this place he was attacked by one or two hundred
Comanches, who stampeded fifty-one head of his horses and
killed two men. The determined resistance of the Texans,
however, soon forced the Indians to fall back. Thirty men,
or all that had arms, mounted and followed them. After a
chase of several miles the Texans overtook the Indians and
a furious contest ensued, which lasted until night put an
end to it. The Texans were then compelled to return to
camp, with the loss of several horses killed and several men
wounded. The loss of the Indians were some ten or fifteen
killed and several wounded. This unlucky affair put an end
to all hopes of capturing Armijo. Had it not been for the
unwarranted interference of Captain Cooke there is no doubt
that Armijo would have been captured and dealt with as he
deserved.

Colonel Snively's Fight at Antelope Creek.

AFTER the fight on Owl creek, Colonel Snively and party
started on back, homeward bound. As previously
stated, he only had sixty-three men in his company,
but only about half of them were armed. After traveling eight or ten days, they halted on Antelope creek, a
small tributary of the Canadian river, for the purpose of
grazing and resting their animals. When they were
1843   to move on again, Colonel Snively ordered his guide,
Mr. James O. Rice, who was an experienced frontiersman, to ride on ahead and keep a sharp lookout for Indians.
Rice was mounted on a little mule about three and a half
feet high   He had gone but a few hundred yards when he
came to a deep, boggy ravine. He had a long staking rope
tied to the mule's neck. He dismounted, and holding the
end of the rope in his hand he drove the animal across, and

then began to look for a place where he could cross himself. While thus occupied he discovered five Indians coming down the path he had just traveled. They did not observe Rice, and four of them crossed over on a log below him, and the fifth, in attempting to cross at another place bogged down and was unable, at least for a time, to extricate himself. As soon as the four Indians who crossed over on the log discovered the mule, they ran forward and caught hold of the rope, while Rice was holding on to the other end of it. Both parties struggled to get possession of the mule, and no doubt the superior numbers of the Indians would have prevailed if the mule, with the perversity of its kind, had not sided with the weaker party. With a sudden plunge it broke loose from the Indians and started back towards Rice. The moment the mule broke away from them, the Indians began to let drive their arrows at Rice as thick as hail, and at the same instant he heard a volley of firearms in the direction of camp, and he knew that an attack had been made upon the company. With Indians behind and Indians shooting at him in front, Rice was compelled to let go his mule, which he did, and fly to a small dogwood thicket about a hundred yards distant. This he succeeded in reaching unhurt, although the arrows were whizzing past his head every step he took.

By this time the four Indians had recrossed the ravine, and they watched the thicket for more than an hour, expecting to catch Rice as he came out, but knowing he was armed, they were afraid to enter it. All this while a furious battle was going on at camp between three or four hundred Comanches, and the little band of Texans under the command of Colonel Snively, but the Indians finding they could not drive them from their position, at length withdrew, for a time.

When the firing ceased, Rice crept cautiously from the thicket, and seeing no Indians, he started towards camp. On his way he discovered an Indian boy sitting on his pony, and evidently acting the part of a spy. Rice concluded he would stop long enough to put an end to the existence of this young warrior. He raised his gun to his shoulder—one of the old flint lock style, took deliberate aim—and didn't fire. The young Indian hearing the gun snap, looked around and discovered Rice. He immediately put whip to his animal and went off at a speed that was quite astonishing, considering the broken character of the ground. Captain Rice then proceeded to camp, where he was met by his comrades with shouts of welcome, for his mule had returned riderless, and they supposed he had been killed. A little while afterwards, the Indians renewed their attack on the camp with greater fury than ever, but finally they were so much worsted that they ceased firing, and their chief advanced alone in front of their lines, and called out "popatino," meaning Americans. Colonel Snively answered him in Spanish, and asked him what he wanted. The chief replied they wanted to quit fighting, make friends, and have a big smoke. To this Colonel Snively agreed, and proposed that four from each side should meet half way between their positions for the purpose of having the desired "talk." The proposition was accepted, and Colonel Snively and three others went out and had a "confab" with the like number of Indians. They professed a wish to cease fighting and be good friends, and Colonel Snively told them that he was perfectly willing to be friends, and would only fight in self defense. They all then had a "big smoke" together, and separated. But the Texans had not much more than reached their camp, when the treacherous Indians made a sudden charge upon them, hoping, no doubt, that their professions of friendship had thrown them off their guard. But the Texans stood firm, and made every shot count one more of the enemy slain. The Indians were again repulsed with heavy loss and withdrew, carrying their dead and wounded with them. The cry of "popatino" was again heard. and answered by Colonel Snively. Another parley ensued, after which another treacherous onset was made upon the Texans, but was once more gallantly repulsed. The Indians then went off out of sight, and did not make their appearance again until sunset, when the Indian chief hailed the Texans, and said: "We all now go to sleep—you go to sleep, and in the morning we get up—all have big smoke and all go home."

To this Colonel Snively agreed. After a little while the chief called out, "All your men asleep?" "No, answered

THE MULE SIDED WITH HIS MASTER.

56

Colonel Snively, "but they soon will be." "My men all asleep," replied the chief.

Colonel Snively knowing well that the object of the Indians was to delay him until they could receive reinforcements, for which, no doubt, they had despatched couriers, determined to leave the dangerous locality as soon as possible. He therefore ordered his men to mount their horses and march off as quietly as they could. But at the crossing of the creek the ground was very rocky, and the Ind ans heard the rattling of the horses hoofs as they passed over.

The Indians knew at once that Colonel Snively and his men were retreating, and they made a final charge on them; but by the time they came up, the Texans had taken a strong position, and drove them back out of gun shot.

When all became quiet once more, Colonel Snively ordered his faithful guide, Captain Rice, to pass over the creek alone at the best crossing he could find, and that each m·n should follow him one at a time, until all were over. The strictest silence was enjoined while the movement was going on. Colonel Snively stood sentinel himself whilst his men were crossing the creek. As soon as they had gained the opposite side of Antelope creek, where the ground was smooth and free from stone, Colonel Snively ordered the men to follow Captain Rice at double quick time. When they had gone, perhaps, a mile, they heard the chief calling out to them again, but this time there was no answering voice, and the Indians then discovered that they had been out generaled—that the birds had flown.

When they realized the fact that their coveted prey had escaped, they made the night hideous with their terrific yells, and scattered around in every direction trying to find the route the fugitives had taken.

Captain Rice led the men into a deep, narrow canon, having a smooth surface well coated with grass, over which they could pass swiftly without making any noise. When the Texans reached the head of this canon, about two miles from where they started, they could hear the Indians thundering down the valley of the creek, in hot pursuit of them —but all to no purpose. Colonel Snively and his men traveled all night, and at day light they reached a place called Cotton Wood Island, where they halted in a strong position. But the Indians did not follow them—at least they saw nothing more of them.

The loss of the Indians in the many charges they made upon the Texans in the fight, must have been very great, for although the Texans had but one gun for every two men, they were far superior to the bows and arrows of the Indians.

The Texans' loss, owing to the strength of the position they held, was exceedingly small—only a few being wounded and none seriously.

The San Marcos Fight of The Burlesons.

THE traveler who passes San Marcos will see north of the road, perched on the high bluff which overlooks the San Marcos head spring a rude log house, built by General Burleson when he was at that place, the outside settler. Hither came, from time to time, Placido, the Tonkawa chief, and his son, who were the friends of Burleson. Placido was a lithe, active Indian, every 1848 inch a warrior, who boasted that he had never shed the blood of a white man. When Placido made with his squaws his annual visit, General Burleson, who valued his services to Austin's early settlers, always made him presents of ammunition and sometimes of ponies. During one of his visits in 1848 Placido and his son were sitting down in Burleson's family room at his San Marcos spring house, conversing with General Burleson and his son Ed, who was about the age of the younger Indian. About nine o'clock at night what seemed to be the hooting of an owl was heard. Placido, whose quick ear detected the cheat, rose instantly and covered up the blazing fire with ashes, at the same time whispering the word "Comanche." As soon as all had been made dark he crawled upon the floor to the door and disappeared in the darkness. Quickly returning he whispered to Burleson: "Scurry stole, Comanche steal 'em."

Scurry was the name of a splendid horse presented to General Burleson by his friend, General Dick Scurry, a horse
ridden by Scurry at the battle of Monterey. Fortunately,
in a small stockade adjoining the house, were the horses of
Placido and two other horses belonging to the General.
Though it was quite dark these were quickly saddled and
the Burlesons, with young Placido, followed the old Indian
chief noiselessly around the mountain. Those who have
been on that mountain will remember the level space
near its summit, which belted it for more than a mile,
varying from twenty to sixty feet wide, on which no bushes
grew, while on each side was the dense cedar brake, through
which no horseman could ride at night. Placido led the way
in this open space, for he knew every foot of the mountain
and the openings that led to the head of the Blanco as well
as the Comanches. In about half an hour the moon rose
and Placido quickened the pursuit, sometimes through
dense brush, where the rider could not see an arm's length
before him and then suddenly emerging in an open glade.
The pursuit was continued without a word being spoken
until after day break. The Comanches never dreaming that
pursuers were on their trail had gone leisurely along until
just before sun up, when they were crossing an open prairie,
the pursuers were discovered close behind them. Then began the race for life. There were three Indians, one rode
Scurry and the others were mounted on ponies. Burleson's
heavy weight, for he had then become corpulent, gave Placido and the two boys an advantage in the race, for he fell
behind. The rider of Scurry could have escaped, but he remained in the chase close by his companions, though in the
lead. As Placido and the two young men approached near
the Comanches General Burleson shouted, "big beef for
Scurry, Placido, big beef for Scurry." Placido was slightly
wounded by an arrow from one of the rear Indians, both of
whom were quickly slain, when the rider of Scurry stood at
bay and was killed by a lance thrust by the Tonkawa chief,
when the horse was taken back unhurt. The combatants
were few, but seldom was ever a race ridden on Texas soil
with more desperate resolve or more tragic end.

Captain York's Fight.

ON the eighth of October, 1848, a party of Indians came down the Cibolo river and entered Gonzales county. On their way down the Cibolo they came across and murdered the little son of the Reverend John S. Mc-Gehee, a Methodist minister. Near the settlements on the Sandies in the western part of the county they encountered Doctor George Barnett, who was out deer hunting, 1848 and finally succeeded in killing him, though it was evident he had made a determined resistance. It appears he had only been wounded at first, and afterwards that he had taken his position in some thick brush, from which the Indians were unable to dislodge him, and there subsequently died from the effects of the wound he had received. It was evident the Indians had retreated before he died, as otherwise they would have scalped him and taken his gun. He had apparently been dead about two days when his body was found. About this time another party of Indians, probably belonging to the same band, crossed the San Antonio river and struck the Cibolo lower down the country. On their route they had killed Mr. Lockhart and a young man by the name of Vivian near where the road from San Antonio to Goliad crosses the Ecleto creek. Subsequently this upper and lower band formed a junction, and the entire force then amounted to about forty warriors.

To pursue and chastise this band of raiders and murderers, a company was raised in DeWitt county, consisting mainly of inexperienced young men and boys, and placed under the command of Captain John York, an old soldier who had distinguished himself at the storming of San Antonio in 1835. Some thirty miles above Goliad Captain York struck the Indian trail going in a southerly course towards the mouth of the Escondido creek, one of the tributaries of the San Antonio river. This trail they followed as rapidly as possible, and after a forced march of about twenty hours, their intrepid spy, Captain Tumlinson, who had been sent ahead to reconnoiter, returned and reported that the Indians were encamped on the Escondido creek.

Hoping to take them by surprise, Captain York and his men pushed ahead, but the Indians discovered their approach in time to take a strong position in some thick brush from whence they opened fire upon Captain Tumlinson, who, with a few men, was in advance of the others. They returned the fire, but Captain Tumlinson called out to Captain York, telling him it was impossible to hold his position against the Indians, protected, as they were, by the thick brush in which they were concealed. Captain York then ordered him to fall back to a mott of timber about sixty yards from where the Indians had taken position. This was done, but the retrograde movement, together with the diabolical yells of the Indians, caused a panic among the inexperienced young men, who had never before been under fire, and it was with difficulty that a portion of them were rallied at the mott. A fight at "long taw" then ensued, lasting about an hour, during which three brave Texans lost their lives—Captain York, James Bell, his son-in-law, and a man by the name of Sykes. The latter was killed in open ground whilst advancing upon the thicket where the Indians were concealed, and two of them rushed out for the purpose of scalping him, but both were immediatly shot down. Finally, however, it seems that both parties got tired of fighting about the same time, the Indians leaving their position in the thicket and going up the creek, whilst the Texans moved a short distance below.

J. Floyd.

SOME time in the year 1835, Mr. Floyd in company with two others were traversing a section of country between the Trinity and Sabine rivers.

On their way they discovered a small party of Indians some distance in their rear, who were evidently fol-

lowing them. The Indians very gradually approached
them, no doubt to induce Floyd and his companions
1835 to believe they were not in pursuit of them until they
were in a short distance, when on looking both to
their right and left they discovered they were flanked by
other parties of Indians they had not previously noticed.

As soon as they made this discovery Floyd and his companions put spurs to their horses and went off at full speed.
Before them there was a long level prairie, on which, about
three miles distant, was the house to which they were going.
The Indians who were flanking them endeavored to get
ahead of them to prevent them from reaching the house.
Floyd alone was riding a good horse. His two companions
were mounted on very inferior animals, which, when within
a mile of the house, began to fail rapidly.

Floyd, seeing there was no chance for them to escape, reluctantly left his two companions and urged his horse as
fast as possible towards the house. At the foot of the hill
on which the house was situated there was a deep ravine,
and when he came to it he drove the spurs into his horse,
leaped it and gained the opposite bank in safety—a feat, he
said, he could not possibly have performed if a troop of yelling savages had not been following closely at his heels.

After he had crossed the ravine the Indians fired at him a
number of times but without effect and Floyd made his way
safely to the house. There was no person in the house but
a woman and he asked her if she had any bullets. "No,"
said she, "but I can soon run some," and she did. Floyd
said he never saw bullets moulded as fast in his life as they
were by this woman when she heard the Indians shooting
and yelling outside.

One of Floyd's companions reached the ravine a little
ahead of the Indians, and knowing it would be impossible for
his wearied animal to leap it, he quickly dismounted and
made his way across on foot. As he rose to the opposite bank
the Indians fired a volley at him but fortunately none of their
shots took effect and he also made his way safely to the
house. But the other poor fellow's horse failed completely
before he reached the ravine. He was overtaken, surrounded and shot and speared to death. The Indians did

not venture to cross the ravine, as they knew it would bring them within rifle range of the house.

Whilst Floyd and his companion were watching their maneuvers around the man they had killed, they were startled by cries for help from some one in the distance, and looking in the direction of the sounds, they discovered a white man coming at full speed on horseback, closely followed by half a dozen Indians. Seeing the perilous condition of this man, they quickly remounted their wearied horses and started out as fast as the poor animals could go to his assistance. As soon as the Indians saw the two men coming from the house, armed with guns, they came to a halt, and the man they were pursuing reached the ravine dismounted and gained the opposite bank in safety. It seems he was riding the range in search of stock when the Indians discovered him, and he also had turned his course towards the house; but the Indians no doubt would have overtaken and killed him if Floyd and his companion had not come to his assistance.

The three men returned to the house to prepare for its defense, supposing the Indians were in such force that they would make an attack on it; but they did not venture to do so, and finally went off with the three horses they had captured and the scalp of the poor fellow they had killed.

Captain John S. Sutton.

CAPTAIN SUTTON was a native of the State of New York. About 1836, whilst yet but a youth, he came to Texas, and from that time until his death, at the battle of Val Verde, in New Mexico, he was almost continuously in the service of the State. During what is known as the Cherokee war he commanded a company, and was present at the last decisive battle with the Cherokees, 1836 in which the head chief, Bowles, and many of his men were slain, and the survivors driven beyond the limits of the Republic.

Captain Sutton subsequently settled at the city of Austin, which was his home for a number of years. In every expedition that was organized at Austin to protect the frontier against Indians and Mexicans he was always among the first to proffer his services.

When it was determined by the authorities to send a force to take possession of New Mexico, Sutton obtained a commission as captain and raised a company for the expedition. On their way to Santa Fe the Texans were surrounded by a large body of Mexican cavalry, and finally surrendered. Previous to the surrender, the Texan officers held a consultation, in which the majority, believing it impossible to contend successfully against such odds, were in favor of capitulating. Sutton was strenuously opposed to surrendering upon any terms, but his advice was overruled. The Texans were taken prisoners, marched to Santa Fe, and from thence to the City of Mexico. Many died on the way from hardships and exposure and want of sufficient food and clothing. Several were brutally bayoneted by their guard, merely because they were unable from physical weakness to keep up with their more robust companions.

On their arrival at the City of Mexico, the prisoners were set to work on the public buildings and fortifications. Whilst at work, one day, Sutton said or did something that displeased the sergeant of the guard, who struck him a severe blow with the flat of his sabre. He instantly grasped the sword, wrenched it from the sergeant's hand and broke it across his knee. This act of insubordination infuriated the sergeant, and he commanded his guard to bayonet Sutton on the spot; and no doubt this would have been done if, fortunately for Sutton, an officer who had witnessed the whole affair had not just then come up and ordered the guard to desist. He reprimanded the sergeant for his brutal conduct, and told Sutton to go to his quarters. From that time and until the prisoners were liberated and sent back to the United States, Sutton was never compelled to perform any manual labor.

He returned to Texas, and when the war between Mexico and the United States broke out he enlisted in Colonel Jack Hays's regiment of mounted volunteers, with which he served until it was disbanded after the battle of Monterey.

Shortly after he came back to Texas, a call was made for volunteers to go to the assistance of General Taylor, known as the "Curtis call," under which Governor P. H. Bell raised a mounted regiment of Texans. Sutton joined this regiment, and was elected captain of one of the companies. The regiment marched to the Rio Grande, but on their arrival there General Taylor ordered Governor Bell to station it along the frontier to protect the settlers against Indians and Mexicans. That this was effectually done, it is only necessary to say that until Governor Bell's regiment of rangers was disbanded (and for months afterward) not one scalp was taken within the limits of Texas.

When the civil war began, Captain Sutton, although a Northern man, promptly took sides with his adopted State. I do not know in what capacity he entered the service, but when he was killed at the battle of Val Verde, in New Mexico, he was the lieutenant colonel of his regiment. In that battle his leg was shattered by a grape shot. The surgeon who attended him told him his life could not be saved unless the wounded limb was amputated. But Sutton would not permit him to perform the operation, saying, "he did not intend to hobble round the balance of his days on one leg, and that when his leg went that he would go with it."

Many a chivalrous son of Texas has given his life in her defense, but none more brave or more true and loyal to his country ever died on the battlefield than Captain John S. Sutton.

The last Legislature (1887) gave his name to one of the newly created counties.

Colonel H. L. Kinney.

AMONG the many marked and original characters who have figured in Texas none perhaps deserve a more conspicuous place than Colonel Kinney. He was a a Northern man, but we do not know the particular State of his nativity. He emigrated to Texas about the

close of the war with Mexico when quite a young man, and
in 1838 he settled on the Corpus Christi bay, at the
1838 place where the thriving city of Corpus Christi now
stands.   He established a trading house there, which
was long known to Texans as Kinney's Ranch.

As he was a man of indomitable energy and enterprise
he accumulated means enough in a few years to enable him
to control most of the trade from Mexico and from all the
towns of any importance along the Rio Grande.

In a country where horsemanship was almost a universal
accomplishment Colonel Kinney was noted for his equestrian
performances.   He always kept on hand for his own use a
number of the best blooded horses that could be had in
Texas, and in his frequent journeys over the State, it was
well known that it was no unusual thing with him to ride
one hundred miles without dismounting in less than twenty-
four hours.

In 1844 a great riding match came off at San Antonio between Colonel Hays's Texas Rangers, fifty Comanche warriors and some Mexican rancheros   The performance took
place on what was then a smooth open prairie just west of
San Pedro creek, and all the officers of the garrison with
their families and all the citizens of San Antonio assembled
at the appointed time to witness it.

I had seen what I thought to be many astonishing equestrian performances in the ring but none of them could compare with those I witnessed that day on the prairie near
San Antonio.   The Comanches were famous riders and so
were the Mexican rancheros, and some of Hays's rangers
were fully equal if not superior to them.   Judges were appointed to determine upon the merits of the performances
and quite a number of valuable prizes were distributed on
the occasion.   The first prize for horsemanship was awarded
to John McMullen, one of Hays's Texas rangers, and the
second to Colonel H. L. Kinney, who was a competitor.
The third, I think, was awarded to a Comanche Indian.

For several years Kinney's Ranch, on Corpus Christi bay,
was the extreme frontier settlement on the southwest, and
as it was exposed to frequent raids by the Indians, Colonel
Kinney and his employes had many contests with them.
He was one of those cool and fearless men who are espe-

cially fitted by nature for a life of wild adventure, and his many exploits among the Indians would afford material for a most interesting narrative. We will give one instance as a fair sample of others.

The Comanche Indians are (or perhaps I should say were) one of the most warlike tribes on the American continent, and were greatly dreaded by Americans, Mexicans and other Indians. Seventeen of these warlike savages, under one of their chiefs, on one occasion attacked some houses near Colonel Kinney's ranch, and after killing or driving off the inmates, they hastily retreated.

Colonel Kinney, in company with eleven others, mounted upon their fleetest horses and gave immediate pursuit. After going a few miles they overtook the Indians on an open prairie. Both parties dismounted, and began the fight at a distance less than fifty yards. Each individual on both sides singled out his particular antagonist and did his best to destroy him. After the fight had continued for some time in this way, Santa Anna, the Indian chief, suddenly dashed to the front, and holding his shield of buffalo hide before him, he ran along the line of his opponents. The whites all fired at him, but their balls only rattled harmlessly on his tough rawhide shield.

The object of this bold maneuver was soon apparent. The chief having drawn the fire of his antagonists, the Indians rushed upon the whites before they had time to reload their guns. Colonel Kinney alone succeeded in mounting his horse before the Indians, with spears and tomahawks in their hands, were upon them. One of the whites was instantly killed, and another was speared and shot in several places with arrows. A young Mexican, a clerk of Colonel Kinney's, was speared and had his horse killed under him, which he had finally succeeded in mounting. The Colonel dragged the young Mexican up behind him on his own horse. Just at that juncture an Indian stuck his spear with such force into the Mexican's body that the blade went entirely through it and wounded Colonel Kinney in the back, and at the same moment a second Indian aimed a blow at the Colonel which missed him, but went through both sleeves of his buckskin hunting shirt. Whilst he was endeavoring to extricate himself from the spear, a third Indian rushed upon them and drove his spear through the bowels of the unfortunate Mexican youth behind him, who relaxed his hold and fell dead from the horse—but not unavenged, for Colonel Kinney instantly turned upon his assailant, drew a pistol from his holster and shot him dead on the spot.

All this while similar contests were going on between other Indians and Colonel Kinney's men, but at length finding that this hand to hand conflict was a losing game to them, the Indians sullenly withdrew from the field, leaving seven of their warriors dead on the ground, and there is but little doubt that the remaining ten were all more or less severely wounded. Of the eleven white men engaged in this fight, three were killed and all the rest wounded.

Certainly taking into consideration the small number of both parties, this was one of the hardest and most obstinately contested fights that ever took place between the whites and Indians on the Texas frontiers.

The great error of Colonel Kinney and his men was in shooting simultaneously at the chief, Santa Anna, protected as he was by his tough rawhide shield, which was impenetrable by the round balls in use at that day. Many Texans have lost their lives by imprudently wasting their shots on such shields. But since the introduction of improved fire arms and the conical ball, the Indians generally have laid them aside as useless incumbrances.

When the war broke out between the United States and Mexico, Corpus Christi became a rendezvous for troops and a depot of supplies. Whilst that State of affairs existed there, Colonel Kinney's energy and enterprise enabled him to take advantage of it, and he reaped a rich harvest. When the troops moved onward into Mexico, he accompained them, and accumulated a large fortune, through favorable contracts for supplying them with beef cattle, forage, etc.

After the war ended, he added greatly to it by buying up at nominal prices, Government teams, wagons, and other public property sold at auction where there were but few if any other bidders, which he afterwards disposed of in Texas at a handsome profit.

I can not vouch for its truth, but at the close of the war with Mexico, it was generally supposed that Colonel Kin-

ney was one of the wealthiest men in Texas; and certainly
he lived in a style that would lead one to suppose he thought
so himself. He seemed to think that his "strong box"
was like the widow's cruse, and that it would replenish
itself automatically whenever it was emptied. He built a
fine residence at Corpus Christi where he kept open house
for his friends and all comers, and a retinue of retainers
about him who were generally paid high salaries for doing
nothing.

Some time after the close of the war he married a
daughter of Judge James Webb, one of the most able law-
yers who ever practiced at the bar in Texas, and subsequently he represented his section for several terms in the
State Legislature, with credit to himself. The advancement of Corpus Christi was an especial hobby with the
Colonel, and he expended money without stint in building
tanks, wharves and warehouses, and otherwise improving
the place. Among other improvements he had an artesian
well bored to the depth of several hundred feet within the
city, from which I believe there is yet flowing a stream of
beautiful water, clear as crystal.

An old friend of mine—an acquaintance of Colonel Kinney—in furnishing me with a sketch of the life and character of the latter, gives quite an interesting and ludicrous
description of his first experience with this artesian water,
and at the risk of offending some of the good people who
now reside in Corpus Christi, I will conclude this narative in
the language of my friend. He says: "But unfortunately this
water is a veritable whited sepulchre, beautiful to the sight,
but salts and senna to the taste." Some of the citizens of Corpus Christi, however, assert that this water is a cure for all
the ills that flesh is heir to, and I believe them, for certainly
a few draughts of it would either cure or kill, and in either
event disease would be eradicated effectually; and here,
though somewhat out of place, I will venture to relate a
little incident descriptive of my first introduction to this
artesian well.

One very hot day many years ago I reached Corpus Christi
tired and thirsty after a hard day's travel on horseback,
and espying a clear sparkling stream of water pouring from
the well I rode up to the door of a neighboring house in

which a man was standing and asked him if he would loan me a cup to get a drink. He replied, "certainly," and when he handed me the cup I thought I saw a quizzical smile on his face, but at the time I did not suspect the cause of it. I rode up to the well, dismounted, placed the cup beneath the stream of clear, crystal water, and when it was full I hastily gulped down the whole contents, for I was very hot and thirsty. My first impression was that I had been struck by lightning, but as there was no cloud in sight I concluded I had been merely poisoned by an infernal mixture brewed in the depths of the earth by some malicious gnome. I was clawing wildly and frantically at my neck and going through various other undignified motions in my agony, when I happened to cast my eyes towards the door in which the man who had loaned me the cup had been standing. He was still there, but leaning doubled up against the door sill apparently in the last stages of uncontrolable laughter. He had evidently been watching my proceedings the whole time in expectation of the denouement. I quickly remounted my horse, returned him the cup I had borrowed, and then with tears in my eyes inquired of him the nearest way to the nearest drug store. When he had given me the desired information as well as he could between his paroxysms, I hurried to the nearest drug store, bought a bottle of Number Six, swallowed its contents, and then tapered off with three or four doses of cold pressed castor oil before I could get rid of the farewell left by that artesian water.

Since then I have often wondered that the citizens of Corpus Christi have not long ere this erected a monument to the memory of Colonel Kinney, not because he was the founder of their city, but because he has furnished them with an ample supply of the most economical water in the world, one drink of which will satisfy a man for a life time.

By his extravagant mode of living, his profuse hospitality and the money he expended in improving his town, Colonel Kinney in a very few years ran through the greater portion of the large fortune he had accumulated. When all was gone, he left Texas and went to Mexico, as he said, for the purpose of retrieving his fallen fortunes, and knowing him as well as I did, his indomitable energy and perseverence, I have but little doubt he would have succeeded in doing so had he lived a few years longer. But shortly after he went to Mexico one of those periodical local revolutions occurred, for which our sister Republic is somewhat famous, and as Colonel Kinney was not one to stand idly by when a fight was going on, he was easily induced to take sides, and was killed in some trifling skirmish that took place between the contending factions.

Colonel Kinney had his faults, possibly some glaring ones, and the one who has not let him be the first to throw a stone at his memory, but they were largely counterbalanced by many sterling qualities. He was a brave man, staunch to his friends and loyal and true to his adopted State, in defense of which he was always ready to peril his life. His generosity was unbounded, his purse was always at the service of the needy, and no one ever applied to him for aid who did not get more than he asked.

When the news of his death reached his numerous friends and acquaintances in Texas, I will venture to say there was not one among them who did not sincerely regret his untimely fate.

Colonel Jack Hays.

AMONG the many noted Indian fighters who have figured in the border wars of Texas none perhaps hold a more conspicuous place than Colonel Jack Hays, the subject of this little sketch. He was a native, I believe, of Tennessee, and came to Texas when quite a young man some time previous to its annexation to the United States. He brought with him letters of recommenda-

1841 tion from prominent people to President Houston, who, not long after his arrival in this country, gave him a commission to raise a ranging company for the protection of the western frontier. This company was, I believe, the first regularly organized one in the service of the country, at least in the west. With this small company, for it never numbered more than three score men, Colonel Hays effectually protected a vast scope of frontier country, reaching from Corpus Christi, on the gulf, to the head waters of the Frio and Nueces rivers.

It may seem incredible to those not acquainted with the facts that one small company of rangers should have been able to protect such an extended frontier against Indians and marauding parties of Mexicans. But it must be borne in mind that this small company was usually divided into squads of ten or twelve men each, who were almost always constantly in the saddle scouting over all parts of the country, and consequently the Indians never knew where or at what moment one of these squads would pounce down upon them. And besides the rangers had so much the superiority of them in arms and horses that one of them was fully equal on any ground to five or six Indians, armed as they were at that time with only bows and arrows or old flint and steel guns still less effective.

Shortly after the invention of the five shooter by Colonel Colt he furnished the navy of Texas, under contract with the government, with fifty or sixty of these improved fire arms. Subsequently, as it was supposed they were more needed on the frontier than in the navy, they were turned over (or at least a portion of them), to Colonel Hays's ranging company. With these improved fire arms in their hands, then unknown to the Indians and Mexicans, I have not exaggerated in the least in stating as I have done that one ranger was a fair match for five or six Mexicans or Indians.

Colonel Hays was especially fitted by nature for this frontier service. He was a man rather under the medium size, but wiry and active and gifted with such an iron constitution that he was enabled to undergo hardship and exposure without perceptible effect, which would have placed the majority of men completely *hors de combat.* I have frequently seen him sitting by his camp fire at night in some exposed locality, when the rain was falling in torrents, or a cold norther with sleet or snow was whistling about his ears, apparently as unconscious of all discomfort as if he had been seated in some cosy room of a first class city hotel;

and this, perhaps, when all he had eaten for supper was a hand full of pecans or a piece of hard tack. But above all, he was extremely cautious where the safety of his men was concerned, but when it was a mere question of personal danger his bravery bordered closely on rashness.

When the war between the United States and Mexico broke out Colonel Hays was elected to the command of a regiment of Texas mounted volunteers, and at the storming of Monterey he and his regiment rendered effective service. Some time after the conclusion of the war he moved to the State of California, where he died several years ago; but his name has not been forgotten by the people of Texas, and will long be a household word among them.

As an appropriate place for them, I will herein relate a few of his battles with the Indians when in command of his ranging company, and also one or two of his personal exploits.

In the fall of 1840, a party of Comanche Indians numbering about two hundred came into the vicinity of San Antonio, stole a great many horses and made their way off toward the Guadalupe river.

Colonel Hays with about twenty of his men followed in pursuit of them. He overtook this formidable force at the crossing of the Guadalupe river. The Colonel, who was riding in front, as he usually did, was the first to discover the enemy. He rode back to his men and said "Yonder are the Indians, boys, and yonder are our horses; the Indians are pretty strong, but we can whip them, and recapture the horses; what do you say?" "Go ahead," the boys replied, "and we'll follow if there's a thousand of them." "Come on then, boys," said Hays, and putting spurs to their horses, this little band of twenty men boldly charged two hundred warriors who were waiting for them, drawn up in battle array.

Seeing the small number of their assailants, the Indians, made sure of victory, but in this they were badly mistaken, for the Texans charged them so furiously, firing a volley into their midst as they did so, that their line of battle was thrown into confusion. For a while, however, they stood their ground, and strove to overwhelm the Texans by mere force of numbers, but at length their braves began to

fall so rapidly before the continuous fire poured upon them
that they wavered and commenced to give way. At this
juncture their head chief while endeavoring to rally them,
received a fatal shot and fell dead from his horse. The fall
of the chief completely discouraged them and the retreat
soon became a total rout, each one fleeing for his life before
the victorious Texans.

Colonel Hays and his men pursued the retreating enemy
vigorously for several miles, inflicting still further loss upon
them and recapturing the greater portion of the stolen
animals.

It was for such feats of personal prowess and daring as
the following that Colonel Hays received from them the
appellation of "Capitan Yack" (Captain Jack.)

In the fall of 1841, he was one of a party of fifteen or
twenty men employed to survey some lands near what is
called by the Indians "The Enchanted Rock." This rock
forms the apex of a high round hill very difficult to climb.
In the center of this rock there is a circular hollow sufficiently large to allow a small party of men to lie in it, and
i.s perpendicular sides formed an effective breastwork.
While the surveyors were engaged in work not far from the
base of this hill, they were attacked by a party of Indians.

At the time the attack was made, Colonel Hays, who was
at some distance from the rest of his companions, ran up
this hill and took his position on the top in the little hollow
we have mentioned, determined to sell his life at the "highest market price." He was well known to the Indians, and
they were anxious, if possible, to get possession of his scalp.
They mounted the hill, surrounded the rock and prepared
to charge him. Hays was well aware that his life depended
more upon tact and strategy than mere courage, and he resolved to reserve his fire as the last alternative.

The Indians rushed towards him, hoping to draw his fire
when they were yet at such a distance as to render it in-
effective, but the Colonel was too wily to be caught in any
such trap, and all he did was "to lay low and keep dark,"
and whenever the Indians came near enough to see the
muzzle of his gun protruding from the walls of his little
fortress their hearts would fail them and they would fall
back. Several times they repeated this maneuver but always

CAPTAIN JACK HAYS.

with the same result, for the Colonel was reserving his fire until they should come to close quarters, when he could make every shot tell. Finding there was no prospect of obtaining the Colonel's scalp without running some risk to get it, the Indians made a charge upon his little fortress in earnest. The Colonel cooly waited their approach until they were so near that he could see the whites of their eyes when he suddenly rose up, presented his rifle, fired at the foremost Indian, who fell dead in his tracks. The others, thinking he had his revolver in reserve (and in fact he had two of them) halted for a moment and then fell back again, giving the Colonel time to reload his gun. At length, however, seeemingly furious at being kept at bay in this manner by a single man, the Indians made another charge upon him, yelling loudly as they came on. But as far as their yelling was concerned they might just as well have saved their breath, for the Colonel had been too often in the woods to be frightened by the hooting of owls. He let them advance until they came even nearer than they had been before, when he "upped" one of them with his gun, and then seizing his revolvers he emptied their contents so rapidly among the others that they hastily fell back again. Just at this moment his companions, who, all this while, had been fighting the main body of the Indians and at length had compelled them to retreat, hearing the firing at the summit of the enchanted rock, and suspecting the cause of it, hastened to the Colonel's relief.

As soon as the Indians, who were beleaguring him in his little fortress, saw them coming, they retreated, dragging with them their wounded comrades, but leaving the dead behind. The surveys finished their work without any further interruption from the Indians.

In the year 1844 Colonel Hays, with fifteen of his company, was out on a scout, the object of which was to discover the rendezvous or haunts of certain bands of Indians who had recently been raiding the settlements. When about eighty miles distant from San Antonio, near the Perdenales river, they came in sight of fifteen Comanches, who were mounted on good horses and apparently eager for battle.

As Colonel Hays and his men advanced towards them, the Indians slowly drew off in the direction of a thick growth of underwood, which convinced the Colonel that the Indians they saw were but a portion of a larger party who were concealed in the thicket. He therefore restrained the ardor of his men, who were anxious to charge upon those they saw; and, taking a circuitous route around the thicket, he drew up his little force on a ridge, with a deep ravine between them and the Indians. The Colonel was satisfied the Indians were in such force they would make the attack, and he wanted to secure an advantageous position or to choose his own way of beginning the fight.

Finding they had failed to draw the rangers into the trap they had set for them, the Indians then showed themselves to the number of seventy-five. As soon as they did so, Colonel Hays moved his men slowly down the ridge until they reached the ravine, where they were concealed from view by the thick bushes that grew along the bank. When they reached this point the rangers started at a full gallop, turned the ridge and gained the enemy's rear. The Indians, who were watching the place on the opposite side of the ravine where they had last seen them, had no intimation of their danger until they were startled by the sharp reports of a dozen rifles in their rear.

This created some confusion among the Indians, but they soon rallied and made a furious charge upon the rangers. To resist this, Colonel Hays formed his men in a square and ordered them to draw their five shooters. The Indians charged on all sides and fought bravely for a while, but after twenty-one of their warriors had fallen before the rapid fire of the five shooters, the remainder drew back. Colonel Hays then charged them in turn, and the fight was renewed. The battle lasted nearly an hour, both parties advancing and retreating alternately. At last the ammunition of the rangers was exhausted and their fire slackened. The chief, perceiving this, rallied his warriors for a final effort. As they were advancing, Colonel Hays discovered that the rifle of one of the rangers (Mr. Gillespie) was still loaded. He ordered him to dismount at once and shoot the chief. Gillespie did so, and at the report of his gun the chief dropped dead from his horse. This so demoralized the Indians that they fell back again and made no further attempt to charge the rangers.

In this fight two rangers were killed and five wounded. Thirty of the Indians were left dead on the field. For good generalship, as well as for the cool, unflinching bravery of Colonel Hays and his rangers, and great disparity of numbers, etc., this fight is certainly one of the most remarkable that has ever occurred in Indian warfare.

In 1845 a large party of Indians, to the number of two or three hundred, made a descent on the settlements west of San Antonio. After killing some people and stealing a large number of horses, they left for their mountain rendezvous. Colonel Hays having received information of this raid, went in pursuit of the Indians, determined, if possible, to overtake them, and by a forced march he came up with them near the Frio river. The Indians numbered between two and three hundred, as previously stated, whilst Colonel Hays had but forty two men.

When the Indians saw the small number of rangers they had to contend against, they immediately drew up in line of battle and waited for the attack. Hays and his men were not in the least intimidated by the superior numbers of the enemy, and without waiting to form in line, they rapidly advanced towards the Indians.

When they were first discovered, Colonel Hays happened to be in the rear of his company, mounted on a mule, and as soon as those in front commenced firing on the Indians he hurried forward as rapidly as he could on his slow going charger. On his way he passed one of his men mounted on a fine horse, and who was evidently trying to hold him back. He called out to him and asked him why he did not let his horse go ahead. The man replied that if he did so his horse would run away with him. "Then," said Colonel Hays, "let me have your horse and you can ride my mule." The man readily agreed to this, and they quickly exchanged animals.

Colonel Hays being now mounted on a good horse, soon reached the front where the missiles of death were flying thick and fast. Here, however, he discovered that the man who owned the horse had told him the truth, for, in spite of all his efforts he found it was impossible to check his excited and unruly charger. On he went, right into the thickest of the Indians, ahead of all others except Flacco, a young

Lipan chief, who was also mounted on a splendid horse, and stuck closely to the Colonel's side. These two alone charged the Comanche line of battle with their five shooters in hand, passed entirely through it, and came out unhurt on the opposite side. The Comanches were so astounded at their reckless bravery that they opened a way for them as they advanced.

The rest of the company seeing this gallant feat of the Colonel and the young Lipan chief, and that it had thrown the Indians into some confusion, took advantage of it and rushed right in among them, each one with his five shooter in hand. The warriors stood their ground for a while, but seeing the numbers that were falling on every side before the rapid and continuous fire of these fatal five shooters, a panic at length seized them and they fled and scattered in every direction.

Not long after this fight Colonel Hays, with fifteen men of his ranging company, encountered and totally defeated the famous chief Yellow Wolf at the head of eighty Comanche warriors. Among the men Colonel Hays had with him on this occasion were Ad. Gillespie, Samuel Walker, Samuel Luckie, Kit Ackland, and several others who subsequently figured conspicuously during the war with Mexico. After a hand to hand fight, lasting for some time, the Indians were totally routed, with the loss of one-half their number. Among the slain was the chief, Yellow Wolf. The loss of the rangers was but one killed and three wounded.

The report of Colonel Hays as to the efficiency of the five shooter on this and former occasions, induced Colonel Colt to present him with one of his improved six shooters, on the cylinder of which there is an engraving representing a Texas ranger charging a party of Indians.

The battle above described with Yellow Wolf and his eighty warriors took place at the Pinta crossing of the Guadalupe river, between San Antonio and Fredericksburg.

Flacco and Castro.

FLACCO (heretofore mentioned) and Castro were chiefs of the Lipan tribe, and both were well known to the old settlers of Texas. They were both staunch friends to the whites, and were always ready to accompany them in the capacity of trailers and spies on any expedition against their hereditary foes, the Comanches. In this way they frequently rendered valuable service to their white allies.

Flacco was a large, fine looking Indian, and a man of veracity and undoubted courage. He was often with Colonel Hays on his expeditions against the wild tribes and made himself conspicuous on many occasions by his daring feats. It was generally believed that Flacco was the man who killed the celebrated chief "Yellow Wolf" in the battle previously described. Castro's character was somewhat dubious, and he was rather cowardly, but withal shrewd and intelligent. On a certain occasion he paid a visit to President Lamar, accompanied by several of his wives. The President remarked to him, "I suppose, Castro, these are your daughters." "No," he replied, "dem feller my wife." "Why," said the President, "are you not too old to have so many young wives?" "No," said Castro, "old womans, young womans, ugly womans, any womans good for young mans, but young womans good for old man." Flacco was eventually killed near San Antonio by a marauding party of Mexicans; and Castro, too, has long since gone the way of all flesh.

As a general rule the Lipans were unreliable, deceitful and treacherous. They always professed to be friendly to the whites, but it is well known that they frequently depredated upon their property, and would occasionally take a scalp when they thought they could do so with impunity The tribe is now extinct.

Colonel Karnes.

O N the tenth of August, 1838, Colonel Karnes, with a
company of twenty-one men, was attacked by a party
of one hundred Comanches near the Arroyo Seco. The
savages were defeated, losing a number of their warriors, whilst the Texans escaped without further damage
than the wounding of Colonel Karnes. About this time
there was a strange rebellion, if such it might be
1838 termed, at Nacogdoches. On the fourth of August
several citizens went in pursuit of some stolen horses
which they found secreted in a Mexican settlement. On
their way back they were fired on and one of their party
killed. Some few citizens followed the murderers, but they
soon ascertained from the size of the trail that the number
of Mexicans, as they supposed them to be, was too great to
be attacked with any hopes of success, and they abandoned
the pursuit.

On the seventh of August Colonel John Durst reported to
General Rusk that there were a hundred or more Mexicans
on the Angelina river, under the leadership of Nathaniel
Norris, Cordova and Cruz. General Rusk made an immediate requisition for men. A company of sixty volunteers
from the town of Gonzales were stationed at the lower crossing of the Angelina river. On the ninth of August they
reported that they had been fired on, and asked for assistance. This report proved to be incorrect, but the enemy
were found posted on the right bank of the river.

On the tenth it was reported that the Mexicans had been
joined by about three hundred Indians, and on the evening
of the same day that their whole force amounted to six hundred. The same day President Houston, who was then at
Nacogdoches, received a letter from the Mexican leaders in
which they disclaimed allegiance to Texas. Shortly afterward they set out on their march to the Cherokee nation.
As soon as President Houston was advised of this move-

JACK HAYS AND CHIEF FLACCO CHARGE THE COMANCHES.

ment he ordered General Rusk not to cross the Angelina. Major Augustine was detached with one hundred and fifty men to follow the Mexican trail, while the main body of Texans under General Rusk marched to the headquarters of the Cherokee chief, whither he learned the enemy had gone.

On reaching the Sabine river General Rusk discovered that the insurgent leaders had fled to the upper Trinity, and that their followers had dispersed.

This emuete was a very strange one. The object of these leaders was unknown, nor did any subsequent discovery throw any light upon it. They must have known that a successful revolution was an impossibility.

On the twenty-fifth of October, 1838, at Jose Maria village, subsequently Fort Graham, a bloody battle was fought by some Texans under Colonel O'Neal and a party of Comanches settled at that place. After a fierce conflict the Indians fled, leaving many of their warriors dead upon the field.

The twentieth of the same month a party of surveyors were attacked by the Comanches within five miles of San Antonio and two of them killed. Some twelve or thirteen citizens went out to ascertain the intentions of these Indians and when within three miles of San Antonio they were attacked by more than a hundred Indians. These citizens very imprudently charged this large body of Indians, who at first gave way before them and then closed in around them. Eight of these citizens were killed and four wounded, only one man escaping unhurt.

On the eleventh of October of the same year General Rusk, at the head of two hundred men, arrived at Fort Houston, on the Trinity river, in pursuit of a motly crowd of Mexicans and Indians, who had been committing depredations on the frontier. Learning that the marauders were at the Kickapoo town he marched to that place and encamped at sun set on the fifteenth instant.

At daybreak, on the sixteenth, he attacked the enemy, who stood their ground for about fifteen minutes, when General Rusk ordered his men to charge them, which they did in such gallant style that the enemy were thrown into disorder and were finally completely routed, the Texans pursuing them for nearly a mile. The enemy left eleven dead on the field and about the same number of the Texans were wounded but none killed.

Thus the whole frontier in this year, 1838, was lit up with the flames of savage warfare. The immediate cause of hostilities was the opening of the land office in the beginning of the year. Surveyors and locators who were anxious to secure the best lands had gone out beyond the settlements and began their operations. The Indians seeing them at work believed that the Mexicans had told them the truth when they said that the white people would take all their hunting grounds and drive them from the country. The hostilities of the Indians was undoubtedly in a great meas-use caused by this state of affairs, and the Mexicans who had not forgotten their defeat at San Jacinto and the capture of Santa Anna, sought to revenge themselves by induc-ing the Indians to wage a border war upon the Texans

[See 2 Yoakum, 245.]

John Nolin.

MR. NOLIN was employed by the United States gov-ernment in 1871 to haul supplies from Jacksboro to Fort Griffin. He had in his charge ten teamsters with their wagons and teams. On his way, and when about sixteen miles north of Salt creek, where he had encamped, his train was attacked by ninety or one hundred Kiowa Indians. The men were not aware of the pres-1871 ence of the Indians until they were pouring a deadly fire in their midst. Four of the teamsters were killed at once, leaving only seven men to defend the train. Elated at this success, the Indians rapidly closed in upon them. One of the teamsters was so badly frightened that he ran away, hoping to escape by flight, but some of the Indians followed him and soon killed and scalped him. Three team-sters only were fortunate enough to escape. One poor fel-low, who was so badly wounded that he was unable to walk, was tied to the wheel of his wagon, which was then fired by the Indians and he was slowly roasted alive.

After the Indians had plundered the wagons of their contents they collected the horses and mules, about forty in number, and left. The gallant Colonel McKenzie started in pursuit of these Indians, intending if necessary to follow them into the nation, but was prevented from doing so by order of his superior officer

Samuel Robertson

MR. ROBERTSON was a resident of Bastrop county. In the latter part of the summer of 1838 Mr. Robertson and a man named Dollar were employed by Mr. Thomas Glasscock in getting out timber from a pinery near the town of Bastrop. One day whilst engaged at this business their attention was suddenly drawn to their horses, which were snorting loudly at some-**1838** thing that had alarmed them. Their horses were tied close by for the purpose of riding to and from their work. Looking around to see what it was that frightened their animals they discovered a large party of Indians within a few rods of them. The two men instantly mounted their horses and endeavored to escape, but the Indians, who were coming at full charge when they first discovered them, soon overtook them. Both men were unarmed. The Indians fired on them and shot a ball through Mr. Robertson which brought him to the ground and so disabled him he could make no resistance. The Indians soon dispatched him. Mr. Dollar was more fortunate and escaped unhurt. His horse was a very fleet one and the Indians were unable to come up with him. However, as he was not well acquainted with the country he soon came to a deep ravine which could not be crossed on horseback. There was no time to be lost. He sprang from his horse, left him, and took down the ravine on foot and thus succeeded in making his escape. These Indians were followed but were not caught.

Johnson's Station.

THIS station was on the overland mail route leading from St. Louis, Missouri, to San Francisco, California. At this station the contractors had several hands employed —seven men and one woman. It was the business of three of these men to take care of the horses belonging to the stand. On the twenty-seventh of March, 1857, a body of about two hundred and fifty Comanches attacked **1857** the station. The parties who had charge of the horses at the time had them grazing outside the inclosure. They were hoppled or side-lined with chains fastened by locks, so that only those who had the keys could take them off.

The Indians first attacked the three men outside and drove them from the horses they were guarding into the station. Supposing there was a considerable number of men in the station, the Indians did not make an immediate attack upon it, but hastened to secure the horses left outside. To their surprise and vexation, however, they found it impossible to remove the hopples. They tugged and pulled at them for some time, but finding it was all to no purpose, they cut off the poor animals' legs and left them in that condition.

As they had not been fired on from the station, the Indians came to the conclusion that there were but few men to defend it, and that they could take it without running any great risk. The station was merely a double log cabin, with a ten foot hall between the two rooms. One room was used for a kitchen or cook house and the other for a dwelling. When the Indians approached, the six men and the woman took refuge in the dwelling room, as it was more solidly constructed than the other, and barred the door securely; but, for want of time, the door of the cook room was left unfastened. The Indians, therefore, entered it without any opposition and plundered it of everything they thought would be of any use to them. They then concluded it was time to take the scalps of the occupants of the other room. But they were somewhat at a loss as to how they should proceed in this undertaking, as they knew from experience it was a very dangerous matter to attack even a small number of armed men when protected by the walls of a house.

However, they gathered all their forces around the station and made their arrangements to take it by a general assault. The men within seized their guns and presented them through the port holes of the house. The Indians, not fancying that kind of a demonstration, retreated back for some distance, and then challenged the whites to come out and give them a fair fight, but the whites could not see exactly how there was to be anything like a fair fight between six men and two hundred and fifty Indians, and consequently they declined to leave their fort. Finding they could not induce the occupants of the building to come out, they attached burning torches to the heads of their arrows and shot them upon the roof. In this way they finally succeeded in setting the house on fire. The men inside the building then called to the Indians in Spanish, which they all understand, and told them that they were coming out well armed, and if they would let them pass they would leave and not fire upon them, but if they did not agree to this, that they would kill as many as they could. To this the Indians consented, mainly, no doubt, for the reason that they supposed there was rich spoil in the building, and they wished to secure it before it was burnt.

The door was then opened and the six men and one woman marched out in line to a neighboring grove with their rifles in their hands, and their thumbs on the hammers, ready for action. As they advanced the Indians made a wide opening in their ranks to permit them to pass, and did not attempt to interfere with them. But just as the whites were entering the grove before mentioned, they met an Indian coming out who looked intently at Mrs. Evaness, the wife of one of them, and said in plain English that he would like to have that woman, and that he would have her before he left.

Mr. Evaness, the lady's husband, heard what he said, and instantly presenting his rifle, he drove a bullet through the scoundrel's body, killing him on the spot. Immediately the

other Indians rushed to the assistance of their fallen comrade and opened fire upon the little band of whites. One
bullet struck Mr. Evaness on the side of his face and came
out of his mouth. Mrs. Evaness was also shot in the side,
but not dangerously. At this juncture the United States
mail coach came in sight, and the Indians fled, thinking
probably that a body of dragoons were close at hand.

The stage took the party of whites on board and conveyed
them to the next station where they were properly cared for.
Mr. and Mrs. Evaness both recovered from their wounds.

Michael Young.

IN the winter of 1842, five Indians came in the settlements
on the Colorado river on a horse thieving expedition.
They spent the night in search of them, but only succeeded in stealing one. Finding that day was approaching and fearing discovery, they concluded to leave with the
one horse they had secured. A dense fog was prevailing at
the time which prevented them from pursuing a direct
1842 course from the settlements, and when day broke,
they found themselves near the residence of Mr.
Michael Young. Mr. Young's little son was out at the time
driving up the calves, and the Indians discovered him.
They slipped up slyly behind him, and one of the Indians
threw a lasso over his head intending to take him prisoner,
but the little fellow was too quick for them. He slipped
the rope from his neck and made towards the house with
such speed that the Indians did not dare to follow him. As
soon as he reached the house, he told his father what had
occurred, who mounted his horse at once, collected some of
his neighbors and pursued the Indians. There had been
heavy rains for several days previous, and as the ground
was soft, the Indians could be readily trailed. After pursuing them about twelve miles, they caught sight of the
Indians as they were passing over a high hill. They waited
until they were out of view, and then charged after them.

Arriving at the top of the hill, they discovered that the Indian on horseback was in about two hundred yards of them at the head of a deep ravine. The whites at first were a little dubious about charging him, as they thought it probable it was his intention to lead them into an ambuscade, but as the ground around was all open prairie, they determined to attack him and take the chances, which they did. When the Indians saw them coming, one of those on foot sprang up behind the one who was riding, but a shot from one of the Texans brought the horse down, and thus all the Indians were left afoot. They then separated and ran in every direction. There were fifteen Texans on horseback in pursuit of five Indians, and yet it took them about four hours to get them all. They ran until all were killed. The last one was killed at least twelve miles from where the chase began.

A Mr. Haynes, who had shot down one of the Indians, and supposed he had killed him, walked up incautiously near him while his gun was empty. As he approached the Indian suddenly raised up and was about to shoot an arrow at him, when Haynes sprang quickly forward and struck him a heavy blow on the head with the breech of his rifle. This only knocked the Indian down, and he soon rose again with his bow in his hand. But before he could fit an arrow to the string Haynes struck him another tremendous blow, this time with the barrel of his gun, and killed him instantly.

Mr. Young also made a very narrow escape under similar circumstances. He also had shot one of the Indians down and walked up to him just as Mr. Haynes had done, with his empty gun on his shoulder. The Indian was only "playing 'possum" to get a chance to kill one man before he died. He lay perfectly still until Young was in a few feet of him, when he suddenly rose and shot an arrow at him, striking Young just below the breast bone. But the Indian's strength was too far gone, and he could not shoot with sufficient force to send the arrow home. The wound, however, though not mortal, was a very painful one, and it was some time before Young recovered from it. He is now an old man, and is truly one of the veterans of Texas. No one ever served his country with more zeal and fidelity than he.

John Eagleston.

JOHN EAGLESTON immigrated to Texas at an early
day, passed safely through all the dangers incident to
frontier life and the war against Mexico, and was killed at
last by Indians on the streets of Bastrop.   In the winter
of 1838 the Indians were exceedingly hostile, and their raids
were of frequent occurrence.   People were compelled to
keep their stables and lots well locked and guarded to
1838, prevent their horses from being stolen, and even such
precautions often availed but little, for whenever the
Indians found it impossible to effect an entrance into stables
and lots, they often revenged themselves by shooting the
animals through crevices and bars with arrows.   This they
could easily do without causing an alarm, for, unlike the
gun, the bow and arrow did their fatal work unaccom-
panied by any report.

Near Eagleston's residence, one of his neighbors, Carter
Anderson, had picketed in a large lot, for the safe keeping
of his stock, the gate of which was fastened every night
with a chain and pad lock.

One very dark night in January, 1838, Eagleston happened
to be walking on the street near Anderson's lot.   Hearing
a rattling of the chain at the gate and thinking probably
some one was trying to enter it he concluded to investigate
the matter.   As he approached the gate he heard, as he
thought, the grunting of hogs, and seeing several dark objects moving in the vicinity, he naturally supposed they
were hogs and turned to retrace his steps.   Just as he did
so an arrow struck him in the breast. Eagleston fled, crying
out "Indians" as he went.   There were a few men on guard
at the time, who heard his cries and hurried to his assistance, but they were unable to pursue the Indians, for the
night, as we have said before, was a very dark one, and
they made their escape.   Mr. Eagleston lived only three
days after he was shot.

Taylor Smith.

IN the winter of 1838 a company of men started from Bastrop to go to the buffalo range, in the same county, that part of it then known as Young's settlement. One portion of the company was to start from the town of Bastrop and the other portion from a point on the river five miles above the town. They had agreed to meet at a certain watering place, but the party that started five 1838 miles above town failed to come to time. Those that had arrived were eager to go ahead, so they went on the same evening to the buffalo range, filled their wagons with meat and encamped for the night. ·

The other party coming afterwards to the appointed place of meeting encamped there. About 1 o'clock in the night the fire had pretty well burned down and Mr. Taylor Smith got up to rekindle it. As he was stooping over it an Indian fired at him from a distance of not more than twenty paces. The ball passed through Mr. Taylor's arm but did not break the bone. The report of the gun awakened the other men, who seized their arms and a regular fight then ensued between them and the Indians. The fight lasted about two hours, the Texans sheltering themselves behind a wagon filled with corn and the Indians behind trees.

One of the Indians, in order to get a fair shot at the boys, crawled up slyly behind them under cover of some bushes. An old gentleman, a Mr. Con, hearing a rustling of the leaves, discovered the Indian crawling upon the ground. He had a large English shot gun in his hand, and waiting until the Indian raised to fire he leveled his gun and perforated his hide with about a dozen buckshot. The Indian sprang up, crying out "wah! wah!" several times, and then pitched forwards upon the ground. As nothing was seen of him afterwards it was supposed he had got his quietus.

The Indians finding they could not dislodge the little band of Texans, gathered their forces and left. That same night they went on to the town of Bastrop. The day previous had been wash day and many people had left much of their clothing hanging upon the lines. The Indians stole the whole of it and about sixty head of horses. On their way out they fell in with the other party who were returning from the buffalo hunt. The writer of this sketch was one of them. There were seven men in the party, and they had to contend with about sixty Indians. Seeing there were but seven of us, they gave a yell and charged upon us at once, anticipating no doubt an easy victory; but in this they were badly mistaken, for we received them with such a deadly volley from our rifles that they fell back in disorder and finally retreated without making another attempt to renew the fight.

One Indian had a large white bed quilt crammed full of clothing before him on his horse, and a little boy he had taken prisoner behind him. During the row the little boy tried to jump down, and to prevent him from doing so the Indian was compelled to let go the bed quilt. In falling one end of it caught on the horn of the saddle and the clothing was strewn along the ground for a quarter of a mile. We gathered it up and returned it to the owners.

William Weir.

M R. WEIR was a resident of Hood county. In the fall of 1871, eight Indians, seven men and one squaw, came into Hood county. They succeeded in stealing fifteen head of horses and left. A company was raised and went in pursuit of them. The company followed them one day and night, and on the second day they overtook the Indians and attacked them. The 1871 Indians took their position in a deep ravine. While the Texans were consulting as to the best plan of dislodging them, twenty-five more citizens came to their assistance. They maneuvered for some time to draw the Indians from their position in the ravine, but all to no purpose. At this juncture a very heavy rain fell, which so swelled the little stream at the bottom that the Indians were compelled to show themselves. As they came into view the Texans charged them and poured a deadly fire into their midst. The Indians defended themselves with desperation and let fly their arrows thick and fast among the Texans. Mr. William Weir, the subject of this sketch, marched boldly up to the edge of the ravine and shot down the Indian chief, who fell into the water. Mr. Weir stepped down to see if he was killed, and having satisfied himself that he was dead, he was about returning, when the squaw, who was standing near, let fly an arrow and shot him in the breast, inflicting a fatal wound. The Indians also wounded a Mr McKenzie, but not seriously. The fight continued until the last Indian was killed—not even excepting that bellicose squaw.

Bowie's Victory.

THE following desperate battle, an account of which we are about to relate, was one of the fiercest conflicts of which we have any record in Indian warfare, and considering the number engaged on each side the result was something wonderful. On the second day of November, 1831, General Rezin P. Bowie, James Bowie, David Buchanan, Robert Armstrong, Jesse Wallace, Matthew Doyle, Cephas Hamm, James Coryell, Thomas McCaslin and two servant boys, Charles and Gonzales, started from San Antonio in search of the old silver mines of the San Saba mission. We give the narrative in the language of General Bowie:

1831

Nothing of interest occurred until about ten o'clock a. m. of the nineteenth day, when we were overtaken by two Comanche Indians and a Mexican, who stated that they belonged to Isaonie's party, a chief of the Comanche tribe, whose followers were about sixteen in number, and that

they were on their way to San Antonio with a drove of
horses they had taken from the Wacos and Tehuacanas,
and that they intended to return them to their owners, who
were citizens of San Antonio.

After smoking and talking with them about an hour and
making them a few presents of tobacco, powder and shot,
etc., they returned to their party, who were waiting at the
Llano river.

We continued our journey until night closed in upon us,
when we camped. The next morning, between daylight and
sun rise, this same Mexican came to our camp. His horse
was much fatigued. After eating and smoking he stated to
us that he had been sent by the Indian chief, Isaonie, to inform us that we were followed by one hundred and twenty-
four Tehuacana and Waco Indians, and that forty Caddos
had joined them, and that they were determined to have
our scalps at all hazards. Isaonie had held a conversation
with them the previous evening and had endeavored, without success, to dissuade them from their purpose; that they
left him enraged and had gone on our trail.

As a voucher for the truth of his statement the Mexican
produced his chief's silver medal, which is common among
the natives in such cases. He further stated that his chief
requested him to say that he had sixteen men, badly armed
and without ammunition, but if we would return and join
him he would give us such assistance as he could. Knowing that the enemy lay between us and him we deemed it
more prudent to resume our journey and endeavor to reach
the old fort on the San Saba river about night, a distance
of thirty miles.

The Mexican then went back to his party, and we went on
our way. We encountered bad roads. the same being quite
rocky, and our horses' feet were considerably worn. We
were disappointed in not reaching the fort in the evening,
and had some difficulty in finding an advantageous place to
camp. We, however, made choice of the best that offered,
which was a cluster of live oak trees, some thirty or forty
in number, and about the size of a man's body. To the
north of them there was a thicket of live oak bushes about
ten feet high, forty yards in length and twenty in breadth.
To the west, at the distance of thirty or forty yards, ran a

stream of water. The surrounding country was an open prairie, interspersed with a few trees, rocks and broken land. The trail that we came by was to the east of our encampment.

After taking the precaution to prepare for our defense by cutting a road inside the thicket of bushes about ten feet from the outer edge all around, and clearing the prickly pears from among the bushes, we hoppled our horses and placed sentinels for the night.

We were now distant about six miles from the fort Nothing occurred through the night. and we lost no time in the morning in making preparation for the continuance of our journey. When in the act of starting, we discovered three Indians on our trail to the east, about two hundred yards distant, and a footman about fifty yards in advance of the main body, with his face to the ground, tracking along on the trail. The cry of "Indians" was sounded, and all hands began to prepare for defense.

We dismounted and fastened both saddle and pack horses to the trees. As soon as they saw we had discovered them they gave the war whoop, halted and commenced stripping preparatory to action. A number of mounted Indians reconnoitered the ground. Among them were a few Caddo Indians, whom we knew by the cut of their hair. These Indians had always claimed to be friendly towards the whites.

Their number being so much greater than ours, one hundred and sixty-four to eleven, it was agreed that Rezin P. Bowie should be sent out to talk with them, and endeavor to compromise with them rather than attempt a fight. He accordingly started, accompanied by David Buchanan, and walked up to within about forty yards of where they had halted, and requested them, in their own tongue, to send forward their chief, as he wanted to talk with him. Their answer was, "howde do, howde do," in English, and a discharge of twelve shots, one of which broke Buchanan's leg. Bowie returned their salutation with the contents of a double barreled gun and a pistol. He then took Buchanan on his shoulder and started back to the encampment. As he did so, they opened a heavy fire on them, which wounded Buchanan in two other places, slightly piercing Bowie's

hunting shirt in several places, but did him no injury. Seeing the shots did not bring Bowie down, eight Indians on
foot took after him with their tomahawks; and when they
had gotten close to him, the rest of Bowie's party rushed to
his assistance and brought down four of the Indians and the
other four retreated to the main body. We then returned
to our position, and all was still for about five minutes,
when we discovered that a hill northeast of us, and about
sixty yards distant, was covered with Indians. They
opened a heavy fire on us, accompanied with loud yells.
We could hear their chief as in a loud and audible voice, he
urged them to charge us. He was walking his horse and
appeared perfectly composed. When we first discovered
him, our guns were all empty with the exception of Mr.
Hamm's. James Bowie cried out, "Whose gun is loaded?"
Mr. Hamm answered "Mine is." He was then told to shoot
that Indian on horseback. He did so, breaking his leg and
killing his horse. We now discovered him hopping around
his horse with his shield on his arm to keep off the balls. At
this time four of our party having their guns loaded, all
fired at him at once, and all the balls took effect through his
shield. He fell and was immediately surrounded by his
warriors, who picked him up and bore him off. Several of
these were shot while carrying away their dead chief. The
whole party then, with the exception of a few, retreated
over the hill out of sight. There were a few that dodged
about from tree to tree to avoid our shots.

The Indians soon covered the hill the second time, bringing up their bow men who had not before been in action, and
began a heavy fire with bows and arrows, which we returned with a well directed fire from our rifles. At this
instant another chief appeared on horseback near the spot
where the first had fallen, and again the question was
asked, "whose gun is loaded?" and the answer was, "nobody's;" when little Charles, the mulatto servant, came running up with Buchanan's rifle, which had not been discharged since he was wounded, and handed it to James
Bowie, who instantly fired and brought the chief from his
horse. He also was surrounded by six or eight of his men,
as was the first, and borne off under our fire.

While we were thus defending ourselves from the Indians

on the hill, some fifteen or twenty of the Caddos succeeded in getting under the bank in our rear, and about forty yards distant. From this cover they opened fire on us, wounding Matthew Doyle, the ball entering the left breast and coming out at the back. As soon as he cried out that he was wounded Thomas McCaslin hastened to the spot where he fell and called out, " Where is the Indian that shot Doyle?" He was told by a more experienced hand not to venture there, as from the reports of their guns they must be riflemen. At that instant they discovered an Indian, and when in the act of raising his gun he was shot through the center of the body and instantly expired. Robert Armstrong exclaimed, " Damn the Indian that shot McCaslin, where is is he?" He was told not to venture there, as they must be riflemen; but he discovered an Indian and just as he was raising his gun to shoot him he was fired at, the ball cutting off a portion of the stock of his gun and lodging in the barrel.

During this time the enemy had formed a complete circle around us, occupying the points of rocks, scattering trees and bushes. The firing then became general from all quarters. Finding our situation too much exposed among the trees, we were obliged to leave them and take to the bushes. The first thing necessary was to dislodge the riflemen from under the bank of the creek, who were now within close shooting distance. We soon succeeded in doing this, as we had the advantage of seeing them when they could not see us. The road we had cut around the thicket the night previous gave us great advantage over the enemy, as we had a fair view of them in the prairie, while we were completely hid.

We baffled their shots by moving six or eight feet the moment we fired, as their only mark was the smoke of our guns. They would put as many as twenty holes in a place the size of a pocket handkerchief where they had seen the smoke. In this manner we fought them for two hours and had one man wounded, James Coryell, who was shot through the arm, and the ball lodged in his side, the ball having first struck a small bush, which prevented it from penetrating deeper than the size of it.

They now discovered that we were not to be dislodged

from our position. They suffered very much from the fire of our rifles, which brought down a half dozen at every round. They now resorted to the stratagem of firing the dry grass for the double purpose of routing us from our position and, under cover of the smoke, to carry off their dead and wounded, which lay near us. The wind was now blowing from the west, and they placed the fire in that quarter. It burnt all the grass down to the creek, and then bore off to the right, leaving a space of about five acres around us untouched by the fire.

Under cover of this smoke they succeeded in carrying away a portion of their dead and wounded. In the meantime our party were engaged in scraping away the dry grass and leaves from around our wounded men and baggage to prevent the fire from passing over them. We also gathered together rocks and bushes and made a breastwork of them.

They now discovered that they had made a failure in routing us by fire, as they anticipated. They then reoccupied the points of rocks and trees and commenced another attack. The firing continued for some time, when the wind suddenly shifted and blew very hard from the north. We saw that we were in a critical position, if the Indians succeeded in putting fire to the small spot around us. We kept a strict watch all around, and had our servant boys employed in scraping away the dry grass and leaves from around the baggage and in piling rocks around the wounded men. The point from which the wind now blew being favorable to fire our position, one of the Indians succeeded in crawling down the creek and setting fire to the grass that had not been burned; but before he could retreat back to his party, Robert Armstrong shot and killed him.

We saw no hope now of escape. The flames were about ten feet high, and bearing directly to the spot where we were! What was to be done? It seemed that we were compelled either to be burned alive or driven out into the prairie among the savages. This so encouraged the Indians that they fired volley after volley at us, shouting and yelling like so many demons. They fired about twenty shots to the minute.

As soon as the smoke hid us from their view, we collected

together and held a consultation as to what was best to be done. Our first impression was that they might charge on us under cover of the smoke, as we could make but one effectual fire, since the sparks were flying about so thickly that no man could open his powder horn without the risk of being blown up. We, however, determined that if they charged us we would give them one fire, then place our backs together, draw our knives and fight them as long as one of us was left alive. We also decided that, if they did not charge us, we would retain our position, every man taking care of himself as best he could, and when the fire arrived at the ring around our baggage and wounded men, that we would smother it with buffalo robes, deer skins, blankets, etc. The Indians not charging us, we had to carry out the latter proposition, in which we succeeded after a great deal of exertion.

Our thicket was so much burned and scorched that it now afforded but very little shelter. We all got into the ring that was made around our wounded men and baggage and began building our breastworks higher, using the loose rocks from the inside, and the dirt which we dug up with our knives and sticks. During this last fire the Indians had succeeded in removing all their dead and wounded. It was now sundown, and we had been fighting ever since sunrise in the morning. The Indians, seeing us still alive and ready for fight, drew off at a distance of three hundred yards and there camped for the night with their dead and wounded. Our party now commenced the work of raising our breastworks still higher, and by ten o'clock p. m. we had succeeded in building it breast high. We then filled our vessels with water, expecting another attack next morning.

We could distinctly hear the Indians crying nearly all night over their dead, which is one of their customs. At day light they shot one of their wounded chiefs, it being also a custom to shoot any of their tribe that are mortally wounded. They afterwards took their dead and wounded and went to a mountain about a mile distant, where they deposited them in a cave in the side of the mountain. At eight o'clock in the morning two of our party went out from the fortification to the encampment where the Indians had a'n the night previous, and counted forty-eight bloody spots in the grass where the dead and wounded had lain. Finding ourselves much cut up, having one man killed and three wounded; five horses killed and three wounded, we recommenced strengthening our little fort and continued our labors until one o'clock p. m., when the arrival of thirteen Indians drew us into it again. As soon as they discovered we were fortified and ready for action they left. We after that remained in our fort eight days, when we set out for San Antonio, where we arrived in safety, bringing our wounded, after a journey of twelve days. Up to this time there had been no encounter between the Indians and whites so protracted and desperate as the one just related. Three tribes had allied, and, counting on their numbers, had expected an easy victory over the handful of whites, but the brave Bowie and his gallant followers taught them the important lesson that, "The race is not always to the swift, nor the battle to the strong." The savages lost three of their chiefs killed on the ground, and probably about one-third of their entire number. There is not a single instance in Indian warfare on this continent where more skill and valor were displayed than in the one we have recorded.

[See Holley, 161.]

Jesse Burnam.

WE do not know the native State of this venerable pioneer, but we know that he came to Texas with the first immigrants to Austin's old colony. He settled in Fayette county, on the Colorado river. At that time the section of country where he lived was constantly exposed to Indian depredations, and as settlers were few and far between, he was compelled to rely mainly 1830 upon his own good right arm and his trusty rifle for protection against them. In the summer of 1830 or 1831, a party of raiding Indians came into Burnam's neighborhood, and finding he had a *caballada* of very fine horses, which were pastured on a beautiful prairie near the house, they concluded to take possession of them. In order to make sure of getting the whole *caballada* the Indians boldly entered the pasture in open daylight, in full view of the house, and drove the horses off.

One of Burnam's little children, who happened to witness their proceedings, ran into the house and told him the Indians were driving the horses away. At the time Burnam was sick in bed with fever, but this bare faced robbery of his fine stock of horses provoked him to such a degree that he got up immediately, saddled his riding horse, and taking his gun, started off solitary and alone in pursuit of the Indians.

He soon came to the trail made by his horses and those of the Indians, and after several hours hard riding he caught sight of his *caballada*, moving on rapidly before a dozen Indians in the rear. He reined up his horse a few moments to consider what was best to be done. After resting his horse a little, he came to the conclusion that he would either recapture his *caballada* or lose his scalp in the attempt. He was satisfied his only chance of success against such odds was to charge the Indians boldly, give them a volley, as he advanced, from his double barreled shot gun, and thereby endeavor to throw them into confusion by his sudden onset, and to stampede the horses so completely as to render it impossible for the Indians to control them; and in that event he was confident the horses would take a bee line for their old range.

The horse Burnam was riding was a very fleet animal, and he thought if he should fail to stampede the *caballada* that at any rate he would be able to make good his escape. So he set spurs to him, and almost before the Indians were aware of his proximity he let fly both barrels of his gun at them and dashed through them, whooping and yelling as he passed, right into the midst of the frightened horses, which were stampeded so badly the Indians were unable to check them, and they went off like the wind, with Burnam in the lead, in the direction of home.

The Indians pursued them for some distance, vainly endeavoring to turn them in their mad career, but finding it was not possible to do so they finally abandoned the chase and left in disgust. A few hours afterwards Burnam arrived safely at home without the loss of a single animal. This is the only instance I know of in which a dozen Indians were charged upon in open prairie by one man alone, and all their stolen property recaptured from them.

Some one asked Burnam how it was he ventured alone to attack such a number of Indians, and he replied that he was sick and mad at the time, and had been so provoked by their previous depredations upon his property that he had made up his mind to foil them at all hazards on this occasion. We can understand this, as we have been very sick frequently as well as angry, and no doubt if we had been in Burnam's place we would have done some desperate charging too—but it would have been in the opposite direction from the Indians.

Mrs. Jones.

AMONG the early settlers in Western Texas was a man by the name of Rabb. He was one of those restless adventurous men so frequently met with on the frontier who are never satisfied except when they are in advance of all other settlements. The nearest neighbor to Mr. Rabb was fifteen miles below. His family consisted of his wife and three small children and a female friend, whom we shall designate as Mrs. Jones (as we are not authorized to give her name to the public). Mrs. Jones having recently lost her husband was living with the Rabb family. She was a fair specimen of those hardy, self-reliant heroines of the border, who are undaunted by dangers, and who bear unflinchingly the hardships and exposures incidental to life in new and sparsely settled countries. Born and reared in Texas, she inherited a good constitution, to which her active life in the open air, a great portion of which was spent on horseback, gave unusual vigor. From an early age she had been a fearless rider,

1867

and her life on the frontier where all traveling was necessarily performed on horseback, had given her better and more practical knowledge of the equestrian art than she could have acquired by training for the same length of time at Astley's.

One morning in June, 1867, Rabb started off to a distant market with some cattle, leaving his family at the ranch without any one to protect them against the Indians. He did not apprehend any danger, however, during his absence, as no Indians had been seen for some time in the vicinity. Everything went on as usual for several days, until one morning while the women were occupied with their domestic affairs in the house, one of the children who were playing in the yard called out to its mother and told her that some men on horseback were coming over the prairie. Mrs. Rabb stepped to the door and saw, to her horror, that these men were Indians, coming at full gallop towards the house. She ordered the children to run in at once, as she wished to bar the door, knowing that Indians seldom ventured to attack a house when barred against them, fearing that armed men might be within who would give them a warm reception. But the children did not obey their mother, thinking, no doubt, that the Indians were cow hunters, and the door was left open.

As soon as the alarm of Indians was given, Mrs. Jones ran up a ladder leading to a loft, and concealed herself, where through a crack in the floor, she could see all that passed beneath.

The Indians rushed up, seized and bound the two children in the yard and then entered the house. They took the young babe from the arms of the terrified mother, in spite of her struggles to retain it, and threw it on the floor. One of them then caught the poor woman by her hair, drew back her head and cut her throat from ear to ear with his butcher knife.

Mrs. Jones, who was watching their proceedings through a chink in the floor above, when she witnessed this cold blooded murder of her friend, involuntarily uttered a cry of horror which betrayed her place of concealment to the Indians. Several immediately sprang up the ladder, dragged her down and out of the house, placed her and the two chil-

dren on horses, and then hurried off with them, leaving the
infant unhurt by the side of its murdered mother.

For several days and nights, fearing pursuit, they traveled
rapidly, only making an occasional halt to rest and graze
the animals. Their unfortunate captives suffered indescribable torments from harsh usage and the want of sleep and
food as they moved on day after day and night after night
towards the staked plains, crossing the Brazos, Wichita and
Arkansas rivers by swimming them, as they were all too full
to be forded.

The Indians kept a close watch upon their captives until
they had gone a long way beyond the frontier settlements,
when they somewhat relaxed their vigilance and permitted
them to walk about camp, but gave them to understand
that death would be the certain result of any attempt to
escape. In spite of this threat, Mrs. Jones was determined
to seize the first opportunity to escape from them that might
present itself. Having thus resolved, she carefully noted
the qualities of different horses in order that she might be
able to make a good selection when a chance of escaping
should occur.

One dark night after a long hard day's ride, while the
Indians were sleeping soundly, she cautiously crept away
from the lodge occupied by herself and the two children,
who were also fast asleep, and going to where the Indians
had staked their horses, she selected one of the best, sprang
on his back, without saddle or bridle, and with nothing to
guide or control him but the rope around his neck. She
started off slowly in the direction of the north star, thinking that course would lead her to the nearest white settlements, but as soon as she was out of hearing of the camp,
she put her horse into a trot and then into a gallop, and continued thus to urge him on as fast as he could go during the
whole night.

At the break of day the following morning she reached
the crest of a considerable eminence overlooking a vast expanse of bald prairie, and there, for the first time after leaving the Indian camp, she halted, turned around with fear
and trembling and cast a rapid glance to the rear, fully expecting to see the savage bloodhounds on her trail, but to
her great relief not a living thing was visible except a herd

of antelopes quietly grazing on the prairie below. Still her uncertainty in the midst of dreary trackless plains as to the course she ought to pursue in order to reach the nearest settlements filled her with gloomy forebodings as to her ultimate fate. Perhaps nowhere does one realize utter helplessness and dependence upon the Almighty Ruler of the universe than when bewildered and lost on the almost boundless plains of the west and Mrs. Jones raised her thoughts to heaven in fervent supplication. She knew that one of the many points embraced within the horizon could lead to safety and that the direction to this one point must be kept without road, tree or other land mark to guide her. But the indominitable spirit of the heroine of this narrative did not succumb to the imminent perils that surrounded her. All day long she urged forward her generous steed until she was so worn out with fatigue and want of sleep that it was with great difficulty she could keep her seat on his back. To add to the horrors of her situation a new danger stared her in the face as the shades of night began to darken around, a danger quite as much to be dreaded as recapture by the merciless savages. Hearing the howling of wolves behind she looked back and discovered that a large gang were closely following on her trail. They seemed to know instinctively that the wearied horse and his rider must soon fall a prey to their voracious appetites. The idea of being devoured by wolves was so horrible that it gave her the strength of desperation and all through the gloomy hours of that dismal night she continued to urge on her faithful steed until she became so exhausted that it was with difficulty she could keep awake. Frequently she found herself in the act of falling from the horse just in time to save herself from being left alone on foot among the ravenous wolves, whose dismal howlings could be heard in every direction.

At length her horse, too, began to fail rapidly until at last the poor animal was scarcely able to drag one foot after the other and she momentarily expected he would drop dead beneath her. The failure of the horse seemed to encourage the wolves and they finally rushed upon him, snapping at his heels and endeavoring to drag him and his rider to the ground. This so terrified the horse that he went on for a while with renewed vigor, and fortunately before the wolves could come up with him again daylight began to show in the east and the cowardly beasts skulked away in their dens.

For the first time in thirty-six hours Mrs. Jones now dismounted, and knowing that sleep would soon overcome her, as there was no tree or bush to which she could fasten the horse, she tied the end of his rope around her waist, threw herself on the ground and in a moment was fast asleep. How long she had slept she does not know, but the sun was high in the heavens when she roused by the clattering of horses feet. Looking up she was terror struck to find that she was completely surrounded by a large party of Indians. Worn down as she was by her long ride and her nerves unstrung by anxiety and the hardships she had undergone the shock was too great for her and she fainted. When she regained consciousness the Indians placed her on a horse and started with her to their camp, which was not far off. On their arrival there they left her in charge of the squaws, who prepared some food for her and gave her a buffalo robe for a bed. It was several days before she was able to walk about camp. She soon learned that her last captors belonged to Lone Wolf's band of Kiowas. These Indians treated her much more kindly than the Comanches, but as she did not think they would ever voluntarily release her, and although she had not the remotest idea of her locality or of the direction or distance to any white settlement she was determined to take advantage of the first opportunity to make her escape from them.

Some time after she was captured by these Indians a party left camp, going off in a northerly direction, and in five or six days they returned bringing back with them some ears of green corn. She knew the prairie tribes did not plant corn, and she felt confident this party had visited a white settlement in a northerly direction not more than three days travel from where they were encamped. This was encouraging to her, and she anxiously watched for a favorable chance to leave.

Late one night after all was quiet in camp and everything seemed auspicious for carrying out her purpose, she cautiously crept from her bed and went to where she knew the Indians had staked their horses. Having caught and saddled one, she was in the act of mounting him, when several dogs rushed out after her and by their barking created such a disturbance in camp that she thought it most prudent to return to her lodge, which she reached without having been seen by any one.

On a subsequent night, however, fortune favored her, and selecting a good horse she rode off in the direction the Indians had taken when they brought back the ears of green corn. Guided by the sun, and the stars at night, she was able to keep her course, and after three days of hard riding, anxiety, fatigue and hunger, she came to a large river. The stream was swollen to the top of its banks, the current coursed like a torrent along the channel, and she thought her tired horse would be unable to stem it; but after surmounting the many difficulties she had already encountered, she was not to be turned aside by this formidable obstacle. She let her wearied animal rest and graze for a while, then mounting him again the dauntless woman dashed into the turbulent stream and with great difficulty the faithful steed bore her in safety to the opposite bank.

Giving her horse a few moments rest, she again set forward, and had gone but a short distance when to her inexpressible delight she struck a broad wagon road, the first and only trace of civilization she had seen since she left her home in Texas. Nothing, she said, ever gave her as much pleasure as the sight of this road, for she felt confident that it would lead her to some settlement of people of her own race; and her anticipations were more speedily realized than she looked for, for a little while afterwards she saw a long train of wagons slowly coming along the road towards her.

At the sight of this train her feelings overpowered her, and she wept tears of joy while offering up sincere thanks to the Almighty for delivering her from a bondage more dreadful than death. She hurried on, and soon met the foremost wagon, which was driven by a Mr. Robert Bent, who had charge of the train. He was very much astonished to meet a young woman traveling alone on horseback in that wild country, with no covering on her head save her long hair, which was hanging in disheveled locks upon her shoulders.

When she came up, Bent stopped his wagon and asked her where she lived and to what place she was going. She replied that she lived in Texas, and that she was on her way to the nearest settlement. At this response he shook his head incredulously, and said she must be mistaken, as the nearest point in Texas was some five or six hundred miles distant. She, however, reiterated her statement, and described to him briefly the leading incidents of her capture and of her escape from the Indians. Still, he was inclined to doubt the story she told him, thinking possibly she might be insane. He informed her that the river she had just crossed was the Arkansas, and that she was then on the Santa Fe road, fifteen miles west of Big Turkey creek, where she would find the most remote frontier settlement. He then gave her some provisions, and after thanking him for his kindness, she proceeded on her way.

When Bent reached Fort Zara he called on the Indian agent there and told him about meeting Mrs. Jones on the road. By a curious coincidence it happened that the agent was at that very time holding a council with the chief of the identical band of Indians from whom Mrs. Jones had just escaped, and the chief had given him a full history of the whole affair, which seemed so improbable to the agent that he was not disposed to credit it until his account was confirmed by Mr. Bent. The agent at once dispatched a man to follow the woman and conduct her to Council Grove, where she was kindly received, and remained for some time hoping through the agent to gain some intelligence of the two children she had left with the Comanches, but no tidings of these children could be obtained. They were eventually found, however, ransomed and sent home to their father.

By reference to the map of the country over which Mrs. Jones traveled, it will be seen that the distance from the place of her capture to where she struck the Arkansas river, could not have been less than five hundred miles, and the greater part of her route was through an immense desert plain unvisited except by occasional bands of Indians.

Her escape from the Indians and her equestrian feats were most remarkable, and the account herein given of them seems almost incredible, and yet there are those still living in Texas to whom the facts are well known, and who can authenticate the truth of the foregoing narrative.

Wd. p. Brashear.

SOME very remarkable escapes have been made from Indians in Texas, of which I will mention one or two instances. Mr. Brashear was one of the very few men I have met with in my life who never took any precautions against danger, and yet was perfectly cool and collected when danger came. I do not believe he ever felt the sensation of fear. He had a brother killed at Fannin's massacre, and, in consequence, he entertained the most inveterate hatred towards the Mexicans, and especially for Santa Anna.

1839

After the battle of San Jacinto, and while Santa Anna was a prisoner at Velasco, Brashear went there as he told me himself, for the express purpose of shooting him on sight, but General Houston, in anticipation of some such attempt upon the life of his illustrious prisoner, had him surrounded constantly with a strong guard, whose orders were that no one with arms should have access to him; consequently, when Brashear applied for permission to see him, he was searched, and the pistol with which he intended to revenge the death of his brother was found upon his person, and his request to see Santa Anna being refused, he remained at Velasco until Santa Anna left for the "States," hoping by some means to get a pop at him, but the opportunity never occurred.

In 1839, Brashear went to Lavaca county for the purpose of locating lands, and whilst there he boarded at the house of a gentleman by the name of Henseley, who resided at one of the extreme frontier settlements. Although that section of country was frequently visited by marauding bands of Indians, Brashear would often, in spite of Henseley's warnings, go out alone and unarmed, to examine lands, ten, fifteen or twenty miles from the settlement. Whenever Henseley told him he ran a great risk of having his hair lifted in riding about the country alone, his reply invariably was that he had no fear, as there was not an Indian in Texas who could catch him when mounted on "Git Out," as he called his half-breed Mexican horse.

One morning he left Henseley's with the intention of examing a tract of land about ten miles west of the settlement, and, as usual, he had no arms with him more formidable than a pocket knife. He reached the locality he wished to examine, and was busily engaged in tracing a line with a pocket compass, when, on turning a point of post oak timber, he discovered about twenty Comanche warriors mounted upon their mustang ponies not more than a quarter of a mile distant. As soon as the Indians saw him they gave the war whoop and came swooping down upon him. Brashear instantly wheeled his horse and started towards the settlement, the Indians following him and yelling and whooping like so many devils. Brashear said he was not at all frightened although he was unarmed, as he felt confident that Git Out could easily run away from the Indians on their ponies, but to his astonishment, before he had gone a mile he found the Indians were gaining upon him, and if something was not done and that pretty quickly they would overtake him long before he could reach the Henseley settlement. About a mile ahead of him he knew there was a creek called Boggy, which could only be crossed at a few localities. He therefore determined to push Git Out to his utmost speed until he struck Boggy six or seven hundred yards below a crossing, and as soon as he was hid from view by the skirt of timber bordering the creek, to make a crossing and get back as quickly as possible opposite the point where he had entered the timber. He therefore plied whip and spurs to Git Out, in order to carry his plan into execution, and soon had the satisfaction of seeing that he was rapidly forging ahead of the Indians. The moment he struck the timber on Boggy and his movements could not be seen by the Indians he made for the ford, crossed it, and galloped down the creek until he supposed he was about opposite the place where the Indians had lost sight of him. He had hardly reached this point when the Indians made their appearance, and seeing Brashear going off in a direct line, they naturally concluded he had crossed at that place.

Without halting for a moment they plunged into the creek, and instantly their horses went down to their necks in the treacherous quick sand.

While the Indians were vainly endeavoring to extricate their horses from the bog, Brashear said he could not resist the inclination to crow over them a little, which he did by some very expressive pantomime. This made the Indians furious, and one or two who had scrambled out of the bog on foot commenced shooting at him, whereupon Brashear bid them adieu and rode off leisurely, as he knew it would take some time to extricate their horses from the embraces of old Boggy.

On another occasion Brashear had a very "close call" from Indians while out hunting. He had just killed a deer and had dismounted from his pony for the purpose of butchering it. He was in the act of doing so when he discovered a party of Indians half a mile distant coming towards him on their ponies at full speed. Leaving his deer to be butchered at a more convenient opportunity, he hastily mounted his pony (he was not riding the redoubtable "Git Out" on that occasion) and started towards home, but he soon found the Indians were rapidly overhauling him. About a half a mile ahead there was a considerable elevation on the prairie, covered in places with a thick growth of chapparal, and Brashear made for it with all the speed he could get out of his pony with whip and spur. As soon as he entered this chapparal and was hid from the view of his pursuers he hastily dismounted, tied his pony to a bush and continued his retreat on foot. His idea was, when the Indians came up and discovered his pony they would naturally conclude he was secreted somewhere in the vicinity, and that before they found out their mistake he would have sufficient time to make his escape. His plan worked admirably and Brashear reached the settlement without seeing anything more of the Indians. The next morning, in company with five or six men from the settlement, he went to the place where he had left his pony and found him still there. It was evident, as Brashear had anticipated, that the Indians, when they came up and discovered the pony, supposed that his rider was concealed near by, and knowing that he was armed, they had not dared to venture within gunshot.

Young Saunders.

ONE of the most remarkable escapes ever made from Indians was that of a young man by the name of Saunders, who settled in Erath county at an early day. As he was pretty well educated, and there were quite a number of families where he had taken up his abode, they built a school house and employed him to teach their children. Not long after his arrival in the
1839 county he made the acquaintance of a young lady who lived at a settlement ten miles distant from the one where he resided, whilst she was visiting a family in the neighborhood. It was another case of love at first sight, or in back woods parlance, he fell dead at the first fire.

After the young lady returned home, as regularly as Saturday came round young Saunders was off to see his sweetheart, and as the emoluments of his school were not sufficient to enable him to keep a horse, he usually made his weekly trips on "shanks's mare," and as the sequel will show, a better never lifted leg.

Young Saunders was as green as a cut seed water melon in everything pertaining to frontier life, and as the Indians had not made a raid into the county since his arrival he thought he could travel the short distance between the two settlements safely on foot.

One Saturday morning when he was about starting on his customary trip, some of his friends told him that traveling on foot and unarmed in that country was a very risky business, but he supposed they were merely trying to intimidate him for their own amusement, and paid no attention to their warning. He had gone about half way between the two settlements when he heard the most diabolical yells behind him, and turning to look he discovered about twenty mounted Indians coming after him at full speed.

There was a dense body of timber a half a mile or so to

the left of the road he was traveling, and towards it young Saunders, now realizing the emergency of the case, put off at a two-forty lick. As he was young and active, and badly scared besides, he made such good speed that for a while the Indians gained but little on him; but unfortunately (or perhaps I should say fortunately), when within a few hundred yards of the timber, he struck his foot against a stone and pitched head foremost upon the ground. As he fell his hand came in contact with a stick, and for the same reason, I suppose, that a drowning man will catch at a straw, he instinctively grasped it.

By the time he had regained his feet, still holding the stick in his hand, the Indians had come up with him, and began to let their arrows fly at him thick and fast. Young Saunders turned and presented his stick towards them, which proved to be a black, half burnt sumach root, about the length of a six shooter, and with a crook at one end resembling the handle.

The Indians, of course, at a little distance, supposed it was a six shooter, and drew back. The young man, taking advantage of their halt, again put in his best licks to reach the timber, but the Indians soon came up with him, and he was forced to turn and present his formidable sumach root at them, which demonstration was followed by the same result. By repeating this maneuver whenever the Indians pressed him closely, young Saunders finally succeeded in reaching the timber and made his escape without having received a scratch, although his clothes were cut in many places with arrows.

The Indians did not follow him any further, no doubt concluding it would not be safe to follow a man into the thick timber who was armed with a sumach root, and reserved his fire until he could make sure of his enemy.

The parties to whom I am indebted for this account of Mr. Saunders's escape from the Indians did not inform me as to the finale of his love affair; and, knowing as well as I do the chivalrous character of "young Texas," I did not think it worth while to make any inquiries about it. I am perfectly confident that the young man did not discontinue his weekly pilgrimage to the shrine of his lady love for fear of meeting Indians on the way. On the contrary, I feel assured that he purchased a horse and a six shooter with the first available funds he acquired, and that he did not cease to pay his Saturday visits to his inamorata until she became Mrs. Saunders. It is said that "the course of true love never does run smooth," but at least in Mr. Saunders's case it ran fast enough to save his scalp, and I do not think I am running myself before the hounds when I assert that in all probability Mr. and Mrs. Saunders are now numbered among the cattle kings and queens of old Erath, and that from the stoop of their hospitable and palatial ranch they can now count a hundred bovine herds grazing upon a hundred hills. At least, no other conjecture is compatible with the known chivalry of the young America of Texas. "Vive l'amour. Cigars and cognac!"

William A. Wallace.

WILLIAM A. WALLACE, better known by the name of "Big Foot Wallace," was born in Lexington, Rockbridge county, Virginia, in the year 1816, and came to Texas in 1836, arriving a few months after the battle of San Jacinto. He had a brother—Major Wallace—who was a graduate of West Point, and also a cousin killed in the Fannin massacre at Goliad. For the 1836 murder of these two men, Wallace says he came to Texas to take revenge out of the Mexicans. He landed at Galveston, but soon left for LaGrange, Texas, where he resided until 1839, when he moved to Austin, but moved to San Antonio the following spring, in 1840. He was at the battle of the Salado, in 1842, when General Woll captured San Antonio. He was also in the Mier expedition, but was one of the lucky ones who drew a white bean, and after returning to Texas, he joined Colonel Hays's ranging company and was with him in many of his exciting Indian campaigns, and in 1846 was with Hays at the storming of

BIG FOOT WALLACE.

Monterey, where, to use Wallace's own language, he took "full toll" out of the Mexicans for killing his brother and cousin at Goliad in 1836. After the termination of the Mexican war, he commanded a ranging company which was organized to protect the frontier of Texas, and subsequently had charge of the mail from San Antonio to El Paso, which was probably the most dangerous mail route in all Texas; for, according to the statement of old Texans who were living in that section of the State, the road is lined on either side from San Antonio to El Paso with graves of those who had fallen by the way side at the hands of the Indian savage, or of the maurauding Mexicans. Wallace's frontier life was fraught with many perilous adventures and narrow escapes. In 1837, while out with a party of surveyors in what is supposed now to be Palo Pinto county, he became separated from his party, was chased by the Indians, the foremost one of whom he killed, and after making his escape, and was making his way back to the settlements, had the misfortune of spraining his ankle, and was compelled to lay up alone from the twenty-eighth of October until the twentieth of November, before he was able to travel. He subsisted alone on wild game and pecans, while he remained in his little cave which fortunately he had found and camped in the night before the morning he sprained his ankle, which accident occurred near by, and he returned to the cave. On his way back to the settlements, he was captured by the Indians, taken to their village, and after a council had been held among the warriors, he was condemned to be burnt and had been taken out, tied down to the stakes with the wood piled around him, but just before the Indians were ready to apply the torch to the flames, Wallace was rescued by an old squaw. Through the kindness of this old squaw and her son "Black Wolf," he was enabled to make his escape from the Indians after remaining with them a few months.

Wallace was able to defend his little ranch out on the Medina river, some thirty miles southwest of San Antonio, from the ravages of Indians, Mexicans, cut throats and thieves, who would occasionally dispute his right of possession, but when civilization spread out in that section of Texas and lands became valuable, he was unable to hold his own against the manipulations of the shrewd land shark, and we have been informed that recently some one discovered a flaw in Wallace's land title and succeeded in ejecting him from his little ranch, which he had occupied for some fifteen or twenty years without any one ever disputing the right of his occupancy except the class above referred to, and now, like the wandering Arab, he pitches his tent wherever night overtakes him.   He is still camping around in Southwest Texas.

Some years ago a little book entitled "The Adventures of Big Foot Wallace"—the well known Texan ranger—was published, having been written by John C. Duval, an old Texan, messmate of Wallace under Hays, and to-day we believe the only survivor of Fannin's Massacre at Goliad in 1836.   From this little book we have concluded to take some extracts for the following reasons: First, because we believe they will vary to some extent the unavoidable sameness of the scenes and incidents narrated in this work; and, secondly, because as but few copies of the book referred to ever reached Texas, we believe they will be new to most readers of this book.   We would not have the reader infer from the quaint and laughable style in which "Big Foot" describes his Indian exploits that the incidents referred to by him are based upon fiction.   He vouched for the truthfulness of the facts, and while the author of "Big Foot" may have dressed up the language in a few instances to amuse the fancy of the reader, the incidents referred to actually occurred, some of which were witnessed by the author of "Big Foot," who, on several occasions, was with Wallace.   The following piece, as will be seen, gives an account of an attack by the Indians on the United States mail coach while Wallace was in charge of the mail route between San Antonio and El Paso. This as well as other extracts will be given in Big Foot's own peculiar language.

Indians Attack the Mail Coach.

SAID "Big Foot," I have been in many tight places, but when I was in charge of the mail line running from San Antonio to El Paso I got into one I thought I should never squeeze out of, but I did. In all the scrapes and difficulties I have encountered since coming to Texas I never was severely wounded either with an arrow or a ball, which, considering my size, is something truly wonderful. I 1849 have known a great many men who, as General Scott said of General Johnson, "had an unfortunate knack of getting wounded in every fight they went into," but I have not been one of that sort. They say "those who are born to be hung won't be shot or drowned;" and perhaps that may account for it. But I am flying off of my story before I have fairly commenced it. We had been traveling hard ever since twelve o'clock at night in order to reach the watering place at Devil's river, where I intended to noon it and graze our animals for two or three hours. After daylight I noticed several Indian smokes rising up and disappearing, but they were apparently a long way off, and once passed a considerable trail where we discovered that fifteen or twenty head of horses had crossed the road. Although I did not like the sign, and I told the boys to keep a sharp lookout, as I was satisfied the Indians were hatching some devilment for our benefit. We, however, reached the water hole in safety, about noon, watered our animals and hoppled them out to graze. I had eight men with me, most of them old frontiersmen who had seen much service, and were as good fighters, with the exception of one, as ever drew a bead upon an Indian, for I had seen them tried on several occasions before.

There was about a quarter of an acre of thick chapparal near the watering place, and after we had taken a bite to eat, I told the boys to draw the coach up to the edge of this thicket and they could lie down on their blankets and take a snooze, for they had been awake all of the night before, and were pretty well worn out.

I felt considerably fagged myself, but somehow uneasiness pervaded me so I could not sleep. Although I had seen nothing in particular to excite my suspicions since we stopped at the watering place, I felt uneasy and determined to watch while the others slept. If there had been nothing else, the appearance of the country around our encampment was enough to make one uneasy, for it had a real "Injiny" look. The country was composed of broken, rocky hills, with here and there little clumps of thorny bushes, stunted cedars, with little narrow valleys or canons between the hills, in which there was nothing but a few patches of withered grass from which our animals were picking a scanty repast. We could see but a short distance in any direction.

I picked up my rifle and walked off about fifty yards to a little mound to the right of our encampment, where I could have the best view of the approach of the enemy. * * *

I don't know how it is with others, but there are times when I feel low spirited and depressed without being able to account for it, and such was the case on this occasion. The breeze rustled with a melancholy sound through the dead grass and stunted bushes around me, and the howling of a solitary cayote among the hills appeared to me unusually mournful. Nothing else could be heard except the snoring in camp of Ben Wade, who was one of the most provident men, where eating and sleeping were concerned, I ever met with. Ben's motto was, "never refuse to eat or sleep when you are on the plains, if you should have a chance forty times a day, for you can't tell how soon the time may come when you will have to go forty days without any chance at all. In that way," says Ben, "you can keep up and stand the racket a good while." * * * *

And before I proceed further I must diverge a little and give an anecdote concerning Ben. He could eat more and sleep more than any man I ever saw. When he was out on the plains he would eat forty times a day if he had a chance. It may be, says Ben, forty days before we will get any more, and in this way, by being sure to keep eating when I have it, it enables me to go without a long time.

Ben was always on hand when there was anything to eat, and the moment he was off guard you could hear him snoring like a wild mule. One night Ben and I went on a spying expedition in one of the villages of the Wacos. The dogs discovered us, and their barking soon aroused the whole Indian tribe, and in a little while they began to pour out of their lodges with their bows and arrows in their hands. We concluded about that time we could find a healthier locality a few miles off, and we made for the river bottom, about two miles distant, and just as we passed the last Indian lodge, Ben discovered a side of buffalo ribs roasting before a fire in front of the lodge.

"Cap," says Ben, "let's stop and take a bite, there is no telling when we will get another chance," and at that very moment we could hear the red devils yelling behind us like a pack of hungry wolves. "Well," said I, "Ben, if you are willing to sell your life for a mess of pottage you can stop, but I set a higher price on mine and can't tarry just now." "But," says he, "Cap, it is a rule I always stuck to, never to let a chance slip of taking a bite when I am on the warpath and I do not like to break through it at this late day." Seeing I made no signs of stopping, for some of the Indians were then within a hundred yards of us screaching like so many catamounts, he said, "if you won't wait I must take the ribs along with me," and I wish I may be cut up into bait for mud cats if he didn't grab them up and sling them over his shoulder, though a half dozen of the foremost Indians were then in sight of us. Ben and I were both pretty hard to beat in a foot race them days, but those Indians compelled us to put in our best licks for a mile and a half. The darkness of the night, however, was in our favor, and we finally got safely within the bottom. As soon as I thought we were out of immediate danger I stopped a little while to catch my breath, and said to Ben: "As you would bring the ribs along I believe I will take one of them now, my run has given me an appetite." "I am sorry, Cap," says he, "but you spoke too late, I've polished them all," and if you will believe me it was a fact. While we were running for dear life, with a dozen red skins after us, Ben had plucked the ribs as clean as the ivory handle of my six-shooter. Notwithstanding this, Ben was as true blue as ever fluttered and would do to "tie to" when danger was about. Thinking Ben had slept enough I determined to go and wake him and get him to help me bring in the horses and mules. Just at that moment I saw one of the horses raise up his head and look for a long time in a certain direction and soon afterward I saw a deer come running as if something had frightened it. I waited long enough to see there were no wolves after it and hurried to camp and gave Ben a shake by the shoulders and told him to get up. I spoke to him in a low voice, for I did not want to wake up the other boys. "Hello," said he, raising himself on one hand and rubbing his eyes with the other. "Hello, Cap," said he, "what's the matter, is dinner ready?" "No," I replied, "you cormorant, it has'nt been half an hour since you had dinner enough for six men. Get up and help me to bring in the horses, Indians about." Says Ben, "I have'nt seen any yet." I said, "but they are about here certain." "Why, Cap," said he, "if I did not know you so well I would say you are over-cautious, but if you say fetch in the horses here goes," and between us we brought them all in and fastened them securely in the chapparal without waking any of the other boys.

After we had got them well fastened, Ben lay down again to finish his nap, but scarcely had he coiled himself in his blanket when he sprang up as suddenly as if a stinging lizard had stung him. "Cracky!" says he, "Cap, I hear their horses' feet; they are coming!" I listened attentively, and sure enough, I could hear the clatter of their horses' feet, clattering on the rocky ground, and the next minute saw twenty-three Comanche warriors coming towards our camp as fast as their horses could bring them. We aroused the boys in an instant and were ready for them. They had evidently expected to take us by surprise, for they never checked their horses until they had charged up within a few feet of the chapparal in which we were posted, and began to pour in their "dogwood switches" among us as thick as hail. But we returned the compli· ment so effectually with our rifles and six shooters that they soon fell back, taking off with them four of their warriors that had been emptied from their saddles. They wounded one of our men slightly, a Mr. Fry, and killed a pack mule.

They went off out of sight behind a hill, and most of our men thought they had gone for good, but I told them they were mistaken, and that we should have a lively time of it yet, and that the Indians had only gone off to dismount, and that they would come back again soon and give us another "turn;" and so it turned out, for we had scarcely reloaded our rifles and six shooters when they rose up all around the little thicket in which we were, yelling and screeching as if they thought we were all a set of green horns, to be frightened by such a noise. But I saw very plainly that they were in earnest this time, and I told Ben Wade to take three of the boys and keep them off from the far side of the thicket while I kept them at bay with the rest of the men on the side next to the coach.

We had our hands full, I can tell you. I think we killed one of their noted chiefs in the first charge they made on us, and that they were bent on revenge, for I never saw the red rascals come up as boldly to the scratch before. Three or four times they charged us with great spirit, and once they got right in among us, so that it was a hand to hand fight. The boys never flinched, but threw the six shooter bullets in among them so fast that they could not stand it long, and they retreated out of sight behind the hill.

When the Indians were charging us so firecely I saw one of my men skulking behind a clump of prickly pears. I went to him and told him to come out and fight like a man. "Cap," said he, "I would if I could, but I can't stand it." I saw by the way his lips quivered and his hands shook that he was speaking the truth. I replied, "well, stay there then if you must, and I will say nothing about it;" but some of the rest noticed him, and if I had not interposed they would have killed him, and I might just as well let them, for the poor fellow had no peace of his life afterwards. I have seen two or three men in the course of my life who were naturally scarey, and could not help it any more than they could help having bandy legs or snub nose. They are born so and are more to be pitied than blamed. You might as well blame a man for not being as smart as Henry Clay as to blame him for not being brave as Julius Cæsar; all the same, it is very aggravating to have them act in that way when the service of every one is needed as it was on this occasion. But after all, bravery is about as safe from harm as cowardice. This man was the only one that was wounded, with the exception of Fry. An arrow flew where he was hiding, struck him in the arm and pinned him to the prickly pear behind which he was concealed.

After the Indians retreated the second time, the boys of course thought that was an end of the fight, but I told them I did not think so, that my idea was that the Indians would try to delude us in the belief that they were gone, when in fact they were waiting for us to start off on our journey. I told them that we could soon satisfy ourselves as to the facts of the case. Accordingly I ordered every man to take his gun and lie down under the coach and keep perfectly quiet. The boys were beginning to get a little tired of this position, all but Ben, who was fast asleep, when we saw an Indian cautiously poke his head out of the chapparal about seventy yards from where we were. He looked for a long time towards us and seeing no sign of life there, he ventured out and straightened himself up to have a better view. "Don't fire, boys," said I, "there will be more of them out directly, and we can get two or three of them." In a little while another Indian came and stood by the first one, and then another, and so on until there were five of them standing side by side, all looking intently toward the coach, and wondering, I suppose, what had become of us.

"Now, score 'em boys," said I, and we let them have it. Four of them fell dead, and the fifth one scrambled back into the chapparal as fast as if he had bet his life on accomplishing the feat in a second of time.

I ordered the men to reload, telling them that some more Indians would come out presently to carry off the dead. But I was mistaken that time. Nothing could be seen of them for fifteen or twenty minutes, when we saw an arm rise up out of the bushes on the edge of the chapparal and make a sort of motion, and the next instant one of the dead Indians was "snaked" into the thicket, and I wish I may be kicked to death by grasshoppers if they didn't rope every one of them and drag them off in that way, and we could never see a thing except that Indian's arm motioning backward and forward as he threw the lasso.

"Boys," says I, "that gets me! I have been in a good

many scrimmages with the Indians, but I never saw them 'snake off' their dead in that way before." However, I continued, "it shows they have had enough of the fight, and I think now we might venture to make a start without any fear of being attacked by them again." While the boys were harnessing up the horses, I took my rifle and went out for the purpose of reconnoitering, and well for us that I did, for on reaching the top of the little rise where I had first taken my stand, I counted forty warriors coming down a canon not more than four hundred yards off. I was satisfied it was not the same party we had been fighting, but a re-enforcement coming to their assistance. They were slowly coming along directly toward me, and when they had arrived within about one hundred yards, I rose from where I was sitting, and showed myself to them. They halted instantly, and one of them, who I supposed was a chief, rode forward thirty or forty yards in advance of the rest, and in a loud voice asked me in Mexican, which most of the Comanches speak, "What we were doing there?" There is nothing like keeping a stiff upper lip and presenting a bold front when you deal with Indians. So I told him we had been fighting Comanches, and that we had flogged them genteely too. "Yes," said he, "You are a set of sneaking Cayotes. and are afraid to come out of the brush; you are afraid to travel the road; you are all squaws, and you don't dare to poke your noses out of the chapparal." "If you will wait until we eat dinner," I answered, "I'll show you whether we are afraid to travel the road. We shall camp at the California springs to-night in spite of the whole Comanche nation." And with this, I turned slowly around and walked back to the coach, as if I didn't think they were worth bothering about any further.

I was satisfied that if I could only make them believe we did not fear them, and that we intended to camp at the California springs that night, that they would hurry on there for the purpose of waylaying us at that place; and so it turned out, for they immediately set off for the springs, eight miles distant, leaving only three warriors behind to watch our motions. When I got back to the coach I told the boys what I had said to the Indians, and that I had no doubt they would hurry off to the springs with the intention of waylaying us there, and that my intention was to wait where we were until they had time enough to reach the springs, and we would then put out and take the back track to Fort Clark.

"They are too strong for us, boys," said I, "for they have had a reinforcement of forty warriors and they will fight like mad to revenge the deaths of those we have killed."

"Cap," said Ben Wade, "I heard you make one sensible remark to that Indian you was a talking with." "What was that, Ben?" I asked. "Why," says Ben, "you told him that as soon as we got dinner we would go to the California springs, in spite of the Comanche nation." "Yes," said I, "I told him that because I wanted him to think that we were delaying here of our own accord, and not because we were afraid of him and his warriors, and I believe they have gone off under that impression."

"It was a pretty smart dodge in you, Cap, to put 'em on the wrong scent in that way, I'll admit, but you see as we may not be able to get to the California springs, after all, *and we can get dinner*, we had better make sure of doing what is in our power. Besides, Cap," he continued, hauling out a chunk of venison and some hard tack from his wallet, "they have probably left a spy to watch us, and as you told them we would eat before we left, I will make pretense to eat a bite, so he will have no reason to think we are throwing off on them."

"There will be no danger of that, Ben," said I, "if he is where he can get a good look at you. There is no throw off in you when eating and sleeping is to be done." "Nor fighting either," he said. "If I hadn't shot that Indian on the last charge they made on us, just as he was drawing his bow on you, not six feet off, you would have a quill sticking out of your back now as long as a porcupine."

"That's a fact, Ben," I replied, "and it is not the first time you have done me a good turn in that way, and I am not the man to forget it, and when we get to Fort Clark I will stop over a day just to give you a fair chance to lay in a good supply of provender." Ben was mollified, and as soon as he had finished the venison and hard tack he tumbled over on his blanket and was fast asleep in two minutes.

After waiting about half an hour longer we took the back track to Fort Clark instead of going on to the springs and traveled as fast as we could urge on the animals. Just as we started we saw two of the Indians that had been left to watch our movements put off at full speed toward the springs, doubtless for the purpose of informing the main body of our movement. The other—for they had three— was left to watch us, followed on after us at a safe distance from our rifles for seven or eight miles, when we lost sight of him. We had so much the start of the Indians and the road was so firm and good and we rattled along at such a rate they had no chance to overtake us even if they pursued us, which I suppose they did. The next morning we reached Fort Clark, where our wounded were taken care of. The command out at the fort furnished us with an escort of twelve men and a sergeant and we made the trip back to San Antonio without any further trouble.

Wallace's Fight With the "Big Indian."

IN the fall of '42 Indians were worse on the frontiers than they had ever been before or since. You couldn't stake a horse out at night with any expectation of finding him next morning, and a fellow's scalp wasn't safe on his head outside of his own shanty. The people on the frontier at last came to the conclusion that something had to be done or else they would be compelled to fall back on 1842 the settlements, which would have been reversing the natural order of things, so we collected by agreement at my ranch, organized a company of forty men and the next time the Indians came down from the mountains we took the trail, determined to follow it as long as our horses could hold out. The trail led us up toward the head waters of the Llano, and on the third day out I discovered a great many signal smokes rising up a long distance off in the direction we were traveling. That night we camped near a water hole and put out a double guard. Just before the sun went down I saw a smoke apparently about three miles to the northeast of us and felt satisfied there was a party of Indians encamped there. So I went to the Captain and told him if he could give me leave to do so I would get up an hour or two before daylight and find out whether there were any Indians there or not.

He was willing enough to let me go, and told the guard to pass me out whenever I wanted to leave. I whetted up Old Butcher a little, rammed two bullets down the throat of Sweet Lips, and left camp about two hours before daylight, and started off in the direction of the smoke I had seen the evening before.

The chapparal was as thick in some places as the hair on a dog's back, but I scuffled through it in the dark, and after traveling through it a mile and a half I came to a deep canon that seemed to head up in the direction I had seen the smoke. I scrambled down into it and waited until day began to break, then slowly and cautiously continued my course along the bottom of the canon. It was crooked, and in some places so narrow that there was scarcely room enough in it for two men to travel abreast.

At length I came to a place where it made a sudden bend to the left, and just as I turned the corner I came plump up against a big Indian, who was coming down the canon, I suppose with the intention of spying out our camp. We were both stooping down when we met, and our heads came together with considerable force, and the Indian rolled one way and I the other. We both rose about the same time, and so unexpected was the encounter that we stood for a moment uncertain what to do, and stood glaring upon one another like two catamounts when they are about to dispute the carcass of a dead deer.

The Indian had a gun as well as I, but we were too close to each other to shoot, and it seemed we both came to the conclusion as to what was best to be done about the same time, for we both dropped our rifles and grappled each other, saying not a word. You see, boys, I am a pretty stout man yet, but in those days, without meaning to brag, I do not believe there was a white man west of the Colorado river that could stand up against me in a regular catamount, bear hug, hand-to-hand fight, but the minute I hefted that Indian, I knew I had undertaken a job that would bring the sweat from me, and perhaps blood too. He was nearly as tall as I am, say six feet one or two inches, and would weigh, I suppose, about one hundred and seventy-five pounds net, for he had no clothes on worth mentioning. I had the advantage of him in weight, but he was as wiry and active as a cat, and as sleek as an eel; and no wonder, either, for he was greased from head to foot with bear's oil. At it we went in right down earnest, without a word being spoken by either one of us—first up one side of the canon, down in the bottom, then up the other side, and the dust flew in such a way that had one been passing along the bank above, they would have supposed that a small whirlwind was raging below. I was, however, a little the stronger of the two, and when we rose to our feet I could throw him easily enough, but the moment he touched the ground the "varmint" would give himself a sort of a squirm, like a snake, and pop right up on top of me, and I could not hold him still a moment, he was so sleek with bear's grease.

Each one of us was busy trying to draw his butcher knife from the sheath all the time, but neither could get a chance to do it. At last I found that my breath was failing me, and I came to the conclusion that if I did not do something soon I should have my note taken to a certainty, for the Indian was like a lobos wolf and was getting better the longer he fought. So the next time we rose I put out all my strength and gave him a back-handed trip that brought his head with great force against a sharp pointed rock that was lying on the ground. He was completely stunned by the shock for an instant, and before he fairly came to I snatched my knife from the sheath and drove it with all my strength up to the hilt in his body. The moment he felt the cold steel he threw me from him as if I had been a ten year old boy, sprang upon me before I could rise, drew his own butcher knife and raised it above his head with the intention of plunging it into my breast.

I tell you what, boys, I often see that Indian now in my dreams, particularly after eating a hearty supper of bear meat and honey, grappling me by the throat with his left hand and his glittering butcher knife raised in his right—

his two fierce eyes gleaming like a panther's in the dark. It is astonishing how fast a man can think under such circumstances. He thinks faster than words can fly along one of these new-fangled telegraph lines. I looked toward the blue sky above me and bid it a long farewell, and to the green trees, the sparkling water and bright sun. Then I thought of my mother as I remembered her when I was a little boy; the old home, the apple orchard, the brook where I used to fish for minnows, and the commons where I used to ride every stray donkey and pony I could catch; and then I thought of Alice Ann, a blue-eyed, partridge built young woman I had a "leaning to," who lived down in the Zumwalt settlement. All these, and many more thoughts besides, flashed through my mind in the little time that knife was gleaming over my breast. All at once the Indian gave a keen yell, and down went the knife with such force that it was buried to the hilt in the hard earth at my side.

The last time I had thrown the Indian down a deep gash had been cut in his forehead by the sharp pointed rock, and the blood running down into his eyes from the wound, blinded him so that he missed his aim. I fully expected he would repeat the blow but he lay still and made no effort to draw his knife from the ground. I looked at his eyes and they were closed hard and fast, but there was a devilish sort of grin still about his mouth as if he had died in the belief that he had sent me before him to the happy hunting grounds. I threw him off of me and he tumbled down to the bottom of the canon stone dead. My knife had gone to his heart. I looked at him some time, lying there so still and stiffning fast in the cool morning air, and said to myself: "Well, old fellow, you made a good fight of it anyhow, and if luck had not been against you you would have 'taken my sign in' to a certainty, and Alice Ann would have lost the best string she's got to her bow." And now said I to myself: "Old fellow, I am going to do for you what I never did for an Indian before, I am going to give you a decent Christian burial." So I broke his gun into a dozen pieces and laid them beside him, according to the Indian custom, so it might be handy for him when he got to the happy hunting grounds (though if they havn't firstrate smiths there I don't think it will be fit for use soon) and then I pulled up some pieces of rock from the canon and piled them around and over him until he was completely covered and safe from the attacks of the cayotes and other animals, and there, I have no doubt, his bones are to this day. This is a true account of my fight with the big Indian in the canon.

Wallace's Maverick.

INDIANS are sometimes monstrous impudent, and will run the greatest risks without anything to gain by it. Would you believe that not more than six months ago a party of five Tonkawa warriors came within half a mile of my ranch and in broad daylight killed one of my fattest mavericks [an unmarked yearling calf], pitched their camp, and set in for a general jollification? It happened 1867 that morning that Tom Jones, Bill Decker, Jeff Bonds and myself were out looking after the stock, when all at once Jeff remarked that he smelt meat roasting on the coals. I then turned up my nose to windward and smelt it too, as plainly as I ever whiffed fried middling of a frosty morning with the breeze dead ahead when I've been coming into camp after a three hours hunt before breakfast. Talk about your Hostetter's bitters and your patent tonics! The best tonic that I know of is a three hours hunt among the hills of a frosty morning. It gives a fellow an appetite that nothing less than a mule and a hamper of greens can satisfy.

Well, as I was saying, just as soon as I smelt roasted meat I knew there were Indians about, although the last place I should have looked, if I had been hunting for them, would have been the vicinity of my ranch. Still, I was certain they were there somewhere, for wolves, and panthers, and catamounts, and other varmints, you see, always take their meat raw. So I told the boys to keep quiet, and get down and fasten their horses. We then recapped our guns and revolvers and cautiously crept along through the bushes until we discovered the Indians, not more than fifty yards from us, where they were making themselves as much at home and as comfortable around their fire as if they were in the mountains about the head of the Guadalupe river, which is undoubtedly the roughest little scope of country to be found in the State of Texas. I whispered to Jeff, who was nearest to. me, and said: "Well, don't this beat you! Did you ever know such impudence before in your life? To kill one of my fattest mavericks and barbecue it in broad daylight within half a mile of my ranch! Well, if I don't let 'em know I am the landlord·of these diggins yet, and bring in a bill for the entertainment they have had, you may call me short stock, if I am six feet three in my stockings!"

All this time the Indians never suspected we were near them. There was one big fellow among them who must have been six feet two or three inches high in his stockings, though, of course, he never had on a pair in his life, and he was making himself very prominent around the fire, broiling the fat steaks of my "maverick" upon the coals, and turning and toasting the joints of meat on the spits; all the while laughing and talking just as if he did not know he was within a mile of Big Foot's ranch. I don't think I ever felt less like giving quarter in my life but once, and that was when a big buck nigger, with a nose like dormant window, and a pair of lips that looked like he had been sucking a bee gum and got badly stung in the operation, objected to my registering as a voter. He was one of the board of registers at Clarksville, but he was not in a condition to object to any one else registering that day, and probably the next, for I took him a clue over the head that would have stunned a beef, but he never winked; I changed my tactics and gave him twelve inches of solid shoe leather on the shins that brought him to his milk in short order. The "buro" fined me fifty dollars and costs, but the amount is not paid yet, and probably won't be until they can get a crowd that is good at traveling and fighting Indians to pilot the sheriff to my ranch.

But, to come back to the Indians that were barbecuing my maverick. I determined to take the impudent chap that was making himself so prominent around the fire into

my special keeping, and I whispered Jeff to draw a bead
on the one sitting down, and to tell Bill and Tom to shoot
at the three standing up. At the word, all four of our rifles
cracked like one gun. Just as I drew the trigger on him
the big Indian was lifting a chunk of my maverick from
the fire. At the crack of the rifle the chunk flew up in the
air, and the big Indian pitched head foremost on his face
right among the hot coals and ashes, and before we left
there was a stronger smell of roast meat than ever, but it
was not my maverick. Jeff also killed his Indian dead in
his tracks, but only one of those that Bill and Tom fired at
was wounded, and not very bad at that. They retreated
into the thick chapparal, and we never saw them again.
However, we got all their bows and arrows, and one first
rate new flint and steel rifle, to say nothing of the maverick,
which was done to a turn; for, to give the scamps their due,
they do understand roasting meat to perfection. The big
Indian that I got must have been a sort of chief, for he had
about twenty pounds of brass rings on his arms, and a
"cue" that reached down to his heels, that "nipped and
tucked" in the hot ashes like a burnt foot. The other Indians took the little hint I gave them and have never
camped on my premises since.

The Indian Hater.

SAID Big Foot, did I ever tell you about a curious sort of
character I fell in with at the "Zumwalt settlement," on
the Lavaca, a year or so after I came out to Texas? I
have met with many a good, honest hater in my time,
but this fellow hated Indians with such a vim that he hadn't
room left even for an appetite for his food. But he had
a good reason for it, and if they had served me as they did
him, I am afraid I should have taken to scalping Indians
myself for a livelihood, instead of being satisfied with
"upping" one now and then in a fair fight.

A party of eight of us had been out on an exploring expedition to the Nueces river, which was then almost unknown to the Americans, and the night we got back to the Lavaca we encamped on its western bank, and all went to sleep without the usual precaution of putting out a guard, thinking we were near enough to the settlements to be safe from the attacks of Indians. I told the boys I thought we were running a great risk in not having any guard out, as I had already found that where you least expected to meet with Indians, there they were sure to be; but the boys were all tired with their long day's ride, and said they didn't think there was any danger, and if there was, they were willing to take the chances. So, after we had got some supper and staked our horses, we wrapped our blankets around us, and, as I have said before, were all soon fast asleep.

I was the first one to rouse up, about daylight the next morning, and looking in the direction we had staked our horses, I discovered they were all gone. I got up quietly, without waking any of the boys, and went out to reconnoiter the "sign." I had gone but a little way on the prairie when I picked up an arrow, and a few yards further on I came across one of our horses lying dead on the grass, with a dozen "dogwood switches" sticking in various parts of his body. This satisfied me at once that Mr. John had paid us a sociable visit during the night, and, with the exception of the one they had killed (he was an unruly beast) had carried off all our stock when they left.

I went back to camp, stirred up the men and gave them the pleasing information that we were ten miles from wood and water and flat afoot. There was no use crying; so we held a "council of war" as to what was best to be done under the circumstances. At length it was decided that each man should shoulder his own plunder or leave it behind, just as he preferred, and that we should take a bee line for the Zumwalt settlement above us on the river, there borrow horses if we could, follow the Indians, and endeavor to get back from the Indians the ones they had stolen from us. So we hastily got a snack, each man shouldered his load and put out at a dog trot for the settlement. It was a pretty fatiguing tramp, hampered as we were with our gun and rigging, but we made it in good time. Fortunately for us, a man had just come into the settlement from the Rio Grande with a large *caballada,* and when we made known our situation to him, he told us to go into the corral and select any of the horses we wanted. They were only about half broke, and it took us fully an hour to catch, bridle and saddle them, and then fifteen minutes more to get on their backs. I was more lucky than the most of the boys, for I only got two kicks and one bite before I mounted mine. When all was ready, we put spurs to our steeds and galloped back to our camp of the previous night. We took the trail of the Indians, which was plainly visible in the rank grass that grew at that day along the river bottoms. Several men who lived in the settlement volunteered to accompany us, so that our number, rank, but not file (for we were all colonels, majors or captains except one chap, and he was a judge), amounted to thirteen men, all armed and mounted.

As long as the Indians kept to the valley, we had no trouble in following their trail, and pushed on as rapidly as we could. When we had traveled eight or ten miles, I had to halt and dismount for the purpose of fixing my girth, which by some means had become unfastened. While I was engaged at this, I heard the tramp of a horse's hoofs behind me, and on looking back the way we had come, I saw a man riding up rapidly on our trail. When he got to where I was, he reined in his horse, evidently intending to wait for me, and I had a chance of observing as curious a looking specimen as I ever saw before in any country.

He was a tall, spare built chap, dressed in a buckskin hunting shirt and leggins with a coonskin cap on. He had a long old fashioned flint and steel Kentucky rifle on his shoulder and a tomahawk and scalping knife stuck in his belt. His hair was matted together and hung around his neck in great uncombed swabs and his eyes peered out from among it as bright as a couple of mesquite coals. I have seen all sorts of eyes, of panthers, wolves, catamounts, leopards and Mexican lions, but I never saw eyes that glittered, flashed and danced about like those in that man's head. He was mounted on an ugly, rawboned, vicious looking horse with an exceedingly heavy mane and tail, but notwithstanding his looks any one could see with half an eye that he had a great deal of "let out" in him on a pinch. As soon as I had patched my girth I mounted my horse and rode along sociably with this curious specimen of an individual for a mile or so without a word passing between us. I got tired of this, and although I felt a little skittish of the strange looking animal, I at length made a pass at him and inquired if he "was a stranger in these parts?" "Not exactly," he replied, "I have been about here off and on for the last three years and I know every trail and water hole from this to the Rio Grande, especially those that are used by the Indians in going and coming." "Ain't you afraid," I asked, "to travel about so much in this country alone?" He grinned a sort of sickly smile, his fingers clutched the handle of his tomahawk and his eyes danced a perfect jig as he said: "No, the Indians are more afraid of me than I am of them. If they knew I was waylaying a particular trail they would go forty miles out of their way to give me a wide birth, but the trouble is they never know where to find me. And besides, the best horse in the country this side of the Brazos can't come along side of Pepper Pod when I want him to work in the lead." As he said this he gave his horse, Pepper Pod, a smart touch with his spurs, when he gave a vicious plunge and started off like a shot out of a shovel, but was soon reined in and we rode on together again in silence for some time.

Finally I said to him: "Man of family, I suppose?" Gracious! If a ten pound howitzer had been fired off just then at my ear I couldn't have been more astonished than I was at that chap's actions. He turned pale, his lips quivered, he fumbled with the handle of his butcher knife, and his eyes looked like two lightning bugs in a dark night. He didn't answer me for awhile, but at length he said:

"No, I have no family now. Ten years ago I had a wife and three little boys; but the Indians murdered all of them in cold blood. I have got a few of them for it, though; and if I am spared long enough I will get a few more of them before I die."

As he said this he clicked the trigger of his gun and pushed the butcher knife up and down in its scabbard. His eyes danced in his head worse than ever; he gave Pepper

Pod another dig in the ribs, who reared and plunged in a way that would have emptied any one out of the saddle except a number one rider.

After awhile he and Pepper Pod both quieted down a little, and he said to me:

"You mustn't think strange of me. I always get in these flurries when I think of the way the Indians murdered my poor wife and my little boys. But I will tell you my story," said Jefferson Turner—for that was his name—and he thus began:

"Ten years ago I was as happy a man as any in the world, but now I am miserable except when I am waylaying and scalping an Indian. It's the only comfort I have now. I had a small farm in Kentucky, not far from the mouth of the Beech fork, and, though we had no money, we lived happily and comfortably, and had nothing to fear when we laid down at night.

"But, in an unlucky hour for us, a stranger stopped at my house one day, on his way to Texas, and told me about the rich lands, the abundance of game and the many fortunes which had been made in this new country. From that time I grew restless and discontented, and I determined that I would as soon as possible seek my fortune in that promised land.

"The next fall I had a chance to sell my farm for a good price, and I sold it and moved off to Texas; and, after wandering for some time, we finally settled on the bank of a beautiful little stream that runs into the Guadalupe river.

"My wife had left Kentucky very unwillingly, but the lovely spot we had chosen for a home, the rich lnnds, the beautiful country around and the mildness of the climate, at length reconciled her to the move we had made. One lovely morning in May, when the sun was shining brightly and the birds were singing in every tree, I took my rifle and went out for a stroll in the woods. When I left the house my wife was at work in our little garden, singing as gaily as any of the birds, and my three little boys were laughing, shouting and trundling their hoops around the yard. That was the last time I ever saw them alive.

"I had gone perhaps a mile entirely unsuspicious of all danger when I heard a dozen guns go off in the direction of

my house. The idea flashed across my mind in a moment
that the Indians were murdering my family, and I flew to
the house with the speed of a frightened deer. From the
direction I approached, the house was hid from view by a
thick grove of elm trees that grew in front. I rushed
through this and hurried through the open door of my
house, and the first thing I saw was the dead body of my
poor wife, lying pale and bloody upon the floor, with the
lifeless form of my youngest boy clasped tightly in her
arms. She had evidently tried to defend him to the last.
My two eldest boys lay dead close by, scalped and covered
with blood from their wounds.

"The Indians, who had left the house for some purpose, returned at that instant, and before they knew I was there I
shot one of them through the heart with my rifle, and drawing my butcher knife I rushed upon the balance like a tiger.
There were at least a dozen of the savages, but it would
have made no difference if there had been a thousand, for
I was desperate and reckless of my life, and thought only
of avenging the cruel and cowardly murder of my poor
wife and children.

"I have but a faint recollection of what happened after
this. I remember hearing the yells of fright and astonishment the Indians gave as I rushed upon them, and that I
cut to pieces several of them with my butcher knife before
they could escape through the door, and then all was a
blank and I knew nothing more.

"I suppose some of them fired on me from the outside and
gave me the wounds that rendered me senseless, but I gave
them such a scare that they evidently never entered the
house again, as otherwise, you know, they would have taken
my scalp and taken off the dead Indians.

"Some time during the day one of my neighbors happened
to pass by the house, and noticed the unusual silence that
prevailed, and seeing no one moving about, he suspected
something was wrong and came in, when the dreadful sight
I have described to you met his eyes.

"He told me afterwards that he found me lying on the
floor across the dead body of an Indian still grasping his
throat with one hand and my knife with the other, which
was buried to the hilt in his breast. Near by lay the bodies

of three other Indians, gashed and hacked with the terrible wounds I had given them with my butcher knife.

"My kind neighbor, observing signs of life in me, took me to his house, dressed my wounds and did all he could for me. For many days I lay at the point of death and they thought I would never get well, but gradually my wounds healed up and my strength returned; although for a long time afterwards I wasn't exactly right here (tapping his forehead), and even now I am more like a crazy man than anything else when I have to go a long time without lifting the scalp of an Indian, for then I always see (especially when I lie down at night) the bloody corpses of my wife and poor little boys."

"I hope, my friend," I said, for I didn't like the way his eyes danced in his head and the careless manner he had of cocking his gun and slinging it around, "I hope you have had your regular rations lately and you don't feel disposed to take a white man's scalp when an Indian's can't be had handily." The fellow actually chuckled when I said this, the first time I had heard anything like a laugh from him.

"Oh, no;" he said, "I have been tolerably well supplied of late, and can get along pretty comfortably without a scalp for a week or so yet. I have forty-six of them hanging up now in my camp on the Chicotile, but I shan't be satisfied unless I get a cool hundred before I die; and I will have them too, just as sure as my name is Jeff Turner."

Again his eyes glared out of his bushy locks, and his fingers fumbled about his knife handle in a way that if I had had a drop of Indian blood in my veins, it would have made me feel exceedingly uneasy. At length, to change the subject, I asked him which way he was traveling, though, of course, I knew very well he was going along with us. "Any way," he replied, "that these Indians go; I'd just as soon go one direction as another; I always travel on the freshest Indian trail I come across. You and your company may get tired and quit this trail without overtaking the Indians, but I shall stick to it until I get a scalp or two to take back with me to my camp on the Chicotile."

By this time we had come up with our companions, and all rode on in silence. At length we came to a hard, rocky piece of ground, where the Indians had scattered, and we lost the trail altogether, for not the least sign was visible to our eyes. You see at that time none of us had much experience in trailing and fighting Indians except Jeff Turner, "The Indian hater." We soon discovered that he knew more about following a trail than all of us put together, and from this time on we let him take the lead, and we followed him wherever he went. Sometimes where the ground was hard and rocky, and the Indians had scattered, he would hesitate for a little while as to the course to pursue, but in a moment or so he was all right again, and off at such a rate that we were compelled to keep in a full trot to keep up with him.

About half an hour before sun down he came to a halt, and when we had all gathered around him, he told us to keep a sharp look out, and make no noise, as the Indians were close by. In fact, we had scarcely traveled three hundred yards until we saw their blanket tents in the edge of some post oak timber about a quarter of a mile to our right. We put spurs to our horses, and in a few minutes we were among them. The Indians did not see us until we were within fifty yards of their encampment; but still they had time to seize their guns and bows and give us a volley as we charged up, but luckily without damage, with the exception of slightly wounding one of our horses.

We dismounted at once, and began pouring a deadly fire into them from our rifles. Just as I sprang from the saddle to the ground, a big Indian stepped from behind a post oak tree and drew an arrow on me that looked to me as long as a barber's pole. I jumped behind another tree as spry as a city clerk in a dry goods store when a parcel of women come around shopping. I had no time to spare either, for just at that moment an arrow grazed my head so closely that it took a strip of bark from the tree about the width of one of my fingers. I drew a bead upon him as he started to run, but the arrow had so unsettled my nerves that I missed him. The fight kept pretty hot for about fifteen minutes, when the Indians soured on it and retreated into a thick chapparal, leaving several of their warriors dead upon the ground.

I noticed my friend Jeff Turner several times during the fight, and each time he was lifting the scalp from the head of an Indian that either he or somebody else had shot down.

It is said that "practice makes perfect," and it was astonishing to see how quickly Jeff would take off an Indian scalp and load his rifle in readiness for another. One slash with his butcher knife and a sudden jerk, and the bloody scalp was soon dangling from his belt. At the same time he never seemed to be in a hurry, and was as cool and deliberate about everything he did as a carpenter is when he is working by the day and not by the job. When the Indians began to retreat, one of them jumped on one of our horses which was tied hard and fast to a post oak near the camp, forgetting in his hurry to unfasten the rope. Round and round the tree he went until he wound himself up to the body. Just at that instant Jeff plugged him with a half ounce ball, and had his scalp off before he was done kicking.

After the Indians retreated to the chapparal, a little incident occurred that shows the pluck of these red rascals when they have been brought to bay. We were standing all huddled up together, loading our guns, for we did not know but that the Indians had retreated on purpose to throw us off our guard. All of a sudden we were startled by a keen yell and the firing of a gun, and at the same instant a tall chap named B——, who had come with us from the settlement, dropped his rifle. and clapping his hands to his face, cried out: "Boys, I am a dead man!"

I looked around to see where the shot came from and discovered an Indian lying in the grass about thirty yards from us, with his gun in his hand and sinking slowly back to the earth from which he had partially raised himself by a dying effort to take a last pop at the enemies of his race. I had seen this Indian fall in the fight and supposed he was dead, which he was in fact an instant after he yelled and fired his gun; for I went up immediately to where he lay and found him as dead as a door nail, with his gun tightly clasped in his hands. When he fired at B—— he had seven rifle balls through various parts of his body, for the wounds were plainly to be seen, as he had nothing on worth speaking of but his powder horn and shot pouch. Our Indian hater, Jeff Turner, came up to him about the time I did and lifted the hair from his head before you could say Jack Robinson, and strung it on his belt to keep company with three other scalps that were already dangling from it. These scalps

served to ease the mind of Jeff considerably, as he told me
they would, and he became quite sociable after the fight
and once laughed outright when one of the men told a
funny story about shooting at a stump three times for an
Indian before he discovered his mistake. But the unusual
sound of his voice frightened him, or else he had used up
all the stock he had on hand, for I never saw him crack a
smile afterward. As it turned out, B—— was worse scared
than hurt, for the Indian's bullet had only grazed his head,
but stricking the black-jack tree near which he was standing, it had thrown the rough bark violently in his face causing him to suppose that he was killed. The Indians had
killed a fat buck, and when we pounced upon them they
had the choice pieces spitted before the fire, and after the
fight we found them done to a turn. We had not eaten a
bite all day, and seized upon the venison as the lawful spoil
of war, and made a hearty supper of it, together with some
hard tack which we had brought along with us in our hav-
ersacks. While I was eating supper I could not help but
feel sorry for the poor creatures who had cooked it only a
half hour before, and who were now lying around us cold
and stiff on the damp grass of the prairie, so soon to be devoured by vultures and cayotes. However, these reflections
did not take away my appetite, or if it did, a side of roasted
ribs and about five pounds of solid meat disappeared with
it. As soon as we had finished our supper we changed our
saddles from the horses we had ridden to those the Indians
had stolen from us, which had been resting for some time,
and mounting, we took the trail back toward the settlement,
where we arrived about sunrise the next morning; making
seventy-five miles we had traveled in part of a day and
night without ever getting off our horses, except for a few
moments when we fought the Indians.

Jeff, the Indian hater, left us here for his camp on the
Chicolite, and I never saw him again. I was told when I
was at the settlement several years after this that he stayed
around there for a good while, occasionally coming into the
settlement for his supplies of ammunition, etc., and always
bringing with him four or five scalps. At length he went
off and never returned, and it is supposed that the Indians
finally caught him napping. At any rate that was the last
that was ever seen of Jeff Turner, the Indian hater.

Mrs. Simpson's Children.

THE following account of the capture of Mrs. Simpson s children will illustrate the audacity of the Indians as late as 1842, in what is now the heart of the city of Austin. In the latter part of the summer of 1842, Mrs. Simpson, a widow lady, was living in the city of Austin, on West Pecan street, about three blocks west of the avenue. She had three children, two sons and one 1842 daughter, but when the following incident occurred her eldest son had gone down to Fayette county, and was in the employment of his uncle, trying to make something with which to support his poor widowed mother. Late one afternoon in the summer of 1842, when the sun was about two hours high, Mrs. Simpson's two youngest children, the daughter about fourteen years of age, and her little son, Tommie, about twelve years of age, went out in the valley (for there were no houses there at that time) about one hundred and fifty yards from the residence of Mrs. Simpson to drive up the cows for their mother to milk, it being a custom in those days to milk very early for fear of the Indians. When the children had reached the little branch where the house of Major C. S. West now stands, and started to drive the cows home, which they found grazing on the banks of the branch, a bunch of Indians sprang out from behind the bushes growing along the banks of the branch, where they had concealed themselves, seized the children, mounted their horses and made off for the mountains. Mrs. Simpson screamed and gave the alarm, when a body of citizens immediately put out in pursuit, some on foot, not taking time to get their horses, while others saddled their horses and gave hot chase. The Indians passed out about where the residence of Governor Pease now stands, going in the direction of Mount Bonnell.

At one time the citizens came within sight of the redskins just before reaching Mount Bonnell, but the Indians, after arriving at that place, passed on just beyond to the top of the mountain, which being rocky, the citizens lost the trail and were never able to find where the savages went down the mountain.   After the Indians had gone some six miles from Austin and had arrived at Spicewood Springs, which is situated in the edge of the mountains, opposite where the poor farm of Travis county is located, they brutally murdered the little girl in a horrible manner. They kept Tommie a prisoner for some eighteen months, when he was traded off to some Indian traders, who returned him to his mother. It was learned from Tommie after his return home that his little sister fought the Indians so desperately they determined to kill her.   Tommie stated that he did all he could while at the springs to persuade his sister to calm down and not make such resistance, but all to no purpose.   The Indians, he says, after remaining at the springs awhile, took his sister up on a hill some distance and in a short while came back with her scalp hanging to the saddle of one of the bucks. Judge Joseph Lee, in company with Tommie and a number of citizens, went out and succeeded in finding the remains after obtaining the above information from Tommie, which they had no trouble in identifying.

Judge James Smith.

JUDGE SMITH was a resident of the city of Austin. On the ninth day of January, 1841, he rode out north of Austin to feed and look after his hogs, taking his little boy nine years old behind him on his horse. When about two miles from town he was discovered by a prowling band of Indians, who immediately gave chase. Judge Smith was well mounted, and would have made his escape, 1841   but his horse, becoming unmanageable, ran under the limb of a tree and knocked him and his little boy off. They jumped up and ran into a thicket near by, but were overtaken by the savages and Smith was killed and his

JOSEPH LEE COMING TO THE RESCUE OF JUDGE JAYNES' FAMILY.

little son taken prisoner. Judge 'Smith's brother, on the same day, and only a few miles from where the judge was killed, was pursued by the same band of Indians, but his good horse saved him.

Just ten days after the killing of Judge Smith, his father-in-law went·alone into the country four miles south of Austin to cut a bee tree, and while out was discovered by the Indians and killed. It seems strange to us at this day that men could become so reckless of danger. Judge Smith's little son was returned to his mother under a treaty about a year after his capture.

Judge Jaynes.

JUDGE JAYNES immigrated with his family to Texas in the year 1840, and settled north of the city of Austin, near where the Lunatic Asylum now stands. In the fall of 1842 a number of Indians made their way into the settlement and came very near the city limits. They were first seen on the eastern slope of College Hill, where the University now stands, by a Mr. Davis. Davis had 1842 been out riding, and had alighted from his horse to· let him graze in the valley east of College Hill, when he discovered Indians making towards him at a rapid rate. He had no time to bridle his horse, but lit into the saddle and put spurs to his animal. He fled down the valley, crossed Waller creek, passed over the hill where the Blind Asylum now stands, and made his way into town. Judge Joseph Lee, who had been to Mr. Raymond's, about one mile north of town, as he returned to town, saw the Indians pursuing Davis. He ran into town and gave the alarm.

The Indians did not pursue Davis very far, but turned back in a northwesterly direction towards the mountains. As they passed on they discovered a Mr. Larrabee on foot, and chased him a short distance, but he gained a thicket and eluded them. When the Indians got to Judge Jaynes's house they rode up to the fence and saluted Judge Jaynes and family, and claimed to be friendly Indians, saying they were Tonkawas. Judge Jaynes walked out to the fence, carrying his little son in his arms. His son about fourteen years old went out with his father, and got outside of the fence and began to talk to the Indians. A hired hand of Judge Jaynes's also went out into the yard. When Judge Jaynes reached the fence, one of the Indians reached out and took hold of his little boy and tried to pull him out of his father's arms. The father became alarmed, pulled his child away and started into the house. As he did so an Indian drew his gun and shot him through the body. They then shot and killed the Irishman in the yard, and one of the Indians snatched up the fourteen year old boy behind him. The whole band then fled as fast as they could. Judge Jaynes reached his door and fell down, and died in a few minutes. His wife and little boy, who was also wounded by an arrow shot, were all that remained of what a few minutes before had been a happy family. Judge Lee arrived at the house but a few minutes after the Indians left, and just as Mrs. Jaynes, with her little child in one arm, was attempting to pull her husband in the door with the other.

William Bell and Captain Coleman.

ON the first day of January, 1843, Captain Coleman and William Bell accompanied Mrs. W. M. Thompson from her residence in the city of Austin to the farm of James Smith, about two miles below town on the Colorado river. They left Mrs. Thompson at Mr. Smith's, promising to return for her in the afternoon. About sundown, they started from Austin in a carriage for Smith's for 1843 the purpose of bringing Mrs. Thompson back with them. After crossing Waller creek, and when about one-half mile from town, they were suddenly attacked by a party of twenty-five or thirty Indians. They jumped out of their carriage and ran into a small field. The Indians pursued and overtook them in the field where they killed and scalped Bell and captured Coleman. They stripped Coleman of his clothes and started off with him, driving him before them by prodding him with their spears. While this was taking place, a part of the Indians had passed by the field and gone near Nolan Luckett's house, about two hundred yards distant. Nolan's little son and a negro boy were driving up the cows when the Indians swooped down upon them. They captured the negro, but seeing that the little white boy would reach the house before they could overtake him, one of them shot him in the back with an arrow, from which wound he died in a few days. Before the Indians who captured Coleman had gotten out of the field, and while they were driving him before them, they were discovered by Joseph Hornsby and James Edmonson, two young men who lived down the river several miles below Austin, and who had started home on the same road that Bell and Coleman were traveling. They had no arms except one pistol, but they did not propose to allow these dusky devils to take off an acquaintance and friend before their eyes. It was growing late and there was no time to procure arms or arouse the citizens. If Coleman was to be rescued, it must be done at once. So without delay and with a reckless courage which heaven delights to honor, they put spurs to their horses and charged right down among the savages, yelling at the top of their voices and firing the old pistol. The Indians were taken so by surprise that they did not take time to kill Coleman, but fled precipitately, not knowing perhaps, how many were after them, and thinking it best to collect their divided forces. Coleman ran off in another direction and made good his escape. The yelling of Hornsby and Edmonson and the firing of the pistol had given the alarm in town, and the citizens were gathering for pursuit. The Indians fled along what is now the eastern part of the city of Austin and crossed Waller creek about two miles above town. Hornsby and Edmonson, though they had emptied their pistol and could do the Indians no harm, followed close on their rear and kept constantly yelling so that the pursuing party might keep track

of them. The few citizens of Austin who had hastily gathered together could tell from the yelling which way the
Indians were going, and they rightly concluded that they
were making for the mountains northwest of Austin; so
they made up Waller creek along the west side, and where
the fair grounds are now situated, about two miles from
town, they intercepted the Indians about dusk. The Indians
halted and made a short resistance, but a few volleys from
the citizens rifles again routed them, and they were closely
pursued to the mountains. Mr. Hornsby had a horse killed
in this fight. Three horses were captured from the Indians,
with their saddles and equipments, and it is supposed as
many Indians were killed or wounded.   Judge Joseph Lee,
who still lives in Austin, was in this fight, and he speaks in
the highest praise of the courage of Hornsby and Edmonson
in rescuing Captain Coleman from his savage captors.

Colonel Moore's Expedition.

IN the year 1839, the Lipan Indians who were almost constantly at war with the Comanches, were so hard pressed
by them that they took refuge among the whites.   In the
winter of 1839, some Lipans who were hunting on the
San Saba river, discovered that a large body of Comanches
had established their winter quarters on that stream. They
immediately returned to the settlements and notified
1839 the whites of the fact.   The Texans knowing that
this would be a very convenient base from which the
Comanches could depredate upon the settlements, determined to oust them from it. A force of sixty Texans was soon
raised and immediately started for the San Saba, accompanied by forty or fifty Lipans as allies and guides. The
whole force under the command of Colonel John H. Moore,
an old frontier fighter. The Colonel, with his Texans, proceeded up the Colorado river, having previously sent forward the two Lipan Indians, Malcom Hornsby and Joe Mar-

tin, to act as spies. Before reaching the Comanche encampment some of these spies rejoined Colonel Moore's command, and informed him that the Comanches had been largely reinforced by other bands who had established their winter quarters at the same locality. Colonel Moore, however, determined to attack them at all hazzards, and continued his march until within a mile or so of the encampment, where he halted until night. After dark he led his forces quietly to within a short distance of the Comanche camp and again halted them, intending to make an attack upon it as soon as daylight appeared.

The plan of attack was as follows: The Lipan Chief Castro, with a portion of his men were to drive off the horses belonging to the Comanches, while Colonel Moore with his own men and the rest of the Lipans was to charge upon their encampment. The encampment was composed of a large number of tents made of buffalo skins and many temporary wigwams, all filled with warriors, women and children. At the dawn of day the Texans charged and fired a volley into these tents and wigwams, killing indiscriminately a number of all ages and sexes. In a moment the wildest scene of confusion ensued—warriors yelling, women screaming and children crying—all running hither and thither and against and over each other in their fright. In this charge the Lipans used their bows and arrows with considerable effect.

The Texans in the excitement of the moment, and their eagerness to make short work of the enemy, got mixed up in the tents among the Indians, and in this way they were frequently in danger of shooting each other. Owing to this and the fact that Colonel Moore perceived at this juncture that the Indians outnumbered his little force considerably he very reluctantly ordered a retreat. He fell back and took a position in a ravine, where he continued the fight until night came on. As soon as he retreated the Indians rallied several hundred strong and made charge after charge upon his little band, but in every instance they were driven back by a deadly volley from the rifles of the Texans. In one of these charges a Comanche warrior was shot so severely that he was unable to retreat when the others fell back. He laid himself flat on his back and shot arrows high up in the air, so that when falling they would come down point foremost among the Texans. As he lay close to the ground it was some time before the Texans could give him his quietus and put an end to his boomerang performance.

Castro, the Lipan chief, whose part of the programme it will be remembered, was to run off the Comanche's horses, was too greedy and attempted to take the whole drove, some two or three thousand head, but not having men to manage so many, the Comanches came up with him and succeeded in retaking the most of them. The few horses the Lipan's got away with were not brought into Colonel Moore's camp, so that while he was fighting they were securing the plunder. Had Colonel Moore's force been larger no doubt he could have captured a large amount of stolen property and some prisoners. Miss Matilda Lockhart, a sketch of whose life among the Indians has already been given, was at that time a prisoner in the Comanche camp and her father was with Colonel Moore when the attack was made upon the Indian village. This battle was fought on the fourteenth of February, 1839.

The Battle of Brushy

JUST as Colonel Moore's party were returning from their expedition against the Comanches upon the San Saba, about the eighteenth of February, 1839, citizens along the Colorado valley, from Bastrop to Austin, were thrown into a high state of excitement by the report that the Indians had made an attack upon the settlers of Well's, or Webber prairie, or, perhaps, both. The news going 1839 up and down the river as rapidly as the facilities of the day would permit soon brought together squad after squad of citizen soldiers, all eager to ascertain the cause of the alarm, which proved to be a large body of Indians variously estimated at from two to three hundred, who had made a sudden attack upon the upper end of

Well's prairie, killing Mrs. Captain Coleman and her son Albert, a lad about fifteen years old, and robbing the house of Doctor J. W. Robertson, who, at the time, happened to be on a visit with his family at the residence of his neighbor and brother-in-law, Colonel Henry Jones. Mrs. Coleman, early in the morning, was with her family out in a small field or garden patch, which lay between the bottom timbers of Coleman branch and the Colorado bottom, when they were suddenly charged upon by a large body of Indians, who came up whooping and yelling as they emerged from their hiding places, near by the residence. James Coleman and a man by the name of Rogers made good their retreat to the Colorado bottom, while Mrs. Coleman with the rest of the family ran towards the house, which all succeeded in gaining, but little Tommie, a boy about five years old, who was taken prisoner. The attack was so sudden and the panic so complete that Mrs. Coleman did not, perhaps, think of the fate of her children until she reached the door of her humble cabin, when her mother's love induced her to look back to see what had become of them—only to receive an arrow wound exactly in the throat, from the effects of which she soon expired, but before expiring she exclaimed, "Oh, children, I am killed;" then turning to her eldest son, said: "Albert, my son, I am dying, get the guns and defend your sisters." Albert, a mere lad about fifteen years of age, and his little sisters were the only persons left to defend the house, and their already murdered mother from further injuries of the inhumane, brutal savages.

Young Albert fought with heroic bravery for a while, killing and wounding some three or four of the enemy; but finally he received a wound which in a very short time proved fatal, and he breathed his last with his head pillowed in the lap of his oldest sister, the last words he uttered being, "Sister, I can't do any more for you. Farewell." This left his two little sisters to take care of themselves as best they could. The little girls, who had taken refuge under the bed, after the death of their brother, kept up a conversation with each other, as they had been told to do, which doubtless deterred the Indians from entering the house, thereby saving their lives and the house from being plundered.

The Indians now began to withdraw, halting at the house

of Doctor J. W. Robertson, robbing it of its contents, ripping open the feather beds in the open air, thus giving the country around a very singular appearance, and carrying off captive seven of the Doctor's negroes.

About noon the citizens from above, twenty-five in number, had collected, and, electing Jacob Burleson their captain, began immediately to reconnoiter, and some two hours later they were joined by twenty-seven men under the leadership of Captain James Rogers, from below, brother-in-law of Captain Burleson, making in all fifty-two men. So eager were the men for the chase that they concluded not to go into any further election of officers, but to march in double file, and for Rogers and Burleson to ride each at the head of one file and command the same. "About ten o'clock the next day," says Mr. Adkisson, who was present and participated in the battle, "we descended a long prairie slope leading down to a dry run, a little above and opposite Post Oak Island, and when about three miles north of Brushy, we came in sight of the enemy."

On the run, and directly north and in front of us, was a thicket, and the enemy, when first discovered, were about one-half mile above, and to the west of the thicket, bearing down towards the same, and as we thought, with the intention of taking possession of and giving us battle from it. We immediately agreed to charge up, open file, flanking to the right and left, cutting the Indians off from, and we taking possession of, the thicket ourselves. The larger portion of the enemy being on foot, and we all well mounted, we could, and ought to have, taken possession of the thicket, and would have done so but for the flinching of a few men, which threw the whole command into a state of confusion, resulting in the death of Captain Burleson and our inglorious flight from the field, leaving his remains to the mercy of the enemy. There were those of us who dismounted and hitched our horses as often as three times, but at last had to retreat, and in doing so the horse of W. W. Wallace became frightened, pulled away from him and ran among the Indians, leaving the gallant Texan on foot in the midst of the conflict. His horse was soon mounted by one of the Indian warriors, who appropriated him for his own use. Just at this time Captain Jack Haynie, observing the perilous situation of Wallace, made a dash for him, pulled him up behind him on his horse, and both made good their retreat.

[NOTE.—For the rescue of Wallace by Captain Haynie, the latter was presented with an elegant rifle, handsomely mounted, by the father of Wallace, who was then living in Tennessee. Owing to the handsome appearance of this rifle, it will be remembered by many old Texans. William Wallace is the father of John Wallace of Travis county.]

The whole command fell back to Brushy (the Indians making no attempt to follow us), in a line one mile in length; the main body of us mortified at the result of the morning's conflict. unwilling and ashamed to return to the settlements without a fight, and being loath to leave the dead body of the gallant Captain up on the field, we halted at Brushy, not knowing what to do. But while halted here in a state of indecision, General Ed. Burleson, who had heard of the raid made by the Indians, raised thirty-two men, followed our trail, halted and brought back those of our men who had so precipitately fled in the morning. This reinforcement swelled our number to eighty-four men, with General Edward Burleson in command, assisted by Captain Jessie Billingsley, who had distinguished himself at the battle of San Jacinto. After a general consultation and exchange of opinions, the whole command moved on sorrowfully yet determined to retrieve the fortunes of the morning. About two o'clock p. m., we struck the enemy, but not where we expected to find them. Instead of occupying the thicket, they had selected a very strong hold in the shape of a horseshoe, with very high and rising ground at the toe—the direction we would approach them, unless we changed base, which, after reconnoitering for a while and exchanging a few shots we did, dropping down, crossing the run and dividing our command, one party under the command of Captain Billingsley, taking possession of the run below the Indians, while the other party went above and gained possession of a small ravine which emptied into the main one just above the Indians. Our intention being to work our way down and drive the enemy before us, while Captain Billingsley was to work his way up the ravine, thus securing a complete route of the Indians.

But nature and fortune seemed to favor the enemy; the
ravines leading from each of our little commands to where
the enemy lay massed behind high banks on either side,
spread out into an open plot forty or fifty yards before
reaching him, which would have made it extremely dangerous for us to carry out our plans.   Thus failing in our
attempt to route and chastise the enemy and recapture the
prisoners they held in possession, we were forced to select
safe positions, watch our opportunities, and whenever an
Indian showed himself, to draw down on him and send the
messenger of death to dispatch him.   In this manner the
fight lasted until sundown, the Indians retreating under
cover of night, and leaving us in possession of the field,
putting up the most distressing cries and bitter lamentations
ever uttered by mortal lips or heard by mortal ears.   We
camped on the battle field that night, and early next morning the sad duty devolved upon us to make litters to convey
our dead and dying to the settlements.   How many Indians
were killed, we have no means of knowing.   Their bitter
wails indicated that their loss was great, either in quantity or quality, perhaps both.   We lost during the day
four of our best and most prominent citizens, to wit:
Jacob Burleson, Edward Blakey, John Walters and Rev.
James Gilleland.   The last named lived some ten days after
receiving his wound.   I have been thus particular in mentioning the names of those who fell in the days conflict,
that their names may be enrolled high up in the temple of
Texas liberty, and find a niche in the hearts of an apprecia-
tive people.

> For no slab of pallid marble,
>   With white and ghastly head,
> Tells the wanderers in our vale,
>   The virtues of our dead.

> The wild flowers be their tombstone,
>   And dew drops pure and bright,
> Their epitaph, the angels wrote
>   In the stillness of the night.

The Cordova Fight.

THE historian is familar with the character and history of Vicente Cordova, a Mexican who lived at the Mexican settlement at Nacogdoches, Texas, and of his insurrectionary movements prior to the date of the happening of events which we are about to relate; but in order to prepare the reader for a full understanding of the importance and significance attached to the battles fought 1839 by the Texans with Cordova and Flores, we deem it best to introduce the subject by quoting from Yoakum, who wrote with all the necessary data from the war department before him. Commencing on page 257, volume 2, he says:

"Prior to the attack of the French on Vera Cruz and the civil war in Mexioo, that government had begun a system, which if it had been carried out as intended, would have resulted very disastrously to Texas. The object was to turn loose all the Indians on her borders from the Rio Grande to the Red River, on the citizens of Texas. Of this fact the Texas government received undoubted evidence. Before the revolt of the Mexicans at Nacogdoches, Vicente Cordova had been in correspondence with the enemy at Matamoras. In July, 1838, he addressed a letter to Manuel Flores, the Indo-Mexican agent, at Matamoras, stating that he held a commission from Filisola to raise Indian troops as auxiliaries to the Mexican army, and that he had already entered on his duties. He desired to co-operate with Flores, and wished to have an understanding in the matter; and for that purpose he desired to have a meeting and personal consultation. Cordova also wrote to Filisola on the twenty-ninth of August and the sixteenth of September, 1838, from the head waters of the Trinity, giving him an account of his progress. The departure of Flores from Matamoras, was, from some cause, delayed until the opening of the following year.

"In the mean time, on the twenty-seventh of February, 1839, Brigadier General Canalizo, who had succeeded Filisola at Matamoras, sent instructions to Cordova—the same that had been given to Flores—to excite the frontier Indians to make war on Texas. He said it was in the power of the Indians, and also for their interest, to prevent the Texans from taking advantage of the troubles in Mexico; that they must not trust to flying invasions, but to operations having a more permanent effect; causing, if not daily injury, at least perpetual alarm and inquietude to the enemy, and depriving them of their commerce, the spoils of which were to go to the Indians. While the savages were to be cautioned not to go near the boundary of the United States, they were to occupy the line of Bexar about the Gaudalupe, and from the Leon to the mouth of the San Marcos. This position, continues Canalizo, is the most favorable for the friendly Indians (as well as for the friendly Mexicans), in order that they shall have the enemy in front only, keeping a friendly and generous nation, as Mexico, in the rear. They were to harrass the Texans in every conceivable manner; they were instructed to burn their habitations, lay waste their fields; and if they assembled in bodies, the Indians were to hang around about them in small parties, and, if possible, steal their horses. The instructions to Cordova were to be sent to him, and he and Flores were to have an interview as soon as possible. They were to spare the defenseless of all ages and sexes; and to pursue and punish all Indians friendly to the whites, and all Mexicans who traded with the whites.

"Canalizo, in his letter to Cordova, informed him that as soon as hostilities with France had terminated, the Mexican army greatly increased, would proceed to recover Texas. Flores had messages from Canalizo to the chiefs of the Caddos, Seminoles, Biloxas, Comanches, Kickapoos, Brazos, Tehuacanas, and perhaps others, promising them the lands on which they had settled; and assured them that they need 'expect nothing from those greedy adventurers for land who wish to even deprive the Indians of the sun that warms and vivifies them, and would not cease to injure them while the grass grows and water runs.' Such were the instructions under which Commissioner Flores set out on his mission. Cordova had been hanging about the Indian camp high up on the Trinity and Brazos rivers, his followers greatly reduced."

From the above we readily see the object of the visit of Flores and Cordova to Mexico, and the reader is now prepared to follow the movements of these two men, who had entered into a conspiracy with the officials of Mexico upon one hand and the Indians of Texas on the other, to urge an exterminating war upon the Texans. With this object in view Cordova, in the early part of the spring of 1839, started on his way westward with a party of Mexicans, Indians and negroes, numbering about sixty or eighty, all told, with the intention of crossing a few miles above the city of Austin and thus avoid the Hornsby settlement, some ten or twelve miles below, (which, at that time was the largest in that section of country, but it seems he missed his bearings and struck the vicinity of the settlement before he was aware of his whereabouts. He then changed his course up the Colorado river, in the direction of the mountains. This was about the twenty-fifth of March, 1839. It so happened that George Davis and Reuben Hornsby, who were riding out on the prairie that day, came across this trail, and supposing that it had been made by the Indians, at once spread the news among the settlers, who collected immediately and set out in pursuit of their unknown enemy. The Texans rendezvoused at Austin and organized in the afternoon of the twenty-fifth, with Colonel Burleson as commander, Captains Billingsley and Andrews each being in charge of a company under Burleson. The entire force now consisted of about one hundred men, and the spies who had been sent out to reconnoiter for the enemy having returned late in the afternoon, reported that the trail crossed the Colorado river between the falls and Austin and leading in the direction of Seguin. Colonel Burleson at once took up the line of march and camped that night on Bears creek, about ten miles southwest of Austin. Early the next morning, before leaving camp, a runner came from the Hornsby settlement, saying a large Indian trail had been discovered in the neighborhood and that the men were wanted to protect the families. This information caused the party to abandon the trail and the whole force proceeded with as much dispatch as possible on the back track to protect their families, whom they had left the day before. Arriving at the settlement it was soon discovered that a false alarm had been given, and that the trail which had been found, was the identical trail Burleson and his men had been following. This caused a good deal of dissatisfaction among some of the men and several declined to return and take up the trail again, so that when Burleson reached the spot where he had camped the night previous, he found himself with a force not exceeding seventy or seventy-five men. Night having come on by this time, Burleson pitched his camp at the same place where he had bivouacked the night before.

About ten o'clock that night Tom Moore, known generally as "Black Tom," and Roberson arrived at Burleson's camp, and made known to them for the first time what character of enemy they were pursuing.

It seems that Roberson, who had started out with Cordova on his journey to Mexico, had for some reason fallen under the displeasure of his superior, whereupon Roberson was court martialed, sentenced to death, and was to have been shot the next day, being the same day on which he arrived at Burleson's camp; but while Cordova's party was crossing Onion creek Roberson made his escape, made his way down the creek bottom, succeeded in reaching the house of Moore, whereupon they both immediately set out to notify Burleson of Cordova's mission to Mexico. This man Roberson was an American, and had evidently enlisted under Cordova, expecting to receive a good share of the spoils should Cordova be successful in his undertaking, but becoming somewhat conscience stricken on account of his treachery toward his own race, and having shown some weakening on the way, became a fit subject for suspicion among his allies, and no doubt the fear of being betrayed by Roberson more than any other cause, was the real secret of Cordova's displeasure to him and the cause of the court martial. Be this as it may, it was certainly a most fortunate incident for Texas, as the reader will soon learn. Roberson freely stated to General Burleson that Cordova was on his way to Mexico to obtain munitions of war with which to equip the Indians for the purpose of making a well directed warfare upon the Texans, and that he would return to Texas so soon as he had accomplished the object of his mission. It will be remembered that Burleson and his command had lost one day by reason of the false alarm which had been given, and it was afterward learned that Cordova's party had likewise lost a day in hunting for Roberson, so that in fact the Texans had neither lost nor gained any on the enemy since starting in pursuit.

Early the next morning Burleson started out with his command in the pursuit of the enemy, but failed to overtake them that day. In the following afternoon, however, about one hour and a half by sun, the spies who had been sent on in advance came in sight of Cordova's party, who had halted for a rest, and the men were lying around carelessly on the grass while their horses were grazing around them with their saddles on. The enemy, it seems, had halted for another purpose than rest, as it was ascertained afterward from prisoners taken by the Texans that Cordova had sent spies on ahead for the purpose of spying out the situation of Seguin with the view of sacking the town that night. As soon as Burleson's spies had returned and made their report, he pushed forward rapidly with his forces and was soon within sight of the enemy, who, unaware of the Texans, were ensconced within a few miles of Seguin in the open post oaks, through which ran a little ravine.

Colonel Burleson, before making an attack, divided his command into two divisions, Captain Andrews commanding the right wing and Captain Billingsly the left, and when these two divisions had taken their respective positions, their line of battle assumed the form of an inverted V, and with one more company to have closed up the rear a complete triangle would have been formed, thus rendering escape impossible for the enemy without cutting their way through; but only two companies being present to participate in the battle, and their positions having been taken as above stated, left one side open as a means of escape for the enemy. Burleson gave the command to charge and open fire, and at the first volley fired by the Texans the enemy took to flight in the direction from which Burleson approached them, when a running fight of five or six miles took place. The exact number of Mexicans, Indians and negroes killed in this battle is not known, but the number killed, as near as could be ascertained by actual count, was about eighteen; a considerable number were wounded, among whom was their leader, Vicenti Cordova, and some three or four were taken prisoners. The Texans sustained no losses in this fight.

There were one or two rather amusing incidents which occurred, one during and the other after the fight, and it may not be out of place to mention them here. During the chase one of the Indians became unhorsed, whereupon he immediately ran back to a little mesquite tree with his gun presented, and came up face to face with about a half dozen of the Texans, who were following in close pursuit. Doctor Ventress, who happened to be one of the party, dismounted, raised his gun, but gave the Indian the first fire, which, fortunately, missed him, whereupon the doctor immediately fired, and at the crack of his gun the Indian fell dead. Doctor Ventress, in after years, when alluding to this incident, always spoke of it as his duel with the Indian. In the fight some three or four prisoners were taken, among them there was a big French negro, weighing about two hundred pounds. Colonel Burleson turned him over for safe keeping to Tom McKennon, an Irishman who was along with the Texans.

When Burleson returned to the place he had left them, he found that Tom had crossed and tied the negro's hands behind his back and had tied the end of his horse's stake rope to the Indian's hands, thus using the captive as a stake for his horse rope; and as Burleson rode up, Tom cried out: "Faith and bejasus, Colonel, I've got him fast." This negro claimed to have always been free, but would not acknowledge any allegiance to the Texan government; on the contrary, claimed to have always maintained a hostile attitude toward the Texans, and as he still manifested a disposition, which was very distasteful to them, he was accordingly court martialed and sentenced to be shot the next day. There were six men detailed to execute the sentence, and they were to shoot by threes. James O. Rice, who was along with Burleson on this expedition, seemed exceedingly anxious to shoot the negro, and offered five dollars to any one of the men who had been detailed, for his place, and one of the three men who were to fire first, not having any special fondness for such sport, accepted the proposition, where-upon Rice, elated at his good luck, as he considered it, took his position in the first file, and at the command "fire!" only two guns fired. Rice's gun, it seems, from some cause had failed to fire, and feeling disgusted and crestfallen, he said: "There, by G—d, my gun has snapped, for the first time in my life." From the fact that Rice had manifested so much anxiety to shoot the negro, the failure of his gun to fire amused some of the boys very much. Thus ended the Cordova fight which occurred about the twenty-eighth of March, 1839.

Cordova, though pretty severely wounded, finally made his way to Mexico with the balance of his followers. Flores, it seems, was with Cordova at the time, but made good his escape.

The Rev. A. J. Adkisson and General William P. Hardeman, both citizens of Austin, Texas, are among the few surviving Texans who participated in the Cordova fight. But few there are of the present day who stop to think for a moment when these two silvery haired old veterans are seen passing along the streets of Austin, of the valuable services they have rendered Texas on numerous occasions, both as a Republic and as a State.

⚓be jflores jfigbt.

WE have never seen in print a full and complete account of the Cordova fight, which we have just given, nor of the Flores fight, which we are about to narrate. Mr. Yoakum, in his History of Texas, briefly refers to both, but he reverses the order in which they should come; and while he attaches considerable importance to them, as has been seen in our extract from his work, which appears in our account of the Cordova 1839 fight, he has not entered into a detailed account of either. In view of the inestimable value to Texas of the information obtained from the Mexicans when these two battles were fought, insignificant as they may seem to some; we have concluded to give a minute or detailed account of each while there yet survive a few—a mere handful—of those worthy pioneers who participated in both engagements, and who can vouch for the accuracy of our statements; for it was from them that we obtained the information that enables us to write intelligently upon the subject.

After the return of Colonel Burleson's forces from the Cordova fight, in the latter part of March, 1839, it was deemed prudent by the citizens settled along the Colorado river to organize for the protection of their families. The Indians were not only extremely troublesome to the whites, but it became evident now, from the information obtained from the man Roberson, who escaped from Cordova, an account of which has been given in our sketch of the Cordova fight, that the Mexican government had entered into a conspiracy with the Indians to make an incessant warfare upon the whites, lay bare their homes and their fields, and drive them from the country. Austin at that time had not arisen to the dignity of a town—much less a city—and was just beginning to build up. The largest settlement in the vicinity of Austin then was down the river some ten miles, and was known as the "Hornsby settlement." The reader can judge from the above how much exposed this section of country was to the ravages of the Indians and marauding Mexicans at that day. Consequently, in order to protect themselves and their families, a ranging company was organized, consisting of about twenty men, with Mike Andrews as captain, and James O. Rice, lieutenant, and it was while this company were out scouting on Onion creek, south of Austin, on or about the fifteenth of May, 1839, and about where the San Antonio road crosses the creek, that Flores and his party were discovered, as they were returning from Mexico, making their way back to eastern Texas, to carry out the enterprise inaugurated by Cordova, Flores and others, as previously related. Captain Andrews's company, as stated, only consisted of about twenty men: but on this occasion six civilians, as they were called, had joined him. While out on Onion creek, and reconnoitering, Lieutenant Rice and ——— Castleberry, on

the evening mentioned, had ridden over the hill south of the
creek to kill a deer for supper. They had only been gone a
short time when they came galloping back, apparently
somewhat excited, and reported that they had seen in the
distance a large *caballada* of horses, but owing to the distance they were from them, and it being very late in the
afternoon, about dusk, they could not tell definitely whether
the horses were mounted or not, but they were satisfied
some of them were, from the fact that some of the animals
were white, and there appeared to be dark looking spots on
their backs.

On the south side of Onion creek there was a range of
hills lying up and down the creek for some distance, and
when Rice and Castleberry discovered Flores and his party
(who, at that time, were unknown to the rangers, but the
latter strongly suspected from the first that it was Cordova
and Flores returning from Mexico) they were traveling
almost due north while the rangers were traveling almost
due east. Owing to the range of hills just mentioned the
Mexicans could not be seen by the rangers, but the latter
pushed on, expecting to intercept the enemy at the crossing
on the creek, but when they arrived at the foot of this range
of hills the Mexicans had crossed the creek and had entered
a thick post oak and cedar country on the north side. The
rangers took their trail and followed it a few miles, but dark
overtaking them pretty soon they halted for the night, leaving their horses all saddled, and they themselves sleeping
upon their arms. At daylight they renewed the pursuit,
determined to overtake the unknown enemy at all hazards,
though the Texans were becoming more and more confident
all the time that it was a return of the Flores party from
Mexico with munitions of war, etc., to place in the hands of
the Indians; consequently the rangers felt the importance
of overhauling them. After following the trail about two
miles, and just as they were beginning to enter the cedar
brake they met the enemy face to face, and were within
forty or fifty yards of each other when both parties halted.
The cedar brake was a very large one, and evidently Flores
and his party had been rambling around in it all night,
until tired and worn out, they concluded to take the back
track and disentangle themselves from the meshes of the

forest. Before reaching the cedar brake and coming up with Flores's party, however, there had been considerable dispute among the Texans as to the number of the enemy, some contending that it was a large party, while others maintained that there were not over twenty-five or thirty, and in support of their theory gave a very plausible reason, as will soon be seen, which illustrates the perspicacity and keen perception of an experienced frontiersman. While following the trail they came to a stooping tree, which was rather too low for a man on horseback to ride under, and upon a close inspection of the trail made by the horses of the enemy it was discovered that all of them, with the exception of some twenty-five or thirty, passed under the stooping tree while the others went around it. This method of reasoning proved afterwards to be reliable, but it was not convincing to those of the party who were disposed to be a little weak kneed. So when the enemy were run upon suddenly, the Texans were divided in their opinions as to whether or not an attack should be made. The Mexicans were so concealed by the brush and timber, that their number could not be ascertained definitely. Perceiving that the Texans were hesitating and parleying over the matter, the Mexicans put on a bold front and cursed and dared the the rangers to charge them. Some of the Texans who could speak Spanish retorted in similar language. Wayne Barton, one of the civilians who had gone along with the rangers, was decidedly opposed to giving battle, and thus addressed Captain Andrews:

"Captain Andrews, if you take your men into that thicket it will be equivalent to leading them into a slaughtering pen, for they will every one be killed."

This little speech had a telling effect upon those who had been wavering, and the captain seemed also to be considerably impressed with the force of the remark, and ordered a retreat. While this parleying was going on, the enemy moved off into the heart of the cedar brake. The Texans now turned their course homeward; but there was great dissatisfaction among most of the men at the conduct of the captain, and they did not hesitate to express their disapprobation in unmistakable language—some of which will not do to repeat here.

After riding about three miles in the direction of home, and discussing the matter pro and con, a portion of the company grew very indignant and considerable feeling was being engendered, when one of the party, A. J. Adkisson— known then as "Ad.," but now as the Rev. A. J. Adkisson— told the boys to hold up a little and he would ride ahead and ask permission of Captain Andrews--who at that time was some little distance in advance of the company—to give those who desired it, permission to return and follow the enemy, for it was now known beyond a doubt who they were. To this proposition the boys consented; whereupon Adkisson rode up to the captain, informed him of the sentiment of the men, and asked him if he would give those who desired to do so, permission to return and continue pursuit of the enemy; that they did not wish him to assume any of the responsibility, and all they asked was simply permission to return. The captain hesitated a moment and then, with an oath, replied: "Yes; and I'll go back, too." This was joyful news to all of the party except six of the men, who continued their course homeward, and who, no doubt, about that time felt like the poor private soldier during the late civil war, when he was found by his colonel in the rear of his command, crying like his heart would break, and was asked "what he was doing there crying like a baby, that he ought to be ashamed of himself;" whereupon the poor fellow said, as he wiped away the tears which were trickling down his cheeks: "I wish I was a baby, and gal baby at that."

It is but fair to say, however, that those who turned back were not all civilians, for it was one of this class who did the most effective fighting that was done when finally the enemy were overhauled.

The little band of Texans now only numbered twenty, and instead of returning to the place where they had left the Mexicans, they cut across the country in a westerly direction with the intention of intercepting them as they came out of the cedar brake, but when they arrived at the point where they expected to intercept them, the enemy had passed out some little time in advance of them. It was about nine o'clock in the morning, and the Texans put out in a brisk gallop, but they had not gone far before learning

that the enemy were also traveling at a rapid gait. The
trail was followed all that day without overtaking the Mexicans, and night coming on the Texans camped on a spur of
the mountains on the north side of the Colorado river, and
within about a mile of the same until the next morning.
During the night a heavy rain fell rendering it very difficult
to follow the trail the following morning. At this point
Captain Andrews's horse being quite lame, and he being a
large man, weighing at that time about two hundred pounds,
it' became necessary for him to return home, and accordingly two men whose horses were the lamest, were detailed
to go back with him. This left us a force of only seventeen
men, with Lieutenant Rice in command, and notwithstanding many of the horses were quite lame, some of which
were scarcely able to travel with their bruised and bleeding
feet, caused from climbing the rough and rugged mountains
the previous day, this gallant little band of Texans pushed
on in pursuit of the enemy. By traveling slowly and ex
amining closely every sign, they succeeded in following the
trail through the mountains out into the prairie on the
waters of the San Gabriel where the Mexicans had camped
the night previous. Here the sign was fresh and plain, and
could easily be followed in a gallop, and the horses of the
rangers, which, up to that time had shown signs of being
much fatigued, now seemed to take on new life and vigor,
and spurted off at a lively gait without being urged on
much by their riders. After following the trail until about
two o'clock in the afternoon the south fork of the San Gabriel was reached at a point where is situated a celebrated
spring, not far from where the residence of "Uncle" Billy
Johnson now stands. At this point Flores and his party
had nooned and cut down a bee tree, and when the Texans
arrived the bees had not yet settled, and the camp fires,
four in number, left by Flores, were still burning. There
being only four camp fires, was another point of circum-
stantial evidence going to show that the force of the enemy
could not be large. The Texans, knowing from these signs
that they were on a hot trail, did not halt, but pushed on
with renewed zeal and enthusiasm.

After going about a mile further, the Texans were sig-
naled by their spies, Felix McClusky and —— Castleberry,

who were about a quarter of a mile in advance of the
party, to hold up, dismount and cut switches. To the
average reader it may seem strange that the latter signal
was understood; but it was, and just as clearly as the other,
and both signals were obeyed. It becomes necessary for
frontiersman to go by signals a great deal of the time, and
they become very expert in interpreting them. The party
having provided themselves with switches, were then sig-
naled by the spies to advance, which was done, and on
coming up with them, they were informed that the enemy
had just passed over the hill. The Texans then started
off in a steady gallop, and within another quarter of a
mile were within sight of the enemy which they had been
following for two days and nights. Flores would make
a stand occassionally as if he intended to make battle, but
the Texans never checked their speed for a moment, but on
the contrary, would push forward more rapidly, raise the
Texan yell, whereupon the Mexicans would turn and retreat. Flores kept up this character of maneuvering for
some little time, and in these temporary halts made by him,
he could be seen riding up and down in front of his men
with sword in hand apparently counting our force. The
Texans kept up the charge, however, until they had driven
the enemy on to a steep bluff on the banks of the North San
Gabriel, which was so steep that it was impossible for the
enemy to descend. At this crisis, Flores, evidently for the
purpose of giving his men an opportunity of finding a crossing, rallied a few of his companions and made a charge
upon the Texans, who discovered him just in time to take
advantage of a live oak grove near by. Flores with some
eight or ten men, charged up within fifteen or twenty paces
of the Texans, and fired a volley at them, but without
effect. The Texans, who had just dismounted, did not have
their horses hitched, and were, therefore, not prepared to
properly receive the enemy; but William Wallace (heretofore mentioned as having participated in the Brushy creek
fight), who happened to be a little quicker than the balance,
had gotten in position ready for action, and just as Flores
was in the act of wheeling his horse to retreat, Wallace
took good aim, fired, and at the crack of his gun, Flores
rolled off of his horse upon the ground, shot through the

heart. Upon the death of their commander, the little party
who had accompanied him in the charge immediately fled
and joined their comrades who in the meantime had succeeded in finding a crossing, but leaving behind them all
their horses, mules, baggage, munitions of war, etc. The
last seen of the enemy, they were making their way as
rapidly as possible to the mountains beyond the Gabriel.
The Texans then gathered up the horses and mules, numbering one hundred·and fifty-six or seven, several hundred
pounds of powder and lead, seventeen dollars in Mexican
silver dollars, besides a good deal of Mexican luggage, all
of which had been abandoned by the enemy in their fight.
Everything having been collected together, and the Texans
being in high glee over their victory, they struck out for
home, arriving at the spring on South San Gabriel, just in
time to camp at the same spot where the ·Mexicans had
camped the night previous. The Flores fight occurred on
·the seventeenth day day of May, 1839.

While on their way, however, between the battle ground
and South Gabriel, the Texans were met by Captain Owen
in command of about thirty six-months rangers, well provided with a bountiful supply of provisions, and going out
to the relief of the heroic band of seventeen. It may be
well to state here that upon the return to the settlement of
those who had originally started out in pursuit of the enemy,
but from causes previously stated abandoned the pursuit,
had circulated the report up and down the river that Rice
with only sixteen men was in hot pursuit of a large body of
Mexicans, and that if he should overtake them it was highly
probable that the entire party of Texans would be slain.
This report is what caused Owen as well as Burleson and
others to start out to the relief of Rice's party. When Captain
Owen first discovered the Texans returning with a large
caballada of horses, and observing that some of the men
were wearing Mexican sombreros, the Texans having captured a few from the enemy and were wearing them when
the two parties met, he mistook them for Mexicans, and ordered his men to dismount and fire, but was finally prevailed
upon by one of his men, who strongly suspected that they
were Texans, to countermand the order. Rice's party having come up within a short time, and, the usual salutations

having been exchanged, some of Owen's company began talking about a division of the spoils, one fellow laying
claim to one horse, another to that one, and so on, until
finally the gallant little band of seventeen, began to think
that they were in earnest about the matter, which up to this
time had been looked upon as a mere joke. Perceiving that
Owen's men were serious in their claims, Rice's party
told them that they had fought the Mexicans for the property, and before dividing it out they would fight again for
it. This very much offended the Owen party, and perceiving that they were not to share in the division of the
spoils, refused to divide even a crust of bread with Rice's
party, notwithstanding they had been without anything to
eat for three days and nights. That was not all. The little
band of seventeen, who had been on the go ever since they
had struck the trail of the enemy, tired and worn out as
they were with fatigue, were denied the privilege of camping with those who came out to their relief, and they were
thus forced, tired and hungry as they were, to stand guard
all night long to protect their horses. The next morning
early Rice's party pulled out for Austin, and after traveling
some distance, and just as they were ascending Pilot Knob,
on Brushy, they met up with Colonel Ed Burleson, in command of a party going out to their relief, who generously
furnished them with all the provisions they needed. After
eating dinner, Burleson and Rice's forces came on back to
Austin, and after reaching there Colonel Burleson, Sam
Highsmith and one other gentleman whose name we have
forgotten were selected as arbitrators to determine upon the
division of the spoils, over which there had arisen a contro-
versy with Owen's company. They were out but a little
while before they decided that "to the victors belong the
spoils." Rice's party then proceeded on down to Hornsby's
Bend, and after reaching there the horses captured from
the enemy were all put in a corral and divided off into seventeen different bunches by disinterested parties, and each
drew lots for choice. This division having been made among
the men, they then proceeded to open a lot of leather sacks
which they had captured from the enemy. One of these
sacks contained the correspondence between Cordova and
the Mexican officials, and several official communications

from the latter addressed to quite a number of Indian chiefs, perhaps a dozen in all. One of the communications was addressed to Bowles, chief of the Cherokees, and one to Big Mush, another Indian chief. There happened to be a Mexican on the place—Francisco, who was possessed of some education, and by means of his translation the Texans were advised of the importance of the documents they had captured.

This is the correspondence referred to by Mr. Yoakum, and to which we have made frequent mention heretofore in our account of the Cordova fight. The summer previous to this, Cordova headed an insurrectionary movement in the Nacogdoches settlement against the whites, and, being subdued, he sought refuge, it was supposed, among the Indians, and while there no doubt sent emissaries to Mexico, offering his services to co-operate in hostile movements against the whites.

This correspondence revealed beyond the cavil of a doubt the Cordova-Flores plot, and verified the statement of the man Roberson who escaped from Cordova on Onion creek and came to Burleson's camp with Tom Moore. This valuable information was at once transmitted to the Texan government, then located at Houston, Texas. President Lamar sent out commissioners to effect, if possible, a peaceable removal of the Indians, but nothing satisfactory being accomplished, he ordered out troops against them under the command of Rusk, Burleson and Douglas.

The only survivors to-day of Rice's party are Jonathan Davis, who resides in Milam county, Texas, the Rev. A. J. Adkisson, a resident of Austin, and —— Harness, who is a resident of Burnet county. While Texas has remembered her veterans and confederate soldiers by granting pensions and land donations, this handful of hardy pioneers who accomplished so much for the republic have not only been neglected, but, with the exception of their gallant lieutenant, their names have never even been mentioned by the historian. At this late day, when we contemplate the ruin and destruction to property and the loss of life to the Texans, which might have resulted had Flores not been killed and this valuable correspondence captured, we can not but think that the fight on the San Gabriel was second only

in importance to Texas to the battle of San Jacinto. Can
it be that Texas has grown so populous, wealthy and so ar-
rogant as to be unmindful of the heroic acts of her humble
private citizens while she boasts of her gallant leaders of
the past in both war and peace? Surely the statesman of
'39, who guided the ship of State and shaped the destiny of
the infant republic, were he present to-day sl a ping and con-
trolling the legislation of our empire State would not withhold from the few survivors of this little Spartan band that
just recognition which their heroic conduct merits. Then
let the sons of Texas to-day, especially those who delight in
perpetuating the memory and heroic valor of those worthy
Texans who risked their lives and their property in the defense of their country, when next they assemble within
those spacious granite walls to legislate upon the different
questions of the hour, remember that had it not been for
Rice and his brave followers thay might not to-day be enjoying the blessings of American government upon Texas
soil, much less the honor of a seat in our magnificent capitol structure. Let them not, ere it is too late, delay in hon-
oring these surviving veterans, whose heads are fast
whitening for the grave.

The Cherokee War.

THE Texan government were now in possession of the
correspondence between Cordova and the Mexican
officials—General Canalizo and Filisola—captured by
Rice's party, as heretofore related, in the fight with
Flores on the San Gabriel, and of course were fully posted as
to the intended movements of the various tribes of Indians
who at that time inhabited eastern Texas, conspic-
1839 uous among whom was Bowles, chief of the Cherokees,
and who was looked upon by his associated tribes as
a kind of leader or head man among them all. The Cherokees and their associated tribes—the Delawares, Kickapoos,

Seminoles, Shawnees and others, numbering some twelve tribes—had settled in eastern Texas as early as 1822, and had established a village north of Nacogdoches, the town at that time being a waste, lately swept by the forces of Long and Perez. These Indians owned a considerable number of stock, had cultivated the lands to some extent, and had made some progress in the direction of civilization. As late as 1835 there were no settlers in northern Texas except a few on Red river. While the revolution was going on, from September, 1835, to April, 1836, great uneasiness was felt among the whites lest Cordova and other Mexican emissaries, who were known to be among the Indians, should per- suade them to take an active part against Texas in her war with Mexico. To avert such a threatening danger General Sam Houston sent Commissioners—John Forbes and Doctor Cameron—among the Indians to negotiate a treaty with them and if possible get them to assume a neutral position. Their mission was only partially successful, however, and the whites were still distrustful. During all this time General Houston's little army had all they could do to attend to Santa Anna, who was marching upon Texas with vastly superior forces, laying waste the country on his entire line of march. The settlers, fleeing from the invading army of-Santa Anna, were moving along the frontier, scattered all along from the Trinity river to the Sabine. It was at this critical juncture that Major General Edmond P. Gaines, U. S. A., crossed the Sabine at the head of five hundred men and established headquarters at Nacogdoches. He imme- diately sent messengers to the Indians with instructions to say to them that, if any of the Texan women and children were killed by them, he would at once attack them with his whole force. This bold move of the patriot and soldier General Gaines, had its desired effect, and restrained the Indians, if they had any intention of depredating at that time. The memory of this gallant soldier and true patriot should be held dear by all Texans for the generous and timely aid he rendered them in this hour of need.

The battle of San Jacinto was fought soon after this, which gave the Texans great prestige, and the defeat of Santa Anna saved the people of eastern Texas from im- mediate danger from the Indians, though the feeling of enmity still existed between them and the whites. It was not long before the families of Pierce and Killough were murdered, only three or four of the latter escaping, and these were brought into the settlements by the Cherokees, who cunningly represented to the Secretary of War that these murders had been committed by the prairie Indians and treacherous Mexicans. To prevent such occurrences, "Major Walters (see Yoakum, vol 2, p. 267, and reference to Report of Secretary of War, November, 1839, p. 6) had been ordered, with two companies, to occupy the Neches Saline, not only to watch the Cherokees, but to cut off their intercourse with the Indians of the prairies. Bowles, the Cherokee chief, notified Major Walters that he would repel by force such occupation of the Saline. As the Major's force was too small to carry out his orders, he established his post on the west bank of the Neches, out of the Cherokee territory."

General Sam Houston, while President of the Republic, did all in his power to allay the growing excitement and preserve peace. Having spent his early boyhood in the mountains of Tennessee, in close proximity to the Cherokees, and, previous to his coming to Texas, having lived among them for four years, he was familiar with their character and customs, and in addition to this, being very popular with this tribe, he necessarily exercised great influence over them. This being generally known, caused many to suspect that General Houston had delayed in taking any decisive steps against the Cherokees because he was more favorably inclined to them than to his own people. "Indeed," says an old Texan, "so strongly was this opinion entertained at the time by many of the Texans, that nothing but General Houston's great personal popularity could have sustained him in the almost neutral position he occupied in regard to the troubles then existing between his quondam friends, the Cherokees, and their white neighbors." However this may be, it is evident that he naturally felt kindly towards them, and was anxious to preserve peace between them and the Texans. Moreover, Houston was aware that it frequently happened that lawless whites upon the border, in some instances, were to blame for the outrages committed by the Indians in a spirit of retaliation,

and no doubt he adopted a conciliatory policy and delayed
taking any decisive action until he could definitely ascertain, first, who were the guilty parties, and to what extent
the Indians were to blame, and he would then be in a condition to deal fairly with both parties.

However, General Houston's forbearance toward the Indians seems to have been exhausted, and in the latter part
of his administration General Rusk, commander in chief of
the militia forces of the republic, was ordered out. It seems
that on the fourth of August, 1838, a party of citizens went
in pursuit of some stolen horses, and after going some distance found them secreted in a Mexican settlement, and on
their return they were fired upon and one of their number
killed. Several persons set out on their trail in pursuit of
the murderers, but after traveling some distance they became convinced from the size of the trail that there were a
considerable number of Mexicans and they returned home.
About the seventh of August it was ascertained that about
one hundred or more Mexicans were encamped about the
Angelina under the command of Nathaniel Morris, Cordova
and Cruz General Rusk made an immediate requisition
for men. On the evening of the tenth it was reported that
the Mexicans had been joined by about three hundred Indians and that the enemy, consisting of Mexicans and Indians, now amounted to about six hundred men. On the
same day General Houston. who was then at Nacogdoches,
received a letter from the Mexican leaders, headed by Vicenti Cordova—the same to whom we have made frequent
allusions heretofore—disclaiming allegiance to Texas, and
then set out on their march for the Cherokee Nation. Houston having been posted as to their movements directed General Rusk not to cross the Angelina. Major Augustine,
with one hundred and fifty men, was detached to follow the
Mexican trail, while the main body of the Texans under
General Rusk made for the headquarters of Bowles, where
he suspected the enemy had gone. On reaching the Saline,
however, he discovered that the insurgent leaders had fled
to the upper Trinity, and that their followers had dispersed.
Thus ended this little expedition, but during the month of
October of the same year General Rusk was found marching at the head of about two hundred men on his way to

Fort Houston, on the Trinity, in pursuit of a motley crowd of Mexicans and Indians, who had been committing depredations on the frontier.

Learning that the enemy were at the Kickapoo town, he marched to that place and encamped there on the fifteenth. At daybreak, on the morning of the sixteenth, he attacked the enemy, and after the engagement had lasted about fifteen minutes, Rusk ordered a charge. The enemy were completely routed and were pursued about a mile, leaving eleven of their dead upon the field. This closed the engagements with the Indians in eastern Texas for the year 1838, and after having thus discussed the policy of General Houston towards the Cherokees and their allies, we now return to the beginning of the Cherokee war proper. General Mirabeau B. Lamar having been inaugurated president of the Republic on the ninth of December, 1838, and being in full sympathy with the whites, it was quite apparent that his policy toward the Indians would be an aggressive one. After his inauguration he attempted a reconciliation of the existing troubles, but failing to effect a peaceable removal of the Indians, or to get any satisfactory assurances from them that they would cease depredating upon the whites in the future, he determined to drive them from the country, nor did he lose any time in making the necessary preparations. Major Walters having been stationed on the west bank of the Neches as previously noted; Colonel Burleson, who at that time was collecting a force on the Colorado river to operate against other Indians, was directed to march his force in close proximity to the Cherokee territory so that he might be prepared to enter the same on short notice. Burleson reached the Neches on the fourteenth of July with four hundred men. He was accompanied on this expedition by Vice President David G. Burnet, General Albert Sidney Johnston, Secretary of War, and others holding high official positions. Colonel Landrum with a regiment from eastern Texas, arrived about the same time. General Rusk, with a regiment from Nacogdoches, had arrived a few days previous. The entire force was placed under the command of General K. H. Douglass.

In the afternoon of the fifteenth of July, the combined forces of Burleson, Rusk and Landrum, under the command

of General Douglass, attacked the Cherokees and their allied
bands who had taken up a strong position about seven miles
up the river above the "Council Grounds," and were awaiting the attack. The Texans coming up in the open prairie,
were fired on by the Indians who occupied a hill near a
ravine, and then retreated in the ravine. The engagement
then became general. The ground was stubbornly contested by the Indians, and from a little before sunset when
the fight began, until dark, the conflict was sharp and fierce.
Finally, however, the Texans made a determined charge
upon the Indians and the latter fled, leaving behind them
on the field eighteen of their warriors dead. The Texans
only had three killed and five wounded. During the night
the Indians retreated several miles, and when the Texans
came upon them in the afternoon of the sixteenth, they
found the enemy strongly posted in a wooded ravine about
half a mile from the Neches, ready for battle. The Texans
were compelled to advance through an open country, and
consequently were greatly exposed to the fire of the enemy,
but they continued to advance, pouring hot shot into the
red skins. The Indians, after standing their ground for a
while, finally fled into the Neches bottom and sought protection in the swamps and thickets, not attempting to make
another stand. This was a hotly contested battle, and
during the engagement which lasted about an hour and a
half, the Indians had about one hundred of their warriors
killed and wounded, and among the former was their distinguished chief, Bowles. The Texans lost five killed and
twenty-seven wounded; among the latter were Vice President Burnet, General Albert Sidney Johnston, Adjutant General McLoud and Major Kaufman. The Indians were completely routed in this engagement, and notwithstanding
they had an estimated force of about eight hundred, against
five hundred Texans, they were taught by this engagement
the superior generalship of the whites over the Indians.

Their trail was followed for several days by the Texans
who passed many of the Indian villages and cornfields; all
of which were destroyed by the Texans. On the evening of
the twenty-fifth, pursuit was abandoned, whereupon the
troops were all marched home and mustered out of service.
This was the last fight between the whites and the Chero-

kees in eastern Texas, but notwithstanding the crushing defeat they had sustained, they continued for several months depredating upon the lives and property of the frontier people. After the death of Bowles, his son John, and an Indian named Egg, became the head chiefs of the allied tribes, who now took refuge on the head waters of the Trinity river, where they remained for a few months.

In the fall of 1839, John Bowles and Egg attempted to lead their followers into Mexico, passing entirely above the settlements. But Colonel Burleson, who happened to be out on a campaign against the wild tribes, came across their trail, followed it, and attacked them on Cherokee creek near the mouth of the San Saba river, some seventy-five miles above Austin. This was on Christmas day. John Bowles and Egg were both killed in the engagement and several of the warriors, and twenty-seven women and children captured, among whom was the wife of Chief Bowles, who had been killed in eastern Texas. All their camp equipage was also captured. The Indians fought desperately for a short time in this engagement, but they could not stand very long the hot fire that was being poured into them by the Texans. Those of the red skins who escaped from this fight retraced their steps and joined their kindred in the Indian Territory. This was the last fight with the Cherokees in Texas. We believe that it was in this engagement that the gallant Captain John L. Lynch was killed whilst leading a charge against the enemy. The Indian prisoners were all delivered by Colonel Burleson to the agent of the government.

Desperate Battle Between Cherokees and Wacos.

THE reader, ere this no doubt has grown tired of reading the many blood curdling incidents recited herein, and will be relieved to know that the Indians sometimes perpetrated outrages and murders upon each other as well as the whites. During the year 1829 the Cherokees who had crossed Red river from the Cherokee Nation into Texas, determined to remain in that portion of the State until 1829 they could make a crop and then move to a more suitable locality next spring. They settled in two villages a short distance apart, planted their crops, and everything was going on prosperously, when a body of Wacos who were on a robbing excursion, discovered the new settlement, and also noticed the fact that there was a large number of fine horses coralled in the vicinity. They determined to appropriate these fine horses for their own use and benefit, and they therefore concealed themselves in the vicinity until night, when they slipped up and succeeded in stealing the whole drove. As the Cherokees could not well leave their crops, and the Wacos besides, had carried off their best horses, they thought best to postpone following the thieves to a more favorable opportunity. It was resolved in council, however, that as soon as their crops were laid by they would visit their red brethren, recapture the stolen horses, and inflict such punishment on the Wacos as would teach them a lesson they would not soon forget.

Accordingly, in April, 1829, fifty five well armed Cherokees left on foot to visit and punish the Wacos, whose principal village was at the place where the city of Waco is now situated. Close by their village they had built a kind of fortification by scooping out the ground and raising a circular embankment ar und the depression thus formed, several feet high. The remains of this fortress were still visible a few years since on the outskirts of the city of Waco.

The Cherokees came to the Brazos river, about forty miles above the Waco village. Finding no signs of the enemy at that point, they continued on down the river until they discovered that they were in close proximity to the village. They then concealed themselves in the brush until night, and sent out scouts to ascertain its exact position.

About day break the spies came back, having obtained the desired information, and the chief told his men that the time had come to wreak their vengeance upon the thieving Wacos and to recover from them the horses they had stolen. In order to take them by surprise the Cherokee chief led his men quietly and cautiously down the bank of the river to a point about four hundred yards from the village. This was done a little before daylight, when the Wacos were asleep, and the Cherokees were thus enabled to approach very near them without being discovered. They here halted until daylight.

As soon as it was light enough to see distinctly the Cherokees moved forward as noiselessly as possible, each one with his rifle in his hand. But one of the Waco warriors, it seems, was an early riser, and while in the act of building his camp fire, his keen Indian ear detected the sound of approaching footsteps. Raising to look, he discovered the Cherokees advancing within rifle shot of the village. He gave one loud, shrill yell, which brought every Waco to his feet and ready for action.

At this juncture the Cherokees fired a volley in their midst which laid many a Waco on the ground. The Waco's, however, outnumbered greatly the Cherokees, and for some time they made a stubborn resistance. The fight lasted for several hours without intermission. At length, however, the Wacos finding that their bows and arrows availed but little against the deadly rifles of the Cherokees and a considerable number of their warriors having already fallen they retreated to the fortress before mentioned, where they had a great advantage over their assailants. They could lie down behind the embankments and shoot their arrows at the Cherokees without being exposed to the fire of their rifles. The Cherokees held a council of war as to what was best to be done. One proposition was to strip themselves naked, rush into the fort, discharge their guns and then with

tomahawks in hand kill every man, woman and child inside
of it. The Cherokee brave who made this proposition, in
order to incite his comrades, did actually strip himself, and
fastening several belts he had found in the Waco village
around his body, he boldly charged up to the breastwork
surrounding the fortress, sprang on top and cursed the
Wacos for being a set of cowardly thieves. After performing this act of bravado he jumped down and returned unhurt to his comrades amid a shower of arrows that were
hurled at him.

Just as the Cherokees had brought their council to a close
they heard the clattering of horses feet on the opposite side
of the river, and to their astonishment they discovered a
large body of mounted Indians rapidly approaching. It seems
that the Wacos, at the commencement of the fight, had dispatched a runner to the camp of the Tehuacanas, who were
their allies, to tell them to come as speedily as possible to
their assistance. The Tehuacanas promptly responded to
the call and dispatched two hundred warriors to the assistance of their allies. These were the Indians the Cherokees
saw approaching. The Wacos being now reinforced by
these two hundred Tehuacana warriors, fresh and ready for
the fray, changed the aspect of affairs considerably, and as
there was no possibility of fighting with any hopes of success the combined forces of the Wacos and Tehuacanas
there was no alternative left the Cherokees but to retreat.
The Tehuacanas immediately crossed the river and took up
their position in some post oak timber, where they kept up
a continuous yelling, but prudently did not venture within
range of the Cherokee rifles.

Just before they had taken position in the post oaks they
had captured a young Cherokee lad about twelve years old
and killed him. They then scalped him, and tying the
scalp to the end of a spear, they held it up in view of the
Cherokees. This boy was the only son of one of the Cherokee warriors, and when he beheld the scalp of his murdered
boy he was frantic with rage. His eyes flashed fire, and
without a moment's hesitation he threw off his apparel and
seized a knife in one hand and a tomahawk in the other.
The chief, who noticed this, said to him: "What are you
going to do?" "Die," replied the Indian, "with my brave

A CHEROKEE WARRIOR DEFYING THE WACOS.

boy—die slaying the cowardly thieves who have killed the only one that was left to me of all my kindred!" and saying this, and without heeding the remonstrances of the chief, he rushed, solitary and alone, upon the two hundred Tehuacana warriors. His onset was so sudden and unexpected that he succeeded in killing and wounding several before he was killed himself.

The Cherokees, having lost two men and the boy before mentioned, retreated to a cedar brake, remaining there until night, when they crossed the river and traveled down it a mile or two. They then turned into the river, which was quite low, and waded up it six or seven miles, thus effectually hiding their trail from the Wacos and Tehuacanas. Although they failed to recapture their stolen horses, as they had anticipated doing, they carried back with them to their villages on Red river fifty-five scalps taken from the heads of Wacos slain in battle.

The Cherokees Get Even.

THE Cherokees, chagrined at failing to whip the Wacos for stealing their horses, an account of which we have just given, attributed their defeat to the arrival of the Tehuacana reinforcements, and they determined to whip the latter for their interference. Accordingly, in the early part of the summer of 1830 they fitted up a party of about one hundred and twenty effective warriors for this 1830 express purpose.

The Tehuacanas were divided, living in different villages. One of their finest being situated in what is now Limestone county, and where the residences of Messrs. Lloyd and Moore now stand. There are some springs at this place around which there is quite an amount of loose limestone, on the surface as well as in the ground. The entire country round is one of great beauty. Here these Tehuacanas had erected small enclosures of these stones, about three feet in height, leaving occasional spaces about two feet square resembling the mouths of furnaces. These they rudely covered with buffalo skins and poles. The enclosure served as a place of retreat in time of an attack.

The Cherokees having learned the situation of this place, and the great estimate the Tehuacanas placed upon it, they determined to attack it. The Cherokees were led by an Indian well acquainted with the country, and soon reached the place.

When the Cherokees first discovered the Tehuacanas they were playing ball around the fortress. The Cherokees prepared for action, while the Tehuacanas rushed the women and children into their retreat and prepared for defense. They greatly outnumbered the Cherokees, but this did not check the latter. The shooting now began, the Cherokees taking position behind trees and advancing from tree to tree. They took good aim, resting their guns against the trees. Their shots told with deadly effect, and one by one the Tehuacanas were melting away beneath their unerring aim. Whenever one was wounded he would take refuge among the women and children.

The Tehuacanas becoming sick of this, they all rushed into their place of retreat behind their breastworks. The Cherokees now rushed forward to complete their work of destruction. The besieged party were lying flat on the ground, and, as the Cherokees advanced, the Tehuacanas let them have a number of arrows, which laid many of them low.

The Cherokees now fell back and drew off a short distance. One of their old warriors advised that they hold a consultation before they proceeded further. Accordingly they held a council, whereupon one of the leaders said that their business there was revenge, and have it they must, and as long as there was a live Cherokee left they would continue their efforts; that it would never do to return and report a defeat—it would be a lasting disgrace.

The old warrior who advised holding the consultation made the following proposition: That a party of them should go a short distance off and cut some dry grass; that they load themselves with this grass, which would be a good shield, and then approach each hole in the fortress from the sides, and stop up the port holes with this grass. This they would set on fire, and they would in this way roast the inmates alive. The plan was agreed on and carried out. The smoke and flame rolled into the fortress in such quantities as to produce complete strangulation, and the inmates were forced to unroof the fortress and leap out amid the blinding columns of smoke. The Cherokees were stationed around, and slew them as they leaped out. The Cherokees would rush on the frightened and smothered Tehuacanas, and with their tomahawks and scalping knives they dealt death on every hand. A great number of warriors, women and children were suffocated to death on the inside. Many of the women and children were made prisoners, and but few of the men escaped. All the horses, buffalo skins, camp equipage, etc., fell into the hands of the Cherokees, who returned to their camp, making a wonderful display of their booty.

The facts in the above case were obtained from a Spaniard who had passed much of his time with the various tribes of Indians. In the year 1840 he came to Gonzales, and fought with the Texans at Salado, and at Mier in 1842, he being one of those who escaped on that memorable occasion. He came back to Gonzales, and, we have been informed, made the house of General Henry E. McCulloch his home. This unfortunate man was captured in 1843 by a body of robbing Mexicans and being aware of his great fidelity to Texas, they suspended him by the heels, and in this position he was found dead, a fine lesson on Mexican morals.

Scalped by Proxy.

THE following narrow escape by our old friend, John C. Duval, is given in his own language: In the spring of 1838, my friend W. P. Brashear and myself left the city of Houston for the purpose of locating lands in the southwestern part of the State. At that time the whole

country, from the very suburbs of Houston to the Rio
Grande, was infested by marauding parties of Co-
1838 manches and other Indians, and we knew that our
trip would be a dangerous one, but as we were
both well mounted and armed, we concluded that with
proper caution we could save our scalps, either by fighting
or running, if we should encounter one of these hostile
bands.

The day before we reached Goliad we encamped at a deep,
clear pool of water, some twelve or fifteen miles to the east
of that place. I told Brashear I thought we would run great
risk in stopping there, as I had been informed it was a favorite camping ground with the Indians, and proposed that we
should travel on until night and then leave the road before
we encamped. But Brashear, who had but lately recovered
from a severe attack of fever and was still very weak, said
it was impossible for him to travel any further, and that he
would have to camp there and take the chances. This, of
course, settled the matter, and we dismounted and staked
our horses upon the grass that grew luxuriantly in the
vicinity of the pool. As the sun was still more than an
hour high, by way of passing the time I improvised some
fishing tackle out of a bent pin and a few hairs out of my
horse's tail and amused myself in catching perch, with
which the pool was literatly swarming. In less than half
an hour I had as many as I wanted, and, returning to camp,
I broiled them on the coals, and they made a very welcome
addition to our hard tack and cup of black coffee.

After supper, while we were lazily reclining upon the
green turf smoking our pipes, I happened to look toward a
slight elevation a hundred yards or so from our camp, and
I perceived some dark object cautiously creeping behind a
tuft of bushes growing on top. At first I took it to be a
wolf or some other wild animal, but I kept my eyes fixed
upon the spot, and in a few moments I saw an Indian slowly
raise his head above the top of the bushes. "Look at that
little hill to the west," said I to Brashear, "and tell me what
you see." Brashear turned his eyes in the direction indicated: "By Jove, there's an Indian there watching us from
behind that clump of bushes," and he made a movement as
if he was about to get up. "Keep quiet," said I; "and don't

let him suspect we have discovered him. There is no doubt a band of Indians somewhere in our vicinity and they have sent that fellow to spy out our position. As soon as he leaves we will determine upon the best course to pursue. In the meantime," I added, "to convince him that we intend camping here for the night, I will go out and restake the horses upon fresh grass." Saying this, I leisurely got up, threw a quantity of wood on the fire and then went out and restaked the horses. Having done so, I returned to camp, took a seat near Brashear and began puffing away at my pipe.

"Now," said I, "that fellow watching us out yonder is satisfied we are going to remain here for the night, and he will soon leave to join his comrades and report to them what he has discovered." And, in fact, I had scarcely spoken when we saw his head slowly descend behind the bushes, and in a few moments his crouching form disappeared behind the hill.

As soon as he was out of sight Brashear said: "Now, let's bring in the horses and leave here as quickly as possible." "No." said I, "that spy will report we are encamped here for the night, and our best plan will be to remain here until dark, when we can leave without any fear of being seen." Brashear agreed to this, and while we were talking the matter over I said to him: "When I was a boy, my father once told me how some hunters in the early settlement of Kentucky outgeneraled a party of Indians who were in pursuit of them." He said by some means the hunters had found out the Indians were following them, and a little before night they encamped near a dense thicket. After they had eaten supper, they wrapped their blankets around them and lay down before the fire as if they had no suspicion of danger, and had fixed themselves for the night. But as soon as it was dark they quietly got up, and each one placed a log of wood where he had been lying, and covered it with his blanket in such a way as to make a pretty good imitation of a man asleep on the ground. They then hid themselves in the edge of the thicket and waited patiently for the denouement.

For more than two hours not a sound was heard except the distant howling of a pack of wolves, and the hunters finally came to the conclusion that the Indians, from some cause, had abandoned the idea of attacking them. But just as they were about to return to camp they descried a dozen dusky forms creeping stealthily towards it. The Indians approached to within a few yards of the camp, and until they could distinctly see (as they thought) by the light of the fire, that the hunters were all fast asleep, when they suddenly rose to their feet, fired a volley at the logs and then rushed upon their supposed victims with tomahawks and knives. Before they discovered their mistake and while they were crowding around the camp fire, the hunters rose up from their ambuscade and poured a deadly volley in their midst, killing all but two, who made their escape under cover of the darkness.

"Now," said I, "I am going to see if we can't play the same game upon the rascals who are plotting to get possession of our scalps, but as there are only two of us and we do not know how many Indians may be in the vicinity it will be more prudent for us to change our base as quickly as possible after night sets in."

We therefore went to work, and among some fallen timber we found a couple of logs of the requisite size which we laid near the fire and covered them with leaves and several old newspapers so as to resemble somewhat the bodies of men sleeping on the ground. As soon as it was dark we brought in the horses, saddled them and took the road with as little noise as possible. We had traveled perhaps a m le or more when we heard a half dozen guns go off in the direction of our camp

"The boys are catching it now," said Brashear, as he pushed ahead at a lively gait and I followed his example

When we had gone perhaps six or seven miles we turned off from the road, where it passed through a body of timber and where we knew it would be impossible for the Indians to follow our trail in the night. In half an hour or so we came to a dense growth of chapparal, through which we forced our way until we reached a small open piece of ground, where we dismounted and staked our horses. After we had fixed ourselves comfortably for a snooze on the soft green grass Brashear said: "Your old Kentucky plan of being shot and scalped by proxy is an admirable one and I shall recommend it to all those who are compelled to travel in this wooden country." "Yes," said I, "it is, and I have no doubt that hundreds who have been burnt or hung in effigy would concur in the same opinion."

Three years ago I was traveling with a party of friends in southwest Texas and I proposed we should encamp on a certain night at the "watch hole," from which the Indians had routed Brashear and myself in 1838. I told them the pool was deep and clear and filled with fish. What was my astonishment when we came to it, or rather the place where it had been, to find it overgrown with weeds and as dry as a doodle bug's hole, with the exception of a small muddy puddle in the center filled with tadpoles instead of fish. The tramping of numerous herds of stock had entirely destroyed the beautiful clear pool that existed there in 1838 But it's an ill wind that blows no good and if we had no fish for supper and nothing but muddy water to drink we were not compelled, like Brashear and myself, to change our base for fear of Indians.

Colonel Moore's Expedition

AFTER the battle of San Jacinto and the capture of Santa Anna, the Mexicans smarting under the crushing and humiliating defeat they had sustained, and thirsting for revenge upon the Texans, did all in their power as we have already shown to incite the Indians to commit further depredations upon the whites. The war waged by Texas in 1839, upon the semi-civilized Cherokees and 1840 their associated tribes, as related in our account of the "Cherokee War," had been a very effective one, and practically put an end to further outrages and murders by them upon the whites. The Texans, however, had a more formidable enemy in the Comanches and other wild tribes, and it was not until they had been almost entirely exterminated, that they left the country and ceased their

murderous and thieving raids along the borders of our frontier. The government was determined, however, to show
these marauding scoundrels that it had the power and would
chastise them whenever the occasion required.

Says Mr. Yoakum (whose account of this expedition
being rather full and complete, we have concluded to
reproduce here): In September, 1840, Colonel John H.
Moore had orders to raise a volunteer force in Fayette
county, and march up the Colorado in pursuit of those that
had escaped at Plum creek. [An account of this fight having already been given is familiar to the reader.] On the
fifth of October he set out with ninety Texans and twelve
Lipan Indians. After passing the head waters of the San
Gabriel he proceeded to the San Saba and up that stream.
Continuing his march for two days up the latter river without finding the enemy, he diverged to the Concho, and
thence to the red fork of the Colorado, passing over a
country of surpassing richness and beauty. On reaching
Red Fork, Colonel Moore came upon the trail leading up the
river; this he followed until the signs indicated that the Indians were at no great distance. He halted and sent out
two of his Lipan spies, they returned on the evening of the
twenty-third of October, and reported that they had discovered the Comanche village. The troops were ordered to
get their supper and be ready to march. At half-past five
o'clock in the afternoon they set out and proceeded ten
miles due north, when they reached the river. · Continuing
on their way about four miles further up the stream, they
found where some beef cattle had been herded very recently
in a mesquite thicket, and four miles further on the troops
were ordered to dismount. This was at night. The spies
were again sent forward to discover the force and position
of the enemy.

The scouts returned at three o'clock and reported that the
Comanche village was situated on the south bank of the
river and from its appearance they judged it to contain about
sixty families and about a hundred and twenty-five warriors.

At daybreak on the twenty-fourth of October the Texans,
leaving their pack mules, proceeded on their way to the
village. It seems that they were not discovered until they
had ascended the hill, about two hundred yards from the

village. Colonel Moore immediately made a charge on the enemy and the Comanches fled to the river, which bent around the village in the shape of a half moon. A murderous fight was opened and continued upon the flying enemy. After passing through the village the Texans dismounted and continued to pour a deadly fire upon the enemy as they attempted to cross the river. Some of the Indians were killed before they reached the river, while others were shot or drowned in the stream. A portion of them succeeded in crossing and reaching the prairie on the opposite bank, but Lieutenant Owen, who had been ordered with fifteen men to cross over and cut off their retreat, succeeded admirably in this business. As this was a war of extermination the bodies of men, women and children were seen on every hand dead, wounded and dying. The fight around the village lasted for about half an hour and the pursuit extended some four miles. The work was done. The butcheries of Victoria and Linville were avenged. There were forty-eight of the Comanches killed in the village and eighty more either shot or drowned at the river and thirty-four prisoners remained in the hands of the victors. The latter only had two men wounded. The village was then destroyed by fire; and Colonel Moore collected a *caballada* of five hundred horses taken from the enemy and returned to the capital of Texas, where he arrived with all his force (except one man, who had died on the way out), on the seventh of November.

This, the severest chastisement which the Comanches had received, was inflicted on them in their distant home, at least three hundred miles from Austin. Little did these blood thirsty monsters think they could or would be sought out in their distant home and such severe retribution meted out to them They had been heretofore pursued but a short distance and often succeeded in eluding pursuit altogether, and they would go on to their villages with stolen property, gloating with fiendish exultation over the bloody scalps at their saddles. Too much honor can not be bestowed on the gallant Colonel and his heroic soldiers for the great and signal victory achieved by him upon this occasion. From the description of the country, this fight must have occurred near where the town of Ballinger, on the Gulf, Colorado & Santa Fe railroad, now stands.

A Comanche Princess.

THE follqwing interesting narrative from General H. P. Bee, which appeared some years ago in the "American Sketch Book," edited by Mrs. Bella French Swisher, of Austin, Texas, will, no doubt, be of interest to the reader, and we therefore reproduce it here:

In the spring of 1843, the Republic of Texas, Sam Houston being president, dispatched Colonel J. C. Eldridge, 1843 Commissioner of Indian Affairs, and Mr. Tom Torrey, Indian Agent, to visit the several wild tribes on the frontier of Texas, and induce them to make peace and conclude treaties with the Republic. General H. P. Bee accompanied the expedition, but in no official capacity. A recent conversation with him disclosed to us the following touching scene as one of many incidents of that perilous and adventurous trip: At the house of a frontier settler, near where the town of Marlin stands, the commissioners received two Comanche children who had been captured by Colonel Moore, a famous and valiant soldier of the old Republic, in one of his forays on the upper waters of the Colorado in 1840. These children had been ordered to be returned to their people One of them, a boy fourteen years old, named Bill Hockley, in honor of the veteran Colonel Hockley, then high in command of the army of the Republic, who had adopted the boy and taken care of him; the other was a girl eleven years old, named Maria. The parting of the little girl from the good people who had evidently been kind to her, was very affecting; she cried bitterly and begged that she would not be carried away. She had forgotten her native tongue, spoke only our language, and had the same dread of an Indian that any of the white children had. Her little nature had been cultivated by the hand of civilization until it drooped at the thought of the rough Indian life, as a delicately nurtured flower will droop in the strong winds of the prairies. There being no excuse, however, for retaining her among the white people, a pretty, gentle Indian pony, with a little side saddle, was procured for her, and she was taken from her friends. On arriving at a camp in Tanaconi, above where the town of Waco is now located, the party met the first Indians, a mixture of Delawares, Wacos, etc. The appearance of the little girl on horseback created great amusement among the Indians. She was so shy and timid, and the very manner in which she was seated on the side saddle was different from that of the brown skinned woman of her race. The next morning after the arrival at the camp, Bill Hockley came out in full Indian costume, having exchanged his citizen clothes for buck skin jacket, pants, etc. He at once resumed his Indian habits, and from that day during the long trip of months, Bill was noticed as the keenest eye of the party. He could tell an object at a greater distance, a horse from a buffalo, a horse without a rider, etc., quicker than an Indian in camp.

The journey proceeded with its varied scenes of excitement, danger and interest for four months, and the barometer of the party was the little Comanche princess. The object of the expedition was to see the head chief of the Comanches, and of course, as the search was to be made in the boundless prairies, it was no easy or certain task; yet they could tell the distance from or proximity to the Comanches by the conduct of the little girl. When news would come that the Indians were near, the childish voice would not be heard in its joyous freshness, caroling around the fire; but when news arrived that they could not be found, her spirits would revive, and her joy would show itself in gambols as merry as those of the innocent fawn that sports around its mother on the green bosom of the prairie.

At last the goal was reached, and the party was in the Comanche camp, the village of Pay-ha-hu-co, the head chief of all the Comanches. Maria's time had come, but the little girl tried to avoid notice, and kept as close as possible. Her appearance, however, was the cause of great sensation, and a few days fixed the fact that she was the daughter of the former head chief of the nation, who died on the forks of the Brazos from wounds received at the battle of Plum creek, in 1840. Thus, unknown to her or themselves, they had been associating with a royal princess, No-sa-co-oi-ash, the long lost and beloved child of the nation. This extraordinary good luck for the little girl brought no assuagement to her grief. Her joy was gone. She spoke not a word of Comanche, and could not reciprocate the warm greetings she received. On arriving at the village, Bill Hockley determined he would not talk Comanche, although he spoke it perfectly well, not having, like little Maria, forgotten his native language. During the week they remained in the village, Bill, contrary to his usual custom, kept close to the party, and did not speak a word to those around him; nor could he be induced to do so.

On one occasion a woman brought a roasting ear, which was of great value in her eyes, as it had come probably one hundred and fifty miles, and presented it to Bill, who sat in one of the tents. The boy gave not the slightest attention to the woman or her gift, but kept his eyes fixed on the ground. Finally, she put the roasting ear under his eyes, so that, as he looked down, he must see it. Then, talking all the time, she walked off and watched him. But Bill, from under his eyes, noted her movements, and not until she was out of sight did he get up and say: "That ugly old woman is not Mammie, but I will eat her roasting ear."

When the chief came home (he was absent for several days after the party arrived) he asked to see the children, and when they were presented he spoke to Bill in a very peremptory tone of voice, and Bill at once answered, being the first word of Comanche he had spoken since his arrival. This broke the ice, and the boy went among his people, not returning to his white friends until he was wanted to take part in the ceremony of being finally delivered over to his tribe, and afterward never going to tell them good bye. So there and then Bill Hockley passed from the scene. The day before the grand council with the Comanches the skill and ingenuity of the party of three white men were taxed to its fullest extent to make a suitable dress for the Comanche Princess, whose clothes, it may be supposed, had become old and shabby. Their lady friends would have been vastly amused at their efforts. There was no " pull-back," to be sure. Whether the body was too long or too short we are unable to say, but it was one or the other. The skirt was a success, but the sleeves would not work, so they cut them off at the elbow. The next morning they dressed the little princess in a flaming red calico dress, put strings of brass beads on her neck, brass rings on her arms, a wreath of prairie flowers on her head, tied a red ribbon around her smooth, nicely plaited hair, and painted her face with vermilion, until she looked like the real princess that she was. All this, however, was no pleasure to poor Maria. She was like a lamb dressed in flowers for the sacrifice.

Finally, the time came when in the full council, Colonel Eldridge stood holding the hands of the two children, in front of the chief, and said to him that as an evidence of the desire of the Great White Father (Houston) to make peace, and be friendly with the great Comanche nation, he had sent them two children, captives in war, back to their people. After these words he attempted to place the hands of both in the extended hand of the chief, but at that moment the most distressing screams burst from Maria. She ran behind Colonel Eldridge and begged him for God's sake not to give her to those people—to have mercy, and not to leave her. Then the poor child fell on her knees and shrieked, and clung to him with all the madness of despair. A death-like silence prevailed in the council. The Indians stood by in stern stoicism, the voices of the white men were silent with emotion, and nothing but the cries of the poor lamb of sacrifice pierced the distance of the bloom scented prairies. Her white friends, as soon as possible, attempted to quiet the child. Of course the comforting words were spoken in their own language, but they were evidently understood by all, for their's was the language of nature. Finding their efforts useless, the chief said:

" This is the child of our long-mourned chief; she is of our blood; her aged grandmother stands ready to receive her, but she has forgotten her people. She does not want to come to us, and if the Great White Chief only sent her for us to see that she is fat and well taken care of, tell him I thank him, and she can go back."

This was an opportunity, and General Bee suggested to Colonel Eldridge to save the child; but although the latter's heart was bursting with grief and sympathy, his sense of duty told him his work was unfinished, and he replied to the chief: "I have been ordered to give you this child. I have done so, and my duty is fulfilled. But you see she is no longer a Comanche. Child in years when she was taken from you by the stern hand of war, she has learned the language of another people, and I implore you to give her to me, and let me take her to my home and care for her all the days of my life." "No," said the chief, "if she is my child I will keep her;" he swung her roughly behind him into the arms of the old grandmother, who bore her, screaming, from the council tent. And thus the princess was delivered to her people; but the last sound the party heard on leaving that Comanche camp was the wail of the poor, desolate child.

Years after, General Bee received a message from Maria, and sent her a few presents by way of remembrance. She had become the main interpreter of her nation, and often met our people in council. So it ended well at last. She became an instrument of good, and fulfilled her destiny on the stage of action for which she was born. But the remembrance of the bright but desolate child, and her prayers and tears when she was forced to be left with her stranger people, is fresh in the memory of at least one of the party, and will last him through life.

We presume the princess was captured in the fight by Colonel Moore, on the red fork of the Colorado, just related.

Margaret McLellan.

THIS lady was a native of the State of Florida. Her parents immigrated to Texas in the year 1835, and settled in Robertson's colony, from whence they afterwards moved to what is now Williamson county. There were no other settlers in the new country to which they moved. The nearest settlement being seventy-five miles distant. The family consisted of Mr. McLellan, wife, 1835 two small boys and an infant. On their arrival at the place of destination, and before they had unloaded their wagon, they discovered they were out of meat. Mr.

McLellan took his gun and went into the woods for the purpose of hunting some game, leaving his wife to keep camp. McLellan being unacquainted with the country, lost his way, and did not reach his camp until nearly dark, when he discovered his wife and children were gone. During his absence the Indians had attacked his camp and captured his entire family. The first act of barbarism committed by these red devils was to strip the entire family of their clothing and then tie them fast. They next proceeded to plunder the wagon. In unloading the wagon they bursted open a large trunk in which they found a looking glass, this so engaged their attention that they entirely forgot the prisoners. This was a new invention to them, and they began viewing themselves alternately, yelling and laughing. Mrs. McLellan took advantage of this and untied herself and the children. She took her infant in her arms and motioned to her little boy to follow. She crawled off in the brush out of view of the enemy, who were still enjoying themselves over the looking glass. She moved off to the San Gabriel bottom and there found a sheltering rock, forming a kind of a cave. In this she concealed herself and two children.

When dark came and the Indians could no longer see themselves in the glass, they turned toward the spot where they had left their prisoners and found they had gone. They made a thorough search for them, but the darkness prevented their being found. Mrs. McLellan says they came so close to her once that she could have spit on them. She was in dreadful suspense, fearing her infant would cry out, and thereby reveal their place of concealment. The Indians failing to find the objects of their search departed for other fields. Soon after they left, McLellan came back to camp, and what must have been his feelings to find that his wife and children were gone, and his wagon robbed. He naturally enough supposed that his family had been taken off by the Indians and perhaps had been murdered. So he took his little son who had accompanied him when he started hunting and set out toward the settlements, a distance of seventy-five miles. Mrs. McLellan and the two children remained in her hiding place all night. It being in the fall of the year, and the Indians having stripped them of their clothing, they suffered considerably from cold.

The next morning she ventured forth and went back to her desolated camp. There she found a few rags of clothing, with which she endeavored to hide the nakedness of herself and children, but could do but little in that direction. She also found a little shattered corn in the dust around the wagon. She ate a portion of this and gave the remainder to her children. This poor woman remained in this horrible condition for several days, or until her husband had returned from the settlements with a company which he raised for the purpose of pursuing the enemy and recapturing his family, if still alive.

When the company approached the camp Mrs. McLellan was scratching about in the dust to see if she could find any more corn. When she discovered them she supposed they were Indians, and ran off. The men immediately gave chase, not knowing who she was, and they had to run her down before they caught her. The poor woman had become almost wild. She and her children were terribly emaciated. They were very much reduced in flesh for the want of food, in so much that they appeared almost like living skeletons.

It is said that the meeting between Mr. McLellan and his wife was quite an affecting scene. This lady has now gone the way of all creation, and rests where no savage can ever again trouble her calm repose.

The Stone House Fight.

ON the eighth of October, 1837, sixty-three Texans left Fort Colorado, which was situated on Walnut creek, six miles from where the city of Austin now stands. This gallant little band was under the command of Captain William Eastland. They proceeded up the Colorado river to the head of Pecan bayou, where, from some dissatisfaction the men separated, and eighteen hardy **1837** young men under the command of Lieutenant Van-thuysen went off in a northerly direction towards a large Indian camp on the Walnut creek, about forty miles from a notable place called the Stone Houses. This was three stone mounds which at a distance resembled houses, hence the name. It was near the place where the last of these mounds was situated that this gallant little band was attacked by one hundred and fifty Indians, consisting of Wacos, Caddos and Keechis.

The little party of Texans took their position in a deep ravine. The savages took their position about seventy yards in front of the ravine. The Texans sent out a Mr. Nicholson, who understood the Indian language, to treat with them. In order to make them hear him, he climbed up a tree and opened conversation with them. They obstinately refused to talk, but opened a fire on the Texans from their horses, from which they had not dismounted. Finding they could effect nothing in that way, the chief commenced riding rapidly up and down the ravine for the purpose of drawing the shots of the Texans at himself, holding his shield between him and the men.

One of the men in the party, an old Indian fighter, knowing how to shoot at him despite his shield, took good aim at him, fired and killed him. The rest of the Indians crowded around the body of their dead chief, and as they did so the Texans poured a volley in their midst which made it pretty hot for them. They threw a rope around the body of the chief and galloped off out of reach of the shots. After depositing the dead body in a neighboring ravine, they returned on foot and took a position within about sixty or seventy yards of the ravine. Here there occurred one of the most terrific fights that ever took place in Texas. For one hour and a half did these savages keep up an incessant fire at the whites. The Indians had an advantageous position in a clump of timber thickly settled with underbrush and tall grass. The Texans had to shoot at them in that secluded place as best they could. They would raise their heads above the ravine, spy out the position of an Indian, then drop back and slip their gun over the bank and fire. Every time one of them shot, the Indians would throw a volley at him. After fighting for an hour and a half, and having fifty of their number killed, the Indians found they could not oust the whites in this way, so they resorted to one of their pieces of strategy, and that was to set the prairie on fire and burn them out. We omitted to state that there were about fifty Delaware Indians with the others at first, but when the fight began, they left and passed around on the opposite side of the Texans and there took a position out of shot gun distance and watched the fight. These Indians always claimed to be friendly with the whites.

The savages set the prairie on fire within a few rods of the ravine, and it threw such a cloud of smoke and heat among the men that they could neither see the enemy or breathe freely. What were they to do? To remain in the ravine was certain death. They thought the Delawares opposite them were a portion of the enemy, and supposed they were placed there on purpose to cut off their retreat. So believing, they thought retreat in that direction impossible. Had they not been there the Texans could have mounted their horses and made their escape. The Indians had now gone down the ravine to cut off their retreat, and what chance of an escape was there? The only alternative, and that was a slim one, was to charge right through the Indian lines down the ravine. After a hurried consultation they settled on this plan. Joseph Cooper, Alexander Bostick, William P. Wills and a Doctor Sanders having been killed, there were but fourteen men left to make the desperate venture. As soon as they advanced the Indians fired, and the men thinking there was no chance of an escape through their lines, turned out of the ravine up the line, thereby completely exposing themselves to the fire of the Indians. As they ascended the hill six more of them were killed.

One individual, Captain Rice, determined he would carry out the plan that had been agreed upon, and dashed on by himself into a briar thicket. Just as he was entering it, to his surprise he met a tremendous Indian with his gun raised to shoot him. He made a long leap in order to stop his accelerated motion, and at the same instant threw his gun over and shot the Indian through the body, killing him instantly. He then dashed on through the thicket and made his way out into the post oak with an empty gun. He here halted behind a tree to reload. He supposed that he and all the rest would be killed. He soon saw a man leaping towards him. He supposed it was an Indian, and raised his gun to shoot him, but found out that it was one of his own party. Soon after six more men came from the same direction and joined them. Here were eight survivors out of eighteen and three of them wounded. They were more than two hundred miles from the white settlements in an Indian country, completely stripped of everything except their arms. They had lost their horses, provisions, clothing and blankets. They had nothing to eat, and no blankets to lie on. Fletcher, Clish and John Zekee were the names of the wounded ones. The wounds of these men were bound up as well as they could fix them and were greased with buffalo tallow. Neither the well nor the wounded had anything to eat for four days. Late in the evening of the fourth day they killed four buffalos, which saved them from utter starvation. On the tenth day they arrived at a Kickapoo camp where the city of Dallas now stands. From there they traveled on for seven days to Samuel Henges in the Cherokee Nation, from thence to Lacy's cross roads on the old San Antonio road where they came to the first white settlement. Captain Rice, Lieutenant Vanthusen and Felix McClusky made their way to the city of Houston.

There was one man in the company who professed an entire disbelief in the existence of a God. His name was Bostick. He and Captain Rice had several arguments on the subject. One day Rice said to him, "You believe that you are no more than a log or a tree. I may yet see you die on this trip."

After the fight began Rice discovered there was something the matter with Bostick. He approached and asked him what was the matter. He replied that he was badly wounded. In a moment more he sank down on one knee, still holding to his gun, and exclaimed in the most piteous accents: "Lord, must I die?" He then began praying in earnest, and expired in a few moments.

The heroism, bravery and endurance of this little band speaks for itself. Although defeated, they killed about sixty of the enemy—ten times almost the number they lost—and the few remaining ones made their escape in the presence of the whole array of Indians, who had been so badly handled that they would not follow them.

The Joy Family.

W E do not know from what State this family emigrated, the year they came to Texas, nor when they
settled in Kerr county, but that they were among
the earliest settlers in that county is certain.   One
morning in the year 1865, Mrs. Joy and her daughter started
out in a buggy for the purpose of visiting a family residing
at some distance.   After spending the greater portion
1865   of the day with their friends, they reharnessed the old
buggy horse and started to return home; but alas! on
arriving at about the half way ground, near a little ravine
where a dense thicket of underbrush grew, they were suddenly charged upon by a party of Indians, who caught the
horse by the bridle and took the helpless women prisoners.
Usually, whenever women were made prisoners by the Indians, they either carried them off into captivity, or killed
and scalped them on the spot, but on this occasion they
simply killed them.   They severed the young woman's head
from her body, and cut her mother's throat from ear to ear.
After committing this atrocious murder, they seemed to
have fled in a hurried manner; doubtless supposing that relief was close at hand, for they not only failed to scalp the
women, but left the horse hitched to the buggy.   After the
Indians had fled, the faithful old buggy horse took the road
home, with the mutilated bodies of the women still lying in
the vehicle, and carried them home.   The people at the
house, seeing the buggy approach without any occupants,
ran out to see what was the matter, and were horrified to
find the lifeless bodies of both mother and daughter lying
on the bottom with the warm blood still flowing from them.
At first they supposed the daughter's head had been carried
off by the Indians, but when unloading the buggy they
found it under the seat.   A more sorrowful sight, an eye
witness said, was never beheld.

Mr. Joy was wild with grief, and swore eternal vengeance against the Indians. He determined to make them pay for this dastardly murder of his wife and daughter, and it was not long before an opportunity for doing so occurred. Late one night his dogs kept up a continuous and fierce barking, and suspecting that Indians had been around the house, the next morning early he took his gun and started out to reconnoiter. He had not gone far when he discovered several fresh moccasin tracks. He followed these tracks cautiously for several miles beyond the settlements. The Indians, three in number, supposing they were out of danger of pursuit, and being hungry and tired, had stopped, made a fire, cooked and eaten a lunch, and then went to sleep. Mr. Joy, having followed their trail nearly all day, at length caught sight of the smoke rising up from their camp fire. He sat down to rest himself a little and determine upon a plan of attack. He finally concluded to attack the camp at all hazards, whether the occupants were few or many, and putting his arms in good order, he crawled to within a short distance of it.

Finding there were but three Indians, and that they were lying down asleep, he advanced to within a few paces of them, deliberately raised his gun, blew out the brains of one, and before the others got fairly to their feet he killed one with his six shooter. The third one took to his heels, with Joy close after him, but it was not *joy* to the Indian. Not being fully awake, and being terribly frightened besides, the Indian ran into some brush, which so checked his speed that Joy came up with him and drove a bullet through him with his revolver. On this occasion he sent three of the red skins to their happy hunting grounds, and many times subsequently he made them pay dearly for the murder of his wife and daughter. Some of the Joy family are still living in Kerr county.

The Caranchua Indians.

THE Caranchua Indians (or the "Cronks," as the old
Texans called them for short) differed in many respects
from all the other native tribes of Texas. They inhabited the gulf coast from Galveston bay to Corpus Christi,
and but seldom went any great distance into the interior of
the country. They were the Ishmaelites of Texas, for their
hands were against every man, and every man's hand
1821 was against them. They were continually at war
with all the other tribes, and never failed to attack
them whenever they encroached upon what they considered
to be their special domain—the gulf coast. It is true they
sometimes professed to be friendly to the whites who had
settled near the coast, when it suited their purpose to be on
friendly terms with them, but no one had any faith in their
sincerity, as it was well known that they always took a
white man's scalp whenever they thought they could do so
with impunity. Physically they were much superior to any
of the native tribes of Texas. This, probably, was due in a
great measure to the fact that, unlike the interior tribes,
they never suffered for want of food, for the waters of the
gulf afforded them at all seasons abundant supplies of fish,
oysters, clams, etc. The vast artificial shell mounds to be
seen in many places along the coast of Texas not only prove
that the "Cronks" were at one time a numerous and powerful tribe, but that they were also as partial to oyster stews
and clam bakes as any of our down east countrymen.

Owing to their constant warfare with other tribes and the
white settlers, the "Cronks" were nearly exterminated before the revolution in Texas. In the fall of 1835, I saw the
remnant of this tribe in their camp below Refugio. It consisted then of about fifty warriors, with their squaws and
papooses. Out of this number of warriors I do not believe
there were a dozen under six feet in height, and many of
them, I am sure would have stood six feet two or three

inches in their stockings, if they had worn such articles of apparel.

The old settlers universally asserted that the "Cronks" were cannibals, and certainly their looks strongly corroborated the assertion. Their great stature, their hideous physiognomies besmeared with splotches of red and white paint and their peculiar guttural language agreed perfectly with my preconceived ideas of man eaters. Their language was the strangest jargon I ever heard. Their words, or, rather, grunts, seemed to issue from some region low down, and were uttered in spasmodic jerks, apparently without any assistance from the tongue or lips.

This remnant of the "Cronks" took refuge in Mexico in 1835 or 1836, but in doing so, they jumped out of the frying pan into the fire; for shortly afterwards they were either exterminated by the Mexicans, or else they perished for want of oyster stews and clam bakes. When La Fitte, the noted pirate, abandoned Galveston Island, which had been for a long time a rendezvous for his piratical craft, it was rumored that he had left considerable treasure buried there. In 1821, a Doctor Parnell raised a company of about twenty men, and went to the island in search of this supposed buried treasure. They did not find it, but whilst searching for it, they discovered that there was a party of one hundred Caranchua Indians encamped at what was known as the "Three Trees." These "three trees" were a small grove of pines situated twelve or fifteen miles below where the city of Galveston now stands, and were so called because there were three large pine trees in it showing above the rest, which were notable land marks to vessels passing along the coast. The Caranchuas had recently captured a schooner that had been driven into the bay by stress of weather, which they had plundered of its cargo. Of its sails they had made commodious tents which they had spread in the shade of the grove mentioned, where they were having a jolly time generally feasting on the stores taken from the schooner. Doctor Parnell and his men concluded to attack these Indians in place of making further search for the mythical buried treasure. They therefore embarked in their boat and proceeded to the mouth of a bayou which ran very near the point where the

Indians were camped. Remaining at the mouth of the bayou until dark, they cautiously and noiselessly poled their boat up it, until they reached a point not far from the encampment, from whence they could see the Indians by the light of their fires, singing and dancing in the grove. Here they landed and divided into two squads, and then marched up to within forty yards of the Indians, who were totally unaware of their proximity. Waiting until a large number were huddled together around the fires, Parnell and his men suddenly opened fire upon them with deadly effect. The Indians seized their bows, fired one volley of arrows at their assailants and then fled to a marsh covered with tall salt grass, carrying their dead and wounded with them.

None of the whites were injured in this skirmish except Doctor Parnell, who was slightly wounded in the head. [1 Yoakum, 221.]

Loy, Alley and Clark.

IN the summer of 1823, three young men, Loy, Alley and Clark, went down the Colorado river in a canoe, for the purpose of buying corn. A part of the Caranchua tribe were encamped at the time near the mouth of Skull creek, and waylaid these young men on their return. When near enough, the Indians suddenly rose up from their place of concealment near the bank of the river, and fired 1823 upon the canoe. Loy and Alley were both instantly killed, but Clark, although wounded in seven places, sprang into the river, swam to the opposite shore and escaped.

The same evening a Mr. Botherton, another colonist, who was coming down from a settlement fifteen miles above, fell in with these Indians. Thinking they were friendly, he incautiously approached them, when they fired upon him, wounding him severely. He, however, quickly dismounted and took to the brush, thus saving his life, but left his horse and gun behind him.

News of these murders and outrages having reached the settlements, a company of fourteen men was raised that night, who at once marched to the Indian encampment and secreted themselves near it. As soon as it was light enough to see, they opened fire upon the Indians, killing nineteen out of the twenty-one composing the party. The Indians were taken completely by surprise, and made but little resistance.

In 1824, several emigrants from the mouth of the Brazos, on their way to the colony, were killed by Indians. As the colonists were satisfied that these murders had been committed by the Caranchuas, Colonel Austin ordered Captain Randall Jones, at the head of a company of twenty-three men, to proceed down the Brazos and along the coast as far as Matagorda bay; and if he learned that these Indians had committed these murders, or if they made any hostile demonstrations, to attack them at once. Accordingly, in September, Captain Jones and his men started in boats for the mouth of the river. On his way down he was visited by several parties of the Caranchuas, who, finding he was on his guard and well prepared for battle, professed great friendship for the whites. Captain Jones soon learned that about thirty of the tribe were encamped on Jones creek, seven miles distant, and that ten or twelve more had gone higher up on the Brazos to purchase ammunition. On receipt of this information, he despatched two of his men to the settlements above to raise an additional force. When these two men reached Bailie's they found eight or ten colonists already collected there, watching the motions of the Indians who had come to purchase ammunition. These colonists were so well satisfied of the hostile intentions of the Indians that they attacked them the next morning, killed some of them and drove the rest away. In the mean time Captain Jones, without waiting for reinforcements, returned up the river to the Caranchua camp on Jones creek, and disembarked his company near it. They concealed themselves in the brush, and sent out spies to ascertain its exact locality. The spies returned about midnight, but they had not gained such accurate information of the precise

situation of the camp as would enable the company to proceed with certainty against it.

Captain Jones therefore remained quietly in his position
the next day. Just at sun set the war whoops and howlings
of the Indians were heard at their camp. This was caused
by the return of the Indians who had been defeated that
morning at Bailies, bringing with them their dead and
wounded. Having by this means discovered the position of
the Indian camp, which was on the west bank of the creek,
Captain Jones led this company to a crossing half a mile above
the camp and came down on the opposite side. When
within sixty yards of it he halted and waited for daylight.
As soon as day broke they discovered the camp, which was
immediately on the margin of the creek, and surrounded by
weeds and tall grass.

Captain Jones formed his men and made a vigorous
charge upon the camp. At the report of their guns the Indians hastily seized their arms and took shelter in the tall
grass from whence they returned the fire of the whites.
The whites being in an exposed place and having one of
their number killed finally fell back, returned up the creek
and recrossed it. The Indians pursued them until they had
crossed the creek. Just as they were about to cross Captain
Jones discovered an Indian in the act of letting fly an arrow
at him. He quickly presented his gun, fired and killed him
on the spot. In this skirmish the whites had three men
killed, Bailey, Spencer and a man named Singer. The Indian loss was fifteen killed and some wounded. [1 Yoakum, 223.]

Among those who participated in this fight was Captain
Horatio Chriesman, a noble and generous hearted old Texan,
who came to Texas in 1822, and was surveyor of Austin's
colony. He died in Burleson county, November, 1878.

John White and Captain Burnham.

JOHN WHITE settled on the Colorado river at quite an early day. In the year 1824, he and some Mexicans went down to the mouth of the river in a yawl for the purpose of purchasing some corn. They were there captured by the Indians. Mr. White, to save his life, told the Indians he would go up the stream, purchase some corn and return to trade with them. To this the Indians consented. They retained the two Mexicans and furnished Mr. White his yawl in which to make the trip. The understanding was that Mr. White should set the prairie on fire ten miles above there on his return so they would know when he was coming.

1824

Mr. White went on up the river and reported the fact in the settlements. Captain Burnham raised a company of thirty men and went down the river. They found the two Mexicans in a yawl, who reported that the Indians were either at the mouth of the river or across the bay on the peninsula.

Captain Burnham then divided his company—one-half remaining where they were, while the other half marched about a mile lower down the river. Those above gave the signal to the Indians they were expecting from Mr. White by setting the prairie on fire. In a short time a large canoe filled with Indians was seen coming up the river. When they arrived opposite the company, they were attacked and all killed.

A short time after this, this tribe of Caranchuas, tired of this unprofitable war, in which their numbers were rapidly melting away before the rifles of Austin's colonists, sued for peace. They proposed to meet Colonel Austin at La Bahia and make a treaty. Colonel Austin collected a hundred volunteers and met them at the creek four miles east of La Bahia. Peace was made, and the Indians obligated themselves not to come east of the San Antonio river. This

pledge they ever afterwards observed. (1 Yoakum, 226.)
Thus the troubles with the Caranchuas was at an end east
of the San Antonio river. We believe this is the only tribe
that ever carried out one of their treaties. The Comanches
will make a treaty of peace on purpose to spy out and take
some advantage.

Captain Tumlinson.

THIS venerable pioneer was a native of North Carolina,
and immigrated to Texas at an early day. He settled at
the Falls of the Brazos, where he remained but six
months and then removed to the Colorado river where
the town of Columbus now stands. This town is located
upon his head right. As he was a man of fair intelligence
and good business habits he was appointed an al-
1824 calde by the Mexican authorities. In the summer of
1824, Mr. Tumlinson left his house in company with
a gentleman named Newman, and started to San Antonio
on business. They had gone as far on their way as where
the town of Seguin is now situated, when they were attacked by a party of Waco Indians. Tumlinson was instantly killed, but Newman, who was on a good horse, fled,
and succeeded in escaping. Diligent search was subsequently made for Captain Tumlinson's body, but it was
never found.

A little while after this a party of thirteen Waco Indians
were discovered approaching the settlements, and it was
supposed to be the same party who had killed Captain Tumlinson. The news was communicated to Captain John J.
Tumlinson (a brother of the murdered man), who raised a
company of eleven young Texas boys and went in pursuit
of them. His youngest brother, Joseph, was despatched in
advance to spy out the position of the enemy. He discovered they were encamped about fifteen miles above where
the town of Columbus now stands, on the east side of the

river, near the bank of a deep ravine. Returning to the
company he gave Captain Tumlinson the information he
had obtained. The Captain then, with his men, advanced
cautiously, and late in the evening reached the vicinity of
the Indian camp, where they concealed themselves. Their
plan was to defer the attack until morning, and the firing of
Captain Tumlinson's gun was to be the signal for the onset.
But his brother Joseph, who was a little nearer the Indian
camp than the rest, seeing an Indian in fair shooting distance, could not resist the temptation to take a "pop" at him,
and fired away. The Indian uttered a loud "wah!" and fell
dead. Seeing this, the rest of the boys opened fire, and
with such fatal effect that in a few moments twelve of the
thirteen Indians soon lay dead upon the ground. The remaining one sprang off like a frightened deer and made his
escape.

Captain John J. Tumlinson will long be remembered, at
least as long there are any old Texans still living, for his
gallant services in the defense of the frontiers against the
murderous savages.

James Tate.

M R. TATE was among the first colonists who came to
Texas. He had no family and made his home at
the house of Captain Sims, in Burleson county. In
the year 1827, a party of Comanches came to the
house of Captain Sims and stated they were on their way
down the Brazos to steal horses from the Lipans and requested Captain Sims to give them an instrument of
1827 writing to the effect that they had stopped at his house
and behaved themselves. Captain Sims requested
Mr. Tate to give them the paper they wanted. He did so,
but added: "From all appearances I am induced to think
these Indians are going down the Colorado to steal from the
settlers." The Indians, when they reached the Brazos,
showed their letter of recommendation to Colonel Ross. He

immediately collected a party of men, attacked the Indians and killed all but two and one of these was wounded. These two Indians, on their arrival at the Comanche camp, re-ported the fate of their comrades. The Comanches at once despatched a party of warriors to revenge the death of their comrades, who proceeded down the Brazos river to where Captain Sims lived. Near his residence they came across Mr. Tate, who was riding out in company with another gen-tleman, and he was recognized by one of the Indians who had made his escape at the time they were attacked by Colonel Ross, as the man who had given them the lying let-ter of recommendation. The entire party of Indians, eight or ten in number, then fired at Mr. Tate, breaking one arm and one of his legs. There was a densely timbered bottom near by, into which Mr. Tate ran his horse and thus saved himself. The Indians supposing they had wounded him mortally did not pursue him. A party of whites went in search of him and soon found him. They carried him to Captain Sims's house, where he remained until he recovered from his wounds. He left Texas soon afterwards for fear the Indians would kill him.

Thomas Thompson.

DURING the years 1828–29 the Indians were quite trou-blesome to the settlers on the Colorado and Brazos rivers. During the winter of 1828, Thomas Thompson opened a small farm near the present town of Bastrop and occasionally visited it to see that everything was going on right. In July, 1829, he went to visit his farm and found it in possession of Indians. He went below for as-1829 sistance, and, raising a party of ten, he returned, ar-riving there just at daylight, when a battle ensued. Four of the savages were killed and the others fled.

Colonel Austin raised two companies of volunteers, of fifty men each, under the command of Captains Oliver Jones and Bartlett Sims, the whole force being placed under the command of Colonel Abner Kuykendall. About the same time the depredations and murders by the Indians in the vicinity of Gonzales induced the raising of another company which was placed under the command of Captain Harvey S. Brown. Learning that a party of Wacos and Tehuacanas were encamped at the mouth of the San Saba, the two commands marched for that point. When they came near the above named place they halted and sent out scouts to ascertain the locality of the Indians. The Indian scouts discovered them and gave notice to the others, so that when the Texans charged the camp of the enemy they found it deserted. They only killed one Indian. Captain Sims and fifteen others pursued the Indians some distance and took from them many of their horses. The troops returned home after a scout of thirty-two days, during which time they suffered for the want of provisions. They subsisted for three days on acorns and persimmons. [1 Yoakum, 261.]

James Alexander.

JAMES ALEXANDER was one of the early settlers in Texas. In the summer of 1835, he and his son, a youth about sixteen years old, were engaged in hauling goods from Columbus to the town of Bastrop, where they resided. On their way, they halted one day to "noon it" at the head of Pin Oak creek on the Wilbarger trace, near where it crossed the old La Bahia road, and whilst 1835 there, were surprised and killed by a party of Indians.

It appears that the Indians approached them unperceived under cover of a ravine, so closely that when they fired on them, their clothes were scorched with powder.

After killing Alexander and his son, the Indians mutilated their bodies in a terrible manner, plundered the wagons and destroyed them as well as all the goods they could not carry off. They also killed the oxen. The Indians then departed, going off in the direction of the falls of the Brazos.

The dead bodies of Alexander and son were found within a few hours after the Indians had committed the bloody deed, whereupon a small party set out in pursuit of the savages, following them as far as Little river, and having lost the trail, they continued in the direction of the Falls of the Brazos, and when some fifty miles above same, they captured a Caddo Indian, who informed the Texans that his camp was about five miles distant and that there were two Caddo Indians, two Cherokees and two squaws there. The party at once set out with the Indian guide, and soon reached the Indian camp. They killed the five men and left the squaws unharmed.

William Cooper.

WILLIAM COOPER was the son of the well known William Cooper who for some reason had acquired the soubriquet of "Cow" Cooper. He was born in Red River county, Texas. In the fall of 1830, Mr. Abner Lee went some distance from his house, hunting deer. He had discovered a deer feeding, and was slowly and cautiously approaching it to get a shot, when the deer
1830 manifested signs of alarm. He had the wind of the deer, and knew it had not seen him, and whilst he was wondering what could have alarmed it, it suddenly sprang forwards, ran a few rods and fell. Then, to Mr. Lee's great surprise a party of Indians rose up out of the tall grass and went to where the deer had fallen. Mr. Lee retreated without having been discovered by the Indians. He quickly raised a party of men, returned to the place and took their trail. The Texans overtook the Indians on Caney creek, where they had encamped in a deep ravine. As it was near daylight, the Texans dismounted and waited until they could see distinctly. They then cautiously approached

HE MAKES AN UNEXPECTED TUMBLE IN THE MIDST
OF THE INDIANS.

the Indian encampment, hoping to take them by surprise. They had advanced within thirty or forty paces of the camp, when an Indian, who was sitting with his gun in hand, discovered them. The Indian raised his gun and fired, shooting William Cooper through. He, thinking it was some one in his own party who had shot him by missake, exclaimed: "Lord! boys, what did you shoot me for?" A battle then ensued between the Texans and Indians, and continued for half an hour, when the latter fled, carrying off with them one of their dead comrades.

The Texans carried the body of young Cooper home, buried him, and returning, took the Indian trail again. After they had gone a short distance they found a blanket. A little further on they found a buffalo robe, some arrows and a new pair of leggins. Still further on they found the dead bodies of four Indians. At a treaty made with the Indians the following spring at Tinosticlan, they acknowledged they had lost seven of their braves in this fight. These Indians were Wacos and Keechies.

Mr. William Cooper, the father of the young man killed in this fight, was one of the first settlers in the country. He was quite wealthy, and one who was ever ready to share what he had with his neighbors. His house was always a home for the needy and suffering

---

Charles Cavina.

CHARLES CAVINA was one of the first emigrants to the first colony of Stephen F. Austin. He resided near Live Oak bayou, on Old Caney creek. It was in the year 1830 that seventy Carancbua Indians made an attack on Cavina's house, killed his wife and three daughters and wounded the fourth. Cavina was at some distance from his house when the Indians attacked it, 1830 and on his return he found it in their possession. He had two or three negroes with him, but as they were unarmed he was compelled to retreat. Near the house of

Cavina there lived another family by the name of Flowers. Mrs. Flowers and one of her daughters were visiting his house when it was attacked. She attempted to escape but was pursued and killed. Her daughter was also wounded. The Indians took her and the wounded daughter of Cavina and threw them into a brush pile. Both of them recovered from their wounds.

Mr. Cavina raised a company of sixty men and pursued the savages. They were under the command of Captain Buckner, who had seen much service on the frontiers. They came up with the Indians on the ground where the city of Matagorda now stands. They had taken their position on the bank of the Colorado river. Captain Buckner sent forward Mr. Moses Morrison to reconnoiter their position. He crawled up to a bank overlooking a small plateau below where the Indians had stationed themselves. This bank was of a crumbling nature, and as he leaned over it to get a better look, it gave way under him and precipitated him downward about forty feet right among the Indians. He clung to his gun, however, and crawled into a hole in the bank, where he fought and killed five of the Indians.

Captain Buckner and his men hearing the reports of his gun, supposed he had been attacked, and hurried to his assistance. As soon as they caught sight of the enemy they made a charge upon them. The Indians had their squaws and papooses with them, and some of them were killed by the promiscuous firing that ensued. The fire of the Texans was so rapid and deadly that many of the Indians endeavored to escape it by plunging into the river, but even after they had succeeded in reaching the opposite shore many were shot and fell back in the stream. An eye witness of the scene says that the river was literally red with blood. Between forty and fifty of this band of savages were killed, a just retribution for the atrocious crimes they had committed.

John Walker.

JOHN WALKER was another one of the early settlers in Texas. He settled on Little river, where he lived for several years without being molested by Indians.

In the year 1830 a party of hostile Indians came down Little river and made an attack on Mr. Walker's house. They killed one of his family and then plundered the house of its contents. They then passed through a thickly 1830 settled neighborhood, killed several others and sacked their dwellings. They also collected and drove off all the horses, cattle and sheep they could find. They were pursued by a few citizens a short distance but the Indians had got so much the start of them that they failed to overtake them.

The Maden Massacre.

THE Maden family came to Texas in the year 1832, and settled in Houston county. In order to secure themselves against the attack of Indians, Maden and two or three of his neighbors, as was frequently the custom in those days, jointly built some strong log cabins close together, in which they might take refuge in case of necessity. In the fall of 1833, in the "light of the moon," 1833 the time usually chosen by the Indians for making raids into the settlements, the families of Mr. Maden and others, had collected at these log buildings for common defense. The house in which they were, was a double log cabin, consisting of two rooms with an entry between them. The men, three or four in number, were in one room,

and the women and children in the other. The men were
engaged in moulding bullets and making preparations for
defense. All the fire arms were in the room occupied by
the women and children. A while after dark they were
suddenly startled by the shrill yells of a large party of Indians. The Indians had crept up cautiously, and had found
out that the inmates of the house were divided in the manner
above mentioned. Some of the Indians rushed to the room
in which the women and children were, while others stood
guard at the door of the room occupied by the men. The
former, with tomahawks and butcher knives in hand easily
effected an entrance, while one of their number guarded the
door by placing one hand on each side of the door frame
above, and one foot on each side below, thus preventing the
inmates from escaping whilst the work of death was being
carried on. The Indians who had entered the room immediately attacked Mrs. Maden, wounding her severely in the
face and other parts of her body. Finally, from the effects
of repeated wounds she fell, and in falling she happened
to roll under the bed near by. One of her little sons, seeing
her lying under the bed, crawled to her for protection. One
of the Indians struck another lady a terrible blow on the
head with his tomahawk, fracturing the skull and knocking
her into the fire place. The blood flowed so profusely from
the wound as to extinguish the flames, and the Indians were
compelled to carry on their work of destruction in the dark.
At this juncture Mrs. Madden, who had previously noticed
the position of the Indian guarding the door, strange as it
may seem, actually crawled out of the room between his
feet, followed by her little son, without being seen by him,
as his attention was drawn to what was going on in front.
As it was then dark, she crept to a negro cabin some distance from the house, unobserved by the Indians outside,
where she hid herself under some old clothes. Seven women and children were slain in this dreadful affair. When
the Indians had finished their diabolical work they set fire
to the house which was consumed with the bodies of their
victims.

Strange to relate, the men in the other room remained
there some time listening to the dying groans of their wives
and children, and because they were unarmed did not at-

tempt to go to their relief. They watched for an opportunity and fled, leaving the poor women and children to their sad fate—the only instance probably of such shameful cowardice recorded in the bloody annals of Texas. It does seem strange that these men, although unarmed, could have resisted the dying appeals of their wives and children. They might have rushed forward together with sticks or clubs, pocket knives, anything, and made an effort to rescue their helpless families. It would have been far better and much more honorable than to have acted as they did. Mr. Maden, when he left the house, was discovered and pursued by two Indians. He had the same little boy with him who had crept out of the room with his mother between the Indian's feet at the door. This somewhat retarded his movements, but as he passed through the corn field he pulled up a stalk and presented it at the Indians who were pursuing him. In the dark they supposed it was a gun and stopped. Taking advantage of this, he and his little son hurried on and finally entered a dense cane brake, where they concealed themselves. Mrs. Maden came very near bleeding to death but after a protracted illness she eventually recovered from the wounds she had received.

It appears the Indians were so close to the house before they attacked it that they had learned the minutest particulars in regard to the situation of the inmates. This is evident from the fact that one of the men who had been in the room occupied by the women and children remarked as he started to leave, "that he must have more bullets." He had been but a little while in the men's room when the attack was made and one of the Indians exclaimed in broken English, "more bullets, ha?" plainly showing he had been near enough to overhear the remark. The Indians took all the firearms in the house, and when they had gone perhaps a quarter of a mile they threw their own guns away and retained those they found at the station. They then made their way back to their mountain retreats without being pursued.

Daniel Gilleland.

M
R. Gilleland was one of the original "three hundred" that first settled in the colony of Stephen F.
Austin. He was a native of Tennessee. Upon his
arrival in Texas, he settled in what is now Whar-
ton county. He was a successful farmer, and generally
raised more corn than any of his neighbors, and the Indians
were aware of the fact.

1833   The Caranchuas, who were a lazy, shiftless tribe of
Indians residing on the coast, were in the habit whenever they needed corn, of levying "black mail" from the
settlers, who usually gave them what they demanded, for
fear of incurring the hostility of these savages.

A party of Caranchuas called at Gilleland's house, told
him they knew he had an abundance of corn, and that they
had come for a portion of it, and must have it. But the old
gentleman could not see the matter in that light, and he
told them they should not have a grain. At this, the chief
of the party flew into a rage, drew his bow upon him, and
told him if he did not give up the corn instantly, he would
kill him on the spot. Gilleland, however, was not a man to
be intimidated by threats. He seized his gun, presented it
at the chief and told him to shoot if he dared. Mrs. Gilleland was so much frightened that she begged her husband
to give up the corn, rather than provoke the Indians, but
the old gentleman was firm in his purpose, and positively
refused to come to terms. The Indians finding they could
not frighten him into submission, left his house, went a
short distance and encamped. Gilleland then collected a
few of his neighbors, went to their camp and attacked them
at once. A pretty severe fight ensued in which several of
the Caranchuas were killed and wounded. None of the
whites were injured. This taught the Caranchuas a good
lesson, and they ceased their attempts at levying "black
mail" on the settlers.

DeWitt Lyons.

YOUNG DeWitt Lyon's father was one of the very first immigrants to Stephen F. Austin's colony. He settled in what is now Lavaca county. In the summer of 1835, while Mr. Lyons and his son, a small lad, were at work in his cow lot, a party of Comanches made an attack upon the defenseless old man and his little son, shooting him dead on the spot. They then scalped him and took 1835 his son prisoner, and carried away with them a large stock of horses belonging to Mr. Lyons. The little boy DeWitt remained with the Comanches until he was nearly grown, although many unsuccessful efforts were made by his friends to get him back. They persevered, however, until eventually they succeeded. But the young man had become so much attached to his savage companions, and to the wild, roving life they led, that it was with the greatest difficulty he could be persuaded to leave them. He had forgotten his own name, and had almost entirely forgotten his native language. At first, after his friends had succeeded in getting him from the Indians, they had some doubts as to his identity, so greatly had he changed during the many years he had lived with the Indians. But all doubts were removed when, on approaching his father's residence, he showed unmistakeably that he knew the country he was passing over. When he came near the lot where his father was killed, he pointed to it and said: "Dar me fadder kill—dar me take off." Mrs. Lyons, his mother, seeing the party approaching, walked out to meet them. Never in all his captivity had the features of his mother been eradicated from his memory. During all his wanderings in the wild woods, over hills, mountains and valleys—or in the chase, hunting the buffalo, elk and deer—that mother's features were indelibly stamped upon his memory. As soon as he saw her he cried out: "Dar me mudder! Dar me mudder!" This left no doubt as to his identity—that he was in truth her long lost son, whom she had mourned for years as for one that was dead.

James Coryelle.

CORYELLE was a native of the Sate of Tennessee. He came to Texas in the year 1822, being then quite a young man. In the year 1833 a party of survey-ors went up the Leon river as far as the mouth of Cory-elle creek, ten miles from where the town of Gatesville now stands. James Coryelle and George B. Erath were among

the party. They moved cautiously, keeping a good
1833 lookout for Indians, and selecting the best lands as
they went on. In spite, however, of their watchful-ness they were finally surprised by a party of Indians. The Indians charged upon them and the whites retreated. In the charge young Coryelle was captured and killed.

The Italian Trader.

IN the year 1835 an Italian with several Mexicans in his employment was engaged in transporting goods from the coast to the interior settlements. They were attacked one morning by about seventy Indians, on the road fif-teen miles west of Gonzales. They (the Italians and Mexi-cans) made a breastwork of their goods, behind which they

fought the Indians until evening; but gradually their
1835 numbers were thinned by the fire of their savage
foes, and they were no longer able to defend their po-sition. The Indians then made a general charge upon them, and the survivors were butchered and scalped.

Kitchens's Station.

THE Kitchens family came to Texas at an early day, and settled in Fannin county. In order to secure themselves against the attacks of Indians, Mr. Kitchens built a kind of fort, to which they could retreat in case of necessity. Several other families settled near this fort subsequently for protection. Thus situated they lived for several years without being disturbed by the Indians. But in the year 1835 a large party of Indians came into Fannin county and determined to attack Kitchens's station. They selected a dark night for their purpose, but the settlers had found out that Indians were in the neighborhood, and when they made the attack they were "forted up" and ready for it. A fire, however, was left burning in one of the rooms, and the Indians could see from the outside any one within. Young Kitchens was sitting in this room and an Indian shot him through the window with an arrow, killing him instantly. The lights were immediately put out, and both parties fought in the dark, the Indians attacking the station on all sides. Among the Indians there was a negro man who had run away from his master and joined them. Wishing to perform some feat that would give his new friends an exalted opinion of his prowess, he advanced to the house and began to climb up the wall, in order that he might fire upon the inmates through an open window; but, unfortunately for him, he was discovered before he effected his purpose, and instantly shot down. An Indian attempted to enter the stable, but was killed by a man who had been stationed there.

Another one was discovered creeping near the house under cover of the fence and he was also shot and killed. The fight continued for several hours with no other harm to the inmates of the station except the killing of young Kitchens. At length finding it was impossible to take the station the Indians withdrew, carrying their wounded with them. They had gone but a little way when one of the wounded died and he was afterwards found buried under a pile of logs. The.two young Misses Kitchens were so exasperated at the death of their brother that they cut off the head of the negro man who had been killed and stuck it on a pole, where it remained for several months.

Colonel Coleman.

COLONEL COLEMAN was one of the early settlers in Texas, and was well known in the section of country where he lived. Whenever Indians or Mexicans made their raids in his vicinity he was always ready to lead where any dared follow. In the summer of 1835 the Keechi nation were living on the Navasota river. They pretended great friendship for the whites, but they were in fact 1835 most consummate thieves, and were constantly depredating upon them. They kept up their robberies for years on the credit of other tribes, but at length the settlers became satisfied of their guilt, and Colonel Coleman was authorized in the summer of 1835 to raise a company to go to the Keechi village and induce them, if possible, to discontinue their theft. The Indians had notice of Colonel Coleman's approach, and knowing they were guilty, they took it for granted that his intentions were hostile; they therefore selected a strong position and fortified it by digging pits in the ground, to which they could retreat when attacked.

When Colonel Coleman and his men came in sight, the Indians, without waiting to have a "talk" with him, opened fire upon them as soon as they were within range. Colonel Coleman and his men were in open ground, and much exposed to the fire from the Indians' guns, whilst they were well protected in their pits. They made every effort to dislodge the Indians, and fought them for several hours, but their position was too strong to be taken without great sacrifice of life.

At length, after one of his men had been killed and several wounded, Colonel Coleman withdrew and sent for reinforcements. In a few days he was reinforced by a party of men under Colonel John H. Moore, and as soon as the Keechies were informed by their spies of Colonel Moore's approach, they abandoned their fortification and fled. The Texans followed them out beyond the head of the Trinity river, where they discovered their camp. Supposing the Indians were all there, the Texans charged upon it, but found only two warriors and the women and children, the rest of the men having gone off on a hunting expedition. The two warriors were killed and the women and children taken prisoners and afterwards sold to the settlers.

David Ridgeway.

RIDGEWAY was from Tennessee and came to Texas in 1835. He was a transient man and had no permanent home. He, in company with another young man whose name we know not, started from Fort Marlin to go to the falls of the Brazos. When they had gone about half way they were ambuscaded by some Indians, and the first intimation they had of their presence was a volley of arrows. Ridgeway fell mortally wounded and the Indians followed his companion some distance but failed to overtake him. They were pursued by a party of citizens without success. Quite a number of people about this time were killed around Fort Marlin by the Indians. They also robbed the settlement of an immense amount of property and did all they could to break it up. For some reason the Indians fought harder to retain the Brazos country than any other portion of the state. The soil of no state in the Union has been crimsoned with the blood of so many brave defenders as that of Texas—not even excepting Kentucky, the "dark and bloody ground."

r835

Sarah Hibbins.

THE Hibbinses were among the early settlers in Texas, and settled in DeWitt's colony. In 1835 Mrs. Hibbins went on a visit to Tennessee. After remaining there a few months, she started home, coming by water, and landed in Houston in January, 1836, in company with her mother, who had come from Tennessee with her. Her husband met her there with a wagon to carry her home, to what was known as DeWitt's colony. They had crossed the Colorado river and were nearing home, when a party of Indians suddenly rushed from an ambuscade, and instantly killed Mr. Hibbins and the mother of Mrs. Hibbins. They took Mrs. Hibbins and her two children, one an infant and the other three years old, and lashed them to a horse. After robbing the wagon, they left for the mountains. They confined Mrs. Hibbins every night, laying her down with her children on each side, and throwing a buffalo robe over them. Two large Indians would then lie down by them, one on each side, so as to guard her. The infant was a sucking babe, and consequently when the poor little thing became hungry it would cry. The Indians took this babe from her, and she supposes killed it.

After they had crossed the Colorado they allowed Mrs. Hibbins and her child to lie by themselves, thinking escape on her part impossible. The first night after they crossed the Colorado they camped where the city of Austin now stands. Here for the first time Mrs. Hibbins and her child were permitted to lie together without being guarded. She lay awake until the Indians and child were sound asleep, and then gently arose and noiselessly crept from the camp. Near the mountain was a creek whose banks were quite steep. She went down the channel of this. There was running water at the bottom, and in order to leave no trail behind, she waded the stream. Having travelled, as she supposed, about two hours, at least a sufficient time to have gone about five miles, she found herself still near the camp, by hearing her child call out "oh! ma!" Should she go

1835 (margin note)

back? Should she succumb to the maternal prompting, and again place herself within the grasp of these demons? She reflected that if she were to return she could do her child no good, and she knew the settlements could not be more than ten miles away. No, she would go on, save herself, and find some good men who would go and rescue her child. She then followed the channel of Shoal creek down to the Colorado river. She passed through brush, and vines, and water all that night. She continued her travels the next day until she saw some home cows. She remained with these until they went home, and followed them. In the evening she became so exhausted with hunger and fatigue, and knowing she must be near the settlements, she commenced hallooing as loud as she could. There were some men in the river bottom who heard her, but not distinguishing her voice, they concluded it was Indians and would not answer her.

Late in the evening, the poor woman without uttering a word, went into the house of Mr. Jacob Harrell, and took a chair, still not uttering a word. It seemed that her joy in discovering a house and knowing that she was safe at last, completely took from her the power of speech.

The family were all very much astonished, as they had not seen her until she sat down. Finally, Mrs. Hibbins broke silence and in a distressed tone, gave Mr. Harrell a history of her case. She was immediately removed to the house of Reuben Hornsby, where she was supplied with clothing and food. It so happened that Colonel Tumlinson, who was commanding a company of rangers on the frontier, arrived at Mr. Hornsby's a few minutes after Mrs. Hibbins came.

After hearing her sad story, and as soon as he could take some refreshments, they mounted their horses just at dark and went in pursuit of Mrs. Hibbin's child; she having first given them a description of the kind of mule that the Indians kept her child lashed on. They camped that night in eight or ten miles of the Indian camp, and the trail being quite plain next morning, they soon overtook them. They opened fire on the Indians, who broke and fled. They killed two of them and succeeded in recovering all their stolen horses, camp equipage and arms; but best of all, Mrs. Hibbin's little son.

When her child was returned to her, she was so over-joyed that she wept and laughed by turns. Her heart went out in deep gratitude to the noble men who had secured her darling boy. Colonel Tumlinson came very near being killed on this occasion. An Indian was shot down, and, as was supposed, dead. As Colonel Tumlinson was passing, he raised his gun and fired. The Colonel seeing the movement in time, sprang to one side, and the shot missing him, killed his horse.

Captain William Hill.

CAPTAIN HILL commanded a company of rangers in the service of Texas. One day, in the summer of 1836, while out scouting, he discovered an Indian trail on the waters of the San Gabriel leading towards the settlements. Captain Hill followed it at once, and after traveling twenty-four hours at twelve o'clock the next day he came up with the Indians. They were encamped 1836 in a dense thicket. As Captain Hill and his men approached the thicket they met an Indian, who was returning on the trail to ascertain if any forces were in pursuit of them. He was immediately shot down and Captain Hill ordered his men to charge the encampment. There were fifty of the rangers and about seventy Indians. The Indians were not only superior to them in number but their position in the thicket gave them a great advantage over the rangers, who were compelled to cut their way through it in order to reach them. The Indian spy who was shot before the charge was ordered was only wounded and he called loudly for his comrades to come to his assistance. Some of them did so, but as they advanced two of them were shot down and the spy was also killed. Owing to the density of the thicket the rangers were compelled to fight at a great disadvantage. They succeeded, however, in wounding some of the Indians and in driving them from their camp. They took all their camp equipage, and among the trophies was a large number of white scalps taken from people of both sexes and all ages.

Joseph Reed.

MR. JOSEPH REED was a native of Virginia. He and his brother, Braman Reed, immigrated to Texas in the year 1829, and settled in the town of Bastrop. After remaining there a short time, they moved to Burleson county and settled on Davidson's creek, where they followed the business of stock raising. In the spring of 1836, Mr. Joseph Reed rode out one day to **1836** the range for the purpose of driving up some cattle.

When he had gone about half a mile he was attacked by a large party of Indians, forty or fifty in number. Mr. Reed put spurs to his horse and endeavored to reach his house, the Indians following and shooting their arrows at him. He succeeded in reaching his yard gate, and there fell. Mrs. Reed saw her husband galloping towards the house, with the Indians pursuing him, and ran to the yard gate to meet him. She met him just as he fell dead from his horse. The brave and heroic woman was determined he should not be scalped by the savages; so, taking the body of her husband in her arms, she dragged him to the house and reached it unhurt, although the Indians were shooting at her the whole time. The Indians then left, but encamped not a great distance from the house.

The brother of the murdered man, as soon as he heard of the affair, raised a small party of whites and attacked the Indians in their camp. A hard fight ensued, in which the brother was killed and several others wounded. The chief was killed finally, and the Indians then fled, leaving their dead behind them. It was not often that the whites took the scalp of an Indian, but on this occasion they were so much exasperated that they followed the example of the savages, and scalped the dead chieftain.

Thomas Norris.

THOMAS NORRIS was a native of Kentucky and immigrated to Texas in 1836. Immediately on his arrival he entered the army under General Houston, in which he served as a private during the war between the Republic of Texas and Mexico. Near the close of the war he and two other men whose names are not known to the writer, were furloughed to attend to some business at 1836 a distance from the army. While passing up the Guadalupe river on their way to their destination they discovered considerable recent signs of Indians, which alarmed them a good deal, as they were on foot and unarmed. While consulting as to what was best to be done, to their great consternation a body of Indians rushed from an ambuscade and charged on the three defenseless soldiers. They fled for life and kept pretty well together for about a mile. As there was a very tall growth of grass on the ground, they were enabled now and then to dodge their pursuers and thus to keep some distance ahead of them. Finally, however, seeing the Indians were gaining on them, Norris suggested that they should gather up some sticks about the size of guns and carry them on their shoulders to make the Indians believe they were armed. They did so, and as they were partially hidden in the tall grass that covered the ground, their ruse for a time had the desired effect of checking the advance of their pursuers. But as the Indians approached nearer they discovered the trick, and then dashed after them with increased speed, determined on having their scalps.

Norris, seeing that the Indians had found out their ruse and that his two companions were rapidly failing, dashed off in another direction by himself, a part of the Indians following him and a part following his companions. Being quite active as well as crafty, Norris dodged into a deep ravine, which led him into a large swamp in which there was a heavy growth of tall water grass.

When he left Kentucky he had been presented with a very fine suit of clothes and other things as tokens of affection and respect by his relatives and friends. When he entered the swamp he found that his clothes and the things he carried impeded his progress through the tall grass, and he cast them away one by one, until his pantaloons and shirt were all that remained, and thus relieved of their weight he made better speed through the swamp. In places the mud was knee deep, in others the water was waist deep, and everywhere the grass was from four to six feet high. While forcing his way through these obstacles he could hear now and then the splashing of his pursuers, who were following like blood hounds on his trail.

Through this dismal swamp he continued his course for the rest of the day, until finally when night set in his pursuers lost the trail and abandoned the chase Night overtook him in the swamp, where the water in the shallowest place he could find was at least a foot in depth and the grass five or six feet high.

In order that he might be able to get a little sleep he cut a quantity of the long grass with his pocket knife, bound it in bundles and upon this he laid down and thus managed to keep his head above water. It may readily be imagined that he did not sleep very soundly on this uncomfortable couch, particularly as he knew he was in great danger, not only of Indians but of being bitten by snakes or devoured by alligators, both of which abounded in the swamp. Having spent the night in the manner described the morning found him in a state of bewilderment He was completely "turned round" and did not know which way to go. However, as it was necessary to make a move in some direction he set out in search of solid ground. He had gone but a short distance when he heard the beating of a drum at a camp then occupied by a portion of General Houston's army. He turned his course towards the point from whence the sound proceeded, and after traveling several miles through mud and water he reached the camp well nigh exhausted by fatigue and want of food. We did not learn what became of his two companions.

John Rover.

THE nativity of Mr. Rover is not known to the writer. He was a soldier in the army of Texas during the war with Mexico. In the spring of 1836 he went up the Colorado into what is now Travis county, with his wagon and team, to move one of his friends from there to some other point. On his way he stopped at the residence of one

1836 of the early pioneers, Thomas Moore. The night previous a party of Indians had come into the neighborhood and had concealed themselves near Mr. Moore's house. As Mr. Rover was saddling his horse for the purpose of going out to hunt his team, the Indians shot and killed him. They then showed themselves, ten in number, and threatened to attack the house, and doubtless would have done so had not several men at that moment made their appearance. The night before these Indians killed Mr. Rover, they robbed the house of Nathaniel Moore. Fortunately neither he nor any of his family were at home.

This portion of the country suffered terribly from Indian raids during the war with Mexico, as nearly all the men were away in the army.

Captains Robinson and Robbins.

AUGUST, 1836, these two officers, belonging to the Texas army, under the command of General Thomas J. Rusk were ordered out in charge of a small force of men to reconnoiter the position of some Indians who were encamped on a little stream called Sandy. While engaged in carrying out this order, they were boldly attacked by a

1836 large body of Indians at night, who had surrounded them under cover of the darkness. The Texans stood their ground and defended themselves bravely until eight were killed and nearly all the rest wounded. There was but one out of the sixteen men that escaped unhurt. The Indians captured all their horses and camp equipage. The loss of these brave men at this juncture was severely felt, as it was during the time that the thirty thousand inhabitants of Texas were battling for life and liberty against eight millions of Mexicans, aided by their Indian allies, and the services of every man were needed.

Captain Harvey.

MR. HARVEY came to Texas in the year 1836. He was a surveyor by profession and was employed by the State of Texas to survey out a large tract of country on the San Saba river granted by the State to a colony of Germans. His company comprised about twenty men, the most of whom were as green as a cut seed watermelon, and Mr. Harvey found it a very 1836 difficult matter to persuade them to take even ordinary precautions against being surprised by the Indians, although it was evident from their camps they had recently been in the country. In spite of all his remonstrances, his men would scatter about hunting, or looking for "bee trees," which were abundant in the region where they were working. On one occasion when the weather was very hot, his men being thirsty, scattered around in every direction in search of water, leaving Mr. Harvey alone. As he was very thirsty himself, he started off alone and on foot, and took his course down a ravine in which he hoped to find a pool of water. He continued his course down this ravine for a mile or so, when suddenly a number of Waco Indians rose up from the bushes on each side of it, and rushed upon him. Their appearance was so unexpected that he was in their clutches before he had time to make any resistance or attempt to escape by flight. Having secured their prisoner, the Wacos started for their camp. As they were out of provisions and very hungry, they stole a pony from a Comanche camp near which they passed, butchered and ate it, or at least as much of it as they wanted. They then tied a hindquarter of the pony on the back of their unfortunate prisoner, and forced him to carry it all day on foot over mountains and across canons and gulches. The Comanches from whom the pony was stolen discovering its loss, determined to follow the thieves and wreak their vengence on them. They knew that there were Wacos in the vicinity, and they quickly came to the conclusion that they were the guilty parties. The chief ordered his men to mount their horses at once, and in a few moments they were on the trail and in hot pursuit of the Wacos. They followed the trail like blood hounds over mountains and through forests without losing it for a moment, for it is a very difficult matter for an Indian to baffle the pursuit of another Indian who follows his trail persistently. The Wacos traveled hard, and when they stopped to camp for the night about an hour before sunset, Harvey was completely exhausted. Without a moment's rest from the time he was captured until then he had been compelled to move forward at a rapid rate, with at least one hundred pounds of meat upon his back.

The Wacos had just begun to make preparations for encamping, when they heard the clattering of horse's hoofs, and the next moment they were as much alarmed as their prisoner had been, when they found themselves completely surrounded by the Comanches.

The poor Wacos offered no resistance to their dreaded enemies, the Comanches. The Comanche chief told them to bring forward the Waco who stole the pony. He was pointed out, and the chief ordered some of his men to seize him, stake him down upon the ground and give him three hundred lashes with a raw hide quirt, which was promptly done. He then called for the Indian who took the white man prisoner. The Wacos pointed to their chief, and his highness was also staked down and treated to a dose of three hundred lashes on his naked hide.

The Comanches then released Mr. Harvey from his burden of horse flesh, and ordered him to take a butcher knife and kill the Indian who captured him. Declining to do this, they told him to cut his ears off, but he told the chief he did not wish to do it. Finding they could not get Harvey either to kill or "crop" the Indian, they turned him loose, telling him to go back to his camp; and at the same time they strictly charged the Wacos not to molest in any way again either him or his men. For some unknown reason, it seems the Comanches were friendly disposed towards Harvey, and considered him and his men under their special protection. Had it not been for this, Harvey could not have carried out his contract with the government.

John Taylor.

JOHN TAYLOR came to Texas at an early day, and settled in Grimes county, near where the town of Anderson now stands. He was a brave and daring man, but was deficient in caution, the want of which has resulted in the death of so many on the frontiers of Texas. On one occasion, Taylor started from home for the purpose of attending to some business in an adjoining neighborhood. While on his way he was attacked by a large party of Indians who were ambuscading the road he was traveling. Seeing the impossibility of defending himself against such fearful odds, he endeavored to save himself by flight, but he was soon overtaken and killed by the Indians, and his body mutilated by them in the most barbarous manner. He left a devoted wife and several small children to mourn his untimely fate.

1836

Not long after the death of her husband, Mrs. Taylor determined to visit the spot where her husband was slain. Her friends endeavored to persuade her from doing so, telling her the country was full of Indians, and that she would be in great danger of losing her life if she should venture outside of the settlements. She persisted, however, in making the attempt, and, strange to say, she was killed by Indians at the very spot where they had previously slain her husband. No doubt, she had been moved to visit the scene of her husband's death from the most praiseworthy motives; nevertheless, we can not commend her judgment in persisting to gratify a mere morbid whim, at the imminent risk of her life.

The Harvey Massacre.

MR. HARVEY was a native of the State of Alabama. He immigrated to Texas in 1835 and settled in what is now Robertson county. He was a stock raiser and farmer. It was in the month of November, 1836, and about the time of the evening that people in the country are usually at supper when a party of Indians approached unobserved and attacked Harvey's house.

1836 He ran to get his gun that lay on a rack above the door and as he did so a bullet struck him in the neck, killing him instantly. His wife attempted to conceal herself under one of the beds in the room, but the keen eyed savages discovered her, dragged her out and killed her. They then scalped her as they had previously done her husband, cut her heart out and laid it on her breast. One of their little children, a lad about ten years old, was also killed, his coat being found with at least twenty bullet holes through it. The little daughter, nine years old, was carried off prisoner, and for more than a year suffered all the privations and hardships, and was subjected to all the insults and indignities her brutal captors could inflict upon her. She was finally taken over to Mexico by the Indians and sold to the Mexicans. Her uncle, James Talbert, was then living in Alabama and was written to by the citizens informing him that his neice was still alive and in Mexico. "Her uncle," says Rev. Z. N. Morrill: "After long search and a large expenditure of money found the child. She had been sold by the Indians and had become greatly attached to its Mexican mother. Her arm had been broken during the killing of her parents. She was carried by the uncle to Alabama and by him was afterwards brought to Texas. They settled near where her parents were killed. She has since married and when recently heard from was living. I have often since been at her house and used the family Bible at worship, owned by her father, and which yet has upon its pages the blood of her parents spilled by the hands of the Indians on that fearful night." (Flower and Fruit, 68.)

John Edwards.

JOHN EDWARDS was also one of the pioneers of Texas. On his arrival in Texas he stopped for some time at the town of Bastrop, where he made the acquaintance of the venerable Bartholomew Manlove, one of the oldest settlers in the place. Some time after his arrival, whilst he was traveling with Mr. Manlove to the town of Washington, on the Brazos, they encountered a large party 1836 of Indians on the way. These Indians, in order to get the advantage of them, made signs to them on their approach signifying that they were friendly, and beckoned them to come on. But Manlove, who was well acquainted with the treacherous character of these Indians, halted and advised Edwards to do likewise, but he paid no attention to his warning, and allowed the savages to approach him. Manlove, who was riding a fine horse, then bore off rapidly to the left. The Indians observing the movement, some of them applied quirts and spurs to their horses and started after him. They ran him several miles, but his horse proved too fleet for them, and he succeeded in making his escape. But the unfortunate Edwards was thrust through with a dozen spears, after the Indians had shaken him heartily by the hand as a token of friendship. They scalped him and took his horse and rifle.

Many have thus been murdered in Texas by imprudently permitting Indians to approach them who pretended they were friendly. Of late years, however, they have not been very successful in playing this little game, as their treacherous character has long since been pretty well known.

John Marlin.

JOHN MARLIN was an experienced frontiersman, and rendered efficient service on many occasions in defense of the settlers against their savage foes. In the spring of 1836, Marlin, Jarrett Menifee and Lahan Menifee went into the woods for the purpose of cutting bee trees. They were going along a trail which was so narrow they were compelled to ride in single file, when an Indian, who was concealed near the path, suddenly raised up and presented his gun, but it missed fire. Before he could take aim again Marlin and Lahan Menifee both raised their guns and fired at him. The Indian leaped in the air and fell dead. Menifee cried out. "I've saved him" Marlin replied, "No, it was I who killed him;" but Menifee still contended that he was the one who shot him. Jarrett Menifee then said to them: "You had better quit quarreling and load your guns, for it is not probable one Indian would attack three men by himself." On an examination of the Indian they had killed, they found that the bullets of both Menifee and Marlin's guns had penetrated his breast not over two inches apart. The two men had fired so nearly at the same moment that neither of them had heard the report of the other's gun.

1836

The men reloaded their guns and had gone but a short distance further when they were fired upon by Indians in ambush near the trail. Marlin and his companions returned their fire with fatal effect, killing two more Indians and driving the rest from their hiding place. They, however, ran but a short distance to a mot of timber, where they concealed themselves. At this juncture Marlin and his companions d scovered another white man riding directly toward the Indians who was evidently unaware of their presence. Marlin called aloud to him not to go near the mot, as there were Indians concealed in it. As Marlin and his companions were dressed in buckskin hunting shirts, the man they had called to supposed at first they were Indians, and seemed at a loss what to do. He finally satisfied himself, however, that they were white men, and turned his course toward them. After he came up, Mr. Marlin told him there were Indians in the mot he was going to, and they at once proceeded to attack them. The Indians (there were but two of them) defended themselves bravely for some time, but at length one was killed and the other one rushed from the mot and ran like a quarter horse. The whites pursued him for some distance, but he made his escape. They killed four out of the five Indians they had found that day, leaving only one to tell the tale—a pretty fair day's work.

John McClellan.

THE nativity of John McClellan is unknown to the writer. His father was among the first of the early settlers in Texas, and was a well known character where he resided. He settled on the Brazos river near where the city of Waco now stands. He had many conflicts with the Indians who then frequently raided that section of country, but always came out unhurt. But he was doomed to be slain by them at last. A party of Indians attacked his house when he was unsuspicious of danger and unprepared to meet it, and murdered him as well as several others of his family, and took his little son John McClellan, the subject of this sketch, who was then a lad eight or ten years of age, a prisoner. They then left for the mountains, taking with them a number of horses they had stolen from Mr. McClellan and others. They did not halt until they reached the villages where they lived on Red river. The Indians kept young McClellan until he was a grown man. In 1846 a treaty was made with these Indians and young McClellan was restored to his relatives. He had almost forgotten his native tongue, and when interrogated as to his capture he could only describe the massacre of his father and family by the aid of signs. He had become greatly attached to the Indians, among whom he had lived so long, and it was with much difficulty that his friends and relatives prevented him from going back to them at once. However, they finally persuaded him to stay with them for one moon (a month.) During that moon, (and it proved to be a honey moon to McClellan), several pretty young ladies paid a visit to the relatives with whom he was staying and he fell desperately in love with one of them, and abandoned his intention of returning to his savage friends. He postponed his departure until he persuaded this young lady to marry him, and after that he settled down contentedly at the old homestead, and we believe he is still living there.

This is only one instance among a number of similar ones of the capture of children by the Indians, who, when restored to their relatives, became restless under the restraints of civilized society, and desired to return to the wild life they had led with the denizens of the forest and prairie, which goes to prove that civilization is an artificial condition of society, and that men are naturally prone to revert to their normal state of savagery. This remark, however, applies only to men, for but few women who were captured and held for any length of time by the Indians ever showed the slightest inclination to place themselves again in the power of their cruel task masters.

Crouch and Davis.

THESE two gentlemen were men of worth, and were well known in the country where they resided. Mr. Crouch was a Baptist minister and Davis was a physician. The latter was from the city of New Orleans. Mr. Crouch's nativity is not known to the writer. Immediately after the battle of San Jacinto, the settlers in western Texas began to return to their homes, from which 1836 they had fled on the approach of Santa Anna and his army. It was at that time that a Mr. Goldsberry Childress started with his family for his home on Little river, in Bell county. He had scarcely arrived and settled down at his old home when the Indians, taking advantage of the disbandment of the Texas army and the defenseless condition of the frontier, began to raid the country at many points, spreading terror and desolation wherever they went. As the government was powerless at the time to give protection to the settlers, they were ordered to rendezvous at Nashville, on the Brazos, for their mutual safety, until some measures could be adopted by the government to protect them against the incursions of the Indians.

Mr. Childress, among others, proceeded to obey the order of the government, and with his family, and Dr. Davis and Mr. Crouch accompanying them, he started for the designated place of rendezvous. The country through which they had to travel was infested with prowling bands of savages, and Dr. Davis and Mr. Crouch remained with Mr. Childress and his family until they supposed they were out of danger. On the morning of June 4, they told Mr. Childress they did not think there was any further danger to be apprehended from the Indians, and that they would ride on ahead. Accordingly they saddled their horses and started. They had gone but two or three hundred yards—not out of sight—when that portion of Mr. Childress's family who were in the rear driving the loose stock saw a cloud of dust rising behind them. At this they became alarmed and called to Childress. By this time the Indians were in view, advancing towards them. Childress called to Dr. Davis and Crouch, who were in hearing, and warned them of danger.

In a little while the Indians came up and surrounded the wagon. Pretty soon they discovered Doctor Davis and Mr. Crouch returning, and a portion of the Indians charged upon them whilst the balance attacked the wagon. Doctor Davis and Mr. Crouch were both armed with guns and pistols, and planting themselves squarely in the road, they stood their ground, and fought the Indians face to face, in regular old Texan style. They emptied their guns and pistols at them, and knocked several from their horses, but the Indians were too numerous to contend against, and both these gallant men were eventually killed. The Indians that killed them then fell back to the main body, and the combined forces made a furious attack upon the wagon.

There were five Texans with Mr. Childress, all well armed, and they took shelter behind the wagon. The fact that they were well armed, and protected in a measure by the wagon, and the gallant fight made by Davis and Crouch caused the Indians to be a little cautious in approaching Childress's party, and for that reason they remained at some distance, but kept up a continuous fire upon them at "long taw." They did no damage, however, with the exception of wounding one of the horses. Whilst this shooting at "long taw" was going on, one of the Childress party became so frightened he mounted a horse and fled, leaving only five men to contend against a horde of savages. After consulting with his men, Childress determined to move from where they were and take a better protected position in a small mot of timber a short distance from them. This movement was safely accomplished, and while a portion of the men kept the Indians at bay with their guns, the rest went to work with axes and quickly built a temporary breast work for the protection of the women and children. Each man then took a tree, firmly resolved to fight it out on that line. But the Indians seeing how advantageously they were posted, and knowing full well if they charged them that many of their braves would bite dust, did not venture to attack them, but contented themselves with killing the cattle. Childress, who was well acquainted with the country, knew there was a settlement within three miles of them, and he determined whilst the Indians were occupied in killing his stock, to retreat to it with his family. He and his men then unloosed the oxen from the wagon, drove them on to a piece of low ground, and mounted the women and children on the few horses they had been able to save. These horses were only partially broken and were hard to manage, but they had no others. After the women and children had started, Childress mounted the best horse he had and kept between his family and the Indians for the purpose of watching their movements. But the Indians did not attempt to follow them into the thickly timbered bottom. They were compelled to make their way through this bottom without a road, and when they reached the settlements, they were nearly naked, their clothes having been torn off by briers and bushes through which they passed.

Mrs. Yeargin.

THIS lady was of German descent. She came to Texas prior to the war with Mexico and settled on Cummins creek, in Fayette county. In 1836, when Santa Anna's army was spreading terror and devastation throughout the country all the people in the settlement where Mrs. Yeargin lived abandoned their homes and fled.

She, however, very imprudently, concluded to remain 1836 where she was. One night an unusual noise was heard around the house. Mrs. Yeargin awoke her husband, who went out to discover the cause of it and found the yard filled with Indians. He ran back to the house, notified the family of their danger and then made his escape. The poor old man was so frightened that he ran ten miles before he halted. Mrs. Yeargin did not have time to dress herself but fled in her night clothes, and as they were white they could be easily seen. She was discovered by the Indians and captured, who also captured her two little sons. After she had been with the Indians about three months they took her to Coffee's trading house, on Red river, and there sold her for three hundred dollars and eventually she was returned to her relatives in Fayette county. The Indians refused to sell her two little boys and they have never been heard of since. The ill treatment Mrs. Yeargin had undergone while a captive among the Indians and the loss of her two little boys came near costing her life. The old man, her husband, who was very infirm, never recovered from the effects of his long run and died shortly afterwards. Mrs. Yeargin is still living in Fayette county or was when this article was written.

Captain McCullom.

MR. McCULLOM was a native of the State of Alabama. He came to Texas in 1837, and settled in Bastrop county, where he followed the trade of blacksmith. He made his home with the family of a well known citizen of Bastrop county, Captain James Rogers, one of the first settlers in Austin's new colony. In the month of November, 1837, McCullom and a son of Captain Rogers left the house and went some distance across a creek, for the purpose of building a wolf pen or trap. Having cut the timber, they were busily engaged in hewing the logs, when they were fired upon by a party of Indians who had crept up close to them in the underbrush, attracted by the sound of their axes. When the Indians fired on them, McCullom hallooed to young Rogers, who was chopping at some little distance from him, to run towards the house, and at the same time he started himself, forgetting, in his hurry, to take his gun, which he had placed near by. Near where they were at work was a new cut road at the crossing of Wilbarger creek, and McCullom and young Rogers took this, as being the nearest way to the house. The Indians pressed them closely, and just as they were ascending the steep bank on the opposite side of the creek, several of the foremost Indians fired at McCullom, and he fell dead, pierced with bullets. When McCullom fell, young Rogers ran up the bank and down the other side until he was hid from the view of the Indians, when he turned his course, dodged his pursuers and succeeded in making his way home.

1837

Bartholomew Manlove

BARTHOLOMEW MANLOVE was a native of Kentucky, and immigrated to Texas at an early day. He lived in eastern Texas for several years, and then moved to Bastrop, where he subsequently did good service in protecting the frontiers of that county from marauding bands of Mexicans and Indians. He had an extraordinary large horse—perhaps the largest horse that could

1836 have been found at that time in the whole of Texas, and he valued him very highly, not for his speed —for a burro could beat him in a fair race—but for his strength and docility.

One night an Indian crept slyly up to the place where the horse was tied, cut him loose and led him away without being seen. The next morning, when the old man found out that his horse was stolen, he was "mightily put out" about it, and was threatening dire vengeance against the thieving Indians, when some of his neighbors happened to come in, and asked him what was the matter. "Why," said he, "the cussed Ingins have stolen my horse, and I wouldn't have sold him for the best league of land on old Caney." Now, among the people who had just called in was a young man who was very attentive to Mr. Manlove's youngest daughter, Dolly, and when he heard the old gentleman protest that he would give the best negro on his farm to anyone who would bring back his horse, he inquired if Dolly was included in the reward he offered. "Yes," replied the old man, "Dolly, too." "If that horse is this side of the Rocky mountains," said the young fellow, "I'll have him." He immediately left, and in a little while raised a party of five or six young men, who agreed to go with him in search of Mr. Manlove's big horse. They first went to the camp of some friendly Tonkawa Indians in the neighborhood, and engaged several of them to act as spies and to assist them in trailing.

By the aid of these Indians, they soon found the trail which they knew was the right one by the unusually large hoof prints of Mr. Manlove's horse. After following it for some miles the party stopped awhile to eat and rest themselves. A few moments afterwards to their astonishment, a Comanche warrior made his appearance on a hill near by, mounted upon Mr. Manlove's big horse. He shook his spear at the young men, made some contemptuous gestures towards them and rode off. Dolly's young man proposed to give chase to him at once, but the others declined doing so, because they believed the Indian had been sent there to draw them into the an ambuscade; but this was not so for the Indian was alone. He had, it would seem, taken up the idea that the speed of his horse was in proportion to his size, and that he could readily make his escape from the young men if they should attempt to pursue him.

Evidently, under this impression, the Comanche again made his appearance on the brow of the hill. He there stuck his spear in the ground as a sign that he would do so to them if they dared to follow him. Then after cursing the Tonkawas for being with the whites and telling them they were cowards and squaws, he made some more concontemptuous gestures at the crowd, and rode off leisurely again. This was more than the young men could bear, and as soon as he disappeared behind the hill, they mounted their horses and started in pursuit. They rode on very cautiously until they reached the summit of the hill, when they discovered the Comanche riding carelessly along not more than a hundred yards from them. The young men immediately clapped spurs to their horses and dashed after him. After running three or four hundred yards, he found that he had greatly overrated the speed of the big horse, as the young men were then within a few paces of him. He then sprang to the ground and took to his own heels for safety. Coming to a mud hole on the way, he hastily snatched a handful of mud, smeared his face and arms with it and continued his flight.

But although he made better speed on foot than he did on the big horse the party soon overtook him and the young men turned him over to the tender mercies of their Tonkawa guides. They, as well as the Comanche, were armed with bows and arrows, and a regular arrow fight ensued between them. The Comanche fought like a tiger and hurled his arrows at his assailants with astonishing rapidity, but finally one of the young men, fearing he might kill or wound one of their Tonkawa guides raised his gun and shot him dead. The Tonkawas then scalped him, cut off his feet and hands, trimmed the flesh from his legs, thighs and hips, and said they would leave the balance of him for the wolves and buzzards.

Mr. Manlove, of course, was greatly rejoiced when his big horse was brought back to him, but whether or not the young man received his promised reward this deponent saith not. But as Mr. Manlove was a man of his word and Dolly married shortly afterwards it is reasonable to suppose that he got the reward and Dolly in the bargain.

Captain James G. Swisher.

JAMES G. SWISHER was born in Knoxville, Tennessee, on the sixth of November, 1794, was a member of Captain John Donelson's company, under General Jackson, and participated in the battles of New Orleans on the night of the twenty-third of December, 1814, and eighth of January, 1815. He moved from near Franklin, Williamson county, Tennessee, to Texas in 1833. Captain Swisher, 1834 in January, 1834, settled at the town of Tenoxtitlan, on the Brazos river, not now in existence, but which up to the year 1832 had been garrisoned by two hundred Mexican troops.

Captain Swisher rented the residence lately occupied by the commander of the post. He obtained fifty or sixty acres of cleared land from different parties in the vicinity, and soon had a splendid crop growing. Everything looked lovely. The seasons were fine, the climate was charming. He and all his family were delighted with the move to

Texas. But there is no elysium on earth. Good and evil,
joy and grief, happiness and sorrow are mixed in all that is
served up to us.

One dark, foggy morning, about day light, in the latter
part of April, 1834, the whole town was aroused by a wild
Indian alarm, not the savage war whoop of the terrible Comanche, but the cry of citizens in different portions of the
town, yelling at the tops of their voices, "Indians!" "Indians!" "Indians!" "Where?" "Where?" "Where are they?"
resounded in trembling accents, and men, women and children, clad principally in night apparel, ran hither and
thither in the wildest confusion. Attention was quickly
drawn to Captain Swisher's horse lot, located about twenty
yards from his dwelling, and near the center of the town.
In an incredible short space of time the lot was surrounded
by the citizens. There a sickening sight awaited them. All
the horses were gone except two; one of these stood trembling in one corner of the lot, with an arrow sticking in its
side; the other, a favorite animal, lay weltering in his blood,
and from his carcass large pieces of flesh had been cut.—Indians are fond of horse meat.

In less than an hour after the alarm had been given fifteen or twenty hardy pioneers, all good citizens, and as
brave Indian fighters as ever settled a new country, assembled, and announced themselves ready for the pursuit. It
is to be regretted that the names of these persons can not be
given. Only a few are remembered. Among them were
Mike and Joe Boren, Mr. Teel and two sons, fifteen to
eighteen years of age. Mr. Mumford, Robert Barr, afterwards postmaster general during General Houston's first
administration, and Major William H. Smith, who commanded a cavalry company and was wounded at San Jacinto.

They started without delay and soon struck the trail of
the Indians, which, after coming into the open country,
took a bee line in the northwest direction. They pursued it
with all the speed possible for persons on foot for several
miles, when a halt was called, and it was agreed unanimously that it was unnecessary to continue the march any
further, as the Indians had got such a start, and were
traveling with such speed that it would be impossible to

overtake them that day. It was decided to abandon the chase and return home.

Captain Swisher was willing that the party should return but he refused to do so himself. He said: "As from the best information we can gather the Indians do not number more than two or three it is unnecessary for so many to pursue them. But I must get my horses; without them I shall be unable to raise a crop, for I have no money to buy others with. Besides, the horse they killed belonged to my wife. He was faithful and reliable and I was very much attached to him, and would like to avenge his death. I shall continue the pursuit as long as there is the possibility of a chance of overtaking the thieves. I would like to have one of you go with me—one who knows the country, who is a good woodsman and can follow an Indian trail." "I will go," "I will go," rang out at once from a dozen voices.

Either Mike Boren or Joe Boren—I forget which one of the brothers—was elected to go.

Having replenished their knapsacks with all the provisions they could conveniently carry, supplied from the rations of their returning companions, Swisher and Boren set out with renewed vigor upon the trail. The ground being moist, the track made by six horses, all shod with iron, was not a difficult one to follow.

They took a brisk step, and kept it up all day until it became too dark to see the trail. They camped and slept all night. They awoke next morning, bright and early, feeling quite refreshed, and again took up their line of march. About ten o'clock they came to a place where the Indians had halted, perhaps to spend the night or to let the horses graze. No signs of their having camped were observable. They had kindled no fire. This point was supposed to be about forty-five or fifty miles from Tenoxtitlan, and the distance had been made by the Indians without stopping. Swisher and Boren continued on the trail with unabated zeal, and late in the afternoon they had the pleasure of knowing that they were fast gaining upon their enemies.

The Indians evidently thought they were out of danger, as they had halted several times during the day to let the horses graze, showing they had no fears of being pursued. As the Indians became more careless, Swisher and Boren became more circumspect. Boren marched in front with his eyes on the trail, Swisher in the rear, with his rifle in hand ready to fire at a moment's warning, with his eyes searching every nook and corner of the post oak woods. About sun down they came to quite a large creek, and the muddy water just below the crossing and the fresh tracks showed that the Indians must have crossed only a few mo· ments before. On account of the lateness of the hour the pursuers concluded to stop where they were until morning. Accordingly they moved down the creek a few steps and established their head quarters in a little clump of bushes, where it would have been hard for even a wolf to have discovered them. As soon as it was. light enough to see how to travel, they crossed the creek, and believing that the Indians might have camped any where in the immediate vicinity, they took the trail, observing the same precaution and plan of march they had adopted on the previous evening. They traveled for about an hour, and just as the sun was about to rise they crossed a dry ravine. At the moment they ascended the bank a small column of smoke shot up suddenly from the edge of a little thicket not more than twenty steps to the left; almost instantly a tall Indian arose, exposing himself from his hips upwards, to plain view; scarcely had he straightened to his full height when Swisher's gun fired. With only one loud "wah!" the Indian fell.

The other one did not attempt to rise but started off half bent, running like a scared wolf, when bang went Boren's gun, and down went the Indian. But he scrambled to his feet again and ran with great speed to the nearest thicket with one hand pressed to his side. Swisher and Boren did not move from their tracks until after they had reloaded their rifles. They then went to the camp. The fire had by this time commenced to burn nicely, and within a foot-or two of it the Indian lay perfectly dead. He had been shot through the heart and evidently never knew what hurt him. They were taken completely by surprise while engaged in kindling their fire. They were at least sixty-five or seventy miles from Tenoxtitlan and never dreamed of being followed to that distance. The horses were all found within a few hundred yards of the Indian camp securely hoppled. The trail of Boren's Indian was followed some little distance into the thicket. It was evident that he was badly wounded, judging from the quantity of blood which marked his re-treating footsteps. But as he was no longer setting up any claim to the horses, and had deserted his camp without taking his bow and arrows with him, they lost all interest in further pursuit of him. They then collected the horses preparatory to setting their faces homeward, taking, before leaving, a last look at the Indian they had slain—

And they left him at rest on the spot where he died,
With his horse meat, his arrows and bow by his side,
Never more, with his wild war whoop, to dash on his prey,
Or to sneak into lots and steal horses away.

It was yet early in the morning when they set out for home, which they reached about the middle of the afternoon of the next day without further adventure. They were met with joy and gladness by their families and friends; indeed, the whole village assembled to offer their congratulations.

Captain James G. Swisher was the father of James M. Swisher and John M. Swisher, both of whom now live in Travis county. The former was for many years captain of a ranging company and most generally known as Captain Mon Swisher. The latter, who resides in the city of Austin, and known all over the State as Colonel Milt Swisher, was in the employ of the republic from 1839 up to annexation, and from that time until 1856 in the employ of the State. In 1841 he was chief clerk and acting secretary of the treasury of the republic, and in 1847 was appointed auditor to audit and settle up the debt of the late republic.

Captain George B. Erath.

THE following sketch of Captain Erath's life was taken by permission from his unpublished memoirs. It is to be hope that ere long he will give these memoirs to the public, as they would make an exceedingly interesting book, especially to Texans; but it would be out of place in

such a book as this to give more than a bare outline or synopsis of what is related in these memoirs. Captain
1813　Erath was born January 1, 1813, at Vienna, Austria,
and was educated in the Polytechnic Institute in that
city. After arriving at a certain age he would have been
liable to conscription for fourteen years in the Austrian
army, and to evade this his mother sent him to Wurtem-
burg, Germany, where he resided with his relatives for some
time.

But being disgusted with the tyrannical government of
his native country, after remaining a year in Germany, he
determined, instead of returning home, to emigrate to free
America. As he could not leave Germany with the pass-
port he had, except to go back to Austria, he traveled dis-
guised as a servant with a retired French officer, who was
on his way to Paris. He says he traveled in style with this
old officer, in his coach and four, and contrasts it in an
amusing way with his next journey in Texas—bareback on
a mustang from Velasco to the interior. From Paris he
went to Havre, and there took shipping to New Orleans,
where he arrived on the twenty-second of June, 1831. From
New Orleans he traveled by steamboat to Cincinnati, where
he remained a short time, and then went to Florence, Alabama. Returning to New Orleans, where he saw for the
first time a railroad, and hearing much said there about
the advantages of Texas and the inducements to settle in
that new country, he concluded to try his fortunes in that
favored region. He therefore took passage on board of a
schooner bound for Velasco, at the mouth of the Brazos,
where he safely landed, and from thence went on horseback
to Brazoria, and shortly afterward to Robertson's colony,
where he opened a farm in conjunction with a Mr. Porter,
varying his occupation as a farmer by an occasional surveying expedition, in which he often came into conflict with
Indians, who were especially hostile to those who were engaged in surveying their lands. When it became impossible to survey on account of Indian hostilities he enlisted in
a company commanded by John H. Moore, and was with
him in what is known as "Moore's expedition," which accomplished nothing, for reasons given by Captain Erath.

In making a charge upon what was supposed to be a large

party of Indians posted in some thick woods, though in fact there were but six of them, who fled precipitately, the Captain says he and one other man were mounted upon unruly mustangs, which they were unable to control, and which took them far ahead of their companions in spite of their efforts to check them, seemingly detetermined to give them a reputation for valor which they by no means deserved. He adds: "In this charge we captured one broken down pony, one hundred strong as we were." Returning from this warlike expedition, he went off on another surveying trip about the head waters of San Gabriel and Brushy creeks. On this trip one of his men, Lang, was killed in a fight with Indians. Subsequently he was out on a number of scouts after Indians.

In March, 1836, he joined the Texan army under General Houston, enlisting in Captain Billingsley's company from Bastrop. He was at the battle of San Jacinto, and remained in the service until the army was disbanded, when he returned to his farm in Robertson's colony. Shortly afterwards the massacre of Parker's fort occurred, and he again entered the frontier service, and was out on several expeditions into the Indian country. Subsequently he resumed his occupation of surveying, and whilst out with a small party in 1838, one of his men, Curtis, was killed in a fight with the Indians.

In January, 1841, he was with the Morehouse expedition, and had command of the friendly Indians and spies. After his return home he was elected captain again of the Milam County Rangers. In one of his scouts he had a fight with a party of Indians, killed several and wounded Jose Maria, a noted chief. He was with the Altier expedition, but, owing to lameness caused by an accident, he, with others, was left in charge of the camp and horses, on the east side of the Rio Grande, and they made their escape after the battle and surrender at Mier.

After he returned home he was twice elected to Congress, and at the last election for members of Congress he was re-elected by a large majority over his opponent; but in the mean time annexation to the United States had been consummated, and Congress never assembled. He was elected a member of the first Legislature by a large majority, and was re-elected in 1857. In 1861 he was elected State senator. Subsequently he raised a company, and was attached to Colonel Speight's Fifteenth Texas Infantry regiment, under whom he served until the collapse of the Confederacy.

While acting as surveyor, he laid off the city of Waco, Cameron, the county seat cf Milam, and several other towns. Such, in brief, are the outlines of Captain Erath's life, from which it will be seen that almost continuously from the time of his arrival in Texas until some years after the close of the civil war, he was in the service of the State, either in a military or civil capacity. But few men, in our opinion, have done more than Captain Erath towards laying the foundations of the great commonwealth of Texas, and in all the positions he has occupied, both civil and military, his bravery, honesty and unimpeachable integrity always commanded the respect of his opponents, and the esteem and admiration of his friends. In the halls of Congress or of the Legislature his straightforward course and his practical views always gave weight to any measure he advocated. If he had only studied his own interests half as much as he did the interests and welfare of his adopted country, with the many opportunities he had of amassing a fortune, Captain Erath would to-day be ranked among the millionaires of the land, and anyone who may read his memoirs will be convinced of the truth of this statement. As it is, he owns nothing, we believe, in the way of this world's goods except his little farm and homestead in McLennan county.

Captain Erath's Fight on Elm Creek.

THE following is Captain Erath's account of his fight with Indians on Elm creek, in Milam county. He was in command, at the time, of a small company of Rangers, about twenty in number. On the fourth of January, 1837, Sergeant McLochlan arrived at camp, bringing

CAPTAIN GEORGE B. ERATH'S GUN "KNOCKS DOWN BEFORE AND BEHIND."

the information that he had seen the tracks of some dozen Indians, on foot, going down the country about twelve 1837 miles from the fort, on the waters of Elm creek. It was all bustle now during the night, as we were determined that these Indians should not be allowed to go down the country to do mischief. There were but ten horses belonging to the company, besides mine and that of Lieutenant Curtis, who was properly in command at the fort and outranked me. He did not intend to go himself or let his horses go, but wanted me to go and take eight or ten men on foot. I was quite eager to go, but opposed to taking men on foot. During the night it began to rain, and continued to rain until the middle of the afternoon the next day, by which time all our arrangements had been satisfactorily made. In the morning, as early as all the horses could be gotten out of the woods—perhaps by ten o'clock—we started. I had ten men from the company, with their horses, and a man by the name of Lishely, who was looking at the country, who had been but a short time in Texas, and of whom I never heard afterwards, and the two Childers boys, constituted my force. There were also four young men from the settlements below, who, before the war, had lived with their parents in the country near the fort. They had come to look after their affairs, and were about starting home. They agreed to accompany me as far as I was going down toward the settlement. Three of them were on horseback and one on foot. This would have made an aggregate of eighteen men. We started together and went five or six miles eastward, but, as I continued to bear further from the course those four men wanted to go, they left me and started for their home at Nashville, sixty miles below Little river fort. I was now left with fourteen men, rank and file, whose names were as follows: Lishely, Frank and Robert Childers, volunteers; Sergeant McLochlan, Lee R. Davis, David Clark (an elderly man), Empson, Thompson, Jack Gross, Louis Moore, Maurice Moore and Gree McCoy. The three latter were mere boys, two of them not fifteen years of age, but all were expert in the use of arms and had good rifles. Davis had two good pistols and Lishely had one. There were two others— one, Jack Houston, a grown man, who had a musket, and John Folks, a mere boy, with a shot gun, and not much used to a woods life. I had a very good rifle and a fine pistol, and McLochlan and myself were better mounted than the others. Four of our number had never been in a battle before.

After we were abandoned by the four men, as previously mentioned, we traveled but an hour or so until we struck the trail, but, behold! instead of a dozen Indians, it was evident from the sign, that there were a hundred, all on foot, going down toward the nearest settlement. Following for two or three miles, we came to where they had encamped the day before during the rain, and had left there that morning. Their fires were still burning. They had built ten or twelve shelters with sticks and grass, each one sufficient for eight or ten men. The trail as they went on made a plain road which could be easily followed. Indians and Indian hunters can tell by the cut of the soles of the moccasins to what tribe those wearing them belong, but we did not possess that art and were perplexed accordingly. It was agreed that if they were wild Indians we could handle them, but if they proved to be the half civilized Caddos or northern Indians we would have our hands full. At night fall we were about twenty-three miles from the fort, and eight miles from where Cameron now stands, and had lost the trail, but heard the Indians calling to each other in the bottom not half a mile distant. Knowing they were around the camp, I fell back about half a mile to reconnoiter. In the early part of the night I sent out McLochlan and Robert Childress for that purpose, but they returned before midnight and reported that they could not find the camp, and that all was silent. About four o'clock the men were called up. They saddled and tied their horses to trees and we marched off on foot.

We got to the place where we left the trail the night before, and about the dawning of day found it going into a a ravine. It followed that ravine, which ran parallel with the creek some three or four hundred yards distant, several hundred yards when it came into another ravine at right angle where the Indians turned and went square down the creek. Following on we heard the Indians coughing, and coming within a hundred yards of the creek where the trail took up a bank, we came in full view of the Indians less than a hundred yards distance, all well dressed, a number of them with hats on, busy breaking brush and gathering wood to make fires. We dodged back to the low ground to keep out of sight as quick as possible, but advanced, it being not broad day light.

I must remark here that this last move developed that we had to deal with the formidable kind of Indians about a hundred strong. There was not time to retire or consult. Up to this time there had been no contradiction, very little said, everybody willing to acquiesce in my actions and orders. If apprehensions were expressed I answered that we were employed by the government to protect the citizens and let the result be what it might, the Indians at least would return—not go any farther down the country toward the settlements for fear of the alarm—having once been discovered.

They were camped in a small horse shoe bend. We took a position at a point under the bank of the creek. It was not light enough to see the sight of the guns. Our distance from them we thought to be fifty yards but it proved to be not more than twenty-five after the battle. We fired and some of them fell about the burning brush. Most of them stooped to grab their guns and immediately took posts behind trees beyond the fire from us, commencing a yell, and to return our shots and flanked out from both sides to get into the creek where they could see our strength, especially on our right wing, where the creek was wider and opened down to where they were. Half of us had jumped on the bank. If we all had had pistols or the six shooters of the present day we could have charged them and kept them running, but as it was we had to keep our position to reload our guns. By this time the Indians commenced opening a heavy fire with their rifles. Their powder out cracked ours. If a shot gun was heard it was but once or twice out of the five or six hundred shots. No bows and arrows were seen among them. After keeping our position five or six minutes they mortally wounded Clark and Frank Childers on my right flank from firing up the creek. Telling the wounded to go back as far as they could I ordered my men to fall back on the other side of the creek in two squads to gain the top of the bank and to post themselves behind trees, which

they did, while I stood in my old position under the bank
loading my gun and watching the approach of the Indians.
As the men got posted the Indians came charging with a
terrific yell. I retreated to the other side of the creek channel but found myself under a steep bank six or seven feet
high. The Indians came charging and jumped down the
bank of the creek. One had his gun within a few feet of
me, firing, but missed me. I could not miss him and he fell
right before me. This caused the others to dodge back a
few feet behind trees as my men were now firing from their
new position. I made an effort to get up the bank with my
back to it and my face toward the Indians, having hold of
a root with one hand. I swung myself partially up it but
slipped and fell back, which caused my men to ask if I was
was hurt. I answered no and said "help me up the bank."
Louis Moore and Thompson laid down on the ground,
reached their hands down and pulled me up with my gun.
I called my men and ordered Davis to fall back with one of
the squads fifty or sixty feet and take a new position, while
I, with the rest covered the movement, and when they had
reached the place fell back beyond them about the same distance to take still another position, and in this manner we
succeeded in retiring several hundred yards through an open
bottom, the trees being only elms about six inches in diameter and the balls of the Indians kept striking trees. [I was
in that neighborhood last year and was told that several of
the trees were standing showed the scars.]

But at this juncture my left had reached the bank of the
gully we had just descended into. There was a big thicket
on the opposite side. The Indians charging on us with great
fury and terrific yells, we could not be blamed for seeking
shelter; but it extended my line, and, seeing Indians on my
right dashing up toward us, McLochlan and myself took to
a big tree standing on the extreme right. McLochlan presented his gun, but could not shoot. I had my gun loaded,
took good aim at a bunch of Indians close by, who were dodging off obliquely but advancing. I had no time to see the
effect of my shot, but running to another thicket with Mc-
Lochlan, the Indians got between us and the other men and
kept up their yelling. Fifteen or twenty steps more, we
reached the ravine that went square up from the creek.

Here we found Clark going up the bed of it, just about exhausted and sinking. He said something about fighting to the last or we would all be killed. Mac said he had nothing to fight with, as his gun was broken. Clark told him to take his gun, but Mac declined it, though it was a good rifle and in good fix. Mac kept on up the gully, and after a while found the other men. I stopped a few seconds longer with Clark, who was then getting down, and seeing a half dozen Indians coming up the gully, I went up the gully and kept up a different prong, and two or three hundred yards more got into open ground, reloading my gun as I went. I saw some of my men, a hundred and fifty yards ahead, among some lone elms, called to them and they waited. I joined them and we reviewed the situation. The Indians were advancing no more, but rather falling back to where the fight had commenced, some of them yelling round Clark, whom they butchered up; but they never found Frank Childers, who had sat down by a tree, leaning his gun upright against it, and died there, in twenty five steps of where the hottest of the fight had been going on. I collected my men directly. There was still another one missing, whom we all knew had not been injured, but had taken advantage to get out of the way while the others were covering his retreat.

The Indians turned their yell to a howl. I knew they would not stay there an hour, and late in the day we could go back there and look after my dead men. I made such a proposition, but can not blame my men for not accepting it. Several of them told me then that only but for impeachment for cowardice and insubordination, they never would have gone into the affair.

Now, it is unnecessary to give all the precise details of our movements, which I well remember at present, but will close this communication by giving the immediate effects. We arrived at the fort that night, it being Saturday night, the seventh of January, 1837. I took four men next morning and started to Colorado fort to carry out my orders, without ever going back to the battle ground since.

Lieutenant Curtis sent McLochlan with about fifteen men back down there next day to bury the dead. They arrived near the ground after sun down, heard divers and sundry noises, saw the carcass of a wild cow which the Indians had

killed the evening before the fight, and concluded the Indians were still there. The four men who had left me on
the morning of the seventh were with them. They immediately hurried down to the settlements d raised an
alarm there. McLochlan sent one of the men by a round
about way to the falls of the Brazos to inform Major Smith,
and returned with the rest of his men to Little river fort.
Considerable consternation ensued down at Nashville and
the few settlements below, clear down to Washington
county. But on the night of the ninth, just after I got to
Colorado fort, and McLochlan got to Little river fort, and
the news diffused to the places where it was sent, a big
snow storm came up, sleet and ice delaying all movements.
I got back on the sixteenth, and was told by Curtis of what
had taken place; that a dozen men from there had gone
down to meet perhaps as many more from the falls, and
whatever volunteers could be brought from the settlements,
to give the Indians a big battle. It was on the same eve of
the sixteenth when Major Smith and some of his men from
the falls and those from Little river fort, came back and
stated that they had found Childers untouched by Indians
—that the Indians could not have stayed there half an
hour—only remained there long enough to gather up their
dead, which, according to their own confession later, was
ten, and carried them up about a mile above and threw
them into a big water hole.

The Indians at the time were in eight miles of Walker's
house where old Niel McLennan's family and his son-in-law
were living. He, himself, with his son and two negroes,
one of whom was captured by the Indians a month later,
were at work twelve miles higher up on Pond creek. Women and children left in a great measure by themselves,
would have been killed next day, perhaps, if we had not
attacked the Indians. There were several narrow escapes
during the action—balls going through men's clothes, bruis-
ing them slightly. A ball broke McLochlan's ram rod, another one his gun lock, another one went through his powder
horn and let the powder out, another through a handkerchief on his head, cutting his hair, and another through his
coat.

The term of serving of all the rangers enlisted expired

in the year 1837 and during the early part of 1838, and
until General Houston's term expired there were hardly
fifty men enrolled into the service of the republic either by
law or under his authority. The citizens had to do their
own defending. The frontier settlements were rather retired than made further out. All the houses built on Little
river in 1835 were evacuated and the settlers from the falls
of the Brazos had to retire, leaving plenty of empty houses.

NOTE.—In the account we had of this fight previous to
seeing that of Captain Erath, it was stated that in his
hurry to reload his gun he had overcharged it, and was
knocked down by the recoil when he shot the Indian; that
one of his men, supposing he was wounded, ran to his assistance and asked if he was hurt. "No;" replied the captain, "I'm not hurt, but you see my gun knocks down before and behind." Whether this anecdote be true or not, it
is certainly characteristic of the captain's well known cool-
ness and bravery.

Williams and Haggett Murdered at Reuben Hornsby's.

REUBEN HORNSBY was among the earliest settlers of
Austin's upper colony. There were only a few who
preceded him, possibly only two or three families.
Jacob Howell was his nearest neighbor, we believe,
and in 1836 there were only five families living in what was
generally known as the Hornsby settlement. These families were headed respectively by Reuben Hornsby,
1836 Jacob Harrell, Joe Duty, —— Casner and —— Webber. The latter lived at Webber's prairie, some six or
seven miles from Hornsby, but in those days that would be
considered near neighbors. It was in the spring of 1836
when the settlers were fleeing from the invading army
of Santa Anna, that Captain John Tumlinson sent three
young men, named Williams, Haggett and Cain, to the

Hornsby settlement to assist in protecting and moving the families above named out of reach of the invading Mexicans. The settlers had finished planting their corn, and upon the arrival of the escort sent out by Captain Tumlinson the settlers at once prepared for flight. They struck Little river and proceeded down that stream beyond the mouth of the same until they reached the old town of Nashville, on the Brazos, where the International & Great Northern Railroad now crosses the Brazos river. Upon arriving at this point they learned for the first time that Santa Anna had been defeated and captured at San Jacinto on the twenty-first of April. They immediately, upon the receipt of this glorious news, proceeded on down the Brazos until they struck the old San Antonio road at the historic little village of Tenoxtitlan, on the Brazos river, and, taking the San Antonio road, came on back to the town of Bastrop, and from thence up the Colorado river to the Hornsby settlement. They had only been home a few days when about ten o'clock one bright morning in the early part of May, while Williams and Haggett were in one part of the field hoeing and thinning corn, and the Hornsby boys and Cain were working in another portion, about one hundred Indians rode up to the fence near where Williams and Haggett were at work, threw down the fence and marched in, bearing a white flag hoisted on top of an Indian lance, the wily red skins expecting by this means to throw the young men off their guard, and in this they were successful. They rode up to where the young men were at work, forming a circle around them as they drew nearer, shook hands in an apparently friendly manner with the boys and then commenced their bloody work. One of the young men was speared to death where he stood, but the other succeeded in breaking through the circle, but was shot to death before he had run but a few steps.

While this bloody work was being carried on by the red devils the young men working in the other part of the field were fast making tracks in another direction. When the attack was made Billy Hornsby was plowing a yoke of steers and was about midway of the row when his brothers, Malcom, Reuben and Joe, and Cain, who had been down to the river to get some water, discovered the Indians just as they

were rising to the top of the bank. Billy had his back to the
Indians and had not seen them, and the first intimation he
had of their presence was the alarm given by the boys as
they ascended the river bank. He left his team standing
hitched to the plow and made for the river to join his
brothers and Cain. Before proceeding further let us take a
peep into the little log cabin, the home of Mr. Hornsby, and
see what was going on there all this time. Hornsby was sitting in the house in company with his wife, and his little
son Thomas, a lad some five years of age, and Miss Cynthia
Casner. In playing around the child happened to go out on
the porch—or old fashioned gallery, as they were usually
called—and discovered the Indians in the distance. He ran
back into the room and said: "Pa, come see what a heap
of Indians out yonder on the hill," but the old gentleman
paid no attention to the little fellow. He again went out
and looked and by this time the number of men had greatly
increased. He ran into the room again and said: "Pa,
there is a heap more; come see." He kept on repeating this
until Mrs. Hornsby said to her husband: "Do go and look
what it is the child has seen." "Oh," replied Mr. Hornsby,
"I don't suppose he has seen anything," nevertheless he got
up and went to the door, and then to his astonishment he
saw that a large party of Indians were in close proximity
to the house. Seeing them approaching Williams and Haggert, he gathered up his gun and the two guns of the young
men and started to their assistance, but he had gone but a
short distance when he turned back. seeing that all attempt
to aid the unfortunate young men would be useless, as the
Indians had already surrounded them.

Mrs. Hornsby and Miss Cynthia Casner in order to induce
the Indians to believe that the house was well guarded,
dressed themselves in men's apparel and walked about
the yard with Mr. Hornsby with guns in their hands.
No doubt the warlike appearance and demonstrations of
these courageous women dampened the ardor of these blood-
thirsty villains and prevented an unslaught on the house,
for, after riding around and shooting off a few guns they
departed, carrying with them all the stock they could gather
up in the neighborhood, amounting to some seventy-five or
one hundred head of cattle, some of which got loose from

the Indians and came back home about three weeks afterwards. But we will now return to the Hornsby boys and
young Cain, who took to the bottom upon seeing the treatment the two young men in the other portion of the field
had received at the hands of the Indians. Billy was the
eldest son, being about eighteen or nineteen years of age;
Malcom, seventeen; Joe, about fifteen; and Reuben, Jr., about
twelve years of age; while Cain was about the age of Billy.
They all broke for the river and swam across, Billy and
Malcom putting Reuben, the youngest, between them in
order to assist him. Upon reaching the opposite bank of
the river they struck out for the thickest brush they could
find in the bottom and made their way up the river until
arriving at a point about Burdett's old ford, they swam back
across the river and traveled down the same until within
about a mile of home, where they concealed themselves in
the brush until sun down, and then went on a little further
until they reached an old deserted cabin where they remained until good dark. Here they picked up some old
pieces of saddle skirts or leather and made temporary soles
for the feet of some of the party who had thrown away
their shoes or moccasins when they first swam the river.
They did not know what had taken place at the house, and
they were preparing for a long journey. When the attack
was made upon Williams and Haggert the Indians were so
far away from the boys who were working down about the
river bank that they could not tell whether they were Indians or Mexicans. They supposed them to be Mexicans
from the fact that the settlers had but recently been fleeing
from them, and the talk of the whole country at that time
was more about the war with Mexico than about the Indians.
Dark having set in, and the boys by this time being good
hungry, they determined to return to the house, see what
had become of the family, and if possible get something to
eat. Billy and Malcom were deputized to go to the house,
while the others remained concealed in a thicket within a
few hundred yards of the house and within hearing distance. Billy and Malcom, after agreeing with the other
boys upon a designated place to rendezvous in case they
should find the house occupied by the enemy, started out on
their mission. They approached the house with great cau-

tion, expecting to find that the family had all been slaughtered and the premises probably occupied by Mexicans. As
they came near it they stopped for awhile and listened, but
hearing no noise they moved on to the smoke house, when
Malcom crawled up on the side of the house, peeped through
the crack and seeing there was still something left, reached
in and pulled out a piece of meat, and in doing so, a board
fell off and made quite a little noise. This aroused Mrs.
Hornsby and a slight noise was made inside of the house.
The boys were determined to ascertain who the occupants
were, so Malcom threw a rock on the house, whereupon
Mrs. Hornsby called to her husband to "get up, that the Indians had returned." The voice was at once recognized,
the boys made themselves known, and after hallooing to
those who were hid in the bushes to come on, walked in the
house. The joyful meeting can better be imagined than
described, for up to this time neither party knew what had
been the fate of the other.

It was in the fall or winter of the same year that three
men — Harris, Blakey, and another whose name is not
known to the writer—came up from Webber's prairie, one
day, spent the night at Hornsby's, and started out the next
day to kill a wild fat cow or two, of which there were a
great number ranging on the river at that time, and belonged
to whoever might be lucky enough to kill them. Having
crossed the river and passed through the bottom on the opposite side, they soon reached their hunting ground, where,
just as Harris and the man whose name is unknown were
ascending the bank of a ravine, Blakey being somewhat in
the rear, they were fired upon by Indians and both killed.
The Indians scalped them, tore out their entrails and strewed
them on the bushes around. They then cut off their arms,
cut out their hearts, and, after going a few rods, they built
a fire, where it is supposed, from the bones scattered around
it, they had roasted and eaten them. Blakey, who as before
stated was in the rear, wheeled his horse when the Indians
fired, put spurs to him and made his escape. Such was the
unsettled state of affairs in the "Hornsby settlement" in
1836; nor did the Indians cease their murders for many years
afterwards in this section of country, as has been shown,
and will be shown further on.

Even as late as the year 1845, Daniel Hornsby, another son of Reuben Hornsby, and William Adkisson, a brother of the Rev. A. J. Adkisson, who resides in Austin, were brutally murdered by the Indians while fishing on the Colorado river. It was in the month of June, 1845, that these two young men left Hornsby's house to have a little fishing frolic all to themselves. They had proceeded up the Colorado river some little distance, and while fishing, some cowardly Indians crawled up behind them and thrust a spear in each of their backs. This caused them to pitch forward into the river, and as they did so the Indians shot several arrows in young Hornsby, producing instant death, and he sank in the river. Adkisson attempted to escape by swimming the stream, and from all appearance he was followed by two of the savages, as the tracks of two were discovered on the opposite bank of the river. Adkisson reached the opposite shore, and had evidently crawled out some ten paces, where he breathed his last. From the character of the wounds in his side, it seemed that one of the Indians had swam along by his side and jagged him in the side with an arrow. After killing and scalping him, they threw him in the river.

The Indians then took up the Colorado, and when they had reached about where the cotton seed oil mill now stands they made representations of two coffins in the sand and stuck an arrow in each, which was evidently intended as a sign for some of their roving companions, indicating the number who had been slain by them. Young Hornsby and Adkisson failing to return at night, search was made for them. The body of Hornsby was found about one mile and a half from where he was murdered. The body of Adkisson was found right where he was killed. It is hard to realize at this day that "Hornby's Bend," as it is now called, all dotted with beautiful farms and an industrious people was, within less than a half century ago, the scene of so many blood curdling murders at the hands of the red man. The Reuben Hornsby league is situated not more than eight or ten miles below the city of Austin, on the Colorado river, and upon it now reside many of the children and grand children of the old pioneer Reuben Hornsby. He has long since passed over the river, but his services rendered in the defense of the frontier will not be forgotten while there are any of that hardy class left to tell over and over again the scenes and incidents which took place in the early settlement of this country. When the author first made his acquaintance with Reuben Hornsby his house was the farthest up the Colorado river. His eldest son, William, whose name we mentioned above, still lives at a ripe old age upon his father's headright league in Travis county. He was in many exciting skirmishes and battles with the Indians at an early day, among which may be mentioned the battle of Brushy, on North Gabriel. He was also in the Cordova fight, near Seguin.

Joseph Rogers.

ROGERS immigrated to Texas at an early day, and settled on the Colorado river about ten miles above the town of Bastrop. In the fall of 1837, Rogers, Craft and a stranger whose name is unknown, went to a small fort on Walnut creek, now called Fort Prairie, six miles below where the city of Austin now stands, for the purpose of procuring ammunition for the settlers on the lower 1837 Colorado. They accomplished the object of their mission, and had gone about five miles on their way home, when, at a place known as Hornsby's Bend, they were charged upon by two parties of Indians, one party coming up behind them, and the other on their right. The Indians were close upon them before they were aware of their presence.

The men were in open prairie, where there was no possibility of defending themselves, and sought safety in flight. All but Rogers succeeded in making their escape. The savages were mounted on good horses, but Rogers was upon a very poor animal, and they soon overtook and killed him. While being pursued he threw away the ammunition to prevent the Indians from capturing it. They also ran Mr.

Craft for several miles, but failed to come up with him. The Indians then proceeded to the residence of Mr. Reuben Hornsby, who was out at work on his farm. They attempted to cut him off from his house, but fortunately his son, who had seen the Indians approaching, ran to him with a fleet horse, which enabled him to escape.

A Mrs. Harrell, who lived near Mr. Hornsby, seeing the Indians approaching the house, took her two little sons and her niece and fled to the river bottom, and remained there until they had gone. These Indians were pursued by some soldiers who were at the fort, but they did not overtake them. Mr. Rogers was a brave and good man, and beloved by all who knew him. He left a wife and several children, as well as numerous friends and relatives, to mourn his sad fate. He was the uncle of Ed. and J. B. Rogers, of Travis county, and the father of Joe Rogers, who lives on Onion creek.

Ten Surveyors.

DURING the summer of 1838 a party of ten men went from Bastrop county up the Gaudalupe river, above the town of New Braunfels, on a surveying expedition. Having reached the locality where they intended to begin work, without seeing any sign of Indians, they thought there was no danger, and neglected to take the ordinary precautions to guard against surprise.

1838 Among these men there was one old frontiersman who endeavored to convince them of the necessity of standing guard at night and keeping a good lookout in the day time, but finding his advice fell upon the heedless ears he became disgusted, left the party and returned home. On his arrival in the settlements he stated the reason why he had left the surveyors and prophesied that none of them would ever return home. His prophesy was fulfilled to the letter.

HE CARVED HIS NAME UPON A TREE FOR A TOMBSTONE
AND THEN EXPIRED.

The surveyors having been out considerably over the time appointed for their return a party was organized to go in search of them. After hunting in vain for several days to find some trace of the surveyors they accidentally struck the very spot where they had all been murdered by Indians. It appears from all the indications that the party had found a number of bee trees close together, and that they had felled six or seven of the trees before they attempted to take the honey. About the time the last tree fell it is supposed they were suddenly attacked by a large party of Indians. Though taken, no doubt, by surprise it was evident the surveyors had fought to the last. Nothing certain, however, is known about the fight, as not one of that little band was left to tell the story. There were the big trees untouched just as they had fallen, and there also were the skeletons of the nine men. Only one of the skeletons could be identified, that of a young man by the name of Beatty, which was found lying at the root of a tree, on which, with his pocket knife, he had rudely carved his name. It is supposed he had been mortally wounded by the Indians and left for dead, but had revived sufficiently to carve his name upon his own tombstone before he died.

Captain John Harvey.

CAPTAIN HARVEY was a Tennesseean. He came to Texas in 1834, and settled temporarily in San Augustine county. He remained there two years and then moved to Bastrop. He was a surveyor. In the month of June, 1839, the captain made a surveying expedition up the Colorado river into Burnet county. He had ten men with him. After reaching the section of country they 1834 intended to survey, they went to work, and for several days nothing occurred to interrupt their labors. One evening the party encamped on the Colorado river. The captain was not only a brave, but cautious man, and in

an Indian country caution is more essential than bravery.
He always had a guard out at night, even when there was
no sign of Indians in the vicinity, for, as he used to say,
"When you least expect Indians, there they are." On the
night mentioned the captain and a Mr. Burnet were on
guard. About midnight one of the pack mules commenced
snorting, and it attracted the Captain's attention. He asked
Mr. Burnet if he didn't think the mule had seen or smelt an
Indian. Burnet replied that probably a wolf had frightened
the mule. All remained quiet, however, around camp until
just before day, when Captain Harvey said he would wake
the boys, as he wished to make an early start. He was just
in the act of doing so, when they were fired upon by a party
of Indians that had crawled up unperceived to some bushes
very near the camp. As it was still too dark to aim with
certainty, the Indians hit no one except Mr. Burnet, whose
arm was broken.

This unexpected fusilade of course threw the surveyors
into some confusion, but Captain Harvey soon rallied them.
He ordered his men to take to trees, and each defend himself
as best he could. They did so, and the fight began. One
Indian, being anxious to capture a fine horse that was tied
near camp, ventured from his place of concealment, and
was in the act of cutting the rope when three guns were
fired at him, wounding him mortally, and he fell. The chief
at this ordered a retreat; and his men, in spite of the rapid
fire from the guns of the surveyors, ran to where their comrade had fallen and carried him off. None of the surveyors
were wounded except Mr. Burnet.

As soon as the Indians retreated, Captain Harvey collected
his men, to ascertain if any had been killed or wounded.
Three were missing. The captain and his men then began
to search for them, but not finding them, they hallooed
loudly to see if any one would reply. One of the men answered from the opposite side of the river, having "taken
water" during the fight. He recrossed the river and returned
to camp—but his life was a burden to him afterwards.

The other two men were so badly frightened that they ran
clean away and got lost. They endeavored to get back to
camp, but on their way they met the retreating Indians, who
charged upon them, and they fled across the Colorado river,

where they hid all day in a deep gulch, nearly famished for water. They never found the surveying party, and, after wandering among the mountains for eight days without any food, they finally reached the settlements near where the city of Austin is now located.

But for the bravery and good management of Captain Harvey, there is but little doubt his men would have been surprised by the Indians and probably all of them killed.

Kinney's Fort.

DURING the summer of this year Kinney's fort was attacked by Indians. Thomas Kinney, one of the early pioneers of Texas, and who had fought through the Mexican war, moved from Bastrop county to a place about forty miles distant on Brushy creek, known as Brushy cove, within about eighteen miles from Austin. He there built a fort and block house as a protection against Indians. 1840 It is well known to all old frontiersmen that an Indian can imitate perfectly the cries of nearly all animals that inhabit the forest, such as the howling of wolves, the scream of the wild cat, and even the hooting of owls, etc.

One morning in August, 1840, Mr. Joseph Weeks, an inmate of the fort, heard a number of owls hooting and others in the distance answering back, in such rapid and regular succession as to excite his suspicions that the hoots came from Indians. He told the people in the fort that Indians were around and advised them to prepare for an attack. They had not fully completed their preparations for defense when the Indians made their appearance and rushed upon the fort, firing a volley of bullets and arrows as they came. The fight then commenced in earnest, the Indians seemingly determined on storming the fort, and the whites equally as determined to defend it to the last.

While the fight was going on, a courier was despatched from the fort to the nearest settlements for reinforcements, and he succeeded in making his way safely through the Indians outside. A company of fifty men was soon raised, but on their arrival at the fort they found that the Indians had left, carrying with them their dead and wounded. Only one man in the fort was wounded.

White's Negro

IT was in the fall of the same year that White's negro was killed by the Indians while hauling lumber from Bastrop to Austin. When the city of Austin was first settled lumber for building purposes was very scarce. There was a good "pinery" however, below, in Bastrop county, from which the people of Austin obtained supplies. A gentleman by the name of Hamilton White had a contract for 1839 hauling lumber to Austin, and he kept his negro boy, a young fellow about twenty years old, pretty constantly engaged in hauling. The distance was about thirty-five miles.

In the fall of 1839, Mr. White started his negro boy from Bastrop with a load of lumber and three hundred dollars in money to pay a debt due in Austin. The negro was alone. He went on his way unmolested, and the second day he reached the house of Mr. Reuben Hornsby, eight miles below Austin. He remained there all night and loitered around for some time the next morning, saying he was afraid to go on, as there was no settlements between there and Austin. Mrs. Hornsby told him if he was afraid he had better remain until he could get company. He said he was afraid but his master had told him not to delay on the road, and evidently with great reluctance he went on. When he arrived at Walnut creek bottom, about six miles from town, he was shot and killed by Indians, who were concealed in a dogwood thicket near by.

The writer of this, in company with another gentleman, happened to pass the spot shortly afterwards, and when we discovered the negro we supposed at first that he was asleep,

A LIVELY TUSSLE BETWEEN A PACK OF DOGS AND AN INDIAN.

but upon a nearer approach we found he was killed and scalped. My companion became greatly alarmed when he found the negro had been killed by Indians. I told him there was no cause for alarm as the danger was over and the Indians gone, but he paid no attention to what I said. He put spurs to his horse and was soon lost sight of in the brush.

The Gonzales Horses.

IN collecting such a vast amount of material for the numerous incidents narrated herein, in some instances the names of the individuals who participated in the different engagements could not be procured at the time most of the material for this book was obtained, without considerable expense and loss of time. It is not to be expected, therefore, that every incident occurred just as related 1839 here in all of its details, for it would be next to an impossibility to give the exact facts in every instance where there are so many different incidents to be enumerated. While we are not able to give names of the parties who participated in the little raid which we are about to narrate, the source from which it was obtained was sufficient to convince us of its authenticity, hence it finds a place among the many incidents mentioned in this volume.

A party of Indians, in the year 1839, came down from the mountains, went to the town of Gonzales and stole a number of fine horses. A company was soon raised and the marauders were speedily followed. The stolen horses had been freshly shod, and the trail was therefore easily found. There was an old bear hunter in the company, who had his pack of dogs with him, as he intended to hunt "cuffee" as well as Indians.

The company pushed ahead pretty rapidly on the trail, and after traveling a couple of days they ascended a high

hill and discovered their horses about a mile distant, hoppled out to graze, but no Indians were visible. This somewhat puzzled them, but the company moved on slowly and
cautiously, supposing the Indians were encamped under the
river bank, and that they could approach them unobserved.
They went on cautiously until they came within about
forty yards of a large live oak tree, under the shade of
which they found the Indians all fast asleep. The Texans
deliberately raised their guns and disturbed their peaceful
slumbers by a general fusilade, killing three of them and
wounding a fourth. The rest ran off, followed by the old
bear hunter's dogs. The dogs overtook one of them, and a
lively fight ensued. The Indian was naked, and the dogs
had a splendid showing at his legs. He jumped about,
slapped, kicked and yelled furiously, but the dogs finally
"doubled teams" on him and dragged him to the ground.
But the Indian still battled bravely for his life, and when
no longer able to kick, he seized a dog by the nose with his
teeth, and never did a raccoon or a wild cat make a dog
howl worse than the one the Indian had gripped. After
the dogs had pretty well torn him to pieces, the men put an
end to the combat by shooting the Indian through the head.

The Texans recovered all the stolen horses, and destroyed
all the camp equipage of the Indians. Only one Indian
made his escape.

Claiborne Osborn.

CLAIBORNE OSBORN, his brother Lee and two or
three others, in about the year 1840, went out on Brushy
creek for the purpose of hunting buffalo. After they
had reached the hunting ground, the party divided,
Osborn and James Hamilton going in one direction and the
rest in another. Shortly after they separated, Osborn and
Hamilton were fired upon by a party of Indians from
1840 an ambuscade, and Osborn's horse was badly wounded.
Both men wheeled their horses and started back towards the place where they had separated from their com-

panions; but Osborn's horse soon fell, throwing him violently to the ground. Hamilton continued his course, and fortunately a few moments afterwards met the rest of the party, who had heard the firing of guns and had turned back to ascertain the cause. Hamilton told them the cause, and they hurried to the assistance of Osborn. When his horse fell with him, as before stated, Osborn was stunned by the violence of the shock, and the Indians rushed upon him. They seized his gun and beat him severely over the head with it, and stabbed him in several places with their butcher knives. One of them passed his knife around his head, and had partially taken off his scalp, when just at that moment Hamilton and the rest came up and fired upon them. The Indians hastily fled, leaving Osborn seriously but not fatally injured. The scalp which had been partly torn from his head was carefully replaced, and in a few months the wound healed over; but it was some time before he recovered from the severe beating the Indians had given him and the stabs from their butcher knives.

Mr. Osborn is still living to tell of his many "scapes and scrapes" in times gone by. He lives at New Webberville, in Travis county, and has a large family.

Clopton's Negro.

THE murder of Clopton's negro girl occurred also in the year 1840. During the days of slavery the Indians very seldom killed a negro. They preferred to capture them, in the hopes of obtaining a high ransom for them, and in this they were not often disappointed. On the fourth of July, 1840, a party of Indians made their appearance on Gilleland creek, in Travis county.

1840 They failed to get any white scalps or horses, and, it seems, concluded to wreak their vengeance on a poor negro girl belonging to a Mr. Clopton. He sent this negro girl out, late on the evening mentioned, to drive up the cows. As no Indians had been in that section of country for some time, no danger was apprehended. The girl found the cattle and began hallooing at them to drive them home. This drew the attention of the Indians to her, who were concealed near by in the bottom, and several of them crept up to her under cover of the tall sedge grass, and shot the poor creature a number of times with arrows until she fell dead. They then scalped her and concealed themselves again in the bottom.

Michael Nash.

ABOUT two months after this, Michael Nash was killed by the Indians in Bastrop county. Mr. Nash immigrated to Texas about the year 1830, and settled in or near the town of Columbus. He remained there until after the war with Mexico, and then moved to the town of Bastrop, where he followed the carpenter's trade. He was a great hunter, and his fondness for the sport eventu-1840 ally cost him very dearly. On Saturday, the first day of September, 1840, Nash took his gun and went out on one of his usual hunts. After he had gone several miles he succeeded in killing a deer, which he butchered and tied behind his saddle. He then started home, and as he was about crossing a creek he was fired on by some Indians who were concealed in a thicket near by.

Nash failing to return home that night, the alarm was given, and early the next morning a party went out to search for him, and found his body where the Indians had killed him. His scalp had been taken; the buzzards had picked out his eyes, and his body was so mangled by wolves or by the Indians that it was with difficulty his friends could identify him. He left a wife and five children.

John Wahrenberger.

WAHRENBERGER was a native of Switzerland. He was in the employment of Colonel Louis T. Cooke, of Austin city, as a gardener, who, at that time, was secretary of the navy of the republic of Texas. One night in the fall of 1841, Mr. Wahrenberger took a sack and went to a mill on the edge of town for the purpose of securing a supply of meal. On his way back to the house **1841** of his employer he was attacked by Indians. As he was unarmed he fled for his life, but hung on to his sack of meal, and it was fortunate for him he did so, for the sack had several arrows sticking in it, which otherwise would have pierced his back. The Indians continued to follow him until he arrived at Colonel Cooke's house. He, hearing the noise, came out with his gun in hand, and fired upon the Indians, wounding one of them pretty badly, as was evident from the blood found upon the trail the next day. When Wahrenberger reached Colonel Cooke's house he was so exhausted that he fell at the door, but was unhurt with the exception of an arrow wound in the arm. As soon as he recovered his breath sufficiently to speak he exclaimed: "Oh! mine Got! what a Texas dis is! I tink I go back to Sweetzerland!" These Indians were pursued the next day but were not overtaken. This affair occurred right in the city of Austin, and from this fact the reader can form some idea of the boldness of the Indians when hungry for scalps and plunder. Wahrenberger died many years ago and his widow still resides in the city of Austin and owns considerable property.

William Barton's Strategem Saves His Scalp.

WILLIAM BARTON was one among the earliest of
those who settled high up on the Colorado river. He
immigrated to Texas at quite an early day, and lived
in various portions of the State, but finally settled in
1837, near where the city of Austin now stands, at the foot
of the Colorado hills, on the south side of the river, at what
is now known as Barton Springs. At that time, says
1842 Joseph Barnhart, who made Barton's house his home,
there was not a single house where Austin now stands,
though there were three families camped on the ground who
were preparing to erect cabins. Settlers soon, however, began to come and it was not long until quite a little settlement had congregated at the foot of the mountains on the
banks of the Colorado. The Indians, nevertheless, kept up
their accustomed visits for many years after. It was in
about the year 1842 that Mr. Barton sent one of his sons to
Bastrop on some business, and the young man failing to return as soon as he was expected, the old gentleman shouldered his gun and walked up the hill to look across the
prairie in the direction from which he expected his son to
return. As he passed a thicket some Indians rose up and
shot at him, one bullet grazing the rim of his hat. Mr. Barton raised his Kentucky rifle, fired and wounded one of the
Indians. The balance made a charge upon him, whooping
and yelling like a pack of wolves. The old gentleman had
pressing business at home about that time and started at a
full run in the direction of the house, the Indians right after
him. Being an old man, some sixty or seventy years of age,
his strength began to fail him and he called out to his some
half dozen deer dogs to come to his assistance. They
promptly responded to the call, but unfortunately for the
old man, just before they reached him a deer ran across the
path in front of the dogs and they put out after him. The
old gentleman's ingenuity was now taxed to the utmost.
There he was by himself, deserted by his dogs, almost within

"HERE THEY ARE BOYS, COME QUICK."

the grasp of the wily sons of the forest who were thirsty for fresh blood and another scalp to dangle at their sides. The full resources of the mind are never fully developed except in such stringent cases as this, and it was just at this critical moment when a bright idea struck the old frontiersman, and he was none too quick in availing himself of it. The Indians were fast gaining on him and if anything was to be done it had to done quickly, *if not a little quicker.* Urged on by the bright idea which had occurred to him, he made an almost superhuman effort for a man of his age until he finally reached the brow of the hill, and it was here that he practiced with good results his little game of stratagem upon the red skins, and played the "bluff" for all there was in it. Now that he was upon the summit of the hill and could see down into the valley, while the Indians who were pursuing could not, he suddenly stopped, hallooed in a loud voice, "here they are boys, come quick," at the same time beckoning with one hand to the boys who were not coming to his assistance, and pointing with the other towards the Indians.

The latter naturally supposed there was a party of whites on the opposite side of the hill who were hastening to the relief of Mr. Barton, and did not wait to catch a glimpse of their mythical enemy, but turned and fled in hot haste back in the direction from which they had come, prompted no doubt by the same feelings which a few moments before had accelerated Mr. Barton's movements. The old gentleman, feeling somewhat helped up by this little piece of strategy, could now draw a long breath; but the wild hyacinth and sweeter scented roses were not enough to "tone up" the atmosphere in that immediate vicinity sufficiently to induce the taking of many long breaths. Seeing the Indians rapidly retreating in the rear over the same ground upon which he had just a moment before made such a fine record, he went tearing down the hill like a regular quarter horse in the opposite direction. Judge Joseph Lee and some three or four other gentlemen were in the house at the time, who, startled by the report of the gun, were on the look out. They heard the rumbling in the forest, coming in the direction of the house, but at first could not tell what it was, until finally old Mr. Barton heaved in sight. He rushed into the midst of the crowd, completely exhausted, saying: "Boys, its a good thing it wasn't one of you, or you would have been killed shore!" It was thus the old man saved his scalp.

Thomas Shuff.

IT was during the spring of this year that Thomas Shuff was killed and scalped by the Indians on Barton's creek. Mr. Shuff was one of the pioneers of Texas .He first settled in the county of Washington, on the Brazos river, where he lived for several years. He then moved to Travis county and settled on Barton's creek, about one mile and a half from the city of Austin, and within about half a mile of the venerable gentleman whose narrow escape 1842 we have just related. One day in the spring of 1842 he went to the house of a neighbor (possibly Mr. Barton) after a cow. He had a son, a small lad, and told his wife that he would take him along, but she said: "No, don't wake him, he is asleep." He then went off alone. On his way home, and when within hearing of the house he was attacked by a party of Indians, who had secreted themselves near the road for that purpose. They shot him, but failing to kill him at once he called aloud for help. His wife heard him and recognized his voice, but supposed he was merely hallooing to the cow he was driving, and never suspected for a moment that he had been attacked by Indians. The Indians killed and scalped him but failed to get his horse, which ran to the house, thereby revealing the story of his untimely death to his bereaved wife. A company was soon formed, who went in pursuit of the Indians, but did not succeed in overtaking them. How fortunate it was that the little boy was asleep that morning when his father left! If he had gone with him he would certainly have been killed or captured.

Baker and Souls were killed by the Indians during the summer of the same year while out on the prairie south of Austin. These two gentlemen were natives of the State of Indiana. They came to Texas in the year 1838 and settled in Travis county. Their occupation was farming and stock raising. In the summer of 1842 these two men were out one day on the range, near Manchaca springs, hunting some of their cattle, when they were fired upon by a party of Indians from an ambuscade. The Indians then charged them, yelling and shooting as they came.

It is supposed that Baker fell at the first fire, but Souls seems to have fought like a tiger, and from the indications, he must have killed or wounded several of his assailants before he fell. Barker was merely scalped after he was killed, but Souls's body was literally hacked to pieces and his heart taken out, showing how enraged the Indians had been at his determined resistance, and for the loss of some of their comrades.

It was a common custom with the Indians of Texas to eat the hearts of those who had fallen fighting bravely in battle against them, under the belief that by doing so they would become braver themselves, and for this purpose it was supposed they had cut out Souls's heart. Judge Joseph Lee, with a number of others, visited the place where these two brave men made such a heroic defense, and brought in a great number of arrows.

There were quite a number of murders committed in Travis county during the year 1842. Gideon White was another who fell a victim to the preying bands of Indians who were continuously scouring the country around Austin. Mr. White was a native of the State of Alabama, and came to Texas in the winter of 1837, at which time the writer of this sketch made his acquaintance. He returned to Alabama the same winter, and in 1838 he moved his family to Texas and settled in Bastrop county, where he remained for one or two years. After the seat of government was located at Austin, Mr. White moved to Travis county and settled near that city, at Seider's springs, where he lived until the time of his unfortunate death, which occurred in 1842.

Judge Joseph Lee and others of his friends at Austin had frequently told him that he ran great risk of losing his life

in going about the country on foot, but he paid no attention
to their warnings.

One beautiful spring morning he started out on foot in
search of some stock. As he had his gun with him, and as
no Indians had been seen for some time in the vicinity of
Austin, he apprehended no danger. But, as the French say,
"it is the unexpected that happens," and where you least
expect to find Indians there you are sure to meet them.

When the Indians made the attack they were on horseback, and had Mr. White been on horseback, as he should
have been, he could easily have made his escape from them.
He ran for some distance, but finding the Indians were
gaining on him rapidly, he sprang behind a tree, in a thicket,
and defended himself as best he could. The Indians, however, finally killed him, in sight of and within a quarter of a
mile of his house.

From the number of bullet and arrow marks upon the tree
behind which Mr. White had taken position, it was evident
that he had made a desperate resistance to his foes; and that
he had succeeded in killing at least one of them before he
fell, was proven by the fact that a place was found near by
where the grass was trampled down and clotted with blood.

The tree behind which Mr. White fought the Indians
was still standing a few years ago, and the marks of many
bullets and arrow heads are still plainly to be seen on the
bark. The place is within two or three miles of the locality
where now stands the magnificent capitol building of the
State of Texas. And yet to-day it is hardly probable that
a single Indian (with the exception of a small remnant of
Caddoes on Trinity river) could be found within the boundaries of the State. Alas for the red man! Like the buffalo
that once roamed the broad prairies of Texas in countless
numbers, from the mountains to the gulf, they have disappeared forever.

Some time in the fall of 1842, a Mr. Newcomb and another
gentleman were hunting buffalo on the waters of Brushy
creek. They had just killed a buffalo, and as it took both
of them to handle and cut up so large an animal, there was
no one to keep watch while they were at work. After they
had butchered their game they cut it up, tied the choice
pieces to their saddles, and then took a seat on a log with

DO YOU HEAR THE OWLS HOOTING? YES, BUT
OWLS DON'T COUGH.

the intention of resting themselves after their labors, before leaving. Just as they did so, they perceived a single Indian coming towards them, who evidently was unconscious of their proximity. Barnhart hailed him, and as soon as he did so the Indian turned and ran, yelling loudly at every jump. The two men then came to the conclusion there was a party of Indians somewhere near by; that the one they had seen would soon return with his companions, and therefore that it would be best for them to quit the locality as speedily as possible. Untying the meat from their horses, they mounted them hastily, and scarcely had they done so when the Indians made their appearance, whooping and yelling as they came. The two men instantly clapped spurs to their horses and fled for their lives. The Indians followed them for about four miles, and at one time got so near to them that Barnhart said he could distinctly see the whites of their eyes. Newcomb was mounted on a very fine horse, and could easily have distanced the Indians, but his companion was riding a Spanish tacky, not much better than the mustangs of the Indians, but he stuck by him, until finally they both succeeded in making their escape.

James Boyce.

THE father of James Boyce immigrated to Texas with his family in 1837, and settled in Bastrop county, where the writer of this sketch made his acquaintance. After remaining there one year, he located land on the frontier, on which he settled in 1839, in what is now Travis county, on a small stream, a tributary of the Colorado, called Gilleland creek. He was eminently fitted for frontier

1842 life, for he was a man of caution, as well as one of cool, determined bravery. He had three sons, whose ages were respectively twelve, fourteen and sixteen years. These youths became thoroughly inured to the hardships of frontier life, and had learned to guard themselves so well against the wiles and strategy of the Indians that they often ventured beyond the settlements in search of mustangs or hunting the buffalo. They were so vigilant and watchful that they really ran but little risk in doing so, as an Indian could not make a track in their vicinity that was not detected by their prying eyes. We will give one instance of their adroitness in detecting the presence of Indians.

They were out in the woods on one occasion, and in company with them there was a young man whose experience of frontier life was very limited. Night coming on, they encamped, and soon after dark they heard the hooting of owls in various directions. One of the young Boyces, when he had listened to them attentively for some time, said to his companions: "Boys, I am going to move; we must get away from here." Being asked why, he replied, "I believe those are Indians who are hooting, and not owls." At this the "green horn" who was with them laughed and said: "You are a fool; it is nothing but the hooting of owls." "Maybe I am," replied Boyce, "but I've got sense enough to know that owls don't *cough*, and we must get away from here." His keen ear had detected a cough from an Indian in the vicinity. They did leave, and the next morning when they returned they discovered a great many fresh moccasin tracks about the place where they had encamped. Notwithstanding his great caution and his knowledge of Indian wiles and their mode of warfare, one of these young men, James Boyce, was fated to fall by their hands.

In the year 1842, Mr. James Boyce rose one morning before day, with the intention of going to the city of Austin. He had only gone about three miles from his father's house when, just before reaching Walnut creek, at a little ravine, he was attacked by a party of Indians who had secreted themselves near by for the purpose of killing any one who might be traveling the road. Boyce was riding a mule, and when attacked he took the back track for home, and had gotten within about a mile from home before he was overtaken by the Indians. They killed him, scalped him, pierced him in many places with their lances, and otherwise horribly mutilated his body. It was universally believed that this murder was the work of Lipan Indians, who pretended

to be friendly to the whites and often visited the settlements to obtain their supplies or to claim protection of the
whites when hard pressed by their inveterate enemies, the
Comanches.

Some of the Lipan Indians were among the first to find
the dead body of young Boyce, and told some of the settlers
about it, at the same stating that they had seen a party of
Comanches in the vicinity. A company was raised in the city
of Austin and the adjacent country, who, taking several of
the Lipans with them as guides, went in pursuit cf the murderers of young Boyce, but not the least sign of retreating
Indians could be found. The Lipans pointed out many
horse tracks, but a close examination always proved that
they had been made by mustang ponies. All the circum-
stantial evidence went to show that the perpetrators of this
murder were the Lipans themselves. As no positive proof,
however, of the fact could be obtained, they were permitted
to depart unpunished.

William S. Hotchkiss.

I N the spring of 1843, about twenty Caddo Indians came
down from the upper Brazos mountains, and on Salado
creek, a tributary of the Brazos, they surprised and
killed three men, Henry, Castleberry, and Courtney.
They scalped them, stripped them of their clothes and
mangled their bodies in a horrible manner. They then proceeded on their way to the Colorado river and struck
1843 it about twelve miles below the city of Austin, at
what is known as "Moore's Prairie." Here they collected together a large number of horses belonging to a Mr.
Puckett, and were in the act of driving them off, when they
were discovered by five men who were out in search of
stock, namely, W. C. Reager, William S. Hotchkiss, Nathaniel Gilleland, Joseph Hornsby and Dow Puckett, a son
of the Mr. Puckett whose horses had been stolen. Perceiv-

ing the Indians were armed only with bows and arrows, and although they had no arms themselves, these brave men determined, if possible, to prevent them from driving off Mr. Puckett's horses. The Indians, when discovered, were all on foot, driving the stolen animals before them. The Texans hastily dismounted, and each cut a heavy mesquite club, then springing into their saddles again they charged upon the Indians just as they were entering a prairie. As they were running down a long descent, free from all underbrush, the Texans closed in on them, with the intention of getting between them and the horses. The Indians, when they found that the Texans were about to succeed in this in spite of the numerous arrows they let fly at them, resorted to a singular plan to rid themselves of their assailants. Suddenly six of them dropped upon their knees and began to rub their arrows across their bow strings in such a way as to produce a sound that seemed to be a sort of hybrid between the caterwauling of half a dozen tom cats and the yelping of as many cayotes. The horses the Texans were riding took fright at the unearthly sounds, wheeled and dashed off at full speed in the direction they had come, despite all their riders could do to restrain them. They ran about a mile before they were able to check the frightened animals. As soon as they did so they returned, and again and again endeavored to force their horses "up to the scratch," but to no purpose, for, whenever they got within a short distance of the Indians, the latter would again drop to their knees and begin to "fiddle" upon their bows and always with the same result. Whilst the Texans were thus vainly attempting to get in between the Indians and their horses, a settler who lived near by, and who was armed with a gun, came up their assistance. He succeeded in getting his horse near enough to shoot, but just as he drew his gun to fire, the Indians threw themselves flat upon the ground and began to "fiddle" again.

His horse instantly stampeded, whirled and dashed off in the wildest terror, and endeavoring to check him he dropped his gun in the tall grass. When he finally succeeded in stopping his horse he returned to where Hotchkiss and his companions were waiting for him, and then half an hour was lost in searching for his gun. In the meantime the Indians kept on rapidly and were soon joined by six others. A little afterwards a party of settlers who were armed came up, but they did not arrive until the Indians had entered the timber, where they could not successfully be followed by the whites on horseback. The Texans continued to pursue them, however, to Brushy creek, a distance of about twenty miles, and then abandoned the chase. The Indians shot Mr. William S. Hotchkiss under the left shoulder with an arrow, which he carried for some distance without having it extracted, so anxious was he to overtake them.

This mode of warfare adopted by the Indians was certainly a very strange and novel one, but in this instance it seemed to accomplish their object with satisfaction to themselves and that, too, without the loss of much blood to the Texans

Leroy Williams.

IT was in the spring of the same year that a lot or Indians attacked and killed Leroy Williams in Bastrop county while plowing. Williams was a native of Georgia, came to Texas at quite an early day and settled in Bastrop county, in that portion known as Young's settlement. He had no family, but was of industrious habits and followed teamstering for a living. He followed this occupation 1843 for several years until he had accumulated some means, when he purchased a tract of land from Michael Young, who was the founder of Young's settlement, and from whom it took its name. When the Indians made the attack on Williams he was plowing some ground for Young.

The Indians, who had been watching his movements from an ambuscade, attacked him in the following manner: Mr. Williams had his gun, but the wily savages noticed that he always left it at the end of the row, thinking, we suppose, there would not be much danger for an attack before he got back. As soon as they saw him leave the end of the

row where his gun was placed one of the Indians slipped
around under cover of some bushes and got possession of it.
They then charged upon him from both sides of the field
at once, thus preventing him from making his retreat to the
house. It is believed by Mr. Young that the Indians shot
him with his own gun. After he was wounded he ran a
shot distance towards the house, but fell on the way. The
Indians then gathered around him and killed him with their
arrows. A party pursued the Indians the next day but
failed to overtake them.

During the Fall of 1843.

DURING the fall of 1843, Captain Pyron, Donovan,
John Gravis, Jim Berry and Harrell went out to
Brushy creek, at a place called Kinney's fort, to get
a load of corn from a little field which they had cultivated that year in the vicinity of the fort. After having
loaded their wagon they all started home, and when within
a few miles of the city of Austin—then a mere vil-
1843 lage town in point of population—about where the
lunatic asylum now stands, they were attacked by
a party of Indians, about fifty in number, supposed to
be Lipans; in fact there was no doubt in the minds of
those who were attacked upon this point. In the afternoon, and before the attack was made, a heavy rain had
fallen and had so thoroughly drenched the guns of the
whites that they were almost unfit for use. When the Indians charged upon them they were traveling in the direction of the timber. The whooping and yelling of the savages
so frightened the oxen that they changed the course which
they had been traveling and started out into the open
prairie While Pyron was attempting to change the course
of the lead steers back in the direction which they had been
traveling towards the timber, an Indian rushed upon him
and thrust him through the side with a lance, producing in-

stant death. Donovan was also killed in the engagement, but the other three made good their escape to the timber, came on down Shoal creek into Austin and notified the citizens, who immediately set out in pursuit of the Indians. Of course some little time intervened between the attack and the notification of the citizens by those who escaped, and by the time the crowd had collected together and arrived upon the battle ground the Indians had reached the cedar brakes of the mountains near by, which always afforded them a secure hiding place after committing their fiendish murders and outrages upon the settlers. This was the first positive evidence that the citizens of Travis county had that the Lipan Indians were hostile towards the settlers, though they have been strongly suspected by some who did not place much confidence in any tribe of Indians.

Captain George M. Dolson.

CAPTAIN DOLSON was a native of the State of Ohio. He immigrated to Texas in 1840, and settled in Travis county, in the city of Austin. In the spring of 1843 a party of Indians came into the vicinity of Austin, stole a number of horses and murdered two men. A company of citizens was raised, commanded by Captain Dolson, who started in pursuit of the murderers. The Indians 1843 having considerably the start of the citizens, they did not overtake them until they had reached the Leon river. As soon as the Indians were discovered, Captain Dolson ordered his men to charge them, and led the way himself. The great speed of his horse soon carried him beyond his men, and not knowing he was so far in the advance, he dashed in among the Indians alone and opened fire on them. They turned upon him and wounded him severely. In attempting to check his horse, he lost his balance and fell to the ground. The Indians rushed upon him with their spears to despatch him, and undoubtedly would have done so, when just at that moment the gallant Lewis P. Cook came up, and kept the Indians at bay until the balance of the company arrived. A general fight then ensued, the Indians taking their position in a thick clump of brush. They fought with desperation, as they were unwilling to abandon the large number of fine horses they had stolen. At length, finding that their warriors were rapidly falling before the deadly fire of the citizens, they precipitately fled, leaving all the stolen horses in their possession.

The citizens constructed a litter for their wounded captain, and carried him by turns, four at a time, until they reached the city of Austin, a distance of about one hundred miles. Captain Dolson finally recovered from his wound, and lived for many years afterwards.

The Manchaca Fight.

A PARTY of Indians, in the spring of 1844, came down from the Colorado mountains and followed the course of the river until they came to Hill's Prairie, where they succeeded in stealing a large number of valuable horses. They then started back to the mountains. The settlers raised a company of sixteen men, which was placed under the command of Captain Wiley Hill, father of 1844 Robert Hill, of Austin, who pursued the Indians. The latter went up a divide between the Colorado river and one of its tributaries, leaving a very plain trail behind them. The settlers were able to follow this trail with ease, and they spared neither themselves nor their horses to overtake the red skins.

Just before the Indians reached the mountains, they encamped for the night at or near a noted watering place known as the Manchaca springs, supposing they were beyond the reach of pursuit. The Texans attacked their camp early the next morning. The Indians fought for a while, but the rifles of the Texans told so severely upon them that they finally fled in every direction.

Captain Hill and his men pursued them into the mountains for some distance, but the country was very rough, and the Indians so scattered, that it was impossible to come up with them. They then returned to the Indian camp near Manchaca springs, where they took possession of all the horses the Indians had stolen, and all their camp equipage.

Joseph Manor.

IT was in the winter of this year that Joseph Manor killed his Indian. In the latter part of the winter of 1844, Mr. Manor and a Mr. Nash formed a partnership in the mercantile business. They had received their first supply of goods at Webberville, where they had established their house, and were engaged one night in marking and invoicing them, when their attention was attracted by the **1844** snorting of a mule that Mr. Manor had staked near his room for safe keeping. He stepped out to see what it was that had alarmed the mule, and discovered three Indians approaching it. As the Indians drew near it the animal snorted loudly, and endeavored to break the rope by which it was staked, whereupon one of the Indians let fly and shot it through the body. Mr. Manor slipped back into the house, seized his gun, and said to Mr. Nash: "There are Indians out yonder. They have killed my mule. Take my pistol on the counter and let's go out and fight them." But Mr. Nash did not hear what he said about the pistol, and followed him without any arms. As they turned a corner of the house they saw an Indian standing at the opposite one, and Mr. Manor fired at him, killing him on the spot. When the Indian fell, Mr. Nash drew his knife from his pocket and started to go to him, saying he wanted to scalp him in revenge for their scalping his father, but Mr. Manor held him back, telling him there were other Indians near, and that he might lose his own scalp. At this juncture the two other Indians rushed up, seized their fallen comrade and carried him off.

Bartlett Sims.

CAPTAIN BARTLETT SIMS immigrated to Texas in the year 1826. He first settled on the Brazos river where he lived for several years and then moved to Bastrop county. He followed the business of surveying. In October, 1846, he, in company with a nephew of the same name, and two other men, Clark and Grant, started on a surveying expedition to the Pedernales river. While 1846 engaged at work, they were attacked by a party of Indians, who had concealed themselves in some tall sedge grass near the line the surveyors were running. They did not discover the Indians until they were right among them. There were but four in the party, and the Indians were about fifty in number. As the surveyors were on foot there was but little chance of escape. The first one attacked was young Sims. He shot one and knocked another down with the breech of his gun, but at that instant he was killed. Clark and Grant, the two chain carriers, were roped by the Indians and then shot to death with arrows. Captain Sims succeeded in reaching his horse, and mounted him, but had hardly done so, when a powerful Indian seized the bridle and attempted to stop him. The Captain had no arms but a small derringer pistol. He drew this from his pocket and shot the Indian through the neck, probably cutting the jugular vein, as his clothes were covered with blood when he reached home, showing that the blood had spurted out of the Indian when shot. The Captain was the only one of the party who made his escape. There is no man more familiar in Bastrop county than Bart Sims, as he was called. In fact, he was pretty generally known over the State, especially to old settlers.

Captain Ben McCulloch.

THE following incidents of the life of Captain (afterwards General) Ben McCulloch, occurred prior to the war between Mexico and the United States, and are taken from an interesting biographical work by Victor M. Rose, Esq., but recently published. Of course any mention of his military career during the war with Mexico and the war between the States would be without the scope and purpose of such a book as this, and besides would be superfluous, as the events of his life during those wars are now a part of our national history and well known to all.

1839

General Ben McCulloch was born in Rutherford county, Tennessee, November 11, 1811. He entered the service a short time previous to the battle of San Jacinto, in which he participated, having the command of one of the "Twin Sisters," as they were called, the only field pieces then in possession of the Texans. That his gallantry was conspicuous at this battle is evident from the fact of his having been promoted to a first lieutenancy in the artillery the day after the fight.

When the war ended he settled at Gonzales and engaged in the occupation of surveying and locating land scrip.

In 1839 he was elected to the Texan Congress by a large majority over his opponent, Colonel Sweitzer. Colonel Sweitzer, from some cause, took occasion to insult General McCulloch publicly, who, on their return from a scouting party, proposed to Colonel Sweitzer to settle the difficulty between them with their rifles. A fight was prevented for the time, but as soon as they returned to the settlements and the scouting party was disbanded, Colonel Sweitzer sent McCulloch a challenge by Colonel Reuben Ross, which he declined to accept for reasons stated. Therefore Colonel Ross, according to the established rule of the "code of

honor," took the quarrel upon himself. Mr. Rose says:
"They met about two miles north of Gonzales, with rifles,
at forty paces. Colonel Ross, being a trained duelist, fired
at the word, his ball striking the under portion of McCulloch's right arm and drew his fire, which doubtless saved
his life, for Ben McCulloch at forty paces could drive a nail
into a tree with a ball from his rifle." McCulloch and Ross
afterwards became friends.

After annexation, General McCulloch was elected a member of the first State Legislature, representing the Gonzales
district.

In the winter of 1838-9, Colonel John H. Moore, of Fayette
county, made a campaign against the Comanches on the
upper Colorado, and Ben McCulloch, taking advantage of
the favorable opportunity thus presented for chastising the
the hostile Indians who so frequently disturbed the quiet of
the Gonzales settlement, concerted measures with "Captain
Jim," chief of the Tonkawa tribe, to act with a small party
of whites consisting of himself, Henry E. McCulloch, Wilson Randle, David Henson and John D. Wolfin; Ben agreeing to furnish the Tonkawas with salt and one hundred
rounds of ammunition for ten or twelve rifles (all the firearms in the tribe), the remaining warriors, to the number of
thirty or more, being armed with spears and bows and
arrows. After much difficulty, occasioned by a fall of snow
and very cold weather, McCulloch succeeded in getting the
Tonkawas from their camp on Peach creek, some fifteen
miles from Gonzales, and the command marched some
twenty-five miles up the creek and encamped for the night
in a dense thicket. The next morning a fresh trail was
struck, indicating a raid upon the settlement by a combined
force of Wacos and Comanches. Knowing that they could
be but a short distance ahead, Ben persuaded Captain Jim
to give pursuit. Two fleet Tonkawas were ordered by their
chief to push on in a run along the trail; and Ben, who was
as fleet on foot as they and possessed of as much endurance,
accompanied the spies. Ben correctly judged that the hostiles would conceal themselves in the dense brush which
grew upon a deep branch which was ahead, during the day,
and sally forth at night to perpetrate their atrocities on the
unsuspecting people. After accurately examining their

CAPTAIN BEN McCULLOCH.

position, Ben fell back to give directions to "Captain Jim."
The enemy was surrounded, and a most obstinate fight ensued, which continued till near night fall, and but for dis-
obedience of McCulloch's orders on the part of the Tonkawas, the whole party of the hostiles would have been captured. As it was, ten Wacos and Comanches were killed on
the field, and but one of McCulloch's party—a Tonkawa.
But the expedition ended here. "Captain Jim" alleging
that his people would have to return to their camp, to re-
joice over their victory and bewail the death of their
brother. The Tonkawas scalped the dead and dying Comanches and Wacos, and while life was not yet extinct in
some of them, cut off their hands and feet, arms and legs
and fleeced the flesh off their thighs and breasts, which
horrid booty the cannibal monsters bore away with them to
their camp, in which, doubtless a revolting, ghoulish feast
was celebrated."

Ben and his brother Henry both were present at the battle with the Comanches on Plum creek in 1840, where they
were conspicuous for their gallant conduct.

The spring of 1841 was rendered remarkable by the fre-
quency of Indian raids, and Ben McCulloch was constantly
on the war path. In one of his many expeditions at this
period, he followed a band of Comanches up the Gaudalupe
river to its source and down the Johnson fork of the Llano
river to its confluence with the main stream, where he found
the Indians resting in fancied security, and entirely unap-
prehensive of danger. He surprised them at day light by
firing into and immediately making a rush upon the camp,
killing four and dispersing the remainder. Their horses,
mules and camp equipage fell into the hands of the Texans.

Soon after General Wall's raid upon San Antonio, a company was organized for service in the plains and mountains north and west of that place, which will always rank
as the very gamest of all the many organization whose
knightly deeds enveloped the name of "Texan Ranger" in
wreathings of glory, of which John C. (Jack) Hays was
Captain and Ben McCulloch first lieutenant. Soon after the
organization of this ranging force, Ben McCulloch was compelled by business engagements to resign, but rejoined it
again in the capacity of a private soldier, and continued

with it in all its battles, scouts and skirmishes until the Lone Star of Texas was added to the glorious galaxy of the Union. The fight with Yellow Wolf on the Pedernales, in which sixteen of this troop fought in open prairie seventy-five Comanches, will always remain one of the most remarkable episodes of border warfare to be found in the annals of any land   This was the first engagement with Comanches in which Colt's revolvers were used, and the engraving so familiar for many years on the cylinders of those of subsequent manufacture, was designed to represent this battle.

One of General McCulloch's old friends who was intimately acquainted with him thus speaks of him: "Ben McCulloch was one of the most admirable characters I have ever known. Brave as a lion himself, he was ready at all times to take any risks personally, and yet he was cautious almost to timidity when the safety of others was concerned. He was courteous, friendly and affable to all—perfectly unassuming and unpretentious—never exaggerating his own deeds, or even speaking of them unless there was some necessity for doing so.   In a word, he was one of nature's noblemen—a prieu chevalier sans peur et sans reproche. When he fell at the battle of Elk Horn, Missouri, the Confederacy, in my opinion, lost another Stonewall Jackson— for, in fact there was in many respects a marked similarity between the two men. No doubt, McCulloch had his faults, as the best of us have, but as long as I knew him, I never discovered what they were."

Riding Match Between Rangers and Comanches.

THE following account of the famous riding contest between the Texas Rangers and Comanche Indians, which took place in the suburbs of San Antonio in the year 1843, was written by Captain John C. Duval some years ago for a book then contemplated by him to be called "Early

Times in Texas," which we hope yet will see the light soon.

Captain Duval was an eye witness to this celebrated 1843 equestrian contest, and the narrative is strictly true, as well as highly interesting.

We had often heard of the astonishing equestrian feats performed by the Texas Rangers, as well as the Comanches, and we were all anxious to see them. Uncle Seth told us they could beat the circus riders "all hollow," and the sight would be worth the loss of a day. The next morning we found the whole population of the city, men, women and children, all preparing to leave for the scene of the great riding match which was to take place in a beautiful prairie about half a mile west of the plaza. Gaily dressed caballeros were prancing up and down the street. Rangers mounted on their barbs, dressed in buck skin hunting shirts, leggins and slouched hats, and with pistols and bowie knives stuck in their belts, galloped hither and thither through the crowd, occasionally charging horse and all, into some bar room or grocery, and calling for mescal or red eye, by way of preparing themselves for the expected contest. All the strangers in the place, and the citizens with their wives and families crammed into all sorts of vehicles, were seen hurrying through the streets in hot haste to reach the scene of action before the "show" began. Mounting our horses, and leaving Uncle Seth in charge of the camp, who declined going with us, because he said he had seen "Ingens often enough cuttin' up their didos" on horseback, we followed the crowd, until we came to the San Pedro. a little stream that flows through the western suburbs of the city. But just then an incident occurred that apparently afforded a great deal of amusement to all present, except ourselves, who were the actors, and which prevented us from reaching our destination as soon as we anticipated by half an hour. A Mexican had come meeting us, mounted on a "burro" or donkey, which was covered from head to tail with mesquite branches and limbs, so that nothing of the animal was visible as it moved along, except its huge ears and portions of its legs. The moment our horses caught sight of this strange looking object, they all suddenly stopped and stood as if they had been rooted to the spot; then snorting like mustangs, they quickly wheeled about and went off like

the wind, through the streets, the way we had come. So
completely were they "stampeded," that we found it im
possible to check their headlong course, until we had go
back to camp on the east side of the river. Uncle Seth seeing
us returning so hurridly and unexpectedly, came out of the
tent to enquire what was the matter: "Oh, nothing much,"
answered Lawrence, who was the first to bring his frightened horse to a stand, "we met a burro on the road, and
our horses stampeded and brought us back, whether we
would or no."

"Well!" said Uncle Seth, laughing heartily at our discomfiture," them ar' burros, when they are kivered up with
wood or grass, and nothing to be seen of 'em except their
legs and ears, are pretty tolerably scary looking fellows, its
a fact; and its no wonder they should stampede a decent
American horse that aint accustomed to 'em, but I 'spose
you'll try it over agin."

"Of course we will," replied Lawrence, "but if we meet
another burro, you may look for us back again in a few
minutes."

However, we encountered no more "burros," and at
length safely reached the locality where the riding match
was to be held, and where we found the whole population
of the town already assembled on the ground. It was indeed, a strange and novel scene that presented itself to our
view. Drawn up in a line on one side of the "arena," sitting like statues on their horses, were the Comanche warriors, decked out in all their savage paraphernalia of paints,
feathers and furs, and looking with Indian stoicism on all
that was going on around them.

Opposite to them, drawn up in single file also, were their
old enemies upon many a bloody field, the Texas Rangers,
and a few Mexican Caballeros, dressed in their steeple
crown, broad brim sombreros, showy scarfs and 'slashed'
trowsers, holding gracefully in check their fiery mustangs,
on which they were mounted.

After some preliminaries, the space selected for the riding
was cleared of all noncontestants, and the "show" began.
A Mexican lad mounted on a "paint" pony (piebalo) with a
spear in his hand, cantered off some three or four hundred
yards on the prairie, and dismounting, laid the spear upon

the ground. Immediately a Comanche brave started forth
from their ranks, and plunging his huge spurs into his
horse's flanks, dashed off in an opposite direction for a hundred yards or so, then wheeling suddenly, he came rushing
back at full speed, and as he passed the spot where the
spear had been deposited, without checking his horse for an
instant, he swerved from his saddle, seized the spear, and
rising gracefully in his seat again, continued his headlong
course some distance beyond, then wheeling suddenly, gal-
lopped back, dropp ng the spear, as he returned, at the same
spot from which he had taken it, and resumed his position
in the ranks. The same feat was then performed by every
warrior, Ranger and Caballero on the ground, without a
single failure.

A glove was then substituted in place of the spear, which
in like manner was picked up from the ground by the riders
while going at full speed and without checking their horses
for an instant. A board with a "bull's eye" painted
upon it was then set up at the point where the spear
and glove had been placed. A warrior with his bow in one
hand and half a dozen arrows drawn from his quiver
charged at full speed towards the mark, and in the little
time he was passing it planted two arrows in the board.
All the rest of the Indians followed suit, none of them failing to strike the board with one or two arrows as they went
by. The rangers and caballeros then took their turn, using .
their pistols instead of bows, and all of them struck the board
as they passed, and often the very center of the "bull's eye."

A great many other extraordinary feats were done, such
as hanging by one knee to the horn of the saddle in such a
way that the rider was invisible to those on the opposite side,
and while in that position discharging arrows or pistols at
an imaginary foe, dismounting from the horse, running a
short distance by his side and then springing into the saddle
again without checking his course for a moment, passing
under the horse's neck and coming up into the saddle again
from the opposite side, etc., etc , all of them performed
while the horse was going at full speed. No feats of horsemanship we had ever seen exhibited by the most famous
knights of the ring could compare with these for daring and
dexterity.

The last and most interesting and exciting performance
of all was the breaking in of several wild steeds of the
desert that had been lately captured and which were teth-
ered to strong stakes driven firmly into the ground by ropes
of rawhide or lariats, as the Mexicans call them. Young
McMullen, of Florida, who had already been voted by general acclamation the most daring and graceful rider of all,
was the first chosen to perform this dangerous feat. Approaching cautiously the most perfectly formed and powerful of these unbroken steeds, he at length succeeded, in spite
of the furious lunges and struggles of the terrified animal,
in binding a strip of cloth over its eyes; when, instantly, as if
transfixed by the wand of an enchanter, the animal ceased
its struggles and stood as still as if it had been hewn out of
solid stone. McMullen then slipped the bit into its mouth,
strapped the saddle securely on its back, and placing his foot
in the stirrup, sprang into the seat. All this time the animal never moved but the quivering of its well formed muscular limbs plainly showed that its terrors were still unabated. McMullen fixed himself firmly in his seat and gathering up the reins of his bridle with his left hand he leaned
forward and quickly drew off the blind he had placed over
the eyes of the horse. The instant the blind was drawn up
the wild horse, snorting and bellowing like a mad bull with
mingled rage and terror, gave one tremendous bound and
then darted off at head long speed across the prairie, but instead of trying to check him McMullen urged him on with
whip and spurs until he had gone perhaps a mile, when he
reined him round and brought him back within fifty yards
of the point he had started from. Here, suddenly coming
to a halt, the horse began to pitch or plunge in such a violent
manner that no one but the most perfect rider could possibly have kept his seat in the saddle. But McMullen stuck to
him as if he had been part of the animal itself, and the horse
in vain attempted in this way to get rid of his unwelcome
burden. At length, frantic with rage and fright, the horse
reared straight up and threw himself backwards upon the
ground. A cry of horror broke from the lips of the crowd
around, who supposed that McMullen would inevitably be
crushed beneath the weight of his wild steed; but he was on
the qui vive and sprang from under just in time to save

himself, and the instant the horse rose to his feet we saw him seated again in the saddle as calm and composed as if he was bestriding the gentlest hack that ever bore a country curate to his parish church. Again the horse darted off at the top of his speed, and again McMullen urged him on with quirt and spurs, as he had done before until they had dwindled to a mere speck on the prairie. Before long, however, he came galloping back, and after cantering leisurely around the arena he drew up his foam covered and panting steed at the place he started from and the black eyes of many a senorita smiled admiringly upon the daring and handsome young ranger. The wild steed of the desert had been effectually subdued.

Several more were broken in the same way by Mexicans and then followed the distribution of the prizes, consisting of handsomely mounted pistols and bowie knives. The first prize was awarded by the judges to McMullen, the second to Long Quiet, a Comanche warrior, the third to Colonel Kinney of Corpus Christi and the fourth to Senor Don Rafael, a ranchero from the Rio Grande. Presents of various kinds were distributed generally among the Comanches, which ended the show, and we returned to camp highly pleased with all we had seen.

The Fate of Judge Martin.

By J. T. DeShields.

DURING the month of June, 1834, Judge Gabriel N. Martin, with his son and a negro man servant, went out on a buffalo hunt high up on the False Washita. After enjoying several days of exciting sport in this delightful region the trio were suddenly surrounded by a band of eleven Pawnee Indians. A desperate struggle ensued and Martin and the negro were overpowered and 1834 tortured to death, the Indians piercing them with lances until life was extinct. After horribly mutilating the already perforated bodies of the two men and scalping Martin, the Indians took the lad prisoner, carrying him to their village on Red river. Judge Gabriel N. Martin is described as being a very respectable, independent and fearless man, who lived high up on Red river. For several years he had been in the habit of taking his little son and a negro man servant to live in this wild region every summer. He would pitch his tent upon the prairie and spend several months in hunting and killing buffalo and other wild game for his own amusement.

The news of the shocking tragedy soon reached the settlements and Mr. Martin's brother-in-law, Travis G. Wright, with three companions, started to recover the captive boy. They fortunately fell in with a company of United States soldiers under Colonel (now General) Dodge, who was on his way to the Pawnee village to negotiate a treaty with them. After a four day's march they arrived at the Pawnee village. The day after their arrival Colonel Dodge opened a council with the chiefs in their council house, where he had most of his officers around him. He first explained to them the friendly views with which he came to see them, and of the wish of our government to establish a lasting peace with them, which they pretended to appreciate and highly estimate. Leh-Toot-Sah, the head chief of the tribe, a very old and venerable looking man, several times replied to Colonel Dodge in a very eloquent manner, assuring him of the friendly feeling of the people towards the pale faces in the direction from whence he came—Texas. After explaining, in general, the objects of his visit, Colonel Dodge told the Indians that he should expect from them some account of the foul murder of Judge Martin and his servant on the False Washita, which had been perpetrated but a few weeks before, and which the Comanches had told him was done by the Pawnees. The Colonel told them also that he had learned from the Comanches that they had the little boy, the son of the murdered gentleman, in their possession, and that he should expect them to deliver him up to his friends, who were present. They positively denied all knowledge of the murder or of the boy. The demand was repeatedly made and as often denied, until at length a negro man, who was living with the tribe, and who spoke good English, came into the council house and stated that such a boy had recently been brought into their village and was now a prisoner among them. This excited great surprise and indignation in the council and Colonel Dodge then informed the chiefs that the council would rest here, and certainly nothing more of a peaceable nature would transpire until the boy was brought in. In this alarming dilemma all remained in gloomy silence and stoical indifference for several minutes, when Colonel Dodge further stated to the chiefs that as an evidence of his friendly intentions towards them, he had, on starting, purchased, at a very great price from their enemy, the Osages, three (two Pawnee and one Kiowa) girls, who had been stolen from them several years before, and whom their enemy had held as prisoners for a high ransom. He stated that he had the girls with him, but would not give them up until the boy was produced. He also made another demand, which was for the restoration of a Texas ranger by the name of Abbe, who had been captured by the Indians during the present summer. They acknowledged the seizure of this man, but all declared that he had been taken by a party of Comanches, over whom they had no control and carried beyond the Rio Grande into Mexico, where he was put to death. After a long consultation about the boy, seeing their plans defeated by the evidence of the negro, and also being convinced of the friendly disposition of the whites by bringing home their prisoners from the Osages, they sent out and had the boy brought in from the middle of a corn field, where he had been hid. When brought in he was entirely naked, with the exception of the scanty dress worn by the children of the tribe. He was a very bright and intelligent little fellow of nine summers. His appearance caused considerable excitement and commotion in the council, and as he passed among the crowd he looked around and exclaimed in great surprise: "What are these white men here for?" to which Dodge replied by asking him his name. He promptly answered: "My name is Mathew Wright Martin." He was then received into the arms of Dodge, who embraced him with tears in his eyes. The three little Indian girls were then brought in and soon recognized by their overjoyed friends and relatives, who embraced them with the most extravagant expressions of joy. The heart of the venerable old chief was

melted at this evidence of the white man's friendship.   He
at once embraced Colonel Dodge and all the other officers in
turn, with tears streaming down his cheeks.   From this mo
ment the council, which before had been a very grave and
uncertain one, took a pleasing and friendly turn.   The stoical old chief now ordered the women to supply the dragoons
with something to eat.   This kind and generous hospitality
was highly appreciated by the hungry soldiers, as they had
consumed their rations twelve hours before.   After several
days of counseling a treaty was formed and for some time
the Pawnees remained friendly toward Texas.

Heroic Defense of the Taylor Family.

THIS full and authentic narrative of the wonderful heroism of the Taylor family, in Bell county, in 1835, has
been kindly contributed by James T. De Shields.

As early as 1833 and 1834 the brave and hardy pioneers of Robertson's colony or "Old Milam Land District,"
as it was known, had pushed as far west as the present
county seat of Bell county.   Among the first who
1835 came was the Taylor family, who settled in the
"Three Forks of Little River," a place since known as
"Taylor's Valley," about three miles southeast of the present town of Belton.

The home of the Taylors consisted of two rude but substantial log cabins, with a covered passage between.   The
family consisted of Mr. and Mrs. Taylor, two youthful sons
and two daugters.   One of the latter, Miss Frances, being
a daughter of Mrs. Taylor by her first husband, and who af-
erwards became the wife of a noted citizen in the early
history of Bell county, George W. Chapman.

At this time the surrounding country was very sparsely
settled.   Indeed, the nearest neighbors of the Taylors were
a few brave and adventurous persons who were forted up in
log cabins several miles further down Little River.   The

thrilling incidents that I will now narrate, occurred some time in the month of November, 1835. As usual, the family had retired for the night, the parents and girls in one room, and the boys in the other; little dreaming that their rest would soon be broken, and that they would soon participate in some dangerous and stirring scenes. But then, as now, life was a mixture of joys and sorrows, hidden dangers were always lurking around the unprotected and lonely cabins of the brave pioneers. Some times they were deluded into a sense of security, when suddenly their hopes were blighted. But when danger presented itself they were quick to take in the situation, and they always prepared to defend themselves, or fight to the bitter end, no matter how fearful the odds were against them. The Taylors were no exception to this rule—especially the heroic Mrs. Taylor—as we shall see.

It was a bright moonlight night about ten o'clock, when eleven Indians made an attack on the house. The first intimation that the family had of the presence of the enemy was the fierce and continued barking of a faithful watch dog, which the Indians soon quieted, by sending an arrow through his heart. The attack now commenced in earnest. A stalwart savage presented himself at the door; violently shaking the shutter and demanding admittance. "Silence gave no consent," and he next inquired, in broken English, "how many men in house? Open door and give poor Indian some tobacco. Friend, no want to fight." Mr. Taylor then answered, saying there were "ten men in the house; that he would open no door, and had no tobacco for red devils," at the same time through a crack in the wall giving him a terrible thrust with a sharp board in the stomach, which caused him to yell and hastily retreat. At this instant Mrs. Taylor threw open the door leading across the hall and commanded the boys to come into her room, which they hastily did, amid a perfect shower of balls and arrows. The door was now securely fastened and a table placed against it, upon which the youngest boy—only twelve years old—was mounted with a gun and instructed to shoot through an open space about four inches over the door, whenever an Indian should appear. For once the child found this space a great convenience. He often thought no doubt the wind whistled

unmercifully through the opening, but now it was a blessing. A big Indian who had procured an axe from the wood
pile, started towards the door, and had reached the passage
between the two rooms when, remembering his orders, the
child fired and the Indian dropped dead. Seeing the fate of
his comrade, another demon rushed up and attempted to
drag the dead one away, but with the same accuracy of his
little son the father fired, felling his Indian, who fell mortally wounded, across the first one. At this juncture the
family found that they were without bullets, but they were
equal to the emergency—a few live coals remained in the
fire place, and Mrs. Taylor and the girls immediately commenced to mold bullets. However, the two last shots of the
Taylors had been deadly, causing the surviving Indians to
be more cautious, and change their tactics. They now set fire
to the farthest end of the vacated room, and immediately
commenced to yell and dance while the flames made rapid
headway to the roof and towards the adjoining room. In
the covered pass way, before referred to, and suspended
to the "joists," was a large amount of fat bear meat.
The burning roof soon began to cook the meat, and blazing
sheets of the oil fell upon the wounded savage, who writhed
and hideously yelled, but was powerless to extricate himself from the torture. Mrs. Taylor had no sympathy for
the wretch, but, peeping through a crack, expressed her
feelings by exclaiming: "Howl! you yellow brute! Your
meat is not fit for hogs, but we'll roast you for the wolves!"
But the flames were rapidly spreading and soon the entire
building would be consumed, with its inmates. Something
must be done, and that too, at once. Mr. Taylor now gave
up all hopes, declaring his wish to rush out and surrender.
To this proposition the heroic Mrs. Taylor would never consent, preferring to perish in the flames, bravely fighting,
rather than place herself and chidren in the hands of a
band of blood thirsty and merciless demons to be tortured
to death. The brave woman was equal to the emergency—
great as it was. Fortunately there was a supply of "home
made" vinegar, and milk in the house, and with this she
declared she could put out the fire. Suiting her action to
the thought, and with a bravery evinced by few men, she
mounted a table, from which she could reach the roof, and

immediately commenced to tear away the boards, (the same not being nailed) making an open space in advance of the near approaching flames Baring her head and body through the opening, she commanded her daughters to pass the fluids, which she cooly and judiciously distributed, and soon succeeded in quenching the flames. During all this time the Indians were yelling like so many demons and shooting arrow after arrow at her exposed form, while the brave woman worked away seemingly undaunted. Surely Mars smiled on her, for while many arrows were hanging in her clothing, she was unharmed. This was indeed a true heroine—a woman rushing into the very jaws of death to save her children. While Mrs. Taylor was thus engaged, Mr. Taylor and the eldest boy were not idle, each succeeding in wounding an Indian as they came within the range of their guns. Having accomplished her hazardous mission, Mrs. Taylor came down from the roof and soon discovered an Indian in the outer chimney corner, endeavoring to start a fire, and peering through a considerable hole burnt through the "dirt and wooden" jam. Seizing a wooden shovel, she threw into his face and bosom a shovelful of live coals and embers, causing him to retreat, uttering the most agonizing screams, to which she responded: "Take that, you yellow scoundrel!" It was said afterwards that her warm and hasty application destroyed his eyesight.

Seeing their plans thus defeated; two of their braves barbecued, two severely wounded, and one suffering considerably in the abdominal regions, and another much disfigured in the face and defective in eyesight, the Indians withdrew a short distance, held a council of war, and soon concluded it was best to beat a hasty retreat, and "seek others more easily devoured."

An hour or so later the heroic family might have been seen wandering about in the darkness of the forest, making their way down Little River towards their nearest neighbors at the log fort above mentioned. Their thrilling and seemingly marvelous escape was soon related, all of which was fully verified by a small company of men who visited the scene of the late terrible action on the following day, finding everything in statu quo, as described by the Taylors.

This thrilling episode in the bloody history of old Bell

county, occurred more than fifty-three years ago. To-day a thriving town of five thousand population bursts upon the vision of the writer as he stands upon the spot once covered by the Taylor cabins, meandering over the bloody past, wondering at the present, and guessing at the future.

Reverting thus far in the misty past, reminds us of the fact that Bell county has an unwritten history of its own, bathed in the blood of its noble old pioneers, nearly all of whom have long since passed away from the scenes of action. But the strife is over, and their gratuitous services are no longer required. Sacred be the memory of the dead —all honor to those who still survive those troublesome times.

Mrs. Chapman (now of Atascosa county, Texas), is the only surving member of the Taylor family, and as she was a witness to the scenes here described, she will fully verify the above statements.   G. T. D.

Parker Fort Massacre.

THE following graphic account of Parker fort massacre has been gathered from several reliable sources, but the greatest portion of same has been by the kind consent of James T. DeShields, copied from a little book published by him entitled " Cynthia Ann Parker." In fact everything from the conclusion of the extract from Mrs. Plummer's diary to the conclusion of the history of 1836 Quanah Parker, is intended to be a literal copy from said book.

Among the many tragedies that have occurred in Texas the massacre at Parker's fort holds a conspicuous place. Nothing that has ever happened exhibits savage duplicity and cruelty more plainly than this massacre of helpless women and children.

In 1833 a small colony was organized in the State of Illinois for the purpose of forming a settlement in Texas. After their arrival in the country they selected for a residence a beautiful region on the Navasota river, a small tributary of the Brazos. To secure themselves against the various tribes of roving savages was the first thing to be attended to, and having chosen a commanding eminence adjacent to a large timbered bottom of the Navasota, about three miles from where the town of Springfield formerly stood and about two miles from the present town of Groesbeck, they, by their joint labor, soon had a fortification erected. It consisted of a stockade of split cedar timbers planted deep in the ground, extending fifteen feet above the surface, touching each other and confined at the top by transverse timbers which rendered them almost as immovable as a solid wall. At convenient distances there were port holes, through which, in case of an emergency, fire arms could be used. The entire fort covered nearly an acre of ground. There were also attached to the stockade two log cabins at diagonal corners, constituting a part of the enclosure. They were really block houses, the greater portion of each standing outside of the main stockade, the upper story jutting over the lower, with openings in the floor, allowing perpendicular shooting from above. There were also port holes cut in the upper story so as to admit of horizontal shooting when necessary. This enabled the inmates to rake every side of the stockade. The fort was situated near a fine spring of water. As soon as it was completed the little colony moved into it. Parker's colony at this time consisted of only some eight or nine families, viz.: Elder John Parker, patriarch of the colony and his wife; his son, James W. Parker, wife, four single children, and his daughter, Mrs. Rachel Plummer, her husband, L. M. S. Plummer, and infant son fifteen months old; Mrs. Sarah Nixon, another daughter, and her husband, L. D. Nixon; Silas M. Parker (another son of Elder John), his wife and four children; Benjamin F. Parker, an unmarried son of the elder; Mrs. Nixon, Sr., mother of Mrs, James W. Parker; Mrs. Elizabeth Kellogg, daughter of Mrs. Nixon; Mrs. —— Duty; Samuel M. Frost, wife and two children; G. E. Dwight, wife and two children—in all thirty-four persons. Besides those above mentioned, old man —— Lunn, David Faulkenberry and his son Evan, Silas Bates and Abram Anglin had erected cabins a mile or two distant from the fort, where they resided. These families were truly the advance guard of civilization on that part of our frontier, Fort Houston, in Anderson county being the nearest protection, except their own trusty rifles. Here the struggling colonists remained, engaged in the avocations of a rural life, tilling the soil, hunting buffalo, bear, deer, turkies and smaller game, which served abundantly to supply their larder at all times with fresh meat, in the enjoyment of a life of Arcadian simplicity, virtue and contentment, until the latter part of the year 1835, when the Indians and Mexicans forced the little band of compatriots to abandon their homes and flee with many others before the invading army from Mexico. On arriving at the Trinity river they were compelled to halt in consequence of an overflow. Before they could cross the swollen stream the sudden and unexpected news reached them that Santa Anna and his vandal hordes had been confronted and defeated at San Jacinto, that sanguinary engagement which gave birth to the new sovereignty of Texas, and that Texas was free from Mexican tyranny.

On receipt of this news the fleeing settlers were overjoyed and at once returned to their abandoned homes. The Parker colonists now retraced their steps, first going to Fort Houston, where they remained a few days in order to procure supplies, after which they made their way back to Fort Parker to look after their stock and prepare for a crop. These hardy sons of toil spent their nights in the fort, repairing to their farms early each morning. The strictest discipline was maintained for a while, but as time wore on and no hostile demonstrations had been made by the Indians they became somewhat careless and restive under confinement. However, it was absolutely necessary that they should cultivate their farms to insure substance for their families. They usaally went to work in a body, with their farming implements in one hand and their weapons of defense in the other. Some of them built cabins on their farms, hoping that the government would give them protection, or that a sufficient number of other colonists would soon move in to render them secure from the attacks of Indians.

On the eighteenth day of May, 1836, all slept at the fort,

James W. Parker, Nixon and Plummer repairing to their field, a mile distant, on the Navasota, early next morning, little thinking of the great calamity that was soon to befall them. They had scarcely left when several hundred Indians (accounts as to the number of Indians vary from three hundred to seven hundred—probably there were about five hundred), Comanches and Kiowas, made their appearance on an eminence within three hundred yards of the fort. Those who remained in the fort were not prepared for an attack, so careless had they become in their fancied security. The Indians hoisted a white flag as a token of their friendly intentions, and upon the exhibition ot the white flag, Mr. Benjamin Parker went out to have a talk with them The Indians artfully feigned the treacherous semblance of friendship, pretending that they were looking for a suitable camping place, and inquired as to the exact locality of a water hole in the vicinity, at the same time asking for a beef, as they said they were very hungry. Not daring to refuse the requests of such a formidable body of savages, Mr. Benjamin F. Parker told them they should have what they wanted. Returning to the fort he stated to the inmates that in his opinion the Indians were hostile and intended to fight, but added he would go back to them and try to avert it. His brother Silas remonstrated, but he persisted in going, and was immediately surrounded and killed, whereupon the whole force—their savage instincts aroused by the sight of blood—charged upon the fort, uttering the most terrific and unearthly yells that ever greeted the ears of mortals. The sickening and bloody tragedy was soon enacted. Brave Silas M. Parker fell outside of the fort while he was gallantly fighting to save Mrs. Plummer. Mrs. Plummer made a desperate resistance, but was soon overpowered, knocked down with a hoe and made captive. Samuel M. Frost and his son Robert met their fate while heroically defending the women and children inside the stockade. Old Granny Parker was stabbed and left for dead. Elder John Parker, wife and Mrs. Kellogg attempted to make their escape, and in the effort had gone about three-fourths a mile when they were overtaken and driven back near to the fort, when the old gentleman was stripped, murdered, scalped and horribly mutilated. Mrs. Parker was stripped, speared and left for dead, but by feigning death escaped, as will be seen further on. Mrs. Kellogg was spared as a captive. The result summed up as follows: Killed—Elder John Parker, aged seventy-nine; Silas M. and Benjamin F. Parker; Samuel M. and his son Robert Frost. Wounded dangerously—Mrs. John Parker, old Granny Parker and Mrs. —— Duty. Captured—Mrs. Rachel Plummer, daughter of James W. Parker, and her son, James Pratt Plummer, two years of age; Mrs. Elizabeth Kellogg; Cynthia Ann Parker, nine years old, and her little brother, John Parker, aged six years, children of Silas M. Parker. The remainder of the inmates making their escape, as we shall narrate.

When the attack on the fort first commenced, Mrs. Sarah Nixon made her escape and hastened to the field to advise her father, husband and Plummer of what had occurred. On her arrival Plummer hurried off on horseback to inform Faulkenberry, Lunn, Bates and Anglin, who were at work in their fields. Parker and Nixon started to the fort, but the former met his family on the way and carried them some five miles down the Navasota, secreting them in the bottom. Nixon, though unarmed, continued on towards the fort, and met Mrs. Lucy, wife of Silas Parker (killed), with her four children, just as they were intercepted by a small party of mounted and foot Indians. They compelled the mother to lift her daughter Cynthia Ann and her little son John behind two of the mounted warriors. The foot Indians then took Mrs. Parker, her two youngest children and Nixon towards fort. As they were about to kill Nixon, David Faulkenberry appeared with his rifle and caused them to fall back. Nixon, after his narrow escape, from death, seemed very much excited and immediately left in search of his wife, soon falling in with Dwight, with his own and Frost's family. Dwight and party soon overtook J. W. Parker and went with him to the hiding place in the bottom. Faulkenberry thus left with Mrs. Parker and her two children, bade her to follow him. With the infant in her arms and leading the other child she obeyed. Seeing them leave the fort the Indians made several attempts to intercept them but were held in check by the brave man's rifle. Several mounted warriors armed with bows and arrows, strung and drawn, and with terrific yells, would charge them, but as Faulkenberry would present his gun they would halt, throw up their shields, right about, wheel and retire to a safe distance. This continued for some distance, until they had passed through a prairie of some forty or fifty acres. Just as they were entering the woods the Indians made a furious charge, when one warrior more daring than the others, dashed up so near that Mrs. Parker's faithful dog seized his horse by the nose, whereupon both horse and rider somersaulted, alighting on their backs in the ravine. At this moment Silas Bates, Abram Anglin and Evan Faulkenberry, armed, and Plummer, unarmed, came up, causing the Indians to retire, after which the party made their way unmolested.

As they were passing through the field where the three men had been at work in the morning, Plummer, as if aroused from a dream, demanded to know what had become of his wife and child. Armed only with a butcher knife, he left the party, in search of his loved ones, and was seen no more for six days. The Faulkenberrys, Lunn and Mrs. Parker, secreted themselves in a small creek bottom, some distance from the first party, each unconscious of the other's whereabouts. At twilight Abraham Anglin and Evan Faulkenberry started back to the fort to succor the wounded and those who might have escaped. On their way, and just as they were passing Faulkenberry's cabin, Anglin saw his first and only ghost. He says: "It was dressed in white, with long white hair streaming down its back. I admit that I was more scared at this moment than when the Indians were yelling and charging us. Seeing me hesitate, my ghost now beckoned me to come on. Approaching the object, it proved to be old Granny Parker, whom the Indians had wounded and stripped, with the exception of her under garments. She had made her way to the house from the fort, by crawling the entire distance. I took her some bed clothing, and carrying her some rods from the house, made her a bed, covered her up, and left her until we should return from the fort. On arriving at the fort we could not see a single individual alive, or hear a human sound. But the dogs were barking, the cattle lowing, the horses neighing, and the hogs squealing, making a hideous and strange medley of sounds. Mrs. Parker had told me where she had left some silver, one hundred and six dollars and fifty cents.

This I found under a hickory bush by moonlight. Finding no one at the fort, we returned to where I had hid Granny Parker. On taking her up behind me, we made our way back to our hiding place in the bottom, where we found Nixon, whom we had not seen since his cowardly flight at the time he was rescued by Faulkenberry, from the Indians."

In the book published by James W. Parker, on pages ten and eleven, he states that Nixon liberated Mrs. Parker from the Indians, and rescued old Granny Parker. Mr. Anglin in his account contradicts, or rather corrects this statement. He says: "I positively assert that this is a mistake, and I am willing to be qualified to the statement I here make, and can prove the same by Silas H. Bates, now living near Groesbeck."

The next morning Bates, Anglin and E. Faulkenberry, went back to the fort to get provisions and horses, and look after the dead. On reaching the fort, they found five or six horses, a few saddles and some meat, bacon and honey. Fearing an attack from the Indians who might still be lurking around, they left without burying the dead. Returning to their comrades in the bottom, they all concealed themselves until they set out for Fort Houston. Fort Houston, an asylum, on this, as on many other occasions, stood on what has been for many years, the farm of a wise Statesman, a chivalrous soldier and a true patriot, John H. Reagan, two miles south of Palestine.

After wandering around, and traveling for six days and nights, during which they suffered much from hunger and thirst, with their clothing torn into shreds, their bodies lacerated with briars and thorns, the women and children, with unshod and bleeding feet, the party with James W. Parker reached Fort Houston.

An account of this wearisome and perilous journey through the wilderness, given substantially in Parker's own words, will enable the reader to realize more fully the hardships they had to undergo and the dangers they encountered. The bulk of the party were composed of women and children, principally the latter, and ranging from one to twelve years old. "We started from the fort," said Mr. Parker, "the party consisting of eighteen in all, for Fort Houston, a dis-

STARVING FUGITIVES OF FORT PARKER MASSACRE PREPARING TO EAT A SKUNK.

tance of ninety miles by the route we had to travel. The feelings of the party can be better imagined than described. We were truly a forlorn set, many of us barefooted and bareheaded, a relentless foe on the one hand and on the other a trackless and uninhabited wilderness infested with reptiles and wild beasts, entirely destitute of food and no means of procuring it." Add to this the agonizing grief of the party over the death and capture of dear relatives; "that we were momentarily in expectation of meeting the like fate, and some idea may be formed of our pitiable condition. Utter despair almost took possession of us, for the chance of escaping seemed almost an impossibility under the circumstances." * * * * "I took one of my children on my shoulder and led another. The grown persons followed my example, and we began our journey through the thickly tangled briars and underbrush in the direction of Fort Houston. My wife was in bad health; Mrs. Frost was in deep distress for the loss of her husband and son, and all being barefooted except my wife and Mrs. Frost, our progress was very slow. Many of the children had nothing on them but their shirts, and their sufferings from the briars tearing their little legs and feet was almost beyond human endurance.

"We traveled until about three o'clock in the morning, when the women and children being worn out with hunger and fatigue, we laid down on the grass and slept until the dawn of day, when we resumed our perilous journey. Here we left the river bottom in order to avoid the briars and underbrush, but from the tracks of the Indians on the high lands it was evident they were hunting us, and like the fox in the fable, we concluded it best to take to the river bottom again, for though the brambles might tear our flesh they might at the same time save our lives by hiding us from the cruel savages who were in pursuit of us. The briars did in fact tear the legs and feet of the children until they could have been tracked by the blood that flowed from their wounds.

It was the night of the second day after leaving the fort, that all, and especially the women, who were nursing infants, began to suffer intensely from hunger. We were then immediately on the bank of the river, and through the mercy of Providence a polecat came near us. I immediately pursued and caught it just as it jumped into the river. The only way that I could kill it, was by holding it under the water until it was drowned. Fortunately we had the means for striking a fire, and we soon had it cooked and equally divided among the party, the share of each being small indeed. This was all we had to eat until the fourth day, when we were lucky enough to capture another skunk and two small terrapins, which were also cooked and divided between us. On the evening of the fifth day I found that the women and children were so exhausted from fatigue and hunger that it would be impossible for them to travel much farther. After holding a consultation it was agreed that I should hurry on to Fort Houston for aid, leaving Mr. Dwight in charge of the women and children. Accordingly the next morning I started for the fort (about thirty-five miles distant), which I reached early in the afternoon. I have often looked back and wondered how it was I was able to accomplish this extraordinary feat. I had not eaten a mouthful of food for six days, having always given my share of the animals mentioned to the children, and yet I walked thirty-five miles in about eight hours. But the thought of the unfortunate sufferers I had left behind dependent on my efforts gave me the strength and perseverance that can be realized only by those who have been placed in similar situations. God, in his bountiful mercy, upheld me in this trying hour and enabled me to perform my task.

The first person I met was Captain Carter, of the Fort Houston settlement, who received me kindly and promptly offered me all the aid in his power. He soon had five horses saddled and he and Mr. Jeremiah Courtney went with me to meet our little band of fugitives. We met them just at dark, and placing the women and children on the horses we reached Captain Carter's about midnight. There we received all the kind attention and relief that our condition required and all was done for our comfort that sympathetic and benevolent hearts could do. We arrived at Captain Carter's on the twenty-fifth of May. The following day my son-in-law, Mr. Plummer, reached there also. He had given us up for lost and had started for the same settlement that we had."

In due time the members of the party located temporarily as best suited the respective families, most of them returning to Fort Parker soon afterwards. A burial party of twelve men from Fort Houston went up and buried the dead. Their remains now repose near the site of Old Fort Parker. Peace to their ashes. Unadorned are their graves; not even a slab of marble or a memento of any kind has been erected to tell the traveler where rest the remains of this brave little band of pioneer heroes who wrestled with the savage for the mastery of this broad domain.

Of the captives we will briefly trace their checkered career. After leaving the fort the two tribes, the Comanches and Kiowas, remained and traveled together until midnight. They then halted on an open prairie, staked out their horses, placed their pickets, and pitched their camp. Bringing all their prisoners together for the first time, they tied their hands behind them with raw hide thongs so tightly as to cut the flesh, tied their feet close together, and threw them upon their faces. Then the braves, gathering around with their yet bloody, dripping scalps, commenced their usual war dance. They danced, screamed, yelled, stamping upon their prisoners, beating them with bows until their own blood came near strangling them. The remainder of the night these frail women suffered, and had to listen to the cries and groans of their tender little children.

Mrs. Elizabeth Kellogg soon fell into the hands of the Keechis, from whom, six months after her capture, she was purchased by a party of Delawares, who carried her into Nacogdoches and delivered her to General Houston, who paid them one hundred and fifty dollars, the amount they had paid, and all they asked.

Mrs. Rachel Plummer remained a captive about eighteen months, and to give the reader an idea of her suffering during that period, we will give an extract from her diary: "In July and a portion of August, we were among some very high mountains, on which the snow remains for the greater portion of the year, and I suffered more than I had ever done before in my life. It was very seldom I had any covering for my feet, and but very little clothing for my body. I had a certain number of buffalo skins to dress every day, and had to mind the horses at night. This kept me em-

ployed pretty much all the time, and often I would take my
buffalo skins with me to finish them while I was minding
the horses. My feet would often be frost bitten while I was
dressing the skins, but I dared not complain for fear of being punished. In October I gave birth to my second son. I
say October, but it is all guess work with me, as I had no
means of keeping a record of the days as they passed. It
was a beautiful and healthy baby, but it was impossible for
me to procure suitable comforts for myself and infant. The
Indians were not as harsh in their treatment towards me as
I feared they would be, but I was apprehensive for the safety
of my child. I had been with them six months and had
learned their language, and I would often beseech my mistress to advise me what to do to save my child, but she
turned a deaf ear to all my supplications. My child was
six months old, when my master, thinking, I suppose, that
it interfered too much with my work, determined to put it.
out of the way. One cold morning, five or six Indians came
where I was suckling my babe. As soon as they came I felt
sick at heart, for my fears were aroused for the safety of
my child. I felt my whole frame convulsed with sudden
dread. My fears were not ill grounded. One of the Indians caught my child by the throat and strangled it until
to all appearances it was dead. I exerted all my feeble
strength to save my child, but the other Indians held me
fast. The Indian who had strangled the child then threw
it up in the air repeatedly and let it fall upon the frozen
ground until life seemed to be extinct. They then gave it
back to me. I had been weeping incessantly whilst they
were murdering my child, but now my grief was so great
that the fountain of my tears was dried up. As I gazed on
the bruised cheeks of my darling infant I discovered some
symptoms of returning life. I hoped that if it could be
resuscitated they would allow me to keep it. I washed the
blood from its face, and after a time it began to breathe
again. But a more heart rending scene ensued. As soon
as the Indians ascertained that the child was still alive,
they tore it from my arms, and knocked me down. They
tied a plaited rope around its neck and threw it into a bunch
of prickly pears and then pulled it backwards and forwards
until its tender flesh was literally torn from its body. One of

A COMANCHE WARRIOR DRAGGING TO DEATH
MRS. PLUMMER'S CHILD.

the Indians who was mounted on a horse then tied the end of the rope to his saddle and galloped around in a circle until my little innocent was not only dead, but torn to pieces. One of then untied the rope and threw the remains of the child into my lap, and I dug a hole in the earth and buried them.

"After performing the last sad rites for the lifeless remains of my dear babe, I sat down and gazed with a feeling of relief upon the little grave I had made for it in the wilderness, and could say with David of old 'you can not come to me, but I must go to you;' and then, and even now, as I record the dreadful scene I witnessed, I rejoiced that my babe had passed from the sorrows and sufferings of this world. I shall hear its dying cries no more, and fully believing in, and relying on the imputed righteousness of God in Christ Jesus, I feel that my innocent babe is now with kindred spirits in the eternal world of joys. Oh! that my dear Savior may keep me through life's short journey, and bring me to dwell with my children in the realms of eternal bliss."

Mrs. Plummer has gone to rest, and no doubt her hopes have been realized.

After this she was given as a servant to a very cruel old squaw, who treated her in a most brutal manner. Her son had been carried off by another party to the far west, and she supposed her husband and father had been killed at the massacre. Her infant was dead, and death to her would have been a sweet relief. Life was a burden, and driven almost to desperation, she resolved no longer to submit to the intolerant old squaw. One day when the two were some distance from, although still in sight of, the camp, her mistress attempted to beat her with a club. Determined not to submit to this, she wrenched the club from the hands of the squaw and knocked her down. The Indians, who had witnessed the whole proceedings from their camp, now came running up, shouting at the top of their voices. She fully expected to be killed, but they patted her on the shoulder, crying: "Bueno! Bueno!!" (Good! Good!! or Well Done!) She now fared much better, and soon became a great favorite, and was known as the "Fighting Squaw." She was eventually ransomed, through the agency of some

Mexican Santa Fe traders, by a noble hearted American merchant of that place, Mr. William Donahue. She was purchased in the Rocky mountains, so far north of Santa Fe that seventeen days were consumed in reaching that place. She was at once made a member of her benefactor's family, where she received the kindest of care and attention. Ere long she accompanied Mr. and Mrs. Donahue on a visit to Independence, Missouri, where she had the pleasure of meeting and embracing her brother-in-law, L. D. Nixon, and by him was escorted back to her people in Texas.

During her stay with the Indians, Mrs. Plummer had many thrilling adventures, which she often repeated after her reclamation. In narrating her reminiscences, she said that in one of her rambles, after she had been with the Indians some time, she discovered a cave in the mountains, and in company with the old squaw that guarded her, she explored it and found a large diamond, but her mistress immediately demanded it, and she was forced to give it up. She said also here in these mountains she saw a bush which had thorns on it resembling fish hooks, which the Indians used to catch fish with, and she herself has often caught trout with them in the little mountain streams.

On the nineteenth of February, 1838, she reached her father's house, exactly twenty-one months from her capture. She had never seen her little son, James Pratt, since soon after their capture, and knew nothing of his fate. She wrote, or dictated, a thrilling and graphic history of her capture and the horrors of her captivity, the tortures and hardships she endured, and all the incidents of her life with her captors, with observations among the savages. This valuable and interesting little book is now rare, scarce and out of print. The full title of the volume is: "Narration of the perilous adventures, miraculous escapes and sufferings of Rev. James W. Parker, during a frontier residence in Texas of fifteen years. With an impartial geographical description of the climate, soil, timber, water, etc., of Texas." To which is appended the narrative of the capture and subsequent sufferings of Mrs. Rachel Plummer, his daughter, during a captivity of twenty-one months among the Comanche Indians, etc. 18 mo, pp. 95-35, boards. Louisville, 1844.

In this book she tells the last she saw of Cynthia Ann and John Parker. She died on the nineteenth of February, 1839, just one year after reaching home. As a remarkable coincidence, in may be stated that she was born on the nineteenth, married on the nineteenth, captured on the nineteenth, released on the nineteenth, reached Independence on the nineteenth, arrived at home on the nineteenth, and died on the nineteenth of the month.

Her son, James Pratt Plummer, after six long and weary years of captivity and suffering, during which time he had lived among many different tribes and traveled several thousand miles, was ransomed and taken to Fort Gibson late in 1842, and reached home in February, 1843, in charge of his grandfather. He became a respected citizen of Anderson county. Both he and his father are now dead.

This still left in captivity Cynthia and John Parker, who, as subsequently learned, were held by separate bands. The brother and sister thus separated, gradually forgot the language, manners and customs of their own people, and became thorough Comanches as the long years stole slowly away. How long the camera of their young brains retained impressions of the old home within the fort, and the loved faces of their pale faced kindred, no one knows; though it would appear that the fearful massacre should have stamped an impress indelible while life continued. But the young mind, as the twig, is inclined by present circumstances, and often forced in a way wholly foreign to its native and original bent.

John grew up with the semi-nude Comanche boys of his own age, and played at "hunter" and "warrior" with pop guns made of the elder stem, or bows and arrows, and often flushed the chaparal for hare and grouse, or entrapped the finny denizens of the mountain brooks with the many peculiar and ingenious devices of the wild man for securing for his repast the toothsome trout which abounds so plentifully in that elevated and delightful region, so long inhabited by the lordly Comanches.

When just arrived at manhood John accompanied a raiding party down the Rio Grande and into Mexico. Among the captives taken was a young Mexican girl of great beauty, to whom the young warrior felt his heart go out. The affection was reciprocated on the part of the fair Dona Juanita, and the two were soon engaged to be married, so soon as they should arrive at the Comanche village. Each day as the cavalcade moved leisurely, but steadily along, the lovers could be seen riding together, and discussing the anticipated pleasures of connubial life, when suddenly John was prostrated by a violent attack of smallpox. The cavalcade could not tarry, and so it was decided that the poor fellow should be left all alone in the vast Llano Esticado to die or recover, as fate decreed. But the little Aztec beauty refused to leave her lover, insisting on her captors allowing her to remain and take care of him. To this the Indians reluctantly consented. With Juanita to nurse and cheer him up, John lingered, lived, and ultimately recovered, when; with as little ceremony, perhaps, as consummated the nuptials of the first pair in Eden, they assumed the matrimonial relation, and Dona Juanita's predilections for the customs and comforts of civilization were sufficiently strong to induce her lord to abandon the wild and nomatic life of a savage for the comforts to be found in a straw thatched jackal. "They settled," says Mr. Thrall, the historian of Texas, "on a stock ranch in the far west." When the civil war broke out John Parker joined a Mexican company in the Confederate service, and was noted for his gallantry and daring. He, however, refused to leave the soil of Texas, and would, under no circumstances, cross the Sabine into Louisiana. He was still on his ranch across the Rio Grande a few years ago, but up to that time had never visited any of his relatives in Texas.

Of Cynthia Ann Parker (we will anticipate the thread of the narrative). Four long years have elapsed since she was cruelly torn from a mother's embrace and carried into captivity. During this time no tidings have been received of her. Many efforts have been made to ascertain her whereabouts, or fate, but without success; when, in 1840, Colonel Len. Williams, an old and honored Texan, Mr. —— Stoat, a trader, and a Delaware Indian guide, named Jack Harry, packed mules with goods and engaged in an expedition of private traffic with the Indians.

On the Canadian river they fell in with Pa-ha-u-ka's band of Comanches, with whom they were peaceably conversant.

And with this tribe was Cynthia Ann Parker, who, from the day of her capture, had never seen a white person. She was then about fourteen years of age and had been with the Indians nearly five years.

Colonel Williams found the Indian into whose family she had been adopted, and proposed to redeem her, but the Comanche told him all the goods he had would not ransom her, and at the same time "the fierceness of his countenance," says Colonel Williams, "warned me of danger of further mention of the subject." But old Pa-ha-u-ka prevailed upon him to let them see her. She came and sat down by the root of a tree, and while their presence was doubtless a happy event to the poor stricken captive, who, in her doleful captivity, had endured everything but death, she refused to speak a word. As she sat there, musing, perhaps, of distant relatives and friends, and the bereavements at the beginning and progress of her distress, they employed every persuasive art to evoke some expression. They told her of her playmates and relatives, and asked what message she would send them, but she had doubtless been commanded to silence, and with no hope or prospect to return, was afraid to appear sad or dejected, and by a stoical effort, in order to prevent future bad treatment, put the best face possible on the matter. But the anxiety of her mind was betrayed by the perceptive quiver of her lips, showing that she was not insensible to the common feelings of humanity.

As the years rolled by, Cynthia Ann speedily developed the charms of womanhood, as with the dusky maidens of her companionship she performed the menial offices of drudgery to which savage custom consigns women, or practiced those little arts of coquetry maternal to the female heart, whether she be a belle of Madison Square, attired in the most elaborate toilet from the elite bazars of Paris, or the half naked savages, with matted locks and claw like nails.

Doubtless the heart of more than one warrior was pierced by the Ulyssean darts from her laughing eyes, or charmed by the silvery ripple of her joyous laughter, and laid at her feet the game taken after a long and arduous chase among the Antelope hills. Among the number whom her budding charms brought to her shrine was Peta Nocona, a Coman-

che war chief, in prowess and renown the peer of the
famous and redoubtable Big Foot, who fell in a desperately
co. ,ted hand to hand encounter with the veteran ranger
and Indian fighter, Captain S. P. Ross, now living at Waco,
and whose wonderful exploits and deeds of daring furnished
themes for song and story at the war dance, the council and
the camp fire.

Cynthia Ann, stranger now to every word of her mother
tongue save her own name, became the bride of Peta Nocona, performing for her imperious lord all the slavish
offices which savageism and Indian custom assigns as the
duty of a wife. She bore him children, and, we are assured, loved him with a species of fierce passion and wifely
devotion; "for, some fifteen years after her capture," says
Victor M. Rose, "a party of white hunters, including some
friends of her family, visited the Comanche encampment
on the upper Canadian, and, recognizing Cynthia Ann—
probably through the medium of her name alone, sounded
her as to the disagreeableness of a return to her people and
the haunts of civilization. She shook her head in a sorrowful negative, and pointed to her little, naked barbarians
sporting at her feet, and to the great, greasy, lazy buck
sleeping in the shade near at hand, the locks of a score of
scalps dangling at his belt, and whose first utterance upon
arousing would be a stern command to his meek, pale faced
wife. Though, in truth, exposure to the sun and air had
browned the complexion of Cynthia Ann almost as intensely
as those of the native daughters of the plains and forest.

"She retained but the vaguest remembrance of her people
—as dim and flitting as the phantoms of a dream; she was
accustomed now to the wild life she led, and found in its re-
pulsive features charms which 'upper tendom' would have
proven totally deficient in. 'I am happily wedded,' she
said to these visitors. 'I love my husband, who is good and
kind, and my little ones, who, too, are his, and I can not
forsake them!' "

* * * * * * * * * * * *

What were the incidents in the savage life of these children which in after times became the land marks in the
train of memory, and which, with civilized creatures, serves
as incentives to reminiscence?

"Doubtless," says Mr. Rose, "Cynthia Ann arryed herself in the calico borne from the sacking of Linnville, and fled with the discomfited Comanches up the Guadalupe and Colorado, at the ruthless march of John H. Moore, Ben McCulloch and their hardy rangers. They must have been present at the battle of Antelope Hills, on the Canadian, when Colonel John S. Ford —"Old Rip,"— and Captain S. P. Ross encountered the whole force of the Comanches; perhaps John Parker was an actor in that celebrated battle; and again at the Wichita.

"Theirs must have been a hard and unsatisfactory life; the Comanches are veritable Ishmaelites, their hands being raised against all men, and every man's hand against them. Literally, 'eternal vigilance was the price of liberty' with them, and of life itself. Every night the dreaded surprise was sought to be guarded against; and every copse was scanned for the anticipated ambuscade while upon the march. Did they flaunt the blood drabbled scalps of helpless whites in fiendish glee, and assist at the cruel torture of the unfortunate prisoners that fell into their hands? Alas! forgetful of their race and tongue, they were thorough savages, and acted in all particulars just as their Indian comrades did. Memory was stored but with the hardships and the cruelties of the life about them; and the stolid indifference of mere animal existence furnishes no finely wrought springs for the rebound of reminiscence."

* * * * * * * * * *

The year 1846, one decade from the fall of Parker's fort, witnessed the end of the Texan republic, in whose councils Isaac Parker served as a senator, and the blending of the Lone Star with the galaxy of the great constellation of the American Union—during which time many efforts were made to ascertain definitely the whereabouts of the captives, as an indispensable requisite to their reclamation; sometimes by solitary scouts and spies, sometimes through the medium of negotiation, and sometimes by waging direct war against their captors, but all to no avail.

* * * * * * * *

Another decade passes away, and the year 1856 arrives. The hardy pioneers have pushed the frontier of civilization far to the north and west, driving the Indian and the buffalo

before them. The scene of Parker's fort is now in the heart
of a dense population; farms, towns, churches and school
houses lie along the path by which the Indians marched
from their camp at the "water hole" in that bloody May of
1836. Isaac Parker is now a representative in the Legislature of the State of Texas. It is now twenty-nine years
since the battle of San Jacinto; twenty years since John
and Cynthia Ann Parker were borne into captivity worse
than death; the last gun of the Mexican war rung out its
last report over the conquered capital of Mexico ten long
years ago; but John and Cynthia Ann Parker have sent no
tokens to their so long anxious friends that they even live.
Alas! time even blunts the edge of anxiety, and sets bounds
alike to the anguish of man, as well as to his hopes.

The punishment of Prometheus is not of this world!

THE BATTLE OF ANTELOPE HILLS.

Brave Colonel Ford, the commander and ranger bold,
On the South Canadian did the Comanches behold,
On the twelfth of May, at rising of sun,
The armies did meet and battle begun.

The battle of the South Canadian, or "Antelope Hills,"
fought in 1858, was probably one of the most splendid scenic
exhibitions of Indian warfare ever enacted upon Texas soil.
This was the immemorial home of the Comanches; here they
sought refuge from their marauding expeditions into Texas
and Mexico; and here, in their veritable city of refuge,
should the adventurous and daring rangers seek them, it
was certain that they would be encountered in full force.

Pohebits Quasho, Iron Jacket, so called from the fact that
he wore a coat of scale mail, a curious piece of armor, which
doubtless had been stripped from the body of some unfortunate Spanish knight slain, perhaps, a century before—
some chevalier who followed Coronado, De Leon, La Salle—
was the war chief. He was a big medicine man, or pro-
phet, and claimed to be invulnerable to balls and arrows
aimed at his person, as by a necromantic puff of his breath
the missives were diverted from their course, or charmed,
and made to fall harmless at his feet.

CYNTHIA ANN PARKER.

Peta Nocona, the young and daring husband of Cynthia Ann Parker, was in command.

About the first of May, in the year above named, Colonel John S. Ford ("Old Rip,"), at the head of one hundred Texan rangers, comprising such leaders as Captain S. P. Ross (the father of General L. S. Ross), W. A. Pitts, Preston, Tankersley, and a contingent of one hundred and eleven Tonkawa Indians, the latter commanded by their celebrated chief, Placido—so long the faithful and implicitly trusted friend of the whites—marched on a campaign against the marauding Comanches, determined to follow them up to their stronghold amid the hills of the Canadian river, and if possible surprise them and inflict a severe and lasting chastisement.

After a toilsome march of several days the Tonkawa scouts reported that they were in the immediate vicinity of the Comanche encampment. The Comanches, though proverbial for their sleepless vigilance, were unsuspicious of danger; and so unsuspected was the approach of the rangers that on the day preceding the battle Colonel Ford and Captain Ross stood in the old road from Fort Smith to Santa Fe, just north of the Rio Negro, or False Washita, and watched through their glasses the Comanches running buffalo in the valleys still more to the north. That night the Tonkawa spies completed the hazardous mission of locating definitely the position of the enemy's encampment. The next morning (May 12) the rangers and reserve, or friendly Indians, marched before sun rise to the attack.

Placido claimed for his red warriors the privilege of wreaking vengeance upon their hereditary enemies. His request was granted, and the Tonkawas effected a complete surprise. The struggle was short, sharp and sanguinary. The women and children were made prisoners, but not a Comanche brave surrendered. Their savage pride preferred death to the restraints and humiliations of captivity. Not a single warrior escaped to bear the sorrowful tidings of this destructive engagement to their people.

A short time after the sun had lighted the tops of the hills, the rangers came in full view of the hostile camp, pitched in one of the picturesque valleys of the Canadian, and on the opposite side of the stream, in the immediate vicinity of the famous Antelope Hills.

The panorama thus presented to the view of the rangers was beautiful in the extreme, and their pent up enthusiasm found vent in a shout of exultation, which was speedily suppressed by Colonel Ford.   Just at this moment a solitary Comanche was descried riding southward, evidently heading for the village which Placido had so recently destroyed. He was wholly unconscious of the proximity of an enemy. Instant pursuit was now made; he turned and fled at full speed toward the main camp across the Canadian, closely followed by the rangers.   He dashed across the stream, and thus revealed to his pursuers the locality of a safe ford across the miry and almost impassable river.   He rushed into the village beyond, sounding the notes of alarm; and soon the Comanche warriors presented a bold front of battle line between their women and children and the advancing rangers.   After a few minutes occupied in forming line of battle both sides were arrayed in full force and effect.   The friendly Indians were placed on the right and thrown a little forward.   Colonel Ford's object was to deceive the Comanches as to the character of the attacking force and as to the quality of arms they possessed.   ·

Pohebits Quasho, arrayed in all the trappings of his war toggery—coat of mail, shield, bow and lance, completed by a head dress decorated with feathers and long red flannel streamers and besmeared in war paint—gaily dashed about on his war horse midway of the opposing lines, delivering taunts and challenges to the whites.   As the old chief dashed to and fro a number of rifles were discharged at him in point blank range without any affect whatever, which seeming immunity to death encouraged his warriors greatly and induced even some of the more superstitious among the rangers to enquire within themselves if it were possible that Old Iron Jacket really bore a charmed life?   Followed by a few of his braves he now bore down upon the rangers, described a few charmed circles, gave a few necromantic puffs with his breath and let fly several arrows at Colonel Ford, Captain Ross and Chief Placido, receiving their fire without harm.   But as he approached the line of the Tonkawas, a rifle directed by the steady nerve and unerring eye of one of their number, Jim Pockmark, brought the Big Medicine to the dust. The shot was a mortal one. The fallen chieftain was instantly surrounded by his braves, but the spirit of the conjuring brave had taken its flight to the happy hunting grounds.

These incidents occupied but a brief space of time, when the order to charge was given; and then ensued one of the grandest assaults ever made against the Comanches. The enthusiastic shouts of the rangers, and the triumphant yell of their red allies greeted the welcome order. It was responded to by the defiant "war whoop" of the Comanches, and in those virgin hills, remote from civilization, the saturnalia of battle was inaugurated. The shouts of enraged combatants, the wail of women, the piteous cries of terrified children, the howling of frightened dogs, the deadly reports of rifle and revolver, constituted a discordant confusion of infernal noise.

The conflict was sharp and quick—a charge; a momentary exchange of rifle and arrow shots, and the heart rending wail of discomfiture and dismay, and the beaten Comanches abandoned their lodges and camp to the victors, and began a disorderly retreat. But sufficient method was observed to take advantage of each grove of timber, each hill and ravine, to make a stand against their pursuers, and thus enable the women and children to make their escape. The noise of battle now diverged from a common center like the spokes of a wheel, and continued to greet the ear for several hours, gradually growing fainter as the pursuit disappeared in the distance.

But another division, under the vigilant Peta Nocona, was soon marching through the hills north of the Canadian, to the rescue. Though ten miles distant, his quick ear had caught the first sounds of battle; and soon he was riding, with Cynthia Ann by his side, at the head of five hundred warriors.

About one o'clock of the afternoon the last of the rangers returned from the pursuit of Pohebits Quasho's discomfited braves, just in time to anticipate this threatened attack.

As Captain Ross (who was one of the last to return) rode up, he inquired "What hour of the morning is it Colonel?" "Morning!" exclaimed Colonel Ford, "it is one o'clock of

the afternoon." So unconscious is one of the flight of time
during an engagement, that the work of hours seems comprised within the space of a few moments.

"Hello! what are you in line of battle for?" asked Ross.
"Look at the hills there, and you will see," calmly replied
Colonel Ford, pointing to the hills some half a mile distant,
behind which the forces of Peta Nocona were visible; an
imposing line of five hundred warriors drawn up in battle
array.

Colonel Ford had with two hundred and twenty-one men
fought and routed over four hundred Comanches, and now
he was confronted by a stronger force, fresh from their
village still higher up on the Canadian. They had come to
drive the "pale faces" and their hated copper colored allies
from the captured camp, to retake prisoners, to retake over
four hundred head of horses and an immense quantity of
plunder. They did not fancy the defiant state of preparations awaiting them in the valley, however, and were waiting to avail themselves of some incautious movement on
the part of the rangers, when the wily Peta Nocona, with
his forces, would spring like a lion from his lair, and with
one combined and desperate effort, swoop down and anni-
hilate the enemy. But his antagonist was a soldier of too
much sagacity to allow any advantage to a vigilant foe.

The two forces remained thus contemplating each other
for over an hour; during which time a series of operations
ensued between single combatants illustrative of the Indian
mode of warfare, and the marked difference between the
nomadic Comanche and his semi-civilized congeners, the
Tonchua. The Tonchuas took advantage of ravines, trees
and other natural shelter. Their arms were rifles and "six-
shooters." The Comanches came to the attack with shield
and bow and lance, mounted on gaily caparisoned and
prancing steeds, and flaunting feathers and all the gor-
geous display incident to savage finery and pomp. They
are probably the most expert equestrians in the world. A
Comanche warrior would gaily canter to a point half way
between the opposing lines, yell a defiant war whoop, and
shake his shield. This was a challenge to single combat.

Several of the friendly Indians who accepted such challenges were placed *hors de combat* by their more expert

adversaries, and in consequence Colonel Ford ordered them to decline the savage banters, much to the dissatisfaction of Placido, who had conducted himself throughout the series of engagements with the bearing of a savage hero.

Says Colonel Ford: "In these combats the mind of the spectator was vividly carried back to the days of chivalry; the jousts and tournaments of knights; and to the concomitants of those scenic exhibitions of gallantry. The feats of horsemanship were splendid, the lances and shields were used with great dexterity, and the whole performance was a novel show to civilized man."

Colonel Ford now ordered Placido, with a part of his warriors, to advance in the direction of the enemy, and if possible, draw them in the valley, so as to afford the rangers an opportunity to charge them. This had the desired effect, and the rangers were ready to deliver a charge, when it was discovered that the friendly Indians had removed the white badges from their heads because they served as targets for the Comanches; consequently, the rangers were unable to distinguish friend from foe. This necessitated the entire withdrawal of the Indians. The Comanches witnessed these preparations, and now commenced to recoil. The rangers advanced; the trot, the gallop, the headlong charge followed in rapid succession. Lieutenant Nelson made a skillful movement, and struck the enemy's left flank. The Comanche line was broken. A running fight for three or four miles ensued. The enemy was driven back wherever he made a stand. The most determined resistance was made in a timbered ravine. Here one of Placido's warriors was killed, and one of the rangers, young George W. Paschal, wounded. The Comanches left some dead upon the spot, and had several more wounded. After routing them at this point, the rangers continued to pursue them some distance, intent upon taking the women and children prisoners; but Peta Nocona, by the exercise of those commanding qualities which had often before signalized his conduct on the field, succeeded in covering their retreat, and thus allowing them to escape. It was now about four p. m.; both horses and men were almost entirely exhausted, and Colonel Ford ordered a halt and returned to the village. Brave old Placido and his warriors fought like so many demons. It was difficult to restrain them, so anxious were they to wreak vengeance upon the Comanches. In all of these engagements seventy-five Comanches bit the dust. The loss of the rangers was small—two killed and five or six wounded.

The trophies of Pohebits Quasho, including his lance, bow, shield, head dress and the celebrated coat of scale mail, was deposited by Colonel Ford in the State archives at Austin, where, doubtless, they may yet be seen, as curious relics of bygone days.

The lamented old chief, Placido, fell a victim to the revengeful Comanches during the latter part of the great civil war between the North and South, being assassinated by a party of his enemies on the reservation, near Fort Sill. The venerable John Henry Brown, some years since, paid a merited tribute to his memory through the columns of the Dallas *Herald*. Of Placido it has been said that he was the "soul of honor," and "never betrayed a trust." That he was brave to the utmost, we have only to refer to his numerous exploits during his long and gratuitous service on our frontiers. He was implicitly trusted by Burleson and other partisan leaders, and rendered invaluable services in behalf of the early Texan pioneers; in recognition of which he never received any reward of a material nature, beyond a few paltry pounds of gun powder and salt. Imperial Texas should rear a monument commemorative of his memory. He was the more than Tammany of Texas! But I am digressing from the narrative proper.

"Doubtless," says Rose, "Cynthia Ann rode from this ill starred field with her infant daughter pressed to her bosom, and her sons—two youths of about ten and twelve years of age—at her side, as fearful of capture at the hands of the hated whites, as years ago, immediately after the massacre of Parker's fort, she had been anxious for the same."

GENERAL L. S. ROSS — BATTLE OF THE WICHITA.

It is not our purpose, in this connection, to assume the role of biographer to so distinguished a personage as is the Chevalier Bayard of Texas—General Lawrence Sullivan Ross. That task should be left to an abler pen; and, besides, it would be impossible to do anything like justice to the romantic, adventurous, and altogether splendid and brilliant career of the brave and daring young ranger who rescued Cynthia Ann Parker from captivity, at least, in the circumscribed limits of a brief biographical sketch, such as we shall be compelled to confine ourself to; yet, some brief mention of his services and exploits as a ranger captain, by way of an introduction to the reader beyond the limits of Texas, where his name and fame are as household words, is deemed necessary; hence we beg leave here to give a brief sketch of his life.

"Texas, though her annals be brief," says the author of Ross's Texas Brigade, "counts upon her roll of honor the names of many heroes, both living and dead. Their splendid services are the inestimable legacies of the past and present, to the future. Of the latter, it is the high prerogative of the State to embalm their names and memories as perpetual examples to excite the generous emulation of the Texan youth to the latest posterity. Of the former, it is our pleasant province to accord them those honors which their services in so eminent a degree entitle them to receive. Few lands since the days of the Scottish Chiefs have furnished material upon which to predicate a Douglas, a Wallace, or a Ravenswood; and the adventures of chivalric enterprise, arrant quest of danger, and the personal combat were relegated, together with the knight's armorial trappings, to the rusty archives of Tower and Pantheon, until the Comanche Bedouins of the Texan plains tendered in bold defiance the savage gauntlet to the pioneer knights of progress and civilization. And though her heraldic roll glows with the names of a Houston, a Rusk, Lamar, McCulloch, Hays, Chevellier, which illumine the pages of her history with an effulgence of glory, Texas never nurtured on her maternal bosom a son of more filial devotion, of more loyal patriotism, or indomitable will to do and dare, than L. S. Ross."

Lawrence Sullivan Ross was born in the village of Bentonsport, Ohio, in the year 1838. His father, Captain S. P. Ross, immigrated to Texas in 1839, casting his fortunes with the struggling pioneers who were blazing the pathway of civilization into the wilds of a *terra incognita*, as Texas then was.

"Captain S. P. Ross was, for many years, pre-eminent as leader against the implacable savages, who made frequent incursions into the settlements. The duty of repelling these forays usually devolved upon Captain Ross and his neighbors, and for many years his company constituted the only bulwark of safety between the feeble colonist and the scalping knife. The rapacity and treachery of his Comanche and Kiowa foes demanded of Captain Ross sleepless vigilance, acute sagacity and a will that brooked no obstacle or danger. It was in the performance of this arduous duty that he slew, in single combat, Big Foot, a Comanche chief of great prowess, and who was for many years the scourge of the early Texas frontier. The services of Captain S. P. Ross are still held in grateful remembrance by the descendants of his compatriots, and his memory will never be suffered to pass away while Texans feel a pride in the sterling worth of Texas's greatness and glory." (Vide Ross's Texas Brigade, p. 158.)

The following incident, as illustrative of the character and spirit of the man and times, is given: "On one occasion Captain Ross, who had been visiting a neighbor, was returning home, afoot, accompanied by his little son, Sul, as the general was familiarly called. When within half a mile of his house he was surrounded by fifteen or twenty mounted Comanche warriors, who commenced an immediate attack. The captain, athletic and swift of foot, threw his son on his back and outran their ponies to the house, escaping unhurt amid a perfect shower of arrows."

Such were among the daily experiences of the child, and with such impressions stamped upon the infantile mind, it was but natural that the enthusiastic spirit of the ardent youth should lead him to such adventures upon the war path, similar to those that had signalized his honored father's prowess upon so many occasions.

Hence we find Sul Ross, during vacation from his studies at Florence, Wesleyan University, Alabama, though a beardless boy, scarcely twenty years of age, in command of a contingent of one hundred and thirty-five friendly Indians, cooperating with the United States cavalry under the dashing Major Earl Van Dorn, in a campaign against the Comanches.

CAPTAIN L. S. ROSS.

32B

* * * * * * * *

Notwithstanding the severe chastisement that had been inflicted on the Comanches at Antelope Hills they soon renewed their hostilities, committing many depredations and murders during the summer of 1858.

Early in September Major Van Dorn received orders from General Twiggs to equip four companies, including Ross's red warriors, and go out on a scouting expedition against the hostile Indians. This he did, penetrating the heart of the Indian country where he proceeded to build a stockade, placing within it all the pack mules, extra horses and supplies, which was left in charge of the infantry.

Ross's faithful Indian scouts soon reported the discovery of a large Comanche village near the Wichita Mountains, about ninety miles away. The four companies, attended by the spies, immediately set out for the village, and after a fatiguing march of thirty-six hours, causing the men to be continuously in the saddle the latter sixteen hours of the ride, arrived in the immediate vicinity of the Indian camp just at daylight on the morning of October 1.

A reconnoissance showed that the wily Comanches were not apprehensive of an attack and were sleeping in fancied security. The horses of the tribe, which consisted of a caballada of about five hundred head, were grazing near the outskirts of the village. Major Van Dorn directed Captain Ross, at the head of his Indians, to round up the horses and drive them from the camp, which was effected speedily, and thus the Comanches were forced to fight on foot—a proceeding extremely harrowing to the proud warrior's feelings.

" Just as the sun was peeping above the eastern horizon," says Victor M. Rose, whose graphic narrative we again quote, "Van Dorn charged the upper end of the village, while Ross's command, in conjunction with a detachment of United States cavalry, charged the lower. The village was strung out along the banks of a branch for several hundred yards. The morning was very foggy, and after a few moments of firing the smoke and fog became so dense that objects at but a short distance could be distinguished only with great difficulty. The Comanches fought with absolute desperation, and contended for every advantage, as their women and children, and all their possessions, were in peril.

"A few moments after the engagement became general, Ross discovered a number of Comanches running down to the branch, about one hundred and fifty yards from the village, and concluded that they were beating a retreat. Immediately Ross, Lieutenant Van Camp, of the United States army; Alexander, a regular soldier, and one Caddo Indian, of Ross's command, ran to the point with the intention of intercepting them. Arriving, it was discovered that the fugitives were women and children. In a moment another posse of women and children came running immediately past the squad of Ross, who, discovering a little white girl among the number, made his Caddo Indian grab her as she was passing. The little pale face, apparently about eight years of age, was badly frightened at finding herself a captive to a strange Indian and stranger white men, and was hard to manage at first.

"Ross now discovered, through the fog and smoke of the battle, that a band of some twenty-five Comanche warriors had cut his small party off from communication with Van Dorn and were bearing immediately down upon them. They shot Lieutenant Van Camp through the heart, killing him ere he could fire his double barrelled shot gun. Alexander, the United States cavalryman, was likewise shot down before he could fire his gun, a rifle. Ross was armed with a Sharp's rifle and attempted to fire upon the exultant red devils, but the cap snapped. Mohee, a Comanche warrior, seized Alexander's rifle and shot Ross down. The indomitable young ranger fell upon the side on which his pistol was borne, and though partially paralyzed by the shot, he turned himself, and was getting his pistol out when Mohee drew his butcher knife and started towards his prostrate foe, some fifteen feet away, with the evident design of stabbing and scalping him. He made but a few steps, however, when one of his companions cried out something in the Comanche tongue, which was a signal to the band, and they broke away in confusion. Mohee ran about twenty steps when a wire cartridge, containing nine buck shot. fired from a gun in the hands of Lieutenant James Majors afterwards a Confederate general), struck him between the shoulders, and he fell forward on his face, dead. Mohee was an old acquaintance of Ross, the latter having seen him frequently at nis father's post on the frontier, and recognized him as soon as their eyes met. The faithful Caddo held on to the little girl throughout this desperate melee, and, strange to relate, neither were harmed. The Caddo, doubtless, owed his escape to the fact that the Comanches were fearful of wounding or killing the little girl. This whole scene transpired in a few moments, and Captain N. G. Evans's company of the Second United States cavalry, had taken possession of the lower end of the Comanche village and Major Van Dorn held the upper, and the Comanches ran into the hills and brush; not, however, before an infuriated Comanche shot the gallant Van Dorn with an arrow. Van Dorn fell and it was supposed that he was mortally wounded. In consequence of their wounds the two chieftains were compelled to remain on the battle ground five or six days. After the expiration of this time Ross's Indians made a litter after their fashion, borne between two gentle mules, and in it placed their heroic and beloved boy captain, and set out for the settlements at Fort Belknap. When this mode of conveyance would become too painful, by reason of the rough, broken nature of the country, these brave Caddos—whose race and history are but synonyms of courage and fidelity— would vie with each other in bearing the burden upon their own shoulders. At Camp Radziminski, occupied by United States forces, an ambulance was obtained and the remainder of the journey made with comparative comfort. Major Van Dorn was also conveyed to Radziminski. He speedily recovered of his wound and soon made another brilliant campaign against the Comanches, as we shall see further on. Ross recovered sufficiently in a few weeks so as to be able to return to college at Florence, Alabama, where he completed his studies and graduated in 1859."

This was the battle of the Wichita Mountains, a hotly contested and most desperate hand to hand fight in which the two gallant and dashing young officers, Ross and Van Dorn, were severely wounded. The loss of the whites was five and several wounded. The loss of the Comanches was eighty or ninety warriors killed, many wounded, and several captured; besides losing all their horses, camp equipage, supplies, etc.

The return of this victorious little army was hailed with

enthusiastic rejoicing and congratulation, and the Wichita
fight, Van Dorn and Ross were the themes of song and story
for many years along the borders and in the halls and ban-
queting rooms of the cities, and the martial music of the
"Wichita March" resounded through the plains of Texas
wherever the Second Cavalry encamped or rode off on scouts
in after years.

The little girl captive—of whose parentage or history
nothing could be ascertained, though strenuous efforts were
made—was christened "Lizzie Ross," in honor of Miss Lizzie Tinsley, daughter of Dr. D. R. Tinsley, of Waco, to
whom Ross at that time was engaged, and afterwards married—May, 1861.

Of Lizzie Ross, it can be said that, in her career, is afforded a thorough verification of Lord Byron's saying:
"Truth is stranger than fiction!" She was adopted by her
brave and generous captor, properly reared and educated,
and became a beautiful and accomplished woman. Here
were sufficient romance and vicissitude, in the brief career
of a little maiden, to have turned the "roundelays" of
"troubadour and meunesauger." A solitary lily, blooming
amidst the wildest grasses of the desert plains. A little Indian girl in all save the Caucasian's conscious stamp of
superiority. Torn from home, perhaps, amid the heart rending scenes of rapine, torture and death. A stranger to race
and lineage—stranger even to the tongue in which a mother's lullaby was breathed. Affiliating with these wild Ishmaelites of the prairie—a Comanche in all things save the
intuitive premonition *that she was not of them!* Finally
redeemed from a captivity worse than death by a knight
entitled to rank, for all time in the history of Texas, *"primus
inter pores."* (Vide Ross Texas Brigade, page 178.)

Lizzie Ross, accompanied General Ross's mother, on a
visit to the State of California, a few years since, and while
there became the wife of a wealthy merchant near Los Angeles, where she now resides.

Such is the romantic story of "Lizzie Ross"—a story that
derives additional interest because of the fact of its absolute truth in all respects.

The following letter from General L. S. Ross, touching
on the battle of the Wichita Mountains and the re-capture
of "Lizzie Ross," is here appropriately inserted:

LIZZIE ROSS.

WACO, TEXAS, July 12, 1884.

MR. JAMES T. DE SHIELDS—*Dear Sir:*—My father could give you reliable data enough to fill a volume. I send you photograph of Cynthia Ann Parker, with notes relating to her on back of photo. On the twenty-eighth of October, 1858, I had a battle with the Comanches at Wichita Mountains, and there re-captured a little white girl about eight years old, whose parentage, nor indeed any trace of her kindred, was ever found. I adopted, reared, and educated her, giving her the name of Lizzie Ross; the former name being in honor of the young lady—Lizzie Tinsley—to whom I was then engaged and afterwards married—May, 1861.

Lizzie Ross grew to womanhood, and married a wealthy merchant living near Los Angeles, California, where she now resides. See History of Ross's Brigade, by Victor M. Rose, and published by Courier-Journal, for a full and graphic description of the battle and other notable incidents. I could give you many interesting as well as thrilling adventures of self and father's family with the Indians in the early settlement of the country. He can give you more information than any living Texan, touching the Indian character, having been their agent and warm and trusted friend, in whom they had confidence. My early life was one of constant danger from their forays, and I was twice in their hands and at their mercy, as well as the other members of my father's family. But I am just now too busy with my farm matters to give you such data as would subserve your purpose. Yours truly,   L. S. ROSS.

BATTLE OF PEASE RIVER—CYNTHIA ANN PARKER.

For some time after Ross's victory at the Wichita mountains the Comanches were less hostile, seldom penetrating far down into the settlements. But in 1859–60, the condition of the frontier was again truly deplorable. The people were obliged to stand in a continued posture of defense, and were in continual alarm and hazard of their lives, never daring to stir abroad unarmed, for small bodies of savages, quick sighted and accustomed to perpetual watchfulness, hovered on the outskirts, and springing from behind bush or rock, surprised his enemy before he was aware of danger, and sent tidings of his presence in the fatal blow, and after execution of the bloody work, by superior knowledge of the country and rapid movements, safely retired to their inaccessible deserts.

In the autumn of 1860 the indomitable and fearless Peta Nocona led a raiding party of Comanches through Parker county, so named in honor of the family of his wife, Cynthia Ann, committing great depredations as they passed through. The venerable Isaac Parker was at that time a resident of Weatherford, the county seat; and little did he imagine that the chief of the ruthless savages who spread desolation and death on every side as far as their arms could reach, was the husband of his long lost niece; and that the commingled blood of the murdered Parkers and the atrocious Comanche now coursed in the veins of a second generation —bound equally by the ties of consanguinity to murderer and murdered; that the son of Peta Nocona and Cynthia Ann Parker would become the chief of the proud Comanches, whose boast it is that their constitutional settlement of government is the purest democracy ever originated and administered among men. It certainly conserved the object of its institution—the protection and happiness of the people—for a longer period, and much more satisfactorily, than has that of any other Indian tribe. The Comanches claimed a superiority over the other Texan tribes; and they unquestionably were more intelligent and courageous. The reservation policy —necessary though it be—brings them all to an abject level, the plane of lazy beggars and thieves. The Comanche is the most qualified by nature for receiving education and for adapting himself to the requirements of civilization of all the southern tribes, not excepting even the Cherokees, with their churches, school houses and farms. The Comanches, after waging an unceasing war for nearly fifty years against the United States, Texas and Mexico, still number sixteen thousand souls, a far better showing than any other tribe can make, though not one but has enjoyed privileges to which the Comanche was a stranger. It is a shame to the civilization of the age that a people so susceptible of a high degree of development should be allowed to grovel in the depths of heathenism and savagery. But we are digressing.

The loud and clamorous cries of the settlers along the frontier for protection induced the government to organize and send out a regiment under Colonel M. T. Johnson, to take the field for public defense. But these efforts proved of small service. The expedition, though at great expense to the State, failed to find an Indian until returning, the command was followed by the wily Comanches, their horses stampeded at night. and most of the men compelled to reach the settlements on foot, under great suffering and exposure.

Captain "Sul" Ross, who had just graduated from Florence Wesleyan University, of Alabama, and returned to Texas, was commissioned a captain of rangers by Governor Sam Houston, and directed to organize a company of sixty men, with orders to repair to Fort Belknap, receive from Colonel Johnson all government property, as his regiment was disbanded, and take the field against the redoubtable Peta Nocona, and afford the frontier such protection as was possible from this small force. The necessity of vigorous measures soon became so pressing that Captain Ross determined to attempt to curb the insolence of these implacable enemies of Texas by following them into their fastnesses and carry the war into their own homes. In his graphic narration of this campaign, General L. S. Ross says: "As I could take but forty of my men from my post, I requested Captain N. G. Evans, in command of the United States troops at Camp Cooper to send me a detachment of the Second cavalry. We had been intimately connected on the Van Dorn campaign, during which I was the recipient of much kindness from Captain Evans while I was suffering from a severe wound received from an Indian in the battle of the Wichita. He promptly sent me a sergeant and twenty well mounted men. My force was still further augmented by some seventy volunteer citizens, under the command of the brave old frontiersman, Captain Jack Cureton, of Bosque county. These self sacrificing patriots, without the hope of pay or regard, left their defenseless homes and families to avenge the sufferings of the frontier people. With pack mules laden down with necessary supplies, the expedition marched for the Indian country.

On the eighteenth of December, 1860, while marching up Pease river, I had suspicions that Indians were in the vicinity, by reason of the buffalo that came running in great numbers from the north towards us, and while my command moved in the low ground, I visited all neighboring high points to make discoveries. On one of these sand hills I found four fresh pony tracks, and, being satisfied that Indian videttes had just gone, I galloped forward about a mile to a higher point, and, riding to the top, to my inexpressible surprise, found myself within two hundred yards of a Comanche village, located on a small stream winding around the base of the hill. It was a most happy circumstance that a piercing north wind was blowing, bearing with it clouds of sand, and my presence was unobserved and the surprise complete. By signaling my men as I stood concealed, they reached me without being discovered by the Indians, who were busy packing up, preparatory to a move. By this time the Indians mounted and moved off north across the level plain. My command, with the detachment of the Second cavalry, had outmarched and become separated from the citizen command, which left me about sixty men. In making disposition for attack, the sergeant and his twenty men were sent at a gallop, behind a chain of sand hills, to encompass them in and cut off their retreat, while with forty men I charged. The attack was so sudden that a considerable number were killed before they could prepare for defense. They fled precipitately right into the presence of the sergeant and his men. Here they met with a warm reception, and finding themselves completely encompassed, every one fled his own way, and was hotly pursued and hard pressed.

"The chief of the party, Peta Nocona, a noted warrior of great repute, with a young girl about fifteen years of age mounted on his horse behind him, and Cynthia Ann Parker, with a girl child about two years of age in her arms, and mounted on a fleet pony, fled together, while Lieutenant Tom Kelliheir and I pursued them. After running about a mile Killiheir ran up by the side of Cynthia's horse, and I was in the act of shooting when she held up her child and stopped. I kept on after the chief, and about half a mile further, when in about twenty yards of him I fired my pistol, striking the girl (whom I supposed to be a man, as she rode like one, and only her head was visible above the

buffalo robe with which she was wrapped) near the heart,
killing her instantly, and the same ball would have killed
both but for the shield of the chief, which hung down, covering his back. When the girl fell from the horse she pulled
him off also, but he caught on his feet, and before steady-
ing himself, my horse, running at full speed, was very
nearly upon top of him, when he was struck with an arrow,
which caused him to fall to pitching or 'bucking,' and it was
with great difficulty that I kept my saddle, and in the
meantime, narrowly escaped several arrows coming in quick
succession from the chief's bow. Being at such disadvantage he would have killed me in a few minutes but for a
random shot from my pistol (while I was clinging with my
left hand to the pommel of my saddle) which broke his
right arm at the elbow, completely disabling him. My horse
then became quiet, and I shot the chief twice through the
body, whereupon he deliberately walked to a small tree,
the only one in sight, and leaning against it, began to sing
a wild, weird song. At this time my Mexican servant, who
had once been a captive with the Comanches and spoke
their language fluently as his mother tongue, came up, in
company with two of my men. I then summoned the chief
to surrender, but he promptly treated every overture with
contempt, and signalized this declaration with a savage
attempt to thrust me with his lance which he held in his
left hand. I could only look upon him with pity and admiration. For, deplorable as was his situation, with no chance
of escape, his party utterly destroyed, his wife and child
captured in his sight, he was undaunted by the fate that
awaited him, and as he seemed to prefer death to life, I
directed the Mexican to end his misery by a charge of buckshot from the gun which he carried. Taking up his accou-
trements, which I subsequently sent to Governor Houston,
to be deposited in the archives at Austin, we rode back to
Cynthia Ann and Killiheir, and found him bitterly cursing
himself for having run his pet horse so hard after an 'old
squaw.' She was very dirty, both in her scanty garments
and person. But as soon as I looked on her face, I said:
'Why, Tom, this is a white woman, Indians do not have
blue eyes.' On the way to the village, where my men were
assembling with the spoils, and a large caballada of 'Indian

ponies,' I discovered an Indian boy about nine years of age, secreted in the grass. Expecting to be killed, he began crying, but I made him mount behind me, and carried him along. And when in after years I frequently proposed to send him to his people, he steadily refused to go, and died in McLennan county last year.

"After camping for the night Cynthia Ann kept crying, and thinking it was caused from fear of death at our hands, I had the Mexican tell her that we recognized her as one of our own people, and would not harm her. She said two of her boys were with her when the fight began, and she was distressed by the fear that they had been killed. It so happened, however, both escaped, and one of them, 'Quanah' is now a chief. The other died some years ago on the plains. I then asked her to give me the history of her life with the Indians, and the circumstances attending her capture by them, which she promptly did in a very sensible manner. And as the facts detailed corresponded with the massacre at Parker's Fort, I was impressed with the belief that she was Cynthia Ann Parker. Returning to my post, I sent her and child to the ladies at Cooper, where she could receive the attention her situation demanded, and at the same time despatched a messenger to Colonel Parker, her uncle, near Weatherford, and as I was called to Waco to meet Governor Houston, I left directions for the Mexican to accompany Colonel Parker to Cooper in the capacity of interpreter. When he reached there, her identity was soon discovered to Colonel Parker's entire satisfaction and great happiness." And thus was fought the battle of Pease river, between a superior force of Comanches under the implacable chief, Peta Nocona on the one side, and sixty rangers led by their youthful commander, Captain L. S. Ross, on the other. Ross, sword in hand, led the furious rush of the rangers; and in the desperate encounter of "war to the knife" which ensued, nearly all the warriors bit the dust.

So signal a victory had never before been gained over the fierce and war like Comanches; and never since that fatal December day in 1860 have they made any military demonstrations at all commensurate with the fame of their proud campaigns in the past. The great Comanche confederacy was forever broken. The incessant and sanguinary war which had been waged for more than thirty years was now virtually at an end. The blow was a most decisive one; as sudden and irresistible as a thunder bolt, and as remorseless and crushing as the hand of Fate. It was a short but desperate conflict. Victory trembled in the balance. A determined charge, accompanied by a simultaneous fire from the solid phalanx of yelling rangers, and the Comanches beat a hasty retreat, leaving many dead and wounded upon the field. Espying the chief and a chosen few riding at full speed, and in a different direction from the other fugitives, from the ill starred field, Ross quickly pursued. Divining his purpose, the watchful Peta Nocona rode at full speed, but was soon overtaken, when the two chiefs engaged in a personal encounter, which must result in the death of one or the other. Peta Nocona fell, and his last sigh was taken up in mournful wailings on the wings of defeat. Most of the women and children, with a few warriors escaped. Many of these perished on the cold and inhospitable plains, in an effort to reach their friends on the head waters of the Arkansas river.

The immediate fruits of the victory was some four hundred and fifty horses, and their accumulated winter's supply of food. But the incidental fruits are not to be computed on the basis of dollars and cents. The proud spirit of the Comanche was here broken, and to this signal defeat is to be attributed the measurably pacific conduct of these heretofore implacable foes of the white race during the course of the late civil war in the Union—a boon of incalculable value to Texas.

In a letter recognizing the great service rendered the State by Ross in dealing the Comanches this crushing blow, Governor Houston said: "Your success in protecting the frontier gives me great satisfaction. I am satisfied that with the same opportunities, you would rival, if not excel, the greatest exploits of McCulloch and Hays. Continue to repel, pursue, and punish every body of Indians coming into the State, and the people will not withhold their praise."

[Signed]   SAM HOUSTON.

CYNTHIA ANN PARKER—QUANAH PARKER.

From May 19, 1836, to December 18, 1860, was twenty-four years and seven months. Add to this nine years, her age when captured, and at the latter date Cynthia Ann Parker was in her thirty-fourth year.   During the last ten years of this quarter of a century, which she spent as a captive among the Comanches, no tidings had been received of her. She had long been given up as dead or irretrievably lost to civilization.

Notwithstanding the long lapse of time which had intervened since the capture of Cynthia Ann Parker, Ross, as he interrogated his blue eyed but bronzed captive, more than suspected that she was the veritable Cynthia Ann Parker, of which he had heard so much from his boyhood.   She was dressed in female attire, of course, according to the custom of the Comanches, which being very similar to that of the males, doubtless gave rise to the erroneous statement that she was dressed in male costume.   So sure was Ross of her identity that, as before stated, he at once despatched a messenger to her uncle, the venerable Isaac Parker; in the meantime placing Cynthia Ann Parker in charge of Mrs. Evans, wife of Captain N. G. Evans, the commandant at Fort Cooper, who at once, with commendable benevolence, administered to her necessities.

Upon the arrival of Colonel Parker at Fort Cooper interrogations were made her through the Mexican interpreter, for she remembered not one word of English, respecting her identity; but she had forgotten absolutely everything, apparently, at all connected with her family or past history.

In despair of being able to reach a conclusion Colonel Parker was about to leave when he said: "The name of my niece was Cynthia Ann."   The sound of the once familiar name, doubtless the last lingering memento of the old home at the fort, seemed to touch a responsive chord in her nature, when a sign of intelligence lighted up her countenance, as memory by some mystic inspiration resumed its cunning as she looked up, and patting her breast, said: "Cynthia Ann! Cynthia Ann!"   At the wakening of this single spark of reminiscence, the sole gleam in the mental gloom of many years, her countenance brightened with a pleasant smile in place of the sullen expression which habitually characterizes the looks of an Indian restrained of freedom.   There was now no longer any doubt as to her identity with the little girl lost and mourned so long.   It was in reality Cynthia Ann Parker—but, oh, so changed!

But as savage like and dark of complexion as she was,, Cynthia Ann was still dear to her overjoyed uncle, and was welcomed home by relatives with all the joyous transports with which the prodigal son was hailed upon his miserable return to the parental roof.

As thorough an Indian in manner and looks as if she had been so born, she sought every opportunity to escape and had to be closely watched for some time. Her uncle carried herself and child to his home, then took them to Austin, where the secession convention was in session. Mrs. John Henry Brown and Mrs. N. C. Raymond interested themselves in her, dressed her neatly, and on one occasion took her into the gallery of the hall while the convention was in session. They soon realized that she was greatly alarmed by the belief that the assemblage was a council of chiefs, sitting in judgment on her life. Mrs. Brown beckoned to her husband, Hon. John Henry Brown, who was a member of the convention, who appeared and succeeded in reassuring her that she was among friends.

Gradually her mother tongue came back, and with it occasional incidents of her childhood, including a recognition of the venerable Mr. Anglin, and perhaps one or two others.

The civil war coming on soon after, which necessitated the resumption of such primitive arts, she learned to spin, weave and to perform the domestic duties. She proved quite an adept in such work and became a very useful member of the household. The ruling passion of her bosom seemed to be the maternal instinct, and she cherished the hope that when the war was concluded she would at last succeed in reclaiming her two children, who were still with the Indians. But it was written otherwise and Cynthia Ann and her little barbarian were called hence ere the cruel war was over. She died at her brother's, in Anderson county, Texas, in 1864, preceded a short time by her sprightly little daughter, Prairie Flower. Thus ended the sad story of a woman far famed along the border.

*   *   *   *   *   *   *   *

How fared it with the two young orphans we may only imagine. The lot of these helpless ones is too often one of trials, heart pangs and want, even among our enlightened people; and it would require a painful recital to follow the children of Peta Nocona and Cynthia Ann Parker from the terrible fight on Pease river, across trackless prairies and rugged mountain ways in the inhospitable month of December, tired, hungry, and carrying a load upon their hearts far heavier than the physical evils which so harshly beset them. Their father was slain and their mother a captive, doubtless they were as intent upon her future recovery, during the many years in which they shared the vicissitudes of their people until the announcement of her death reached them, as her own family had been for her rescue during her quarter of a century of captivity. One of the little sons of Cynthia Ann died some years after her recapture. The other, now known as Captain Quanah Parker, born, as he says, in 1854, is the chief of the Comanches, on their reservation in the Indian Territory.

Finally, in 1874, the Comanches were forced upon a reservation, near Fort Sill, to lead the beggarly life of hooded harlots and blanketed thieves, and it was at this place that the war chief Quanah learned that it was possible he might secure a photograph of his mother. [Mr. A. F. Corning was at Fort Worth in 1862, when Cynthia Ann Parker passed through there. He (Mr. C.) prevailed on her to go with him to a daguerreotype gallery (there were no photographs then) and have her picture taken. Mr. Corning still has this daguerreotype, and says it is an excellent likeness of the woman as she looked then. It is now at the Academy of Art, Waco, and several photographs have been taken from it, one of which was sent to Quanah Parker and another to the writer, from which the frontispiece to this work was engraved.] An advertisement to that effect was inserted in the Fort Worth Gazette, when General Ross at once forwarded him a copy. To his untutored mind it seemed that a miracle had been wrought in response to his paper prayer, and his exclamations, as he gazed intently and long upon the faithful representation of Preloch, or Cynthia Ann, were highly suggestive of Cowper's lines on his mother's picture, and we take the liberty of briefly presenting a portion of the same in verse:

> My mother! and do my weeping eyes once more—
> Half doubting—scan thy cherished features o'er?
> Yes, 'tis the pictured likeness of my dead mother,
> How true to life! It seems to breath and move;

Fire, love and sweetness o'er each feature melt;
The face expresses all the spirit felt;
Here, while I gaze within those large, dark eyes
I almost see the living spirit rise;
While lights and shadows, all harmonious, glow,
And heavenly radiance settles on that brow.
What is the "medicine" I must not know,
Which thus can give to death life's bloom and glow,
O, could the white man's magic art but give
As well the happy power, and bid her live!
My name, me thinks, would be the first to break
The seal of silence on those lips, and wake
Once more the smile that charmed her gentle face,
As she was wont to fold me in her warm embrace.
Yes, it is she, "Preloch," Nocona's pale faced bride,
Who rode a matchless princess at his side,
'Neath many a bloody moon afar,
O'er tortuous paths devoted alone to war.
Long since she's joined him on that blissful snore,
Where parting and heart breaking are no more,
And since our star with him went down in gloom
No more to shine above the blighting doom,
'Neath which my people's hopes, alas, are fled,
I, too, but long that silent path to tread—
A child, to be with her and him again.
Healed every wound an orphan's heart can pain!

Quanah Parker is a Nocone, which means wanderer, but on the capture of his mother, Preloch, and death of his father, Quanah was adopted and cared for by the Cohoites, and when just arrived at manhood was made chief by his benefactors on account of his bravery. His name before he became a chief was Cepe. He has lived among several tribes of the Comanches. He was at one time with the Cochetaker, or Buffalo Eaters, and was the most influential chief of the Penatakers. Quanah is at present one of the four chiefs of the Cohoites, who each have as many people as he has. The Cohoite Comanches were never on a reservation until 1874, but are to-day further advanced in civilization than any Indians on the Comanche reservation. Quanah speaks English, is considerably advanced in civilization and owns a ranch with considerable live stock and a small farm, wears a citizen's suit, and conforms to the customs of civilization—withal a fine looking and dignified son of the plains. In 1884, Quanah, in company with two other

prominent Comanche chiefs, visited Mexico. In reporting
their passage through that city, the San Antonio Light thus
speaks of them:

"They bear relationship to each other of chief and two
subordinates. Quanah Parker is the chief, and as he speaks
very good English, they will visit the City of Mexico before
they return. They came from Kiowa, Comanche and Wichita Indian Agency, and Parker bears a paper from Indian
Agent Hunt that he, Parker, is a son of Cynthia Ann Parker, and is one of the most prominent chiefs of the half
breed Comanche tribe. He is also a successful stock man
and farmer. He wears a citizen's suit of black, neatly fitting, regular "tooth pick" dude shoes, a watch and gold
chain and black felt hat. The only peculiar item in his appearance is his long hair, which he wears in two plaits down
his back. His two braves also wear civilization's garb, but
wear heavy boots into which their trousers are thrust in
true western fashion. They speak nothing but their native
language."

In 1885 Quanah Parker visited the World's Fair at New
Orleans.

The following extract from the Fort Worth Gazette is a
recent incident in his career:

"'HE BLEW OUT THE GAS'—AND ON THAT BREATH THE SOUL
OF YELLOW BEAR FLEW TO ITS HAPPY HUNTING
GROUNDS—ANOTHER INSTANCE IN WHICH THE
NOBLE RED MAN SUCCUMBS TO THE
INFLUENCE OF CIVILIZATION.

"A sensation was created on the streets yesterday by the
news of a tragedy from asphyxiation at the Pickwick hotel,
of which two noted Indians, Quanah Parker and Yellow
Bear were the victims.   *   *   *   *   *   *   *
"The circumstances of the unfortunate affair were very
difficult to obtain, because of the inability of the only two
men who were possesseed of definite information on the
subject to reveal it—one on account of death, and the other
from unconsciousness. The Indians arrived here yesterday
from the territory on the Fort Worth & Denver incoming

CHIEF QUANAH PARKER.

train. They registered at the Pickwick and were assigned
an apartment together in the second story of the building.
*   *   Very little is known of their subsequent movements, but from the best evidence that can be collected it
appears that Yellow Bear retired alone about ten o'clock,
and that in his utter ignorance of modern appliances he
blew out the gas. Parker, it is believed, did not seek his
room until two or three o'clock in the morning, when, not
detecting from some cause the presence of gas in the atmosphere, or not locating its origin in the room, he shut the
door and scrambled into bed, unmindful of the deadly
forces which were even then operating so disastrously. * *

"The failure of the Indians to appear at breakfast or dinner caused the hotel clerk to send a man around to awaken
them. He found the door locked and was unable to get a
response from the inmates. The room was then forcibly
entered, and as the door swung back the rush of the deathly
perfume through the aperture told the story. A ghastly
spectacle met the eyes of the hotel employes. By the bed-
side in a crouched position, with his face pressed to the floor,
was Yellow Bear, in the half nude condition which Indian
fashion in night clothes admits. In the opposite corner
near the window, which was closed, Parker was stretched
at full length upon his back. Yellow Bear was stone dead,
while the quick gasps of his companion indicated that he
was in but a stone's throw of eternity. The chief was removed to the bed, and through the untiring efforts of Doc-
tors Beall and Moore his life has been saved.

"Finding Quanah sufficiently able to converse, the reporter af the Gazette questioned him as to the cause of the
unhappy occurrence, and elicited the following facts:

" 'I came,' said the chief, 'into the room about midnight,
and found Yellow Bear in bed. I lit the gas myself. I
smelt no gas when I came into the room. When I went to
bed I turned the gas off. I did not blow it out. After a
while I smelt the gas, but went to sleep. I woke up and
shook Yellow Bear and told him, 'I'm mighty sick and hurt-
ing all over.' Yellow bear says, 'I'm mighty sick, too.' I
got up and fell down and all around the room, and that's all
I know about it.'

" 'Why didn't you open the door?' asked the reporter.

" 'I was too crazy to know anything,' replied the chief.

. "It is indeed a source of congratulation that the chief will recover, as otherwise his tribe could not be made to understand the occurrence, and results detrimental to those having interests in the Territory would inevitably follow."

The new town of Quanah, in Hardeman county, Texas, was named in honor of Chief Quanah Parker.

We will now conclude our little work by appending the following letter, which gives a true pen portrait of the celebrated chief as he appears at his home on the "reservation:'

"ANADARKO, I. T., February 4, 1886.
    *   *   *
         "*   *   *   *

"We visited Quanah in his teepe. He is a fine specimen of physical manhood, tall, muscular, as straight as an arrow, gray, look-you-straight-through-the-eyes, very dark skin, perfect teeth, and heavy, raven black hair—the envy of feminine hearts—he wears hanging in two rolls wrapped around with red cloth. His hair is parted in the middle; the scalp lock is a portion of hair the size of a dollar, plaited and tangled, signifying: 'If you want fight you can have it.'

Quanah is now camped with a thousand of his subjects at the foot of some hills near Anadarko. Their white teepes, and the inmates dressed in their bright blankets and feathers, cattle grazing, children playing, lent a weird charm to the lonely desolate hills, lately devastated by prairie fire.

"He has three squaws, his favorite being the daughter of Yellow Bear, who met his death by asphyxiation at Fort Worth in December last. He said he gave seventeen horses for her. His daughter Cynthia, named for her grandmother, Cynthia Parker, is an inmate of the Indian agent's house. Quanah was attired in a full suit of buck skin, tunic, leggings and moccasins elaborately trimmed in beads, a red breech cloth with ornamental ends hanging down. A very handsome and expensive Mexican blanket was thrown around his body; in his ears were little stuffed birds. His hair was done with the feathers of bright plumaged birds. He was handsomer by far than any Ingomar the writer has ever seen, but there was no squaw fair enough to personate his Parthenia. His general aspect, manner, bearing, education, natural intelligence show plainly that white blood trickles through his veins. When traveling he assumes a complete civilian's outfit—dude collar, watch and chain, takes out his ear rings—he, of course, can not cut off his long hair, saying that he could no longer be 'big chief.' He has a handsome carriage, drives a pair of matched grays, always traveling with one of his squaws (to do the chores). Minna-a-ton-cha is with him now. She knows no English, but while her lord is conversing gazes dumb with admiration at 'my lord,' ready to obey his slightest wish or command.

Anglin, Faulkenburry, Douthet Hunter and Anderson.

By J. T. D. in U. S. Service Magazine.

ON the twenty-eighth day of January, 1837, Mr. Abraham Anglin, accompanied by David and Evans Faulkenbury, Douthet, Hunter and Anderson, left Fort Houston, in Anderson county, for the purpose of gathering up some horses that had strayed. Finding some of them on the east side of the Trinity, they sent them back by Dauthet and Hunter, who promised to return on 1837 the following day and bring a canoe for the purpose of crossing the river. Being impatient to accomplish their mission, the remaining four men constructed a raft of logs and crossed the river. After searching all the afternoon without success, they repaired to the place where they were to meet the parties with the canoe. Arriving at the river, they found no canoe but plenty of Indian signs, and, supposing the tracks to have been made by friendly Indians, they went near the river where the bank shielded them from the wind, and lay down to await the coming of their comrades. Being considerably fatigued by their day's tramp, all now fell asleep, but were soon awakened by the war whoop and firing of Indians.

About thirty sneaking redskins had crept up within five or six yards of them, some armed with guns, who now opened a heavy fire upon the sleeping men. David Faulk-enbury received a severe wound, and at once arose with his gun in hand. Anderson had already received a wound, and just as Anglin arose a ball struck him in the thigh, inflict-in a severe wound. David Faulkenbury now handed Anglin a gun, and called out: "Come on, boys, it's time to go," at the same time throwing his gun into the river and plunging into the water, followed by Anderson. Evans Faulkenbury and Anglin sprang behind an ash tree, intending to shoot at the Indians, but they had concealed themselves behind a bluff, and knowing it to be folly for two to fight against so many Indians, who now had every advantage, Mr. Anglin jumped into the river and swam to the opposite side, leav-ing poor Faulkenbury to his fate. As Anglin was swim-ming across, the Indians were discharging their arrows in rapid succession at him, and just as he was making his way out on the opposite bank which was steep and difficult of ascent he received several slight wounds. Weak and ex-hausted, however, as he was, he finally succeeded in mak-ing his way out, where he found David Faulkenbury too badly wounded to travel. Faulkenbury informed Anglin that he was unable to travel, and that it would be best to leave him and make his way to the fort as soon as possible for assistance.

Anglin had only gone about four hundred yards when he met the man Hunter with the canoe. Leaving the canoe, Hunter now took Anglin up behind him on his horse and traveled at a rapid gait towards the fort. They soon over-took Anderson, who, being severely wounded and almost entirely exhausted, insisted on being left until they should return from the fort with assistance. The two men soon reached the fort, where Anglin, whose wounds were pain-ing him considerably, received attention. A company of men went back the same night to look after the remainder of the party who had been left behind, but did not succeed in finding them until the next day. They found the lifeless body of David Faulkenbury near a water hole. He was

lying upon a bed of grass, which he had evidently prepared
to breath his last upon.   Some two miles farther on they
found the corpse of Anderson with two arrows sticking
through his back.   Poor Evans Faulkenbury was never seen
or heard of afterwards.   His footsteps were followed some
distance down the river near the edge of the water, when
suddenly they could be traced no farther.   The river was
sounded for his body but it was never found.   Thus all the
men on this occasion perished, with the exception of Mr.
Anglin, who alone was left to tell the tale of their sufferings.

General Walter P. Lane

WE have compiled the following synopsis of the life
of General Walter P. Lane principally from a biographical sketch of this grand old veteran, written
by Victor M. Rose.   This famous old veteran, "a
hero of three wars," was a native of Ireland, where he
was born in the county of Cork, in 1817.   His parents emigrated to America in 1821, and settled at Fair View,
1838   Guernsey county, Ohio.   Of Walter P. Lane we know
but little prior to his arrival in Texas, whither he came
as a volunteer youth to aid in the war of Independence.
His first appearance was at the battle of San Jacinto, where
his reckless, devil-may-care gallantry brought him into immediate and favorable notice.   On this occasion the intrepid
young Lane engaged a Mexican lancer in single combat,
"and," says Victor M. Rose, "but for the timely interference of Mirabeau B. Lamar, must have succumbed,
wounded as he was, to his more powerful antagonist."   The
day after the battle he was elected to a second lieutenancy
in Captain Henry Karnes's cavalry company.
    His next appearance on the field of battle was in the fa-
mous and sanguinary surveyors' fight on Battle creek, in the
southwestern part of Navarro county, in October, 1838.

This famous and hotly contested fight ranks in stubborn courage and carnage with the bloodiest in our history, the details of which, taken from General Lane's memoirs, will hereafter be given.

In the war between the United States and Mexico Lane was one of the first in the field. As captain of Company A he participated in many of the engagements of that stirring campaign, and added many new laurels to his name as a brave soldier and leader. He was at the battle of Monterey and also at the decisive battle of Buena Vista, where he was distinguished by many gallant acts. During the progress of the war his company had frequent engagements and skirmishes with the guerrillas and renegade Indians, in one of which he was shot through the leg. In the various battles in which he participated in Mexico he had five horses killed under him Says the Encyclopedia of the New West: "One episode in the career of Walter P. Lane will embalm his memory forever in the hearts of Texans. While he was major of Hays's regiment of Texas rangers, under General J. E. Wool, he was despatched by the latter with a small body of men in a southern direction to watch the movements of the enemy. At the hacienda of Salado, where the Mier prisoners were decimated, he seized the alcalde and ordered him to resurrect the bones of the seventeen martyred Texans and to furnish him with mules, sacks, saddles and all things necessary to bear them away. This was done, and Lane carried the relics to General Taylor's headquarters. The old hero deputed Captain Quisenberry, a Texan, with an escort to convey them to Texas. They were taken to La-Grange, on the Colorado, and there interred with all solemnity on Monument Hill in the presence of thousands.

"Few know even to this day that to General Walter P. Lane, Texas is indebted for the possession of these mementoes of a heroism never surpassed."

The names of the seventeen heroes, who drew the black beans and were shot as malefactors for an act of heroism perhaps unparalleled in history, were: James D. Cocke, a printer and lawyer, from Richmond, Virginia; Robert H. Dunham, William M. Eastland, from Tennessee, for whom at a later day Eastland county was named at the instance of John Henry Brown; James M. Ogden, a lawyer from Henry county. Kentucky; Thomas L. James, a native of Louisville, Kentucky; J. M. N. Thomson, a son of Alexander Thomson of Yellow Prairie, Burleson county, who was one of the first settlers of Robertson's colony; Henry Whaling, W. N. Rowan, C. Roberts, Edward Este, brother-in-law of David G. Burnet, J. Turnbull, R. H. Harris, Martin Carroll Wing, a printer from Vermont; Patrick Mahan, L. L. Cash, J. L. Shepherd and James H. Torrey, from Colchester, Connecticut a brother of the Thomas Torrey mentioned in the reunion of General H. P. Bee as one of his two companions whose lives were adjudicated by a council of Comanches in August, 1843.

When the war between the States broke out he was elected early in 1861 lieutenant colonel of the Third Texas Cavalry and served throughout that long and bloody fratricidal strife. We have barely space to enumerate the various battles in which he participated. Was at the battle of Oak Hills, Missouri, August 10, 1861, where his horse was killed under him in a charge on a battery. His next fight was that known as Chustinallah, against the Pin Indians, in the winter of 1861–62, where another horse was killed under him. He was in McIntosh's charge on the masked batteries of the Federals four miles north of Bentonville. He was at the battle of Elkhorn in which McCulloch and McIntosh fell.

Says John Henry Brown: "He was at the battle of Farmington, and on the withdrawal of the Confederate troops from that region Beauregard placed him in command of the rear guard of (if our memory serves us right) only two hundred and forty-six men. Charged by an overwhelming force he met them with such havoc as to cause a panic and route them, killing great numbers." For this brilliant action he was complimented in general orders, read on parade to each regiment of the army and the name of the battle ordered to be placed on the regimental flag. Before the close of the war he was promoted to the rank of brigadier general, which position he held when the fiat went forth announcing the surrender of the Confederate armies.

In June, 1863, General Lane was with the force that captured Fort Defiance and a large amount of property from the Federals. In the attack on Fort Butler, adjoining Donaldsonville, Lane commanded the force which took the town.

On the thirteenth of July, 1863, in the severe battle of La Fourche, Lane commanded the right and General Tom Green the left wing. On the third of November, 1863, Lane commanded a brigade under General Green at the battle of Berheaux, capturing four pieces of artillery, nine hundred prisoners and a large amount of stores. Being in the advance on April 7, 1864, his brigade was the first to encounter the Federals under Banks at Pleasant Hill, Louisiana. From nine o'clock in the morning till four o'clock in the afternoon he held in check a vastly superior force of the enemy, until being completely surrounded and out of ammunition, he charged through the Federal lines, the enemy falling bac< in confusion. He lost sixty out of four hundred men, but the enemy's loss was much greater. On the next day, April 8, Lane, co-operating with General Polignac, led a desperate charge across a field, cut off the right wing of the enemy, captured a great number of prisoners, one hundred and fifty wagons and twenty pieces of artillery. But in the moment of victory he was shot from his horse by a minie ball, which entered the upper part of his hip, when Colonel George W. Baylor succeeded to the command and gallantly completed the triumph of the day.

When "the cruel war was o'er" General Lane returned to his home in the beautiful town of Marshall, Texas, where he still resides, without pretense or ostentation, beloved and honored by all who know him.

Battle Creek Fight in Navarro County

TAKEN FROM GENERAL LANE'S MEMOIRS.

A SURVEYING party being formed at Franklin, Robertson county, I went with William Love and others from San Augustine to join it, all of us having lands to locate. We organized at Franklin—twenty-three of us—electing Neil, captain, William Henderson being our surveyor. We started in September, via Parker's Fort, for Richland creek, where we intended to make our locations. The second day we camped at Parker's Fort, which was then vacated, having been stormed about two months before by a body of Comanches [This is error; Parker's Fort destroyed May 19, 1836], who murdered all the inhabitants or carried them off into captivity, the two historical Parker children being among the latter. We passed Tehuacana hill on our way to Richland creek, and crossed through a dense thicket to the other side of the creek and encamped about a mile on another stream, where we were going to commence operations. We found there some three hundred Kickapoo Indians, with their squaws and papooses, who had come down from their reservation in Arkansas to lay in their supply of dried buffalo meat, for the country then abounded with any amount of game, and from the hills you could see a thousand buffalo at a sight. The Indians received us kindly, as a great many of them spoke English. We camped by them three days, going out in the morning surveying, and returning in the evening to camp in order to procure water.

The third morning at breakfast we observed a commotion in the camp of our neighbors. Presently the chief came to us and reported that the Ionies (a wild tribe) were coming to kill us. We thanked them for the information, but said we were not afraid of the Ionies, and said if they attacked us we would "clean them out," as they had nothing but bows and arrows, anyway. They begged us to leave, saying if the Ionies killed us it would be laid on them. We refused to leave, but asked the chief why, as he took so much interest in our welfare, he could not help us to whip the Ionies. He said he could not do that, as his tribe had a treaty with them. They begged us feelingly to go, but as we would not, they planned a little surprise for us. They knew where we had made a corner the evening before, and knew that we would go back there to commence work. So they put one hundred men in a ravine we had to go by. We started out from our camp to resume our work, several of the Indians going with us. One of them stuck to me like a leech, and succeeded in begging a piece of tobacco from me. Then shaking hands with me, he crossed the ravine, within fifty yards of where his friends were lying in ambush for us. We got opposite to them, not suspecting any danger, when about forty of them arose from the ravine and fired into us, killing some of our horses and wounding several of our men. Captain Neil ordered us to charge them, which we did, and routed them out of the ravine, when they fell back on a small skirt of timber, fifty yards off, from which up sprung one hundred and fifty Indians and confronted us. We retreated back into the prairie. The Indians mounted their horses and surrounded us. They went round in a circle, firing into us. We got to the head of the ravine in the prairie and took shelter in it. The Indians put a force out of gun shot to watch us, while their main force went below about eighty yards, where the ravine widened, and they had the advantage of brush wood. They opened fire on us and shot all our horses except two, which were behind a bush, to make sure that none of us should escape.

The Indians had no hostility towards us, but knew as we were surveying the land, that the white people would soon settle there and break up their hunting grounds, so they wanted to kill us for a double purpose—none would be left to tell on them, and it would deter others from coming into that section of country surveying. We commenced firing into each other up and down the ravine, we sheltered by nooks, and they by brush in their part. Euclid Cook got behind the only tree on the bank, firing at them, when exposing himself, he was shot through the spine. He fell away from the tree and called for some of us to come and pull him down into the ravine. I dropped my gun, ran up the bank and pulled him down. He was mortally wounded and died in two hours. We fought all day without water, waiting for night to make our escape; but when night came, also came the full moon, making it almost as bright as day.

Up to this time we had several killed and some badly wounded. We waited till near twelve o'clock for the moon to cloud over, but as it did not, we determined to make a break for Richland creek bottom. We put our four worst wounded men on the two remaining horses. As we arose upon the bank the Indians raised a yell on the prairie, and all rushed around us in a half circle, pouring hot shot into

us. We retreated in a walk, wheeling and firing as we
went, and keeping them at bay. The four wounded men
on horseback were shot off, when we put other badly
wounded ones in their places. We got within two hundred
yards of the timber, facing around and firing, when Captain Neil was shot through the hips. He called to me to
help him on a horse behind a wounded man, which another
man and I did. We had not gone ten steps further, when
Neil, the wounded man and horse were all shot down together, and I was shot through the calf of the leg, splinter-
ing the bone, and severing the "leaders" that connected
with my toes. I fell forward as I made a step, but found I
could support myself on my heel. I hobbled on with the
balance to the mouth of the ravine, which was covered with
brush, into which four of us entered, the other three taking
the timber on the other side. We had gone about fifty
yards down the ravine where it was dark and in the shade,
when I called to Henderson to stop and tie up my leg, as I
was bleeding to death. He did so—cut off the top of my
boot and bandaged the wound. We saw about fifty Indians come to the mouth of the ravine, but they could not
see us, as we were in the shade, so we went on down the
ravine. They followed and overtook our wounded comrade
whom we had to leave and killed him. We heard him cry
out when they shot him, and knowing they would overtake
us, we crawled upon the bank of the ravine, laid down on
our faces with our guns cocked, ready to give them one
parting salute if they discovered us. They passed us so
closely that I could have put my hand on any of their
heads. They went down the ravine a short distance when
a conch shell was blown on the prairie as a signal for the
Indians to come back. After they had repassed us, we
went down to Richland creek where we found a little pond
of muddy water, into which I pitched head foremost, having been all day without any, and suffering from loss of
blood. We here left Violet, our wounded comrade; his thigh
was broken and he could crawl no further. He begged me
to stay with him, as I was badly wounded, and, he said,
could not reach the settlements—some ninety miles distant.
I told him I was bound to make the connection; so we bound
up his thigh and left him near the water. We traveled

down the creek till daylight, then "cooned" over the dry creek on a log, so as to leave no track in the sand, to a little island of brush, where we lay all day long. In the morning we could hear the Indians riding up and down, looking for us. They knew our number, twenty-three, and seven had escaped. They wished to kill *all* so that it could not be charged to their tribe.

We started at dusk for Tehuacana hill, some twenty-five miles distant. When I rose to my feet, after lying all day in the thicket, the agony from the splinters of bone in my leg was so severe that I fainted. When I recovered consciousness, and before I opened my eyes, I heard Burton tell Henderson that they had best leave me, as I could not get in and would greatly encumber them. Henderson said we were friends and had slept on the same blanket together and he would stick to me to the last. I rose to my feet and cursed Burton, both loud and deep, telling him he was a white livered plebian, and in spite of his one hundred and fifty pounds I would lead him to the settlements, which I did. We traveled nearly all night, but next day got out of our course by following buffalo trails that we thought would lead us to water. The country was so dry that the earth was cracked open.

On the third day after the fight we sighted Tehuacana hill. We got within six miles of it when Burton sat down and refused to go any farther, saying he would die there. We abused and sneered at him for having no grit and finally got him to the spring. We luckily struck the water one hundred yards below the springs, where it covered a weedy marsh and was warm. Just as we got in sight of the water ten Indians rode up to us. I saw that they were Kickapoos. They asked us what we were doing. I told them we had been out surveying, had a fight with the Ionies and got lost from our comrades, who had gone another way to the settlement. They wanted to talk longer but I said: "Water! water!" The chief said: "There is water." So I made for it, pitched headforemost into the weeds and water on my face. and drank until I could hold no more. Luckily for me the water was warm. If I had struck the spring above, the water would have killed me. Henderson and Burton were above me in the water. In a short time they called me. I heard them but would not answer. I was in the water covered by weeds and felt so happy and contented I would have neither moved nor spoken for any consideration. Henderson and Burton got uneasy about me, as I did not answer, and came down the bank to find me. An Indian saw me in the water and weeds, waded in and snaked me out. I asked the chief what he would take to carry me to a settlement on a horse. He looked at me (I was a forlorn object from suffering hunger and want of water—my eyes were sunk nearly to the back of my head) and said: "Maybe so you die to-night!" I told him no, unless he killed me. He replied: "No kill." He asked: "Want eat?" We said "yes." He answered: "Maybe so, camp in two miles; come go; squaws got something to eat." He helped me on a horse and we went to camp. The women saw our condition and would only give us a little at a time. They gave us each a wooden bowl of soup, composed of dried buffalo meat, corn and pumpkins all boiled together. Green turtle soup with all its spicy condiments dwindles into insipidity when compared with my ecollection of that savory broth. When we handed back our bowls they said "bimeby." They waked us up twice during the night and gave us more. They understood our condition, knew that we were famished, and that to give us all we wanted at one time would kill us. We slept till next morning, when we wished to start, knowing that at any moment a runner might come into camp and tell them it was their tribe that had attacked us, and as we were the only ones who could criminate them we must be killed. I traded a fine rifle of Henderson's for a pony and saddle, but when I started to mount him a squaw stopped me and said: "No, my pony." I appealed to the Indian who looked at me ruefully and said: "Squaw's pony"—showing that petticoat government was known even by the Kickapoos.

We started on foot, my leg paining me severely. We had gone about three miles, when six Indians galloped up to us on the prairie. I told my comrades our time had come. We got behind two trees and determined to sell our lives dearly. They rode up, saying: "Howdy. We want to trade guns" —showing an old dilapidated rifle to trade for our good one. We soon found out it was trade or fight; so we swapped, with the understanding that they would take me to Parker's Fort, about twenty-five miles, on a pony, which they agreed to. One Indian went with us, the balance going back and taking the rifle. We got near the fort in the morning, when Burton proposed to Henderson to shoot the Indian—who was unarmed—and I could ride to the settlements. Henderson indignantly refused, and I told Burton that, rather than betray confidence, I would walk in on one leg. Five minutes later I heard a gun fire to the right. We asked the Indian what it meant. He replied: "Cosette, Kickapoo chief, camp there." So, if we had shot the Indian, we would have brought down a hundred on us to see what the shot meant. He then told me: "May be so, you get down. Yonder is Parker's Fort. Me go to Cosette's camp." I did so. We struck the Navasota below the fort, and waded down the stream a mile, fearing the Indians would follow us. We crossed in the night and went out some three miles in the prairie and slept. The Indians that morning had given us as much dried buffalo meat as we could carry, so we had plenty to eat on our way. We traveled all next day and part of the night, having got on the trail that led to Franklin. We started the next morning before day. Going along the path, I in the lead, we were hailed, ordered to halt and tell who we were. I looked up and saw two men with their guns leveled on us, about forty yards off. I answered: "We are friends; white men." I didn't blame them much for the question, for I was in my shirt and drawers, with a hankerchief tied around my head, having lost my hat in the fight, and they thought we were Indians.

They proved to be my old friends William Love and Jackson, who had left our party some six days before for the settlements, to get us another compass. They were horrified when we told them of the massacre. They put us on their horses and returned with us to Franklin, a distance of some fifteen miles. The news spread over the neighborhood like wildfire. By the next morning fifty men were raised, and, piloted by Love, started for the scene of our disaster. I had been placed in comfortable quarters in Franklin, and kindly nursed and attended by sympathetic ladies. Henderson and Burton bade me good-bye and went to their respective homes.

We told Love's party where we had left Violet with his thigh broken, and asked them to try and find him. The party got to Tehuacana Springs, and, being very thirsty, threw down their guns to get a drink. Violet, who had seen them coming across the prairie, thought they were Indians, and secreted himself in the brush close by; but when he heard them talk and found they were white men, he gave a yell and hobbled out, saying, "Boys, I'm mighty glad you have come." He came near stampeding the whole party, they thinking it was an Indian ambuscade.

Poor Violet, after we left him in Richland creek bottom, stayed there three days, subsisting on green haws and plums. Getting tired, he concluded to make for Tehuacana hills, as he knew the course. He splinted and bandaged his thigh as best he could, then struck out and got there after a day and night's travel. Being nearly famished, he looked around for something to eat. In the spring, which was six feet across, he saw a big bullfrog swimming around. Failing to capture him, he concluded to shoot him. He pulled down on him with a holster pistol loaded with twelve buckshot and the proportional amount of powder. Having his back to the embankment down which the water ran, the pistol knocked him over it, senseless, breaking the ligature that bound his thigh. He remained insensible, he thought, about two hours. When he became conscious he bandaged his leg as well as he could and crawled up to the spring to look for the frog. He found one hind quarter floating around, the balance having been blown to flinders. Being very hungry, he made short work of that. In a few hours after that, Love's party came up and supplied him with all he wanted. They left him there until their return, they going up to the battle ground to bury the dead and see if they could find any more wounded.

When they got there, they found the bones of all our killed, the flesh having been stripped off by the wolves. And they also found, much to my satisfaction, eighty piles of green brush, in the lower part of the ravine, from where the Indians were firing at us during the day, and under each pile of brush a copious quantity of blood, which proved that we had not been fooling away our time during the day.

The company returned to Franklin, bringing Violet with them, who recovered from his wound.

Sparks, Barry and Hollano.

D URING the year 1838 three men, Sparks, Barry and Holland, were killed by the Indians on the south side of Rich'land creek, about twelve miles from where the town of Corsicana now stands. These three men belonged to a surveying party and were killed by Indians who had placed themselves in ambush near the line they were running. The rest of the party escaped by
1838 flight. William F. Sparks was a well known land locator from the town of Nacogdoches, and his name as surveyor is attached to a great number of land titles in that region of country. These three men were never buried, as there were no friendly hands near to administer the last sad rites of interment. Some of the surveying instruments of this party were found twelve or thirteen years afterwards about four miles south of Corsicana. About one year after this occurrence there was a battle fought by Captain Chandler and Lieutenant William M. Love at the head of about forty Texans, with a large body of Comanche Indians. This was a running fight and was continued about ten miles. A number of the Indians were killed, while the Texans only lost one man. At the commencement of the engagement the Indians began to retreat and ran to their encampment, which was stormed by the Texans, when nearly four thousand dollars worth of property was captured. The gallant Colonel C. M. Winkler, late of Corsicana, who so nobly won honors under General Lee, of Virginia, participated in this fight. (See narrative of J. Eliot in Texas Almanac for 1868, p. 52.) Colonel Winkler has since been district judge, was a member of the Thirteenth Legislature, and at the time of his death, May 13, 1882, was one of the judges of the Court of Appeals. We are sorry that we are not in possession of a full account of this battle. [We have been informed that it was Richard Sparks that was killed instead of his son, William F. Sparks, who in April, 1886, resided in Johnson county.]

The Morgan Massacre and Bryant's Defeat.

THE year 1839 will long be remembered by all old Texans as one in which they were called upon to pass through many dangers, privations and hardships. The glorious victory gained by Texas heroes over the Mexican army upon the banks of San Jacinto, on April 21, 1836, failed to bring rest and security to the Texans. Marauding bands of Indians constantly raided the white settlements, and 1839 on every such occasion they stole and drove away the best horses of the settlers. In many instances the bow and arrow and tomahawk did their deadly work, and on other occasions women and children were carried away into a captivity worse than death. During this year many important battles were fought, among which may be mentioned that of Colonel John H. Moore with several hundred Comanches, which occurred above Austin, on the San Saba river; the battle of Brushy creek, in Travis county; the Flores and Cordova fights, and Bird's victory in Milam county. But the year opened with the Morgan massacre, the history of which we are about to narrate.

Many years ago, that veteran old Texan frontiersman and statesman, John Henry Brown, of Dallas, contributed to the current history of Texas a number of articles on the Indian wars and fights in Texas. The "Morgan Massacre" appeared among the number. The history of this sad tragedy, and that of the battle known as "Bryant's Defeat," will be given substantially in the language of Colonel Brown. We would here further remark that we are indebted to the same source for the accounts previously given in this book of the battles between the Cherokees and Wacos in 1829, and between the Cherokees and Tehuacanas in 1830, credit for which should have appeared in the proper place but for an oversight. But to the history of the Morgan massacre.

On the east side of the Brazos river, near the Falls, the families of the Morgans and Marlins lived, and with them

the families of some of their married children. Some resided above and others below the present town of Marlin.
There were a number of settlements on the river below
Marlin for a distance of twenty miles, but above that place,
with the exception of the families mentioned, the country
at that time was an uninhabited wilderness—the time to
which we refer was the winter of 1838–9. It was on Sunday night, the first day of January, 1839, that a portion of
the families of James Marlin, Mrs. Jones and Jackson Morgan were passing the night together at the house of George
Morgan, who lived at what is now called Morgan's Point,
six miles above the town of Marlin. The remainder of the
divided families were at the house of John Marlin, seven
miles below the fort. John and James Marlin were brothers,
the others of the same name were their children. A little
after dark the house of George Morgan was suddenly attacked by Indians, who instantly rushed into the dwelling,
thereby giving the inmates no time to prepare for defense.
George Morgan and wife, their grandson, Jackson Jones,
Mrs. Jackson Morgan, Miss Adeline Marlin, fifteen or sixteen years old, were all tomahawked and scalped in the
house in a very few moments. Miss Stacy Ann Marlin, afterwards the wife of William Morgan, was severely wounded
and left for dead. Three children were in the yard when
the attack was made. One of them, Isaac Marlin, a child
ten years of age, secreted himself behind the fence, and remained there undiscovered until the Indians had left. The
other child, Wesley Jones, first ran to the house, but seeing
the red devils entering and tomahawking the inmates, he
ran out unobserved by them, and was followed by Mary
Marlin, another little child. They both escaped together.
The young lady, before mentioned as having been severely
wounded, retained her consciousness and feigned-death.
She was not scalped, but all the rest were. The Indians,
after they had finished their bloody work, robbed the house
of its contents, and then left. When the Indians departed,
the little fellow, Isaac Marlin, who had secreted himself
behind the fence, entered the house and felt the pulses of
each one of the victims to ascertain if they were dead. His
wounded sister, supposing him to be an Indian, remained
motionless until he had left, when she crawled out. The

little boy Isaac then took the path leading to John Marlin's, and ran the distance, seven miles, in a very short time—a swift messenger of death to his kindred there assembled.

Wesley Jones and Mary Marlin, the two little children before mentioned as having made their escape, did not reach Mr. Marlin's house until daylight the next morning, and the wounded Miss Marlin not until noon the next day. John Marlin, his brother James, William and Wilson Marlin, Jackson and George W. Morgan and Albert G. Gholson, after they were told of the terrible massacre by the little boy Isaac, hastened to the scene and found the facts to be as he had stated. The next day a great many came from the lower settlements to their assistance, and the dead were consigned to their graves amid the wailing of their grief-stricken relatives and friends. Ten days later, being the tenth day of January, the Indians, seventy in number, attacked the house of John Marlin and his son Benjamin (the surviving family of the latter are now residents of Milam county). Garrett Menifee and his son Thomas were present also when the Indians made their attack. They killed seven of the Indians and wounded others, without receiving any injury themselves. The Indians, not particularly relishing such a "friendly" reception, withdrew.

When the attack was made Menifee's negro man, Hinchey, was at work a short distance from the house and "put out" for the settlements below at "double quick." He ran twenty-five miles, and reached his destination in less time than a good horse could have traveled the same distance—in fact, as he admitted himself, Hinchey was badly scared. He reported the attack that was being made upon Mr. Marlin's house, and a company was soon raised and started to the assistance of the beseiged party, but before they reached the place the Indians had left.

After some discussion upon the subject, those who were present came to the conclusion that they must either pursue and fight the Indians or abandon their homes and fall back to the lower settlements for safety. They chose the former alternative, and made their preparations accordingly. Their effective force available for pursuit was forty-eight men.

Benjamin Bryant, of Bryant's Station, whose surviving

family now reside in Milam county, was called to the command. The next morning he and his company took ·the trail of the Indians and followed it until it struck the Brazos river near Morgan's Point. They crossed the river at that place, and on the west side they found a deserted camp which the red devils had but recently left. About a mile from this camp they came upon a fresh trail bearing in towards the river and followed it. They counted sixty-four fresh horse tracks upon the trail besides the moccasin tracks of a great number of foot Indians. They crossed the river where the trail entered it, and just as they did so they observed a smoke rising up from the prairie which was on fire, and supposing the Indians had fired Mr. John Marlin's house, they hastened down there with all the speed they could make. As the day was far advanced when they discovered their mistake, they halted and encamped for the night. The next morning, January 16, they started again and found that the Indians had been at the deserted houses two miles above and had plundered them. They then traveled on six miles further to Morgan's Point, where they discovered the Indians in the open post oak woods near a dry ravine.

The noted chief, Jose Maria, who was riding in front in perfect nonchalance, when he saw Bryant and his men coming, slowly rode back to the rear where he halted, pulled off his gauntlets, and taking deliberate aim, fired at Joseph Boren, cutting his coat sleeve. Jose Maria gave the signal for battle, and the action commenced. Captain Bryant ordered a charge, which was gallantly made, and in which he was wounded, and the command was transferred to Mr. Ethan Stroud. The Indians fired one volley at the Texans when they charged, and then fell back into a ravine. Before they did so, however, David W. Campbell fired at Chief Jose Maria, the ball striking him in the breast, but not wounding him seriously. At the same time Albert Gholson fired at the chief and killed the horse he was riding. The Texans followed the Indians to the ravine and fired upon them from the bank. The Indians then commenced retreating down the ravine in order to reach some timber known as the "River Bottom," and as soon as the Texans perceived the movement a number flanked around and got into the ravine below them to hold them in check, which caused the Indians to fall back again to their original position. By this time the Texans had come to the conclusion that they had won the day, and in consequence they became careless and scattered about in all directions, every man acting as his own captain and fighting on his own hook.

The shrewd old Indian chief, observing this state of affairs, suddenly sprang from the ravine at the head of his men and opened a terrible and unexpected fire upon them. This threw the Texans into some confusion, and their commander seeing how matters stood, ordered his men to retreat to a point some two hundred yards distant where he intended to re-form them, and then charge the enemy again. He also desired by this move to draw the Indians some distance from the ravine, so that when he charged them again they could not easily avail themselves of its shelter.

This order, owing to prevailing confusion, was understood by many to mean an unqualified retreat, and a sudden panic seized upon the men. Taking advantage of their disorder, the wily old chief at the head of his men charged furiously upon the Texans, at the same time making the welkin ring with their demoniac yells. Several of the Texans were killed at the first onset, the rest were demoralized and the rout soon became general, and they were hotly pursued by the Indians for four miles. In this retreat ten men were killed and five wounded. All who were killed fell within one and one-half miles of the battle ground—the most of them being dismounted within half a mile. Plummer, Ward and Barton were killed at the ravine before the retreat began. Some individual acts of heroism and bravery deserve especial mention. David W. Campbell, not hearing the order to retreat, was about being surrounded by the Indians when the brave Captain Eli Chandler, who was mounted, rushed to his rescue and took him up behind him. Young Jackson Powers, having lost his horse, mounted on a pony behind William McGrew, and at the same moment his arm was broken by a bullet. Shortly afterwards his brother, mounted on a large horse, came up with him, who told him to leave the pony and get up behind him. He sprang from the pony with the intention of complying with his brother's request, but owing to the plunging of the horse and his own inability to mount quickly, because of his broken arm, the Indians came up with them before he succeeded in doing so. His brother defended him to the last, but when he saw him fall dead, he put spurs to his horse and escaped. William N. P. Marlin was severely wounded in the hip before the retreat began and was unable to mount his horse. David Cobb ran to him and lifted him on his horse at the imminent risk of his own life.

Wilson Reed, a daring young fellow, was knocked from his horse during the retreat by coming in contact with a tree. The Indians were close upon him, coming at full speed, yelling and brandishing their tomahawks, when he cried out: "Oh Lord, boys, Mary Ann is a widow;" but just then some one came riding by, took him up and bore him off unhurt.

The Indians lost about as many in this affair as the Texans although the latter were driven from the field. They were greatly elated by their double victory in that neighborhood, and became more daring than ever until checked by a signal defeat near Little river, known as "Bird's Victory."

The names of those who participated in the battle just described were as follows: A. J. Powers, Washington McGrew, —— Ward, Armstrong Barton, —— Plummer, Alfred Eaton, Hugh A. Henry, William Fullerton, A. J. Webb, —— Doss, Charles Solls (or Salls), William N. P. Marlin, —— Bryant, G. W. Morgan, Enoch M. Jones, John R. Henry, Lewis B. and William C. Powers, Henry Haigwood, Eli Chandler, Ethan Stroud, Joseph Boren, William McGrew, Andrew McMillan, Clay and David Cobb, Richard Teel, Albert G. Gholson, Michael Castleman, Wilson Reed (brother of William and Jeff Reed of Bell county and uncle of Volney Reed of Milam county), Wiley Carter, John Welsh, Britton Dawson, R. H. Mathews, David W. Campbell, Nathan Campbell, —— Smith, Jeremiah McDaniel, Walter Campbell, William Henry, Hugh Henry, John Marlin, Wilson Marlin, Joseph McCandless, John Tucker, Thomas Duncan (then a mere boy and afterwards a citizen of Bell county. He was mysteriously murdered about the close of the war), and one other whose name is not remembered. In the charge and retreat, the ten first names of the company in the preceding list were killed, and the next five were wounded. All who were killed fell within one and a half miles of the battle ground, the most of them within half a mile, being overtaken on foot. Plummer, Ward and Barton were killed at the ravine.

Jose Maria, so long the dread of the frontier, but after-wards the most pacific and civilized chief on the government reserve, has always acknowledged that he was whipped and retreating, until he obseived the panic and confusion among the Texans. There is scarcely any doubt at all that if the Texans had observed the order of their commander to fall back to the designated point and there rallied that they would have gained a complete victory over the Indians, and probably the old chief himself would not have lived to tell the story of that disastrous fight.

Jose Maria visited Bryant's station years afterwards and offered Bryant his pipe to smoke. Bryant insisted that Jose Maria should smoke first as he had won the fight, and the old chief proudly followed the suggestion.

The Famous Bird Creek Fight

BY J. T. DeSHIELDS IN U. S. MAGAZINE.

ON Sunday morning, May 27, 1839, the intrepid Captain John Bird, with a company of thirty-one rangers, well mounted and equipped, left Fort Milam at the falls of the Brazos, on a scouting expedition against the depre-dating bands of Indians who were constantly making forages upon the unprotected settlements around Fort Griffin on Little river, which was at that time on the extreme frontier of Texas in that direction—the Bryants, Marlins and a few others on the Brazos being their nearest neighbors. Captain Bird arrived at Fort Griffin at one o'clock in the afternoon of the same day, and at once learned that Indians had been seen near the fort but a few hours before his ar-

rival. Without dismounting, the rangers proceeded to the
point where the Indians had been seen. After a hurried
march of some five miles upon the freshly made trail, they
suddenly came upon twenty-seven Comanche Indians.
When discovered, the Comanche gentlemen were busy skin-
ning buffaloes, and did not notice the approaching rangers
until they were close upon them. The rangers charged the
redskins, who fled in different directions, thinking to prevent pursuit. Following on in the direction which the main
body had gone for some three miles over the prairie, the
rangers found themselves confronted by the same party of
Indians, who had come together at this point, and were arrayed in battle order and ready for a fight. The Texans
again charged upon them, and after a short skirmish the
Indians again fled, the rangers pursuing them several miles
further, but without overtaking them. Their horses being
considerably jaded, the savages easily outrode them. The
rangers now gave up the chase, and had decided to return
to the fort, but after retracing their steps for half a mile,
and just as they were emerging from a skirt of timber on
the south side of a small stream, since called Bird's creek,
and at a point about seven miles northeast of the present
town of Belton, they were suddenly surrounded by about
forty Indians, who shot their arrows at them from every
direction. The rangers made for a ravine some six hundred yards in front, where there was a spring, which they
succeeded in reaching, despite the desperate attempt made
to prevent them by the savages, who now retired to the top
of a hill about three hundred yards distant. A council of
war was now held, when the Indians sent up three "signal
smokes," which were in a like manner answered in as many
different directions. In about half an hour the rangers saw
a large body of mounted warriors heading in the direction
of their confederates. In a few minutes the hill top seemed
to be literally alive with painted demons. Increased to
about three hundred in number, and led by their famous
chief, Buffalo Hump, the Indians now arrayed themselves
in battle order, ready and eager for the fray. Advancing
a few paces, the entire company halted, and they remained
silent and motionless for several moments, perhaps to give
the little band of Texans in the ravine an opportunity of

PLACIDO, A TONKAWA CHIEF.

counting the enemy; but, as one of the rangers remarked after the fight, "Thar warn't no time for countin' Ingins." The helpless little company of men well knew that this formidable army of red devils would soon swoop down upon them, and they were busy preparing to defend themselves against such fearful odds. Raising the Comanche war whoop all along the entire line, the Indians charged down upon the men in the ravine, uttering the most unearthly yells that ever greeted the ears of mortals, and at the same time pouring in a regular deluge of arrows. The Texans were brave and cool, and gave them a most deadly reception, causing them to retire to the hill top, without carrying off their dead and wounded. Again the enemy charged in overwhelming numbers, this time advancing to within fifty yards of the ravine, but under the galling fire of the rangers, they were once more compelled to retreat, leaving a number of their braves dead and wounded upon the field. Having failed in each attempt to dislodge the rangers from their stronghold, and seeing that several of their number had bitten the dust at each successive charge, the whole company retired some distance beyond the hill and out of sight.

They now divided into two companies, and immediately began making a third and more fierce attack upon the rangers, this time closing in upon them from either side, determined to rout the little garrison at all hazards. The strife became deadly. The gallant little band of rangers in the ravine fought for life, and taxed their energies to the utmost. The field was almost an open prairie, with little or nothing to shield the contending foes against the showers of arrows and leaden hail which were incessantly being sent. Victory trembled in the balance. The Indians repeatedly charged almost to the brink of the ravine, but were as often forced back. The brave Captain Bird was killed early in the fight, and six other rangers were killed or wounded. The remainder, reduced to only twenty-five in number, and exhausted by the long and protracted contest, seemed doomed to almost certain destruction, when James Robinnett, a young German, and upon whom the command now devolved, swore to his comrades that he would kill the chief in the next charge, at the risk of his own life. Young Robinnett had not long to wait before the Indians again charged down upon them, led by their chief, who was arrayed in full uniform, with an immense head dress of buffalo horns, and mounted on a splendid American horse, presenting a most ludicrous and formidable appearance. Taking deliberate aim, Robinnett fired at the chief, and, true to his vow, succeeded in killing him. His lifeless body was at once surrounded by some ten or twelve braves, who immediately carried it out of sight, leaving their comrades to avenge his death.

After one more unsuccessful attempt to dislodge the rangers, and night coming on, the savages retreated to the hill, with a heavy loss of men and horses. The Texans lost five killed—their gallant and lamented captain, a Mr. Gale, —— Nash, —— Weaver, and one other whose name we can not recall, and they had two or three wounded. The loss of the Indians was supposed to be about one hundred.*

Fearing another attack from the savages, the rangers remained in the ravine until the next morning; and, seeing no Indians in sight, they mounted their horses (which had been secured near by in the ravine) and made their way back to Fort Griffin in double quick time. Their story was soon told, and a large force collected and immediately repaired to the battle ground. A huge coffin had been prepared, and into this uncouth receptacle all that was mortal of Captain Bird and his unfortunate comrades was placed and sent back to the settlement for burial. The remains of the five men now repose side by side on the bank of Little river, near the site of old Fort Griffin. After detailing a part of their number to care for the dead, as above referred to, the remainder of the men at once went in pursuit of the Indians, and proceeded as far as Stampede creek, where they camped for the night. From some unaccountable cause, all their horses stampeded about midnight and left the men afoot, which circumstance gave to the creek its present name.

The bullet holes may still be seen in many of the trees on Bird's creek, where the engagement first commenced. The

---

*Nathaniel Brookshire, commanding, in his report of May 31, 1839, states that the supposed number of Indians killed was thirty. This is very incorrect, as it was afterwards ascertained to be a much greater number—some say as many as one hundred.

little spring in the ravine that slaked the thirst of the besieged rangers and cooled the fevered brows of their dying
comrades, still bubbles forth its sparkling water as on that
memorable. day — murmuring an eternal requiem to the
memory of the heroes who so nobly perished to protect their
homes and loved ones. The battle ground is now inclo-ed
in a farm, and all that marks the scene of this desperate
conflict is a clump of alamo blanco trees, living monuments
to the sacred memory of the fallen heroes.

Massacre of Sparks's Surveying Party and Victory of Major Howard.

BY J. T. DeSHIELDS, IN UNITED SERVICE MAGAZINE.

ON the eighteenth of November, 1840, a surveyor by the
name of Dick Sparks, with a company of about forty
men, left San Augustine, in San Augustine county, on
a surveying and land locating expedition to the country
between the head waters of the Red and Brazos rivers.
After fifteen days of traveling the party arrived at their
destination, and having seen no signs of Indians along
1840 their route, and thinking themselves entirely secure
in this wild and desolate region, they immediately
commenced work. On the third day, while the men were
busy surveying, they noticed a large herd of buffaloes coming hurriedly from the north. The animals seemed to be
considerably frightened, and soon passed out of sight, going
south. This was rather unusual and caused the party some
little uneasiness, some of them remarking that there were
surely Indians behind them; but as no Indians came in sight,
quiet was soon restored and the men resumed their work.
Among the party was an old teamster called "Good Eye
Roberts," who had lost one of his eyes by having it shot out
with an arrow in a skirmish with a party of Indians near
San Antonio, and who, it seems, better understood the wily

Comanches than the remainder of his party, for he repeatedly warned the men that the buffaloes had been scared by Indians, and that the Indians had discovered them, and were only waiting for a favorable opportunity to attack them. At this Captain Sparks became impatient with the old friontiersman, telling him that he was a coward, and that he should hold his tongue until he got into camp, and then he could talk all night if he wished to do so. To this Roberts replied: "Very well, captain, you will talk, too, after awhile, and with good reasons." Reaching camp a half hour before sun set, the men soon dispatched a hearty meal of venison steak, flour bread, and some honey which had been secured from a bee tree which had been cut that day. The incidents of the past day were discussed, and, after the usual number of yarns had been spun, the party spread their blankets and retired for the night, each man taking his gun by his side as a bed-fellow. Forgetting the incidents of the previous day, and being somewhat fatigued and worried, the entire party was soon asleep. But "Good Eye's" fears had been well founded, for not long afterwards there came the most horrible yelling and screeching that had ever met the ears of the whites, accompanied witn a prolonged shower of arrows. They had been surrounded by a large party of Indians, and almost every man was killed lying on his blanket.

Robert Wires and another man named Kellogg made their escape, however, and at once left for a more comfortable and safer place, taking nothing but the clothes which they had on and their guns.

The remainder of the story details facts of an interesting nature, and we prefer giving them as narrated by Mr. Wires —not in the same words of the old veteran, but the sum and substance of his narrative as he often relates it. He says: "I had been weakened in strength by having had chills and fever for several days past, and it was not long before I began to feel my weakness. We saw that we were hotly pursued, and, gathering my strength, I ran along beside my comrade and said: "Kellogg, I can't stand this pain in my side, and must rest; save yourself the best you can, and I will try and dodge 'em." Just then we reached a sort of ledge or bluff in the prairie, after which the ground inclined downward to the bed of a creek about half a mile away. As soon as we were over the bluff I turned sharp to the right and ran around a little point that reached out beyond the balance of the bluff, and stopping to look, I saw a kind of shelf of rock or flat edge of a bowlder, under which there was room for me to lie, and without delay I disappeared underneath it, every moment expecting to hear my right disputed by rattlesnakes. Meanwhile Kellogg had dashed ahead, and soon reached the underbrush, making a terrible racket in tearing through them. In a very short space of time our pursuers, of whom there were four, tore past within a few yards, keeping directly ahead after Kellogg. They did not run a very great distance in their pursuit, however, for after a little time they returned and came directly toward the rock underneath which I was lying, and I began to fear that they had mistrusted my whereabouts; but my good fortune had not quit me. They walked up to the rock, and two of them jumped upon it to reconnoitre, the other two standing upon the ground within reach of my ramrod, all of them puffing and breathing hard after their fruitless race. They soon left me, for which little kindness I was grateful. I feared they might still be near, and so lay perfectly still, but heard no more of them, and at the first sign of day I crawled out and made my way cautiously partly on hands and knees, to the stream that ran a little distance from me. As soon as I had gained the cover of the brush, and with the help of my hat got me a drink, I pushed on a little way; and, as soon as the sun was up enough to give me my course, I began making my best time toward the settlements. I had but two bullets left, and held them for an emergency, not daring to use my ammunition upon game. I soon very naturally became pretty hungry. Toward night of the second day I heard the distant tinkle of a cow bell, and made my best time toward it, and, hearing me coming through the brush, the animal became startled and made for the trail leading homeward, and was soon joined by many other bells. You may suppose that this was music to my ears, and I soon reached the settler's house, who proved to be an old acquaintance named Hallmark, and, although a long way from other settlements, he was near the main road from San Antonio to Red river. With blistered feet and famished stomach, I was cared for by my friend Hallmark in the best possible manner. He sat by the table, and every now and then would move the food out of my reach, fearing I would eat too fast and too heartily. I remonstrated with him, but said he: "I have been in your fix myself, and know what you need."

His wife then related how at one time he had a long, hard run from the Indians, and when he reached home he had thirteen arrow points in his back, all of which she removed except two, which were still there.

After a good rest and doctoring my feet, I pushed on to San Augustine, finding Kellogg one day ahead of me.

Later on, in December of this year, Major Howard had another fight with Comanches on Opossum creek, near Georgetown, and by drawing them into an ambuscade suc-ceeded in giving them another chastisement. The rangers had followed the trail of the Indians for several miles, and were fortunate enough to discover them without being dis-covered. Knowing full well that he never could come up with the Comanches in a chase, or provoke them into an open fight on the open prairie—for in numbers the two par-ties were nearly equal—Major Howard resorted to a strata-gem. Secreting his men in a thick grove of timber, he started off alone, well mounted, in the direction of the enemy. The moment the Indians saw him they considered the possession of his scalp as certain as though it was already hanging at their saddle skirts, and, with frightful yells, gave chase. The gallant officer trusted to his steed at a time when a stumble would have been inevitable destruc-tion to both. The Texans in their covert could plainly hear the distant whoops of the savages, and hugged still closer the trees behind which they were sheltered. With almost lightning speed the pursued and pursuers scoured across the prairie, the former leading the savages directly within range of his own men. When at a point opposite the Texans and within a few yards distant, a well directed volley tumbled seven of the Comanches dead from their horses. So sudden and unexpected was this reception that the Indians turned their horses and made a precipitate retreat. One only re-mained behind, whose heroic conduct deserves a passing remark. Among the dead was his brother, and, in endeavoring to save the body from the hands of the Texans, the savage lost his own life. He dismounted and absolutely succeeded in packing his lifeless brother upon his horse, amid a shower of bullets; but, while mounting, a well directed rifle ball pierced him to the heart, and the brothers came together to the ground. Not one of Major Howard's men was injured.

Sketch of the Life of Colonel John Henry Brown.

AMONG the many whose names are now identified with the history of Texas, Colonel John Henry Brown, of Dallas, holds a conspicuous place. He has not only rendered important services to the State as a frontiersman, and in a military and civil capacity, but has done more with his able pen than any one else to preserve from oblivion the achievements and sufferings of the pioneers of Texas. The following sketch of his life is mainly taken from a book lately published by Victor M. Rose, Esq., the biography of Gen. Ben McCulloch. Of course in a book such as ours anything more than a bare enumeration of his services and of the prominent events of his life would be inappropriate.

1839

John Henry Brown was born in Pike county, Missouri, October 29, 1820. Whilst yet but a youth he emigrated to Texas, which has been his permanent and actual home ever since. In 1839, when the city of Austin was laid out. Colonel Brown went there, and, obtaining employment in the office of the Texas Sentinel, he remained there until 1840. He was made Secretary of the Austin Lyceum, composed of nearly all the talented men then in the place, and was a member of the Travis Guards, a fine volunteer company. When the Indians in the winter of 1839–40 made a night raid on the town, killing several people within its limits,

General Burleson, with some Toncahua Indians, pursued them far up the country, and Brown accompanied the expedition. Early in the summer he left Austin on a visit to his uncle, then living on the Lavaca river, where he arrived just in time to take part in the fruitless expedition known as the Archer campaign.

On the sixth of August, 1840, the great Indian raid of about one thousand Indians and renegade Mexicans attacked Victoria, killing a number of persons. On the eighth they sacked and burned Linnville, near where the present town of Lavaca is situated on the bay. On the seventh a small company left Lavaca to unite with others above, to intercept the retreat of the savages, and young Brown was a volunteer in this company. As an account is given elsewhere of the fight with these Indians, it would be superfluous to repeat it. In the battle young Brown signalized himself by killing in a hand to hand encounter one of the Comanche chiefs who had made himself conspicuous in the battle by his daring and the unique dress he wore on the occasion. Brown took possession of his cap, which was surmounted with buffalo horns, and which a friend soon afterward sent to the Cincinnati museum, and for nearly half a century it has remained there, bearing substantially this inscription: "Cap of an Indian chief, killed by a Texas cow boy in the battle of Plum Creek, August 12, 1840."

When Vasquez made his raid on San Antonio in 1842 Brown was among the first who volunteered to repel the invader and served under Jack Hays as first lieutenant of Captain James H. Callahan's company. Subsequent y he served for some months in Hays's spy company, operating west of San Antonio, and was with it on many scouts after Indians and marauding Mexicans. While in this company he took part in the engagement on the Hondo with General Wool's invading force. Afterwards, as lieutenant of a company, he went out on the Somerville expedition, but when there was a division of the party, and General Somerville fell back in obedience to the orders of General Houston, Brown adhered to the commander of the expedition, and thus escaped the fate of those who were captured at Mier.

In 1846, when the Victoria Advocate was started, he removed to that place and was employed on that paper. At this time he began writing historical pioneer sketches of Texas, and has at intervals continued to do so to the present. Many of his contributions have been used in historical works, and quite a number without credit. It was his object to collect and preserve the facts connected with our pioneer history, much of which he has saved from oblivion. When the militia of the new State was organized in 1847 he was appointed brigadier major of the southwest, with the rank of colonel, and held the position for four years.

In 1848 he removed to Indianola, and until 1854 was an active and zealous worker in the interest of that place. He also founded and edited the Indianola Bulletin, an influential journal. In 1854 he purchased an interest in and became co-editor of the Galveston Civilian In 1855 he was unanimously nominated for the House of Representatives, and was elected by a large majority. At the expiration of his term in 1857 he was re-elected without opposition.

In 1858 Colonel Brown was appointed by the Governor commissioner, under the law of 1856, to sell at auction in the respective county seats, and in one hundred and sixty acre tracts, the alternate sections of the large amount of university lands in the counties of McLennan, Hunt, Fannin, Grayson and Cooke. The labor was successfully completed and reported in January, 1859, to the entire satisfaction of the authorities. During the troubles with the reservation Indians in 1859 Colonel Brown was appointed commissioner by the Governor, in conjunction with Richard Coke, Geo. B. Erath, Jos. M. Smith, of Waco, and Dr. J. E. Steiner, of Austin, to investigate the facts. This duty was satisfactorily performed and disturbances ceased. In the autumn of 1859 the Belton Democrat was founded and Colonel Brown became its editor, and so continued until secession was accomplished, in 1861. He was a member of the convention that met on the twenty-eighth of January, by which the ordinance of secession was passed, and was one of the committee who drafted the "declaration of the causes which impel the State of Texas to secede from the Federal Union." After the adjournment of the convention he left for the headquarters of General Ben McCulloch, in southwest Missouri, as he had been requested to do by letter from that officer. He served on his staff through the fall and winter, and until the death of the general on the field of Elkhorn, March 7, 1862. After the death of General McCulloch he alone escorted the remains of the deceased hero, borne in an ambulance six hundred miles to the capitol of Texas, and pronounced his funeral oration in the Hall of Representatives to a vast assemblage. Subsequently he was appointed adjutant general on the staff of General Henry E. McCulloch. When Lee and Johnston surrendered he was in command of the third frontier district, extending from Lampasas to the Rio Grande, in which position he rendered important services. After the fall of the Confederacy he emigrated to Mexico and settled on the Tuxpan, river where he remained for several years. On his return to Texas in 1872, he was unanimously nominated by the Democratic party for the House of Representatives from the district of Dallas, Collin and Tarrant, and was elected by a large majority. In 1875 he was brought forward as a candidate for the constitutional convention and was again elected by a large majority.

In the autumn of 1881, Col. Brown was appointed, by the Governor, commissioner on part of the State to superintend the location and survey of three hundred leagues of land, to be held in trust by the State as school lands. This work was accomplished satisfactorily to the Governor and the State Board, at considerably less expense than the appropriation for that purpose.

This was the last public service rendered by Col. Brown, forty years after he first, a boy of nineteen, went out in defense of the frontier of Texas. He is now engaged, we believe, in writing a history of Texas, and certainly no one in the State is better qualified to undertake the task. His book should be in every household.

Reminiscences of Pioneer Life in Grayson County.

D URING the years 1885-6, Mrs. Mary A. E. Shearer, of Santa Cruz, California, contributed with her able pen several communications to the reading public, in which she gave many thrilling reminiscences of pioneer life in Grayson county. Some fifteen years prior to coming into possession of these interesting articles, we had obtained from other sources accounts of many of the murders 1836 and outrages committed by the Indians (and mentioned by Mrs. Shearer) in that section of country; but we have concluded to lay them aside, and adopt the narratives of this most estimable lady, feeling that the reader will be very considerably the gainer by the substitution. We are not seeking a reputation as an author—our purpose being chiefly to rescue from oblivion the early pioneer history of the country, and put it in such form that it may be preserved for future generations.

Mrs. Shearer has so graphically described the habits and customs of a frontier people—the daily occurrences incident to a newly settled country, etc., that we feel to leave it out would be a great loss to the reader. What she has said of the trials and hardships of the early settlers of Grayson county is true of many others. The counties of Gonzales, Guadalupe, Hays, Travis, Williamson, Bell, Coryell, Brown, Comanche, Hamilton, Parker, Jack, Young, Palo Pinto and many others too numerous to mention, were the scenes of many blood curdling murders, massacres, etc. In giving to the reading public these valuable articles of Mrs. Shearer, in which she has so vividly portrayed all the details of the different incidents about which she writes, each communication will appear in the order in which it was written; and while there are a few in which the bloody hand of the fiendish savage does not appear, yet they are so illustrative of pure and simple frontier life—so true to nature and

so truthful in fact—that we can not refrain from publishing
them all.   Besides, they were written by a Texan lady, a
descendant of a noble pioneer family, and, though reared
upon our frontier, shows a culture in her writings which
might be envied by the ladies of the older States, who were
favored with better advantages.   It can be seen throughout
her writings that, although she claims a domicile upon the
golden shores of the Pacific slope, yet her heart will involuntarily go out occasionally to the old homestead of the
Dugan family in Grayson county.

"In giving these reminiscences of pioneer life in Grayson
county, your readers will pardon the writer if the articles
refer more particularly to the incidents and experiences of
the family of that veteran pioneer, Daniel Dugan, from the
fact that I write wholly from notes furnished me by my
mother, his daughter, Catherine, and from memory of many
a tale told by the fireside of border warfare and of the many
brave deeds of her father and mother and gallant brothers
in their struggle for existence, and a home in the far away
beautiful wilderness of Texas.

Sitting here in far off California, on the shores of the
broad Pacific ocean, with the busy hum of a hurrying world
around me, and the view of many a white winged vessel
sailing afar upon the shining waters before me, it requires a
most vivid imagination and a very retrospective train of
thought to call up to the mind's eye, the scenes of a long
ago.   To picture the broad prairies of another land, the tan-
gle and wild beauty of bloom and brake and the silence of
leafy woods, broken only by the cries of strange animals
and birds or echoing the war whoop of painted savages.

Too much can not be said in praise and honor of the many
brave men and noble women who penetrated those wilds
and by their almost superhuman exertions built their altar
fires; who battled with every foe to mankind; the elements,
wild beasts, hunger and the wily Indian, depending alone
upon their own resources and a firm determination to do and
dare.   As the long years have rolled into eternity and one by
one these pioneers have been called to another world, we
can not help but look back upon their lives and deeds and
give them due credit for having opened the way.   The results of their sacrifice and bravery can be seen throughout

the length and breadth of the land of their adoption. For, coming right along with giant strides in the broad track of civilization, the Lone Star State has long ago swung into place and is now known and honored as one of the brightest stars in the constellation of our Union. Daniel Dugan, one of the foremost of these adventurous spirits, was born in Maryland in 1784, and was early introduced to pioneer life by his parents moving to Ohio when he was but fifteen years of age. In early manhood he went to Kentucky, then its infancy, and there met and married Catherine Vaden, whose parents were among the first settlers of that dark and bloody ground. After living in Indiana, Missouri, Illinois, Louisiana and Arkansas he determined to emigrate to Texas, and in 1836 he started for that comparatively unbroken territory.

It was an undertaking of great importance and he felt the great responsibility of moving his wife and young family to that unknown country. But, imbued with the spirit that characterized the movements of all those brave pioneers, and with an earnest desire for more elbow room he started upon that perilous journey. The family consisted of himself, wife and eight children, viz.: George C., Daniel V., Mary, Emily, William, Catherine, Henry P. and James. all between the ages of three and twenty-four."

"Our first camp fire on that journey," says my mother. "is a bright spot in my memory, and will be as long as I live. I would paint it if I could draw figures. The camp fire was burning low, the wagon, with its white cover, stood near by and the oxen were grazing not far away. Our beds were spread on the grass under the trees, among which were the beautiful dogwood, with its pale green leaves quivering above us in the dim firelight. Mother was sitting in one of the two chairs we had brought with us, holding brother James in her lap, and the rest of us were gathered around her. Father soon came, and, standing by mother's chair, joined us in singing a hymn; then we all knelt down while he prayed for God's mercy and protection."

Proceeding upon their journey without special incident, they arrived at Red river, where occurred the death of the youngest child, little James, and with sorrowful hearts they prepared the little body for burial. "Father took his axe," continued mother, "went into the woods, cut down a tree, and out of the trunk made the little coffin. A man, who happened to be passing, fastened down the lid. Father and brother George dug the grave, and there, far away from home and friends, with dim forebodings of a clouded future, we buried our baby." From there they moved to Bois d'Arc creek, now in Fannin county. Their wagon tracks were the first ever made in Honey Grove and where Bonham now is. Their nearest neighbors were fifty miles away, and for a while they were in very straightened circumstances, owing to a scarcity of provisions. Their principal food for a time was buffulo meat and other wild game, varied by a diet of turnips and water, antedating Colonel Sellers's cholera preventative by about forty years. What a situation to be placed in! Nobody to borrow of when the tea gave out; no news, no gossip and no fashion plates to study! Oh! solitude, where are thy charms?

Roasting ears were substituted for bread, by taking them as soon as hard enough, and grating them on a grater, and then taking this coarse meal or "grits," and making it into pones or loaves. There were no mills, and every family had to have, of a necessity, their own hand mills and graters. Other settlers soon came along and located on Bois d'Arc, among whom were the familes of Josiah Washburne and Micajah Davis. Some of their descendants are now living in Grayson county. Davis's trade was that of a blacksmith, and he opened a shop and established himself at that business as sole monopolist.

Josiah Washburne was the first white man killed by the Indians in northern Texas (the circumstances of which I will write in my next letter) and his murder was the beginning of the hostilities between the settlers and Indians in that part of the State.

This border warfare lasted about three years, the settlers protecting themselves and defending their homes the best they could alone and without aid from the government.

Little do we of the present day and generation know or realize the constant anxiety, suspense and ceaseless vigilance of those harrassed people during that time—ever on guard against a surprise from their restless foes. Plowing, sowing and reaping with their rifles at their sides—constantly on the alert—watching with suspicion every bush and quivering branch. Taking notice of every sign and sound—the uneasiness of cattle and horses, whose keen scent and instinct often disclosed the hiding place of the lurking savage. At night the lone watcher—oftentimes a woman—would listen with eager intentness to every sound borne upon the night air, quick to detect a false note in the cry of the whip-poor-will, and knowing but too well that the answering hoots of the owls in the woods were but the signaliz ng calls of the enemy.

Settlement of the Dugan Family in Grayson County—Murder of Josiah Washburn.

IN January of 1838, the family of Daniel Dugan left Bois d'Arc and settled near Choctaw creek, in Grayson county, not far from a little settlement or town called Warren.

Better land and better location for a land grant were the inducements to move there. They immediately took possession of a league and labor, Spanish measure. This amount of land was granted by the Republic of Texas, 1838 before the declaration of her independence from Mexico, to every man of family who came to Texas. Single men got a third of a league. Texas was then the ideal "happy hunting grounds" for all who loved to hunt, shoot or trap. Buffalo, bears, deer, wolves, panthers and wild turkeys roamed at will through the woods and over the broad and beautiful prairies. Grass grew from three to four feet high, the loveliest flowers variegated the landscape, and in variety and color would set a botanist wild. Wild fruit and nuts were to be had in abundance. The soil was rich, natural springs bubbled and flowed into clear running streams, and our weary travelers felt as if they had reached the "promised land" at last.

Their journey ended, father and sons went to work clear-

ing the land and building their home. The stately walls of
a palatial log house were soon reared, and as they gathered
around the fireside in their new home all felt that notwithstanding the toil and privations of frontier life there was
compensation in the thought that they were anchored at
last, and come what may, that was their home and future
abiding place. And home it has been for the Dugan family
ever since. Many years have rolled by since the first smoke
curled from the chimneys of that humble log house. Its
hospitable roof has sheltered many a weary traveler and
afforded protection to the defenseless settler. Sons and
daughters have grown up and married or wandered away
from the scene of many cherished recollections; but no
home has ever been to them like the old home. To the exile in California it is a satisfaction to know that its roof
still shelters one of the family and that no stranger can
claim any right to it or disturb the resting place of the dead.

There are, probably, a great many changes in the general
appearance of the old place since I last saw it when a child,
but I could map it all out now as it has always appeared in
my fond recollection. No house has ever seemed so grand
and mysterious as that log house where I was born. Its
gun racks, port holes, looms, spinning wheels and many
relics of Indian warfare were ever a source of pleasure and
curiosity. That large, low ceiled kitchen has echoed the
shouts and laughter of many a romping play when all the
grandchildren would meet at "gran' ma's." Then crossing
the plains and sun blistered deserts, at times almost chok-
ing for want of water, my imagination would revel in the
rippling of that "spring branch," and in my fancy I would
take the long handled gourd from where it hung above the
spring, kneel down until I could see my face mirrored in
its crystal depths, dip up the cold, refreshing water and
drink, and drink, and drink.

But I am wandering from the original subject, and I suppose a more interesting one to your readers. Soon after the
Dugan family left Bois d'Arc, Micajah Davis also moved and
settled near Iron Ore creek (we call them rivers here in California), not far from and west of what is now called Denison, Josiah Washburn remaining in Bois d'Arc.

Roving bands of Indians had up to this time frequently

camped near the settlements, and appearing to be friendly and anxious to trade with white people. There seemed to be no occasion for anticipating trouble with them, although some of the men would at times paint their faces a hideous red, act angry, scowl and talk about "the white man killing their cows (buffalo) and turkey." Sometimes the squaws and children would sullenly refuse to talk and finally seldom appear when the Indians visited the settlements. To people better posted on Indian tactics, all these signs would have been sufficient to warn them that the wily red man meant mischief of some kind. But they did not notice it, and took no extra precautions for safety until like a thunder bolt from a clear sky came the startling news that their old friend and neighbor, Josiah Washburn, had been killed by the Indians. And this is how it happened: Some time after Davis left Bois d'Arc, Washburn told his wife one day that he was going over to the old shop to get a chain of his that had been left there by Davis, also saying he would be back by sun down. He got on his horse, and taking his gun for any game he might chance to see, started upon his errand. The afternoon wore away, and at sun set the expected husband and father was not at home or in sight. At dark he was still absent. With increasing anxiety the waiting wife and children watched and listened through the long hours of that night for some sound of his coming, and still no sign of him. At daylight the neighbors were sent for; men armed themselves and started out to hunt for the missing man, who was never more to gladden his home with his presence. They found him not far from the shop, dead. He had been there, had secured his chain, and was on his way back to his home when the Indians attacked him. They had shot and scalped him, and taking his horse and gun had made good their escape. The whole country around was alarmed, and the settlers in every direction were notified to be on their guard.

From that time on the people were harrassed in every conceivable manner that Indian ingenuity and cunning could devise. The Indians would remain quiet for weeks, sometimes months at a time, then suddenly appear, kill a man or two, maybe a whole family, then as suddenly disappear, driving before them all the horses they could find.

The time came when men went armed at all times, even at their work in the fields; and a loaded gun was always left at home, to be fired by the women, either as a signal of distress or in defense should they be attacked.

One of the many methods or tricks resorted to by the cunning red man to take the advantage of the unwary settler was to waylay his cows during the day, tie them out in the woods and take off their bells. The cows would not come home at the usual time, but during the night the tinkling of the cow bells would be heard in the distance. They would approach close to the house, wander around in an aimless sort of way, as cattle generally do, walk around by the cow pen at last, and with a final rattle appear to settle down for the night. The unsuspecting settler would hear the bells, and thinking his cows had come home, would rise early in the morning to attend to them, open his door only to find himself and family confronted by gleaming tomahawks and an implacable foe. A desperate struggle and fight for life and loved ones would ensue, but it would be the vain endeavor of the weak and defenseless against the strong and mighty; and soon the blackened walls and mutilated victims would mutely tell the story of a home destroyed and a few more names added to the bloody list of martyred pioneers.

In the emergencies of no organized help from the government and an uprotected border, there arose the necessity of some kind of reliable help against the repeated attacks of the Indians. A sort of a State militia was formed, composed of laboring men, hunters and trappers, and were known as "Texas Rangers." They were ever ready to answer a call for help or go to the rescue of those settlers who had ventured too far out upon the exposed frontier. Sure shots every one of them, and skilled in all kinds of woodcraft, thoroughly posted and "up to the tricks" of the cunning red man, they were a host in themselves, and the timid felt assured of safety whenever a "ranger" was on hand.

In fighting Indians they did effective work by fighting Indian style. If they had been hampered by red tape and only allowed to "fire and fall back" by military rule, the chances are they would have been several months capturing a few old squaws, while the bucks would be skipping around here and there taking in the scalps.

Take a half dozen of the old original stock of "rangers" and turn them loose on these treacherous Apaches and there would soon be a settlement of the Apache question. The murders of Daugherty on Bois d'Arc and the flight of the settlers to Fort Warren will be the subject of my next letter.

Murder of Daugherty—Flight of the Settlers.

THERE is now living in Grayson county—or was two years ago—an old man whose record for bravery tells that he had once fought the Indians single handed and alone, saving his own life and that of a boy who was with him. It will not be out of place now to narrate the circumstances, for they occurred next in the list of tragedies in that section after the murder of Josiah 1839 Washburn. After that happened, almost in their midst, there was a general scattering and removal of the settlers from Bois d'Arc, and among the first to move away was one by the name of Thomas. He and his father-in-law with their families selected the site for their future home below Bonham, and about twelve miles from Bois d'Arc, taking with them their household goods and cattle, leaving their crops to mature and taking chances of remaining undisturbed until crop time. In the following fall Thomas and his father-in-law, Daugherty, decided to take a trip over to the old place and gather their corn, if there was any, and kill their hogs if they could find them, taking with them a boy about eight years of age. On arriving there they were agreeably disappointed in finding everything in good order and immediately went to work. They had finished the job without molestation from the savages and were about ready to start for home when the little boy came running from the cotton patch, where he had been gathering some stray bolls of cotton, crying that the Indians were coming. Before they could make their escape or defend themselves the Indians fired upon them, wounding the old man, Daugherty. They all ran into the house, where Thomas returned the fire of the Indians with good effect until his ammunition was reduced to one charge. Seeing no way of escape only by taking the most desperate chances he told Daugherty to hide, as he was too badly wounded to travel, and taking an ax handle in one hand and his gun in the other he placed the boy in front of him and started out. With a yell of astonishment and satisfaction the Indians rushed upon him only to be met with blows as they fell thick and fast from hands nerved to desperation. He fought his way right and left through the blood thirsty demons and succeeded in getting as far as the road, some distance from the house, when he told the boy to run for his life! This the little fellow did, although badly wounded by a stray bullet intended for his brave defender. Thomas succeeded in beating back and eluding the Indians and overtaking the boy, they made fast time for home, where they arrived exhausted but with their scalps in good order.

But the poor old man was not so fortunate. While Thomas was fighting his way out he saw Daugherty on his hands and knees creeping under the house and thought he was hiding and would be all right, as the Indians were paying all their attention to him, and were not noticing the movements of the wounded man. But after the Indians had left him—probably thinking he bore a charmed life—he heard the sound of the old man's gun. Knowing that something was wrong, and realizing how powerless he was to aid him, he hastened on for help. Arriving at home he immediately gathered together as many of the settlers as he could and as soon as possible returned to rescue the wounded man. But too late! They found him tomahawked and scalped, the gun and horses gone and no sign of Indians, dead or wounded. They had cleared out, and emboldened by the success of this attack were probably planning where to strike next.

The spring of 1839 found the settlements in an agitated and uncertain state. The Indians—the Cachattas, the Shawnees and Comanches—continued stealing cattle and horses and committing other depredations which kept the settlers in a continual state of alarm. Men in companies would go on expeditions against them, and Rangers would scout around, but they could not succeed in drawing the Indians into a general battle.

As spring opened they could travel around with greater ease, and began bolder operations by directing their attention to the more thickly settled districts, and where they could find the greater number of horses and cattle. The Dugan family had not been troubled very much by the Indians up to this time, but they were constantly on the lookout. Some one, coming or going, would bring news of murder and stealing, and they had no assurance that the next attack would not be upon them. One evening as they were all variously employed, the men securing the horses and cattle for the night and the women preparing the supper, their attention was drawn to the unusual amount of noise made by the owls in the woods surrounding the house. They also remarked that the hooting did not sound quite "owlish" enough, and there was too much regularity in the sounds and directions from whence they came. They would hear a prolonged and mournful "hoo-hoo-ah" out in the woods on the north side of the house, and very soon an answer would come from the south side, followed by another on the west. This was kept up with so much regularity they were certain the Indians were surrounding the house.

After a family consultation, they concluded it would be best, as they were all alone, to get away from there as soon as possible and go to Warren. The evening meal was hastily eaten, and as soon as night and darkness set in the horses were brought out, the mother and daughter placed on them, and with a few bundles of clothes gathered in the hurry of departure, they turned their backs on their home never expecting to see it again. It was the first "scare" they had experienced, and that journey through the woods in the dark night must have been one of thrilling interest. The miles were certainly long, and every bush and tree must have seemed, peopled with the hidden enemy. The father and sons walked beside the horses, and silently and swiftly as possible they traversed that lonely road to Warren and safety. When they reached the grove of trees on the Montague prairie, it was decided that the family remain there until one of the boys, Daniel V., could go to Warren and see what the prospects were for shelter and safety there. He took the swiftest horse, and leaving father and mother, sisters and brothers, to anxiously count the moments until his return, rode away in the darkness alone; his brave young spirit upholding him in the midst of unusual dangers as he sped along in the interest of that lonely group of loved ones, houseless and homeless on the prairie. Arriving safely in Warren, he found the place almost deserted. An Indian panic had struck them also, and the women and children, with a number of fugitives from other settlements near Warren, had been sent across Red river and were camping together in the woods, a few of the men remaining in Warren. Daniel returned immediately and reported the state of affairs, when they hurried on and were also sent across the river that night. Preparations for flight having been so hastily made, there was little comfort for any one that night, and no accommodations at all save the broad bosom of mother earth, under the canopy of the heavens and shelter of the leafy trees. The men stood guard on both sides of the river, expecting an attack by the Indians, but none came, and the next morning the families were brought back into Warren, and a party of men went out to search for the Indians, but failed to find any. It was the opinion of the settlers that the Indians had abandoned the attack on seeing preparations being made by the settlers to resist them, and had retreated to await the time when they could steal upon them in a more unguarded moment; but this time they withdrew from the settlements without destroying property or following their usual course of driving off cattle and horses. A party sent out to the Dugan farm to inspect its condition found everything as the family had left it, so they returned home not much the worse for their trip, but far more than ever inclined to appreciate its humble comforts and shelter.

The principal settlements at this time were on Iron Ore creek, Preston bend on Choctaw, at Warren, and below Warren on the river. Warren was given the precedence as possessing greater commercial advantages, and being the principal trading post for the Indians on both sides of the river. It boasted several stores, and the merchants were Daniel Montague, William Henderson and William and Slater Baker.

There was not much demand for fancy dry goods, high heeled shoes, millinery and "novelties" in those pioneer days. Homemade cloth, "linsey woolsey" and jeans were the prevailing fabrics which clothed men and women, young and old, rich (?) and poor alike. When they wished to put on style—not caring for expenses—the men would indulge in the wildest extravagance of fringed buckskin trowers and hunting shirts, while the ladies would appear at "social gatherings" in the most bewildering toilets of calico. The bright eyes of many a pioneer belle have twinkled merrily beneath the protecting shade of a calico sun bonnet, and as she listened with blushing cheek to the old, old story, her lover forfeited nothing in her estimation because he appeared before her and told his love in homely jeans, and adorned with coonskin cap and moccasins.

There were no schools or school houses in those days, and churches were unknown. Among those who professed a religion the Methodist and Baptist faith predominated, but only in nature's grand cathedral could they praise and worship, and in their daily life and surroundings look from nature up to nature's God.

Their style and manner of living were in strict conformity to the times and circumstances. Until their lands were cleared and their crops were planted, grown and matured, until stock increased and there were returns from their produce and looms, there was of a necessity a scarcity of all luxuries, and their living was of the plainest kind. There were no mills. The corn they grew and grated, or ground by hand mills, furnished their bread. Their larder and store house for meats, fruits and honey was the wild woods.

Sometimes the pioneers had other enemies besides the Indians to contend with. Wild animals were too numerous for comfort, and were too fond of prowling around the premises of their new neighbors. Coons were too fond of chickens, and bears had uncommon appetites for young calves and pigs. It was no uncommon sight to see herds of buffalo near the settlements, and I can't help but think the settlers lived well and dined sumptuously when it could be

"turkey" with them every day if they only took the trouble
to go a short distance in the woods and pop one over.

Mother very graphically describes a bear fight she and
her sister had right in the yard in broad day; but I will have
to reserve it for my next letter as this is already too long.

The Bear Fight and Murder of John Denton.

THE bear fight, as mother relates it, is as follows:
Father had been out hunting one day, had killed two
cub bears and wounded the mother, but not having daylight enough to follow her up and kill her, left her and
brought the cubs home. The bereaved mother, in her
anxiety for her young ones, and guided by her sense of
smell, tracked and followed him home that night, and
1839 for several nights came snuffing and grunting around,
but would get off and away before the boys could get
a shot at her. She finally became so bold in her determined
search, that she walked right into the door yard one day
and began her usual hunt for her babies. Mother and we
girls were alone in the house at the time, and sister Emily,
seeing the bear first, commenced screaming, "a bear! a bear!"
We all rushed pell mell out into the yard, and not stopping
to think of danger, attacked the bear with sticks, shovels,
or anything we could first lay hands on. The dogs joined
in the fracas, and with their barking and snapping at her
heels, and all of us yelling and screaming at once, the poor
bear was too badly scared to show any fight. We chased
her to a tree, which she tried to climb, but the dogs pulled
her back. She then turned and caught hold of our favorite
dog and began biting him on the back, and otherwise using
him too rough to suit us. We redoubled our efforts to make
her let go, setting the other dogs on and we girls whacking
her over the head or wherever we could get in a blow with
good effect. She loosened her hold at last, and turning
started for the orchard, almost knocking me over, as she

passed. She jumped the fence, crossed the orchard and was up a tree before we could catch up with her, and there we kept her snarling and growling, dogs barking and we throwing clods at her until brother William came to our assistance. He shot at her without effect, and in trying to reload broke his gun stick. Brother Dan was off in the field some distance at work, and hearing the gun and our shouting, thought we had been attacked by the Indians. He came running home with all possible speed, expecting to find us surrounded by a howling mob of red skins but, instead, it was only a bear treed by a lot of girls and dogs. He had his gun with him, and a well directed shot brought Mrs. Bruin tumbling to the ground. Of course all we needed was a gun.

The flight of the settlers into Warren referred to in my last letter, was but a foretaste of what was to come. It was not long after that occurrence that the people were compelled to concentrate for mutual protection. The Indians were gathering in a body on the frontier, and a combined attack upon the settlers seemed imminent. Preparations were made by the settlers in the vicinity of Warren to move to that place, and a fort, or stockade of logs stood on end, was built large enough to accommodate a great many, and to be used in case of an attack. But some preferred houses built of logs, or tents, near by to live in, depending upon the fort in time of extreme danger, while others lived inside the stockade until their return to their homes. They brought their cows with them, made butter, spun and wove, and as well as they could under the circumstances, performed their daily routine of labor. Those of the men living near enough to the fort to go and return the same day, worked their farms, some one standing guard always while others plowed. Eternal vigilance was the price of safety. The Shannon brothers, Micajah Davis and the Carothers brothers from Iron Ore creek, the Dugan family from Choctaw, and the families below Warren, were among the first to avail themselves of the protection of the fort until all danger was considered over and they could return to their farms in safety. This unsettled state of affairs necessitated a good many remaining there all summer, and during that time the residents of Warren and the

settlers congregated there concluded to have a school. The
young idea must be taught, as well as the fingers how to
shoot, and extensive preparations were made to forward
the cause. A log cabin that had been used as a stable was
cleared out and furnished for the school house; some split
logs placed therein for benches, a chair furnished by a pa-
tron (richest in chairs) for the teacher, who was a gentleman by the name of Trimble, and all was complete.

A muster roll of all the children old enough to go to school
was called, an inventory taken of all the available books
and then and there the first school in Grayson county was
established. Deponent sayeth not, but suppose there was a
dogwood thicket near by; have a dim remembrance of the ex-
cellence of dogwood switches! The list of text books used
in this pioneer school will compare favorably with those in
present use (theology excepted), but I will leave their classi-
fication to some one better posted. The New Testament
(the old was too historical for new beginners), Life of Nelson, A Methodist Preacher, Bunyan's Pilgrim's Progress,
Fox's Martyrs, a few old spelling books and a Murray's
grammar and arithmetic completed the catalogue.

Among those who were brave enough to encounter this
formidable array of condensed wisdom were: William and
Lee Lankford, Artelia Baker and little sister, Mary and
Louisa Davis, Catherine and Henry Dugan, a Miss Moody
and Martin Hart, brother of Hardin Hart, both well known
by the old residents of Grayson county. Should any of these
pioneer students see this allusion to their early educational
struggles,

> Let memory carry them back once more.
> To the days of Auld Lang Syne,
> When "spellin' skules" were glorious fun,
> As we stood up and "toed the line."

The representative to the Congress of the Republic that
year, 1839, from our district, was Colonel Hollin Coffey, a
very popular man and well liked by every one. When he
returned to his home after the adjournment of Congress he
brought with him a beautiful young wife. They stopped a
few days in Warren to secure a guard to escort them to their
home in Preston, about thirty miles from there, on Red river,

and while there Colonel Coffey made inquiries concerning the movements of the Indians and promised the settlers all the assistance in his power toward establishing a peace treaty with their enemies. To effect this, soon after his arrival in Preston he raised a company of men and went out on the frontier to see what could be done with the noble red man. He succeeded in meeting the Indians without bloodshed and made a treaty of peace with them. This treaty lasted only a few months, but it gave the settlers a little rest and allowed them to return to their homes and neglected farms for a while. The only treaty of peace these red skins and all like them ever paid any attention to was a well directed bullet. They observe that on the same principle a setting hen is made to lay, by wringing her neck. There is no honor, according to our code, in their composition; they only respect a superiority of numbers, and a treaty to them is time given to take breath and make preparations for a more advantageous attack upon the too confiding white man. Consequently it is not to be wondered at that in a few months the settlers were again thrown into a state of terror by a renewal of their terrible atrocities and wholesale stealing.

The next step taken by the pioneers of Grayson county towards civilization was to have "preaching" whenever they could catch a gospel dispenser straying that way. The first sermon they had, and the last for several years, was delivered by a Methodist preacher by the name of John Denton. He hailed from Arkansas, where he was well known by the Dugan family. After his arrival in Texas he located in Clarksville, occasionally visiting Warren to attend court. It was during one of these visits that mother Dugan heard of his presence and sent him a request to preach while there. He cheerfully complied, and made an appointment for the following Sunday at the school house in Warren. An event of so much importance must have filled the little log house to overflowing. What an attentive congregation he must have had, as they listened to the word of God for the first time in the wilderness, and awoke the echoes of the silent forest with their songs of Zion. Would it were my pleasant task to record a long life of usefulness for this good man. But such is not to be. A sacrifice to Indian treachery, his

death fully serves as an illustration of their appreciation
of a "peace policy." When the Indians again commenced
their depredations, Denton was among the foremost to go
wherever the call for help was heard, and to assist in any
movement for the benefit of the settlers. A raid had been
made and a number of horses driven off by the Indians, and
Denton with a party of men started on their trail to try and
recover the stock. When near the crossing of a creek, in
what is now called Denton county, he called a halt. and
pointing to the bushes and brush near the crossing ahead
of them, remarked that he did not think it safe to ride
through there, as the Indians might be lying in ambush
to surprise them, and advised turning back a short distance
and scouting around. Some of the men in the party were
of the same opinion, and thought that the safest plan; but
one objected—didn't see any danger, etc.—and intimated
that Denton was afraid and wanted to turn back. Not
fancying this unmerited attack upon his bravery, Denton
said that he would go as far as any man, and started on
ahead, the others following. When they approached the
crossing and were well opposite the bushes, the Indians
raised from where they had been crouching and watching
every movement, and fired upon them, singling out Denton
as the leader. The whole party turned and retreated in
great haste, to find when they halted at a safe distance that
Denton's riderless horse was with them. Unknown to his
companions he had been mortally wounded, and had fallen
off his horse in the retreat. The man who told of the affair
afterwards, said: "When Denton wheeled his horse around
to retreat, he looked at me with a smile on his face, and an
expression which seemed to say: "What did I tell you?"
Hardly realizing that he was shot, as he had turned with
them, they returned to rescue him if it were possible he had
been thrown. They found his dead body where it had fallen
off in the brush by the side of the trail, and not far from
where he was shot. Strange to relate, the Indians had not
disturbed him, probably not knowing they had killed any
one. His friends carried him to a secluded spot away from
the trail, wrapped him in a blanket and buried him. His
grave they dug with their hatchets and knives and lined
with slabs of slate rock; then they laid him tenderly in,

covering him with another slab, and filled up the grave, carefully smoothing it level and scattering leaves over it, that the Indians might not find and disturb his last resting place.

So perished one of Texas's bravest and best pioneers. A fine orator, far above the average in intelligence, and had he lived, would have proved a blessing to his country and assisted materially in its advancement.

> The pioneer was laid to rest,
> The red man set him free;
> D: turb him not, but let him sleep
> Beneath that old oak tree.

Murder of Doctor Hunter's Wife and Daughter and Abducting Another Daughter.

THERE is but little to chronicle concerning the settlement of Grayson county during the next two years of 1840 and 1841, except attacks, murders and depredations committed by the Indians. It was fight and work, and work and fight, the whole time, the harrassed settlers scattering to their farms for a season, again taking refuge at Warren, or gathering together at the home of some better protected neighbor until danger was over. The weary pioneer could only endure with patience, and hope that immigration and a superiority of numbers would finally effect a peace that the government seemed indifferent to hasten. One instance only can be given when the government came to their relief and that was when a company of regulars were sent out in the fall of 1839. They were thoroughly equipped with baggage wagons, ordnance, military tactics and red tape. It is needless to say they never sighted an Indian. The tardiness of the government and its slow deliberation in aiding and protecting these people is thoroughly in keeping with the course pursued at the present time with New Mexico and Arizona. What other

1840

government under the shining sun would hesitate and
waste precious time in useless forms while a handful of Indians were murdering its subjects, stealing and generally
defying the ruling powers. The prayers of the so called
humanitarians have never saved an innocent settler's life
yet, or so changed the nature of an Indian that he would
not kill and scalp whenever an opportunity offered.

These wars and rumors of wars did not hinder immigration as might be supposed; on the contrary, people were
coming into Texas from all directions and taking advantage
of the liberal inducements offered by the Republic in regard
to land grants—every man of family located wherever the
situation pleased him, and there settled with the intention
of making that place his home. The majority of immigrants were farmers—just what the new country needed—
and not town builders. Warren grew but slowly, and Sherman was yet in the future, and not thought of.

The settlers lived too far apart for much sociability, but
all were united in one common cause, that of making comfortable homes for themselves and of defense against their
common enemy, the Indians. The later immigrants into
Grayson of about 1840 numbered among them one Doctor
Hunter and family, who, tempted by the glowing descrip-
tions of Texas, the fertility of the soil and beautiful land-
scapes, decided to make it their home, locating about eight
miles east of Warren and quite a distance from any neighboring settler. The family consisted of Doctor Hunter, his
wife and four children, one son and daughter grown, and two
little girls of ten and twelve years of age; a colored woman
servant also accompanied them. The first important event
that transpired in this family circle after settling in their
new home was the marriage of their eldest daughter to Mr.
William Lankford, of Warren.

The wedding festivities over, the happy pair departed to
their new home, a few miles west of Choctaw, near Red
river, and the family resumed their daily routine. All
was peace quietude and happy content till, like a cloud
of vampires, the Indians, with one fell blow, forever blasted
that happy home, and thus it was: A few days after the
wedding the doctor and his son had occasion to be away
from home on business and did not expect to return until

evening. Not dreaming of danger lurking in the woods the rest of the family pursued their usual avocation without uneasiness or fear of trouble. Late in the afternoon the two little girls took a bucket and went to the spring, a hundred yards or more from the house, to get some water. Little realizing the dreadful doom awaiting them at the end of their path, they tripped along in unsuspecting innocence, and with merry thoughts and childish chatter, reached. the spring, filled the bucket and started back to the house. But glittering restless eyes were watching every movement and they had taken but a few steps when a hideously painted Indian sprang out of the bushes by the path, and before a sound could be uttered he shot the younger girl with an arrow, killing her instantly. This painted fiend was joined by another and still another until ten of his companions appeared from where they had been concealed in the bushes, and the other poor girl, paralyzed with fright, offered no resistance, when they speedily took her captive and carried her with them to her home to witness the completion of their devilment. So quiet and sudden had been their attack upon the girls that no alarm had been raised and they had no trouble in surprising and killing Mrs. Hunter and the negro woman, scalping the former but not touching the latter.

Then they leisurely commenced ransacking the house for plunder; ripped open the feather beds and poured the feathers all over their victims first, then packed up all the blankets and clothes they wanted, destroying the rest. In their search for valuables, they came across a medicine chest belonging to the doctor which afforded them considerable amusement. They emptied bottles, threw pills at each other, taking good care not to swallow any, and rummaged and smelled of everything in the chest with a good deal of hilarity until they got hold of some assafœtida and aqua fortis That proved too much for them, and with a good deal of snuffing and many grunts of disgust they ceased their investigations and prepared to leave.

It was growing dark and they suddenly seemed to think it was time to leave. So gathering up their spoils in great haste and securing their prisoner they left in a hurry. They had not yet got out of hearing when young Hunter rode up to the fence and called and hallooed for some one to come out. His sister and the Indians heard him, and to get away from that vicinity in greater haste one of the Indians took her on his back and carried her until they considered themselves safe from pursuit. They traveled all that night in a drizzling rain and only halted next day to dry their blankets and rest, then they scattered in parties of two and three to mislead any pursuit, and in a few days reached their villages.

To return to the scene of the tragedy: When young Hunter could get no response to his repeated calls, and seeing no light anywhere, he dismounted and went into the house, wondering where his folks were and why they were absent. All was darkness and silence; the pungent odor of medicines pervaded the air, and a horror of something he knew not what, took possession of him. He hastened to make a light, and in groping around in the dark, hunting for the steel and flint, he stumbled over something lying on the floor. Stooping down to find out what it was, to his horror he felt a body, and feeling feathers all over it his trembling hand sought the face. Brushing aside the feathers, moist and clammy with her life blood, he recognized his murdered mother, and in the same moment felt the dreaded "sign manual" of the blood thirsty savages—his mother was scalped!

What a situation! Alone in the dark, his murdered mother lying cold at his feet, his sisters, perhaps, in the same condition some where, the nearest neighbor miles away. What was he to do? Bewildered and stunned by this awful condition of things, he staggered to where his horse stood, mounted and with all speed possible roused the neighbors and started rangers in pursuit of the Indians. But it was, of course, a fruitless journey, as the Indians had gained a good many hours advantage and had scattered in all directions.

Search was made about the house for the girls, and not finding them it was believed that both had been carried off by the Indians. It was by accident that the body of the murdered girl was found near the spring the next day, and that left the fate of the other one wrapped in mystery and uncertainty. An age of suspense and anxiety passed before

MOODY SHOT FROM AN AMBUSCADE.

400

the broken hearted father and brother could get any tidings whatever of the missing girl, when at last they heard that a white girl of about her age had been sold to the friendly Choctaws by some wild Indians.

Hoping and praying that she might prove to be his sister the brother went over to the Nation and hunted her up. He found her and saw at last his long lost sister; bought her from her owners and brought her back to what was left of home and family circle. In relating her experiences with the savages she said that on that journey from her home to their village the Indians would mark out a circle on the ground every night when they camped, build a fire in the center of it and make her sit by it and scrape and clean her mother's scalp. Night after night the poor girl had to go through this performance until they arrived at the Indian villages. She thought at first their intentions were to burn her alive, but she soon found out that they spared her life only to make a slave of her for the squaws. She was compelled to work early and late with little to eat and exposed to all kinds of weather. For six months they kept her going from one band to another until they saw a good chance to make a trade, then sold her to the Choctaws, and from them she was at last rescued by her brother and taken home.

Murder of Moody, McIntyre's Two Sons and Sewell.

THIS chapter will contain sketches of several massacres committed in Grayson county in the vicinity of Warren and Choctaw—blows made here to-day and there to-morrow by the savage, and serving to keep the settlers in a continual state of alarm and unrest.

A man by the name of McIntyre, settled with his family near Shawneetown, an Indian village several miles 1840 above Choctaw and not far from Red river, but finding his Indian neighbors inclined to be displeased on account of his close proximity to their village he thought it

best to leave there and settle somewhere else. They complained that he was trying to get their land from them, but
they did not dare to trouble him, as any depredations they
might commit would be too easily traced to them. So they
continued their annoyances so as to force him to move, and
subsequent events proved that their object was to get him
away that they might commit their murders without fear of
detection. He moved and settled at what is now known as
McIntyre's crossing, on Choctaw, having for one of his
neighbors a family by the name of Moody. Not long after
McIntyre moved there Moody went to Warren on business,
and on his road he had to pass McIntyre's house about sun
down. When almost opposite the house, and riding along
unconscious of lurking danger he was suddenly fired upon
by a party of Indians lying in ambush by the roadside. He
was instantly killed, scalped, and his face and body horribly
mutilated; then the blood thirsty savages built a huge bon-
fire in the middle of the road, and with the body of their
victim in their midst, danced around it and made night
hideous with their yells and war whoops. McIntyre heard
the shot, and instantly suspecting Indians, gathered his
family into the house and barricaded the doors. They kept
watch all night, fearing, as the anxious hours passed by,
that the savages would next attack them. After a long
night of agony and suspense daylight appeared and the Indians suddenly left; but not until the sun was high in the
heavens did the McIntyres dare to venture out to investigate
the cause of the Indians' great hilarity. When they found
the mutilated remains of their friend and neighbor their
sorrow and indignation knew no bounds. They could only
surmise that the Indians were lying in ambush for them,
but seeing Moody pass in range of their guns they either
thought it was McIntyre or else could not resist the temptation to shoot the first one who came along.

A hunt was made for the Indians, but without avail, they
had vanished like spirits of darkness at the approach of
day. The McIntyre family consisted of himself, wife, three
sons and two daughters, and it was not long after the murder of Moody that two of his sons, aged twelve and fourteen,
were killed and scalped while out hunting below Choctaw.
It was supposed the Shawnees did it but there was no proof.

Two brothers, by the name of Sewell, who lived in War-ren, were aroused one night by hearing a commotion in the horse lot not far from the house. The horses were snorting and running around in great alarm, and thinking the Indians were making a raid on their stock, the younger brother got up, got his gun and started out first to the rescue. When near the lot he heard a voice call out in plain English: "Lay the gap lower." Feeling sure that it was white ras-cals stealing his horses instead of red ones he very un-thoughtedly spoke out: "Oh, yes, I've caught you." The words were no more than out of his mouth when an Indian jumped the fence and came running toward Sewell with his bow drawn, and before Sewell could defend himself twang went an arrow, striking him straight in the breast. He turned and ran back to the house, exclaiming as he passed his brother: "I am shot!" His brother ran toward the In-dian, firing as he ran, and shot the Indian dead; but none too soon, for the Indian had his bow drawn, and as the bul-let from Sewell's gun whistled its way to the Indian the ar-row from the Indian's bow whistled by him and stuck in the end of a log lying near by. At the sound of Sewell's gun the other Indians decamped and he went back to see his brother, but the poor fellow was dead, and it was with great difficulty the arrow was extracted from his breast.

As Kentucky is designated in history as "The Dark and Bloody Ground," and stands foremost among the sisterhood of States, valiantly fought for and nobly won from the sav-age rule of the red man, so ought Grayson county be known as the battle ground of the Lone Star State, and be given precedence by its baptism of blood and human sacrifice.

There is no record in existence to accurately give the number of valuable lives forfeited in those early struggles as the purchase price of your broad acres, flourishing towns and present peace and prosperity; and it would require an abler pen than mine to faithfully portray the sufferings, both mentally and physically, of those pioneer people. They were entitled to every rood of their land, and through suc-ceeding generations, by a patent right greater than can be bestowed by any land office in existence at any time; and how much dearer must their homes have been to them when a father or friend, perchance a husband or brother, yielded

up his life in defense of loved ones, making the very sod
sacred with his life blood.

*   *   *   *   *   *   *   *

My next letter will tell of the murder of Dan V. Dugan
and Daniel Kitchens; also the attack by Indians on the
Kitchens homestead. For the present let us change the
subject, leave the horrors of Indian warfare and turn to
brighter scenes.

In the commercial annals of Warren you will find taking
the lead, the names of Montague and Henderson, merchants. The name of Colonel Montague is synonymous
with the early growth of Grayson county, and he will always be remembered as one of the most stirring and energetic men of the times. He came to Texas from Louisiana,
but was originally from Maine; and at the time of which I
write 1839, his family was composed of himself, wife and six
children. His circumstances were considered very good for
those days, and his residence the finest in the country in
point of finish and architectural beauty. It had two large
rooms with a wide hall between, side rooms and a front
porch which, to a log house, then meant a notch or two
nigher in the scale of aristocracy. The logs were "finished
off," the cracks chinked with morter smoothly put on, and
the whole inside and out treated to a coat of whitewash!
The puncheon floor was made extra smoth, the hospitable
fire place deep and wide, and when all was finished and
complete, invitations were sent out and around about to
friends and acquaintances as far as Honey Grove and Preston Bend to attend a grand ball, a genuine "house warm-
ing" to be given at Montague mansion on the great and
glorious Fourth of July. Extensive preparations were
made for the important event, and I have no doubt the female breast was agitated then, as now, over the all important question of what to wear. "Biled" shirts came up from
the depths of the family chest. Forgotten finery saw the
light once more and "bar's greese" went up in the market
immediately. Turkeys, chickens, pgs and wild game of
all kinds were cooked by the wholesale in every style known
to back woods culinary art. All other edibles to be had,
flanked by drinkables, from persimmon beer to something a
little stronger, were provided with a liberality only known

to the generous hospitable people of the olden time; and a good time generally was anticipated. No "regrets" were sent in, and for two days and nights mirth and good cheer reigned supreme. The lads and lasses tripped the light fantastic toe to the music of fiddles (than which no better can be produced by a string band for dancing) and during the intervals, when the musicians were tuning up and putting a "little more rosin on the bows" what a flutter there must have been among the rustic belles at the call of "choose your partners;" and how many sly glances and daring flirtations carried on from behind those protecting "turkey tail" fans!

For a time troubles and anxieties were forgotten. Scouting for Indians was a thing of the past and skirmishing for partners occupied present time and attention. The memory of whistling bullets and yells of savages was lost amid the intricate mazes of the "Virginia reel" and the inspiring sounds of "Money Musk." It was a never to be forgotten good time, and in society statistics the first ball of Grayson county was a success.

Daniel V. Dugan and William Kitchens Murdered.

A CESSATION of hostilities for about a year was thankfully appreciated by the settlers, and nothing happened during that time to disturb the peace which they earnestly hoped would be lasting. The rangers had been unceasing in their efforts against the Indians, and it was probably owing more to the profound respect the latter were forced to entertain for unerring rifle shots **1841** than to any feeling of mercy, that they ceased their depredations and let weary settlers alone. More immigrants came to Grayson county, and well pleased with the prospect of peace and plenty, settled in different parts. In the spring of 1841 a large company, composed of families

and single men, were temporarily stopping at the Dugan
farm until they could look around for good locations to settle.   Among them were John Kitchens and family, Rev.
Mr. Spivey, a Methodist preacher, and family, and Messrs.
Green and Long with their families.   Mr. Kitchens's family
consisted of wife, two sons, William and Daniel, and three
daughters, Elizabeth, Melinda and Melissa; one son and one
daughter were grown.   He rented a farm situated about a
mile south of the Dugans; moved his family there and proceeded to put in a crop.   The farm was owned by a Mr.
Abred, but was temporarily abandoned by its owner, who
had left at the beginning of the Indian troubles.

The settlers, old and new, were all hopeful of the future,
looking forward to the time when their happy homes,
churches and schools would be established, and they could
once more enjoy the benfits of a civilized life.   The Indians
had cruelly harrassed the earliest settlers, it is true, but now,
peace, with her sheltering wing, sat brooding o'er the
land, promising a full fruition of all their hopes.   They
could go forth with renewed courage and vigor to clear
forests, till the soil, establish homes and lay the foundation
of a great and glorious republic.   The Dugan family especially felt that they had particular cause for thankfulness;
that amid the troubles and bloodshed on all sides of them,
the Indians had passed them by, and their family circle remained unbroken.   But alas, for human hopes; they little
knew how soon the blow would fall, depriving them of one
of the brightest and best of their number, and how soon the
hopes and bright anticipations of all were to be plunged into
the gloom of doubt and uncertainty.

In July, after the crops were "laid by," Daniel V. Dugan,
second son of Daniel Dugan, engaged Wm. Kitchens to help
him get out logs for a house he was going to build on his
land, which lay near Choctaw, about two miles northwest
of his father's place, and where he hoped to bring a young
bride, and establish a little pioneer home of his own.   The
young man made every preparation to camp on the ground,
taking provisions enough, with what game they would kill,
to last them about a week, intending then to return home
on a visit and replenish their larder.

Two days after they left for their camp John Kitchens

went up above Choctaw on business and while there heard
,hat a party of eleven Indians, presumably Cachattas, had
peen seen crossing Red river above Preston Bend and were
making their way down toward the settlements. Knowing
very well that Indians of that tribe were not in that part of
the country with any good intentions he mounted his horse
immediately and turned back to alarm the settlers and warn
everybody to be on their guard. He hurried into camp to
tell his son and Dugan of their danger and have them abandon their work for the present and go home. The sun was
down as he rode up, and as he could see nothing of them
and could get no answer to his calls and loud hallooing he came to the conclusion that they had been warned
in some way and had already gone home. So he turned
and rode away in the fast gathering darkness of the
lonely woods, with no voice to tell him that the night
winds were even then singing a requiem o'er the slain,
that only a short distance from him lay his murdered
son, fast growing cold in the embrace of death. and not far
away was his dead and mutilated friend and companion.
But no, the echoes of the fearful struggle had long since
died away, and ignorant of the horror that yet hovered in
the very air he breathed, he hurried on to his home and
waiting family. He stopped at the young Dugan's to in-
quire about the return of the young men, but to his horror
and the consternation of all he was told that they were not
there and had not been there since leaving two days before.
Such a night of anxiety and suspense as that was to the distracted relatives my pen fails to describe. Everything that
could have befallen the boys from any source was imagined
and discussed. The possibility that the Indians had renewed their attacks upon the settlements after so long a
period of peace came upon them in all of its dreadful meaning and was difficult to realize.

Runners were sent to Warren for rangers and more help
to search for the missing ones. The rangers were off in
another direction, but friends and neighbors soon gathered
together, and at the first glimmer of daylight a party
started for the camp. A few were left to guard the families at the house in case of surprise and attack, for all felt in-
tuitively that it was to be war to the knife once more as long

as an Indian was seen or heard of About nine o'clock Mr.
Henderson, one of the searching party, was seen coming at
full speed toward the house, and before he could dismount
from his panting horse he was surrounded by anxious friends
and relatives, foremost among them the mothers of the
missing boys.   With pallid cheeks and bursting hearts they
listened to his hurried reports; how the party had reached
the woods around the camp, and had found William Kitchens's body lying where he and Dan had been cutting logs.
He was shot and scalped, and it appeared from indications
that the Indians had slipped upon them while at work, unconscious of danger, and had killed him instantly.   The
fate of Dan was yet unknown, as the searching party were
yet searching the woods when he left.   He had returned
for a wagon to bring the bodies home in.   When he got back
to the scene of the tragedy the body of Daniel had been
found about three hundred yards from where Kitchens's
lay.

Evidences of a long and desperate fight were all about
him, also signs which showed that he had made more than
one "noble red" bite the dust. The Indians had either missed
him at the first fire, or had intended taking him alive. They
came upon him so suddenly he had no chance or time to get
his gun, and there, solitary and alone, with no hope of help
from any source, his companion killed, he boldly faced that
band of fiends thirsting for his blood.   He knew he could
expect no mercy at their hands, and he determined to sell
his life as dearly as possible.   Possessing no means of defense save his trusty axe, he fought them off and gained
inch by inch the ground traversed, and it was only when
the murderous devils closed in upon him, and hacked and
stabbed his arms until his axe, bloody to the eye, fell from
his nerveless grasp, did he turn in obedience to the heaven
born instinct of self preservation, and try to get away from
his cruel pursuers.   Then they shot him twice and finished
their bloody work by taking his scalp; then they ransacked
the camp, took the guns and made their escape.

The bodies of the victims were brought to the Dugan
homestead and the following day the impressive funeral
services conducted by the Rev. Mr. Spivey, were attended
by settlers and neighbors from far and near, and as they

looked upon the faces of the dead in their rough coffins one
and all registered the unspokon vow that no mercy would
be shown when opportunity offered to avenge the death of
these promising young pioneers. They were buried side by
side in a beautiful spot on the Dugan farm, a place conse-
crated then and there as "God's acre," and though time has
wrought many a change during this long lapse of years, it
is very probable their graves can be seen there to day. But
you will find there no monument or storied urn commemorative of the bravery and daring of Daniel V. Dugan; nevertheless he was composed of that sterner stuff of which
heroes are made, and I am pleased that it is my privilege
to perpetuate the memory of my gallant young uncle, and
in these Reminiscences tell of his courage in braving unseen
danger and his hand to hand conflict with those savages
who had to disarm him before they could kill him. He was
a devoted son and brother and looked upon by all the
family as an ever present help in time of need. It was a
terrible blow to them and a sad fate for him to be literally
cut down in his early manhood when the brightest and best
years of his life were yet before him.

The Sunday following the burial Mr. Kitchens and family
attended the funeral sermon and remained at the Dugans
until late in the afternoon, talking over the sad events of
the week. After they returned home and had finished attending to their horses and cows Mr. Kitchens, his son Dan
and a young man named Stephens were sitting out in the
yard with their chairs tilted back against the house and their
guns standing near them.

The house was the usual log structure of only one room,
and, as the logs had not yet been chinked or closed with
mortar, the movements of Mrs. Kitchens and the girls could
be plainly seen as they walked around doing up their evening work. All felt quiet and subdued by their sad affliction,
and a Sabbath evening, peace and twilight settling over the
little home, was disturbed only by the distant lowing of cattle
and the tinkling of cow bells. A fine horse, belonging to Mr.
Kitchens, was tied to a wagon standing in the yard. He
suddenly began to show signs of uneasiness, gave a snort
of alarm, squared himself around, threw his ears forward,
and gazed intensely in the direction of a cornfield near the

house. Without other warning or sign of danger, three
shots rang out upon the air, one for each man. The men
jumped to their feet and sprang into the house, forgetting
their guns, yet in the yard, and not even realizing that two
of the shots had taken effect, one in Dan's foot and one in
his father's. But their guns! What could they do without
them? Without a moment's hesitation, Mr. Kitchens
walked out and handed the guns and pouches in, one by
one, while zip, zip! went the bullets into the logs all around
him. Then the fight began in earnest. Bullets and shot
flew thick and fast, and rattled on the roof like hail. Mrs.
Kitchens joined in with an old fashioned pistol, and the
girls moulded bullets. The men aimed and fired between
the logs, changing their position constantly. As Mr.
Kitchens was looking for a chance to shoot, he saw a big
burly negro raise his gun and aim for him. But Mr.
Kitchens was the quicker shot, and down went the negro.
He rolled over, got up, and ran about a quarter of a mile
before he fell, and gave up his African ghost. Then it was
Steven's turn to score one. He saw an Indian trying to un-
tie the horse from the wagon, and took aim; the Indian saw
him, dropped the rope, and in a twinklng raised his gun
and fired; but Stevens got in ahead, and the Indian, with a
convulsive leap backward, also "laid him down to rest."

The bullet from the Indian's gun went through the door
shutter, and buried itself in a log on the other side of the
room. When this "brave" fell, the Indians quit firing, and
disappeared, carrying their dead with them, but leaving the
colored gentleman.

As soon as it was safe enough Mr. Kitchens put Dan on
his swiftest horse and sent him over to the Dugans to tell
the news. Dan got over the ground at a Tom O'Shanter
gait, and as soon as he got within hailing distance he commenced yelling as if the whole Indian nation were after him.
The firing at Kitchens had been heard and active preparations were being made at Dugans to resist an attack. When
they heard Dan coming they at once thought its was Mrs.
Kitchens, and the girls, with the Indians after them, and
the men rushed to the rescue, but it was only fourteen year
old Dan, badly scared and badly hurt. They took him off
his horse and tied up his wounded foot, which was still

bleeding, and heard with great rejoicing the good news that the Indians had been completely licked!

A party of men went back with Dan, and guards were stationed at both places, expecting the Indians would get reinforcements and come back, but none came that night.

Not considering his house safe enough Mr. Kitchens moved his family over to the Dugan farm and camped in the yard, as the rooms, halls and barns were all full. They stayed there until his and Dan's wounds healed and then he moved and settled in Warren, where he engaged in the dry goods business for many years. Many of the old settlers will remember John Kitchens and will remember him as a brave and honest man. The redoubtable man is now living here in California and when he visited us, his Texas friends, in the early 60's, he had to take his boot off and show Kate's children where the Indians shot him in the foot

Attack on the Dugan Residence.

OUR pioneers about Warren and Choctaw had a hard time of it during the summer and fall of 1841. The Indians seemed to feel their defeat and loss at the Kitchens fight, and afterwards directed their attention more particularly to the settlements on the Choctaw. They prowled around continually, watching for a chance to steal and murder, but the settlers were generally successful in driving them off. In this way a skimishing fight was kept up for some time.

1841

A couple of hunters were out about eight miles above Choctaw one day, and observed an Indian sitting on his pony, away off on a high point of prairie. They watched him awhile and concluded that he was a guard or sentinel on duty, watching his campood (that is Piute) somewhere in the vicinity. They came in and reported, and a party of six men, led by G. C. Dugan, started at once on a "raid." They found the camp without any difficulty, attacked it and killed one Indian and captured a number of their own horses, a lot of bows and arrows, and several great cowhide shields. From the appearance of the outfit the men thought they were wild Indians, or those who had not lived long enough near their white brothers to acquire and learn how to use powder and shot. There were many so called tame Indians around who professed great friendship for the white man, but no reliance was placed upon 'their friendly advances, as it seemed a very easy transition for them to be either tame or wild at will. How the Indians disposed of their dead was always a mystery to the settler, as no trace of burial could ever be found. No matter how hard pressed they were, they always, with very few exceptions, managed to get their dead and wounded away. To discover the whereabouts of the latter, every Indian carried a whistle made of bone suspended from a buckskin string around his neck; this was to be blown when one of them was missing, and by the answering whistle discover the wounded one and carry him away. Very frequently run away negroes would join the Indians and render valuable assistance in fighting and stealing, but their dead bodies were never moved, nor was a negro ever scalped by them. Bad medicine in the wool, I suppose.

The first love of an Indian brave, be he a Cachatta or a bow legged Comanche, is a horse. If he has none of his own his first duty is to get one or more if he has to appropriate the property of his neighbor. A lot of fine horses at the Dugan farm were a great temptation to the covetous red skins, and repeated attempts were made to capture them, but without success. A guard was always on watch during the day and at night. George and William Dugan occupied the loft over the log stable, taking turns in watching and sleeping. A number of settlers in the vicinity of Choctaw became very dissatisfied with the prospect of fighting Indians all winter, to say nothing of the chances of losing their scalps, so late in the fall they began moving away to more secure localities. Some went to Fannin county, others to Lamar county, and to counties lower down the river, but the Dugans and several men resolved to stay and fight it out. Of the latter there were Joseph Gordon (afterward a Methodist preacher) and a young man named

Hoover. These two made arrangements to stop at Dugans and hunt and trap all winter. The Green family were about ready to go but lingered a few days to attend the wedding of Mary Dugan and Colonel Montague. His first wife died a year previous. (I should have mentioned in a former letter that Montague county was named for the colonel.) Colonel Montague and Mary Dugan were married on a Sunday afternoon, a large number of relatives and friends from Warren attending and witnessing the ceremony. On Monday morning after breakfast the wedding party left for Warren, the bride accompanied to her new home by her brother George and sister Emily. Green and family also left, but very much against the wishes of his parents. The oldest son William decided to remain. His sisters joined in entreating him to go with them, but the prospect of a winter's pleasure in hunting and trapping with Gordon proved more potent than their pleading, and unfortunately for him he allowed them to go without him.

After the wedding party and visitors were all gone, work was commenced on the house for greater security against Indians and cold weather. William Dugan and young Green worked hard all day chinking the cracks between the logs of the house, cutting port holes on all sides and fitting blocks for the same; also making bars for the doors, as the only fastening was a common wooden pin. Gordon and Hoover went hunting. The house proper was a long log building of two large rooms with a hall between, facing north and south. The kitchen was built at the west end of the house, a part of it projecting beyond far enough to allow a port hole at that end to command a view of the yard and one side of the house. The men slept in the farthest east room, their beds ranged around the room head to head and facing the fire place. About dusk George and Emily returned from Warren, Gordon and Hoover came in from the hunt, bringing a fine fat deer. William and Green had finished their work except one bar intended for the door of their room, and the absence of this particular bar furnishes the tragic events to be related in this chapter. As my mother, Kate Dugan, was a principal figure in the incidents of the evening, I will present the facts in her own words. She says:

The first indications of Indians we had noticed for some time were on that Monday evening. The cows would not stand still long enough to be milked, but would snuff the air, hoist their heads and herd together in the upper part of the pen, gazing very intently towards the woods. We felt certain that Indians were in the vicinity, watching our movements, but it was such a common occurrence we took no extra precautions, depending a good deal on our dogs to keep them at a distance. Our dogs had been of great service to us and I believe they had many times kept the Indians off by barking and extreme fierceness. After supper George and William went to the barn to sleep as usual and the other men went to their room, where they had a good fire burning. Henry Dugan and another boy named William Albert, who was staying at our house, were out in the yard playing until father went to the door and told them to go to bed. Henry slept with Green, and, boylike, wanted to sleep in the front, but when he was ready for bed Green was too sound asleep to be induced to get over, so necessarily Henry had to crawl in behind, and though very unwilling to occupy so undignified a place it was the means of saving his life. Mother went to bed early and father lay dozing by the kitchen fire, as was his habit, being troubled with rheumatism, Sister Emily and I sat near by working by the dim light of a single tallow dip, I sewing and she cording cotton rolls for the next day's spinning. Everything was very quiet, the dogs not even barking as usual. Afterwards we knew they were down behind the smoke house knawing the deer bones that Gordon had thrown there.

Emily and I were talking in whispers about the wedding when we both started and listened to an unusual noise we heard in the men's room. The door pin fell on the floor and some one gave the door a kick. We were about to resume our work and conversation, thinking it was one man, when like a thunderbolt two shots rang out, followed by another, and then all was confusion. Pandemonium let loose, in an instant the yard seemed full of Indians, all yelling and blowing whistles. Emily sprang up and commenced running up and down the room screaming "Indians." I blew the candle out the first thing, then ran for the bucket of water and threw it on the fire, and turned just in time to catch mother, who, half dazed with sleep, was trying to unbar the door and get out. Father was pretty quick, considering his rheumatism, and grabbing his old "flint lock" ran to the port hole and fired at the noise as it was too dark to take aim. The dogs, hearing the noise, came tearing around the house and joined in the row with all their teeth and lungs, and the Indians soon left. Emily kept running up and down the room, and if the Indians heard that puncheon floor rattle they must have thought the kitchen full of men. I have no doubt, though, that they had watched us as we sat there at work, for there was a crack between the logs near the door that one could have put his arm through, and it is very likely they took observations and knew where to find the men first. I don't know what I should have done if I had turned and seen a pair of shining eyes looking at me through that crack. After the Indians left and the noise subsided, we could hear cries and groans in the men's room, which set us almost distracted. Father called out through the port hole to know who was hurt, and Gordon answered that Green was killed and Hoover wounded.

In about half an hour we heard three shots in the direction of the barn, followed by such terrible groans that we were alarmed for fear that one of the boys was hurt, but the whistles and howls of lamentations, a cross between the howl of a wolf and the cry of a human, accompanying the groans, gave us a very correct idea that our enemies were getting the worst of a bad bargain. We did not dare to stir out until morning and, as it was best to keep our forces scattered, we all stayed where we were until sun rise. The men barricaded their door and kept watch in their room, and I took father's gun and remained on guard at that port hole while father slept. I could only listen for strange noises or look out once in a while to see if the Indians were skulking about the house on our side. All night long I could hear their whistles first in one place and then in another, sometimes clear and shrill near the house, then a tremulous quivering note like the plaintive song of a bird would break the silence of the night. It was evident that the Indians were very uneasy about something.

Toward morning, as it began to grow light, I leaned forward once more and looked out on the familiar bushes and trees, thankful that day was at last dawning and this fearful suspense would soon be at an end. My searching eyes took in every object within the circuit of the port hole, and I was about to draw back when I was arrested by a sight that made my heart jump right into my throat. Not twenty feet away stood an Indian by a tree, silent and motionless as a statue; where he came from or how he got there was more than I could tell. I had seen no motion and heard no sound. My first thought was to shoot, and what a fine chance it was! I had a feeling of hatred and a desire for vengeance against the whole Indian race since my brother was so cruelly murdered by them, and now was my time. I raised my gun, but in the excitement of the moment I must have made a noise that gave him the alarm, for, when I looked again down the shiny barrel he was gone. Sun rise came at last, bringing the boys in from the barn, and when in a few hurried questions and replies they learned our situation, George mounted our fleetest horse and went to Warren for a doctor, and to inform Green of the death of his son.

For many years after the print of an Indian's hand could be seen where he leaned against the soft mortar and pulled the peg out of the door on that fatal night.

Two shots were fired towards the beds, one striking Green, killing him instantly. Hoover sprang out of bed and sank to the floor with a very bad flesh wound in his side, while Gordon, as quick as a flash, jumped over the bed, ran in behind the door and pushed it to with such force that he fairly knocked the Indians out of the door. He fastened it with chains and tables the best he could, threw water on the fire that was burning brightly in the fire place and then went to the assistance of the wounded man. Not knowing that Green was shot Henry sprang out of bed and tried in vain to rouse him; he threw back the cover, and taking hold of his hand, told him to "wake up, the Indians were upon them," but no response came from the lips forever dumb, and they soon discovered that the poor boy was wrapped in the slumbers that knows no awakening.

When George and William heard the firing at the house and Emily screaming they hurried on their clothes to come to their rescue; then they heard father's gun and the dogs, and thought they had better stay where they were. A wise resolve, for the Indians next turned their attention to the horses.

The boys made all preparations, for they saw that their guns were in order and ammunition handy. They did not have long to wait. As William was on the lookout at the front side of the barn, he saw a dark form moving about very strangely among the trees. It would appear from behind a tree, jump up and down, and then dart back. After acting in this wild way for awhile, it made a dash for the barn door where it "materialized" to the watching eyes above, as a very stalwart Indian, who had been acting in that way to tempt a shot if any one was on guard at the barn. Seemingly satisfied that no one was around, and that he had everything to himself, he set his gun down by the door and began to work and pick at the padlock, venting his anger in choice English "cuss words" when it would not yield to his manipulations. In a few moments he was joined by two more Indians who had been watching the proceedings. They walked up and stopped within a few steps from the door, talking in a low tone of voice and looking up toward a little window cut in the logs just above the door. Like the colonel of Revolutionary fame, William "waited until he could see the whites of his enemy's eyes and then fired." At a signal George was by his side in a second, and motioning him that it was time to shoot, they rested the muzzles of their guns between the logs and fired. Both Indians were mortally wounded, fell, got up and ran some distance, four to the north and one west of the barn. The former by his groans, attracted his friends who came and carried him off; the other was not heard from and the boys supposed he was taken away too. They reloaded their guns and took their places again to await another attack, for they did not think the Indians would give up the fight without another effort to get the horse; nor were they mistaken. As George was looking out on his side next to the cow pen, he saw the cows very much disturbed, step aside very suddenly and give a wide berth to an object crawling on the ground.

At first he thought it was a hog as it grunted its way toward the barn, but upon closer inspection, and knowing that the hogs could not get in on that side, he suspected it was an Indian and raised his gun to give him a reception worthy of his mission.   As he was taking aim the muzzle of his gun raked on the bark, making a slight noise.   The quick ear of the Indian caught the sound and partly raised up, but he only made a better target of himself and received a ball and twenty-four buckshot full in the breast, cutting in two a hair rope tied around his waist.   He was tracked the next day by his blood to where he died, and where the Indians had found and carried him off, but the continual whistling during the night made all think that they had not succeeded in finding all their dead yet.   When George came back from Warren he brought the doctor, several rangers and the family of Green, who took their boy back to Warren for burial.   As the men were waiting for dinner, some talking and others, who had been up all night, were trying to sleep, a shrill whistle was heard in the woods near the house, which brought every man to his feet and off into the woods in no time.   A fleeting vision of a red skin clearing the ground by flying leaps two yards apart was all they saw and they returned and commenced searching for dead Indians. They found one of the first that was shot, the one that had run west of the barn and had fallen dead without a groan. The men dragged him to the house and laid him out in state in the yard, inviting all to come to the funeral (no flowers).   He was dressed in light marching order, a calico shirt and leather leggins, and as Doctor Rowlett came out with the others to take a last look at the deceased he looked at him for a moment and then exclaimed: "Why, that is Cachatta Bill; he used to work for me; my wife made that shirt he has on!"

Rev. Mr. Brown, a Methodist Preacher who Don't Eat Chicken.

IT was late in the afternoon of a bright sunny day, in the spring of 1844, that a solitary horseman was seen approaching the Dugan farm, on Choctaw, and from his dusty, travel stained appearance and the weary, jaded look of his horse, one could imagine that both man and

beast stood greatly in need of rest and refreshments. Now,
men on horseback, single or in pairs, were no uncom-
1844 mon sight to these dwellers in the woods, and few ever
came near a habitation without stopping at fence or
door and exchange greetings or whatever news there was
to tell, and most every one knew who his next neighbor was
on sight. But this traveler's outfit and general make up
was so foreign to backwoods life and dress, that he could
hardly hope to pass through the settlements without being
closely scrutinized and arousing a curiosity as to who he
was and where he was going. He appeared to be about
forty years of age; his clean shaven face disclosing many
marks of time's ravages, and a careworn expression betray-
ing many a hard tilt in life's tournament. He was a tall
angular man, and mounted upon a tall angular horse; a
tall hat set on a head covered with rather long hair, together
with a high choker and a long tailed coat, completed his
elongated appearance. A pair of well stuffed saddle bags
looked like great excrescences on the horse's back; and, as
the rider urged his animal along in a sort of a jog trot his
elbows and the saddle bags kept up a concerted motion that
threatened a total disarrangement of the internal economy
of both horse and rider.

As he approached the house the dogs, stretched lazily on
the ground, raised their heads and uttered low growls in
warning that a stranger was near; these gave way to a
fierce barking, which brought the family to the door. The
girls, Catherine and Emily, dropped their work of carding
to take a look at the stranger, convinced at a glance that
he was no one they had ever seen, and wondered if he was
going to stop. Mother Dugan gazed at him long and earnestly as he rode up to the fence, slowly dismounted and tied
his horse as if he knew that his welcome was assured. She
then turned, and in a decided tone that admitted of no argument, said: "Girls, that is a Methodist preacher as sure
as I live. Leave your work and get supper quick; kill some
chickens and churn. Henry blow the horn for your father!"
As they flew around to do her bidding the stranger came to
the door and asked if Brother Dugan lived there? On being
assured that he did, and invited to come in, he introduced
himself as the Rev. Mr. Brown, lately transferred from the

Indiana to the Texas Methodist conference and was now ap
pointed to the Red river circuit. He was given, on that account, a doubly hearty welcome and told to make the Dugan
mansion his home; that their doors had always been open
to the Lord's annointed since the time when away back in
Missouri Peter Cartwright had lived and preached at their
house. They also told him what a benighted condition the
settlements were in without religious services, and how they
had longed for the time to come when all could gather together, have meetings, a regularly appointed spiritual guide
and once more live like Christians. The good mother busied
herself to make her guest comfortable, went out to the
kitchen to tell the girls that he was really a Methodist
preacher, to be sure and have plenty of chicken and to see
that the best of everything was set before him. When the
bountiful supper was ready it was a meal fit for a king.
Delicate cream biscuit (in honor of company) offered a
striking contrast to the little mound of golden corn pones
close by; wild honey and preserved wild fruits, pats of fra-
grant butter and cool refreshing buttermilk, while occupying a prominent place stood a dish, whose delicate slices of
pink tinted home cured ham could be seen peeping out from
beneath their thick covering of fresh new laid eggs. But
the crowning dish, the "piece de resistance," was a platter
piled high with nicely browned, crisp, fried chicken, flanked
by a steaming bowl of rich milk gravy. How true to her
early training and Methodist instincts had Mother Dugan
followed the time honored custom in catering to the proverbial appetite of the Methodist itinerancy; instinctively
knowing what would make Brother Brown feel perfectly at
home, though among strangers and in a strange land.

Fried chicken! Magical words, that carry me back
through memory's halls to that same old log kitchen, and I
see that same table bountifully spread and surrounded by
loved ones now dead or scattered—never more to be united.
I see a rosy cheeked little girl, in "linsey woolsey" dress,
sitting at the dear gandma's right hand, and cousin George
on the left, while between the two a jealous rivalry exists
as to who will secure the greater number of drumsticks and
wishbones, requiring great tact and diplomacy on the part
of the white haired, white capped saint, to prevent a blood-

less war, ready to be declared should she give one an extra drumstick more than the other.

Pardon me for this digression; but while wiry fibres all along the taproot of memory cling close to early associations and grandmother's savory dishes, with a love that shows no affinity with fleshy appetite, I can never divorce fried chicken and sentiment. But Brother Brown has asked the blessing some time ago, and all are now waiting in decorous silence until their honored guests shall be helped. Father Dugan picks out the tender brown morsels, and loading the plate with other good things, hands it to Brother Brown, who passes it to the next one, with the remark that "he never eats chicken!" An awe-ful silence falls upon the assembled household, and startled glances are exchanged. Shades of John Wesley and all the apostles! A Methodist preacher and not eat chicken! Has there been a change in the creed since our exile? What manner of man is this, who comes to us in the guise of an itinerant circuit rider, who carries neither purse or scrip, depending alone upon the manna to be found in the wilderness, and who now goes back on the first confession of faith and says he never eats fried chicken! Parson Brown, be careful, be strong and steadfast; it will take your longest prayers and your most eloquent oratory to convince your scattered congregation that you are the genuine article. Don't you know, Brother Brown, that wherever you go along the line of your circuit, your clerical appearance and those saddle bags will be the death warrant of scores of "yaller legged roosters," and if you do not follow the precedent established by your colleagues gone before, you will be regarded with unbounded surprise and suspicion? Brother Brown, take heed unto the hundreds of despairing squawks that will go up from as many severed throats on your account, and reform your heretical appetite before it is everlastingly too late. But the good brother likes ham and eggs, so there is no danger of his starving; and coming full of "Peace on earth and good will to man," he stayed and preached the word. conquering the hearts of his many hearers. After making his appointments for every four weeks at Brother Dugan's and at Warren alternately, he left to travel about three hundred miles before making the round of his circuit. Braving

storms and flood, heat and hunger, wild beasts, and still
wilder Indians, the earth often his bed and his saddle a pillow; all for the sake of Jesus, to carry his messages and
teachings into the barren places.

Verily, I think, such heroism and self sacrifice can never
receive fitting reward in this vain, selfish world. But in the
next, ah! the next, methinks the angels will tune their harps
anew and sing anthems of praise to these noble souls as
they gather around the great white throne to render an account of their stewardship while on this little foot stool of
their Master, especially in one little spot called Texas.

First Camp Meeting in Grayson County.

T HE Rev. Brown, mentioned in the last chapter, minis-
tered faithfully to his scattered flock, and at the end of
the conference year held a camp meeting at Warren,
assisted by Rev. Custer, the presiding elder, and the
Rev. Duncan, a missionary from the Indian Territory.

It is not to be denied that a camp meeting in those days
was a very important event, and anticipated with in-
1847 tense interest by the settlers far and near.   Different
motives actuated people to attend camp meetings, and
the same rule will apply to such occasions of later date.
Some go out of curiosity, to see and be seen, others regard
it as a season of rest and diversion, while many embrace the
occasion to gossip, exchange news, see the latest fashions,
and make new acquaintances.   A few, a chosen few, anticipate the event when in God's natural temples, the leafy
groves, they will feel the "outpourings of the Spirit," or experience that magical "change of heart," granted through
the efficacy of prayer, to those who earnestly seek the Di-
vine blessing.   But we will go as spectators, mere lookers on,
and take a bird's eye view of this panorama in the midst of
nature.   We see first a large shed covered with brush and
limbs of trees; this is to shelter the large audience; while

heavy boards or logs are to serve for seats. Another slab
upheld by stakes, driven into the ground and covered by a
bearskin is the pulpit; a number of chairs, some splint bot-
tomed and some covered with rawhide, the hair left on, are for
the deacons and ministers who are expected to be present.
The "mourners bench" has not been forgotten, neither has
the straw which is scattered around with liberal hand. Little brush shanties have been erected all around in convenient places for the campers, and soon their occupants begin
to arrive. They come "a foot and a horseback," riding single
and double. On carts and wagons drawn by horses are
loaded bedding, cooking utensils and children. Dogs have
not been invited, but they come any way, and make themselves too familiar for comfort, and are all sizes and breeds,
from the long eared deer hound to the common cur. The
camp ground begins to assume the appearance of a picnic on
a large scale; horses neigh as new comers arrive, babies cry,
children shout and play and a hum of good natured conversation, enquiries and greetings all combine to make a vivid
and realistic picture in its setting of living green. I said something about fashions, but it was a far fetched allusion. I
wonder if our dear forefathers and mothers in their coonskin caps and slat sun bonnets ever worried about the
"latest styles," or in their primitive simplicity ever
imagined that succeeding generations would lose sight of
their humble origin, forget what the foundation of American aristocracy really is, and "run" to vanity, selfishness,
patent spring bottom pants, tournieres and pompadour
puffs."

It is now approaching time when meeting is to commence
and to blast or toot on a tin horn brings the scattered congregation together. Those men who, from long habit, carry
their rifles with them, lean them against the nearest tree,
and out of respect to the occasion divest themselves for the
present of shot pouch and powder horn. A dog fight or two
is settled and the yelping curs sent off to crouch under the
wagons; then all gather in and seat themselves on the rough
boards. A few youngsters who are habitually thirsty at
meeting take a last drink out of the bucket near the pulpit,
put the gourd dipper down rather noisily, then make their
way to their mothers, who unceremoniously yank them into

a seat and bid them sit there and be quiet.   At last all is still
and solemn.   Brother Brown rises up. his tall form threatening to bring the top of his head and the brush above in
violent collision.   He casts a searching glance over the
audience and finally all are attentive as the occasion requires and he commences in a sonorous voice to line out the
hymn:

> Children of the heavenly king,
> As ye journey sweetly sing.

Here we will leave them, confident that Brother Brown,
in his fervid zeal, will faithfully warn his interested hearers
to flee from the wrath to come.

*   *   *   *   *   *   *

Thus was the foundation of Methodism laid in Grayson
and adjoining counties.   Brother Brown was succeeded by
Jefferson Schuck, and he by Andrew Davis and others, all
earnest workers in the cause.   The Baptist faith was ably
upheld by two brothers by the name of Hiram and James
Savage.   One lived on Caney creek and the other on Bois
d'Arc, as farmers.   They tilled the soil during the week,
preaching on Sundays; accomplishing great good on the
frontier of Grayson.

The fourth of July, 1847, was the occasion of a grand barbecue and bran dance at Sherman, then in its infancy; and
to a great many who attended the festivities this was their
first view of the new county seat.   A log house about twenty
feet square, used for the court house, and a few rods of
ploughed land comprised the metropolis from one end to the
other.   I will leave it to my readers to picture the contrast
of the city then and now.

For the barbecue a large brush shed was built, under
which were ranged long tables loaded with all kinds of
roasted meats and all the delicacies of the season, welcome
to all to eat, drink and to be merry without money and without price.   The refreshment stand—a rail fence built partly
around a barrel of whisky—stood near at hand, while a tin
cup did frequent duty for a thirsty crowd.   The court house
was thrown open to accommodate the dancers.   Justice took
off her spectacles, laid aside her steel yards, and for once in
her life gave herself up to the intoxicating pleasures of the .
hoe down.   Music was furnished by a ' stalwart darkey

perched on a barrel; when he would give out another stood ready to take his place until he could visit the refreshment stand and counteract the effects of the heat and his violent exertions by looking for the bottom of that tin cup.

As this is my last letter on Reminiscences we want to leave our pioneers prosperous and contented, and it will not be difficult to do so. They have enjoyed peace and security from their enemies, the Indians, for several years now, with a few exceptions of horse stealing.

The little pioneer school started in Warren grew and flourished under the teaching of Mr. Limble, who was succeeded by R. W. Lee, and he by a Mr. Graham and others.

As the settlements increased, other schools were established in different parts of the county. Among the improvements gradually introduced for the benefit of the settlers, the first of importance was grist mills. They could now throw away their hand mills on which they had depended so long, but their looms and spinning wheels stayed with them many years longer.

When we stop and think of the advancements made in every direction since this period of Texas, early settlement, the time seems longer than it really is. When we remember that those pioneers had no newspapers, magazines or any kind of communication with the outside world, save as come by word of mouth; no telegraph, telephone or railroads; that churches and schools barely struggled into existence after long years of patient waiting, it makes one imagine a pre-adamite sort of existence, and not of a time only forty years ago. Think of having no thread except that manufactured at home; no matches, a flint their only dependence, and a log stump in the field set fire to by its sparks was their reserve when the fires at the house would accidentally go out; the neighbors literally coming to borrow a shovel full of coals. I might mention many more instances where improvements have been made to increase the comforts and lessen the toil of the pioneers, but I am certain there are many of my readers who know a great deal more on that subject than I do. One more word and I am done. The future historian of the Lone Star State cannot ignore, if he is a faithful chronicler, the honors due the earliest settlers for services rendered as advance guard to

the great tide of immigrators that peopled a properous land.
It has not been in my power to mention but a very few of
the pioneers of Grayson county, but, however small the
number, they help swell the grand total, and I bespeak a
recognition in the annals of the State.

The pioneers of a country are justly deserving of a niche
in the country's history.

The pioneers who became martyrs to the cause of the development of an almost unknown land deserve to have
a place in the hearts of its inhabitants.   None but the brave
and venturesome, energetic and courageous dare penetrate
the pathless wilderness and trackless forests, and Texas,
with her cultivated fields, wealth and beautiful homes may
well enshrine the memory of her noble hearted pioneers,
path finders, martyrs.

Fannin's First Campaign.

THE following accounts of murders and massacres in
Fannin county were written a few years ago, by the
late Judge J. P. Simpson (an old pioneer of Fannin
county), for publication in a little book entitled, "History of Fannin county," by W. A. Carter. Having been
written by one who was personally familiar with the different incidents related, and whose reputation for verac-
1838 ity was so well recognized by those who knew him,
we have no hesitancy in giving them to the reader
with no other endorsement, and feel perfectly safe in saying
that they will all be found substantially correct.

In 1838, the first volunteer companies for the defense of
Fannin county were raised and organized by Captain
Robert Sloan and N. L. Journey. These two companies
consisted of forty men each. Captain Journey's company
met at Jonathan Anthony's, eight miles south of Fort English, all in high glee under the influence of strong drink.
That night the Captain's charger and two others were stolen

by the Indians. Next day was spent in getting other horses to supply the vacancies; and that night two companies met at what was then called Linsey's Springs, on Bois d'Arc, where Mr. Sears now lives. Beef was slaughtered for rations, and everything made ready for an early start for the Indian village on the west forks of Trinity. Guards were stationed around the encampment for the night, and each went to spinning yarns. In the midst of all this amusement one of the guards fired his gun, in an instant the pickets fled for camp, men ran for their guns; some guns were misplaced, shot pouches and ammunition missing, all hurry and confusion; the captain dispatched to ascertain the cause of alarm; no guard at his post; one of the guards (my mess fellow) dashed into camp, saying he had seen and shot at an Indian trying to steal horses; his heart beating so hard he declared it was the sound of Indians' feet fleeing from the fire of his gun. The officer returned, made his report to headquarters, stated that he found no dead or wounded Indian; he supposed he had found an Indian's blanket, but on examination found he was mistaken; the blanket turned out to be the paunch of the beef slaughtered for rations for the men; no more yarns that night. Next morning we mounted our horses and started for the Indian village, our pilot in front. Marched three days and camped for the last night until the Indian village would be desolated by the heroes of Fannin. An alarm by the pickets during the night, but no one killed or wounded. Next morning a council of war was held, scouts were sent ahead to spy out the village. The scouts returned and reported the village near at hand. Now we must try our bravery or run—three hundred Indian warriors fortified in their huts, to defend themselves, squaws and children, and only ninety whites to attack and enter into deadly conflict with them. Columns of attack were formed and the charge ordered. Many a pale face was to be seen in the ranks. Away we went, but lo! when we got to the scene of action, only a camp of Indians was there. The Indians were soon dispatched by the men and the scalps taken from their heads by Captain John Hart. One white man was wounded and one horse was killed. There we found Captain Journey's stolen horse and others. After the battle one wounded Indian lay concealed in the grass with a tomahawk in his hand. A man by the name of Pangborn (usually called "Brandy," from the quantity of that article he drank) was on the lookout for the wounded Indian and came up on him so close he couldn't shoot. The Indian rose with toma-hawk in hand, striking at Pangborn's head. The latter wheeled and ran, shouting for help at every jump. One gun was fired from our ranks, the Indian fell, and Captain Hart was on him in an instant and took his scalp. The place some years since was occupied and settled by Major Bird, and called Bird's Fort, not far from where Fort Worth now stands. We started for home, and the third night camped on Bois d'Arc near where Orangeville now stands, and found that Indians had been in the settlement and killed and scalped one of our best citizens, William Wash-burn Thus ended our first scout for Indians in Fannin, until a more formidable force could be raised to protect the frontier, which was done that winter under the command of General John H. Dyer, of Red River county.

Massacre of McCarty and Daugherty.

I n 1838–39 the Indians were hostile against the whites in this part of the county and committed many depreda-tions in Fannin county and her territory. The citizens were up in arms and on the lookout for the foe; compa-nies were organized and every man was on the alert. A battalion was formed of the citizens of Lamar and Fannin counties, armed and equipped for service under the 1838 command of General Dyer, of Red River county. The rendezvous was at Fort English, near where Bonham now stands. This settlement, then consisting of eight or ten families, was forted up for mutual protection. When the army left in search of the Indians the writer was left at the fort as lieutenant in command of a squad of twenty men for the protection of the women and children. While the army was out William Daugherty, Andrew Thomas,

Andrew Daugherty and William McCarty's son (the two latter were youths) went in search of their pork hogs near where Kentuckytown now stands, they having lived a short time in that vicinity.

* * * * * * * *

Judge Simpson then relates the killing of old man Daugherty, the heroic defense made by Andrew Thomas and the narrow escape of the latter and young Daugherty, but the full details of the massacre having been graphically described in the articles of Mrs. Shearer, which we have heretofore given to the reader, we deem it unnecessary to go over them again. Judge Simpson, however, mentions the killing of William McCarty, who, it seems, was with the party. In the account given by Mrs. Shearer his name is omitted. Judge Simpson says: "The savages shot young McCarty full of arrows and cut off his head with their tomahawks. The next morning we started to the scene of the slaughter. Arriving at the battle ground there lay old man Daugherty in a pool of blood, three scalps having been taken from his head and the tomahawk having been sunk twice in the naked skull—a sight so horrible and appalling that you can have no conception of it without you had been an eye witness. McCarty's son was not scalped, but his head was cut entirely off except a small ligament on one side. The bodies were brought to the fort next day and deposited in the graveyard at Fort English, being the second burial at that place.'

The Two Old Guards.

BY JUDGE J. P. SIMPSON.

WHILE the white people were forted at Warren, in 1839, Daniel Dugan and Henry Green, two old men, volunteered their services to guard the horses at night. The young men had become worn out by incessant watching and guarding the horses of those citizens who were forted, being kept in an enclosure for safety, where they had to be guarded at night. In the center 1839 of this enclosure, a stable had been built, which answered for a guard house, and was surrounded with shade trees. The stable loft was partly laid with rails which projected over the center joist, and which was for the guard to occupy while watching for the Indians. The two old veterans took their stand in the guard house, on the rails, watching vigilantly for the foe, who, true to their instincts for stealing, made their appearance in the horse lot, secreting themselves behind and in the shade of the trees. The moon shining very bright, gave the old men a chance to see; but the shadows of the Indians as they passed suddenly from one tree to another, gave them no chance to get a shot. They being extremely anxious to sun the Indian moccasins, and in their eagerness to get a position to do execution, they reached beyond the balance on the joists, when their foot holds gave way, the rails turning end upon end, and away went the old men, guns, rails, and all, with a great crash in the stable, making a great noise. The Indians did not take time to see what was the matter, nor what was done, but ran out, and made their escape to the brush, not being accustomed to such charges in warfare. The old men were somewhat bruised by the fall, but had the honor of inaugurating a new way of scaring off Indians. Some time after this three men left the fort to go to Preston; Bushnell Garner, David Alberty and Isaac Camp, two going on horseback and one on foot. When three miles west of the place where Denison now stands, the Indians ambushed and fired on them, killing the two horsemen instantly, pursued Alberty, the footman, some distance, caught him, stabbed him in the heart with their knives and then scalped him and broke his skull in small fragments with their tomahawks. The two other men who were shot, were scalped and tomahawked in a similar manner to Mr. Alberty. They also stripped them of their clothing and mutilated them in a shocking manner. After these murders were committed the citizens ceased to travel in day light, but traveled at night. I knew that J. P. Simpson, the then sheriff of this county, did all his traveling in the west portion of Fannin territory, in discharge of the busi-

ness connected with the office, after night. Then in passing over these lonely prairies, he became accustomed to
hearing the scream of the panther, the howl of the wolf,
and the hoot of the night owl. Many times was he alarmed
by these, taking them for the savages.

A Negro Turns White

By Judge J. P. Simpson.

A FEW days after the killing and scalping of Bushnell
Garner, David Alberty and Isaac Camp, as related by
me in a former sketch, the Indians still continued to
prowl around the neighborhood—we suppose to steal
more horses and murder the whites when they could get a
chance. The citizens were alarmed and carried their
weapons of warfare with them when engaged in their
1839 secular concerns of life. Mabel Gilbert, living two
miles south of Fort English, his being an outside
house, was greatly exposed, and often annoyed by them. He
became greatly excited, and armed and equipped himself
and those about him, so that they were prepared to meet
danger at every emergency. Some Indians had hid themselves in the brush near his fence, watching his black boy
Smith, who was engaged in the field pulling corn; armed
with a holster pistol and large butcher knife, and in order to
deceive and decoy him they imitated and answered the
croaking of wild turkeys. The boy left his work and approached with all the caution and stillness possible to prevent the turkeys from finding him out, with his pistol in
hand ready to shoot, until he approached a dense thicket,
when three Indians arose as quick as thought from an ambuscade and attempted to capture him. He didn't hesitate
a moment, but discharged the load in his pistol into the breast
of the one nearest him; the Indian staggered and fell, and

the other two sprang at him as-if determined to capture him.
The boy drew his butcher knife and ran to a big tree close
by, the Indians in close pursuit, when he made a desperate
thrust with his knife at the Indians who came meeting him
around the tree, but he missed them. He left his knife sticking in the tree and ran for the house; the Indians fired their
guns at him, but missed their aim.   His master and sons
hearing the alarm, ran from the house with their guns to his
rescue.   The Indians retreated, carrying off their wounded
buck, leaving a pool of blood where he laid.   His master
said that when he met the boy he was so frightened that his
complexion had assumed that of a dark skinned white man,
trembling from head to foot as though he had an ague, and
his voice faltering so as to be scarcely intelligible, and for
years afterwards, when talked to on the subject, he would
become so excited that his complexion would change.

Death of Sowell.

By Judge J. P. Simpson.

AFTER the battle with the Cachatta Indians, by the
Dugan family [Note. A full account of the Dugan
fight has been given in the communications of Mrs.
Shearer], the Indians left Dr. Rowlett's and fled to
the Indian Territory, north of Red River. The Texans, being greatly incensed at the course practiced by them while
living in Texas, determined that they should not re-
1841 main so near us. Captain Joseph Sowell, with ten or
twelve men, crossed the river at night, ascertained
where they were camped, charged on them and fired into
their wigwams, killing ten or twelve. This matter was kept
still with the Texans for sometime, the act being a violation of
international law with the United States Government. The
district court for Fannin county was to commence in 1841
at Warren, on Monday morning. Owing to the long dis-

tance those summoned as witness and jury men had to travel to court, many went on Sunday evening, who would put up at the tavern kept by Mr. Sowell and J. S. Scott. After securing lodging for themselves, and their horses cared for, they would indulge in drinking, and engage in a recital of the dangers, narrow escape and bats with the Indians. Captain Sowell had a fine and favorite charger, which he kept to himself securely locked in his stable, his guests' horses in a substantial enclosure close by. That night the Indians had cut the door facing in two with their knives and removed the chains and lock from the door shutters, bridled the fine stallion and mounted him, for the purpose of driving out the horses in the lot. The Indians had lain down in the fence corners and stationed themselves at the bars armed with bows and arrows, with their horseman on the fine charger in the lot driving the horses out. The neighing and tramping of the horses gave the alarm to those at the tavern, notwithstanding by this time they were in high glee and uproar at the house; for they had arrived at that point, that every man was a hero, a general, a statesman, or some great man in his own estimation; hearing the mighty crash and tramp of horses their amusement ended in short meter; all hands ran for their horses, most of them without their guns or pistols. Sowell and Scott ran to the gap, laid down by the Indians; Sowell armed with a pistol, Scott with a double barrel shot gun; Sowell discharged his pistol at them without effect, when they sent a volley of arrows at him, one passing through his stomach and out at his back. He fell at the Indians feet, and called to Scott to shoot the Indian, and expired without a groan. Scott discharged his gun and one Cachatta fell dead with Captain Sowell. The other Indians left the horses and fled in every direction, and collected on the road near Brushy creek beyond where Colonel Bradford now lives, filled the road with brush and other obstructions, and hid themselves on each side of the road, so if any man had gone that way that night, either with dispatches to Fort Smith or to protect his wife and children, he could not possibly have escaped the Indians. From the moccasin tracks next day at the place, we supposed there were twelve Indians. Had I as sheriff went to Warren that evening, which was my usual custom,

instead of morning, I should have tried to return that night
to my family at Fort English with the dispatch to the
people here, and certainly would have fallen a victim to
savage cruelty. Captain Sowell, when I came to the county,
was living on a bluff at Red river, below the mouth of
Sandy creek, in this county, and yet known and called
Sowell's bluff.

Two Boys Captured.

By Judge J. P. Simpson.

IN 1841, General Tarrant raised a battalion of men in the
counties of Bowie, Red River, Lamar and Fannin for the
purpose of driving out the Indians from Fannin's territory. They rendezvoused at Fort English and camped for
the night, and next morning were to take up the line of
march for the Indians. In the evening William Cox, who
lived a few miles north of the fort, sent his son and
1841 another boy, who were about twelve years old, to
drive up his milk cows. They did not return, being
captured by the Indians, and the family were in great distress, not knowing whether the children were captured or
killed by the Indians. A runner was sent to the fort to notify General Tarrant, who sent scouts in every direction in
search of the children and to notify the settlers that the Indians were upon them and to keep a sharp lookout. The
scouts sent to me, delivered the message and wheeled their
horses to go in search of the captured boys. They had not
gone more than fifty steps when they came in contact with
some Indians, who had caught some horses, and were in the
act of mounting to start. The men hailed the Indians, supposing them to be soldiers, when the Indians fled across the
prairie, where Bonham now stands, the troops in pursuit,
without the fire of a gun. I supposed they intended to capture them alive, from the course they pursued. Some lost
their pistols, some horses fell down, riders were thrown off
and the Indians made their escape. All was pell mell and
in a bad fix. The Indians then charged the fort, with the

captured boys behind them on their horses; the picket guards fired at them and wounding one old squaw, who died that night and was buried next morning by the Indians near where Orangeville now stands. This is the statement of the captured boys after their return, having been ransomed by the government for six hundred dollars. After the Indians buried the squaw they started for their village. They had not gone far when they saw a one armed man carrying a saddle, who, from his actions and gestures, they supposed had lost his horse and was looking for him. The Indians concealed themselves in the brush until the man came near; they then shot and scalped him and cut off the arm at the elbow and threw the body in the creek. When they camped at night the Indians roasted the hand and arm and ate it and appeared to be much elated while partaking of the delicious fare, and by signs and gestures showed the little fellows how they would kill, roast and eat them soon, which frightened them so they did not sleep, but spent the night in weeping and thinking of father, mother and home. In six days they reached the village, where the boys were most cruelly treated by the Indians, their backs cut and lacerated in a most horrible manner; they were stripped of clothing and went naked in the cold and chilling northers, getting no bread to eat, and but little meat; their suffering was great. In about six months they were purchased by some traders and sent home. The case of the prodigal son was eclipsed by the return of the two captured boys. The father fell on the neck of his son and wept; the mother ran to meet them, but swooned away with ecstatic joy and fell to the ground, and when returning to consciousness, with deep emotion and tears, exclaimed, when embracing them in her arms: "My son was lost, but now is found; was dead, but liveth again; glory to God on high." One of the boys was the brother to Hugh Cox, who now lives eight miles north of Bonham. The residence of William Cox was then near where the camp ground is located, four miles north of Bonham. Reader, reflect and think of the danger, toil, tears, blood and carnage the first settlers of this country encountered for the purpose of developing the resources of the great State of Texas, which was then a wilderness country, but now is as rejoicing and blooming as the rose.

Massacre of Clemmons and Whisler.

By Judge J. P. Simpson.

IN 1842, Doctor William E. Trockmorton settled in the territory of Fannin county, twenty-five miles from Fort English. This territory was afterwards made a county and called Collin. Many families settled around him—his place being the nucleus for the settlers to rendezvous for protection in case of an alarm of danger from the Indians. Mr. Wesley Clemmons and Mr. Whisler, with their families, 1842 moved from Timber creek, eight miles north of Fort English, and settled some eight miles north of Doctor Throckmorton. Mr. Clemmons had a wife and two children, and Mr. Whisler, a wife, but no children. They found land to suit them for homes, went to work and built themselves houses to live in, and commenced clearing land for a farm that they might make bread for their families. On starting to work one day after dinner, Indians who had concealed themselves in the brush near by, charged upon them when about one hundred and fifty yards from the house, screaming and yelling like demons, and cutting off their retreat to the house. They were shot down, tomahawked, scalped, and their bodies terribly mutilated. The wives of these two victims of Indian barbarity, witnessed the entire scene. One of the women attempted to take a gun to her husband, but had to retreat to the house to save herself. The Indians then hiding in the brush again for the purpose of doing more mischief. The two women and children remained in the house until night, when they repaired to the dead bodies of the murdered men. They did not know but that they themselves would feel the tomahawk and scalping knife, and that the little children be roasted and eaten by the savage cannibals. After drying their tears and quieting their sobs as best they could, they agreed that Mrs. Clemmons and her children should remain with the dead bodies during the night to keep them from being devoured by wolves and other beasts of prey, and that Mrs. Whisler should start for the nearest settlements, eight miles off, and give information of the murder. There being no road from their house, Mrs. Whisler followed the dry channel of a branch until she came to a road movers had made in moving to Doctor Throckmorton's neighborhood. She reached a house in safety, and gave the alarm.

The thoughts and feelings of Mrs. Clemmons that night never have been, nor never can be, described. Alone with her little children in the night, watching over the dead bodies of her husband and Mr. Whisler. Every wolf that howled; panther that screamed, or owl that hooted in that dark and lonely wilderness, she imagined to be the Indians coming to murder her and her children. If possible, she would have wept tears of blood that night. After becoming exhausted she fell asleep, but dreamed that the Indians were scalping her and her children, which aroused her to consciousness to weep and mourn.

Mrs. Whisler having accomplished her mission, the following day the dead were buried, and the women and children taken care of. Wesley Clemmons was a brother of Ex-Governor Throckmorton's step-mother, who is the mother-in-law of the Hon. L. C. Wilson, member of the Legislature from this county, now living in the city of Bonham.

Death of Clubz.

By Judge J. J. Simpson.

IN the year 1842, Judge English, Major Barker, John B. Denton, James S. Baker and others left Fort English on a tour of exploration of the country, on the waters of Trinity river—there being no settlement at that time in the territory southwest of Fort English, out of which Collin, Dallas and other counties were afterwards organized.

They examined critically for the most suitable sec-
1842 tions for location and survey—viewing the rich soil, beauty and grandeur of the Trinity country, together with the romantic scenery spread out before them. Traveling down some of the tributaries of the Trinity until they struck the main river, they selected Cedar Springs, and

where the city of Dallas now stands, and many other choice places for future location. They then started for home, traveling northeast, without a road or path to guide them. In the company was a Polander from Fort Towson, in the Choctaw Nation, whose character, person and manner indicated the perfect gentleman and scholar. His name was Clubz, and his broken English was vastly amusing to the entire company, with whom he was a general favorite. On the way home they discovered not far from them in a dense thicket smoke rising from a camp fire. Indians were instantly suspected, and preparations made at once for examination and attack. The two old men, Judge English and Major Baker, were selected to guard and take care of the horses. Guns were examined, and everything made ready for battle. Then they advanced cautiously and silently—the Polander in front, eager for the conflict. When they arrived at the place, there sat a fine looking Indian with a white shirt on, viewing himself in a looking glass. There were also a number of squaws and children around the camp, the warriors, it was supposed, being out on a hunt. Quick as thought, the whites arose from their ambush and fired at the breast of the Indian, who pitched forward and fell dead. The women and children ran and hid themselves in the brush. Supposing the warriors to be in hearing of the guns and would hasten back to camp and pursue and attack them, the policy of the whites was to get away as soon as possible to their horses, and so they started. But a familiar voice in front imploringly called them not to leave him to be scalped by the Indians. They turned to see what was the matter, when, to their surprise and horror, there lay their comrade, the Polander, writhing in the agonies of death. They carried him back to the horses, but, poor fellow, he was dead, having been shot by some one of the company who was in the rear; they being excited, had fired at random, and a chance shot had pierced him through. Gloom and melancholy sat on every countenance; but no time was to be lost. They lashed him on his horse, and traveled with speed till night, when they halted, and in a point of Brushy Prairie, with their knives and hatchets, they dug a grave and deposited the body of Mr. Clubz, with no mark or sign to designate his last resting place.

The company traveled the remainder of the night, guided by the stars, there being no roads nor paths in the country. Near daylight they halted and camped, considering themselves out of danger of pursuit—in deep gloom on account of the unfortunate death of one of their colleagues. On their return home, when in conversation on the subject, I could see profound sorrow on their countenances. Reader, I have two reasons for writing this sketch. One is, that when reviewing these exciting incidents which transpired thirty-five years ago, it drives from the old man's mind those melancholy thoughts and feelings to which age is subject. The other is, that this sketch may possibly fall into the hands of some friend or relative of the unfortunate Polander who would like to know what became of their lost friend or brother. He was entitled to land under the pre-emption laws, which I presume never has been attended to by any person.

Indian Warfare on the Northwestern Border.

WE are indebted to Captain R. B. Barry, of Bosque county, for the following interesting items:

According to promise, I herewith contribute to your historical compilation a short account of such conflicts with the Indians as have occurred in my own vicinity, and within my own knowledge.

I will commence my narrative with the winter of 1857 1857, for it was in that year that the first blood of my neighbors was shed in their conflicts with Indians. On one occasion, Mr. Renfrew and his son were out horse hunting on the head of Meridian creek, and whilst there they were attacked by Indians. Young Renfrew was killed and scalped on the instant. His father was riding a good horse, and rode four miles after receiving his death wound. He fell off dead, and the horse returning home riderless revealed the sad fact to the family that the father and husband was no more.

A party immediately went in search of the missing ones. Young Renfrew's body was found about two weeks after he

was killed, but the old man—or rather his mutilated remains—were not found until after the lapse of two years.
They were found by a Mr. Rabb. Near by was a saddle
which was identified by the family as the one Mr. Renfrew
was riding when he left home.

In the latter portion of the same year (1857) Mr. Bean, a
relative of the Bean of Texas history, and his negro man,
while returning home to the Leon river from some of the
older settlements, where he had been to buy corn, was attacked by a party of Indians near the same place where
they had killed the Renfrews. From the number of arrow
marks and bullet holes in the wagon bed, it was supposed
that the Indians had paid dearly for their trophies.

The next day the same party of Indians came in sight of
my place and attacked a Mr. Johnson, who was returning
from the lower country with breadstuffs, and who was driving two yoke of cattle. He was murdered at the foot of a
high peak, which has ever since been known as "Johnson's
Peak." They took Mr. Johnson's little boy, a lad eight years
of age, a prisoner. They also killed several of the oxen,
emptied the meal and flour in the road and carried away
the sacks.

Some eight or ten days after this, as Hinson Roberts and
party were following an Indian trail, along which a good
many of their stolen cattle had been driven, they came
across this little boy about forty miles from the nearest
house. The little fellow was nearly dead with hunger and
cold—the Indians having, as they usually do, stripped him
of his clothing. The boy had slipped out of camp one cold
night, in the same apparel that nature gave him, and came
across some cattle that had ropes attached to them; no doubt
some that had escaped from a marauding party of Indians.
He was trying to stay among these cattle, supposing that
they would protect him from the wolves. The little fellow
was taken home, and is still living.

The same party of Indians stole from my settlement about
one hundred and thirty head of horses, sixty of them belonging to me.

During this same year the Indians made a good many
raids into Bosque county, and also the county of Erath. I
will relate one incident that occurred in the winter of 1857.
A party of Indians came down by the upper settlements on

JOHNSON'S LITTLE BOY FOLLOWING THE COWS.

the North Bosque and killed a part of two families. They took two ladies, Mrs. Woods and Mrs. Lemly, some two miles from the house, and, after using them in the most savage and brutal manner, they murdered and scalped both. They also carried off two young ladies, the Misses Lemly, but turned them loose after two days travel. The next day this same party came across two young men, the Monroes, on Spring creek, seven miles from my ranch, where they were opening a farm, and killed both. The Indians met with no resistance, as they took the young men completely by surprise. They left a one hundred dollar bill lying on the ground near where they murdered the young men, probably knowing nothing of its value.

Late the same evening they killed young Knight on Neil's creek, fifteen miles from the scene of their former murders. The next day they wounded two Baptist ministers near the corner of Bell county. One of them died afterwards from the effects of his wound.

These Indians were pursued by the citizens, but owing to their rapid retreat they failed to overtake them.

Whenever such raiding parties of Indians were followed, it was invariably observed that after a time the trail divided, and that a part of the Indians had gone off in the direction of the reservations; and, finding many of our horses on the reservations, we were led to believe that at least a portion of the reserve Indians were concerned in the raids made upon the settlements by the wild tribes.

The feeling of hostility towards the reserve Indians caused by such suspicions was a good deal modified, however, by the soothing story of the interpreter, who told us that we were greatly indebted to these reserve Indians for risking their lives in retaking our stock stolen from us by the wild tribes, and really induced us to believe this, and that they had conferred a favor on us by making us pay ten dollars for every horse returned to us.

However, after Fred Gentry's horse had been found on the upper reserve, in possession of the Comanches, and four of the reserve Indians were killed by Captain Preston and his neighbors, when in the act of driving off a number of stolen horses, we were pretty well satisfied that these reserve

Indians were leagued with the wild tribes in raiding on the settlements.

On one occasion Captain Peter Garland, who was following an Indian trail, came near a camp of the lower reservation Indians, and mistaking them for Caddoes, a fight was the consequence, in which —— Stephens and —— Barnes, two of his men, were killed and ten of the Indians. As this fight took place among the wigwams, some of the squaws and children were killed in the melee.

This was the beginning of the reservation war. The citizens flocked to the protection of those living above, near the reservation; and in a few days there were embodied together seven hundred men, besides some small parties scattered about at different points. Captain Allison Nelson was elected to the command, and it was resolved to make an attack upon the upper reservation, as it was believed our worst enemies were there. Four hundred men were ordered to proceed up the Clear fork of the Brazos, under Colonel John R. Baylor.

While passing up by the lower reservation, Colonel Baylor's men killed and captured some straggling Indians. This brought on a fight with the Indians of the lower reservation. The fight lasted several hours, and was carried on in regular savage style by both parties, each putting to death all the prisoners taken. Many were killed and wounded on both sides, but the Indians having the United States forces under Captain Parmer to fall back upon, there was but one alternative left us—either to draw off or attack Captain Parmer's command.

It is very certain that on this occasion some white men fought against us, but no doubt they were mainly the "dead heads" and hangers on about the reservation, as no United States soldiers were seen in the fight.

During a consultation between Colonels Baylor and Nelson, the Indians of both reservations were thrown together, and, with the United States soldiers protecting them, they left the State of Texas and established their reservation at Fort Cobb, on the upper Wichita, in the Chickasaw nation.

During the most of the time while these events were taking place, I was, with a few well mounted men, reconnoitering the Comanche agency.

As the State Convention that passed the ordinance of secession saw proper to place troops on our frontier after the Federal forces had retired, they ordered Colonel Henry E. McCulloch to proceed at once to the front and take charge of the fort, then occupied by United States soldiers. A portion of my company was at that time encamped on the head of Hubbard's creek, and was ordered out by Governor Houston while I was absent on a scout. Subsequently they were transferred to the Confederate service. When I returned, I found myself in command of a company in the First Texas cavalry, under Colonel Henry E. McCulloch.

Our regiment was stationed in detachments from Red river to the Rio Grande, each about a day's ride apart along the uppermost settlements. The officers were strict in their discipline and drill, with the expectation of soon being ordered to a more glorious field than operating against savages, where every man usually was his own commander Major Edward Burleson and myself both considered that the time wasted in disciplining and drilling troops for service against Indians was costing the frontier people much blood as well as property, and for this or some other reason Burleson resigned his commission as major.

The first scout of any importance was ordered by Major Burleson, who directed me to meet him at a certain big spring on Red river, nearly a day's ride above the Wichita mountain. The night before the morning on which I was to start an express came in, stating that ten of my men whom I had sent to escort some wagons from Camp Cooper, on the Brazos, to Gooch's ranch, on Red river, had been badly used up by the Indians between the Red Fork of the Brazos and Little Wichita, forty-five miles from Camp Cooper, where I was then stationed.

I sent off one-half of my company that night to their relief and all that could be spared from the post the next morning. They met the remnant of the little detachment at the Red Fork. After burying young McKay, one of the wounded who had died, and giving such medical aid as we could to the other wounded, we sent them back with an escort. We then proceeded on our way and had been traveling but half a day when we came up with the same Indians that had attacked the wagon escort. But before mentioning

ιhe result I will here relate the incidents which took place
ιn the fight between these Indians and the detachment
escorting the wagons. The detachment was under the command of Sergeant Erhenback. Eight of the ten men composing it were mortally or seriousiy wounded, the slightest
wound having been received by Sergeant Erhenback, the
bullet passing through his stirrup before it struck him. His
horse was badly wounded. Eight of their ten horses were
killed or wounded. The sergeant reported Corporal Miller
as having acted mutinously. Corporal Miller said that during the hotest part of the contest, while surrounded on all
sides in the open prairie and Indians cross firing at them
from every direction, he (Sergeant Erhenback) had ordered
a retreat, to what he thought a better position. Corporal
Miller persuaded the boys to fight it out where they were,
as they had several dead horses for shelter, and he called
the sergeant a coward, whereupon they attempted to shoot
each other, but were prevented from doing so by the others.

The fight lasted until the Indians had used up all their
ammunition (so they supposed) and fell back. It began at
nine a. m. and continued until three p. m., and extended
over five miles of open prairie. The wounded men rode
such horses as were able to travel, whilst the rest fought
around them on foot against four times their number. We
learned from some of the reservation Indians that their
wild friends lost eight of their warriors in this fight.

We will now relate what occurred after we came up with
these Indians two days subsequent to the fight just described.
Their force had been increased to about one hundred warriors, and they were making their way toward the settlements. Willie Biffle, who was a long way from the command on the right flank, came in and reported Indian signs.
I halted the command and sent twelve men back after the
pack mules that had stampeded. They had scarcely gone
out of sight over the divide when we heard firing. We
hurried to their relief, but not in time to save three of the
twelve men from being killed and others wounded. A general fight then ensued. After a short time the Indians began to fall back, notwithstanding they had three to our one.
The fight extended over some ten or twelve miles of ground
across the divide, and between the Little Wichita and the

Red Fork of the Brazos. Whenever we became somewhat scattered in the chase the Indians would turn and check our advance for a while. They were well armed and equipped and wore a great many savage ornaments. The one the chief wore was composed of feathers, stripped from the quills and tied to his hair, as long as there was a place to tie one, which increased the size of his head until it looked like a large wash tub. He was quite a brave man, but we made his hair and feathers both fly. Many bullets were thrown from their course by his shield, and many were embedded in it. A chance shot from the gun of John L. Hardigree eventually just missed the top of his shield and struck his head, but did not inflict a wound sufficient to kill him. As soon as they perceived that their chief was wounded his warriors rallied around him and moved him away.

Many of our men who were on slow horses had fallen behind, but coming up just then with loaded guns they soon set the Indians traveling again.

We lost three killed in this fight, to wit, Thomas J. Weathersby, Lip Conley and Bud Lane. Two men were wounded. We only killed seven of the Indians that we know of. The next morning our horses were so stiff that we had to help them upon their feet. Lieutenant Bushong's horse was unable to stand, and we were compelled to leave him, expecting he would be devoured by wolves, but when we returned to camp we found him there. We buried our comrades with our butcher knives, placing their bodies in a deep buffalo trail, and carrying earth in our blankets to cover them from the nearest bluff, where it was readily scooped out. After we had thus covered their bodies as well as we could with earth, we laid heavy stones on top of all to prevent wolves from scratching them up. This was in July, 1861. We moved a short distance that day, and the next day our spies on the right flank reported they had seen Indians chasing buffalo. We started out for them at once, but only succeeded in running our horses down. Thinking the Indians would follow us, I left two men on good horses on our trail three miles from where we intended to camp, to keep watch, instructing them to remain there until dark. After night they came in and reported that the Indians were following us. That night I divided my whole

force into fives, and placed them in squads around our
horses, with orders that no one was to speak above a whisper.
Twice during the night the Indians attempted to get the
horses, but failed both times. Some shots were fired at us
but none of us were hurt. It was a dark night, though
clear, and the bushes and vines hanging over from the banks
of the ravine where we were encamped, made it still darker.
Some of the men were encamped below and some above in
the ravine. I inquired if there was any one who was willing to go into the dark hole or canon near by to ascertain
if there were any Indians secreted there, Aaron Burr Brown,
an eighteen year old boy, said: "Captain, suppose you go
yourself, as you are getting the biggest pay for hunting Indians, and here is a good chance to find one if it is dark."
I replied, "you go in with me," and in we went. We felt
along the side of the bank where there was a hole in which
we thought Indians might have secreted themselves, but
did not discover any, although we found a horse. The next
day we continued our route up the Brazos. We found
fresh signs of Indians, and I am satisfied they would have
attacked us had it not been that they discovered Major
Burleson's command on the opposite side of the river.

Two of our men who had been wounded and lost during
our chase after the Indians, supposed, it appears, that the
rest of us had been killed. They made their way to Camp
Cooper and reported that they were the only survivors of
the fight. It was a long time before the report was cor-
rected, as we were forty days in getting back to camp. I
kept one scouting party out during the balance of that year.
No conflicts with the Indians of any importance occurred
until the winter set in. The Indians were depredating all
the time on the settlements, but the settlers found it a very
difficult matter to catch them, as well as we. They almost
invariably managed to elude pursuit.

During the winter Captain Milton Boggess, with near half
his company, and I with about half of mine, were going up
Pecos river, and when near its head waters, we discovered
an Indian camp in the distance, but their keen eyes had
seen us first, and the Indians ran off, leaving their camp
equipage, robes, blankets, etc., and some of their ponies and
a large quantity of meat. We stopped in their camp and

ook possession of all we wanted. The next day we hunted them until night, but with no success. The day following, we discovered them a great distance off. I ordered the men to throw away every pound of extra weight, even including their ropes and hopples, and to run the Indians as long as one was to be seen. I told them if any one should fail to keep up with the rest, he would have to show bloody spurs as evidence that he tried to do so.

After running the Indians about eight miles, they began to leave their worst horses and double up on the best ones. John Hammock, of Gatesville, who was riding one of the best horses in my company, was ahead and fired the first shot at the Indians. The Indians then raised a white flag, but Hammock hallooed to them and told them that he had ridden too far to be swindled out of a fight in that sort of a style. The fight then began and soon grew pretty warm. Many of our horses had broken down in the chase, and it left us rather short of men, but our close, well directed shots soon told with fearful effect on the enemy, and they began to retreat. A running fight was kept up for several miles on the open plains, where not a bush or shrub was to be seen. The Indians were nearly all killed. Our men were well nigh worn out with fatigue, and two of them, Hardigree and Weston, were badly wounded.

I saw two of the Indians make off by themselves, and thought it strange. Sam Stills and I followed them. Our weapons were empty, and by the time we had loaded them we discovered that the two Indians were making for the head of the canon. I fired at one of them just as he went over the bluff into the head of the canon. Stills ran about one hundred and fifty yards below for the purpose of hiding himself in the brush at the bottom and killing the other Indian as he passed. He succeeded in doing so, but the one I shot at could not be found.

After the men who had fallen behind in the chase came up we made a thorough search for the Indian I had shot at, and found that he had been wounded and had secreted himself among the loose rocks that had fallen off the bluff.

While we were sitting on the rocks resting ourselves, Aaron Burr Brown said to me that if I would have him decently buried, and rocks put over him to prevent the wolves from scratching him up, in the event that he was killed, that he would go down among the rocks and try to finish the Indian I had wounded. I promised to do so, and off he went. Soon after disappearing from sight we heard him fire, and in a few moments we saw him coming out backwards from a crevice, the report of the pistol among the rocks having nearly stunned him. He waited until the smoke had cleared away, went in again and dragged out the dead body of the Indian.

On returning to where we had left our pack mules, we came across a fine looking young Indian who had been slightly wounded in the hips. His comrades thinking, we suppose, that he was mortally hurt, had taken all his weapons from him except his butcher knife, but he fought desperately with that. The men scalped him before killing him, because the Indians had scalped Mr. Jackson alive a short time previously. The Indian complained greatly of the manner in which he was treated.

In April, 1862, we were ordered to Fort Mason for the purpose of being mustered out of the service. A party of Indians came in from the settlements with their booty, up the San Saba river, and passed near where we were encamped, Captain Boggess's company and my own. We immediately went in pursuit, and after a chase of ten or twelve miles we came up with them. They had abandoned all the horses they had stolen except those they were riding. As usual, they made fight, and gave us as much as we wanted to do until the men who had fallen behind in the chase came up.

One of the warriors had on a silk dress that had belonged to a lady who resided below on the San Saba. They had killed the whole family, and this scoundrel was wearing the dress of one of their murdered victims. The silk dress rattled as if it had adorned some city belle. Captain Boggess, thinking he was a squaw, called my attention to her, and asked me to notice "how viciously the damned squaw shot her arrows." He soon found out that a warrior's strength was inside that silken dress.

Some of the Indians were killed on the spot where the fight commenced, and the rest ran into a shin oak thicket, from which they fired on us with effect, killing or wounding horses and men at nearly every shot. Sergeant Erhenback was seriously wounded in several places. Mr. Johnston was also wounded, and Lieutenant Nelm's lips were pinned together with an arrow. Three or four of our horses were killed or wounded, one of which was my own. He was shot in the neck and shoulders with arrows. Three Indians were killed and another afterward died of his wounds.

Being now transferred to the Confederate service, I was placed in command of the regiment to fill the vacancy occasioned by the death of Col. Openchain, who had been killed. Colonel Malone was first ordered to take six companies and proceed to Columbus, and I soon afterward was ordered to march with the remaining four companies to Houston, thereby leaving the whole frontier west of the Brazos exposed, with no protection from the raids of the savages save what little the cow hunters could give.

Between six hundred and one thousand Indians soon after this made their appearance at or near Fort Murray, where about thirty families were forted up, inside of pickets driven in the ground, about eight miles from Fort Belknap. Several parties of these Indians raided the settlements below on the Brazos and murdered some families.

The first conflict they had was with Judge Harmison and his son Perry. They fought some sixty Indians for an hour. They retreated into a small mott of brushy timber and being armed with breech loading guns, they fired with such effect that they kept the Indians at bay until they heard the report of guns in another direction, and went off to ascertain the cause. The firing was by another party of Indians who had attacked and killed a man named Myers. When Myers was found afterward, it was evident from the signs that he had defended himself to the last against the fearful odds he had to contend with. He had undoubtedly caused several of the Indians to bite the dust. They butchered him in their usual savage manner, cutting out his heart and cutting off his hands which had hurled such destruction in their midst a few moments before.

The Indians then attacked the houses of Jodine Sprague, Carter, Hamby, and Joe Laker, killing some and capturing others. Susan Durken was left dead in the yard, she having refused to go with them as a prisoner they had to kill her. They captured old Brit Johnson, a slave, who was attending to a ranch for Moses Johnson, near the mouth of Elm creek on the Brazos, in Young county. His family were all killed, excepting his wife and two of his children, who were carried into captivity. After Brit was freed he spent more than three years among the Comanches before he succeeded in recovering his wife and children. The narrative of Brit's exploits, and how he finally succeeded in recovering his family, would be quite interesting had we space to go into details.

Doctor Wilson's wife and children and Mr. Hamby's wife and children, seeing the Indians across the Brazos, became alarmed, and when they heard of the murdering of their neighbors they tried to make their way to Bragg's ranch, known as Bragg's fort. As there was no chance to make fight against three hundred Indians, Wilson and Hamby concealed their families in a cave, hoping by showing themselves and making a feint of fighting by firing at them occasionally, to lead them away from the spot where they had hidden the women and children. In this they would probably have succeeded had it not been for some dogs that were with their families, whose barking led the Indians to where they were secreted. The Indians, not knowing who or how many were hid there, did not venture up, but called out in English to the women and children, telling them they were friends to the whites, etc. But the news they had heard of the previous massacres, and the arrows still sticking in several of the dogs that had run to them for their protection, gave the lie to all such assertions.

About this time some of the Indians attacked the house of Mr. George Bragg, to which Wilson and Hamby had fled after hiding their families, as previously stated. There were twenty-seven women and children and but five men in the house, to wit, George Bragg, Doctor Wilson, Mr. Hamby and his son, who was about grown, and a negro boy about eighteen years old. The rest of the men were off on a cow hunt, so there were but these five men to protect this house filled with women and children against hundreds of Indians. The women and children were directed to lie down upon the floor, so that the bullets and arrows might pass harmlessly over them. George Bragg had just built a small picket house without any shelter to the doors and windows. Many of the bullets and arrows shot by the Indians came through these open doors and windows, and Doctor Wilson was soon killed and Bragg fell mortally wounded, leaving only three to contend against such fearful odds. The Indians made a furious charge on the house before these men fell, but the men had plenty of guns and pistols well loaded, and they were used in such a manner as to kill and wound a number of the assailants. The Indians, however, succeeded in wounding Hamby several times, though not severely, and would have killed or carried into captivity the three remaining men, together with the women and children, but just then another party of about three hundred Indians had attacked Lieutenant Whitesides, of the border regiment, commanded by Colonel James Bourland, who had only forty-seven men and some citizens with him. Those attacking the house hearing the firing, and not knowing the cause, fled in hot haste, leaving their dead and the battle ground in possession of the twenty-seven women and children, the wounded Mr. Hamby, his son and the negro boy.

The fight lasted about an hour. If ever men were heroes and deserved the thanks of their countrymen, assuredly the few who fought so nobly on that day, defending these helpless women and children, should not be forgotten.

The lieutenant, before mentioned, had succeeded in making his escape from the horde of savages that had surrounded him, and he and his party, together with some cow hunters, crossed the Brazos near Fort Murray.

The inmates of Fort Murray estimated the number of the Indians at from six hundred to a thousand. They were around the fort all day, and from their maneuvers it was supposed they intended to attack it. There were about eighty men in the fort, and perhaps about one hundred women and children.

The next day these Indians drove off a large number of cattle, estimated at from five to ten thousand head. A party followed them far enough to satisfy themselves that the cattle were being driven to Kansas for the use of the Federal army.

This formidable raid of the Indians caused a general desertion of the organized northwestern frontier counties. The counties of Stephens, Palo Pinto, Jack, Wise and Montague were almost entirely abandoned by the settlers, only a few cowboys remaining at the large ranches—or, as they were then called, "forts." Not a living soul was left in Clay county. The last scout I made through that section, the houses and yards were as silent as the grave, all being deserted. The thirty-five thousand head of cattle on which this county had paid taxes to the government were all gone —gone to feed our enemies and to strengthen them for further destruction of our lives and property.

But I must not pass unnoticed the narrow escape made by my friend Bill Wooten from the Indians. He was living near Fort Belknap, and went off on a scout with a party of rangers—the same forty-five of the border regiment that fought against the six hundred Indians. The rangers were fighting against an overwhelming force, but when they saw that the Indians had completely surrounded the women and children, they did not stop to calculate the consequences, and rushed right in among them. Wooten having discharged all his shots, and, as it was no place to reload, started to run across a prairie about four miles wide, on foot, his horse having been killed under him. About forty Indians pursued him; but, as they perceived that two of the foremost Indians were pressing him closely, the rest turned back to follow the retreating rangers. After he had crossed the divide one of the Indians overtook him, drew his bow on him and said: "Run, Wooten, run, or I kill you. I know you. Do you know me? Long time ago you drive beef at Cooper; now Comanche drive beef heap."

Wooten made no reply, and the Indian did not attempt to shoot him. He reached home safely, but his clothes were nearly all gone, having been torn off by bushes and briars in his race for life. His run for life however left him an incurable invalid.

Another incursion was made by the Indians in the winter

of 1863, while I was at Fort Belknap in command of six
companies. Captain Guilentine, of the frontier militia, reported that the Kickapoos were in full force, and were passing up the Clear fork of the Brazos, near Phantom Hill.

At that time the Confederate authorities were pressed for
soldiers and there was no force to spare for frontier service,
but my command. The State of Texas exempted the
frontier counties from conscription and organized all the
citizens able to bear arms, for their defense, who scouted in
companies by turns, the whole being placed under the command of Brigadier General James W. Throckmorton.

Captain Guilentine sent an express to the nearest militia
captains at once. I despatched one hundred and ten Confederates under Captain Henry Fossett from the nearest
Fort. Captain Totten, of Bosque county, being the senior
captain of militia, hurried to the objective point with what
men he could collect, numbering over three hundred,
making in all about four hundred and fifty men. This force
pursued the Indians and followed their trail notwithstanding the ground was covered with snow, from a fearful snow
storm. They crossed the Colorado and Concho rivers, and
overtook the Indians at Dove creek. The Kickapoos,
together with refugees from other tribes, numbered as
estimated, about nine hundred. They took their position
in a dense thicket, a deep ravine on one side and Dove
creek on the other with its high bluffs. This left but few
places open to attack.

Our officers held a consultation and the plan agreed upon
was that Captain Totten, with the militia, should charge the
thicket, and that Captain Fossett with his one hundred and
ten men was to approach on horseback, take possession of
the Indians' horses, if possible, and avail himself of any
other advantages that might present themselves. Captain
Fossett and his men captured all the Indian horses, with the
exception of about fifty that were near the camp. They
numbered between six hundred and one thousand head.

Captain Totten meeting with some delay in getting his
men across the deep ravine, got them somewhat out of order.
Just then the Indians opened a heavy fire upon them from
the thicket. The whites being in open prairie, across the
ravine, were thrown into confusion. The most of the offi-

cers. with some of the men. having gained the thicket across the gulch, were nearly all killed or wounded. The Indians would have followed up their advantage with heavy slaughter to Captain Totten's men, but at that critical moment Captain Fossett, seeing the situation, left the herd of horses he had just captured and charged upon the thicket at the opposite side, right amongst the tents, wigwams, women and children, thus drawing the attention of the Indians and preventing them from following up the advantage they had gained over the militia. Their lodges extended along the bank of Dove creek for about a quarter of a mile, and Captain Fossett charged the whole length of the encampment, firing at whatever could be seen from the brush. The Indians, hearing the firing in the direction of their camp, hastened thither and came near cutting off all retreat from the thicket. Captain Fossett's men had discharged all their guns, and there was no time to reload. They were compelled to retreat, in many places in single file, and they suffered considerably. Among the killed of the Confederates was Lieutenant Giddeon, of Captain Rowland's company.

The Indians, having no other force to contend against, pursued them until they reached the open prairie, where another desperate struggle ensued around the horses, extending over several miles of ground. Captain Fossett, having to cover the retreat of the militia, was compelled to abandon a portion of the captured horses, but he succeeded in carrying off about three hundred head. When he came up to where Captain Totten had rallied the militia some ten or twelve miles from the scene of action, they halted there and laid on their arms until the next morning with the determination of renewing the fight next day, but a heavy snow storm set in during the night, which put an end to all further hostilities.

It continued snowing until the ground was covered three or four feet deep. Some of the men came very near freezing to death. Some of the horses, those that had been greatly fatigued in the fight, froze during the night.

Captain Totten returned to the battle ground and buried the dead. There were about fifty whites killed in this fight and probably about as many Indians. The Indians evidently thought themselves badly whipped, as they left their camp equipage and dead on the battle field. They fled across the Rio Grande into Mexico.

Among the last visits the Indians made to this (Bosque) county they stole many horses, and they also raided at the same time several of the adjoining counties. A good many small parties of citizens scoured the mountains in pursuit of the Indians, one of which, my neighbor, Bill Erwin, commanded,. having with him his sons and stock hands, together with my sons and stockmen. He stopped one night near the Leon bottom. He put out two of the youngest boys, Will Barry and Jim Erwin to guard the horses, thinking there would be but little danger while cooking and eating supper, but the boys discovered some Indians reconoitering the camp. They reported the fact to Captain Erwin, who took the older men and placed them in ambush near the horses. He then made the young men build up big fires and dance, sing and wrestle around them for about an hour and a half to make the Indians believe they had not been discovered. They all then laid down around the fires as if they were going to sleep. The ruse had the desired effect. The temptation to steal horses was too strong. About two hours afterwards the Indians crawled up noiselessly and approached the horses. When very near Captain Erwin and his men fired upon them and killed one of the Indians. They think they killed another but supposed he was carried off by his comrades.

Another party of Indians went out through the moun tains and crossed the Paluxy into Hood county. When on the divide between the Paluxy and Brazos they were discovered by a party of whites from Hood and Erath counties. They pursued the Indians, who, after quite a race, took position in a thicket on a small branch. The creek had a hole of water in it about waist deep. The brush and vines hanging over this hole of water from the banks hid the Indians from view, and the whites were compelled to approach within a few yards of them before they could be seen. This gave them a great advantage over the whites. But, after some maneuvering, the whites obtained a favorable position and picked off the Indians one by one, until there was none left to inform Brother Tatum, of the Sill agency, of the massacre.

It finally reached his ears, however, through some cow hunters who were driving beeves to the agency to feed the squaws and pappooses while the warriors were plundering and murdering the settlers. Brother Tatum told the cow men that it was an outrageous act to have killed such an innocent party of Indians; that they were merely a doctor and his escort who were going into the settlements to get roots and herbs for sick Indians, which grew there in greater abundance than anywhere else. This may have been so, but the settlers did not understand what benefit the sick Indians would derive from their stolen horses. There were seven Indians in the *doctor's* party, and all of them were killed. Two of the whites were killed and several wounded.

About the same time this fight took place, twenty Indians were discovered on the Paluxy. Fifteen citizens, under Haley and McDowell, pursued them. They overtook the Indians, and a sharp skirmish ensued, which lasted some time, and resulted in the recapture of all the horses they had stolen. Several of the whites were wounded, but none killed. Several Indians were also wounded, but none killed, as far as known. The Indians fled in haste to some place of safety. This was near Hanna's mill, in Hood county.

[NOTE.—It is but proper to say that the Kickapoo Indians, who were attacked on Dove creek, afterward claimed that they were on their way to Mexico with their families, and that the attack made upon them was unjust and uncalled for.]

Attack of Baggett's house.

By James T. DeShields.

DURING the first week in March, 1857, a large band of marauding Indians came down, and on approaching the frontier divided into squads of eight and ten and simultaneously entered Erath, Brown and Comanche counties, and began depredating in the most

daring and alarming manner. A severe drouth the previous year had caused an entire failure in crops,
1857 which was followed by a severely cold winter, which
had reduced what few cow ponies the settlers had
left, so thin in flesh that very few were able to do any
kind of service; in fact most of the citizens were literally afoot. Breadstuffs had to be bought and freighted
on ox wagons from Fannin, Grayson, Collin and Dallas
counties. While in this helpless condition three different
squads of Indians began depredations at the same time in
different parts of Comanche county.

One squad of ten passed down the south Leon valley in
open day gathering what few horses they could find. And
four miles below old Cora (now extinct) on the third day of
March, 1857, about four o'clock p. m., they came upon Gid
Foreman and killed him, taking off every vestige of hair
with his scalp. Foreman had red hair, which is a great
trophy among Comanche Indians. They stripped Foreman,
save his drawers, and mutilated his body in a most horrible
manner. After butchering the unfortunate man and tying
his reeking bloody scalp to one of their belts they proceeded
down the valley and crossed North Leon, and about five
o'clock p. m. approached John Baggett's ranch, near the
present town of Hazel Dell, driving up into the yard and
catching the only horse Baggett had left. At the time, Mr.
Baggett was not at home and no neighbors nearer than four
miles.

Now come, ye sentimental lovers of Heaven's noblest gift
to man—a wife and mother—and view with me this terrible
tragic scene, no *ignus fatus*, no fiction or imaginary con-
coction of the brain, but a reality. A lone woman, with
nine helpless children, with no chance of escape and no
means of protection, not even a gun (Mr. Baggett had that
with him) and surrounded by ten steel hearted, fiendish savages, in whose veins the milk of human sympathy had
never flowed, with hideous visages made doubly frightful
by being bedaubed all over with war paint, and uttering
fiercely their most diabolical war whoops, their dark bodies
besmeared and their hands still dripping with the life blood
of Foreman, whose gory scalp was still dripping the crim-
son fluid and hanging to a fiendish savage, whose greatest

delight was in torturing his most innocent victim, while the
excruciating suffering and agonizing cries only serve to increase his merriment.

Mrs. Baggett succeeded in getting seven of the children
into the cabin while the savages were catching the horse.
But alas! Oh, horror of horrors! Two of the children, little Joel, twelve, and little Bettie, ten years old, were under
a live oak tree playing some sixty yards from the cabin,
and were intercepted, caught and four of the savages proceeded to strip off every vestige of clothing that the children had on, and proceeded slowly, so as to prolong the sufferings of little Joel and to increase and intensify a mother's
agony, in torturing the little fellow to death by lancing him
with arrows in every conceivable way to produce the most
acute and excruciating suffering, and if possible, to add additional pain and to make his lifeless form appear the more
ghastly and horrible, while his plaintive, piteous shrieks and
cries were still audible to a mother's ears. One of the savages, to whose belt was hanging poor Foreman's gory scalp,
proceeded before life was extinct in little Joel, to scalp him,
and hung the scalp on the opposite side of his belt, as an additional trophy to heighten the pleasure of their fiendish
war dances. But is this all of this frightful tragedy?   '
. No. Not content with torturing, scalping and killing
little Joel, but if possible to add to a mother's already
overflowing cup of sorrow and grief, mentally equal to a
Spanish Inquisition, those barbaric and unfeeling savages
proceeded to lance little Bettie in twenty places, in three
places to the hollow, then turning her loose to go bleeding,
staggering and fainting twice before she reached the house.
On reaching the house, Mrs. Baggett still had the presence
of mind to say: "Bettie go around to the other door; the
Indians will kill all of us if mamma opens this door."

Four of the Indians had followed the child to within
twenty paces of the door, thinking, no doubt, that Mrs. Baggett would be imprudent enough to come out and meet the
child, but she well knew her own life and that of her other
seven children depended upon their remaining in the house.
So, failing in this, the savages remounted and rode off just
before dark, and as soon as they left, Mrs. Baggett carried
in the lifeless and mangled body of her boy, and had washed

and dressed it before the father's return, one hour after dark.

To attempt to describe the feelings of Mrs. Baggett on this occasion would be an utter failure, and a mockery of the sublimest fortitude and courage, known alone to mothers. Indeed, no language, except it be that of angels, is capable of describing such a scene, or a mothers's love. Little Bettie got well, grew to womanhood, married, and is now the wife of a wealthy and respected gentleman (Mr. ————), living at Abilene, Texas. Mr. and Mrs. Baggett are both dead.

On the next night after the killing of Foreman and the tragedy at Baggett's, another squad of Indians that had been depredating in the upper part of the county, were coming into the town of Comanche, but when within about one thousand two hundred yards from the public square they were met by a scout that had been raised to guard the town. Though they knew that the Indians were in the county, and had started out expressly to look for the savages, yet, they were completely surprised; not expecting to meet Indians coming into town. But the unexpected meeting to both parties resulted in a fight at once, in which Kenith McKenzie received a fatal wound, from which he died in a few hours, and James McKenzie received a severe wound, from which he has never entirely recovered, but will always be an invalid.

Some of the boys in this fight had never before been in an Indian fight, and were a little fuller of whisky, perhaps, than courage, just at that particular moment, and while some of them were shooting at the Indians, others were "shooting" back into town in double quick time, carrying each one a whole scalp on top of his own head, but minus two horses, killed by shots, either from the Indians or by their own party.

The Indians held the ground, and left at their leisure, but without carrying away any trophies of victory.

To use the language of one of the men who participated in this skirmish, and who gave us these facts. "Too much whisky and Indian fighting don't mix worth a cent."

Lewis, Brown, Pierce and Elam.

ABOUT the first raids made by the Indians in the above named counties after their organization was during the years 1856 and 1857, when they stole and carried off a large lot of horses belonging to Adams and Gentry, in Comanche (now Hamilton) county, and Mullens, in Brown county. In every instance they succeeded in making their escape without suffering any loss. After the 1857 stealing of these horses the Indians were emboldened by their success, and the correct knowledge gained in making those raids of the whereabouts and conditions of the settlements on Pecan bayou, the Leon, Bosque, Cow House and Lampasas valleys enabled them to operate with great facility. During the fall of 1857 marauding parties of Indians were numerous in Pecan valley, riding over the country in open day in squads of eight and ten and attacking every person that chanced to be out. A squad of 'eight Indians came upon Brooks Lee during the month of November, 1857. Lee was riding a mule and was some half mile from his ranch, in the valley, just below the present city of Brownwood, when the Indians ran upon him. Lee and others had enclosed a small field and he succeeded in gaining the fence and dismounted amid a shower of arrows, the Indians in twenty paces of him; but crossing the fence without climbing, and using it as a breastwork, he opened fire with a sixshooter, his only weapon, and the first shot knocked the nearest Indian *hors de combat,* which caused the others to halt and assist their comrade up again and place him behind another Indian to be carried off. This halt enabled Lee, with the advantage of the fence as a shield, to gain additional distance, and the Indians, not fancying his replies, stopped the chase and struck off for the mountains, leaving the wounded Indian's blanket, which was well saturated with blood, and quite a quantity of arrows sticking in the fence, the ground and some in the mule. The bones, supposed to be the remains of this Indian, were afterwards found in the mountains, a few miles distant from the scene. This was the first Indian that was killed in this part of the frontier after depredations began in 1856.

A short time after the attack upon Lee, Mr. Lewis, who lived three miles lower down the valley, near the mouth of Stepp's creek, had gone out three-fourths of a mile from his cabin to unhopple and drive his horses up, when five Indians ran upon him, captured his horse and killed Lewis, shooting an arrow clear through his body, which killed him instantly. Lewis was the first white man killed by Indians in the territory embraced in this sketch after settlements were commenced in 1854. After killing Lewis, the Indians passed on down the valley, falling in with another marauding party of ten, which increased their number to seventeen.

They then passed on down the country, through Lampasas and on to the head of Nolan's creek, in Bell county; then turning back they passed up through Coryell county, south of Gatesville, some ten or twelve miles. On the head of Owl creek they came upon two men, Brown and Pierce, who, with a little boy, whose name was Dave Elam, were hauling rails to fence a farm. The little boy jumped from the wagon and fled for life. Some of the Indians pursued him and whipped him severely, but seeing one of the men about to get away they left the boy to pursue him. The two men were killed and scalped, but the boy made good his escape, and now lives in Coryell county. He is known as "Indian Dave." In the upper or western part of Coryell county the Indians divided into three squads, each squad having one hundred and fifty head of horses. One squad passed up the Leon Valley, one up Cow House creek, and one up Lampasas river, and were to come together at Salt Creek mountain, some thirty miles west of the town of Comanche, in the northwest part of Brown county. The squad that passed up the Leon Valley was discovered late one evening by the mail carrier en route to Brownwood, as they were passing Mercer's Gap. Fortunately for the mail carrier, he was not discovered by the Indians, and seven miles back to Elisha Barcroft's, the nearest house, he returned as fast as a mule under spur and quirt could travel, arriving at Barcroft's just after dark, with barely enough breath left to detail the facts.

Dutchman as he was, Barcroft soon deciphered his broken

English, and proceeded at once to dispatch the news to all
in reach, and by ten o'clock that night a scout of ten or
twelve Comanche county boys were in the saddle and riding
at a rapid gait. Salt Creek mountain being the objective
point, they thought by reaching that noted land mark before day light, that the Indians could be discovered and intercepted as they passed in the morning. About mid night
a terrific and furious norther blew up, but a freezing norther
was not sufficient to cool or abate the boys' courage; a sure
chance for a fight, as the boys all thought, and as the sequel
proved to be correct, and thinking that the Indians would
stop at a certain water hole ten miles short of the mountain.
But in this they were mistaken. The Indians had traveled
to the mountains without halting, and beat them there. On
approaching the mountain, just before day light, the boys
discoved the horses. The moon had gone down and it was
too dark to see anything correctly. The horses had been
driven over one hundred miles in less than thirty hours,
and did not scare or run as the scouts approached; but where
were the Indians? was the anxious inquiry among all. One
hour's suspense until day would dawn, was disturbed only
by the chilling north wind and chattering teeth and shiver-
ing frames of the boys. But the dawn of day soon relieved
their freezing stillness; all eyes were eagerly scanning in
every direction to discover the lair of the wily, cautious Indian, who never makes a mistake in selecting a fortified
camp. A small curl of smoke ascending from a deep ravine
just in the edge of an impenetrable thicket, some four hundred yards distant, was discovered by the keen eye of Dan
Cox, one of the coolest—not from the effects of the freezing
norther, but from deliberate courage, which made him on
all occasions one of the most successful, and to the Indians,
terrible fighters. A wave of his hat in the direction of the
smoke was the signal for an instaneous hurly burly charge.
Cox being nearest led the charge by at least twenty paces.

The Indians were broiling chunks of horse beef and did
not discover the whites until Cox was within thirty feet of
their fire—neither party could discern objects at a greater
distance through the dense thicket—Cox's shot gun failed to
fire and he threw it down. The Indians sprang to their feet,
but in an instant Cox's revolver rang out and one of the In-

dians, as he sprang from the bush, received the bullet, breaking his back and felling him on the spot. By this time the balance of the boys had gotten up and opened fire, but the brush was so thick that the shots were all ineffectual, save one, and that was from Cox's revolver, which stopped another Indian some thirty feet from the first, and in trying to get him Cox received a slight arrow wound in the face and Jesse Bond a painful wound in the shoulder. The other three Indians got away, but the boys emptied all their pieces in the direction that the brush was seen shaking, and tore their clothes to shreds almost in trying to catch them. When the fight was over and the boys had reloaded their guns and extracted the arrow from Bond's shoulder it was not near so cold as it had been, and if the detail that each one gave of his unerring shots had been correct scores of dead Indians could have been counted instead of two. But every horse was recovered, and the first Indian that Cox killed had on Pierce's hat and boots, and the firing alarmed two other squads, which were camped one and a half miles lower down on Salt creek, and caused them to leave camp in double quick time. The other two squads of Indians went clear, not being overtaken, and getting away with some four hundred head of horses and killing, as before stated, in Brown county, Lewis as they passed down, and Pierce and Brown, in Coryell county, as they passed out. This fight at Salt Creek mountain, in Brown county, was the first Indian fight that any of the boys from Comanche county had been lucky enough to get into, but from this time on until Indian troubles ceased on our frontier they had plenty of such fun, as the boys were wont to call it, and a more untiring or a braver set of men than the pioneers of Comanche county would have been hard to find.

Nathan Holt.

NATHAN HOLT came to Texas at an early day—during those times that "tried men's souls." He settled in what is now known as Hood county, where he lived for a number of years, engaged in the occupation of stock raising. This business exposed him a great deal to the attacks of Indians. One beautiful morning in the summer of 1859, Holt went out on the range to collect some

1859 of his cattle. While he was thus employed, and unsuspicious of any danger, he discovered a party of Indians coming towards him at full speed. As he was alone he sought to save himself by flight. His faithful animal strained every nerve to bear his rider out of danger, but all to no purpose. The Indians were well mounted and soon came up with him. He defended himself for a time against the numbers that surrounded him, but finally fell dead from his horse pierced with a dozen arrows. Holt's body was found the next day and taken to his sorrowing family. Reader, when we thus relate to you the murders of fathers, mothers and helpless children, all destroyed by the tomahawk, scalping knife and death dealing arrows of the savage, it awakens within us the keenest emotions of pity and anger—pity for those who suffered and anger at the perpetrators of these diabolical, hellish outrages. But when we remember that there are none but "good Ingens" now in Texas, and that they have all gone (mostly by the shot gun and rifle route) to their "happy hunting grounds," we can almost, but not quite, forgive them for the atrocious deeds they committed.

Jeremiah Green.

JEREMIAH GREEN was a native of the State of North Carolina.. He came to Texas in 1859 and located in Hood county. In the month of July, 1863, Mr. Green, in company with several of his neighbors, went out on the range for the purpose of gathering cattle. After they had ridden several hours in the hot sun they, as well as their horses, became very thirsty. They went to a stream near by, where they obtained water and then rode to the top of a hill, where they intended to rest awhile and graze their horses. Just as they reached the top of the hill they discovered a party of Indians, sixteen in number, within a few hundred yards of them. The Indians were sitting on their horses, with their weapons in their hands, and were gazing intently at the whites, as if they were debating the question of making an attack. Some of the whites proposed to stay and fight it out if they attacked them. Others thought they had better retreat in time, as there were but five whites altogether and but two guns among them. One of the whites seeing the Indians outnumbered them so greatly became alarmed and fled. Two more of them, who were mounted on good horses, followed him, leaving the other two behind, who were riding rather inferior animals. These two men were hotly pursued by the Indians, and one of them being closely pressed, dismounted from his mule, ran into a thick cedar brake and made his escape. Green was riding a very poor animal, was soon overtaken and mortally wounded. Those who escaped ran into the settlements and gave the alarm. A small company of men was quickly raised, who went to the spot where it was known the Indians had overtaken Green. Here they found traces of blood which they followed through the cedar brake until they came to the dead body of the unfortunate man. It was evident that after he had been mortally wounded he had dismounted and made his way into the brake, where he died. Shortly after this sad

1863

event a man by the name of Hyant was out hunting his stock in the same locality by himself. He was a brave and cautious man, but many men who were both brave and cautious have been killed by the Indians in Texas. The Indians attacked Hyant, and as he was well mounted it was evident from the sign that he ran a long distance before the Indians overtook and killed him. This same party of Indians, when about leaving the settlements, came across an old negro man, who belonged to a Mr. Bryant. He attempted to save himself by running, but the Indians caught and killed (as they supposed) and scalped him. He was found afterwards still alive, and carried home, but died in a few days. This is one of the very few instances where the Indians scalped a negro.

Battle of Lookout Point.

ON the night of the eleventh day of September, 1869, a party of seven Indians came into Hood county, and passing eastward through the southern part of the county, down Squaw creek, they came upon the premises of Robert West and stole all the clothes that had been washed that day and left out over night to dry. This characteristic of the savage seems to have been shown by them when opportunity offered. Years before, they had

1869

sacked Linnville and stolen all the dry goods in the town; and upon another occasion they stole all the clothes washed and left out to dry in the town of Bastrop. But to our narrative. After leaving West's place they continued down Squaw creek to McDonald's place, where they found four or five horses in the horse lot, which they rapidly transferred to their own possession. Having now penetrated nearly to the Brazos river, they hastened to retrace their steps, going westwardly but not over the same trail made in coming down. All along they added rapidly to their stock of stolen horses until they had gathered a herd of some two hundred head. But, unfortunately for the red devils, some one had discovered their presence while passing down Squaw creek, and arousing the neighborhood, a runner was sent over to the Thorp settlement, requesting a posse to meet their posse at or near Lookout point, a point of timber about twelve miles west of where Thorp springs is located. The word reached Thorp settlement about two o'clock in the night of the eleventh of September. The following well known citizens were soon armed and in the saddle, to wit: J. J. Daws, J. B. Sears, T. J. Scott, Mark Herring, W. H. Johns, W. M. Clark, John Clark, Lee Wright, James Parnell and H. P. Thorp. This little party of ten, stuck spurs to their horses and were off about one hour before day, and arriving at Lookout point of timber, they found that the Squaw creek party had run on the Indians in the timber near by, as they were changing horses. The Indians now had about two hundred head of stolen horses. The race for life on the one part and the race for stolen property and the scalp of the red man on the other now began in earnest. As they came past the Point, the Thorp party came up on them and the two parties of whites being joined a furious chase for four miles now took place. But fate frowned on the Indians. By the dint of hard riding they were surrounded and forced into a deep ravine, where they took shelter under the roots of a large tree. It was now about eight o'clock in the morning of the twelfth of September. The news of the chase and the fact that seven live Indians were surrounded in a deep ravine spread rapidly, and about two o'clock p. m. the whites numbered seventy-five or eighty men and boys. About this time a heavy rain came up, and as soon as it was over John Toby rose up and commenced to blow his bugle. This was the signal for the attack. The party who descended into the ravine and attacked the Indians was composed of the ten before mentioned from Thorp settlement and the following men from Squaw creek, to wit: Robert Tramble, Marion Selph, John Toby, Alvin Martin, Clabe Oxford, George Oxford, John Dennis, Wear, McKinsey and perhaps a few others whose names we did not learn. The conflict was short. The terrified Indians made but a feeble resistance against the out numbering white men. They were soon all killed and scalped. It was then discovered that one of the seven was a squaw. Two white men were wounded. Wear was shot with an arrow and died of his wound about two weeks afterwards and McKinsey was wounded with a bullet but recovered. The horses were returned to their respective owners and the whole party dispersed to their several homes, feeling that this had been the most successful haul they had ever known. This fight is remarkable for two things, one that not a single Indian escaped and the other that they were scalped by the white men, something not usually done by them. This is the same party of Indians referred to in Captain Barry's article published elsewhere in this book.

William Willis.

CLOSELY following the close of the "war between the States," and the disbandment of the Confederate troops on the frontier, the thieving and murderous raids of our savage and implacable foe—the Indian— became of monthly occurrence all along the Texas frontier. These raids were generally made about the time of the full moon, and were more than usually frequent and bar- 1866 barous in Hamilton county, during the years of 1866 and 1867. During these years the loss in horses, especially, was enormous. Settlements were scattering and few, and as Hamilton county was about the limit of their predatory incursions, eastward, generally, by keeping well concealed in the chapparal of the mountains, their presence was not known until they had mounted themselves upon fleet horses, and the theft detected or a murder committed; after which, before a pursuing party could be organized, ten or twelve hours had elapsed, giving the Indians much the start. After a short chase, night usually ended the pursuit till morning, thus another advantage was gained by the red man. In 1866, John Hogue Pierson, purchased a fine tract of land on the Leon river, ten miles east of the town of

A FAIR RACE BY WILLIAM WILLIS, AND NO JOCKEYING.

Hamilton, and settled upon it, establishing there a large horse ranch. He had great experience in Indian warfare, having been on the frontier from boyhood to manhood. His father, J. G. W. Pierson, moved to Texas from Union county, Kentucky, in 1822, when the son was five years of age. In the spring of 1836, he shot a young chief, and in the August following was wounded in a battle on the Colette. He realized the disadvantage the settlers labored under in not being able to continue the pursuit at night, and to overcome this he obtained five noted and well trained blood hounds from Falls county, from where he had moved, and turned over the management of them to his elder son, J. G. W. Pierson, then a lad of sixteen. He had one other son, Thomas C. Pierson, four years younger. On Christmas eve, 1866, at about nine o'clock, news was brought to Pierson's ranch that the Indians had shot Will Willis, about sun down, within sight of Captain J. M. Rice's, who lived south of the town of Hamilton, about three-fourths of a mile. None of the family were on the ranch except the elder son, John G. W. Hastily procuring his gun and pistols, he mounted his favorite horse, and sounding the call for the blood hounds, in fifteen minutes from the time the news came he was riding in a swift gallop by the nearest route over the prairies, with a single companion, towards the town of Hamilton. Wishing to have the dogs as fresh as possible when they should "take the trail," they were not forced beyond a good running gait till the place where the shooting occurred was reached. This was, for once, on the dark of the moon A high, cold wind came with freezing breath from the north. A dozen men joined young Pierson at Hamilton, and, with scarcely a halt, the dogs were taken to the trail, which these sagacious animals "took" with such a ferocious howl that each one instinctively tightened his grasp on his gun, and straightened himself in his stirrups as the hot blood went tingling through his veins. The details of the shooting had not been told to young Pierson, for the runner sent for him had not been informed, and he had not taken the time to make any inquiries—to get on the trail was his first desire. As soon, however, as the dogs gave vent to such a howl of rage on "taking the trail," Pierson said to the party, "There is blood on

this trail." "Yes," said one, "Willis said he was certain
he hit the one who seemed to be the chief of the Indians, as
he nearly fell from his horse when he (Willis) fired.

The dogs were soon in full pursuit, heading down Blue
Ridge, in a south east direction. These dogs were trained to
yelp in trailing at long intervals. Young Pierson requested
all the others to ride behind him, fearing that, if they
passed ahead, they might over-ride the hounds. At that
time and season of the year the tall sedge grass brushed the
stirrups of the riders, and was considerably higher than the
backs of the dogs, and very thick. The night grew cloudy,
the wind whistled and moaned across the prairies, and the
sleet began falling, beating mercilessly upon all. It was no
easy task to keep with the dogs in the darkness and gloom;
and, but for the instinct of the horse ridden by young Pierson, which was accustomed to following the hounds in the
chase, with flashing eyes and distended nostrils—the occasional howl of "old Ball"—the lead-dog of the pack—and,
now and then, the "hoo-a-dogs," of young Pierson, as he
urged on the pursuit—the party could not have kept together
at all. But, as it was, like so many weird, spectral phantoms rushing onward, borne upon the furious blast, the pursuit was rapidly continued on into the darkness. When
about fifteen miles had been gone over and horses as well as
dogs were giving evidences of fatigue, suddenly the furious
baying of the dogs convinced every one that the Indians
were overtaken. Dashing ahead to where the dogs were it
was ascertained the Indians were not there, but young
Pierson discovered something stretched upon the ground,
and, in the darkness, not unlike the figure of a man. His
horse plunged about so he could not ride up to the thing, but
dismounting and giving the rein to a comrade, he approached to find only a blanket and an Indian's shield.
These, next morning, were found to be covered with
blood, and from the decorations and figures upon the shield
the conclusion was that young Willis had given an Indian
of high degree his death wound, and that he had died
where his blanket and shield was found. Another thing
was made certain: the Indians had heard the pursuit and
hastily departed with their dead, for at this point the trail
scattered and the dogs went in several directions. The

party, supposing they were upon the Indians, divided into
as many squads as there were dogs, each urging on the dog
nearest. Now all was confusion and the party broken up
and scattered over the prairie. Young Pierson tried in vain
with horn and voice to get the party together and follow the
· leader, "Old Ball." If the other dogs had not been urged
on they soon would have abandoned their trail and have
come to the assistance of the leader, who, no doubt, took
the trail by which the wounded, perhaps dead Indian, had
been carried off. Finally, after two or three hours had been
lost day light began to dawn. Everything was covered with
ice and all nearly frozen. The dogs, after a long run (in all
about th rty-five miles), as they became cold also became
stiffened and their feet began to swell where they had cut
them on flint rocks. The trail was attempted to be followed
by the eye, but having reached a barren section it was soon
abandoned and the party returned home. Will Willis was
shot in the back with an arrow, the spike sticking into the
spine. He was twenty-three or twenty-four years of age
and the son of Robert Willis, who moved from South Arkansas and settled on the Lampasas in 1855. There were
thirteen Indians in the party which attacked him. He was
riding a small mule and was coming· to town to attend a
dance. Everybody in those days carried arms and he had a
Spencer rifle. He was about a mile from Captain Rice's
residence when he saw the Indians and attempted to run.
Vain effort! The Indian he afterwards shot was riding a
large dun horse and this Indian soon ran ahead of him,. cutting off all chance of escape, while the others quickly closed
around him. He then dismounted and pushed on, leading
his mule and protecting himself behind the animal, now and
then pointing his gun at the enemy as they came nearer and
nearer in circling around. Finally his mule was so badly
wounded with an arrow he had to abandon it, but continued
towards town. He was finally struck by an arrow from the
bow of the Indian on the dun horse, supposed to be the
chief. At this Willis lost all patience, and turning upon the
unrelenting savages, who were now pressing him closely,
he knelt upon one knee and took such aim at the Indian riding the dun horse as was possible while he was dashing
around him and fired. The Indian cried out, "Ugh! ugh!"

and came near falling from his horse. Willis said he thought the Indian was tied on the horse, for at the crack of his gun the supposed chief gave vent to that peculiar cry or grunt, which signal generally indicates that an Indian has been hurt. The other Indians abandoned Willis and went to the supposed chief and then rode rapidly off, leaving Willis and his mule, as it subsequently proved mortally wounded on the prairie. There were no men at Captain Rice's, and by the time the neighbors had been notified of Willis's fate it was too dark to follow, so a runner was sent to Pierson's ranch for the blood hounds. Willis's mule was found next morning in a corner of Captain Rice's fence dead. Will Willis received every attention but died at the residence of Dr. W. S Walker, in the town of Hamilton, some three weeks afterwards.

School House Massacre.

MISS ANN WHITNEY was murdered by a party of eleven Indians, about 2 p. m., Thursday, July 11, 1867, just one month after the burial of the veteran, John Hogue Pierson, who, after one week's illness, died at his ranch on the ninth day of June, 1867, on Sunday morning.

The place where Miss Whitney was murdered was at 1867 a small log school house, where she was teaching school, in Hamilton county, situated upon the brink of the south bank of the Leon river. A beautiful valley, three-quarters of a mile wide, and one and one-half miles long, spread out in front—free from every obstacle to the sight. This was called "Warlene Valley." The Howards lived one-half mile west, and John Baggett one-half mile east of the school house. Ezekiel Manning and Alexander Powers lived one and one-half miles south, but behind a high hill. The Massengills, Ganns, Strangeline, Cole and James M. Kuykendall, lived up the river within two miles. J. B. Hendrix and sons, Crockett and Abe, lived two miles, Judge D. C. Snow and Nel Livingston, lived three and four miles, and the Pierson ranch was six miles below. The town of Hamilton is six miles southwest of the place of the murder. This is only one of the many instances of fiend ish cruelty and barbarity practiced by the Indians in the 'cold blooded and cowardly murder of their victims. The logs, of which the school house was built, were unhewn, as was the custom in those days, and the spaces between were left open, so that it was an easy matter for parties outside to fire through them upon the inmates. There was a small window cut out in the north side and was without a shutter, Olivia, the twelve year old daughter of John Barbee, a stockman who lived northeast some ten or twelve miles, was boarding in the neighborhood, and attended the school. Her father was expected to come by that week to see her, while out cow hunting.

On the day and about the hour above named, a daughter of Alex Powers was about the door, which was in the south side of the house, overlooking the valley; while there she saw a party of men on horse back rapidly approaching, and soon became satisfied they were Indians. Miss Whitney, seeing her standing at the door and gazing so intently, asked her what she saw. She replied she was looking at some persons in the valley, who were coming towards the school house, and that she believed they were Indians. Miss Whitney bade her take her seat, telling her not to be so foolish as the men were cow hunters. She believed it was Mr. Barbee, and did not take the trouble to see for herself. Fatal error! Mr. Powers' daughter was still uneasy, and soon took another look, when she cried out, "they *are* Indians," and took her little brother by the hand, and made good their escape through the window. This induced Miss Whitney to go to the door, and immediately told the children they were Indians, and that they were taking "Mary." Mary was the name of a fine saddle animal, the property and pet of the lady. She often made the remark, "if the Indians ever take Mary I want them to take me, too." When she became satisfied who the men were, she shut the door and told the children to escape by the window, which all did except Mary Jane, a daughter of

Ezekiel Manning, who was sick, and two sons of James M. Kuykendall. Miss Whitney was very large and fleshy, weighing about two hundred and thirty pounds, and could neither get out of the window nor hope to escape by running out at the door. Many of the children crawled under the house and thus became unwilling witnesses of the tragedy that soon took place. In a few minutes the Indians had surrounded the house, and one who seemed the leader, said to Miss Whitney, in fair English, "Damn you, we have got you now." She read her doom in the hideously painted faces and blood thirsty looks and menaces of the savage foe. This heroic woman never lost her presence of mind, and desiring to save the lives of the children committed to her care, she implored the Indian who had addressed her in English, to kill her, if that would satisfy them, but not to harm the little ones. Whereupon, the Indian held up three fingers to his comrades, and they began shooting the poor defenseless woman with their arrows, aiming through the chinks. Little Mary Jane Manning clung to the skirts of her beloved teacher, whose life blood soon began to gush from her cruel wounds and to pour over the floor, and upon those beneath, and the fear stricken child that clung to her so resolutely. She walked from side to side of this—her prison of death—marking her footsteps with streams and pools of blood, all the while pleading with the ruthless savages to spare the lives of the little children—a spectacle which should have softened the obdurate hearts even of these devils incarnate. She finally succeeded in getting the two girls (Manning's and Kuykendall's) to get out of the window, and while doing so an arrow was buried in the back of Miss Kuykendall, inflicting a severe but not fatal wound. This left Miss W. and the two Kuykendall boys in the house, and about this time the Indians succeeded in bursting the door open, and an Indian entered to complete the foul murder, but too late to do further harm. The last gasp was given—the last quiver shook the straightening limbs, and a tortured soul was loosed to angels as her hellish enemy crossed the threshold of the doorway.

On perceiving that their victim was dead, the Indian who had entered called to some one outside, whereupon the English speaking Indian entered and asked the two boys if they wanted to go with them.   One, in fright, said yes, the other said no.   And, strange, with a "damn you, sit there," to the one that said no, he took the other and put him on a horse and took him away with them.   This was John Kuyken-dall and was subsequently purchased from the Indians and sent home.

At the time the Indian who had entered the house called to the one outside, the latter had about succeeded in getting Oli-via Barbee up behind him on his horse.   This call saved her from a barbarous and perhaps shameful captivity.   She im-mediately fled and was afterwards found by Josiah Massen-gill.   She had received such a fright and was so terror stricken that she was wild and it became necessary to run her down to secure her, which was not till the succeeding day.   Miss Whitney was not scalped nor were any of the children killed.   Other things were transpiring near by, and so rapidly that, in the opinion of the writer, had more to do in saving the children from slaughter or captivity than the entreaty of the poor school mistress.

At about the time of the attack on the school house two ladies, Miss Amanda Howard and her brother's (Volney Howard) wife, Sarah, rode into the valley from the south, and some nearer John Baggett's, on the east, than to their home on the west.   Miss Amanda, who was a fearless rider, was gentling a young horse for her own use, and her sister-in-law was only keeping her company.   They saw the In-dians at the school house and at first took them to be cow hunters.   They were discovered by the Indians before they had ridden far up the valley and two of the party rode to meet them.   The ladies soon discovered their mistake and turned to run to Baggett's, and the Indians seeing this gave hot pursuit.   Miss Amanda had some difficulty in turning and starting her young horse.   When, however, she did get him whipped into a run, a glance over her shoulder showed the foremost Indian to be so close that she looked into his gleam-ing and gloating eyes.   She dashed away from her pursuers and heading straight for Baggett's fence, determined to try her horse at a leap, and with this purpose she lashed him into furious strides—the horse cleared the fence at a single bound, and on she flew to the house of Mr. Baggett.   Mrs. Sarah Howard did not fare so well; her horse shied and sud-

denly turned to one side, to be caught by an Indian, while
Mrs. Howard was thrown headlong over the fence, so great
was her momentum; being unhurt she quickly escaped also
to Mr. Baggett's.   While Miss Whitney was being murdered at the school house and Miss Howard and Mrs. Howard were being chased east of it, a mover, Mr. Stangeline,
had entered at the west end of the valley, at the Howard
place, and had proceeded to about half way across the valley when he was attacked by some of the Indians as they
were leaving.   He was killed but not scalped.   They shot
but did not kill Mrs. Stangeline, a little girl and the baby.
About this time the brave Miss Amanda Howard, seeing
what was going on, formed the bold design of escaping from
the valley and warning the settlers.   To do this, she would
have to ride obliquely in the direction of the Indians and
outride them in getting to the only road that crossed the
high hill to the south that led to the lower settlement—she
was cut off from those above.   Her plans matured, she
mounted her half wild steed and commenced the perilous
ride.   Dashing at the fence she again cleared it handsomely
and with whip and rein put her steed at his best.   She was
well started before her design became apparent to the
enemy, when, with a yell, well calculated to strike dismay
to the stoutest heart, the band left off the attack upon the
Stangeline family, and being joined by those still lingering
around the school house, they all rushed pell mell to cut off
Miss Howard from the road.   Here again was the heroism
of woman severely tried on this day of murder, rapine and
blood.   Picture, if you can, reader, a woman, surrounded
by hideously fiendish looking foes, thirsting and panting
for her blood, she begging to be killed if that would save innocent childhood!   And, again, a woman, riding into the
very jaws of death, depending alone upon her skill in managing an unbroken horse, not bridlewise, and the speed she
may be able to get from him, to carry the news of the presence of savage foes to distant settlements!   Thank heaven
Miss Howard escaped by a few rods and the cowardly foe
hurriedly turned westward and left the valley, carrying the
Kuykendall boy with them.   The daring of Miss Howard,
scarcely seventeen, no doubt saved many lives.   She it was
who attracted and withdrew the attention of the merciless

savage from the work of blood and warned him that with his longer delay would certainly come retribution for this day's hellish work. She passed Manning's and Power's, stopping at the fence only long enough to tell them that the school house had been attacked by Indians. What awful tidings to parents, who, only a few hours before, had kissed rosy lips good-bye, which, for aught they knew were silent in death, or worse still, captives.

Miss Amanda rode rapidly on to Mr. Hendrix, who immediately sent his son Abe to the Pierson ranch for the bloodhounds. Miss Howard went on as far as Judge D. C. Snow's, and the men being away, a daughter of the judge's, Miss Belle, mounted a horse without taking time to saddle him, and notified Mr. Livingston, who lived a mile south.

When Abe Hendrix reached the Pierson ranch the eldest son, J. G. W. Pierson, was east of the Leon river in company with Chap and Volney Howard (brothers to Miss Amanda), horse hunting, and did not return till night fall, when they were met with the startling news detailed above, or as much as was then known, which was conjectured to be worse than proved to be true, for it was at first supposed all the school children were murdered, also all the movers.

The day had been intensely hot, and young Pierson and the Howard boys were very hot and tired, and their horses badly jaded, after a hard day's riding. There was no time to lose, and no fresh horses at hand, so, with a good bye to mother and his young brother, young Pierson called his dogs by a blast from his horn, and he and the Howard boys and Abe Hendrix, rode rapidly away. They gathered up a crowd of seven men in all, and stopping at Manning's long enough to get information as to the direction taken by the Indians, they got upon the trail about 11 o'clock p. m. It was difficut to get off in good style, for at the west end of the valley, the way the Indians left, it was very brushy and rocky, and the enemy had scattered, apparently every felfellow looking out for himself. The night was close and hot, and as no water was crossed until the party reached the Cow House, which was crossed about twenty-five miles from the school house, it made a run of thirty-one miles for the dogs without water, and in the hottest weather. It was impossible to get them away from the water till they had thoroughly bathed their bodies and drank to their hearts' content. Riders and horses were suffering also, but no more time was lost than was unavoidable, and the pursuit continued on into the mountains, which were covered with a dense growth of chapparal, rendering it almost impossible to get through. It was soon discovered that the Indians had again separated. The day grew intensely hot, and there was no water and no canteens. The feet of the dogs were badly cut upon the sharp flint rocks, and began to swell and become sore after they went into the water. Towards noon it became impossible to urge them on—they fell in their tracks, panting and moaning. The dogs were sent to water by a man whose horse had given out, and the pursuit continued till night put an end to the chase. They had ridden over one hundred miles without stopping. This band of Indians were well mounted. They had abandoned all the horses they were driving, and gave all their attention to getting away. Young Kuykendall says he saw the pursuing party about sunrise, when the Indians took to the chapparal and scattered, one Indian leading his horse, to which he was tied, from which he was not permitted to dismount for the next two days and nights, and when he did the skin pealed from his legs. As well as he could tell, the Indians were some six or seven miles ahead of the pursuers when the Indians took to the mountains and chapparal.

Witcher and Carter.

DURING the year 1860 a scouting party, consisting of eight or ten men under Captain Cotton, left the town of Hamilton upon a scouting expedition, and after having been out for several days, John Witcher, who accompanied the party in the expedition in some way, late one evening became separated from his companions, and while riding leisurely along was discovered by a large 1860 party of Indians, who at once gave chase. The Indians charged upon him, and Mr. Witcher put spurs to his horse, and made all the speed he possibly could towards a thicket at no great distance ahead. The Indians, however, were mounted on good horses, and they soon overtook him, but not before he had reached the thicket to which he had directed his course. Here he quickly dismounted, and leaving his horse to the Indians, plunged into the thicket, and as they saw he was armed, they did not venture to follow him, especially as it was now getting dark and they knew it would be impossible to trail him. As soon as the Indians had gone, Mr. Witcher left his place of concealment, and started to the town of Hamilton, twenty-five miles distant, with the expectation of reaching there before day light the next morning. After traveling about twenty miles he found himself at Hoover's ranch, on the Cow House creek, having gone several miles out of his way; he then changed his course, as he supposed, direct for home, but after he had traveled ten or twelve miles, he found himself back again on the Cow House, ten or twelve miles below the point where he had first struck it. Once more he changed his course, and about sun rise the next morning he reached the town of Hamilton, having traveled altogether about thirty-five or forty miles during the night. He knew nothing of the fate of his comrades, from whom he had separated an hour or so before the Indians attacked him.

Some of the citizens of Hamilton immediately mounted their horses and went out to ascertain what had become of these men. The men were found in the course of the day, and from them they learned the following facts: The party was about one mile behind Mr. Witcher when the Indians attacked him, and knew nothing of it. They reached the place where they intended camping for the night, and were scattered around looking for a good position, when the party of Indians who had attacked Witcher rode up, no doubt, with the intention of camping at the same place. This was a complete surprise to both parties, as neither had any knowledge of the others' proximity. The first thing they knew they were all mixed up together, whites and Indians, and as it was then nearly dark, it was very difficult to distinguish friend from foe, at a little distance.

Like droves of wild turkeys, each party by a peculiar whistle and other signals known to the Indian and frontiersman, soon succeeded in collecting a portion of their scattered forces, and a "helter skelter" fight ensued, in which every man was his own commander, taking his own position and firing at such a time as he thought best. In this way the fight was kept up for a considerable time between the two parties, but at length the Indians retreated and left the "bone of contention," the camping ground, to the rangers. In this night affair there were no doubt several Indians killed and wounded, but as they were carried off under cover of darkness their loss could not be ascertained.

The brave Lieutenant Carter fell, pierced with a dozen bullets, early in the engagement. Grundy Morris was severely wounded but finally recovered, and when last heard from was living on the Lampasas river ten miles above the town of Lampasas. We are not sure, but think he is a son of the venerable old Uncle Davy Morris, who, with ten others, were the first settlers on Bennet's creek, in Hamilton county, and he alone of the entire number escaped the tomahawk and scalping knife of the wily savages. There was another member of the party, John Hurst, who was severely wounded with an arrow, which struck him in the side, glanced around the ribs and embedded the spike in the backbone, where it remained for a day or two before it was extracted. When surgical aid was obtained it was drawn out crooked, resembling somewhat a fish hook. The operation came very near costing him his life, and it was years afterwards, we are informed, before he was able to do any labor. The death of Lieutenant Carter was a great loss to the county, for he was not only a brave man, ever ready to respond to every call in defense of our frontier settlers, but he was a kind neighbor and a useful citizen. He left a sorrowing family and many friends to mourn his loss. If we are correctly informed he originally came from Tennessee, settled in Bell county in about 1855, remained there a year or two and then moved to Hamilton county, where he resided until he met his tragic death just related.

William Jenkins.

WILLIAM JENKINS was born in the State of North Carolina and settled in Texas in the year 1849. He settled in Williamson county, where he resided for some time and then moved to Hamilton county. On the fifteenth day of ———, 1866, a party of Indians came into the settlement and stole his horses. Jenkins, in company with a Mr. Willis, pursued the Indians.

1866 They soon found their trail and followed it for about ten miles towards the Lampasas mountains. On the summit of one of these mountains the Indians had halted for the purpose of resting their animals. The two men discovered the Indians without being seen by them. Jenkins an l Willis, after holding a consultation as to what was best to be done, fired upon the Indians and then charged them. The Indians were taken by surprise, gave way and took to the brush, but there they turned and made fight. Jenkins had fired his rifle and attempted to reload, but after getting the ball down about six inches from the muzzle he could force it no further, and at this juncture the Indians made a charge upon him. He drew a revolver and drove them back and again attempted to load his rifle, but without success. Again and again the Indians charged him but each time he drove them back by a discharge from his revolver. One of the Indians, in order to avoid Mr. Jenkins's shots, slipped around the tree behind which he had taken shelter, but in doing so his body came in full view of Mr. Willis, who shot him down. As Mr. Jenkins was still endeavoring to reload his gun the Indians once more charged upon him, feeling assured that his pistol was empty, which was the fact, but fortunately in passing through their camp he picked up a shot gun they had left in the hurry of retreat, and with this he compelled them to fall back again. Just then Jenkins called out to Willis to retreat, and at the same time mounted his horse and started. But the bridle on Willis's horse had become entangled in some way in the brush, and before he could get it loose the Indians charged him again. His gun and pistol being then empty he called to Jenkins and asked him not to leave him. He turned to look and seeing three Indians close upon his friend he wheeled his horse and charged upon them, killing two on the spot. At the same time he was struck with an arrow shot by the third Indian, which entered his breast just below the nipple. At the moment he only felt a slight sting. As soon as Willis had succeeded in getting his bridle loose he mounted his horse and the two men made good their retreat. When they had gone some distance Jenkins asked his friend if he was hurt and he replied that he was not. Willis then asked if he was hurt in any way and Jenkins said that he had been slightly touched by an arrow. On examination a hole was found in his coat and a puncture in the flesh just under it. "Oh," said Mr. Jenkins, "it is nothing and will soon be well." In a little while, however, he became deathly sick and was compelled to rest several times before reaching home. A further examination of his wound on their arrival there, revealed the fact that the arrow had gone entirely through his body. The fight took place on Sunday and he died the following Tuesday. This was a gallant little fight of two men against the terrible odds they had to contend with. Jenkins could easily have saved his own life by abandoning his companion to his fate, but he was not the man to desert his friends in time of need.

Captain Crawfield.

CAPTAIN CRAWFIELD resided in Hamilton county. In the summer of 1868 a party of eight Indians came into the settlements, on the waters of the Leon. The first house they approached was that of a Mr. Pickett. They sent one of their number as a spy ahead, who took his position on the top of a hill near Pickett's house. In his eagerness to spy out the land, he advanced too far out 1868 of the brush, and was discovered by one of Pickett's children. The child reported the fact to its father. Pickett, knowing well the shrewdness of an Indian walked carelessly for some time about his yard, as if he was unaware of his proximity, and then entered his house. When he came out he was accompanied by another man, both of them with a blanket wrapped around them, and each with a bucket in his hand, and took their way toward a spring a short distance off, as if for the purpose of getting water. The blankets were worn to prevent the Indian from seeing the guns they carried. As soon as they were out of the Indian's sight, they dropped their blankets and slipped around to the opposite side of a hill, and then cautiously crawled up to within a few yards of the place where the Indian was watching their movements and expecting, no doubt, to see them coming back from the spring with their pails of water. Pickett and his companion both fired at him at the same time and he fell dead, pierced by two bullets. They then hastily reloaded their guns and concealed themselves in the bushes near by.

The other seven Indians hearing the report of their guns came running up to see what was the matter and, when within close gun shot, the two men in ambuscade fired upon them, killing two more. The remaining five instantly turned and fled, but, unfortunately for them, they had gone but a short distance, when accidentally they met Captain Crawfield. This gallant officer at once charged them, killed three more of them and wounded the fourth—the fifth one making good his escape. The wounded Indian was disabled entirely and died soon after the fight occurred, but that night the one who had escaped returned to the place and buried him. Of this party of eight Indians only one survived to tell the tale of their unlucky raid.

Griffith and White.

THESE two gentlemen were both Baptist ministers, and both were residents of Coryell county. In the fall of 1857 or 1858, whilst riding in company not a great distance from where they lived, they encountered a party of Indians who peremptorily ordered them to dismount and deliver up their horses. As the two gentlemen did not relish this method of levying "black mail" upon them, they **1858** put spurs to their horses, instead of dismounting, and endeavored to make their escape by flight. The Indians pursued them, firing upon them as they ran, and severely wounding both Griffith and White, and their horses also. Both of them, however, succeeded in reaching a thicket of dense chapparal, in which they concealed themselves, leaving their horses to the Indians, who carried them off. The two gentlemen had separated from each other in their flight—had struck the thicket at different points, and consequently neither knew what had been the other's fate. Their absence was soon made known in the settlement, and every house in the county was visited, to ascertain, if possible, what had become of them, but as no information could be obtained in this way, the settlers started out en mass in search of the missing men   They were eventually found in the thicket where they had taken refuge from the Indians, but so badly wounded that they were unable to travel, and were taken to their respective homes.   Griffith survived the injuries he had received but a few days.   His widow and children, and some of his grand children, were living in Hamilton county when last heard of.   White, though severely wounded in the side with an arrow, eventually recovered, and a few years ago was living in Lampasas county.   He is the father of Martin White, who resides in the town of Lampasas.

J. H. Chrisman.

IN the year 1861 Mr. Chrisman and three others, to wit, T. B. Saunders, Ambrose Lathen and Pat Gallagher, left Camp Colorado to go to Gatesville for the purpose of getting fire arms repaired. Saunders was their guide, and as he was riding in front of the others he discovered on ascending a high hill a number of Indians driving a *caballada* of stolen horses. He waited until his companions **1861** came up and then showed them the Indians, who were coming towards them rapidly. The question was, "shall we fight or shall we run?" Finally they concluded to stand their ground. The point at which the Indians were discovered was between Pecan bayou and Blanket creek, in Brown county. J. H. Chrisman being the oldest man was given the command. He immediately ordered the men to dismount and prepare for the conflict. Having examined their guns and pistols and seen that they were all well loaded and in order the rangers remounted their horses and at once charged upon the Indians, who, by that time, had advanced within one hundred yards of them. The rangers, as they charged upon the Indians, kept motioning back with their hands as if they were beckoning to others behind them to come on, and the Indians supposing they were the advance guard of a company, abandoned their stolen horses and took to flight. Besides, they were only armed with bows and arrows, and when the rangers charged them their bows were unstrung. The rangers pursued them so vigorously they had no time to rally. Finally, however, five of them got together, and having succeeded in stringing their bows they began shooting at the rangers as they advanced, but they were so excited their arrows flew wide of the mark. The rangers then charged upon them furiously, firing as they advanced, killing one and wounding or scaring the others so badly that they fled as fast as their horses could carry them. The rangers followed them about half a mile further, and finding they had completely dispersed the crowd for the time being they made haste to return to the place where the Indians had abandoned the stolen horses before they could collect together again.

There were thirty-six head of these horses, and as it was late in the day and ten miles to the nearest point where they could pen them they started with them, keeping a good lookout for fear the Indians should pursue them. About nine o'clock at night they safely reached the house of Jesse Mercer, where they penned and guarded the horses until day light. It was afterwards discovered that the Indians had found out that they had been stampeded by four men, and that they had followed the rangers and would undoubtedly have taken their scalps if they had been a few minutes later in reaching Mercer's house, on Mercer's creek, Comanche county.

After leaving Mercer's the next day they drove the horses to the town of Hamilton, where they penned and guarded them that night, and the following day drove to Gatesville, in Coryell county, and turned the horses in a pasture. Gallagher, who lived some fifteen miles from Gatesville, was riding a very fine black mare, and being anxious to get home separated from the party before reaching town. The rangers suspicioned that they were being followed by Indians, but of this they were not sure. Subsequent events, however, proved that their suspicions were not ill founded. The night they turned their horses in the pasture near Gatesville, R. B. Wells, who lived within one mile of town, had his horse stolen, and on the same night Gallagher's fine mare was also stolen from his residence. Three days after this, five Indians were intercepted in Lampasas county by some rangers, who killed one Indian and captured a bunch of horses. About one month later, in the light of the moon, while another party of rangers, under Lieutenant Chandler, were guarding one of the passes at Santa Anna mountain, in Coleman county, through which the Indians always passed with their stolen horses in going out of Coryell and Lampasas counties, four Indians were discovered with a large *caballada* of horses while attempting to pass through the gap. The rangers charged the Indians, who at once attempted to save themselves by flight, abandoning all of their horses. Two Indians were killed in the chase that ensued and the other two severely wounded. As an evidence of the fact that they were the same Indians attacked by Chrisman's party, the horse stolen from R. B. Wells was captured and also the fine black mare belonging to Gallagher. One of the Indians was riding the latter animal when he was killed. So out of the six Indians only two finally made their escape and they were badly wounded.

The Killing of Williamson.

MR. WILLIAMSON was a citizen of Coryell county. In the year 1863 he and a man by the name of Hendrickson started together from the Langford setment to go to his residence, on Cow House creek, a distance of about ten miles. On their way they encountered a party of Indians and a fight ensued, in which Williamson was so disabled by a severe wound that he was unable 1863 to make any resistance and the Indians ran him through with their lances. Hendrickson made his escape, collected a party of men and returned as soon as possible. But they were too late. The Indians had left and all they could do was to bury the remains of Williamson where he had been killed. The following year Captain Graham's son was captured. Captain Gideon Graham was a citizen of Coryell county. He had several sons in the Confederate army, and on one occasion he started to where his sons were stationed to carry them a supply of clothing, leaving his youngest son, a lad ten years old, at home to assist his mother. Early in the fall of 1864 Mrs. Graham sent this lad out to hunt some horses. He found the horses a mile from home in an old waste farm on the top of a hill, near Sugar Loaf mountain. As he was unhoppling them preparatory to driving them home he was surrounded and captured by a party of Indians. These Indians, on their way out to the mountains, happened to pass near the ranch of Captain Burleson. He discovered them, raised a company and went in pursuit. The Indians finding him on their trail pushed ahead as fast as possible. He knew a pass in the mountains through which he believed the Indians would go, and he hastened forward to intercept them at that place. He succeeded in getting there before the Indians came, and just as they were entering the pass he opened fire upon them. The Indians made no resistance but fled as fast as they could.

The little boy, seeing the Indians were badly frightened, attempted to jump from his horse, but an Indian caught him by the arm and held him fast. Finally, however, he was so closely pressed by the whites he was compelled to drop the lad, but as he did so he thrust his spear through the poor little fellow's body. Captain Burleson shortly afterwards came up, and seeing the boy was still alive he left one of his men in charge of him while he and the rest followed on after the Indians. They succeeded in killing one of the Indians, and on their return they carried young Graham to a house and sent for his mother, who, of course, hastened to the relief of her wounded boy. The poor little fellow gave his mother an account of the cruel treatment he had received from the Indians. Although they had plenty of venison and buffalo meat they gave him nothing to eat but horse flesh, and on one occasion when he was very thirsty and there was plenty of good water in camp they tried to force him to drink the water from the stomach of a horse they had killed, and when he refused to do so they whipped him most unmercifully. The little fellow lived but a day or two. The Graham family still reside in Coryell county.

Carmeans and Tankersly.

IN May, 1861, these two men were passengers from Camp Collier to Camp Colorado. When leaving Camp Collier, the commanding officer offered them an escort, but they declined taking one, saying they would have company, as some gentlemen had gone on ahead of them, and they would soon over take them. When the two men had gotten about two miles from camp, on Clear creek, 1861 some twenty miles from Camp Colorado, in Brown county, and before they had overtaken the party ahead, they were discovered by ten Indians, who were driving a lot of stolen horses. These Indians were well mounted and well armed, and they at once charged upon the two men.

Instead of running as they should have done, to overtake the party ahead of them, the two men took a position among some trees near by, and made a stand there.

The Indians completely surrounded them and, although the men fought bravely, their courage availed but little against such odds, and both were killed. The party ahead heard the firing of guns, but supposed it was hunters from the camp shooting at game. A young man by the name of Isham Large, who was out hunting his horse, also heard the firing, and concluded to find out the cause of it. As he approached near the spot the Indians espied him, and pursued him hotly, but fortunately he was mounted on a fleet horse, and he made his escape.

From indications where the fight took place, it appeared that Carmeans fell early in the action, but that Tankersly was only wounded at first, and was shot several times afterwards, before he was killed.

Massacre of Mose Jackson's Family.

MOSE JACKSON was a native of North Carolina. He emigrated to Texas and first settled in Harrison county; from there he moved to Brown county and settled in the southeastern portion of said county, on Pecan Bayou. A Kirkpatrick and —— King lived on neighboring ranches several miles from Jackson's. In the fall of 1861 Jackson, Kirkpatrick and King went to the bayou to select some board timber. They found a large pecan tree which suited their purpose, and they decided to come the next day and cut it and make their boards. As

the tree was full of fine pecans one of the number suggested
that they should bring their families along to gather the
pecans and a have a pleasant day in the woods.   This was
unanimously agreed to.   The next day was a beautiful day,
and Mr. Kirkpatrick was the first to arrive on the ground.
He brought with him his children and two or three of his
brothers who were living with him, having left his wife who
was unwell at home.   Soon after he arrived he heard several
shots fired in quick succession up the bayou, in the direction
of Jackson's ranch, but he supposed it to be a party
of hunters.   Soon after King arrived with his family.
Mr. Jackson did not come.   The men spent the day in making boards, and the women and children in gathering pecans
and enjoying their pic nic.   Late in the day they returned
to their homes little dreaming the cause of Jackson's failure
to put in an appearance.   On the next day King and Kirkpatrick, with their brothers, returned to get their boards
and haul them home.   As they were starting home in the
afternoon, Kirkpatrick told his brother and one of the King
boys to ride up the valley and round up the cattle for salt-
ing.   They proceeded a little over a half mile up the valley
when a horrible sight met their view.   Jackson's wagon was
standing in the road, and in it were the dead bodies of Jackson and two of his children, a four year old daughter and
seven•year old son, and a short distance from the wagon
were those of his wife and daughter about fourteen years old.

All had been scalped.   Jackson had started from his home
on the day appointed for the place of their agreed meeting.
When within about one-half mile of the picnic grounds the
Indians, who were concealed in a pecan thicket near the
road, ran out upon him, shooting him several times and
killing him instantly.   They then rushed up to the wagon
and pulled Mrs. Jackson out, when she asked time to pray,
and walked a few steps from the wagon and knelt down,
and while kneeling the Indians went up to her and took her
by the hair and cut her throat.   They then dragged out the
eldest daughter and cut her throat, and next they pulled the
little seven year old boy and four year old girl to the side of
the wagon and cut their throats and left their heads hanging outside with their bodies inside the wagon.   They took
captive Jackson's little son Joshua, about eleven years old,

and his daughter Rebecca, aged nine. When the bodies were discovered about thirty-six hours had passed since the killing. The young men immediately raised the alarm, but as the country was very sparsely settled it was some time before a sufficient number of men to pursue the Indians could be gotten together. As soon as this could be done pursuit began. They followed the Indian trail for several days and finally came upon the little boy and girl, whom the Indians had captured, coming back on the trail. They had suffered much from hunger and cold. The children stated that the Indians had left them in the woods and told them to remain there until they should return. But as soon as the Indians were gone the little children started back on the trail as fast as they could go, and had been coming toward home for more than a day when discovered. They were brought back into the settlement and kindly taken care of and reared by the kind and noble hearted settlers. The girl is now married and is living, we are informed, in Lampasas county. The boy is also living, but his mind never recovered from the shock caused by the murder of his family before his eyes, and a few years after his capture he lost his mind entirely. He is now constantly talking about the murder of his family and wanders about the country, being clothed and fed by those who know and sympathize with his sufferings.

Owen Lindsey Killed.

THE late civil war had called many of her bravest sons to fight her battles in distant States, and during the year 1863, the then frontier county of Lampasas, San Saba and Brown counties was the scene of their almost monthly visitations. The light of the moon was the time most suitable for their forays, and on every such occasion the few settlers had to use the utmost caution 1863 to keep their saddle horses, often tying them to the logs of the house, and not infrequently watching them the night through. In March, 1863, the people of Hanna's

Valley were suddenly aroused by the report that Indians
were in the neighborhood. In a very short time, armed
with rifle and six shooters, the following hardy frontiersmen were in the saddle, to wit: Owen Lindsey, Albert Jones,
John Jones, David Hanna, —— Powell, —— Robbins, ——
Martin, Isaac West, Jim Robbins, Jim Williams and Pick
Moss. The trail was soon found, and by these skillful moun-
taineers, was easily trailed. A. J. Jones and Owen Lindsey being better mounted, outrode the others, and near the
mouth of Pecan Bayou the Indians were discovered dismounted and trying to climb the steep mountain side. Lindsey and Albert Jones still led in the chase, and the other
boys came as fast as they could ride. The Indians numbered eleven, and were well protected by boulders and
projecting cliffs. No halt or parley seems to have been
made by these two fearless leaders, but they charged the
Indians, who stood their ground, and made no effort to escape. Owen Lindsey was shot and instantly killed, his
body being transfixed with an arrow, and his head being
wounded with a stone hurled by the savages, for he was
now within thirty steps of them, and they were still higher
up the mountain side. The blood covered ground near
where Lindsey fell, showed that he too, had brought down
one Indian. Albert Jones was shot in the left leg with an
arrow, which he pulled entirely through his leg, and which
was a most serious wound, but he finally recovered, and is
entirely well. Powell was wounded in the arm, and Robbins in the side, but both recovered. David Hanna's horse
was killed from under him. The Indians escaped and left
some bridles, blankets and lariats as the only trophies for
the whites. If any Indians were killed or wounded, the survivors carried them away with them. The Texans' arms
failed to fire on several occasions, and this fact added to the
fact that they attacked up hill, a well armed body of men,
equal in numbers to their own, and well concealed behind
rocks, make the fight a very unequal and disasterous one to
the frontiersmen. Most all the Texans who were in this fight
are still living in Brown and surrounding counties. Albert
Jones lives on his old place, now, perhaps, in Mills county.
David Hanna and John Jones live in San Saba. These marauding bands of Indians are happily, now unknown in

A RUNNING FIGHT WITH INDIANS.

Texas, but the battle ground where poor Lindsey fell, bleak and barren as it is, remains a lasting monument to the memory of a gallant young man who shed his last drop of blood in trying to rid the frontier of the marauding savages.

Cedar Gap Raid.

THE particulars of this bloody fight have also been fur nished us by Mr. J. T. DeShields. It was in the fall of the year 1866, about the time that the early settlers of a new country are wont to lay in their supplies for the coming winter that Colonel William Stone, an old Texan frontiersman, made ready his wagons and teams and started 1866 them to the San Saba mills, in San Saba county, to procure his supplies and breadstuffs for the coming winter. There were two wagons and three men, Frank Brown, Larkin Stone and another gentleman whose name we no not remember. Larkin Stone was a brother of Colonel William Stone, who died not long since in Comanche county. The road leading from Comanche to San Saba passed through a noted Indian gap. Some sixteen miles southwest from the town of Comanche is a small pool or water hole, the only water on the road from Comanche to the mills. The boys had stopped here to water and graze their teams and to take lunch when up drove John Roach, who was on his way returning from San Saba to Comanche. The friends had soon heartily dined, and after preparing their pipes for their accustomed smoke were lazily grouped around their wagons, admiring the beauty of the surrounding country. Just as they were thinking of renewing their journey they were charged upon by a band of Indian warriors, painted up in the most hideous styles and colors. They were a party of Comanches who were down from Uncle Sam's reservation on a prospecting tour, looking at the country and intent on carrying back to their homes a few white scalps and a bunch of horses to show their kinsmen that the whites were not all gone yet. In other words they were out upon the warpath for the purpose of stealing horses and carrying off captive women and children, to be be reclaimed at a high ransom. Besides this they did not hesitate to murder any helpless victim that they might come upon.

There were twenty-five or thirty of the red devils, all well mounted on the best American horses they could find in Brown, Hamilton, Lampasas and Coryell counties. They were armed with the latest improved guns and pistols. On seeing that there were only four whites, and knowing that they had good teams the Indians thought it would be an easy matter to pounce down upon their unsuspecting victims, kill and scalp them and take four white scalps along with the other booty to their chief as trophies of their valor. In this they were mistaken, for they met with a most determined resistance by the four white boys, who were also well armed with guns and pistols and who were all brave, cool and determined men.

Instead of giving up and suffering themselves to be murdered in cold blood, the boys answered the Indians' volley of shot with powder and lead, that carried death and destruction with them. At the first fire three Indians reeled in their saddles, which showed the accuracy of the Texans' aim. The second volley caused one to fall from his horse. He was immediately picked up and carried away by his comrades, but Frank Brown had taken true aim and his trusty rifle had done good service. The spirit of the Comanches' brave chief had been wafted to the "happy hunting grounds." During the short time the Indians had kept busy and their rapid firing had not been without effect. Roach had been badly wounded and Brown had received an ugly and painful wound in the face. However, the fall of their leader had thrown the Indians into considerable confusion, and seeing that the entire party had withdrawn a short distance, the boys took advantage of the opportunity and securing their animals each man mounted a horse or mule and made a break for liberty.

Brown, Stone and the gentleman whose name is not remembered, each made his escape, and succeeded in reaching the settlements without any further injury, except a few scratches. They, however, had a close ride and a bad scare. Roach was not so fortunate. There he was, thousands of miles away from his home, the Emerald Island, surrounded by a body of Comanche Indians, who were maddened beyond reason by the escape of the other three men, and who were intent upon having his scalp locks and of knowing that one of the white braves had shared the fate of their dead chief. The Indians were too close to him to allow him to get a good start, and after reaching his mule and mounting it the animal became unruly. It was shot with an arrow, and commenced pitching, throwing Roach off. He had already received one or two shots through the body, and after falling he was shot time and again, but he made his way off, and by the hand of God alone succeeded in getting out of the range of the savage's guns, and by crawling and dragging himself along on the ground he succeeded in making his way some distance, where he was found, a bloody, hideous looking mass, shot all over, and suffering a thousand deaths from his wounds, and almost dying for water.

The three other men having reached the settlement of old Captain James Cunningham, Sr., who lived about four or five miles from the scene of the attack, sounded the alarm that Indians were in the neighborhood, and related the tragic death, as they supposed, of their comrade Roach.

Under the leadership of Old Uncle Jimmy Cunningham, a company of tried and true men was soon in readiness, and immediately went in pursuit of the depredators. About one mile from the wagons they found poor Roach more dead than alive, as above described. Arriving at the scene of the attack the party found the broken and demolished wagons still there, but the mules and horses had been carried off by the red fiends, who had left for other scenes. The trail was quickly found and followed up by the scouts, recruits coming in from all quarters. After following the trail some three miles it entered the mountains. Just at the foot of the mountains was found a newly made grave. Upon examination it was found to contain the body of the lamented chief, whose death had been caused by Frank

Brown's superior markmanship. As is their custom, the chief had been buried with all his arms and equipments, among other things was found a very fine iron shield, through which the fatal ball had penetrated, entering the heart of the chief.

After a short pause here the trail was again resumed. The force having now increased to thirty or forty men it was thought best to divide up into two companies, each to go a different route, and to meet at the Salt Creek mountains, in Brown county, and, if possible, to get in ahead of the Indians and cut them off. So, they divided, Old Uncle Jimmy Cunningham taking twelve or fifteen men and going a near way, leaving eighteen or twenty men under command of his son, David, and his company being well mounted, and all being young men who were eager for a fight and an Indian scalp, now began traveling at a rapid gait. Among the company were several good trailers, and as they were assisted by several good blood hounds (negro dogs) they had no trouble in following the trail, and by traveling until far into the night, they found themselves near Salt Creek mountains. Being well acquainted with the locality of the country, and thinking that the Indians had camped in the immediate vicinity, Captain David Cunningham ordered a halt, and at the same time detailing two of his men to go forward and spy out the enemy, reconnoiter their position, and if possible, to ascertain their number. The two spies soon made their rounds and returned to their company, reporting that they had discovered twenty-five or thirty Indians with a herd of about two hundred head of horses, encamped on the creek below the gap in the mountains.

It was now four o'clock a. m. Captain Dave Cunningham ordered his men to keep pefectly silent and to be ready and make a charge at the break of day. They had not long to wait, and with the first faint streams of light the boys charged down upon the Indians with a regular Texan yell. The Indians had just risen, and were busy preparing their breakfast. The surprise was complete, and before the Indians were aware of their presence the boys were among them shooting right and left. At the first charge five Indians fell, and their scalps were soon dangling to the six shooter

GEN. BEN M'CULLOCH IN 1861.

belts of the rangers as trophies of their marksmanship. Among others Larkin Stone had secured a scalp. William Cunningham, one of old Uncle Jimmy's boys, had two. The boys had done good service and continued the fight. But let us see what damage the Indians had done. We find that one of the Indian's bullets had laid one of the rangers—Freeman Clark—low, and just as the Indians commenced to retreat, poor Clark was borne away by his comrades in the last agonies of death. The poor fellow was a brave and daring youth of seventeen or eighteen years of age. He was riding a splendid horse, and was armed with a good shot gun. In the first charge Clark rushed ahead into the midst of the Indians' camp. Singling out a warrior, the youth cocked his gun and took deliberate aim, but the cap snapped and the gun failed to fire. Poor Clark had no chance for his life now. His would-be victim had his pistol cocked and ready to fire, and when Clark's gun failed the warrior placed his pistol within a few feet of the lad and fired. There was a loud report, the aim was fatal, and Freeman Clark reeled in his saddle and fell from his horse. Just at this instant some of the boys came up, and seeing Clark shot they rushed upon the Indian, and in less than a minute his body was riddled with bullets, and his spirit had taken its flight with poor Clark's. The fight lasted about two hours, the Indians retreating for several miles, followed by the rangers, who kept up a running fight.

The Texans killed and scalped seven Indians besides wounding several.

The result was a complete victory for the Texans, with the loss of only one man killed and one wounded.

During the engagement some of the boys had several narrow escapes, which deserve a passing notice. Lark Stone's life was saved by the bullet striking the handle of his six shooter. The wood was shattered to pieces, but the force of the ball was spent. Joel Neighbors, uncle Jack's oldest boy, had his noble horse, Old Smoke, shot from under him. Old Jimmy Cunningham and his party did not reach the place in time to take any part in the engagement. They came up just as the men were returning from the pursuit of the discomfited and fleeing Comanches. This engagement was said to have been one of the best managed fights that has

ever occurred on our frontier, and the honor and management of the well laid plans are due to Captain Dave Cunningham's skill and energy.

Captain Dave Cunningham still lives on his old homestead
place, some seven or eight miles south of Comanche town,
on the waters of the South Leon, in Comanche county. He
is loved and respected by all who know him. He has filled
several important official positions in his county. He was
sheriff of his county one term, during which time he made
a brave and vigilant officer, and it is often said of him that
many of the inmates of the penitentiary can look back and
curse Dave and his vigilance.

Poor Roach lay for weeks and months between life and
death, but having a strong desire to live and have revenge
upon his assailants, he finally recovered and was once more
able to arm and equip himself and to help his country in following up and slaying the devils who had used him up so
unmercifully. The mill trip was abandoned and the provisions were not obtained till a more convenient season.

Colonel William Stone came to Comanche county at an
early day, and settled on his ranch in the county in 1858
or 1859, where he died not long since. Larkin Stone and
Frank Brown still live in Comanche county. The latter has
held several positions of honor and trust in his county, and
is, at this time, a prominent business man of DeLeon, in
Comanche county. Old Uncle Jimmy Cunningham also
still lives in Comanche county, an honored old citizen.

Indian Raids in Erath and Adjoining Counties.

By J. T. DeShields.

DURING the early part of January, 1858, several marauding parties of Indians approached the frontier
again and began depredating in a very bold and daring manner, one squad of eight coming down through
Erath county and entering Comanche county near Jones

Barbee's ranch on Resley's creek. A negro man, belonging to Barbee, was out some half a mile from the house 1853 unhoppling some horses. The Indians ran upon him, lanced him in several places and left him for dead, but the sable son of Africa survived. After the Indians left, the negro got up and went to the house minus the horses, and reported to massa Barbee that "his horses were gone, and nigger too, almost;" and in a half jocular, half serious way, said: "The Injuns kill me for awhile, and they tink I was dead for good, but I wasn't; I played 'possum on 'em, and they didn't skelp dis nigger, shore."

After leaving the negro, the Indians passed on down the valley of Resley's creek, gathering horses as they went. Only a few ranches were in the valley, and it required considerable time to get up a scout. Barbee was left afoot, and the settlements in the valley at that time were like angel visits—few and far between. Eli Picket, the Neals and John Bune were living five miles lower down the valley. Bune had started that morning with his wagon and a negro man to go to Waco, and near the Twin Mountains—then in Comanche but now in Hamilton county—the Indians came upon Bune and the negro man, killing both of them, and rifled the wagon, taking everything they wanted.

After killing Bune and the negro, the Indians turned a northeast course from the mountains and came into the Bosque valley, traveling down the same to Meridian Peak, as it was then called, and which stands fourteen miles west from Meridian and one and a half miles south of the present town of Iredell. Peter C. Johnson and his little ten year old son, Peter C., jr., had been to Waco to purchase breadstuffs and other family supplies and were returning home, and after passing Meridian Peak—since then called Johnson's Peak—some twelve hundred yards, the Indians, eight in number, surrounded the wagon, killed Peter C., sr. and captured little Peter C., jr., rifled the wagon and struck out up the Bosque valley, passing out through the northeast gap in Erath county and the Clear Fork of the Brazos, carrying out a large bunch of horses.

In the meantime a scout from Resley's creek and the Leon valley, consisting of Eli Picket, Dave Roberts, George B. Hasty, Jim Neal, F. B. Gentry and Tom Shockley, had hurriedly taken the trail on Resley's creek. The next morning after, the wounding of Barboo's negro and the finding of Bune and his negro killed on the trail caused considerable delay, as did also the finding, of Peter C. Johnson, senior, next; these two unavoidable delays enabled the Indians to get so far the start that it was impossible for the scout to overtake them. On the Clear Fork of the Brazos, from some cause unknown, the Indians dropped little Peter Johnson, taking his coat, hat and socks, leaving him with nothing on but his shirt and pants, fifty or seventy-five miles from the nearest ranch, in the bleak month of January, with nothing to subsist upon and no means of procuring any, and liable to be destroyed by hungry wolves. He had wandered from the trail, and the scout in pursuit had failed to find him, but in this, as in many other instances, Providence apparently protected the helpless. Little Peter lived five days and nights without a single morsel to eat save grass roots. On the evening of the sixth day he was found by a company of cow boys that Bill Keith had sent out from his ranch to make a "round up." The little fellow had found the cattle and had remained with them, thinking perchance he could procure milk from some of the cows, but in this he failed, the cows being too wild, but the cow hunters found him in time to revive and save him. But fortunate it was that they found him when they did. A cold, drizzling norther was blowing at the time and the poor little fellow would evidently have frozen to death during the night that ensued. When brought to Cora a few days after his being found, says Hon. Frank M. Collier (who gave me these facts), he was the poorest looking object imaginable—a mere skeleton. Mr. Collier says he took the little fellow up in his arms and carried him around over town and procured a present of one dollar from every man in town. Peter grew to manhood and is now a stout, robust man, and a worthy, good citizen of Comanche county.

[NOTE—This is the same Johnson referred to in the report of Captain R. B. Barry, published elsewhere in this work, and while the two stories differ somewhat in the details, the facts in each are substantially the same. We have concluded to publish both, as they appear in connection with other incidents.]

The attack upon Barbee's negro was the first blood drawn by Indians in Comanche county, and Bune and his negro were the first men killed by Indians in Comanche, but now in Hamilton county.

During the spring, summer and fall of 1858, Indian raids into Erath, Comanche and Brown counties were as frequent and regular as the full and change of the moon, and to preserve life and save property required constant vigilance and continuous scouting, and with all that could be done hundreds of men in the counties embraced in these articles lost by Indian raids their entire stock of horses, amounting in many cases to several hundred head. Some time during the month of August, 1858, a squad of Indians approached Eli Pickett's ranch on Resley's creek. One Indian ventured up to within three or four hundred yards of the house and took a position on high ground to spy out the situation. Mrs. Pickett was preparing dinner, and happened to discover the Indian as he was taking his position. Immediately, with gun in hand, Pickett and Dave Roberts started, and taking advantage of a ravine that chanced to lead in the right direction, they were enabled to approach within sixty yards of the Indian, and while the Indian was looking at some hoppled horses hard by in the valley, two unerring rifles rang at the same instant—two balls entered the Indian's breast, killing him instantly. This was the first Indian killed inside the boundary lines of Comanche county.

Kuykendall and Splann.

IT has been impossible to follow a band of Indians upon every raid made by them into the settlements and chronicle each murder in the order in which it occurred. Whenever they made their appearance along the border the work of death was begun, which was carried on so rapidly that you would scarcely be able to recover from the shock of one, before the scalping of another neighbor would 1861 be announced. Of course it is not to be expected that every murder committed by the Indians in their incursions along the border will appear in a volume of this size,

but we have endeavored to have some from each county.
Doubtless those omitted here will be chronicled hereafter
by some one else.   Among the murders committed in Erath
was Samuel Kuykendall, a native Texan and raised upon
the frontier.   His death, as related to us, occurred in the following manner:

In the summer of 1861, young Kuykendall and a youth
named Splann left their homes to go to Hamilton county in
search of some oxen that had strayed off.   Having found
the oxen, they started home.   As they were driving them
along the road, through a thinly settled section of country,
they were attacked by Indians.   The younsters had but one
gun between them, and that was in the hands of Splann.
Seeing the Indians were about to overtake them he halted,
dismounted and sheltering himself from their arrows behind his mule, presented his gun at them.   The Indians
well knowing that one of their number would certainly fall
if they ventured to charge upon him, left him and turned
their attention to young Kuykendall, who unfortunately
ran his horse into a bog.   The Indians instantly took advantage of his mishap and gathered around him.   They literally
filled his body with their arrows.   They then scalped him
and stripped him of his clothing.   In the meantime young
Splann succeeded in making his escape.   These Indians stole
a large number of horses on this raid.   They were followed
but without success.

Some two years later Samuel Rogers was killed.   Rogers
was a native of the State of Tennessee.   He came to Texas
in 1834, and settled in San Augustine county.   He moved
from there to Erath county and engaged in the business of
stock raising.   On the third day of May, 1863, Rogers was
at the house of one of his neighbors, who, having occasion
to leave home, requested him to remain all night with his
family.   He did so, and the next morning started to go to
the house of his son, James Rogers, where he lived.   While
on his way he was discovered by a party of Indians, who at
once gave chase.   Rogers, who was mounted on a small
pony, made all the speed he could towards his son's house,
and probably he would have succeeded in reaching it had it
not been for some Indians belonging to the same party who
were then near his son's house trying to steal his horses, but

in this they had failed, as the horses were so situated they could not get at them. Just as they had started to leave they met Rogers as he was fleeing from the other party. This forced him to turn his course, and as he did so his horse ran into a deep gully, and before he could extricate him the Indians closed in upon the old man and soon killed him.

In the summer of 1867, Cox and Hollis were killed. They and several others went out one day on the range for the purpose of gathering cattle. After they had gone some distance they were attacked by Indians, who, by some means, succeeded in getting between Cox and Hollis and the rest of the company. Both parties were on fleet horses, and they ran for several miles, but the Indians finally overtook the two men and killed them both.

Nathan McDow was killed during the year following. In the fall of 1868, he and his son went into the woods one day for the purpose of cutting timber. Before starting he found that he had but two loads of shot for his gun, and he told his wife if she heard him shoot she might know it was at Indians, as he did not intend to waste his ammunition at any smaller game. Some time after they left, his son returned to the house for some purpose, and he had scarcely more than reached it when he and his mother heard both barrels of McDow's gun fire in quick succession. "There!" exclaimed his son, "father has fired." He instantly mounted his horse and hastened to the spot where he had left his father. The Indians had just killed him, and were in the act of scalping him, when, seeing the boy approaching, and supposing, no doubt, that others were coming behind, they hastily fled. The boy gave the alarm, and a company pursued the Indians, but failed to overtake them.

The Flanagans.

THIS family were among the first settlers in Eastland county. They resided on what was known as the Colony fork of the Leon river. Some time in 1858, Mr. Flanagan had occasion to send some distance for breadstuffs for the use of his family. Accordingly he fitted

up his wagon and team and started his son and another
youth to the settlements on the lower Brazos.   It ap-
1858 pears that a party of Indians had been concealed near
Flanagan's house for several days, watching a favorable opportunity to attack it, and when they discovered
young Flanagan and his companion leaving the house in
their wagon they determined to get their scalps.   They
therefore took their course through the woods, struck the
road the young men were traveling some distance ahead of
them. and hid themselves in a thicket near by.   As the
wagon approached the place near where the Indians were concealed young Flanagan thought he saw the horns of a deer
showing above the brush, and he remarked to his companion: "Do you see that buck?"   At that instant the Indians
rose up and fired upon the youths, killing Flanagan on the
spot and wounding the other young man in the knee.   But
although he was thus partially disabled he leaped out of the
wagon, ran into the brush and made his escape.

Thomas Eubank.

MR. EUBANK was a son of the venerable John Eubank,
one of the first settlers in Shackelford county.   He
was a very cautious man as well as a brave one, and
never permitted any of his family to leave the place unarmed.   In 1866, a large party was organized in his settlement for the purpose of hunting their stock jointly for
1866 mutual protection against Indians.   Eubank sent his son
Thomas, the subject of this sketch, to accompany the
stock hunters on their expedition. He had to ride ten or twelve
miles alone to reach the place of rendezvous, and on his
way he was attacked by a party of Indians. Young Eubank
defended himself bravely, killed one Indian and two horses,
but at last was killed himself. A few weeks afterwards
the party he intended to accompany returned from their
hunt and Eubank called on them to learn what success they

had met with. He then, for the first time, learned that his son had never joined the party.

It was at once suspected that he had been killed or captured by the Indians, and immediate search was made along the road that led to the place of rendezvous. Finally they discovered a dim trail making off towards some mounds and followed it. On the way they came across the carcasses of two horses that had been killed by sixshooter bullets. Keeping on their course they came to the top of some rugged hills, where they halted to examine the surrounding country. While there they noticed a very disagreeable odor as if there was some dead animal in the vicinity, but they could see nothing. At length, however, after a long search, their attention was drawn to some brush that appeared to have been recently piled in a shallow gulch, and beneath it they found the body of an Indian wrapped up in a blanket, which was fastened around it by a belt that had belonged to Eubank's son.

Not finding the body of the young man they took it for granted he had been captured by the Indians. Eubank made every effort to ascertain whether or not his son was still living, but all to no purpose. Time rolled on and Eubank still hoped that his son might have been taken captive and that he would yet be restored to him, until eventually some boys who were hunting stock on the same prairie where the two dead horses were seen came across his skeleton. On examination it was identified beyond all doubt as the skeleton of young Eubank.

George Hazlewood.

GEORGE HAZLEWOOD was one of the early pioneers of this country. Where he first settled we do not know, but the latter portion of his life was spent in Stephens county. In the month of March, 1869, Hazlewood went out one day, as he frequently did, on the range

in search of some of his stock. While thus engaged he was attacked by Indians. It appears that he first at-
1869 tempted to save himself by running, but finding he could not do so, he dismounted, took a stand behind a tree and fought until he was killed. He had a repeating rifle with him, and it was evident he had made the Indians pay dearly for his scalp. All around where the fight occurred a number of empty cartridge shells were found, showing that he had shot many times at his assailants. A party of soldiers went in pursuit of these Indians and soon found their trail. In some places on the trail splotches of blood were seen, clearly proving that Hazlewood had killed or wounded one or more of the Indians. It was evident also from the "sign," that they had constructed some sort of sleds to carry their dead or wounded. Owing to this fact the Indians could travel but slowly, and the soldiers soon overtook them, and at once charged upon them and plied their guns with deadly effect. The Indians stood their ground for some time and fought with desperation, but finally were totally routed, leaving twenty dead on the field and having more than twice that number wounded. The soldiers also captured all their horses and camp equipage. A negro man and a Mexican who had been wounded in the fight with Hazlewood, were also captured. The negro man had run away from his master, had joined the Indians and become quite a conspicuous character among them. The Indians had taken good care of their own wounded, but they had paid no attention to the wounded negro and Mexican. They both died in two or three days. Hazlewood was a most estimable man, and one who had rendered efficient services on many occasions to the frontier settlers.

Henry Martin.

THIS youth was a native Texan. His parents were well known to the author. They were true lovers of their adopted country of Texas. Henry Martin and others were engaged October 5, 1870, in hunting cattle on Palo Pinto creek, in Eastland county. A portion of the

cattle having been gathered, it was necessary for one part
of the company to herd those while the rest of them
1870 went in search of other stock. Martin being a very
expert horseman and huntsman, was singled out as
one of those who should go in search of stock. While hunting he ventured off from the rest nearly a half mile. The
Indians who were in the vicinity, unknown to the party,
finding that the cow hunters were thus scattered, dashed in
among them. All of the hunters fled, leaving young Martin
off by himself. He did all that was possible to save himself. The savages soon surrounded him and cut off all
chance of escape. He fell a victim to their savage cruelty.
He was but nineteen years old. His parents were still living in McLennan county when last heard from.

Killing of Mrs. Woods and Miss Lemley.

IT is to be regretted that we are not in possession of all
the particulars connected with this horrible tragedy,
but after several attempts we finally obtained the following very meagre account of one of the most heartrending scenes that ever occurred along our border. During
the month of January, 1861, Mrs. Woods—whose given name
we do not know—and her three unmarried sisters, the
1861 Misses Lemley, were all congregated in one house.
While in this helpless condition, with no man at the
house to protect them, they were suddenly attacked one day
by a party of Indians, who, it seems, undertook, after out-
raging the ladies in the most brutal manner, to make captives of them all. Mrs. Woods and one of the Misses Lemley, preferring death to such captivity, attempted to escape
by running, when they were pursued by the Indians, and
both were killed and scalped in the presence of their sisters.
The sad fate of the two deceased sisters in endeavoring to
make their escape so terrified the two remaining ones, that
they made no effort to escape by flight, but sought the protection of an old Indian who was in the company, and he,

be it said to his credit, kept his blood-thirsty companions
from killing the unfortunate girls. This most diabolical
tragedy occurred on Rush Creek, in Eastland county. After
the completion of their hellish deeds, the Indians left the
premises, carrying with them the two Misses Lemley. They
passed over into Erath county near Stephenville, and there
the poor unfortunate girls were stripped entirely of all their
clothing, and that, too, in the month of January. They
finally made their way to the house of one of the citizens
of Erath county, where they were furnished clothing and
otherwise provided for.   The poor girls, however, had been
so much abused that it required several weeks treatment at
the hands of their physician—Dr. J. P. Valentine, of Weatherford—before they recovered.

There were quite a number of the Lemleys living in that
section of the country, and they have suffered much at the
hands of the savages.   George Lemley, a brother of the
young ladies above named, now resides in Parker county,
some eight miles from the town of Weatherford.   He is
mentioned elsewhere in this work in the fight which took
place near the line of Palo Pinto and Young counties,
known as the "Rocky Creek Fight."   In this fight he received a wound which left a scar which yet disfigures his
face.

Murders in Palo Pinto County.

WE do not hesitate in saying that there is no territory
upon the face of the earth of equal dimensions to
that embraced within the boundaries of Palo Pinto,
Parker, Young and Jack counties, whose inhab-
tants have suffered as much at the hands of the blood thirst-
savages as have those who, at an early day, peopled the
counties above named.   From 1858 up to 1875, Indian
1858   raids were frequent, and they scarcely ever visited the
settlements without carrying with them a large number of horses, and generally a few scalps of the settlers
ornamented their belts as they passed out of the settlements

to their homes in the mountains or on the staked plains, and not unfrequently these trophies were carried with them to the reservation, where the Indians were being cared for by the United States government. The list of murders which we here present, simply represents a very few of the many outrages committed by the Indians in that section of the country. It may not unfrequently happen that errors will be detected in the following narratives, but this was almost unavoidable, for at the time the data was obtained (some fifteen years prior to going to press) from which these articles were written, there were no railroads in that section of the State and settlers were rather scarce. We have been unable since then to have corrections made in every instance, but trust there will be no serious errors found in any of them. It has been almost impossible to get the correct dates in every instance, but in most cases they will be found correct, as reliable frontiersmen have been found who kept a diary in which the dates of most of the murders have been recorded. The first murder of which we have any account in Palo Pinto county is that of John Edwards, a lad about seven years of age. Young Edwards was playing in the lot when five Indians suddenly rushed upon him, tore his scalp from his head then turned him loose. They took so large a scalp from the boy's head that the skin fell down over his eyes, blinding him, and he was compelled to raise it with one hand to enable him to see. The Indians then started to the house of the boy's parents, but Mrs. Edwards saw them approaching and barred the doors. Fortunately for her at this moment Mr. Edwards and his herders came up, driving some cattle, and as soon as the Indians heard them they fled. The little boy who was scalped lived several months afterwards, but finally died from the effects of the wound.

The next victims of whom we have any account were Benjamin F. Baker, William M. Peters and Henry Welty. These men were all killed by the Indians in 1863. During the winter of 1863 a party of Indians came down the Brazos river on the east side into Parker county. They stole a large number of horses, and to avoid pursuit they crossed to the west side of the river and went out through Palo Pinto county. They had gone but a short distance on the west side when they came across Mr. Baker, who was traveling alone.

The Indians waylaid him and shot him from the brush. This was on Saturday, February 28, 1863. Baker had left his home in the morning and had gone over to a neighbor's, Doctor G. P. Barber, for some pork. After getting the pork he started back home and had gotten about one-fourth of a mile from Barber's house when he was attacked by eight or ten Indians. They ran him back to Barber's, and in the chase shot four arrows into him, two in his back, one in his arm and one in his thigh. He remained on his horse, however, until he arrived at Barber's fence gate, where he fell off his horse, dead. Barber hearing the noise ran out with his gun, which he presented at the Indians and prevented them from scalping him. They did not molest the house but got the horse Baker was riding and then went to Barber's lot and took his horse out and then departed. J. H. Baker, a nephew of Benjamin F. Baker, who then, as now, lived in Palo Pinto county, was the nearest neighbor of Doctor Barber and had seen his uncle pass his house during the morning while on his way to Barber's. The sudden death of his uncle was, of course, a great shock to the nephew (who was notified of the fact during the afternoon) and it devolved upon the latter to communicate this sad intelligence to the family of the deceased. The scene at the household was one never to be forgotten by the kinsman who bore the sad tidings. The following day the remains of Mr. Baker were carried to town for burial by the nephew, who first carried them by the home of the deceased, that his wife and children might take their last look upon the cold, pale face of the husband and father. The death of Mr. Baker cast a gloom over the entire community. He was among the earliest settlers of Palo Pinto county, having come to Texas and settled in the county in 1857, and had passed through many privations and hardships, such as are incident to a frontier life. He was a native of Ashe county, North Carolina.

We will now follow up the Indians after leaving Barber's house. At what point we do not know, but it was during the same day of the killing of Baker that this party of Indians came upon William M. Peters. Mr. Peters also moved into Palo Pinto county in about the year 1857, afterwards married there, and at the time of his death was living about thirteen miles south of the town of Palo Pinto.

On the day mentioned he had occasion to go to the town of Palo Pinto, and from there he intended to go to the residence of his father. The morning he left he seemed uneasy and unwilling to start. He kissed his baby, and before leaving he kissed his wife and told her good bye, as he was going on a long journey. The horse he intended riding was a very poor one, and his wife advised him to ride another; but he replied, no, that it would take too much time to get another one. Whilst on his way, and just as he was entering a large prairie, he was attacked by a party of mounted Indians. His horse being exceedingly slow, there was no chance of escape. The Indians pressed him closely, and finally he dismounted and ran into an old deserted ranch house. As he entered the door many bullets struck the door facing above and on each side. Here he seems to have made a desperate fight and to have kept the Indians at bay for some time, as many bullets were found lodged in the walls, which had been fired at him by the Indians. Finally a ball struck him in the forehead and killed him. The Indians took his scalp and left.

During the fall of the same year Henry Welty met with a fate similar to that of Baker and Peters. He was born in Arkansas in 1818. He immigrated to Texas at an early day and lived for many years in Falls county. In 1846, he moved up the Brazos river into Palo Pinto county, where he followed the occupation of farming and stock raising without being molested to any great extent by the Indians. About the tenth of November, 1863, Welty took his gun and went out on foot in search of some stock. When he had gone about a half or three-quarters of a mile from his residence he was attacked by a party of Indians who had concealed themselves in a clump of shin oak bushes. After shooting him with a gun and several arrows, they cut his throat, scalped him, stripped him of his clothes and slashed the flesh from his limbs with their butcher knives. His body lay in this condition for three days before it was found by some of his neighbors. He was a brave and true man, and loved by all who knew him. He left a wife and three children to mourn his loss

Marcus L. Dalton was one of the earliest settlers of Palo Pinto county, and like most of those who cast their lots in that section of the country engaged in the stock business. By close attention to business and shrewd trading he soon accumulated a considerable stock around him, and made frequent drives to the territories. It was while he was returning home from one of these successful drives, that he met with his tragic death. Dalton was returning home from Kansas, at which place he had disposed of a large herd of cattle and had with him the proceeds of the sale, when he was attacked and killed by the Indians. On his return to Texas, he was accompanied by James Redfield and James Mc-Caster. On the morning of the sixteenth of December, 1870, these three men left the residence of Dr. J. P. Volentine (brother-in-law of Dalton), in Weatherford, for Dalton's home on the Brazos. They had reached about the northeast corner of Palo Pinto county, when they were attacked by a party of Indians. The three men were riding in a buggy or ambulance and, of course, had no chance to escape from the Indians who were on horseback. The Indians soon killed all three of the men—then scalped and butchered them in a horrible manner. They also carried off several head of horses and a pair of mules. Before leaving they broke open the trunk, took out the clothing, and such articles as they did not care for, were scattered around over the ground. They failed to find, however, eleven thousand four hundred dollars, which Dalton had concealed in an old shoe which lay inside the trunk. Mr. Dalton left quite a large family, and many of them reside in Palo Pinto county. His widow, Mrs. Lucinda Dalton, and three of his sons, to wit: Charles A., George W. and Robert S. Dalton, all reside at this time —1888, in Palo Pinto county. His two sons, W. C. and G. L. Dalton, and his daughter, Mrs. Jane Volentine (wife of Dr. J. P. Volentine), are residents of Weatherford, Parker county. His eldest son, John Dalton, lives in the Pan Handle, of Texas, and one of his daughters, Mrs. Mary Hoover, wife of Frank Hoover, lives in Young county, Texas. Prior to the attack upon Dalton and his companions, but on the same day, George and Richard Joel had a fight with the same party of Indians, and forced them to retreat. It was during this retreat that they came up with Dalton's party.

On the following day the bodies of the three men were discovered by Green Lassiter, while passing through Loving's
Valley, and recognizing the body of Dalton, had the remains
of the three men interred, and then carried the news to
Weatherford. Poor fellow! little did he dream then that a
similar fate awaited him only a few months later, but alas!
too true. It was during the fall of the following year, we
believe, that a party of Indians came down from the
Wichita mountains, and began pillaging and plundering in
their usual way. It was not long before they had collected
a large number of horses, but before getting out of the
country were discovered by some one on the range, who
gave the settlers the alarm, and a party was quickly raised
and in pursuit. The Indians were soon overtaken—a fight
ensued—and Lassiter, who was one of the pursuing party
was killed.

Chesley S. Dobbs and Jesse B. Veale were both residents
of Palo Pinto county. The first named was killed in the
year 1872, and the other in the following year. On June 26,
1872, Dobbs left his home and went to the town of Palo
Pinto to buy some goods for his family. He reached the
town in safety, made his purchases, and left for home—but
the poor fellow was fated never to see it again. Failing to
reach home at the appointed time, his wife became uneasy,
and sent one of her sons in search of him. He went to the
town of Palo Pinto, and learned that his father had been
there, made his purchases, and gone home. The son of
Dobbs was satisfied that some accident had happened to the
old man, and raised a small party of men to aid him in
searching for his father. They found the old man about
half way between his house and town, killed, scalped and
stripped of his clothes. The next day his clothes and scalp
were recovered by a party of men who pursued the Indians.
The Indians were taken by surprise and several of them
killed. Clinton Dobbs, who now lives in Shackleford
county, is a son of Chesley S. Dobbs.

Mr. Veale, we believe, was a native of Texas. On the
twenty-fifth day of February, 1873, he, in company with
some others, went on a fishing excursion into Palo Pinto
county. After fishing a while, some of the party, Veale
among the number, went into the woods in search of game,

and accidentally came across some Indian horses that were hoppled. They took the horses and drove them to their fishing camp. One of the parties while driving the horses lost his powder horn, and Veale and J. E. Corbin went back to hunt for it. In the meantime the Indians had returned to the place where they had left their horses hoppled, and finding them gone, they determined to have revenge. They discovered Veale and his companion coming back, secreted themselves, and awaited their approach. As soon as they were within close range, the Indians fired on them, and Veale was so badly wounded he was unable to escape. His companion, being unhurt, made good his retreat. The Indians pressed him closely, but he had a repeating rifle which he fired several times at them with such deadly effect that they finally abandoned the chase, and went back to where they had shot Veale, carrying with them their wounded. They took refuge in a cave near by, and the Texans endeavored to drive them from it, but after several men had been wounded, they found it was impossible to dislodge them. The Texans then went to where Veale had been shot, and found him sitting at the root of a tree, dead. Before he died, however, he succeeded in sending one of the Indians to his "happy hunting ground." The Texans committed a great error in taking the Indian horses. They should have concealed themselves in the vicinity, and when the Indians came for them they could probably have killed them all with but little risk to themselves. Veale was killed at the mouth of Ioni Creek, on the Brazos. His mother and two of his brothers still reside in the town of Palo Pinto. He was a Mason, and was buried with Masonic honors on Wednesday, February 26, 1873.

Massacres in Parker County.

THE name of Parker seems to be an ill-fated one in Texas when taken in connection with the Indian history of our country. Parker county was named for the venerable Isaac Parker, who, in the year 1855, represented that county (which then embraced a much larger territory than now) in the Legislature. He belonged to the Parker family who came to Texas in 1833, and settled 1859 in Montgomery county, now Grimes county. This same family of Parkers, with a few others, settled in Limestone county a little later, and in the year 1835 built Parker's fort, of historic fame, near where the town of Groesbeck now stands. The full history of the "Parker Fort Massacre" appears elsewhere in this volume. It will be seen from the long list of murders at the hands of the Indians as having occurred in Parker county and herein recorded, which list is but a very partial one, that no other county in the State furnishes a history with such a bloody record of barbaric cruelty.

Among the first murders which took place in Parker county and which in after years was never surpassed in savage duplicity and barbaric cruelty was that of Mrs. Sherman. During the year 1859 there lived two families, John Brown and —— Sherman, in the northwestern portion of Parker county, on Rock creek, near the line of Palo Pinto, some three or four miles apart. This was from twelve to fifteen miles from the town of Weatherford, the county eat of Parker county. In the month of December, 1859, a party of marauding Indians made a raid into Parker and adjoining counties, stealing horses and committing murders wherever they went. Their presence was first made known in Parker county when they attacked John Brown, who was on the range, about one-half mile from his house, looking after his horses. He was surrounded by a party of five or six Indians, shot and speared to death and then scalped. The Indians carried off several head of horses. They then proceeded to his residence, but Mrs. Brown seeing them coming barred the doors and thereby saved herself, as the Indians were afraid to attack it, thinking probably there were men inside to defend it. From there they proceeded to Mr. Thompson's farm, at which place they increased their number of stolen horses to some twenty-five or thirty head. The marauding party had divided up into squads and before arriving at the residence of Mr. Sherman they had collected together and now numbered about fifty-six. When the Indians approached the house the family, consisting of six persons, were at dinner (one account we have says they

were at breakfast, this, however, is immaterial). Several
Indians galloped up to the yard fence, alighted from their
horses, went into the house and cordially shook hands with
the family, making the most friendly demonstrations. After
this exhibition of savage duplicity these devils incarnate
told the family to " vamose, vamose, Indians no hurt." The
presence of so many Indians, of course, very much alarmed
the family, but owing to the disadvantage at which they
were placed, both by the sudden appearance and the superior
number of the Indians, resistance was not to be thought of.
Nothing was left for the family but to do as they were directed.

It was a cold rainy day, but the unfortunate family not
wishing to incur the displeasure of these savages, started off
upon their journey through the forests. They had only
gone about half a mile, however, when a party of the fiendish band overtook them and ordered Mrs. Sherman to return
to the house. The bereaved husband and children implored
them not to take away the one they loved so dearly, but
their entreaties were of no avail. The Indians said "they
wanted squaw," and without further ceremony tore the unfortunate woman from the embrace of those she loved so
dearly. She was taken back to the house and subjected to
all manner of torture, barbaric cruelty, and brutal treatment too horrible to relate. Let the *imagination* picture if
it can, this terrible tragedy—a description of it will not be
attempted here.

The agonizing screams of the victim seemed to delight the
heartless monsters, and it was not until they had inflicted
upon this poor woman every character of punishment which
their devilish minds could invent, that they could make up
their minds to leave. Not satisfied to leave Mrs. Sherman
to survive, if she could, the trying ordeal through which
she had passed, they deliberately stripped her of all her
clothing, shot several arrows into her body, and when ready
to leave, two Indians on horseback rode up on either side
and each taking hold of her, dashed off, while a third Indian followed behind and beat her in the back with a
heavy stick. Finally, she fell almost lifeless upon the
ground, when an Indian warrior dismounted, passed his
knife around her head, and tore off her scalp. She was

then left for dead, but after the Indians had departed, she revived sufficiently to crawl to the house, where she was soon found by her husband, who in the meantime had taken his children to a neighbor's, and had gotten a few friends to return with him to look after his wife. She was found in the condition we have just described, suffering a thousand deaths from wounds received, and indignities to which she had been subjected.

When she beheld her husband upon his return, by an effort almost superhuman, she rallied sufficiently to relate to her bereaved companion the sad story of all her sufferings at the hands of these merciless demons. Mrs. Sherman lived four days after this cruel treatment. The day following the perpetration of this outrage, the children were taken back home to take a last look at their dying mother. The meeting was one never to be forgotten by those who witnessed the tragic and heartrending scene. We would be glad that the catalogue of murders might end here, but this is but the beginning in that section.

General Baylor's Fight on Paint Creek.

THE Browning boys were native Texans, and lived with their father on the Clear Fork of the Brazos river, and we think, in Stephens county. But the surrounding cir· cumstances, and the fight of General Baylor with the Indians immediately after their attack upon the Browning boys, all tend to make this a proper place to record this incident among the list of Parker county massacres.

1860 During the month of June, 1860, a large party of Indians came down the Clear Fork of the Brazos on one of their raids. After committing numerous depredations they came upon Josephus and Frank Browing, who were out on the range hunting stock. It seems they had gotten down off their horses for the purpose of letting them graze. The horse of Josephus was hoppled. Upon the approach of

the Indians the boys made for their horses, hoping to escape
by flight, as they had no arms with which to make a defense. The Indians were pressing them so closely that
Josephus saw he would surely be overtaken if he waited to
unhopple his horse, so he mounted him as he was, and
started with his brother. The Indians, of course, soon came
up with him, and quickly despatched him. Frank being on
an unhoppled horse, made better speed, but the Indians
were well mounted, closed in on him and wounded him in
several places. Finally he reached Hubbard's creek, which
was swimming and plunged into it just in time to escape
the foremost Indians, who were rapidly gaining on him.
The Indians seeing that they would have to swim the creek
if they followed him further, gave up the chase and left.

The news of this sad affair soon reached the ears of General John R. Baylor, who happened to be in that section of
the country, with a small party on a cow hunt. We take
the following account of the fight, which ensued from H.
Smythe's Historical Sketch of Parker county:

In June of 1860, General John R. Baylor, who now resides
in San Antonio, with his brother, George W. Baylor, his
two sons, Walker K. and John W. Baylor, and Wat Reynolds, visited the Clear Fork of the Brazos, where the General formerly lived.   While there hunting cattle, these gentlemen were informed of the killing of Josephus Browning,
and the serious wounding of Frank Browning, by a large
body of Comanches.   They immediately went to the Browning ranch, on the Clear Fork, near the mouth of Hubbard's
creek, where they met other gentlemen who had been attracted to the spot by the murderous acts of the Indians.
General Baylor, George W. Baylor, Elias Hale, Minn
Wright and John Dawson started in pursuit of the demons,
and on the fifth day, June 28, overtook them on Paint creek,
where a fierce contest ensued, during which Baylor and his
friends killed thirteen of the Indians. On their return to
Weatherford they brought the scalps of nine of them, together with numerous trophies, including the scalp of a
white woman whom the Indians had killed, several bows
and arrows, darts, quivers, shields, tomahawks and other
paraphernalia of savage warfare. The feeling against the
Indians was so bitter that Baylor and his party were de-

cide'ly lionized for their prowess and daring. The horrible murder of Mrs. Sherman and others in the northwestern portion of the county, in 1859, and other similar outrages, were fresh in the minds of the people, who seemingly delighted in the slaughter of any of the hostile bands. The excitement was very great. The news of Baylor's success extended to the adjoining counties, and the heroic men were honored by a public barbecue on the square, which was participated in by several hundred people. Speeches were made and general rejoicings were universal. In the evening of the day a dance was indulged in at the court house, which was kept up "until broad day light," the following morning. In the long room a rope was stretched diagonally across, and on it were hung the nine Indian scalps, the woman's scalp captured from the defunct Comanches, and all the trophies of the expedition. In the excitement incident to the glorification, those who participated in the festivities evidently forgot that the prominent decorations of the hall were the unmistakable evidences of death and murder, and the relics of a barbarism then very frequent in this section of Texas.

General Baylor took his scalps and other spoils of the victors to various cities and towns, and soon after the people of the southeastern portion of the State sent flour, meal and all kinds of provisions, clothing, boots and shoes, blankets, pistols, guns, etc., to Weatherford for the support and protection of the people of the frontier. These supplies came in large quantities and served a most excellent purpose. There was one universal cry. It seemed to be the heartfelt desire of every person. "Exterminate the Indians," was the watchword, and it is not to be wondered that such was the case, when we fully realize the vast destruction of property and human life. Up to the close of 1875 it is estimated that the Indians captured and destroyed property, within a circle of one hundred miles of Parker county, worth at least six millions of dollars, and killed and took into captivity nearly four hundred persons! The reservations, nine miles below Belknap, and twelve miles above, in Young county, on which were upwards of one thousand Indians, were broken up and the savages driven beyond the Red river on the north and the Pease river on the west. Colonel Robert S. Neighbors was the government Indian agent and Shapley Ross of Waco the reservation agent. Yet, with all the terror and devastation of those days and the insecurity of persons and property in this very section of Texas then, no portion of the great States of New York, Pennsylvania or Ohio can boast of more security than the Texas frontier—even one hundred and fifty miles beyond Parker county—enjoys to-day. The periodic predatory incursions of these wild men are ended. Civilization and population have driven them far away from any possible danger from them and rendered our county and vicinity places of very decided safety. [NOTE.—The book from which this was taken was published in 1877.]

It may not be inappropriate to here narrate an incident that took place possibly the latter part of the same year, or the first of the next. Baylor gave notice to the young men that he was going to take a grand buffalo hunt and wanted the boys to take a hand in it. As this announcement was made about the beginning of the war, a good many thought that Baylor's object was to capture the United States posts along the frontier, but be this as it may, he raised a considerable force with which he proceeded far out on the plains, and although they took no government posts they did have a glorious time in hunting and killing buffalo. When they were tired of the sport they turned their faces towards the settlements and reached Camp Cooper in safety. The Colonel and his men, thinking they were beyond all danger, betook themselves to rest without placing any guards on post, forgetting, it seems, that it was a common practice with the Indians to follow parties returning to the settlements without making any attack upon them until they thought themselves safe from all danger. The Indians were shrewd enough to know that when in or near the settlements they would not naturally be as watchful as when they were within the enemy's country.

Early one morning while the Colonel and his men were taking their ease and enjoying their pipes a large party of Indians that had been watching for a favorable opportunity dashed in on them and stampeded and drove off nearly all his horses, leaving most of them flat afoot. Fortunately for them, Colonel W. C. Dalrymple happened to be near by with

a ranging company. Being notified of Colonel Baylor's
mishap he immediately started with a part of his men in
pursuit of the Indians. They were soon overtaken, and
after a running fight of about twelve miles Colonel Dalrymple and his men succeeded in recapturing nearly all the
stolen horses. Two of the Indians were killed—none of the
rangers were hurt. Colonel Baylor is an old Indian fighter
but for once (and I believe the only time) he was caught
napping. Colonel Dalrymple's services on this occasion
were rendered just in the nick of time, for if the Indians had
succeeded in getting away with Colonel Baylor's horses he
and his men would have had a hard road to travel in getting
back to the settlements. Both these well known gentlemen
are still living, and though they are growing somewhat old,
they are still hale and hearty and give promise of many
years of usefulness to their country.

More Murders in Parker County.

THE details of the following murders of Youngblood,
Killen, Washington and Mrs. Brown, will be given substantially in the language as they appear in Smythe's
Historical Sketch of Parker county, from which they
are taken. In the spring of 1861, the Indians came upon
William Youngblood and killed him. The day previous a
party of Captain M. D. Tacket's rangers, composed
1861 of David Stinson, Bud Slover, John Slover, —— Boyd,
—— McMahan and others, were out on a scout, and
while feeding at noon, eleven Indians were discovered coming out of a deep ravine, twelve miles north of Jacksboro.
The Indians attacked the rangers but were quickly repulsed
with the loss of one, and serious injury to a second. They
made off, hotly pursued by the rangers, but having better
horses, of course made the quickest time, and escaped. The
rangers were distanced; still they followed on all night, but
could not find the objects of their search. Early in the
morning William Youngblood was going into the woods

close by his house to cut and split rails, and while there nine
Indians surrounded the place, scalped and killed him. The
same morning the rangers were reinforced by James Gilleland, Angie Price, Palmer and other citizens. They overtook the murderers and killed the leader, who had Youngblood's scalp in his shot pouch. The scalp was instantly
taken to the deceased's late residence, and placed on his
head a moment before he was lowered into the earthly receptacle of the dead.

In the summer of 1861, John Killen and William Washington, each about twenty-four years of age, who resided
on Grindstone creek, were stock hunting, and while resting
at noon, were pounced upon and a well directed arrow killed
the former, and another badly wounded the latter.

During the same summer Mrs. John Brown was killed,
and possibly by the same party of Indians. This lady also
lived on Grindstone creek. She had twin babies and had
started to visit a neighbor near by, she carrying one of the
children, and a girl about grown (one of the accounts we
have, say she was a daughter, but of this we are not positive) the other. On their way they were attacked by a
party of Indians. The girl who had one of the children
was some distance ahead, and had well nigh reached her
destination. Mrs. Brown, at the sight of the savage monsters, in her fright, for the moment, apparently forgot that
she was the mother of the two children, and clasping the
the child she carried in her own arms, tightly to her bosom,
she ran hastily back to the house, crying "they shan't have
mine, they shan't have mine." She finally reached the
house, but the Indians soon came up, scalped and killed her
on the spot, but spared the child

Marion Tacket—Sarah Mathews.

TACKET settled in Parker county at an early day, near
the line of Jack county. In the spring of 1862, as he
was hunting his stock one day on the range he was
attacked by Indians. Seeing there was no chance of
escape by flight he took a stand behind a sapling three or

four inches in diameter and defended himself to the last.
At length, however, an arrow pierced his lungs and
1862 another struck him in the neck, severing the jugular
vein. But before he fell, he discharged both his gun
and sixshooter at his assailants and it is supposed that he
killed and wounded several. The Indians seeing a son of
Mr. Tacket approaching, and probably thinking that others
were coming, gathered up their dead and wounded and fled.
The sapling behind which Tacket had taken his stand was
stuck full of arrows. The Indians were pursued for some
distance but were not overtaken. On the trail the dead body
of an Indian was found covered over with stones, proving
that one at least had paid for Tacket's life with his own.

We are not positive as to this date, but think it was in the
month of October of the same year that the Mathews's
family were attacked by a party of Indians, who murdered
Mathews and one of his daughters and took Mrs. Sarah
Mathews and four or five of her children prisoners. These
Indians killed and captured the family of Mr. Stovall in the
same neighborhood while Mr. Stovall was absent from home.
There were also two or three captives taken from another
family, whose names we do not know.

The whole number taken from the three families amounted
to ten. Among them were two women and three children.
Mrs. Mathews states that after the Indians captured her
they traveled for thirty-six hours without rest or food.
She carried her young child the whole way on her arm until
it was perfectly numb and dead to all feeling. When the
Indians had arrived at a point where they thought they
would be safe from pursuit they made a halt and tied their
prisoners securely. From thence on and until they reached
the Indian village, the captives suffered terribly from exposure and want of food, and the Indians told them all the
time that they intended to kill all the men and sell the
women and children. These captives were carried about
from point to point, between the Rocky mountains and Kansas. Finally, in 1864, a treaty was made with the Indians
by the government of the United States, and these captives,
with others, were released. Mr. Stovall learning that his
son had been delivered to the government agent sent his
brother after him. The agent turned him over to him and

also the other nine captives. They were in a destitute condition and five or six hundred miles from home, but the government kindly provided for their wants and they were soon restored to their friends and relatives.

Murders in Parker County, 1863-1873.

DURING the year 1863, several families were living in the valley of Patrick's creek, in Parker county, the Rev. John Hamilton among the number. He owned, in connection with his farm, a small tannery. On one occasion he sent his sons, William and Stewart Hamilton, out into the woods to collect material for tanning purposes. While thus engaged the two young men were attacked by Indians. The frightened boys attempted to escape by running, but they were soon overtaken, their bodies pierced full of arrows. They were both killed and scalped, and before leaving, the heartless savages cut off one of the ears of Stewart, together with a portion of his head. During the same day either this or another party of the same band killed Mrs. F. C. Brown, who resided some four miles from Hamilton's, while standing in the yard in front of her door. Mrs. Brown had two daughters, Sarah, aged sixteen, and a younger daughter, whose name we do not know, about fourteen years of age. These two young ladies had been over to visit their neighbor, Mr. Gatling, and were returning home when the merciless red skins fell upon them and seriously wounded both the young ladies with arrows. The eldest daughter, Sarah, died shortly afterwards from the effects of her wounds, but the younger one finally recovered. In September of the following year, 1864, William (or John, we are not positive as to the given name, accounts vary) Berry was killed on Sanches creek.

Berry resided in eastern Texas for several years, and then moved to Parker county, where he settled at what was known as the "Horse Shoe Bend." One day in the above named month, Berry and his little son went with a wagon to a field he had on the opposite side of the Brazos river for a load of pumpkins. When he started his wife insisted that he should take his gun with him, but he did not do so, thinking there was no danger, as no Indians had been seen in that section for a long time. He crossed the river, loaded his wagon and was on his way home when he was attacked by Indians who had secreted themselves in some brush near the road side. As he passed by, they suddenly rose and fired a volley at the wagon. Berry was instantly killed and his little boy was wounded in several places with arrows. The Indians beat his head with clubs until they thought he was dead and then left. But the little fellow was found shortly afterwards and got well of his wounds.

Mrs. Jane Smith was a resident of Parker county, and was also killed about this time. One day in the fall of 1864, while Mr. Smith was absent in the Confederate army, Mrs. Smith discovered a party of Indians about three-quarters of a mile distant coming towards the house. A moment afterwards she saw that they were in pursuit of two boys, whom they soon overtook and killed. Mrs. Smith told her children to run as fast as they could to the house of a neighbor, and that she would follow them in a little while. She did so, but before she could reach the house the Indians came up with her and killed her, and also two of her daughters, whom she had just overtaken in their flight. Mrs. Smith had her infant in her arms, and her eldest daughter who was near, seeing her fall, ran up to her, took the infant from the arms of her dead mother, and fled with the remaining children to an old gun shop that fortunately happened to be very near. There were several old guns in the shop, and when the Indians approached it the children presented them through the windows. The Indians thinking no doubt there was a man in the house, fell back when they saw the muzzes of the guns protruding from the windows, and finally left without making an attack. They then went to the house of Mr. Smith and plundered it of its contents. A near neighbor of Mr. Smith, hearing an unusual noise about his premises, started out to ascertain the cause. He had gone but a short distance when he discovered the Indians, and knowing that in all probability they would attack his own house, he hastily ran back. As soon as he reached it, he told his wife and children to run to the woods and hide themselves, and he would remain at the house to draw the attention of the Indians to himself and thus give them time to escape. They did so, and a few moments afterwards the Indians came galloping up, and seeing the owner of the house standing in front of it, they at once charged upon him. He immediately ran in the house, took his stand in the door, and presented his gun. Seeing he was prepared to defend the premises, the Indians, after some consultation among themselves, evidently came to the conclusion that it would be a risky business to attack him, and rode off the way they had come.

About four miles from this house they stole a number of horses and took a woman prisoner. They were pursued by a party of Texans. The Texans knew a pass in the mountains through which they believed the Indians would go on their way out, and they succeeded in reaching it before the Indians. They secreted themselves in the pass, and a little while after dark the Indians came riding along, totally unsuspicious of danger. The Texans waited until they could see them distinctly, and then fired a volley at them, killing several and wounding others. At the report of the guns, the Indians' horses "stampeded," and the one the captured lady was riding threw her to the ground. She was but slightly hurt, however, and concealed herself behind a large rock to prevent being shot by the Texans. A few moments before she had been a hopeless prisoner in the hands of her savage captors, and one can imagine what must have been her joyful feelings when she found herself among her own people.

Mr. Coldiron resided near Van Buren, in Parker county. If we are not mistaken in the date, it was one morning in the fall of the same year that Mr. Coldiron sent his two children out, a son and daughter, in search of a yoke of oxen. Whilst the little girl and her brother were still in sight of the house, a party of Indians who were concealed in the vicinity, rushed upon them and took them prisoners. They took the children to the top of a neighboring mountain, where they remained a day or two and then went off. A company of citizens pursued them, who after following them about sixty miles, overtook them and at once attacked them. Whilst the fight was going on the two children jumped from the horses they were riding, climbed to the top of a big rock, and amid the yells of the Indians and the firing of guns, the little girl cried out *"Don't shoot us, we are white folks."* One of the men seeing the little girl and thinking she was an Indian, fired both barrels of his shot gun at her, but fortunately did not hit her. This caused the little girl to cry out louder, *"Please don't shoot any more, we are white folks."* The man who had fired at her, discovered from her voice that she was not an Indian, and went to where she was before the Indians retreated; and thus probably prevented them from taking the children with them when they left. They were properly cared for and restored to their family.

In the following year Henry Maxwell was killed near his place on the Brazos. Maxwell came from the State of Arkansas to Texas, in the year 1842, and settled in Collin county, where he resided for about ten years. He then removed to Parker county. In the year 1865, Maxwell and his son-in-law, Mr. Joice, went out on the range for the purpose of hunting and collecting stock. Maxwell was armed with a shot gun and Joice with a rifle. After they had gone some distance on the range they saw a party of Indians coming towards them, who evidently had not dicovered them. Joice proposed that they should fire on them at once, but Maxwell, who, as we have said, was armed with a shot gun, thought it would be best to wait until they approached nearer. The Indians, however, who just then discovered them, cut their discussion short by giving the war whoop and charging upon them.

Maxwell and Joice stood their ground and fired several rounds at the Indians, but the Indians were more numerous than they supposed and they soon surrounded the two men. Seeing the great odds they had to contend with they endeavored to retreat to a better position than the one they occupied, but before they succeeded in reaching it an arrow struck Maxwell in the back, inflicting a mortal wound. Finding his strength was rapidly failing he told his son-in-law to save himself if he could, that he was unable to fight or retreat. Joice then put spurs to his horse and fled, leaving the poor man to be slain by the Indians. The Indians did not pursue Joice, and it is reasonable to suppose from this fact, and the number of shots he and Maxwell fired at them that several of their number had been killed and wounded.

Joice raised a party of men and as soon as possible returned. They found Maxwell still alive and they carried him home, but he died that same evening.

Hugh O. Blackwell was also slain by a party of Indians while returning from Jacksboro to his home on Rock creek. He was killed, scalped and his horse taken. A few years previous to this, the Indians made a raid in that section of country and captured a little boy of Mr. Blackwell's and a little girl of —— Sullivan's. They then went to the house of Samuel Hartfield while he and his family and a number of other persons who were assisting them, were engaged in making syrup.

As soon as the Indians were discovered, the whites being unarmed, all fled to the house. One lady, who had a child in her arms, begged the others not to leave her, whereupon a gentleman ran to her assistance, took the child from her, and by doing so, enabled her to escape.

The Indians then unharnessed the horse that was working in the sugar mill and made off with him. After going about ten miles, the little girl they had captured becoming troublesome to them, they put her to death. Her body was found some days afterwards much decayed, but it was identified beyond all doubt. The little son of Blackwell was retained a captive for several years, after which he was purchased by an agent of the United States government at Fort Cobb and restored to his friends in Parker county.

In July, 1866, a party of whites, while out on the range near West Meek's prairie, encountered a band of Indians, when a severe contest ensued. In this fight A. J. Gorman was killed. He had only returned home from the war about one month previous.

Among the pioneer settlers of Parker county was an old gentleman by the name of Leeper. He lived seven miles northwest of Weatherford. He was a man about seventy years of age, and was a farmer by occupation. In the fall of 1866, while the old man was at work one day on his farm,

DON'T SHOOT AT US; WE ARE WHITE CHILDREN.

he was suddenly fired upon by a party of Indians and instantly killed. They scalped the old man and retreated without venturing to make an attack on the house.

There were two brothers, Bohlen and James Savage, living in Parker county; the first named lived on Sanches creek, the latter on Patrick creek. In the month of November, 1866, while plowing in the field, Bohlen Savage was shot in the neck by an arrow before he was aware of the presence of Indians. He immediately broke for the house but was overtaken, scalped and killed in the presence of his young daughter, who went out to meet him. This little girl was taken captive and remained with the Indians until in 1868. She was recovered at the Fort Sill agency in exchange for a pony. The Indians having killed Bohlen they passed on to his brother's house, where they succeeded in killing him also. The murder was of the most brutal character. We have been informed that the Indians captured three children from these two families. The youngest son was turned loose in the woods to perish only a short distance from where it was captured. The little creature was found the same evening and taken care of. After traveling some distance the Indians murdered one of the other children, whose body was afterwards found and identified by its clothing. Several years ago the widows of the Savage brothers were still living in Parker county.

During the year 1867 Oliver Loving was killed out on the Pecos river. We record his death here, for at that time he was a citizen of Parker county, living in the town of Weatherford, where he was engaged in buying stock for Charles Goodnight to drive to the Territories.

In the year before mentioned, 1867, he and others started to Colorado with a large drove of cattle. They went on without any interruption for about three weeks, and until they had arrived near the line between Texas and New Mexico. Here they halted the cattle, and sent Loving and a one armed man, named Wilson, ahead to pick out a camping place for the night. They had just reached the Pecos river near Horsehead crossing, when they were attacked by twenty-five or thirty Indians.

Wilson, riding an excellent horse, fled and reached the camp in safety; but they cut off the retreat of Loving and forced him to the river's edge. Although one arm was broken by a shot, he plunged bravely into the river and remained in the water under cover of some bushes for several hours. As soon as night came, fearing to come out on the same side of the river, on account of the Indians, who were still searching for him; he swam the Pecos, and took his course towards Fort Sumner.

But weakened by his great loss of blood and stay in the river, he was unable to travel far. He lay down, and from exhaustion fell asleep. He was awakened by some Mexicans who were passing by with a train of wagons.

They took him to Fort Sumner and placed him in charge of a surgeon, but his wounded arm had swollen to such an extent that an artery burst and he bled to death.

Jacob Lopp was a native of the State of Missouri. After immigrating to Texas he lived in several counties, but finally made his permanent home in Parker county, where he was eventually killed. In the month of August, 1868, a daughter of Mr. Lopp rode off one day some distance to visit one of the neighbors, telling him she would be back at a certain time. As she did not return at the designated hour Lopp became alarmed for her safety, and not waiting to get his horse, or his arms, he set out on foot in search of her. The old man had not gone more than half a mile from the house, when a party of Indians rushed upon him just as his daughter made her appearance in the road beyond. The Indians killed the old man in full view of his daughter, who was compelled to witness the terrible sight. Seeing there was no chance to get home, the young lady wheeled her horse and fled for life in the direction she had come, and succeeded in making her escape. It is thought the Indians did not discover her approach, as no attempt was made to pursue and capture her.

In the latter part of the same year Edward Rippey and his wife were both murdered at his residence. Rippey was a native of Tennessee, and had been in Texas but a short time. He was living fourteen miles west of Weatherford. On Christmas day, 1868, he and his wife were rendering lard in their kitchen, forty or fifty yards from the residence. Rippey seeing his dog baying something through the fence one hundred and fifty yards away, took his gun and started out, supposing it to be a varmint. He was almost there when the Indians, which it proved to be, fired upon him. Mrs. Rippey seeing her husband was wounded, took a gun and ran to his side. The fence protected the Indians from the bullets, and in a few moments Rippey and his wife were both killed. The children left the kitchen and ran to the house. An old rusty shot gun remained, and the oldest child taking it presented it at the door. The Indians having been taught some very dear lessons in that section of country, did not dare to approach the house. They plundered the kitchen, took the scalps of Rippey and wife and departed, soon followed by a posse of blood thirsty citizens.

Miss Rippey, a few years ago, was living with her grand father in Tarrant county. A few years prior to this sad event, Rippey's first wife came near being killed near the scene of this terrible tragedy. While carrying dinner to her husband and a lot of hired men, she was attacked by a party of Indians who chased her until she came to a grove of trees near where the men were at work. Here she stopped and threw her gun down on the Indians, but reserved the fire. After all attempts to get Mrs. Rippey to leave her position had failed, the cowardly savages withdrew.

The year following—1869—James Light and wife were scalped and left for dead while returning home from a neighbor's house where they had been passing a pleasant day on the fourth of July. They had two children with them, one was killed, while the other managed to escape during the confusion and hid in a thicket near by.

On Sunday morning, April 23, 1871, Linn Boyd Cranfill, a lad some fifteen years of age, was massacred by the Indians. He was the son of Isham Cranfill, who resided some twelve or thirteen miles from Weatherford. Linn had two favorite ponies, and bestowed upon them much of his time in seeing that they were properly cared for. On the ill-fated morning, says Mr. Smythe, whose narrative we substantially adopt, he arose unusually early and started out for his ponies. He was unarmed, a thing that had possibly never before happened since he was old enough to carry a revolver. While passing along the prairie looking for the objects of his search, and still within sight of his home, a party of Indians suddenly rushed upon him, shot him down and galloped away. An elder sister witnessed the bloody murder of her brother, and gave the alarm before the miserable wretches had time to scalp him. They were pursued for several miles, but, as was too frequently the case, were not overtaken. The lad lingered until the next day, when death came and relieved him of his sufferings. This is but one of the many instances where the youth of our border fell at the hands of the murderous savages, while just budding into manhood. Those who enjoy the peace and blessings civilization brings, have but a poor conception of the trying scenes through which the early settlers of the northwestern border passed, even as late as the period of which we are now writing. While the larger portion of the State was entirely free from the prowling bands of savages, yet they kept up their periodical raids, stealing horses and murdering people all along the northwestern border for several years.

The year following the murder of young Cranfill, they came across Thomas Landrum and shot and killed him while unhitching a span of horses in front of Fuller Millsap's residence, on Rock creek. This was on the morning of March 14, 1872. Mr. Millsap and Joseph B. Loving seized their rifles, followed the miscreants, who were on foot, and killed one. Miss Donnie Millsap, a regular heroine, ran after her father with ammunition and was shot through her clothing several times, but fortunately without serious consequences. The Indians dragged off their dead companion and made good their escape. The young lady above mentioned (Miss Donnie Millsap) deserves more than a passing notice, and her many deeds of valor should some day be recorded by one more familiar with her thrilling adventures of frontier life, in order that the ladies of to-day might see what a conspicuous part their sex took in rescuing the northwestern border from the hands of the savage Comanche, and putting it in line with her sister counties in the front ranks of civilization. On several occasions Donnie Millsap helped to defend the homestead during the Indian raids in that section of country. Her father had but little fear of the hostile fiends, and the daughter seems to have inherited in a large degree the cool and daring bravery which was so characteristic of the father. Several years previous to the event which we have just related (we think it was in June, 1866) Mr. Millsap was engaged in a sharp conflict with two Indians when his daughter, Donnie, ran to him with some ammunition, whereupon the old gentleman spoke sharp to her and said: "For God's sake, Donnie, stay in the house, I'll manage this party." Upon this occasion the Indians were armed with bows and arrows, but when they killed Landrum, several years later, they were armed with improved firearms, and the services of Donnie were not so easily dispensed with by the old gentleman as upon the former occasion. Miss Millsap afterwards became the wife of Jesse Hitson, who, we think, in 1887, was living in Colorado City, Mitchell county, and is well known to the stockmen of northwest Texas.

A few months after the killing of Thomas Landrom, Jackson Hale and Martin Cathy were most foully murdered. These two youths, aged respectively thirteen and eighteen, the first named a son, and the latter a nephew, of Jesse Hale, had been to the town of Weatherford on the fourth of July to attend a circus.

In order to combine business with pleasure they took a wagon load of grain with them to have it ground. After seeing the show, they started in their wagon to return home. They were going along totally unsuspicious of danger, when a party of Indians rushed upon them from an ambuscade. The boys were unarmed and, of course, could make no resistance. The Indians shot them with arrows and thrust them through in many places with their spears.

When their bodies were found it was almost impossible to identify them, so terribly were they disfigured by wounds. One year afterwards the harness cut from the horses was found hanging to a tree two miles distant from the scene of the murder.

Some thirteen months later, John Hemphill was killed. This young man was a native Texan—a citizen of Parker county, and was born near the spot where he was killed. In the month of August, 1873, Hemphill, in company with several others, went one Sabbath to a church some distance from where they resided. As the moon shone brightly they postponed their departure until night. They had traveled but a short distance, when they discovered some people riding ahead of them. Supposing them to be some of their neighbors returning home from church, they spurred up their horses with the intention of overtaking them.

The people they had seen, however, were a party of Indians, who, no doubt, comprehending their mistake, rode rapidly on until they were hidden from view by a turn in the road, when they secreted themselves in some bushes near it, and awaited the approach of the young men. As they rode by totally unsuspicious of danger, the Indians fired upon them, and killed young Hemphill, but his companions were unhurt, and escaped. A company was raised the next day and the Indians were pursued for some distance, but they made good their escape.

This same party of Indians captured and carried off a large number of horses. During the same month George W. McClusky was killed while out in the yard, by an Indian who had crept up and concealed himself behind an oat stack. McCluskey lived with his father-in-law, John Baumgarner, and the two were walking around in the yard totally unsuspicious of danger, when McCluskey was shot and killed. The Indian then attempted to fire the oats but was prevented from doing so. This one instance illustrates the condition of affairs in the northwest, and the insecurity of human life, even as late as 1873. To those who are not familiar with the unsettled condition of Parker and adjoining counties at that time, such bold attacks in broad, open day light, in one's own premises, may seem somewhat incredulous, but nevertheless, they are true.

Murders in Jack County.

IT will be remembered that the Indians commenced their depredations in Parker county during the year 1859, and and so it was in Jack county. There was living in the above named county in 1859 a lady by the name of Mrs. Calhoun. She was the mother of six children and supported herself and family by her own exertions. In the spring of 1859, Mrs. Calhoun had been washing one day at a 1859 spring not far from the house and had left some articles of clothing there. She sent two of her children to get them, a lad about nine years old and a girl seven. As they did not return as soon as she expected she became alarmed and went out to look for them. Imagine the poor woman's horror when she discovered a party of Indians rapidly moving off from the spring. She ran to the place as fast as she could and called to her children, but receiving no answer and seeing nothing of them she hurried back to the house and dispatched one of her children to Jacksboro to tell the people that Indians had carried off a part of her family. A company of fifteen men was quickly raised. Six men from Johnson county joined them, making their total number twenty-one. They took the trail of the Indians, and after following it for about forty-five miles they came up with an old squaw, who was carrying the little girl on her back. She endeavored to hide in the brush, when she made such a desperate resistance that the enraged men killed her.

They then followed on the trail of the Indians who had possession of the little boy, and fifteen miles beyond they overtook them.

The whites charged on the Indians, who retreated as fast as they could, but the horses they were riding were pretty well broken down whilst those of the Texans were comparatively fresh, and they were soon overtaken. The Indians immediately abandoned their horses, and leaving them and the little boy, took to the brush for safety, where they scattered in every direction. Finding it impossible to follow their trail any longer, the Texans started for home, and it was not long until the two little children were soon presented to their distressed mother, who had given them up for lost.

We think it was during the same year, that the Indians attacked the house of Calvin Gage in his absence, killing Mrs. Gage and her infant, and Mrs. Katherine Saunders, mother-in-law of Gage. After committing these murders, the Indians then plundered the house and carried off such articles as they wanted. When they left, they took two daughters and a son of Gage prisoners. After traveling some fourteen miles with their prisoners, lashed fast on horses, they untied the little boy, and deliberately murdered him.

They then stripped the two girls of their clothing, and turned them loose to fare as best they could. These two girls wandered around in the woods for two days, exposed in their nude condition to all the inclemencies of weather and without a mouthful of food. The morning of the third day, they ascended a high hill, and from its top, to their great joy, they discovered a settlement about four miles distant. They directed their course towards it, and when they reached it, were kindly received by the people. They furnished them with clothing, and sent them home to their friends.

Cameron and Mason Massacre.

WILLIAM CAMERON was one of the early settlers in Texas—a farmer by occupation. His family consisted of himself, wife and five children. No other settlers being near, he and Mr. Mason built their houses close together for mutual protection. For some time they were very vigilant and cautious to guard against surprises by the Indians. But at length when no Indian "signs" had been seen in the vicinity for a long while they grew careless and pursued their daily avocations as if there were no danger to be apprehended.

1859

In the spring of 1859, while Cameron and his son, a lad of some sixteen summers, were at work on the farm, the first intimation they had of danger was when they found themselves attacked by a large party of Indians. The father and son attempted to run to the house some three hundred yards away, but were shot down before they had proceeded far.

Mrs. Cameron, seeing from the house the perilous condi-

tion of her husband and that he was attempting to reach
the house, seized a six shooter in one hand and her baby in
the other with the intention of going to him, but finding
the weapon unloaded she turned back and attempted to
conceal herself in the cow lot. But the Indians had discovered and followed her. They treated her in a most brutal
manner, splitting her head open with an ax, but left the little child beside her unharmed.

Cameron's other little son, witnessing the tragedy, started
to the house of Mr. Mason, screaming loudly as he went.
Mason, hearing his screams, took up his gun and ran towards the child, but before he could reach the lad the Indians had overtaken him, speared him and left him for dead.
Mason made several attempts to shoot at the Indians, but
his gun was out of order and failed to fire. Mrs. Mason,
seeing that her husband's gun had failed to fire, ran towards
him with a box of caps, but before she could reach him he
was dead and scalped, and a few moments afterwards she
and her little two year old child were also killed. Having
ransacked both houses they left, taking with them one of
Mrs. Cameron's children. A little girl of six and the baby
two years of age they left unmolested, a thing very unusual.
The little boy, whom they had left for dead, reviving,
glanced at the horror spread around him and then started
to tne town of Jacksboro, ten miles distant, to carry the
news, but he could not go more than a mile owing to his
weakness, where he sat down by the root of a large tree and
died.

The Indians, on their retreat, met a party of Californians,
who, seeing they had a white child prisoner, determined to
rescue it. The child was tied on a horse behind one of the
Indians. The horses of the Californians being fresh, and
those of the Indians pretty well broken down, they were
coming up with them rapidly, when the Indian, behind
whom the child was tied, cut it loose and let it drop to the
ground. The child was unhurt, and the Californians, having gained the object of their pursuit, did not follow the Indians further. This child was the one they had stolen from
Mrs. Cameron.

But now to return to the first portion of our story. The
bodies of Mrs. Cameron and Mrs. Mason, as well as those of

the others killed by the Indians, remained unburied and undiscovered for two or more days. A Mr. Flint, who happened to be passing Cameron's house, seeing no one about,
went in and found the little girl sitting on the bed crying.
The little creature was nearly starved, and could give no
information as to what had become of the rest of the family. The baby, by the side of its dead mother in the cow
lot, hearing Mr. Flint talking to the child in the house, cried
aloud for assistance, lifting up her hands in piteous appeal,
but would not leave the decaying body of her mother.
Neither child had tasted food for three days. They were
taken care of and the bodies of the unfortunate persons
buried. These two families, living as they did, five or six
miles from any other, will account for the fact that their
deplorable condition was not discovered sooner. Both the
fathers and mothers of these two families were slain, also
two sons, and a baby girl taken captive, and the remaining
two left to perish of hunger. As Cameron had twelve
hundred dollars in his house, and many bad men were in
the country, it is supposed the Indians were incited and assisted in the deed by them.

There was a family by the name of Willis, whose reputation was anything but a savory one. There were six or
seven grown men in this family, and from the reputation
they bore in the community in which they lived, it seems
that there was no crime too heinous for them to commit. In
one account which has been furnished us, this family is
charged with being wholly responsible for the Cameron and
Mason tragedy. Their connection with it is explained about
as follows: It seems that the Willises in some way had ascertained the fact that there was a considerable amount of
money stored away in the house of one of these families,
and in order to get possession of it, they went to a camp of
Comanche Indians and persuaded them to assist in the proposed robbery and murder of these two families. As this
was strictly in the line of Comanche business but little per-
suasion was necessary to induce them to aid in any scheme
of which murder and robbery was the object. The account
we have, which connects the Willises with the massacre,
states a little girl some eight years old, a daughter of one
of the families, witnessed the whole proceedings. She had

concealed herself when the Indians made the attack and thus escaped death. She states that when the attack was made on the house in which the money was stored away for safe keeping, a white man broke open the trunk and took the money out. When this terrible massacre became known, some of the exasperated citizens collected together, arrested a party of these scoundrels and gave them a trial, so the story goes, in Judge Lynch's Court. But, for once it would seem, the judge leaned a little too much to mercy's side. When the prisoners were arraigned, the little girl who had witnessed the horrible tragedy was brought forward as a witness. She stated that it was a man with red hair and a sandy beard who had killed her mother, and that the Indians killed the rest of the family. She also stated that she could recognize this man if he were brought before her. The little girl was then taken to the examining committee, and every one of the prisoners who, in any way, corresponded with the description given by the child was brought before her, one at a time. The moment Bill Willis was brought in, she immediately sprang up, and pointing to him, exclaimed: "That is the man who killed ma, and took pa's money from the trunk; but the Indians killed all the rest." Notwithstanding this strong evidence, these demons, for some unknown reason, were turned loose to continue their fiendish course of murder and robbery. But, although "the mills of the Gods grind slowly, they grind exceeding small," and their day of retribution came at last—at least to a portion of them. Subsequently the Willises stole a large number of horses, ran them to Mexico and sold them there. This was during the latter part of the war between the States. During the rebellion they were looked upon as traitors to their country, and were being watched for by the officers of the different counties. In attempting to pass back through the western portion of the State to their home in the northwest, they were arrested by a party, several miles above the city of Austin, brought to the capital of the State, and without court or jury, three of them were lynched by a vigilance committee. Many of the old citizens of Austin well remember the finale of the Willis brothers, and for aught we know, there may be some yet alive of the old residents of the city who could tell, if they would, the full particulars of the last moments spent on this earth by these assassins.

Murders in Jack County, 1864-1874.

WHILE Jack county suffered as much as most of her sister counties from frequent raids of the Indians, yet, comparatively speaking, we have but very few accounts of murders occurring in that county.   The first on the list of which we have any account as having occurred in 1864 is that of John Reasnor.   He first settled in Palo Pinto county, remained there some three years and then moved to Jack county, where he lived until he was murdered by the Indians in 1864.

Jack county is situated high up on the Brazos river, and at the time Mr. Reasnor moved into it, was subject to frequent incursions of the Indians.   It was at a time, too, when the late civil war was raging between the two sections in the United States, and the frontiers were but poorly defended, as most of the men fit for service were absent in the army. Mr. Reasnor, in company with his little son, was at work on his farm when a party of about fifty Indians, who had approached under cover of some thick bushes, suddenly rushed upon them.   Reasnor discovered the Indians before they reached him and he and his little son endeavored to save themselves by flight.   Finding that the Indians were about to overtake them Reasnor ran in among some wheat stacks and hid himself, but they soon found him and put him to death with their spears.   His little son, who was more active, succeeded in making his escape to the house, and the Indians left without venturing to attack it

Some two years later the McKinney family were all murdered by the Indians.   This family consisted of husband, wife and three children.

In the spring of 1866 he and his family went to visit some of their friends in Tarrant county.   On their way home, it seems, they took a wrong road—one that had been but little traveled—and as they approached a deserted house, they were attacked by Indians.   It was evident that the Indians had frightened the oxen so badly that they ran away, and threw the occupants out of the wagon. From all appearances the family were murdered as follows: McKinney took his youngest child, an infant, in his arms, and ran to a deep ravine. But the Indians followed him, and beat him to death with sticks. They then took the infant by the heels and knocked its brains out against a tree. After treating Mrs. McKinney in the most shameful manner, they thrust a spear through her heart, stripped her of her clothing, and scalped her. They killed one of the remaining children and took the other prisoner, but after going several miles they killed it also—thus exterminating the whole family.

We are not advised of the date of the attack on Francis M. Long, nor are we sure that it happened in Jack county, but we will record it here. Mr. Long was a native of Missouri. His parents emigrated to Texas in 1865, and settled in Montague county. Young Long was employed by some United States soldiers to pilot them from Elm creek, in Montague county, to Jacksboro, in Jack county. On his return home, he was discovered by a party of Comanches, who, finding he was alone, immediately gave chase to him. After they had run him about four miles, they succeeded in shooting him through the leg with an arrow, which also wounded his horse severely. Finding his horse was about to fail, young Long dismounted and ran into some thick brush near by. There he took his stand, and fought the Indians until he had emptied his Spencer rifle and two six-shooters at the redskins. The Indians were in open ground, and his shots told with deadly effect. They killed his wounded horse, but concluded, after all, they did not want his scalp, so they left it where it belonged, on the top of his head, and took their departure. Mr. Long suffered a great deal from his wound—had to lay out all night, and walk eight or ten miles the next day before he came to a settlement, but eventually he recovered.

During the year 1871 Charles E. Rivers was killed while gathering stock. Mr. Rivers was a native of Louisiana. His father came to Texas when Charles was but a child. After this young man grew to manhood, he moved to northwestern Texas, where he married the daughter of Mr. Loving. [Note. We are not positive, but think it was a daughter of Oliver Loving, who was killed by the Indians on the Pecos, and whose death we have recorded in the list of Parker county murders.] He engaged in the stock business and was quite successful. He made a contract in 1871 to furnish a large amount of beeves to a company. He was busily engaged in June, 1871, with his herders in gathering stock in Jack county, when he was attacked by a party of Indians.

They fired on his camp, mortally wounding Mr. Rivers. There were more men in the camp than it seems the Indians had supposed; and upon the discovery of this fact they retreated, after having fired, as above stated. As they left they ran through a large herd of horses and mules, causing them to stampede, and succeeded in carrying off some fifty head. Mr. Rivers being a man of fine constitution, lived over a month before he died. Strong hopes were entertained of his recovery, but the wound was too fatal. He had been of great service to the frontier, and was beloved by all who knew him. His widow still resided in the town of Weatherford, in Parker county, several years ago, so the writer was informed.

During the year 1873, the Indians were constantly raiding into Jack county, stealing horses, committing murders and creating terror wherever they went. Not unfrequently, herders upon the range were chased into camp, often barely escaping death at the hands of the pursuing savages. In the month of October, H. Walker and his son were both killed on the Salt fork of Keechi. We are not in possession, however, of the particulars of the killing.

During the month of November of the same year, the Indians killed Harris on the main fork of Keechi. Sorry we are not able to give full particulars in this instance also.

James R. Wright, an employe of J. C. Loving, was killed during the year 1874. Wright was a native of Arkansas. He came to Texas and settled in Loss valley, near the line of Young and Jack counties. He was employed by James C. Loving to assist him in managing his stock. Being an efficient herder and one that could be relied upon, Loving gave him full charge of his large stock and control of his hands. In taking care of so large a stock it often became necessary for the herders to separate and the Indians now and then took advantage of the opportunity thus offered them to add to their stock of scalps.

On the twentieth day of May, 1874, Wright, when at some distance from his men, was suddenly attacked by a party of Indians. When he discovered them they had almost surrounded him, leaving him but a little chance to escape. He was mounted upon a good horse and started towards his men, but, unfortunately, in attempting to leap a gully the animal fell and threw him. He attempted to remount and had just succeeded in doing so when the Indians fired upon him at close quarters, killing him instantly. They took his horse and arms and the much coveted scalp and left for the mountains.

John H. Heath, who was also an employe of J. C. Loving, was killed on the tenth day of July following. Heath first settled in Parker county and subsequently was employed by James Loving to herd horses in Jack county. These horses were, of course, an inducement to the Indians to frequent the locality where they were pastured. Heath, in company with other herders, went out upon the range one day in the month of July, 1874 for the purpose of driving the stock to his ranch. After he had collected the herd he drove it to the ranch and was just in the act of penning them when a party of Indians made a furious attack upon him. At their first fire Heath fell dead with a bullet through his brain.

There were several men in the ranch at the time, who flew to their arms and a fight ensued, lasting for an hour or more. Finding the Texans were too much for them they retreated, and as they carried off their dead and wounded, it was not known what loss they had sustained. None of the Texans except Heath were killed in this fight. About the same time the Indians stole two hundred head of horses and mules from Hensley, Cooper, Lindsey and Rogers.

The Tacket Fight—Young County.

THE first pioneer preacher in Young county was Old Father Tacket, as he was familiarly called. He was of the Methodist creed. He moved his family on Boggy creek, in the western portion of Young county. On the fifteenth of January, 1859, about ten o'clock in the morning, one of his cows came up alone. He thought it strange that she would leave the bunch, and, upon **1859** examination, found an arrow sticking in her neck.

He and his three sons, Jim, George and Lycurgus, arming themselves, each with a shotgun and sixshooter, took the back trail of the wounded cow, which they could easily follow, as the snow lay on the ground to the depth of several inches. They followed the trail for about two miles, where they found the remainder of the heard at the foot of a very rough hill, to which the present occurrence gave the name of "Tacket Mountain." Not daring to follow the redskins into such a place, they rounded up their little bunch of cattle and started for home. The Indians, observing them from the summit of the mountain, concealed themselves in a deep gulch which headed there, and, running to where the path crossed it, they lay in ambush for their approach. The cattle became frightened at the crossing, and Lycurgus, thinking some wild animal was crouched there, cocked and presented his gun. At this moment the Indians sprang up, and Lycurgus shot the only one who had a gun. Eleven Indians more were left, and a general fight ensued. The Indians thought the Tackets were only armed with guns, and when they had emptied them, the blood thirsty demons threw down their bows, leaped from out the gully, knives in hand, to make a charge for scalps. The pistols were then, for the first time, drawn, and with deadly effect. The Indians fled in great confusion, leaving four of their dead on the field of battle. Father Tacket and son Jim were wounded slightly—in the foot and eyebrow, respectively. They did not follow up their advantage and exterminate the whole maurading band, but returned home, without being further molested.

The old man lived in Young county until 1883, when he moved to Parker county, and in 1887 he died. Jim Tacket now has a large cattle ranch in the Texas Panhandle.

A party in the spring of 1860, left Fort Belknap and the settlements close by, to gather cattle on Elm Creek. One day when they had been out about a week, on the thirtieth of April, Newhouse and a Mexican, who were in the company, were left on herd. The others were at their dinner, when a small band of Indians attacked Newhouse and the Mexican. They made fight but to no avail. Both men were killed, and although pursued by the remainder of the party, the Indians made good their escape.

In the summer of 1861, a man by the name of Butoff, left his "clearing" on Elm Creek, in Young county, with a hide press, taking it to Johnson county. Butoff was driving four yoke of oxen, and had proceeded about thirty-five miles on his way, to what is now called Dillingham prairie. He was here riding on the tongue of his wagon, wholly unsuspicious of danger, when a party of six Indians came upon him from behind and killed him. A Mr. Glasinjim who was horse hunting on the range, seeing the man was unconscious of his danger, and thinking he would find a gun at the wagon, put spurs to his mule, intending to reach the spot before the Indians. The Indians rode fleet horses, and his mule was so slow that he found this impossible, so he faced about, thinking to reach his home on Rock Creek, a mile and a half distant. The Indians, after they had murdered Butoff, gave chase. They came within arrow shot of him when in about half a mile of his house. Seeing they would soon overtake and slaughter him, he concluded to sell his life as dearly as possible, so he drew his revolver and faced them, cursing them with every breath. They stopped, laughed at his pluck and impudence, held a consultation, and retraced their steps to plunder the wagon of the murdered man.

Some two years later three Indians were killed in an engagement with Texas rangers.

In the fall of 1863 a party of rangers belonging to Captain White's company, Colonel McCord's regiment, started to carry an express from Loss Valley to Fort Belknap. On their way they came across four Indians. A man named Jim Dozier fired and killed one of the Indians. Whilst he was reloading his gun the rest of the party, six or seven in number, continued the fight with their six shooters, as they had no guns, but failed to do any damage to the enemy. As soon as Mr. Dozier had reloaded his gun he fired again and killed another Indian. The two remaining Indians then fled, and the men with six shooters pursued them. They finally succeeded, after much firing, in killing one of them, but the other escaped. Mr. Dozier killed two Indians with his rifle, whilst the rest of the party only killed one, which clearly proves the superiority of the rifle to the six shooter, especially when in the hands of such an experienced frontiersman and Indian fighter as Dozier.

The sad death of Alf. Lane occurred the following year, which happened under peculiar circumstances. In the month of July, 1864, Goodnight removed a bunch of cattle from Keechi Valley, going with them to the territories. On the second night of their drive, they camped at a place known as Fort Murray, in Young county. In the company was a young man, Alf. Lane, a brother-in-law of Mr. Goodnight. While in camp here at Fort Murray, Lane dreamed that his father and mother, whom he had left at their home on Keechi creek, had been massacred by the Indians, and it appeared to him so vividly that he determined to leave the trail and return. Goodnight reasoned with him, told him how hazardous the attempt, and how foolish his apprehensions. But no, he must go; nothing would satisfy him short of going back to see.

Alas, his vision leads him to his doom! He had gone only some six or eight miles on his return, when he was killed by a band of marauding Indians. When found his body was at the foot of the Cement mountain, ten miles north of the town of Graham, horribly mangled, as though the killing was not enough, but torture had to be resorted to, to satisfy their vicious cravings.

Peveler and Cox.

CAPTAIN PEVELER was a native of the State of Kentucky. On his arrival in Texas he settled at Fort Belknap in Young county. Some time afterwards he was elected captain of the militia. His name was a terror to the red skin race, and well they knew that they could not commit their depredations in reach of him with impunity. In September, 1864, he, in company with **1864** State Cox (who was then sheriff of Young county), Cole Duncan, Perry Harmison and George Hunter, went over to Loss valley, in Jack county, to the annual round up.

They had proceeded on their homeward journey to a spot about ten miles north of the town of Graham, driving a small bunch of cattle, when they saw a band of six or eight Indians ahead and gave chase. They followed them into a dense mesquite thicket and here, as if by magic, fifty or sixty Indians sprang up around them. They would have immediately retreated had not the horse which Cox was riding been unable to run. They all dismounted, determined to share the fate of Cox, be it for weal or for woe. Cox pleaded so piteously for them to save their own lives and let him take his chances that at last a retreat was ordered. It seems that Cox became excited, for he mounted his horse without untying him from the tree and starting off at full speed, the jerk of the rope broke his horse's neck. After falling from his horse he was soon dispatched. Harmison, Duncan and Hunter, who were unhurt when the retreat was ordered, fled precipitately and never halted until they were inside the walls of Fort Belknap, where they reported that the Captain and Cox had been killed. Peveler, however, having received a number of wounds, was much weakened by loss of blood, and his horse also being badly wounded he was compelled to move slowly. He had gone only a few hundred yards and reached a deep ravine when they had almost overtaken him. There was only one crossing to this ravine, which was a narrow path and very deep. Peveler had just crossed over and was ascending the other bank when the howling pack of Indians, headed by their chief, came rushing on him. Just as the chief reached the bottom of the canon, Peveler, seeing his opportunity, shot him dead from his horse. He fell square in the path and not a horse could be urged over the dead body. The Indians, unwilling to leave their horses, held a war dance over the remains of their chieftain and left for parts unknown. Captain Peveler, wounded as he was, and riding a wounded horse, rode eight miles with an arrow sticking in his neck. On arriving at the house of a Mr. Crossman the arrow was extracted with great difficulty, and, notwithstanding he was suffering with no less than sixteen wounds, he lived for fifteen days. These men, expecting no such trouble, were armed only with sixshooters, but with these feeble weapons several Indians were left dead upon the battle ground and many more wounded. A hill near where the occurrence took place now bears the name of Cox mountain, an undecaying monument to the memory of State Cox.

James McCoy and his son were both slain by a prowling band of savages the same year. McCoy came from Missouri to Texas and settled in Hood county. In 1863 he moved to the vicinity of Fort Belknap. On the thirteenth of October, 1864, whilst he and his son were engaged in hauling rails to fence a farm, they were charged upon by a party of Indians. These Indians had just come out of a fight with some State rangers, in which they had got the best of the soldiers. Flushed with their victory, and falling in shortly afterwards with McCoy and his son, they at once attacked them. The rangers, who were still in sight, saw the Indians attack McCoy and son, and knowing it was impossible to aid them, they did the next best thing they could do, hurried to his house took Mrs. McCoy and her niece behind them on their horses, and carried them to Fort Belknap—thereby saving them from death or captivity. McCoy and his son were both killed.

In 1867 a triple massacre occurred near Belknap—Proffitt, Johnson and Carlton, in July, 1867, while branding cattle near Fort Belknap, in Young county, were surprised by a horde of savages. Their Winchesters were on their saddles, and they had, as usual, turned their horses loose to graze. The animals had wandered off some distance from the lot. In attempting to reach the horses all the men were killed. The Proffitt killed in this massacre was a brother to John Proffitt, now, in 1888, a popular ranch man in Young county.

In the fall of the year, 1868, a herdsman for Charles Rivers was out with his stock on Salt Creek prairie, about two miles from camp. He was attacked by several Indians, and for nearly a mile kept them off in a running fight, himself on foot, and with no weapon but his six shooter. Weakened by loss of blood from his wounds, he could run no further, and sank down exhausted. They ran to him, fractured his skull with a club, scalped him, and left him for dead. Soon after they left him he revived, walked a mile to camp, and lived for six days. He was shot three times, his skull fractured, and was then scalped. It was thought that, had not the "screw worms" eaten into his brain, he would have recovered from his wounds.

Rock Creek Fight.

ON Sunday the sixteenth day of April, 1871, near Rock creek, and close to the line between Young and Palo Pinto counties, and not a great distance from Fort Belknap, occurred one of the most desperate and bloody fights that ever occurred on the northwestern border. We are sorry that we are not in possession of the names of all the twelve men who made such a gallant 1871 stand against such an overwhelming force of well armed Indian warriors, and that we have thus far obtained only a meagre account of the particulars of this bloody encounter. During the month of April in the year above named, the stock men of Palo Pinto and adjoining

counties were engaged in their annual spring "round up,"
when a party of twelve men were attacked by about forty
or fifty armed Indian warriors. We have the names of only
a few of the whites who participated in the engagement, and
they are as follows: Jason McLean, who lived on Keechi
creek, in Palo Pinto county; I. E. Graves, who, in 1888,
lived in Weatherford, Parker county; George and John
Lemley who resided, we believe, in either Palo Pinto or Parker county; Shap Carter and Tom Crow. The country
where they were attacked was a level prairie, and the
Texans took their position in a shallow ravine to defend
themselves against the great odds they had to contend with.
The ravine proved to be too shallow to afford them much
protection, and they were greatly exposed to the constant
fire the Indians poured upon them.

It appears that the chief in command of the Indians on
this occasion directed the movements of his warriors
through a negro. The chief took his position about two
hundred yards in the rear of the Indian lines, on an eminence, from whence he could overlook the position held by
the Texans, and every movement they made was communicated through couriers to the negro who was in command
of the fight. The Texans had no arms but six shooters,
and the Indians' long range guns gave them a great advantage. Eight of the horses ridden by the Texans were
shot down in the beginning of the fight. This was a bloody
day to these beleaguered Texans. As they were but poorly
protected from the bullets of the enemy they suffered
severely.

Late in the evening, the Indians, unaware of the damage
inflicted upon the Texans, withdrew, taking with them all
the horses belonging to the Texans, and a large portion of the
cattle. Eight out of the twelve Texans were either killed
or wounded in this fight. Tom Crow was killed dead on the
ground (whereupon the Indians cried out "Wano!") and two
of the wounded died shortly afterwards. The day following John Lemley died, and the next day Shap Carter died.
If the Indians had known that there were but four men
among the Texans not wounded, they, no doubt, would have
attacked them again, and it is probable they would have
discovered the fact had it not been for one of the party, Mr.

Graves. When the Indians withdrew from the field, they ascended an eminence beyond gun shot, from whence they could plainly see the Texans in the shallow ravine. Graves made all the men, who were able to do so, stand up, thereby making the Indians believe they had suffered but little damage. This little piece of stratagem no doubt saved the lives of the few who thus far had survived this terrible conflict. George Lemley, who now—1888—lives near the place where the fight occurred, bears an ugly scar on his cheek to remind him of that direful day.

In the month of May following the Rock Creek fight, Henry H. Helerin was murdered in a most brutal manner. Mr. Helerin, previous to his coming to Texas, had been a great traveler, rambling about over the world. He became tired of traveling, and came to Texas for the purpose of going into the stock business. He went to Parker county, and engaged to work with Mr. Charles E. Rivers, who was also killed in Jack county the following month. He was engaged as Mr. Rivers' book-keeper. He would often go out among the stock, and amuse himself looking at them. One day in the month of May, 1871, he took a long ride, and concluded to rest a while. He alighted from his horse and sat down at the root of a tree. While thus enjoying a rest, a party of Indians discovered him, slipped up to him, and shot him. After this they scalped him, and left him for dead. But he revived. He was perfectly conscious, and knew when they scalped him, but could do nothing. The herders, who were near by, heard the firing, and ran to see what was the matter; but they were too late. The bloody work had been done, and the Indians were gone. The young man lived for thirty-six hours after being scalped.

Gen. Wa. T. Sherman's Tour of Inspection.

D URING the year 1871, General W. T. Sherman made a tour of inspection, which included the military posts in Texas. It was in the same year that Satanta and Big Tree made their famous raid in Northwest Texas, upon which occasion they attacked a wagon train belonging

to Henry Warren, while en route on the military road leading from Jackboro to Fort Griffin, in Shackelford
1871 county. The Indians killed seven out of the twelve
teamsters, then fired the wagon train, with one of the
teamsters chained to the wagon wheel, while yet alive, to
be consumed amid the torturing flames. Five of the teamsters made their escape. The day previous to this fiendish
massacre, General Sherman, with his escort, pas ed along
the same road on his way to Fort Richardson, at Jackboro.
In 1877, when Mr. H. Smythe, of Weatherford, Parker
county, was writing his little book entitled "Historical
Sketch of Parker County, Texas," General Sherman kindly
furnished him with a manuscript copy of the journal kept
on the general-in-chief's tour of inspection, by Inspector
General R. B. Marcy, during the months of April, May
and June, 1871. From Mr. Smythe's book, we obtain the
following data. Much of this journal relates to the attack
on Warren's wagon train and massacre of the teamsters,
the capture of the Chiefs Satanta, Big Tree and Satank,
and the subsequent history of these noted chiefs; besides,
the journal kept upon this occasion shows clearly the condition of our frontier settlements at that time, and coming
from the general-in-chief of the United States army, can be
taken as absolutely true.

General Sherman and party left New Orleans, April 18th,
by rail to Lake Pontchertrain, and thence on the steam reve-
nue vessel, "The Wilderness," for Mobile, arriving there on
the afternoon of the nineteenth. April the 20th, they returned to New Orleans. While there General Sherman examined Forts Jackson and St. Philip; on the twenty-third
the party left New Orleans for Brashear City, where the
party embarked on one of Morgan's steamers for Galveston,
reaching there at day break the following morning, and by
rail arrived at Columbus at 6 p. m. They left Columbus on
the twenty-fifth in a spring wagon, sent forward by the
quarter master at San Antonio. On the twenty-seventh
they arrived at Seguin, and on the following day arrived at
San Antonio, and remained at that place—the headquarters
of the department—until the morning of May the 2d, dining
with General Reynold on the twenty-ninth, and attending a
ball in the evening, given by the German club.

From San Antonio, General Sherman and staff were accompanied by an escort of seventeen men of the Tenth Infantry and camped thirty miles from San Antonio on the evening of May 2. They passed through Boerne and on May 4 reached Fredericksburg. Passing on up the country through Fort Mason, Menardville and Fort McKavett the party camped at Kickapoo Springs, in Concho county, on the ninth, and arrived at Fort Concho, in Tom Green county, May 10. From Fort Concho the party proceeded north, passing old Fort Chadborne, in Runnels county, on the twelfth, and on the following evening reached old Fort Phantom hill. May 14 brought the party to Fort Griffin, in Shackelford county, where they remained during the fifteenth, and on the sixteenth, Fort Belknap, in Young county, was entered. Here General Sherman ordered that a detachment of troops be sent to Fort Belknap from Fort Richardson for picket service, as the Indians came there often and troubled travelers and the two or three families that lived near the fort. On May 17, General Sherman's party set out for Fort Richardson, in Jack county. We now quote from the journal, which shows the condition of the country at that time. "We passed immense herds of cattle to-day, which are allowed to run wild upon the prairies and they multiply very rapidly. The only attention the owners give to them is to brand the calves and occasionally go out to see where they range. The remains of several ranches were observed, the occupants of which have either been killed or driven off to the more dense settlements by the Indians. Indeed, this rich and beautiful section does not contain to-day (May 17, 1871) as many white people as it did when I (General Marcy) visited it eighteen years ago, and if the Indian marauders are not punished the whole country seems to be in a fair way of becoming totally depopulated.

"May 18, 1871.—This morning five teamsters, who, with seven others, had been with a mule wagon train en route to Fort Griffin (Captain Henry Warren's) with corn for the post were attacked on the open prairie, about ten miles east of Salt creek, by one hundred Indians and seven of the teamsters were killed and one wounded. General Sherman immediately ordered Colonel MacKenzie to take a force of one hundred and fifty cavalrymen with thirty day's rations on pack mules and pursue and chastise the murderers."

This brings us up to the date of the attack upon the wagon train; but before beginning the details of this tragedy we will follow General Sherman further on in his tour of inspection. On the nineteenth, General Sherman remained at Fort Richardson and received a delegation of gentlemen from Jack and Parker counties, among whom were W. W. Duke, R. J. Winders, J. R. Robinson, W. M. McConnell, Peter Hart and H. H. Gaines.

They represented the exact condition of affairs, growing out of the infamous and suicidal government policy of rewarding these savage brutes for murdering the whites, and assured him that unless decisive action was taken, and the Indians put down, that Northwest Texas would soon become depopulated, the labor and industry and accumulations of years would be lost, families scattered, important interests sacrificed, society ruined, and a delightful and improving country given over to the blight of these demons. General Sherman listened attentively and grasped the entire situation. He keenly felt the humiliation of the Indian policy of the United States, acknowledged its injustice, and promised to do all in his power to remedy the condition of affairs then existing. The deputation requested authority to go to Fort Sill to recover stock that had been stolen from them by the Indians, when General Sherman invited them to go with him the following day and identify their animals. During that day, Colonel Mackenzie reported that the information concerning the murder of the teamsters in Captain Henry Warren's train was correct; that their bodies were found much mutilated, and one of the Elliott brothers (Samuel) "burned to a cinder."

On the twentieth day of May, General Sherman's party left Jacksboro for Fort Sill, and on the twenty-first crossed Red River at Red River Station, the same being the great crossing for the herds of cattle going from Texas to Kansas. In the afternoon of the twenty-third they arrived at Fort Sill, where they changed their escort, and for the first time after leaving San Antonio, went into quarters. Fort Sill is situated on an elevated plateau, near the eastern extremity of the Wichita mountain, and upon the identical spot, says General Marcy, that he recommended for a military post in 1852. During the twenty-fourth and twenty-fifth, General

Sherman remained at Fort Sill examining into the condition of affairs with General Grierson and others, and on the twenty-sixth visited the signal station, on one of the most easterly peaks of the Wichita mountains. But before following General Sherman further, let us now return to the operations of the three noted Kiowa chiefs while on their raids in Texas.

Satanta, Satank and Big Tree's Raid.

THERE is no act of savage cruelty recorded in the history of our Indian warfare more barbarous and inhuman, than the unwarranted attack by one hundred and fifty warriors under the leadership of the three above named Kiowa chiefs upon Henry Warren's wagon train on the eighteenth day of May, 1871. Warren had a contract for freighting between Forts Richardson and Sill, and 1871 on the above named day, his mule wagon train, while freighting between these two forts was attacked by this prowling band of blood thirsty villains, just as the twelve teamsters were preparing to strike camp. The alarm of "Indians" was given by one of the teamsters, and the wagons were quickly corralled. A short and deadly fight ensued, in which seven of the twelve teamsters were killed and one wounded. The remaining four, together with the wounded teamster, fled to a point of timber close by, where they concealed themselves in the brush, thus narrowly escaping a cruel death, and finally made their way to Jacksboro. To-day, twelve miles northeast of Graham, the county seat of Young county, on or near the old military road leading from Jacksboro to Belknap and Fort Griffin, stands a monument erected to the memory of the seven teamsters who were so foully murdered on that sad day. The balance of the history pertaining to this monstrous outrage perpetrated by savage brutes will all be taken from Mr. Smythe's "Historical Sketch of Parker County."

The burning of the train and massacre of the teamsters must have occurred near the line between Young and Jack counties, but in the latter, as the chiefs were tried and convicted at Jacksboro.

"A MOST CONSPICUOUS YEAR WAS 1871."

During the months of that and the previous year, sad and serious consequences resulted to many persons in this vicinity. Murders were frequent, Indian massacres numerous and society in constant agitation. The whole frontier country was kept in a continual state of excitement and many settlers left for the east temporarily, while others actually returned to the States from whence they emigrated. It was a dark period for Western Texas, and the terrible tragedies enacted made warriors out of many men, women and children who, previously, were anything but adepts in the use of the revolver or the rifle. Tired of the many raids indulged in by the Comanches and the Kiowas, and sick of the consequences of those periodic visitations the people resolved upon action; but, early in the year, learning that General W. T. Sherman was about to visit Texas and make a tour of this frontier country determined to wait his presence. In the meantime other murders were perpetrated and life was considered unsafe, even one single mile from home, while property was at the mercy of these marauding parties. In addition to the several massacres, mentioned elsewhere, seven teamsters in the employ of Captain Henry Warren, on the road to Fort Griffin, were killed by a band of one hundred and fifty Kiowas, commanded by

SATANTA

The chief who signed the very treaty of peace (August, 1869), between his tribe and the United States, under which he and they were being fed and protected by the government, at the Fort Sill reservation. This was on the eighteenth day of May, 1871. The names of the unfortunate men were Nathaniel S. Long, wagon master of the train, John Mullens, James S. Elliot, Samuel Elliot, M. J. Baxter, and Jesse Bowman, teamsters from Clay county, Missouri, and James Williams, teamster from Eastern Texas. Thomas Bazeal, teamster, was seriously wounded, and R. A. Day and Charles Brady, teamster, escaped. [Note. The names of the other two teamsters who made their escape, and not mentioned by Mr. Smythe, were Hobbs Carey and Dick Motor.] This noted chief, Satanta, is described by W. E. Webb, in his "Buffalo Land," page 180, as "the very embodiment of treachery, ferocity and bravado. Phrenologically considered, his head must have been a cranial marvel, and the bump on it maping out the kingdom of evil, a sort of Rocky mountain chain, towering over the more peaceful valleys around. Viewed from the towering peaks of combativeness and acquisitiveness, the territory of his past would reveal to the phrenologist an untold number of government mules, fenced in by suttler's stores, while bending over the bloody trail leading back almost to his bark cradle, would be the shades of many mothers and wives, searching among the wrecks of emigrant trains for flesh of their flesh, and bone of their bone. Satanta was long a name on the plains to hate and abhor. He was an abject beggar in the pale face's camp, and a demon on their trail."

THE LAST DRAW.

We left General Sherman and party at Fort Sill looking into the condition of affairs. We again quote from his journal:

"May 27.—This afternoon about four o'clock several Kiowa chiefs, among them Satanta, Satank, Kicking Bird and Lone Wolf, came to the agency to draw their rations. In a talk with Agent Tatem, Satanta said he with one hundred warriors, had made the recent attack upon the trains between Fort Richardson and Belknap; that they had killed seven teamsters and driven off forty-one mules. This he considered a meritorious exploit and said: "If any other Indian claimed the credit of it, he would be a liar that he was the man who commanded." He pointed out Satank, Big Tree and another chief as having been with him in the action. The agent immediately reported the facts to General Sherman and requested him to arrest the Indians concerned; whereupon the General sent for them and Satanta acknowledged what he had stated to the agent, when the General informed him that he would place them in confinement and send them to Texas for trial by the civil authorities. Sa-

tanta, seeing that he was likely to get into trouble, replied
that, although he was present at the fight, he did not kill
anybody himself, neither did he blow his bugle.

[NOTE BY GENERAL SHERMAN.—The conversation with Satanta was through an interpreter. I understood him to say
he took no part in the fight except to blow his trumpet. At
that instant of time he had an ordinary trumpet slung on
his person.—W. T. S.]

"His young men wanted to have a little fight and to
take a few white scalps, and he was prevailed upon to go
with them merely to show them how to make war, but that
he stood back during the engagement and merely gave
directions. He added that some time ago the whites had
killed three of his people and wounded four more, so that
this little affair made the account square, and that he was
now ready to commence anew—cry quits. General Sherman told him it was a very cowardly thing for one hundred
warriors to attack twelve poor teamsters who did not pre-
tend to know how to fight. That if he desired to have a
battle the soldiers were ready to meet him at any time.
That he would send the three men (Indians implicated) to
Texas for trial. Seeing no escape, Satanta remarked that
rather than be sent to Texas he preferred being shot on the
spot. About this time Kicking Bird arrived. He had seen
the General on the Arkansas river. He is one of the most
influential chiefs of his tribe and has generally behaved
tolerably well. He arose and said that he, as General Grierson and the agent well know, had done everything in his
power to prevent his young warriors from leaving the reservation and going to Texas for marauding purposes. That
he had invariably endeavored to keep his followers in the
right path, and for the sake of the good he had done he now
asked the General to release his friends from arrest—and he
would return the captured mules. General Sherman replied
that he fully appreciated all that he had done and that he,
himself, would be kindly treated so long as he continued to
do well, but that the arrested Indians must be sent to Texas.

"About twenty armed soldiers now came up in front of
the piazza where we were assembled, and the Indians
seemed quite excited, nearly every one of them having a
Spencer carbine or a Colt's revolver. Kicking Bird con-

tinued in the endeavor to persuade the General to release the chiefs—said he was friendly to the whites, and should feel sorry if war ensued from this affair, but of course he should be with his people in the latter event. Another Indian named Lone Wolf also rode up upon a fine horse, dismounted, laid two Spencer carbines and a bow and quiver of arrows upon the ground, tied his horse to the fence, then throwing his blanket from his shoulder, fastened it around his waist, picked up the carbines in one hand and the bow and arrows in the other, and with the most deliberate and defiant air, strode up to the piazza, then giving one of his carbines to an Indian who had no arms, and the bow and arrows to another, who at once strung the bow and pulled out a handful of arrows, he seated himself and cocked his carbine—at which the soldiers all brought their carbines to an aim upon the crowd—whereupon Satanta and some other Indians held up their hands and cried, no! no! no! don't shoot! The soldiers were directed not to fire, but just at this moment we heard shots fired outside the fort, which resulted from the fact that the guard had been ordered to permit no Indians to leave without further instructions. Some Indians, in attempting to go out, had been halted by the sentinels, when one of them shot an arrow, wounding one of the sentinels. The shot was returned, killing the Indian as he was riding off. When the excitement had subsided a little, the General told the Indians that they must return the forty-one mules, which Kicking Bird promised to do, and he went off for them, but on his arrival at the camp he discovered that the squaws had become frightened and ran off with all their animals except eight, which were taken possession of. All the Indians were allowed to leave except the prisoners, who were put in irons and closely guarded. The benevolent, civilizing peace policy, so urgently advocated by a class of people in the eastern States, has received a long and fair experimental trial with these Indians. They have been regularly fed and the kindest treatment extended to them for two years by our authorities, but it has not had the slightest effect upon them. *They have no more conception of gratitude than so many wolves, and they have continually been stealing horses and mules, murdering men, ravishing women and enslaving children. Besides, they have not only openly acknowledged, but have boasted of these atrocities.* There was hardly a day during our trip through the frontier settlements of Texas that we did not hear of some persons who had suffered from Indian raids, and there seems to be no prospect of their ceasing.

"The question has resolved itself into this, *that the border settlers of Texas must all be annihilated, or the Indian chastised and disarmed.* Many of them have the best modern arms, and they know how to use them well, which has given them confidence in their ability to cope with the whites in battle. While they were armed with bows and arrows only, they were comparatively powerless against equal numbers of white troops, but those officers who have encountered them recently, say they fight well, and do not care about meeting them again with any very great odds against them. The prairie Indians seldom ever uses fire arms in hunting; they kill the buffalo with the bow and arrow, and this is about the only animal they hunt. They reserve all their ammunition for war purposes, and it is a well known fact that they will sacrifice anything to get ammunition, moreover, they will not sell their fire arms at any price."

The agent, Tatem, in one of his interviews with General Sherman, remarked that he was glad the General happened here at this particular time, as it gave him an opportunity to witness the actual condition of Indian matters; that he not only approved the course pursued in arresting these Indians, but he would have been glad if Lone Wolf had been arrested, as he is one of the boldest and most troublesome men of his tribe.

"*He also said that it had been his opinion for a year that severe measures should be resorted to towards these Indians, and had so informed the Indian Bureau, but that no attention had been paid to his representations.* He concluded his remarks by saying that, if the Texas people followed Indians, who had stolen their stock, into the reservation, they would not be prevented by him. He is decidedly of the opinion that the Indians should be held to a strict accountability for all their misdeeds, and this sentiment is concurred in by every disinterested sensible man on the frontier."

As before stated, Satanta, Big Tree and Satank were ar-

SATANTA AND BIG TREE WITH THEIR WARRIORS FIRING A WAGON TRAIN IN JACK COUNTY,

rested on May 27, at Fort Sill. They were at once heavily ironed, and on the thirty-first, two of them were safely lodged in the jail at Jacksboro, by Colonel R. S. MacKenzie, under whose escort, with a detachment of soldiers, they were brought from the fort. On the way, and very near the spot where Long, Elliot, Williams and others were so cruelly butchered, Satank loosed his heavy iron handcuffs by gnawing and stripping the flesh to the bone. He immediately, and wild cat like, seized a Spencer carbine, and attempted the life of a soldier in the presence of the guard and his fellow prisoners. He was a large, powerful, muscular man, and thus exhibited his extraordinary will power, and preference for death, rather than take the chance of receiving justice in a Texas court. As quick as he was observed, a file of soldiers instantly poured a volley into the desperado and he fell lifeless at their feet. This sudden and unexpected termination of Satank's existence, created the greatest consternation and alarm in Satanta and Big Tree, and the balance of the trip, while they were perfectly docile, they were placed under the closest surveillance until lodged in, and chained to, the floor of their prison cells.

The arrest of Satanta and Big Tree occasioned general rejoicing throughout northwest Texas; and it is not to be wondered at when the condition of the country and the number of atrocious murders are considered. As soon as the prisoners were taken to Jacksboro, and the fact was made known to Judge Soward, of the thirteenth judicial district, at Weatherford, His Honor fixed an immediate trial at the term then ensuing.

THE TRIAL

Commenced on Wednesday, July 5, 1871, Judge Charles Soward on the bench. The district attorney, S. W. T. Lanham, Esq., of Weatherford, conducted the prosecution. Thomas Ball, then of Weatherford, but now of Jacksboro, and J. A. Woolfork, Esq., of Weatherford, appeared for the prisoners. The court room was densely packed, during the progress of the case, with men, women and children. It occasioned the greatest curiosity and excitement. *The Indians were the first and only chiefs ever tried before a civil*

court in America! The interest, therefore, as might be supposed, was intense. The prisoners were taken to and from
the court room under a military guard, and in the hall of justice the strong arm of military power protected the civil authorities during the trial, conviction and sentence of the
murderers. While there was no attempt on the part of the
citizens or others to interfere in the administration of justice, it was deemed judicious to have the prisoners strongly
guarded so as to prevent the possibility of injury to themselves or to others.

This remarkable cause progressed before Thomas W. Wil-
liams (now mayor of Jacksboro and brother of "Blue Jeans"
Williams, governor of Indiana), John Cameron, Everett
Johnson, H. B. Vernor, S. Cooper, William Hensley, John
H. Brown, Peyton Lynn, Peter Hart, Daniel Brown, L. P.
Bunch and James Cooley, twelve intelligent and conscientious jurors. The principal witnesses were Colonel R. S.
MacKenzie, Lowrie Tatem and Thomas Brazeal. The prisoners were all ably represented by Messrs. Ball and Woolfork, both of whom were faithful to their clients. They
took advantage of every legal technicality and conducted
their defense with excellent judgment and decided impres-
siveness. At the conclusion of the testimony, during which
the witnesses passed through a searching examination, the
counsel for the prisoners talked long and well to the jury. The
learned and eloquent district attorney, S. W. T. Lanham,
Esq. (of the Weatherford law firm of Watts, Lanham &
Roach), then closed with a powerful address, from which we
extract as follows:

"This is a novel and important trial, and has, perhaps, no
precedent in the history of American criminal jurispru-
dence. The remarkable character of the prisoners, who are
leading representatives of their race; their crude and barbarous appearance; the gravity of the charge; the number
of victims; the horrid brutality and inhuman butchery inflicted upon the bodies of the dead; the dreadful and terrific
spectacle of seven men, who were husbands, fathers,
brothers, sons and lovers, on the morning of the dark and
bloody day of this atrocious deed, and rose from their rude
tents bright with hope, in the prime and pride of manhood—

found, at a later hour, beyond recognition in every condition
of horrid disfiguration, unutterable mutilation and death,
lying

Stark and stiff
Under the hoofs of vaunting enemies!

"This vast collection of our border people; this sea of
faces, including distinguished gentlemen, civic and military,
who have come hither to witness the triumph of law and
justice over barbarity and assassination; the matron and the
maiden, the gray haired sire and the immature lad, who
have been attracted to this tribunal by this unusual occasion,
all conspire to surround this case with thrilling and extraordinary interest. Though we were to pause in silence, the
cause I represent would exclaim with trumpet tongue:

" 'Satanta, the veteran council chief of the Kiowas—the
orator, the diplomat, the counselor of his tribe—the pulse of
his race:—Big Tree, the young war chief, who leads in the
thickest of the fight, and follows no one in the chase—the
mighty warrior athlete, with the speed of the deer and the
eye of the eagle, are before this bar, in the charge of the
law !' So they would be described by Indian admirers, who
live in more secure and favored lands, remote from the
frontier—'where distance lends enchantment' to the imagination—where the story of Pocahontas and the speech
of Logan, the Mingo, are read, and the dread sound of the
war whoop is not heard. We who see them to-day, disrobed
of all their fancied graces, exposed in the light of reality,
behold them through far different lenses ! We recognize in
Satanta the arch fiend of treachery and blood—the cunning
Cataline—the promoter of strife—the breaker of treaties
signed by his own hand—the inciter of his fellows to rapine
and murder—the artful dealer in bravado while in the pow-
wow, and the most abject coward in the field, as well as the
most canting and double-tongued hypocrite when detected
and overcome! In Big Tree we perceive the tiger-demon, who
has tasted blood and loves it as his food—who stops at no
crime, how black soever—who is swift at every species of
ferocity, and pities not at any sight of agony or death—he
can scalp, burn, torture, mangle and deface his victims with
all the superlatives of cruelty, and have no feeling of sym-

pathy or remorse. They are both hideous and loathesome in appearance, and we look in vain to see in them anything to be admired, or even endured. Still, these rough 'sons of the wood' have been commiserated; the measures of the poet and the pen of romance have been invoked to grace the 'melancholy history' of the red man. Powerful legislative influences have been brought to bear to procure for them annuities, reservations and supplies. Federal munificence has fostered and nourished them, fed and clothed them; from their strongholds of protection they have come down upon us 'like wolves on the fold;' treaties have been solemnly made with them, wherein they have been considered with all the formalities of quasi nationalities; immense financial 'rings' have had their origin in and drawn their vitality from the 'Indian question;' unblushing corruption has stalked abroad, created and kept alive through

'—— the poor Indian, whose untutored mind
Sees God in clouds, or hears Him in the wind.'

"Mistaken sympathy for these vile creatures has kindled the flames around the cabin of the pioneer and despoiled him of his hard earnings, murdered and scalped our people, and carried off our women into captivity worse than death. For many years, predatory and numerous bands of these 'pets of the government' have waged the most relentless and heartrending warfare upon our frontier, stealing our property and killing our citizens. We have cried aloud for help; as segments of the grand aggregate of the country we have begged for relief; deaf ears have been turned to our cries, and the story of our wrongs has been discredited. Had it not been for General W. T. Sherman and his most opportune journey through this section—his personal observation of the debris of this scene of slaughter, the ensanguined corpses of the murdered teamsters, and the entire evidences of this dire tragedy, it may well be doubted whether these brutes in human shape, would ever have been brought to trial; for it is a fact, well known in Texas, that stolen property has been traced to the very doors of the reservation, and there identified by our people, to no purpose. We are greatly indebted to the military arm of the government for kindly offices and co-operation in procuring the arrest and transference of the defendants. If the entire management of the Indian question were submitted to that gallant and distinguished army officer (General Mackenzie) who graces this occasion with his dignified presence, our frontier would soon enjoy immunity from these marauders.

"It speaks well for the humanity of our laws and the toler-ance of this people, that the prisoners are permitted to be tried in this Christian land, and by this Christian tribunal. The learned court has, in all things, required the observance of the same rules of procedure—the same principles of evi-dence—the same judicial methods, from the presentment of the indictment down to the charge soon to be given by his honor, that are enforced in the trial of a white man. You, gentlemen of the jury, have sworn that you can and will render a fair and impartial verdict. Were we to practice lex talionis, no right of trial by jury would be allowed these monsters; on the contrary, as they have treated their victims, so it would be measured unto them.

"The definition of murder is so familiar to the court, and has been so frequently discussed before the country, that any technical or elaborate investigation of the subject, un-der the facts of this case, would seem unnecessary. Under our statute, 'all murder committed in the perpetration, or in the attempt at the perpetration of robbery is murder in the first degree.' Under the facts of the case we might well rest upon this clause of the statute in the determination of the grade of the offense. The testimony discloses these salient features: About the time indicated by the charge, the defendants, with other chiefs, and a band of more than fifty warriors, were absent from their reservation at Fort Sill; they were away about thirty days—a sufficient length of time to make this incursion and return; that upon their return they brought back their booty—the forty mules, guns and pistols, and camp supplies of the deceased; that Sa-tanta made a speech in presence of the interpreter, Lowrie Tatem, the Indian agent at Fort Sill, and General Sherman, in which he boasted of having been down to Texas and had a big fight—killing seven Tehannas (Texans) and capturing forty mules, guns, pistols, ammunition, sugar and coffee and other supplies of the train; that he said 'if any other chief claimed the credit of the victory that he was a liar; that

he, Satanta, with Big Tree and Satank (who were present
and acquiesed in the statement), were entitled to all the
glory.' Here we have his own admission, voluntarily and
arrogantly made, describing minutely this whole tragic affair.   Then we have the evidence of one of the surviving
teamster who tells of the attack upon him and his comrades,
by a band of over fifty Indians—of the killing of seven of
his comrades and the escape of four others, with himself.
Then we have the testimony of the orderly sergeant, who,
himself, is an old Indian fighter, and familiar with the
modes of attack and general conduct of the savages.   He,
with a detachment of soldiers, went out from Fort Richardson to the scene of blood, to bury the dead.   He describes
how they were scalped, mutilated with tomahawks, shot
with arrows; how the wagon master was chained to the
wheel and burned, evidently while living; of the revolting
and horrible manner in which the dead bodies were mangled and disfigured, and how everything betokened the
work and presence of Indians.   He further describes the
arrows as those of the Kiowas.   We learn from him the interesting fact that Indian tribes are known by the peculiar
manner in which their arrows are made, like civilized nations are recognized by their flags.

"The same amount and character of testimony were sufficient to convict any white men.   'By their own words let
them be condemned.'   Their conviction and punishment can
not repair the loss, nor avenge the blood of the good men
they have slain; still, it is due to law, justice and humanity
that they should receive the highest punishment.   This
is even too mild and humane for them.   Pillage and
bloodthirstiness were the motors of this diabolical deed—
fondness for torture and intoxication of delight at human
agony impelled its perpetration.   All the elements of murder in the first degree are found in the case.   The jurisdic-
tion of the court is complete, and the State of Texas expects
from you a verdict and judgment in accordance with the
law and the evidence."

*   *   *   *   *   *   *   *   *

We regret our inability to reproduce all the speech of District Attorney Lanham.   His pictures of the massacre, the
sufferings of the victims, the piercing shrieks of the dying

teamsters; his delineation of the habits and miserable, wicked existence of the Kiowas and other tribes, led on by such daring savages as Satanta, Big Tree, Satank and others, and his representations of the scenes and incidents surrounding the numerous Indian raids in Texas, with their scalping processes, their destruction of life and property, combined to make up an appeal to the court and jury, such has rarely been listened to in any court of justice.

SPEECH OF SATANTA,

As interpreted by Mr. Jones. It was spoken in the Comanche tongue, that being the dominant vernacular among the Indians of the plains. The Kiowa chief was handcuffed at the time of his speech, which was delivered semi-signal, semi oral, so to speak. Of course the speech can not now be literally reproduced. It is given below as substantially remembered:

"I can not speak with these things upon my wrists [holding up his arms to show the iron bracelets], I am a squaw. Has any thing been heard from the great father? I have never been so near the Tehannas (Texans) before. I look around me and see your braves, squaws and papooses, and I have said in my heart, if I ever get back to my people I will never make war upon you. I have always been the friend of the white man ever since I was so high [indicating by sign the height of a boy]. My tribe have taunted me and called me a squaw because I have been the friend of the Tehannas. I am suffering now for the crimes of bad Indians—of Satank and Lone Wolf and Kicking Bird and Big Bow and Fast Bear and Eagle Heart, and if you will let me go I will kill the three latter with my own hand. I did not kill the Tehannas. I came down Pease river as a big medicine man to doctor the wounds of the braves. I am a big chief among my people, and have great influence among the warriors of my tribe—they know my voice and will hear my word. If you will let me go back to my people, I will withdraw my warriors from Tehanna. I will take them all across the Red river, and that shall be the line between us and the pale faces. I will wash out the spots of blood and make it a white land and there shall be peace, and the Te-

hannas may plow and drive their oxen to the banks of the
river, but if you kill me it will be like a spark in the
prairie—make big fire ! burn heap!"

Judge Soward's charge to the jury was delivered Friday,
July 8. We are told it was in strict accordance, with the
horrible facts of the case, as minutely detailed by the witnesses and the law. Every effort was made to obtain a copy
of the charge, but without success. W. H. Mitchell, clerk
of the district court of Jack county, wrote, May 4, 1877, that
the papers in the Satanta case have been a lost and can not
be found."

THE VERDICT.

The jury was absent but a little while. When they returned and rendered their verdict of "guilty of murder in
the first degree," fixing their punishment at death, there
was a silence, an indescribable feeling of awe for an instant, when the entire audience broke forth in one shout of
rejoicing. The result closed a trial second in importance and
interest to none in America.

It gave instantaneous relief to the populace. It seemed
as if the thraldom and terrors of the Texas frontiersman
were at an end; that business could again resume its wonted
channels; that the community could enjoy a peace unknown
to them for years, and that justice had been meted out to
two of the most devilish of the worst desperadoes of the age.
The prisoners were remanded to the custody of Sheriff
Blanchard. Subsequently they were sentenced to be hung
on the first day of September, 1871.

On May 29, 1871, Lowrie Tatem, the Fort Sill reservation
Indian agent, addressed a letter to General W. T. Sherman,
in which he wrote: "Permit me to urge, independent of
my conscientious views against capital punishment, as a
matter of policy, it would be best for the inhabitants of
Texas, that they (meaning Satanta and Big Tree) be not
executed for some time, and probably not at all, for the reason that if they are kept as prisoners the Indians will hope
to have them released and thus have a restraining influence
in their actions. But if they are executed the Indians will
be very likely to seek revenge in the wholesale murder of
white people."

Indian Agent Tatem also wrote S. W. T. Langham. Esq., district attorney, June 29, as follows: "In view of the trial of Satanta and Big Tree, Kiowa chiefs, of this agency, permit me to remind thee that two characteristic traits of the Indians are to seek revenge and great dread of imprisonment. From my knowledge of the Indians, I believe if the prisoners should be convicted of murder, it would be a more severe punishment to them to confine them for life than to execute them, and it would probably save the lives of some white people; for if they were executed it is more than probable that some of the other Kiowas would seek revenge in the murder of some white citizens. This is judging the case from a policy standpoint. But if we judge it from a Christian standpoint, I believe we should, in all cases, even of murder in the first degree, confine a person for life, and leave to God his prerogative to determine when a person has lived long enough."

COMMUTATION RECOMMENDED.

WEATHERFORD, PARKER COUNTY, TEXAS,
July 10, 1871.

Governor E. J. Davis.

SIR—I have the honor to say　*　*　that the last term is regarded of more interest to our frontier than any court that has ever been held in the State. Upon arriving at Jacksboro, we despatched a posse of five citizens to Fort Sill, for the necessary witnesses, and through the assistance of Colonel MacKenzie, commanding United States army at Fort Richardson, General Grierson, commanding at Fort Sill, and Lowrie Tatem, Indian agent, we obtained the necessary witnesses for the State, and after a fair and impartial trial, the defendants having the best counsel at the command of the court, the jury returned a verdict of murder in the first degree, and fixed their punishment at death.

Mr. Tatem expressed a strong desire that they should be punished by imprisonment for life, instead of death, but the jury thought differently. I passed sentence upon them on the eighth of July, and fixed the time of execution at Friday, September 1, next. I must say, here, that I concur with Mr. Tatem as to the punishment; simply, however, upon a politic view of the matter. Mr. Tatem has indicated that if they are tried, convicted and punished by imprisonment, that he would render the civil authorities all the assistance in his power to bring others of those tribes on the reservation who have been guilty of outrages in Texas to trial and just punishment. I would have petitioned your excellency to commute their punishment to imprisonment for life, were it not that I know a great majority of the people on the frontier demand their execution. Your excellency, however, acting for the weal of the State at large, and free from the passions of the masses, may see fit to commute their punishment. If so, I say amen! Now, while entertaining the opinion that the present policy of the United States toward these wild tribes, is founded on supreme folly, nevertheless, I see in this new phase of the Quaker policy (which has culminated in the trial and conviction of the great chief, Satanta and brave Big Tree, by civil authority) a solution of our difficulties; and, if we only use our vantage ground, I think we will be speedily redeemed from the ravages of all the reserve Indians on our borders.

During the trial of Satanta and Big Tree, it appeared from legitimate testimony that Big Bow, Fast Bear, and Eagle Heart, were in the last raid that resulted in the murder of seven men and the capture of forty-one head of fine mules. Now, I most earnestly request your excellency to issue your requisition for the above named Indians, to be turned over to the sheriff of Jack county. You will please send your commission through General Reynolds, to Colonel MacKenzie at Fort Richardson. Colonel MacKenzie informed me that he is ready and will execute the commission, and Tatem, the agent, is under promise to render all the assistance in his power.

With many wishes for your good health, I remain with much respect. Your very obedient servant,   —

CHARLES SOWARD,
Judge Thirteenth Judicial District, Texas.

GOVERNOR'S OFFICE, ⎱
AUSTIN, August 2, 1871. ⎰

DEAR SIR—Your communication of the tenth ult. has been received recommending the commutation of sentence in the case of Satanta and Big Tree. I have thought your recommendation a good one, and have accordingly directed that the sentence of these two Indians be commuted to imprisonment for life.

Respectfully,

EDM'D J. DAVIS, *Governor.*

To Charles Soward, Judge of Thirteenth District,
Weatherford, Parker Co., Texas.

COMMUTATION OF SENTENCE.

Governor Davis, on August 2, 1871, issued the following proclamation commuting the sentences of Satanta and Big Tree to imprisonment for life:

THE STATE OF TEXAS,
To all to whom these Presents shall come:
WHEREAS, At the July term, A. D. 1871, of the District Court of Jack county, in said State, one Satanta and Big Tree, known as Indians of the Kiowa tribe, were tried and convicted on a charge of murder, and sentenced therefor to suffer the penalty of death on the first day of September, A. D. 1871; and, *whereas,* it is deemed that a commutation of said sentence to imprisonment for life will be more likely to operate as a restraint upon others of the tribe to which these Indians belong; and, *whereas,* the killing for which these Indians were sentenced can hardly be considered as a just consideration of the animus as coming within the technical crime of murder under the statutes of the State, but rather as an act of savage warfare; *now, therefore,* I, Edmund J. Davis, Governor of Texas, by virtue of the authority vested in me by the constitution and laws of this State, do hereby commute the sentence of Satanta and Big Tree to imprisonment for life, at hard labor, in the State penitentiary, and hereby direct the clerk of the District Court of Jack County to make this commutation of sentence a matter of record in his office.

REMOVAL TO THE PENITENTIARY.

HEADQUARTERS DEP'T OF TEXAS AND LOUISIANA, ⎱
SAN ANTONIO, TEXAS, September 12, 1871. ⎰
[*Special Order No. 185.*]

IV. The Governor of the State of Texas, by his proclamation, dated August 2, having commuted the sentence of death of Satanta and Big Tree, Kiowa Indian chiefs, to imprisonment for life, at hard labor, in the State Penitentiary, and having requested the commander of this military department to cause said Indian chiefs to be delivered to the warden of said penitentiary; therefore, the commanding officer at Fort Richardson, Texas, will send, under suitable guard, the prisoners Satanta and Big Tree to Huntsville, Texas, and cause them to be delivered to the warden of the said penitentiary. Receipt for said prisoners will be taken from the warden, and the original forwarded to department headquarters. The commissioned officer in charge of the guard will be held directly responsible for the sure custody and entire personal safety of the prisoners *en route* and until formally delivered to the warden, and to this end all communication of the prisoners by civilians will be carefully prevented and strictly forbidden.

By command of Major J. J. Reynolds.

H. CLAY WOOD, *Ass't Adj't General.*

The sentence of the murderous chiefs had scarcely been pronounced (July 8, 1871) before Enoch Hoag, Superintendent of Indian Affairs, Lawrence, Kansas, was beseeching the President of the United States (July 19, 1871) for executive clemency. He gave as his reasons for asking that the death sentence be commuted to *imprisonment for life,* that if these chiefs were hung, he feard the consequences to the border inhabitants of Texas, as resulting from the executions. As the result of this intercession Governor Davis, under influences brought to bear upon him by the United States Government, on August 2, 1871, commuted the sentences to imprisonment for life. What other influences or motives prompted President Grant to interpose further in behalf of these murderous chiefs, we have not been able to learn, but it is a fact that Governor Davis set them at liberty upon the recommendation of the President, as the following from the records of the penitentiary will show: "Set at liberty by Governor Davis, August 19, 1873, upon recommendation of the President of the United States upon parole." Satanta and Big Tree were accordingly set at liberty upon that day, and escorted from Huntsville back to the reservation. How well these murderous villains observed the "parole," without going into details, can be seen from the following extract from Lieutenant General Sheridan's order of October 30, 1874, written from the headquarters of the military division of the Missouri, in camp at Sheridan Roost, on the North Canadian river, directing Captain C. H. Carlton, commanding at Fort Sill, to return Satanta to prison. The extract is as follows: "That as the Kiowa Chief Satanta, now in the guard house, at Fort Sill, has violated the conditions on which he was released from the State penitentiary in Texas, that you return him in charge of a commissioned officer and suitable guard, to that institution. His Excellency, the Governor of Texas, will give the necessary instructions for his re-incarceration." Satanta was accordingly returned to the penitentiary November 8, 1874. Big Tree has never been captured, although he, too, has flagrantly violated his parole on several occasions. Big Bow is in the penitentiary as a hostage.

Previous to his parole, Satanta did very little work, sometimes picking wool and pulling shucks for mattresses, only working when inclined to do so. After he was returned to prison the second time, he did very little, with the exception of making bows and arrows. Big Tree, before being paroled, worked constantly bottoming chairs, and became very expert, and could put in as many or more bottoms than any other hand.

[NOTE.—Since the publication of the book from which the above data was taken, we find from the report of Adjutant General King, September, 1884, that Satanta either committed suicide or broke his neck in attempting to escape from the penitentiary. The precise facts, the Attorney General did not have.]

The Indians were continually raiding in Young, Jack, Parker, Palo Pinto, and in fact, throughout all the northwestern counties, and both life and property of the citizens were almost at the complete mercy of these bloodthirsty demons. Their depredations became so frequent, and their outrages so numerous that the Fourteenth Legislature of Texas authorized the raising of a battalion, and as will be seen in the succeeding article, Major Jones became commander.

Major John B. Jones.

THE Fourteenth Legislature of Texas, which convened in January, 1874, passed an act authorizing a battalion of rangers to be raised for the frontier service, and Major John B. Jones, of Corsicana, was appointed by Governor Coke, to the command.

We will briefly give an outline of the services performed by Major Jones and his battalion of rangers, taken from his report to General William Steele, Adjutant General of the State.

(The first of September, 1875, the battalion consisted of five companies, of thirty-three men each.)

"During the first six months of the service there were more than forty parties of Indians on the frontier, being about the average, so the settlers say, of what it had been for several years past. We had fourteen engagements with them. During the second six months we had four engagements. On the first of May, 1875, there were eight parties of Indians in at one time. I caught one of these parties and killed five. Since May last only six bands of Indians have visited us, and I have had only one fight. Have had in all, nineteen engagements with Indians, in one of which we killed all but three, and in another two.

"We have killed twenty-seven Indians that we know of and ten or twelve more we have reason to believe have been killed. My losses have been two men killed and six wounded. On the twelfth of July, with two officers and thirty-four men, I met a large war party of well armed and well mounted Comanches, Kiowas and Apaches, numbering between one hundred and twenty-five and one hundred and fifty, commanded, as I have since learned, by the celebrated Kiowa chief Lone Wolf, and in an engagement of several hours duration defeated them and forced them to retreat. My loss was D. W. C. Bailey and W. A. Glass killed, company B, and Lee Conn and George Moore wounded. Twelve horses killed and two wounded.   Three Indians were killed and three wounded.   This fight took place in Loss Valley, Young county."

In his reports, Major Jones says: "About September 15, Lieutenant Telesfero Montes, of El Paso county, frontiersman, with twelve men of his command, attacked a party of seven Indians, killed two and captured five horses."

"On the eighteenth of November Lieutenant B. F. Best, company E, frontier battalion, with sixteen men, overtook a party of Indians near Brownwood, Brown county, after following them from Coleman county, a distance of twenty miles.   Three Indians were killed, one wounded and most of their camp equipage captured.   Two men of company E were slightly wounded and one horse killed.

"On November 21, 1874, Lieutenant D. W. Roberts, company D, frontier battalion, and a detachment of his company, pursued and engaged in Menard county a party of eleven Indians (Comanches), killing five on the field and capturing three horses, guns, pistols, etc.   As his horses were too much fatigued to pursue the remaining five Indians the chase was continued by Lieutenant L. P. Beavert and his men, who succeeded in killing another Indian and wounding one.   The loss on our side in these fights was the wounding of three horses."

It is plainly evident from the foregoing that the gallant Major did all that could be done for the protection of an extensive frontier with the small force at his command. Besides fighting and chasing Indians, much of the time was occupied in quieting bloody feuds among the border settlements, where the civil authorities were powerless to act, and capturing numerous lawless desperadoes by whom at that time the frontiers were greatly infested.   He also recaptured from the Indians in the various encounters he had with them a large number of stolen horses and other property which were restored to the proper owners.   There is no doubt that but for the protection given by Major Jones and his little battalion the settlement of many frontier counties would have been greatly retarded, and many defenseless families murdered by the savages.

Major John B. Jones was born in Fairfield District, South Carolina, December 22, 1834, and with his father, Colonel

Henry Jones, came to Texas in 1838, and settled in Travis county. Thus it will be seen he was only four years of age when he landed in Texas. During the war between the States, he was among the first to enlist in the service of the Confederacy. Although he entered as a private, he did not long remain so, as shortly afterwards he received the appointment of adjutant of the Fifteenth Texas Infantry, which served in the trans-Mississippi department till the close of the war. Recognizing his gallantry and capacity for command. Generals Harrison, Green, Smith, Polignac and Taylor, recommended him for promotion to the rank of major in his old regiment, the line officers waiving their claims in his favor (something unusual). The appointment was made, but owing to the irregularities of the mail his commission did not reach him until after the war had closed.

Without solicitation on his part, he was appointed, as before stated, by Governor Coke, major of the frontier battalion of State troops. We are sorry we are not in possession of the particulars of the various engagements in which Major Jones participated while in command of the troops stationed on the borders. We have only had his reports made to the Adjutant General, to go by, which merely give the general results, and this is our explanation of the very meagre accounts herein contained. One of the Texas journals of that day, in speaking of Major Jones, said: "As an Indian fighter, Major Jones has acquired a reputation unsurpassed, and now that a quietus has been put upon the red man, he is devoting special attention to the rest of the outlaws and lawless characters generally among more civilized classes. In this field he has so far achieved a success no less conspicuous than on the frontier."

While in command of the frontier troops, Major Jones became perfectly familiar with the condition of affairs, which required the strong arm of the government to protect both the citizen and his property, and Governor Roberts, after his election to the gubernatorial chair, recognizing the peculiar fitness of the man, appointed him Adjutant General of the State, which position he filled up to the time of his death, at his home in Austin, July 19, 1881. He was a man suited for private or public—for civil or military life. He possessed the unpretentious, but dignified mein of a chivalrous southern gentleman, and was always armed with the "courage of his convictions." His word was a bond of honor, ever to be respected and never violated. His engagements were sacred and inviolable. He was a man in whom his fellow man had implicit confidence. In short, he was "an honest man—the noblest work of God." In these degenerate days, when honesty seems to be considered a commodity of traffic, it is refreshing to contemplate the character of one upon whose escutcheon rests not even the taint of suspicion. He was a courtly knight, clothed in the panoply of a Christian gentleman.

Heroic Defense of the Dillard Brothers.

WE are indebted to Colonel E. S. Graham for the following account of the heroic defense of two beardless youths (Henry and Willie Dillard) against thirty Comanche warriors.

Early in the autumn of 1869, I arrived in Texas, from Louisville, Kentucky, accompanied by two young men, Dillard and Dorrell, who wished to see Texas, and the 1869 "wild west" generally. Late in the following spring I returned to Kentucky, leaving these young men in Texas to improve a place yet known as Fort Davis, on the Clear fork of the Brazos, about eight miles below Fort Griffin. In 1872, Dillard planted an abandoned farm, mostly in water melons, on the west side of the Brazos, about four miles above Belknap, in Young county. He had written to me previously that he was very anxious to have his brother Willie with him (a lad about eleven years old) who was then in Kentucky. I therefore furnished Willie with tickets to Fort Worth, and gave such directions as would enable him to reach that place, and from thence to Fort Griffin via Belknap. He arrived safely at Henry's lonely abode, and shortly afterwards they went to Fort Griffin with a two horse wagon loaded with watermelons, which they disposed of at from fifty cents to one dollar and fifty cents each. On their way home, and when about six-teen miles from Fort Griffin, Henry was aroused from a slum-ber into which he had fallen by Willie exclaiming "Bro-ther Henry, the Indians have got us." Henry quickly looked up and discovered about thirty mounted Indians ahead of them in the road, painted and in full war costume. He in-stantly seized his repeating rifle, jumped from the wagon and told Willie to follow him. After running a short dis-tance, Henry halted, and turning, fired upon the foremost Indians, but without any effect except to check tempora-rily their approach. Taking advantage of this, the boys ran on in the direction of some timber upon a creek until they were compelled to halt again and confront their pur-suers. Again Henry fired his rifle, and as before, without any effect except to retard their advance for a moment. But just as he was in the act of firing the third time (as he has told me subsequently) the advice I had frequently given to Dorell and himself in our travels came to mind. "In a fight with mounted Indians always aim low, as in do-ing so they are unable to ward off the shot with their shields, at which they are exceedingly expert, and you will be sure to hit either the rider or his horse—and a dismounted warrior is already half whipped." Following my advice he aimed low the third time, and at the report of the rifle, both the horse and the rider fell to the ground. Seeing their com-rade fall, the Indians gave a terrible yell and rushed upon the boys. Soon Willie's piercing shriek, "Oh! brother Hen-ry," caused him to turn round, and he discovered an Indian warrior just in the act of lifting Willie upon his horse. Raising his gun quickly he fired and dropped him dead from his horse. This again checked the Indians momentarily, and the boys once more made for the timber as fast as they could go. But when about twenty paces from the point of timber they were endeavoring to reach, Henry stumbled and fell, but quickly regaining his feet, he turned and shot one of the foremost warriors, who with scalping knife in hand, was in the act of dismounting, thinking no doubt that he was killed or wounded. In another moment the boys reached the timber and this unequal contest came to an end, for the Indians had been so roughly handled, they dared

not follow them further. The boys came out of it without
a scratch. This band of Indians, on their return to Fort Sill,
reported that they had had a fight with a "heap d—d big
captain and his little boy," and that their "medicine" was too
strong for them. When night came the brothers went to
the nearest ranch. There they obtained horses, proceeded
to Fort Griffin, and reported the facts to the officer in command, who at once sent a detachment of dragoons in pursuit of the Indians. They discovered that the band had divided into two parties—one of which had carried off the dead
and wounded. Following the trail of this party in a day or
so they came to a fresh camp, in which they found several
beds of grass covered with clots of blood. On a mound
near by, the bodies of three "good Ingens" were found.
Other bodies were subsequently found, and on his return
the officer in command of this detachment of dragoons,
asserted that he was satisfied that Henry Dillard and is
little brother Willie had killed and wounded eleven Indians
in the fight, besides five horses left dead on the ground.

Brit Johnson, A Negro—His Thrilling Career.

TO COLONEL GRAHAM we are also indebted for the
following thrilling narrative. [This is the same Brit
Johnson incidentally referred to in the article contributed by Captain Barry, published elsewhere in this
book.] The free air of the prairies, the stern trials of frontier life, have always developed a manly, self-reliant and
courageous people in Texas. During the war between
1864 the States there lived in Young county on Peters' Colony, survey number seven hundred and two, situated
on the south side of Elm creek, about three miles from its
junction with the Brazos river, Moses Johnson, grandfather
of Parker Johnson. With Moses Johnson, lived Britton
Johnson (commonly known as Brit), a shining jet black
negro of splendid physique and fine expression of face,

which plainly manifested his kindly and manly character-
istics. Brit had a wife and four children, all of whom he
dearly loved. His master, Moses Johnson, had allowed him
the enlarged liberty which belongs to the frontier, often relying in part upon his strong arm to help defend the family
and neighborhood from the raids of hostile bands of Indians. On the thirteenth day of October, 1864, while Brit
Johnson was absent in Parker county after supplies for his
master's family, one thousand Comanche warriors swept
through the doomed little neighborhood carrying death and
desolation to every hearth stone. They killed Brit's son
Jim, Joel Meyers, Doctor T. J. Wilson, James McCoy and
his son Miles, the widow Durgan and five out of fifteen
Texan rangers, and wounded many others. They carried
away as captives the widow Patrick, her two grand daughters, daughters of the slain widow Durgan, and the negro's
wife and those of his children whom they had not murdered.
They also started with Joe, son of the slain widow Durgan,
but being sick and unable to stand the fatigue of the march,
they killed him on the second day's journey. When the
negro reached home, he shared in and felt the common ruin
to the community, but was not paralyzed by his great grief,
and with a courage possessed by few he determined to
have back his wife and children or perish in the effort.
Under the generous treatment of his master he became the
owner of a large number of horses and cattle, and when
peace, like an angel of mercy, with healing on her wings,
blessed the country and gave him his freedom, he tried
every pathway to recover his lost ones. He visited the
forts in the Indian Territory, and offered for ransom all he
had. He made inquiries of Indian agents, and of Indians
who visited the agencies, but all in vain. Finally he returned to his Texas home cast down and disappointed by
his futile efforts, but not unnerved. He determined to go
alone hundreds of miles through a howling wilderness, infested with hostile savages and find the Indians who held
his wife as a slave. It was useless to ask any one to go
with him on such a perilous mission, so he carefully packed
with provisions one horse, and mounting his favorite black
steed, he started from Young county to seek the villages of
the wild tribes far out on the plains. He traveled for sev-

eral weeks continuously, mostly by night, in a northwesterly direction, through what is known as the Panhandle of
Texas.

One evening when about thirty miles distant from the Indian encampment, where his wife and children were, he discovered upon a mountain peak the Indian pickets. They
discovered him about the same time. Brit signalled them
as a friend, approached them, and informed them as best
he could that his purposes were friendly, that he wanted to
find his wife and be one of the tribe. These pickets detained him for three days—probably awaiting instructions
from the chief of the village—when he was escorted into
the main Indian encampment. Here he was kindly received; did everything in his power to disarm the suspicion
of the Indians; was given his wife and children and became
a member of the tribe. It was the custom of the Indians
when hunting for game to scatter out over the plains in
small squads to kill and cure their meat. The negro took
advantage of this custom, got his wife and children and one
of the captured Misses Durgan in his hunting party, and on a
seasonable occasion, in the summer of 1865, under the
friendly shades of night, set out with his party on horseback for his Texas home, which he finally reached in safety,
guided only by the stars and his general knowledge of the
country. His stay among the wild tribes of the plains gave
him a fund of information as to their manner and mode of
fighting, the meaning of their telegraph smoke signals, etc.,
and after his return home it was Brit's greatest delight to
talk over with his old friends his life spent among the Indians, and relate his adventures, privations and hardships,
incident to his hazardous mission. It was not destined,
however, that Brit should enjoy for a long season the inestimable happiness which the reclamation of his loved ones
brought him. The Indians never forgot or forgave what
they deemed his treachery to their tribe. In the latter part
of January, 1871, while returning from Weatherford with a
couple of colored men, who were to assist him in gathering
in his stock, they camped over night on the old military
road, about four miles east of Salt creek. Unaware to each
other a freight train was camped on the same road about one
mile and a half further west. Early the next morning, be-

tween day light and sun up, while the freighters were rounding in their stock, about twenty-five mounted warriors suddenly appeared and began hostile maneuvres, but about this
time rapid and continued firing began at Brit's camp, to
which this party of warriors hastened.   The freighters, taking refuge on a brush mound, from whence they could see,
witnessed the fight at Brit's camp.   A large band of painted
warriors, once the friends, but now the deadly enemies of
Brit, had surrounded him and his two companions, and were
making the very earth tremble beneath the clattering hoofs
of their horses, while their hideous yells broke the stillness
of the early morning.   Brit's two companions fell early in the
action, but his courage was equal to the occasion, and the
determined negro, who knew his time had come, resolved to
sell his life dearly to his foes.   Like the great king making
Baron on his last bloody field, the negro drew his bowie knife
and deliberately cut the throat of his favorite black steed
that had borne him safely through many perils, and of his
body made a breastwork.   Armed with his own weapon and
that of his fallen comrades, Brit fought with a desperation
almost supernatural, killing and wounding many of his assailants before he went to eternal rest.   When the battle
ground was afterward visited, one hundred and seventy-
three cartridge shells were counted lying around his dead
body.   The savage demons cut off his ears, one of his arms,
disemboweled him, then killed and thrust in his pet little
dog, besides otherwise fearfully mutilating his person, but
his dauntless spirit had taken its flight before one of them
was able to lay his bloody hands upon him.   The remains
of Brit and his two companions lie buried on the north side
of the road, near the spot where they fell.

Captain Curiton's Fight on Wolf Creek.

THE year 1860 was fraught with many thrilling incidents in Texas.   The Indians in that year visited
almost every portion of the frontier, and many lives
were lost and a vast amount of property was stolen.
Several companies were stationed along the frontier border

for the protection of the settlers. The command of one of these companies was given to Captain Jack Curiton.

1860 As soon as the necessary preparations were made, Captain Jack, with his company, started out in search of the enemy. In a few days he came across an Indian trail leading northwest. This they followed beyond the Double Mountain fork of the Brazos and out into the Staked Plains. They continued on in these dreary plains for two days, when they were compelled to abandon the trail for want of water. Their stock of provisions was exhausted, and game was also very scarce in those desolate regions. They therefore turned their course southward, intending to strike the Colorado river or some one of its tributaries. In the meantime they succeeded in finding a little bad water every day, but for five days they had nothing to eat. Finally their hunters killed a fine, fat bear and several deer, and this timely supply relieved their pressing wants, and from thence on they found an abundance of good water and grass. Late in the evening one day they came to an Indian trail leading pretty much in the direction they were traveling. The trail seemed to be several days old, but they followed it until dark and then encamped. The next morning they took the trail again, and about ten o'clock the spies, who had been sent in advance, rode to the top of a small mountain, and from its summit they discovered some objects in the distance, but were unable to tell what they were. They hurried on to find out what it was they had seen, and soon discovered that it was a party of Indians going towards the Colorado settlements. The spies hastened back to the company and told Captain Curiton they had seen the Indians. The company pushed ahead on the trail as rapidly as possible, and about four o'clock in the evening they discovered the Indians on foot, engaged in shooting prairie dogs with their bows and arrows. The Indians had their camp in the bottom on Wolf creek, and were out killing prairie dogs for their supper.

The Texans and the Indians discovered each other about the same time, and the Indians at once began to retreat. Captain Curiton, knowing there was no time to be lost, ordered his men to charge them. The order was promptly obeyed, and the Indians being hard pressed by the Texans fled into the bottom; but before they could reach it, the

Texans poured a deadly fire upon them, killing several and wounding others. Panic stricken, the rest leaped into the creek and concealed themselves among the drift and thickets along the banks. The Texans then began to search for those who had secreted themselves. One had hidden himself under a willow bush, near a large pile of drift. James Lane approached the bush where the Indian was hidden, and stooped down to look under it. At that instant the Indian shot an arrow at him, which passed through his abdomen and lodged in the back bone, and a second arrow went through his hand.

When the fight was over, the Texans went to the Indian camp, and took all their camp equipage, consisting of blankets, buffalo robes, one rifle, nine horses and mules and ten saddles. Only one Indian made his escape, which he did by mounting a pony, bare back. The Texans made a litter on which they carried Mr. Lane to Fort Chadborne. He lived but a few days.

The Butcher Knife Fight.

WE are not positive of the exact year in which this fight occurred, nor are we in full possession of all the minor incidents connected with it, which are essential to make the narrative interesting. In many particulars it is very similar to the fight which Captain S. P. Ross had with Big Foot, which will be found elsewhere in this book; but Mr. Brittain, of Georgetown, who furnished us with the following data, is authority for saying that this fight has no connection whatever with the one above mentioned. The incident we are about to relate took place in Denton county, while the other occurred in Bell. During the spring of the year a large party of Indians came down from the mountains and entered Denton county at what is known as Brittain's spring. A company of rangers were stationed there at the time, but it seems this company, unlike most of our ranging boys—afforded but little protection to the settlements below. In fact, it stated that the rangers scarcely protected themselves; that upon one occasion the Indians came into their camp one night, while the boys were all asleep with not a sentry on post, stole all of their provisions and a good deal of their camp equipage, and every horse they had except the captain's, which was tied to a tree near his tent.

It is no wonder, therefore, that the people of Denton county, when the large party of Indians before mentioned came into it, should have lost all confidence in these redoubtable rangers and taken measures to protect themselves, which they did.

Finding that the Indians had divided up into small squads in order that they might raid the country more effectually, the people collected together at a certain point, and then followed their example by sending out small scouting parties in every direction, who were instructed to follow any Indian trail they might find. While out scouting the country, a squad of four men—Major Witt, his two sons and one other, whose name we did not learn—came across a fresh Indian trail and followed it until they overtook the Indians, whose number was just equal to their own. The Texans charged them so impetuously that they were right on them before they could check their horses—too close, in fact, for either party to make use of their guns. The Indians instantly dismounted, and so did the Texans, and both parties dropped their guns and rushed upon each other with their drawn butcher knives. The Indians, however, were nearly naked, while the Texans were clad in buckskin or heavy cloth, which, in a conflict with knives, gave them a great advantage over their antagonists. Three of the Indians were soon killed, and the fourth no doubt would quickly have been despatched also, but when he saw his companions fall, he dropped his butcher knife and sought safety in flight. Just before the Texans came up with them the Indians had eaten a hearty meal of raw meat. When the fight began, one of them rushed at a Texan with his butcher knife in hand, and as he did so the Texan gave him a stab which made the red warrior bite the dust.

None of the Texans were seriously wounded in this novel combat.

The Menasco and Shegog Families.

BY J. T. DeShields.

AT the time this narrative commences the counties of
Denton and Cooke were sparsely settled, and buffalo,
bear, deer, antelope and other wild game roamed at
will over the beatiful prairies, and sought shelter from
the scorching rays of the sun during the summer and the
cold northers in the winter in the forests that lined the
streams in the far famed cross timbered belt. Fre-
1868 quent incursions were made by the wild Indian tribes
of the upper Red River valley, from the early settlement down as late as 1868, when the last great raid was
made by a band of the Comanches, estimated at three hundred strong.

Among the early pioneers who endured the hardships and
trials to secure a home in the sunny clime of Texas, and
who now (1888) is an esteemed and prosperous farmer, residing near Pilot Point, was Mr. D. G. Menasco, who gave
the writer of these sketches a thrilling account of his experience in the last great Indian raid above mentioned, and
which we will now proceed to narrate.

In the winter of 1858, Mr. Menasco married Miss Sophia
Brown, daughter of Judge Brown, of Navarro, and with
his young wife, located early in January, 1859, on Clear
creek, near the county line which separates Denton from
Cooke, about twenty-five miles west, or a little north of
west, from Pilot Point. There were at the time of the settlement, occasional Indian raids by small bands not sufficiently alarming to drive the hardy pioneers from their
homes, their chief purpose being to stealthily drive away
the settlers' horses, massacre those who perchance came in
their way, and a great many fell victims to their brutal
savagery. In the year 1861, the father, mother, brother and
sister of Mr. Menasco arrived from Arkansas, and shared

his home and hospitality. Himself and brother enlisted in the Confederate service, leaving their families in the care and protection of the father. During their absence the mother died. At the close of the fratricidal strife, Mr. Menasco came home and engaged in the pursuits of farm life. During the period of his army life the Indians continued to make frequent incursions into the vicinity of his new home, but happily without molestation to his family. Hoping that in the near future times would grow better, and the government afford them protection against the savages, they resolved with heroic purpose to defend their homes. The Indians continued their depredations, killing many persons and stealing stock, till it appeared as if they would be forced to abandon their homes and the country.

Then for a period there was a cessation of the hostile incursions until the beginning of the year 1868, when suddenly, on the fifth of January, began the last memorable raid, in which more than three hundred painted warriors took part. The attack being unexpected, the citizens were unprepared to resist the overwhelming number. Mr. Menasco and his brother-in-law, Captain Shegog, who had married the sister named Lizzie, were absent from home on the day mentioned. Mr. Menasco's two oldest children, Lizzie and May, were visiting their aunt, Mrs. Shegog, whose home was one mile west of Menasco's. Hearing that the Indians were in the country, the father of Mr. Menasco went to Captain Shegog's home to bring his daughter and grandchildren over to Mr. Menasco's for safety and better protection. While returning the Indians came upon and surrounded the fleeing party, killing outright the grandfather by shooting him down, making captives of the others. The weather for that season of the year being warm they were thinly clad. The capture occurred about four o'clock in the afternoon on Sunday. The captured party consisted of Mrs. Shegog and her child, but eighteen months old, Lizzie and May Menasco, aged respectively six and four years. The Indians then crossed over the creek and surrounded Mr. Menasco's dwelling with the usual demoniacal yells and whoops, threatening momentarily to enter the house and capture the inmates while Mrs. Menasco with heroic cour-

age, born of a mother's love, defended, gun in hand, her
fireside, while at the same time, with a thrill of horror, she
beheld her two oldest children in possession of the savages.
After maintaining a threatening attitude for some time the
Indians withdrew, taking with them the horses found in the
lot. Mr. Menasco and Captain Shegog returned in time, and
from a distance looked upon the thrilling heroism displayed
by Mrs. Menasco and the departure of the Indians, taking
an easterly course. After traveling about three miles they
killed the little child of Mrs. Shegog by dashing its brains
out against a tree in the presence of the mother. The Indians then pursued their way, passing through the town of
Gainesville to a point six miles east, then turning, retraced
their way through the town, camping one mile west, waiting for daylight, the moon having gone down, the latter part
of the night was dark, During the night a severe norther
came up, and just before day Mrs. Shegog escaped and
wended her way, almost frozen, to the house of Sam Dorres,
where she was kindly received and cared for by the sympa-
thizing family. At day break the Indians started on westward. After going seven miles west of Gainesville, or six
miles from where they had camped, they left the two little
children of Mrs. Menasco. The remains of one was found
one month and the other three months afterward. It is supposed they were frozen to death. Soon afterward Mr. Menasco and Captain Shegog removed to Pilot Point, where
they have since resided. Captain Shegog and wife have
since died. Mr. Menasco and his noble wife are still honored citizens of Denton county.

Captain S. P. Ross Slays the Noted Chief "Big Foot

IN 1842 Captain S. P. Ross lived near where the present
town of Cameron is situated. The Indians had stolen
all of his horses, and he had just returned from Burleson
county with a very fine animal. His wife told him she
believed the Indians were still in the vicinity. As he did

not apprehend any danger, however, he remained in the
house some time before he went out to look for his
1842 mare, which he had turned loose to graze. He could
not find the animal but heard the hooting of owls and
then the whickering of his colt, which was answered by its
mother. Presently he saw the mare going in the direction
of the whickering, when she suddenly stopped and showed
every indication of having seen Indians.

Captain Ross thought it more prudent to return to the
house, as he was satisfied the owls and whickering of the
colt were Indians who were trying to draw him into an ambuscade. His suspicions were not ill founded. Early the
next morning he went to Captain Monroe's and found the Indians had stolen his best horse during the night. Shapley
Woolfork (Captain Ross's nephew) and Captain Monroe
agreed to go with him in pursuit of the Indians. They soon
discovered the trail, in which the tracks of the noted Big
Foot were plainly visible, and they knew if they should succeed in overtaking the enemy, from the well known prowess
of this chief, that some desperate fighting would be the result. The party soon came to where the Indians had encamped the previous night, and from thence trailed them to
the vicinity of a Mr. Bryant, who lived on a high ridge with
a ravine on each side. Here Bryant joined them and the
party divided, two going on one side of the ridge and two
on the other. They supposed the Indians were stealing corn
from Mr. Bryant's field, and that they would meet them as
they returned. Unfortunately, however, the Indians escaped them by returning on top of the ridge instead of following either of the ravines. On the way Captain Ross noticed a horse running up to the fence ahead of them, and
on nearer approach was rejoiced to find that it was his faithful mare, which evidently had escaped from the Indians.
The party then returned to Mr. Bryant's house, where they
stayed all night and the next morning early took the Indian
trail again. By this time two other gentlemen, whose names
we do not know, had joined the party, making six in all.
They traveled in a rain storm about thirty miles, and when
near a noted land mark, known as the "Knobs," in Bell
county, and within a few miles of where the present town of
Temple is situated, they came upon four Indians with the

stolen horses, who, as soon as they saw them, ran off in the opposite direction. All came to the conclusion that as they had been seen, it would be useless to follow them any farther, for their horses were tired, while those of the Indians were fresh. Every one, excepting Captain Ross, was in favor of turning back. He insisted on going farther, but at first the rest were opposed to it. Finally, however, two only went back—those whose names are not remembered—and the others agreed to continue the chase. A short time afterwards they overtook the Indians, who had just killed a buffalo, and had dismounted for the purpose of butchering it. Their guns were covered with a blanket to keep them dry, as it was raining at the time. The Texans immediately charged them, but riding so long in the rain had rendered their old fashioned guns useless and all except Captain Ross's missed fire. His went off but without doing any damage.

By this time the savages had uncovered their guns, and took deliberate aim at the Texans, but their powder also being wet their weapons failed to fire. Notwithstanding the Texans had come upon the Indians so suddenly, the latter had succeeded in catching most of their horses, and were now attempting to escape by flight, when Bryant rushed up and struck one with his big gun, killing him instantly. Both parties then clubbed their guns and the fight began in earnest. Captain Munroe was the next to get in his work, but he only stunned his Indian. Just at this time Captain Ross observed the notorious Big Foot coming towards him. He tried both of his pistols, but neither would fire. He hurled one at Big Foot, hitting him on the shoulder, and then started to strike him over the head with his gun, unaware of the presence of an Indian just in his rear, who, no doubt, would have dealt a fatal blow to the Captain, had it not been for the timely aid of his nephew, who knocked the Indian from his horse, but in falling, the Indian pulled Woolfork from his horse, and then jumped up behind Big Foot, who was riding a fine mare which he had stolen from Captain Munroe. The two Indians were almost out of sight before Captain Ross and his nephew started, as they were considerably delayed in catching Woolfork's horse. Having succeeded in this, Ross and his nephew were quickly in hot pursuit of the fleeing savages, and were fast gaining ground upon them. Captain Ross was riding a fine animal which he had given his nephew, and being fleet of foot, soon put the Captain some distance in advance of Woolfork. Big Foot and his companion were so closely pursued, that when they came to a steep bluff the animal they were riding suddenly stopped, and the two Indians dashed headlong into the mud and water. Ross seeing this, checked his horse when within about forty yards of the Indians, but Woolfork was not so fortunate, and as his horse reached the bluff he made a similar tumble to that of the two Indians, and before he knew it was right in among them. At this juncture Captain Ross rushed up and ran in between them in order to separate the Indians, whereupon Big Foot made for him with his butcher knife. They were both now upon the ground and each had on moccasins. Big Foot had on a pair of leggings and was wearing a checked cotton shirt, while his long plaited hair hung down his back between his shoulders. Captain Ross spoke to Big Foot in sign language, as he was approaching, telling him to surrender and he would not be hurt, but the defiant chief had no idea of being taken prisoner, and shaking his finger at Ross in a taunting manner, began to advance. As he came to close quarters Big Foot made a furrious lunge at him with his butcher knife, but as he did so his foot slipped and he missed his aim, and before he could recover himself, Ross, with one hand grasped his plaited hair, and with the other drove his hunting knife up to the hilt into Big Foot's body, killing him instantly. In the mean time Woolfork had despatched and scalped his antagonist. Just after they had started back to the others, Woolfork asked his uncle what he had done with Big Foot's scalp, and when his uncle replied that it was still on his head, he begged him to go back and take it off, as otherwise the boys would always believe that Big Foot had got away. The Captain then returned and "lifted" the hair from Big Foot's head. When Ross and his nephew had rejoined their two companions they found the bodies of the two Indians whom Bryant and Monroe had despatched. After exchanging congratulations over their hard earned victory, they gathered their stolen horses and returned home. This was indeed a remarkable fight. It was fought without the firing of a gun, and without the shooting of an arrow. Not a white man was hurt and every Indian slain.

A few weeks after this fight, Captain Ross was sick and lying in the yard at home, under the shade of an oak tree, when he discovered some twenty-five or thirty Indians approaching the house. He went into the house and tried to get his wife to take his two daughters and go to his neighbor—Captain Monroe's. This she refused to do, preferring to remain and take her chances with her husband. Captain Ross, who was familiar with the customs of the Indians, and understood to some extent the "sign language" affected a perfectly indifferent manner, and directed his wife to sit beside him and fan him as if she cared nothing for the presence of the savages. This the good lady did, and when the Indians came within the house and perceived the apparent indifference of the family, they no doubt thought very strange of it. The chief ordered Captain Ross to get up. The latter made signs that he could not. The chief then said he had come to make a treaty and wanted watermelons and corn. This was agreeable news and quite a surprise, as a few moments before, Ross thought they had come for scalps instead of watermelons and corn. His surmises might have been correct, had the Indians then known of the fate of Big Foot. Captain Ross then directed his little boy, Sul, to show the Indians to the watermelon patch. This was done and the Indians got all they wanted.

In 1855, while at the agency at Belknap, in Young county, Big Foot's brother stepped up to Captain Ross's tent one day with tomahawk in one hand and pistol in the other, and asked him through an interpreter, if he was the man who killed "Big Foot?" Captain Ross told him "he was." Said he, "my brother was a brave man—you killed him—I have no brother now—he was all I had—I now want you to be my brother." Captain Ross, of course, readily assented to this proposition, and the Indian, in order to show his sincerity, ran a thorn into the fleshy part of his breast, drew up a portion of it and cut off a piece with his butcher knife. This he held up on the point of his knife, and at the same time called on the Great Spirit to bear witness to his sincerity, adding that he would ever obey every command and wish of Captain Ross, and that he would forever after be his friend, which vow was most religiously kept.

CAPT. S. P. ROSS (FATHER OF GOV. L. S. ROSS) SLAYS CHIEF "BIG FOOT."

The Riggs Massacre.

By J. T. DeShields.

THE early history of Bell, like that of all frontier counties, has certainly been an eventful and tragic one. Here, as in all other counties, the rattling hoofs of the Indian's horse and the mournful wail of captive women and children often broke the stillness of the midnight air. Weird sounds they were, foreboding trouble, death and desolation in once happy homes.

1859 Much has been written, and much yet remains to be penned. One by one the old land marks and living witnesses are rapidly passing away, and soon much will be lost in vague, uncertain tradition. With this fact in my mind, and with a desire to rescue a part at least of our unwritten history from oblivion, and place it in permanent form before the facts have entirely passed from the memory of man, we have sifted the following facts from living witnesses.

A true story lisped by many tongues.

There are comparatively few now living who can attest, from personal knowledge. the last atrocious efforts of the brutal savages to check the settlement of Bell county by her hardy pioneers, or who, as they now behold this fair domain in the front rank of all her sister counties, with vast wealth, dense population and enterprising citizens, can realize that her territory was the scene of a shocking Indian massacre. Such, however, is the fact, and that too at a comparatively recent date.

As late as 1859 Bell was a frontier county. West of Belton, which was then a mere village, the settlements were few and far between. For some years previous the county had been comparatively free from Indian incursions, and the settlers, even on the outskirts, were thereby deluded into a sense of security, by reason of which they were rendered more liable to an Indian surprise. In one of the numerous cedar brakes skirting the classic banks of Noland's creek, and near the present residence of the Rev. Ike Scroggins, at the time lived a family named Riggs, consisting of Mr. William Riggs, Sr., his wife and three children—two girls, Rhoda and Margaret, aged respectively about eight and ten years old, and an infant son, William C., Jr.

On a bright and beautiful morning in March, 1859, a band of savages, estimated to number from fifteen to forty, suddenly made their appearance in the settlement and immediately commenced their brutal work. They first met and killed a Mr. Pierce, a member of the Riggs family, about a mile from the house. Next they intercepted Mr. Riggs and a boy named Thomas Elms, who had just left the house with a wagon to go to the cedar brake. Immediately they commenced to strip the boy of his clothing and to whip him with quirts. At this juncture Mr. Riggs succeeded in making his way to the house. Seeing this the Indians left the boy (who now succeeded in making good his escape) and went in pursuit of Riggs. The Indians seeing the doors of the house securely barred, quietly withdrew a short distance, when Mr. Riggs and his wife, with their children, left the house, fleeing towards their neighbors. Seeing this the Indians commenced to yell and rushed upon the unfortunate fugitives. The father and mother were soon killed, scalped and horribly mutilated by the blood thirsty demons, who left the helpless little babe to play in the blood of its murdered parents and carried the the two little girls off captives. We will now quote the narrative of the youngest girl, as detailed to the writer in a letter dated Medina City, Bandera county, Texas, April 25, 1886. She says:

"After murdering and scalping my poor father and mother and leaving little brother crawling about in the blood, the Indians placed sister and myself behind them on the horses and carried us back to the house, which they plundered; carried the beds out of the house and emptied the feathers out and wrapped the ticks around them, dancing and making sport with them. They then started with sister and myself, carrying us behind them on horseback, when they came upon a bunch of horses; they rounded them under a

tree and snared some of them and went on until noon.
When they stopped to eat dinner they separated into two
squads, keeping sister in one and me in the other. I went
to where sister was, but they would not let me stay. After
they had feasted upon the victuals which they had taken
from our home they started on without giving us anything
to eat. They would change me from one to another occasionally. And they traveled on with us until about the middle of the afternoon, when they came upon a man and ran
him on horseback until they caught and killed him, shooting him with arrows. I can remember seeing him bathed
in blood and hearing his piteous groans but they did not
tarry long with him, and going on some distance, came in
sight of some cow hunters, as I afterwards learned, which
surprised and excited them and caused them to ride very
fast, and I fell when they went to change me from one to
another, which, with the ride together, hurt me so that it
was some time before I could walk, and sister seeing this
jumped off from behind the Indian that carried her and he
held on to her until he passed near a stump, which she
caught hold of and freed herself from his savage grasp.
After she recovered sufficiently she came to where I was.
She being about four years older than I was, as you know,
she would carry me all she could and we started back in the
direction we came and I would walk all I could. About
dark we reached an old house where there was no one living. We went in the house and remained there all night.
The night being very cold, sister pulled off her dress and
wrapped me up and nursed me all night. Next morning
we started, and taking a road which led to a house, which
we reached pretty soon, but the people were all gone, being
in fort from the Indians. However, we went in the yard
and stayed a while, when a man came riding up, which
frightened us, and we went round the house from him,
when he came up to the house and hallooed. We went to
see him and found out that it was a white man; then we
went to him and related what had happened and he put us
on his horse and taking us to the next house, which was
the house of Captain Damern, where we stayed until our
friends came after us."

As soon as the news of the murder of Riggs and his wife

and Pierce reached Belton, it, of course, created great excitement, and soon two companies—one under John Henry Brown, and the other under "Uncle Ben" Cox—were formed and went in pursuit. But the Indians were far in advance, and after several hours hard pursuit, the chase was given up as hopeless. The two companies dividing and returning to their homes; and thus ended the last savage raid into Bell county. The two little girls, together with their brother, were cared for by relatives and kind friends, and ultimately grew to man and womanhood. All three are now married. William C. Riggs, Jr., now lives in Colorado, and is a wealthy stockman and useful citizen. Rhoda, the eldest sister, lives in New Mexico, and Margaret, the younger, in Bandera county, Texas. They have many relatives who still live in Bell county.

The heroic endurance and wonderful escape of these tender little children stamp them as true heroines, and the occurence was as remarkable as any written in the annals of Indian warefare, and certainly more richly deserves to be commemorated in marble and brass, than the selfish deeds of many a red handed military despot, in whose memory often times the costly and stately monument has been erected, emblazoned with false and fulsome praise. But long years have elapsed since the events that were connected with that sad tragedy occurred, and with them have passed away most of the gallant spirits who participated in them. Many a brave and generous heart has ceased to beat since then. The then remote and solitary wilderness where the life blood of the poor victims flowed, now teems with wealth and population, and where once its silence was only broken by the yell of the murderous savage, is heard the busy hum of happy thousands, and the shrill whistle of the locomotive as the fiery steed comes thundering along, planting civilization along its pathway. War is over. Peace is king. Those troublesome times will come no more. So may it ever be. Truly the victories of peace are greater than those of war.

Massacre of the Keenon and Paschal Families.

THE story of this sad tragedy is given as related by A. J. Sowell, author of "Texas Rangers." Mr. Sowell, who was in the ranging service at the time, arrived at the scene of the bloody tragedy soon after it occurred, and ought to be prepared to give a true version of all the particulars.

  "While in camp on Big Sandy, news was brought to us of a fearful massacre of women and children on a small creek about thirty miles north of our camp, near the line of Montague and Wise counties. We lost no time in getting off, with eighteen men, well mounted and armed, to the scene of the slaughter, and by rapid riding arrived at the place before night, which was at Keenon's ranch; but we soon discovered that it would be impossible for us to follow the trail, as it had been snowing since the Indians were there. As we rode up we saw seven new made graves on the north side of the cabin, under some trees. The settlers from down the country had buried the dead. There were only two ranches west of there—Colonel Bean's and O. T. Brown's. Bean was absent at the time. His ranch was about two miles from Keenon's. The Keenon house consisted of only one room, about twelve by fourteen feet, made out of logs. There was a small field south of the cabin, at the foot of the hill near the creek. On the northwest side, about two hundred yards from the house, was a small lake of water, at the foot of some hills; on the east was a crib of corn. Keenon himself was not at home when the Indians made the attack on his ranch and massacred the helpless inmates. We dismounted, entered the yard, walked to the door and looked in. It was a horrible sight. The door was torn from its hinges, and lay in the yard covered with blood. Blood on the door steps, blood everywhere, met our sight. The inside of the cabin was like a butcher pen. Quilts and pillows were scattered about over the floor, stiff with clotted

1871

blood. The dress which Mrs. Keenon wore was hanging across the girder which extended from one wall to the other. It had been hung there by some party who buried the victims. The dead were as follows: Mrs. Keenon and two of her children; the widow Paschal, who was living with the Keenon family, and her three children. We obtained the particulars of the attack from one of the Keenon children, a boy about eight years old, who made his escape on that fearful night. He said it was about ten o'clock at night; the ground was covered with snow, and it was very cold. The inmates had all gone to bed except Mrs. Keenon, who was sitting by the fire smoking. On the north side of the cabin was a small window with a shutter which fastened on the inside with a wooden pin entering a hole in one of the logs. The door was in the south side. Everything was still and quiet on that cold winter night. The children were all asleep, probably dreaming sweet dreams, which seldom visit the couch except of innocent childhood; when suddenly crash came the end of a rail through the frail shutter, bursting it wide open, and the hideous painted face of an Indian looked in and began to crawl through into the cabin. One brave man or resolute woman, armed with an ax or hatchet, could have held them at bay; but poor Mrs. Keenon was timid, and instantly sank on her knees and began to pray and beg for her life. As fast as one Indian got through another followed, until nine hideous wretches stood inside. By this time the balance of the inmates were aroused. The children began screaming and the work of death commenced. Pen can not describe the scene. The cold and lonely night, far out in the western wilds; the painted faces of the Indians lit up by the wood fire; the frantic and heart-rending cries of the women and children; the sickening blows of the tomahawks, etc., make one shudder to think of it. Who can blame a Texas ranger for placing his six shooter to the head of a wounded savage and pulling the trigger, as they often do in battle when they are victors. It was during the confusion that the little boy made his escape through the window by which the Indians had entered. He received a severe cut in the hip with a knife as he went through, but succeeded in getting clear of the house, and was able to run off and hide himself until the Indians left.

Crouched in some bushes near the corn crib, and bleeding profusely, he waited and listened until all was still. The work was done; the fiends had reveled in blood. This boy displayed a presence of mind that was truly astonishing for one of his tender years before he made his escape from the house. He noticed the number of Indians that entered, and when they came out to take their departure, counting them to see if they were all leaving. The Indians had left their horses at the lake and came to the house on foot, and as the ground was covered with snow he could plainly see each form standing out in bold relief against the white back ground. He left his place of concealment and watched them until they mounted their horses and disappeared over the snow clad hills towards the west, and being satisfied that they would not return came back to the house and entered. What a sight for a boy of his age to behold. His mother lay near the hearth with three arrows in her breast, toma- hawked and scalped. Some of the children were killed in bed, others lay on the floor in pools of blood; one of his sis- ters was crouched in a corner with her throat cut. There was at least a quart of blood in that corner when we were there. The widow Paschal was lying on the door shutter in the yard. She had three broken arrows in her breast. She had broken them off in attempting to pull them out; she was also scalped. The youngest child, about eighteen months old, was taken by the legs and its head dashed against the wall of the house and then thrown out through the window on the frozen ground. But the boy brought his little sister back in the house and laid her down before the fire and she recovered. While in the house attending to his sister he heard a noise in the yard, and on going to the door saw Mrs. Paschal sitting upon the door shutter, upon which she had been lying. She looked horrible, covered with blood and her scalp taken off. But the brave boy went to her and she asked him for a drink of water, and there be- ing none at the house he took a gourd and went to the lake and brought the water. Mrs. Paschal drank the water and immediately expired. On looking around in the house while we were there I saw the old lady's pipe lying on the hearth, about half smoked out, where she had dropped it on that fatal night. We also saw a bent arrow spike in one of the

logs, just above the bed. It had been shot at some of the
children on the bed and missed. The shaft had been removed. The next evening after the massacre a settler
passed the house and was hailed by the boy, who soon told
his tale of woe.

The man took a hasty view of the victims and then galloped off to give the alarm. The next day the dead were
buried and the news carried to the ranger camp, and when
we arrived the ranch was deserted, the children having been
taken away and cared for until their father arrived, who
was off somewhere with a wagon and had one of his children
with him, which circumstance saved its life, no doubt. As
we could accomplish nothing, the trail being covered with a
fresh fall of snow, after about an hour's stay we mounted
and set out for camp, vowing vengeance if we should ever
meet the red man face to face. Some time after our first
visit to the Keenon place a small party of us returned after
a load of corn. Keenon had returned and was preparing to
move away from the frontier. Our captain hearing of it
had purchased his corn crop, which amounted to about three
hundred bushels. I was detailed on this trip as one of the
guards and saw the little girl who was thrown out of the
window and so nearly killed by the Indians. She was very
lively and when we asked her where the Indians hit her she
would tuck down her head so we could see the back of it,
which still looked discolored and bruised. The boy looked
pale and thin: his wound was not yet healed.

Colonel Oldham's Fight on Cedar Creek.

THE traveler of to-day, who in passing along the almost
abandoned road leading from the Yellow Prairie neighborhood, in Burleson county, to the old town of Nashville, on the Brazos river, in Milam county, passes
through a level little prairie, interspersed with motts of bot-

tom timber and dense thickets of sumac bushes. This little prairie, which is situated on the south side of 1844 Cedar creek, lying up and down the bottom for about a mile, is now known, and has been ever since Colonel Oldham's fight with the Indians, as "Battle Ground Prairie." Just in the edge of Cedar creek bottom proper, and up to the left of the road, a few hundred yards in traveling north, is where Colonel Oldham, with a party of whites, had his fight with a small party of Indians, in which —— Reed and —— Bingham were both killed.

During the year 1844, a party of seven or eight Indians made their appearance on Cedar creek, in Milam county. They were discovered by some citizens, who pursued them, until the Indians finding they would be overtaken, halted in a strong position and made ready for battle. The whites concluded they were too few to attack the Indians in the strong position they had taken, also halted, and sent one of their number back for reinforcements. Colonel Oldham at once raised a company of about thirty men, and hastened to join his comrades. In the mean time the Indians had gone on, and the now combined forces of the two parties pursued them as rapidly as possible. The Colonel had sent a spy ahead, who discovered the Indians about twelve miles north of Caldwell, in Burleson county. The spy, on his return, reported the fact to Colonel Oldham, and the pursuit was continued. The Indians, when overtaken, had camped, and were roasting terrapins for their dinner. As soon as they discovered the whites advancing, they flew to their arms, no doubt thinking they had only to contend against the small party they had seen the day before; but when they perceived the number of the whites they fled to the creek bottom, near by. The whites had several good dogs with them, and put them on the trail. The Indians dashed into Cedar creek bottom, and in order to escape from the dogs, they waded some distance up the creek. But finding that the dogs still followed them, they left the creek and took their position in a small hammock where the soil was very loose and sandy. The dogs trailed them to the edge of this hammock where they stopped and bayed furiously. Messrs. Reed and Bingham went to where the dogs were baying, and the former seeing an Indian partially buried in

the sand (for the Indians had dug holes in it with · their
butcher knives sufficiently deep to protect themselves from
the bullets of the whites) raised his gun and fired on him,
and at the same instant the Indian fired also. His bullet
entered Reed's breast, inflicting a wound from which he
expired in a short time. The bullet from Reed's gun also
struck the Indian. By this time the main body under Colonel Oldham came up and endeavored to route the Indians
from the strong position they had taken. In this attempt
Bingham was killed.

Colonel Oldham, seeing the Indians were so well posted
that they could not be driven out without great loss of life,
drew his men off, leaving the two dead men, Reed and
Bingham, on the battle ground. The next day Mr. Alexander Thomson and a few citizens went to the battle ground,
found the bodies of the two men and gave them a decent
burial in Yellow Prairie, in Burleson county.

Ezekiel Rowland, Captain Stewart and John Gray.

MR. ROWLAND was a native of the State of Alabama. His parents emigrated to Texas in 1836 and
settled for a time in Washington county. In 1837
they moved up the Brazos river to the town of
Tenosticlan. They remained there but a short time and then
moved to Burleson county, near the town of Caldwell. After
his father moved to Burleson county, Ezekiel entered
1853 the ranging service, in which he remained for three
years, discharging all his duties as a true and brave
soldier. In the spring of 1853 he joined Captain Stewart in
an exploring expedition to the Wichita mountains The exploring party were out about three months, and having accomplished their mission started to return. They found
water very scarce on their route, so much so that the entire
party on several occasions were in imminent danger of per-

ishing from thirst. One day when suffering exceedingly from thirst Captain Stewart, in order to search for it, without permitting his men to scatter, detailed Ezekied Rowland and John Gray to go with him in advance of the main body in search of water, and if found they would be notified of the fact by the firing of their guns. After several hours of diligent search they finally succeeded in finding a beautiful stream of running water. It is supposed that after they had quenched their thirst they had seated themselves under a spreading oak that grew near the margin of the stream to rest for awhile when they were attacked by Indians. Their companions hearing the firing of guns, which was the signal that water had been found, hurried forward as fast as possible, and to their surprise and horror discovered the lifeless bodies of their friends weltering in their blood beneath the oak tree we have mentioned. The ground around for some distance was covered in places with stains of blood and the live oak tree under which the bodies were lying was filled with bullet and arrow marks, showing that the men had defended themselves to the last. Their comrades buried them under the live oak tree, where they had fallen. Subsequently they fought their way though various tribes of Indians and finally reached the settlements without the loss of any more men. Joseph Rowland (or Uncle Joe, as he is usually called), the father of young Rowland, still lives in Burleson county, a venerable patriot of more than four score years, loved and honored by all who know him.

[NOTE.—Since this article was written—some twelve or fifteen years ago—"Uncle Joe" has passed over the river to join his veteran comrades on the other shore.]

Mrs. Lance's Son.

MRS. LANCE and family settled in Bastrop county. They engaged in the business of farming and stock raising. Mr. Lance went out on the range one day to hunt some oxen. He spent a large portion of the day in hunting them, but failing to find them in their accus-

tomed range, he ventured out farther than usual. As he
approached a watering place he was fired upon by a
1842 party of concealed Indians and killed. They scalped
him and stripped him of his clothes.

The young man not returning at the proper time, the family became alarmed and went out to hunt him. They called
out to him and were answered by the Indians, who were
endeavoring to decoy them into their grasp; but they knew
the voice of the son too well to be deceived by these demons.
The night passed away in much sorrow to the family, for
they felt positive some evil had befallen the beloved son.
Morning came and he returned not. This confirmed their
fears.

A party of men was raised, and they soon found him.
He had been shot with a ball and his body speared through
in several places. This was in the fall of 1842. His remains
were restored to his distressed mother, who was a widow
lady with another son and two daughters.

Incidents in Southwest Texas.

WE think it was in the fall of 1831 that a party of
Waco Indians came into DeWitt's colony, stole a
lot of horses from Andrew Tomlinson and made off
with them. Tomlinson, in company with four or
five others, pursued the Indians. After following their trail
for about twelve hours they overtook a couple of Waco Indians. They interrogated the Indians pretty closely,
1831 and as they looked guilty and gave contradictory an-
swers, they came to the conclusion that they were the
very ones that had stolen the horses. They therefore took
them prisoners, and told them if they did not point out the
place where they had concealed the horses that they would
kill them. When Mr. Tomlinson and his party arrested
these Indians they took all their arms from them except
their butcher knives. The Wacos strenuously denied know-

ing anything about the horses, but the Texans told them they knew better, and if they did not take them to the place where they were hid that they would certainly kill them. "Well, then," said the Wacos, "we will show you the horses;" and they went off in a certain direction towards the place where they said the horses were tied. After going about a mile one of the Wacos, knowing that death would be certain whether he showed the horses or not, determined to fight it out. He, therefore, suddenly drew his butcher knife and made a furious lunge with it at Mr. Tomlinson, who being on the alert, instantly drew his gun and shot him through the body. The Indian, however, had succeeded in plunging his knife into Mr. Tomlinson's side, and they fell dead together. The remaining Waco then endeavored to make his escape, but was pursued and killed. The Texans found the stolen horses, buried Mr. Tomlinson and returned home.

In the spring of 1840, Joseph Powell, who was then about twelve years of age, in company with his father and an elder brother, went out on the range in search of stock. While thus engaged they were attacked by a large number of Comanches. Powell and his sons attempted to escape by flight, but in vain. The Indians closed in on them, killing the old man and his eldest son, and making a prisoner of the younger one, Joseph. They had gone but a few miles further, when they met and killed another old man who was out hunting his horses. Whilst they were scalping this old man, for some reason they did not wish young Powell to see the operation, and compelled him to look in another direction. After this they continued their journey, and for six nights in succession, they tied young Powell fast, hand and foot. He tried his best at night to get loose, but the Indians watched him too closely. The sixth night, supposing there was no longer danger of pursuit, after tying young Powell securely, as they thought, all except the guard "turned in" early and went to sleep. Towards the latter part of the night young Powell noticed that the guard had gone to sleep also, and he made strenuous efforts to loosen the thongs with which the Indians had tied his hands and feet, and finally succeed in doing so. But just then daylight began to dawn, and he hesitated about leaving the camp for

fear the Indians should discover him, which he knew would
be certain death. Some distance from where he was lying
he saw one of the Indians sitting up, wide awake. He was
doubtful about the course he should pursue. If he attemped
to leave, the Indian who was awake would be almost sure
to see him, and if he remained, he thought it very probable
the Indians would kill him as soon as they discovered that
he had untied himself during the night. It so happened
that the Indian who was sitting up had his back turned towards the youth, whilst all the rest who were lying around
him were still fast asleep. Keeping his eye on the Indian
who was awake, he threw a blanket over his shoulders, and
noiselessly walked off, until he reached the opposite side of a
clump of bushes. He did not dare to look back, and every
moment he expected to hear the whoop of the Indian who
was awake. But if he saw the young fellow passing by
with the blanket thrown over him, he no doubt thought it
was one of his comrades. Be this as it may, young Powell
made his way without being followed, to a large body of
timber, and finding the Indians, as yet, were not pursuing
him, he hurried on as fast as possible. He wandered around
for eight days in the wilderness, suffering terribly for want
of food and for fear the Indians would recapture him. After eight days hard travel, he succeed in reaching the house
of Jose Antonio Navarro, on the Gaudalupe river, in an almost famished condition. There he was kindly cared for,
and eventually restored to his relatives.

During the month of August, 1840, when the thousand
Comanche warriors made their descent upon the coast—an
account of which has been given elsewhere in this book—
mention was made of several murders being committed by
the Indians while en route to the coast. Among those slain
were two men whose names were Foley and Ponton. While
out in the early part of August, rounding up stock, they
were attacked by a party of Indians who belonged to the
invading army but were scouting through the country on
their way down.

The two men were riding ponies, and when they saw the
Indians they attempted to save their lives by flight. Foley's
pony soon began to fail, and finding the Indians about to
overtake him, begged his companion to leave him and if

possible save himself. Ponton took him at his word, put spurs to his horse and left his companion to his fate. Some of the Indians passed by Foley and pursued Ponton. As they were gaining rapidly upon him, he ran to a dense thicket a short distance ahead, dismounted from his horse and made his way into it on foot, barely in time to escape his pursuers. The Indians placed a guard around the thicket to prevent Ponton from leaving it, and then returned to where Foley had been captured by others. They skinned the soles of his feet with their butcher knifes, and compelled him to walk in that condition over stones, thorny shrubs and burned stubble to the thicket in which Ponton had concealed himself. and forced him to call to him several times to come out where he was. Finding that Ponton would not come out, the Indians thrust Foley through with their spears and scalped him. They tried by various maneuvers to make Ponton leave the thicket, but failing to do so, they took his horse and the one they had captured from his companion and left.

As soon as Ponton discovered the Indians had gone he climbed into a tree and watched them until they were out of sight. While there he saw the Rev. Z. N. Morrell pass in his ox wagon. He then left the thicket and made his way safely to the settlements

One day in 1842, Matthew Jett, who lived on the Medina river, in Bexar county, and was one of the early pioneers of that section, discovered three Indians approaching his house. He left the house and walked hastily away. The Indians entered it and began to plunder it at their leisure, supposing that they had frightened Jett so badly that he would not venture to return — which proves conclusively they were not well posted as to the character of that gentleman. Whilst they were busily occupied in plundering the house Jett came back, stepped to the door and deliberately shot one of the Indians down. He then entered the house, knocked another over with the breech of his gun, and shot the third with a pistol as he endeavored to escape. In this way he succeeded in killing the whole party. No man rendered more service to the country than did Mr. Jett while he lived.

He was finally killed by a robber named Schultz. Jett

was traveling in company with a citizen of Gonzales county,
and both of them had quite a large sum of money with
them.   In some way Schultz had ascertained this fact, waylaid them and assassinated them both.

In the spring of 1842 the Indians were very trouble-ome
in Gonzales county, stealing horses and taking scalps
whenever the opportunity occurred.   About four miles
from the town of Gonzales there was preaching one night
at a school house by the Rev. Z. N. Morrell.   During the
sermon most of the men sat with their guns across their
knees, whilst the rest stood guard, and this fact will give
the reader some idea of the constant danger to which the
settlers at that time were exposed.   Just as the sermon was
over and the people were leaving for their homes, they
heard a gun fire, apparently about a quarter of a mile from
where they were, and the report was instantly followed by
a shrill whistle.   It so happened that the people in going
home had to travel the same road, and, fearing the Indians
would attack them, they kept together for mutual protection.   No attack, however, was made upon them, and
they reached their homes in safety.   The next morning
some of the settlers went to the place where they had heard
the gun fire, and a horrible sight presented itself to their
view.   There lay the body of Doctor Witter, weltering in
blood, scalped and otherwise mutilated in the most barbarous manner.   The settlers all attended his funeral and sorrowfully paid the last rites to their beloved friend.   Around
his grave stood his four little children, who had lost their
mother only a few weeks previously.   Doctor Witter lived
within a short distance of Henry E. McCulloch, and was his
family physician.   The doctor had hoppled his horse out
to graze, and before retiring had gone out to look after him
when he was shot.

GENERAL HENRY E. McCU

608

General Henry E. McCulloch.

HENRY EUSTACE McCULLOCH was born in Rutherford county, Tennessee, on the sixth day of December, 1816. He first came to Texas in the fall of 1835, accompanied by his brother Ben, but only came as far as Nacogdoches. At this point an incident occurred which illustrates the high sense of duty of which McCulloch was possessed even in his youth. After the two brothers had retired one night Ben, who was some five years older than Henry, feeling solicitous for the latter's welfare, used every argument in his power trying to prevail on Henry to return home. When he had finished, Henry told him that his argument all counted for nothing, and that he intended to cast his lot with him (Ben) in Texas. Ben, finding his brother fixed in his determination, then told him that it was his *duty* to return home to look after his parents in their old age. "Well, then," said Henry, "if you put it upon that ground, I will do as you say." This ended the discussion. The next morning the two brothers, each of whom was possessed of a fine saddle horse, sold their horses for a good price and then set out afoot, Ben going west and Henry east, retracing his steps homeward. After remaining at home awhile, he accompanied a volunteer company to the the Florida war in 1836.

In the fall of 1837 young McCulloch again came to Texas, landing this time at old Washington, on the Brazos. which was then the seat of government. Here he passed the winter uneventfully, hewing house logs, splitting red oak boards and building board houses. In the spring of 1838 Captain Chance, with a party of fifteen men, composed of Captain James Cook, James Shepard, James Evitts, Sam Evitts, McFall and others, started from Washington with the purpose of exploring the upper Brazos. In this expedition young Henry McCulloch joined. This party proceded up the Brazos to Little river and thence up Little river and explored the country drained by the waters of the Leon, Gabriel, Lampasas and other tributaries of Little river. On this trip, while McCulloch and McFall were out hunting by themselves, they came upon a party of five Indians, upon whom they made an immediate attack. The two white men succeeded in killing two Indians and chased the other three to the bottoms of the Gabriel, where they made good their escape. This was the first fight against Indians Henry McCulloch ever engaged in, but by no means the last, as our readers will see. In the summer of 1838 Henry joined his brother Ben at Gonzales and formed a partnership with him in surveying and locating lands. The partnership formed then, continued in respect to lands, goods, cattle and horses up to the time of the death of General Ben McCulloch, who was killed in defense of the "Lost Cause."

In January, 1839, Ben and Henry McCulloch, Wilson Randle, David Henson and John D. Walfin, accompanied by about thirty-five friendly Tonkawa Indians, started out in search of the hostile Indians, who had, in the light of almost every moon, raided the settlements and driven away the saddle and work horses of the settlers. On the head of Peach creek they came upon a band of Comanches and Wacos and fight was immediately joined. The hostile Indians lost five killed and others wounded and the Tonkawas lost one killed. (In our sketch of the life of General Ben McCulloch we state ten Indians were killed. This was error. General H. E. McCulloch says there were five killed.)

The Tonkawas took the scalps of their inveterate foes and celebrated their victory by the war dance and paid tribute to their dead comrade amid loud lamentations. During the year, Henry McCulloch joined a ranging company, raised and commanded by Captain Mathew Caldwell, for defense against the Indians. In this year, being protected by escort of Caldwell's company, Ben and Henry McCulloch surveyed the road from Gonzales to Austin.

In August of 1840, a large force of Comanches invaded the settlements, penetrating to Victoria and Linnville, on the coast, of which invasion and sacking of Linnville and Plum creek fight an extended account will be found elsewhere in this work. In our account of the last named battle, mention is made of the heroism displayed by Henry Mc-

Culloch on that occasion, and of his saving the life of Doctor Sweitzer, between whom and Ben McCulloch there existed a bitter enmity. The particulars are as follows: "During the battle Henry had dismounted and taken his position behind a small sapling somewhat in advance of the main Texan force and was pouring hot shot into the ranks of the enemy, who, in return, had completely scaled the bark of the little tree behind which he stood. Arch Gipson and Alsey Miller had come up and were sitting on their horses near Henry, who was standing on the ground beside his horse, when suddenly Gipson or Miller cried out: 'They'll catch him; they'll catch him!' McCulloch asked, 'catch who?' His companions .replied, 'Sweitzer.' Glancing over his horse's neck the gallant young McCulloch saw a party of eight or ten Indians closely pursuing the bitterest enemy of his brother, but the life of a human being was involved, and prompted by that magnanimity of heart which has ever characterized his life, he did not stop to calculate the consequences, but in a second was in his saddle going at full speed at the risk of his own life to save that of Sweitzer. The companions of McCulloch joined him in the chase and they reached Sweitzer just in time to save his scalp." The battle over, Sweitzer sent word to McCulloch through Captain Mathew Caldwell that since he (McCulloch) had saved his (Sweitzer's) life he would like to make friends with him. McCulloch replied that he had only done his duty to his fellow man and would not accept frendship on such terms and that he did not feel that Sweitzer was under any obligations to him. Very soon after this battle, to wit, on August 20, 1840, the subject of this sketch was married to Miss Jane Isabella Ashby and he then settled on the place improved by his brother Ben, four miles from Gonzales. Though a man of peace and peaceful habits it seems it soon became necessary for young McCulloch to take up arms again in defense of his home and country. In September, 1842, the Mexican General Woll, with an army of one thousand infantry and five or six hundred cavalry and a battery, had captured San Antonio and taken away as prisoners Judge W. E. Jones, the district judge, and other prominent citizens. Before the retreat of the Mexican forces, however, Captain Mathew Caldwell, at the head of two hundred and two men (himself included in the count) engaged the Mexicans some five or six miles from San Antonio and completely defeated them. While the fight was progressing Dawson's men were massacred in the rear of the Mexican army while trying to make their way to Caldwell. Henry McCulloch was a lieutenant under Jack Hays in this engagement. This bold outlawry on the part of the Mexicans so incensed the Texans that an army of eight hundred was gathered by November and started to invade Mexico, but on reaching the Rio Grande and having taken possession of Laredo they were deterred from further hostile acts against Mexico by command of General Somervell. Lieutenant McCulloch. however, in charge of a detachment of Captain Hays's company, continued down the Rio Grande, where he and his squad acted in the capacity of scouts to a body of three hundred men, led by Colonel W. S. Fisher, who disregarded General Somervell's order and insisted on invading Mexico anyway. This service was gratuitous on the part of young McCulloch, he having refused to connect himself in any official way with the movement. Leaving the Rio Grande McCulloch scouted southeastward, passing by what is now Goliad, thence over to the Guadalupe river, where Cuero is now located, and thence up to Gonzales. In February, 1843, he was elected sheriff of Gonzales county. In 1844 he began merchandising in Gonzales. In the fall of that year he moved to Seguin and went into merchandising there. In June, 1846, he was elected captain of a volunteer company in the Mexican war. In 1847, Captain McCulloch, with his company, operated with Captains Highsmith and Shapley P. Ross in suppressing the Indians. Captain Highsmith being stationed near where Fredericksburg now is. Captain McCulloch, on Hamilton's creek, in Burnet county, a few miles from the present town of Burnet, and Captain Ross near where Waco is now located. In 1848 he was regularly discharged from service in the Mexican war. Again, on November 5, 1850, in the city of Austin, McCulloch was mustered into service as captain of a company of rangers to protect the country west of San Antonio against the Indians. Soon thereafter he established his camp high up on the north fork of the Llano river. In one of his scouts, having with him twenty-two men, he struck a fresh trail of Indians on the head of the north fork of the Llano river. Following the trail they came upon a body of Indians on a branch of the San Saba, who were loitering around, wholly unsuspicious of any danger, their horses grazing off several hundred yards. McCulloch made an immediate attack. Four Indians were killed and two squaws taken prisoners. Captain McCulloch detained the squaws a few hours and sent them away well mounted and supplied with blankets, and requested them to tell the warriors that he was not making war on them if they would not raid the settlements any more, and that if they would return to Fort Martin Scott within one month and make peace he would restore their property. They did return in less than a month and professed peace and Captain McCulloch returned to them all their property. This was the last Indian fight Captain McCulloch ever commanded.

In 1853, McCulloch, as a democrat, defeated Colonel French Smith, a whig, for the legislature. In 1855, he was again returned to the legislature, defeating Thomas H. Duggan. In 1858, he was appointed United States marshal for the eastern district of Texas, which position he held until the breaking out of the civil war. We can not prolong this sketch further in order to follow the brilliant career of this noble man through the four years that followed this beginning of real war. He was first commissioned colonel and was soon promoted to brigadier general, which commission he maintained throughout the war. General McCulloch always showed the greatest desire not to recklessly hazard the lives of his men, but his courage and determination was always apparent. On the first of March, 1876, Governor Coke appointed General McCulloch Superintendent of the Deaf and Dumb Asylum, which position he held until dismissed by Governor Roberts, September 1, 1879. In 1885, he was employed by the State Land Board as their agent in the management of the public school, university and asylum lands. Such in brief is an outline of General McCulloch's past career, and we regret that the limited space we have forbids us doing justice to the old patriot. He was a candidate before the last State democratic convention, which convened in Dallas in the month of August, 1888, for State Treasurer, but was defeated by the present incumbent, Hon. F. R. Lubbock.

Doctor R. M. Swearingen, of Austin. Texas, in language unsurpassed for its beauty and pathos, placed the grand old hero in nomination, and closed his nominating speech with the following eloquent remarks: "Gentlemen of the convention, the people of Texas should never forget the deeds, nor ignore the claims of the old pioneers, who first followed the star of empire into this country, then a splendid boundless wilderness. Conspicuous in that heroic band for courage, for patriotism and for honesty were two brothers, Henry and Ben McCulloch, who hand in hand planted the banner of the white man beyond the picket lines of civilization. One of those brothers went down like a falling star upon a field of glory, and sleeps the dreamless sleep upon a shield as spotless as ever flashed in the light of war. The other brother, quiet and unpretentious in the walks of private life, in the councils of State, upon the Indian trail in the distant west, or when leading victorious columns along the fire lighted valleys of Louisiana, has, with unfaltering devotion, performed all the duties of a citizen and soldier; and he is with us to-day, poor in purse, but rich in glorious memories—a splendid type of that grand race of men who discovered as it were this new world, and laid the foundations of a colossal empire. In his youth, with strong arm and brave heart, he guarded well your border land, and now with the silver dust of some seventy years upon his noble head, by all that is just and generous, let him guard your treasury. I have the honor to nominate for State Treasurer General Henry E. McCulloch."

John L. Wilbarger.

JOHN L. WILBARGER was a native Texan, and son of Josiah Wilbarger. He was born November 29, 1829, in the county of Matagorda. When he was still an infant his parents moved into Austin's new colony, now Bastrop county. The subject of this narrative, who was the eldest son, was noted for his daring and enterprising character. Brought up on the frontier, and skilled in 1850 all the tactics of Indian warfare, he was well qualified to render efficient service when called upon to aid the settlers in defending themselves against their savage foes.

In the summer of 1850, on the twentieth of August, he left the command of Colonel Ford (better known as "Old Rip") with which he was serving, on a furlough, to visit his mother's family in Bastrop county. He remained for some time with his mother, and then, in company with two others, Neal and Sullivan, started back to his command, which was then between San Antonio and the Rio Grande river. On the twentieth day of August, 1850, these youngsters were quietly pursuing their journey, suspecting no immediate danger, when they were discovered by a party of Indians, who at once charged towards them, yelling as they came, like a gang of hungry wolves. Neal and Sullivan were shot down at the first fire. Wilbarger, being untouched, put spurs to his horse and fled for his life. The Indians, supposing that Neal and Sullivan were both killed, continued on in pursuit of Wilbarger. They ran him about two miles before they succeeded in overtaking him. His horse failing, and the country being open prairie, he had but a poor chance to defend himself. He was armed with a gun and two six shooters, and when he found that escape by flight was impossible, he turned upon his savage foes and made them pay dearly for his life. This was evident from the fact that a number of pools of blood were found near the place where the Indians had killed him. His body when found was terribly mangled. The Indians, having slain the brave young fellow, returned to the place where they had shot Neal and Sullivan, fully expecting to find there the bodies of their victims. But Neal had been wounded only, and had recovered sufficiently to make his escape, before the Indians returned, to a chapparal thicket, where he remained undiscovered until they left. After they had gone he made his way to the settlement at San Patricio on foot and told the sad story of the murder of his young companions. The citizens immediately raised a party to go out and search for their bodies. They found

Sullivan lying by his horse, which had also been killed, and they gave him as decent a burial as circumstances would allow. They then went in search of young Wilbarger, whose body was found about two miles from the place where Sullivan had been killed. From marks upon the ground, it was evident he had made a desperate resistance before he fell. His body was literally cut to pieces. They also buried him as decently as they could. Young Wilbarger left a mother, two brothers and three sisters to mourn his untimely fate. He had lived all through the dangers that encompassed the young republic, and fell a prey to the savages after "annexation," when peace and safety were supposed to have been secured by union with the States. At the request of his mother, John H. Wilbarger subsequently took up and carried his remains to Bastrop county, where they were interred in the cemetery near the grave of his father, Josiah Wilbarger, who, it will be, remembered, was scalped by the Indians near Austin. The names of these men deserve to be remembered by Texans, for their blood was shed whilst in the service of the country

---

Major Ed. Burleson's Fight with Foot Indians.

MAJOR, then Lieutenant Ed Burleson, in command of a detachment of Texas Rangers, had one of the most sanguinary and desperate fights with a band of Comanches that ever occurred in Texas. —Burleson was a son of General Ed Burleson. The father distinguished himself not only at San Jacinto, but both he and the son in many a border fight with the Indians.

1850   Not many miles from the Nueces river, on the San Antonio and Laredo road, Lieutenant Burleson, with his command, was riding cheerfully forward thinking, no doubt, of the joyous Christmas frolic they would have at Fort McIntosh, then in command of Captain Sidney Burbank, and occupied by United States troops. It was a cold, cloudy morning, and if the writer mistakes not, in the month of December, 1850, and as the detachment moved forward Burleson discovered three men on horse back nearly a mile from the road, and riding leisurely across the broad prairie, with their backs to the rangers. Burleson's keen eye at once discovered that they were Indians. He directed the largest portion of his command to keep the road, and took with him nine of his men, who volunteered to help him kill or capture the Indians. Over the prairie he went, his men in a gallop, in pursuit, little dreaming of the fierce conflict before him. The three horsemen did not quicken their pace, for the prairie was broad and no timber near. Occasionally an Indian would turn his head to glance at the pursuers, but he showed no impatience to get away. The mystery was soon explained. When Burleson and his men were within fifty paces of the Indians, the Indian horsemen suddenly wheeled, and at the same time thirteen foot Indians, who had been walking in line in front of the mounted Indians, and concealed by the horses wheeled right and left into line, and stood with bows strung confronting Burleson and his men. The rangers were at the moment in line on the lope, but at the sudden revelation every horse was suddenly reined, and Burleson at the same instant cried out, "Well. boys, you see what it is, what do you say?" The answer was, "Say yourself, Lieutenant." His order then was, "Well, boys, light in," at the same time dismounting and opening fire. The words had scarcely escaped his lips until every ranger was on the ground and opening fire. The Indians on horseback dismounted in the same instant, and with bow and lance in hand charged the rangers. In a moment the combatants were mixed, the lance, the six shooter, and arrow doing their deadly work. Burleson received from the bow of the chief an arrow wound which penetrated his hat at the band, and glancing against the skull came out through the hat behind his ear, thus pinning his hat to his head. Almost in the same instant a shot from his six shooter killed the chief. The rangers were outnumbered nearly two to one, and in such close quarters the pistol has small advantage over the bow and arrow. The conflict was hand to hand, on the smooth prairie, where no cover could be

found, and where every man knew that quarter would neither
be asked or given. Warren Lyons, an interpreter, was one of
Burleson's men. He had been raised among the Comanches
and that day wore boots. Accustomed to Indian warfare he
kept continually in motion jumping, dodging and leaping,
and while fighting halloed to Burleson, "my boots are too
heavy." When almost every combatant on both sides was
either dead or wounded, Lyons, who understood the Comanche language, shouted to Burleson, "Lieutenant, they
are whipped, they are saying to one another they will have
to retreat." Four of the Indian warriors lay dead on the
field, eight or ten of the others were bloody with wounds.
The order was given by an Indian to retreat, which was
done by quickly placing those most seriously wounded on the
three horses, whose retreat was covered by the two or three
Indians who remained unhurt. Pursuit was impossible, for
not only Burleson but every one of his men able to stand up
was wounded, and two of his men, Baker Barton and William
Lackey, were killed. Baker Barton received three mortal
wounds, and died on his feet grasping the horn of his saddle. Lackey was wounded in three places. Jim Carr received four wounds. A warrior charged him, lance in hand,
and was killed by Carr with a shot from his carbine. In an
instant his carbine was again up and leveled at another Indian, who sent an arrow through his hand, penetrating the
last joint of his trigger finger and the breech of his gun; the
wood splintered and released his hand. Jack Spencer,
though wounded, was charged by three Indians at the same
time. He used his horse as a cover, but received help from
a comrade just in time. Alf, Tom and Jim Wilkerson, though
desperately wounded, fought until the Indians retreated.
During the fight Leach and a wounded Indian were both
prostrate on the ground, and but a few feet apart. Burleson's quick eye discovered the wounded Indian with a pistol in hand pointed at Leach, and turned his pistol to despatch the Indian when Leach said, "Save your fire Lieutenant. I've been watching him; he is only bluffing; there's no
load in that pistol "

Just as the fight closed Sam Duncan came on the field
and was sent by Burleson to a water hole miles away for
water. Burleson, with his wounded men, some able to ride

and some strapped on their horses, followed slowly, and when nearly famished with thirst met Duncan about one o'clock returning with water. They carried Barton, strapped to a mule, and buried him on a hill some miles from the battle ground. Bill Lackey shot through the lungs, was carried by Burleson, strapped to his horse, and did not die until after he reached the settlements. On reaching the water hole a courier was sent to Laredo for ambulances to convey the wounded rangers. The day following, those able to travel reached Fort McIntosh, where they were kindly cared for by Captain Burbank, but were in poor condition for the Christmas festivities, anticipations of which had cheered them when starting.

Burleson was so concerned for his wounded companions that he neglected the arrow that pinned his hat to his head until the swollen head bursted the hat band. On Duncan's return his rough surgery relieved Burleson by cutting the arrow in two with his butcher knife and drawing it through the scalp wound. Some days after the fight the battle ground was visited by an old Indian fighter. The bodies of the dead Comanches had disappeared, but the desperate character of the fight was revealed by what he saw, for he picked up over two hundred arrows on a space of less than half an acre. This was one of the most desperate Indian fights that has ever occurred on this continent. From the instant when the first shot was fired it did not last three minutes until the Indians were in retreat, yet in that time of the twenty-six rangers and Indians engaged nearly every man was either wounded or killed.

Major Ed Burleson soon afterwards married and spent many happy years with his noble wife on his farm near San Marcos, where he died in 1877. He was about five feet ten inches high, with compact sinewy frame, high, bold forehead, with a full, clear blue eye and a face remarkable for manly beauty. He left seven children, who promise to be useful ornaments in the State he served so well. He was a member of the Constitutional Convention of 1876, and while attending its session heard of the death by drowning of one of his boys. He never recovered from the shock, for, though in perfect health at the time, he began at once to decline in health, and in a few months died. The brave are always gentle, and this man, who began his career as a warrior at the battle of Monterey when a mere boy, and who for years as a ranger, had been inured to scenes of carnage, exhibited in the home circle all the gentleness of a child. None who ever enjoyed his hospitality will soon forget his cheerful face, his solicitude for the comfort of his guests, and the pride with which he regarded his little children.

We enjoy the blessings of peace through the privations and sacrifices of such men, and the few who remain do not receive that public consideration which they deserve.

Massacre of Wood and the Killough Family.

MR. WOOD was a native of the State of Alabama. At the age of twenty he married Miss Jane Killough, and immigrated to Texas in 1836. He settled in Cherokee county, where he followed various avocations, farming, merchandising, and occasionally teaching school. Just before the breaking out of the Cherokee war, the Indians had become so hostile in 1837 that the settlers in Cherokee county were compelled to seek safety by moving into Nacogdoches county. They remained in Nacogdoches county until the fall of the year, when it became necessary for them to return to Cherokee county to gather the crops they had planted before leaving. Accordingly, in the fall of 1837, Mr. Wood, in company with the rest of the refugees, returned to their homes. On their way they met an old friendly Indian who advised them not to go into Cherokee county, as it was full of wild Indians. To this advice the party paid no attention, and proceeded on their journey. On arriving at their homes they found that the old Indian had told them the truth as to the county being full of Indians, but the supposition has always been that they were Cherokees, or some of the tribes claiming to be friendly, instead of prairie Indians. The fences around their farms had all been burnt and their crops exposed to the ravages of stock. It was evident that Indians were or had been recently in the neighborhood, and most imprudently they concluded to remain until they could gather what little of their crops had not been destroyed. Accordingly all hands turned in to work to save what they could. They were making good progress, and were in high hopes that they would be able to finish without being molested by the Indians. One day, however, as they were going to the house for dinner, they were fired upon by a party of Indians who were lying in ambush. Several were instantly killed and the balance fled in disorder, each one trying to save his own family.

Mr. Wood succeeded in getting his family to a place of security but returning to the house afterwards to obtain some provisions for them, he unexpectedly encountered a band of the savages. He was instantly killed. They subsequently found the place where he had secreted his family, captured the whole of them and carried them off as prisoners. Not one of this unhappy family were ever heard of afterwards, with the exception of one little boy. He became a leader of considerable notoriety among the tribe by whom he had been adopted, and upon the death of the old head chief he was chosen to take his place.

Mr. Allen Killough, his wife and five children were lost in the fight. From the best information that could be obtained it is supposed that Killough was killed and his family taken prisoners; though nothing definite has ever been heard of them. Two entire families made their escape, that of another man by the name of Killough and that of a man by the name of Williams.

Old Mr. Killough (of the first family of that name) and his two sons fell dead in the yard, pierced by the bullets and arrows of the savages. There were also two other men killed about one hundred yards from the house, being five killed at the place of attack, six altogether, and ten persons taken prisoners. Among the captives there was a Miss Killough and a Miss Elizabeth Williams. They have never been heard from since.

There were three ladies left in the house unhurt, one of them the wife of old man Killough, who was killed, and two others unmarried. Strange to say, the Indians did not attempt to hurt them. There were several Mexicans with the Indians who could speak broken English. When old man Killough was killed, his wife ran out and begged the Indians to kill her also, but the Mexicans cursed her and told her to go back in the house.

When the Indians departed they left the three ladies before mentioned unhurt to weep over their dying and dead kindred and friends. The ladies were subsequently taken back to Nacogdoches county by a friendly Indian. The above facts were obtained some twelve or fifteen years ago from Mrs. —— Garrett, sister of Geo. W. Wood. This, we presume, is the same Killough family mentioned by Mr. Yoakum in his history of Texas. He states only three or four members of the Killough family escaped, and that they were brought into Nacogdoches by the Cherokees, who cunningly represented that the murder of these families was committed by the prairie Indians. We have been informed that the unfortunate members of the Killough family above mentioned were related to the Killoughs who reside in Fayette county.

Raids and Murders in Burnet County.

THE first white man killed in Burnet county by the Indians, was Robert Adams, a stockman, who lived on Morgan's creek. He was killed in 1857, while out stock hunting. Evidently the Indians had chased him some distance before coming up with him at a ravine at the foot of a mountain. When his body was found the following day it had been fearfully mutilated. In 1859, a small 1859 party of Indians came down into Burnet county, on a raid. They were discovered within a short distance of the town of Burnet, when a party of citizens collected and started in pursuit. General Adam R. Johnson, David Hunter, and Billy McGill, a lad of some thirteen years old, were among those who joined in the chase. A portion of the Indians took to the brush, while others fled across the hills, this side of the town of Burnet. General Johnson killed one of the fleeing party, and he, in turn, was slightly wounded in the nose. Billy McGill soon came up, took aim and fired, and at the crack of his gun, another Indian fell, but it proved to be a squaw. Billy, however, was after Indians, and he was not particular about the sex. The Indian shot by General Johnson was not killed on the spot, but was found the next day, with one leg buried in a pond of muddy water. Here he was despatched after being shot sixteen times. In the spring of 1861, James Gracey, a lad about thirteen or fourteen years old, went to Thomas Dawson's ranch, situated some ten miles southwest from Lampasas, in search of some horses that had strayed from home. The next morning after reaching the ranch, young Gracey, in company with another lad, whose name we do not remember, went out to look for the missing horses. When they had gone a mile or so from the ranch, Gracey's companion left him for the purpose of shooting a turkey that had flown into a tree near by. He had gone but a short distance when he heard the clattering of horses' hoofs, and looking back, he saw a party of fifteen or twenty Indians coming towards him, driving before them a large herd of stolen horses. Just then the Indians discovered young Gracey, and several immediately rushed upon him, and dismounting, they seized him, stripped him of his clothing and scalped him alive. Then telling him to go, the little fellow started off, and as he did so, the Indians followed him and amused themselves by shooting him with arrows until he fell dead. All this time Gracey's companion stood terror stricken, and momentarily expecting that his turn would come next, but at the moment the Indians were about to rush upon him, their attention was drawn to another party coming up the road. It consisted of Mr. George Baker, of Austin, on horseback, his father-in-law, Mr. Austin and his wife and infant, who were in a buggy. Those of the Indians who could be spared from the herd, immediately attacked this party. Mr. Baker, who was well armed, endeavored to cover the retreat of his family to some timber a short distance from the road. The Indians succeeded in wounding him, but Baker killed one of the foremost with his gun, which checked their advance temporarily, and he and his family were enabled to gain the shelter of the timber. Mr. Austin was an old man and unarmed, and of course could render no aid, but Mr. Baker kept the Indians at bay by firing upon them and wounding one or two others of the attacking party. Finally, however, he received a wound himself which disabled him, when his heroic wife seized his gun and used it so effectually as to keep the Indians at a respectful distance. In the mean time young Gracey's companion had taken advantage of this diversion in his favor, to make his escape, and finally reached the house of Thomas Espy, a mile or so from Dawson's ranch.

When Baker's family abandoned the buggy to retreat to the timber the horse luckily took fright and ran off at full speed towards Dawson's ranch. Just before he reached there he was overtaken and captured by several Indians who had pursued him. This, however, was witnessed by Mr. Dawson, who immediately mounted his horse and started for Lampasas to give the alarm. He had gone but a short distance, however, when he met some four or five men, all armed. He told them what had happened and of the probable murder of Baker and his family, whereupon the whole party hurried on to the rescue. When they came in sight of Baker's family, Mrs. Baker was still "holding the fort" bravely against the enemy, and as soon as the Indians saw this reinforcement approaching they hastily abandoned the field. Baker was conveyed to the house of Mr. Espy, where he was well taken care of and finally recovered from his wounds. This incident may have occurred in Lampasas, but must have been near the line if not in Burnet county. In 1862, John McGill, brother of Billy McGill, who killed the squaw, was killed by Indians about five miles west of the town of Burnet. He and his brother Sam, his cousin, Marshal Thomas, and two other boys, the oldest one about fifteen years of age, were out looking for stock. Sam and young Thomas were riding the same horse. They were discovered by a party of Indians, who immediately gave chase, and the boys fled towards the house of Thomas Shepard. Two of the Indians who were pursuing John soon overtook and shot him. The boy fell from his horse just as he reached the road. The other boys made their escape to

Shepard's house. John, when found that night, was still alive, but died soon after his friends reached him. During the spring of the same year Skaggs and Vanhook were killed while out hunting stock on the San Gabriel, in Burnet county. The former lived in Burnet, the latter in Lampasas county. In the month of February, 1863, Jonathan Ragle, Jackson and two young men by the name of Holland, who had been to mill to get their corn ground, on their return home, and within about six miles of the town of Burnet were attacked by a party of Indians from an ambuscade. The men sprang from their wagon and rushed for a mott of timber. Ragle was killed just as he was entering the mott. Jackson was pursued a little farther and also killed. The Holland boys took refuge in a small thicket and defended themselves as best they could with their only weapon, a sixshooter. One of the boys finally received a wound, destroying his eyesight. The younger one, a lad some thirteen years of age, made such a successful resistance that the Indians finally left him. When night came young Holland left his brother in the thicket and made his way to the settlements. Upon repairing to the spot next day the citizens found the bodies of Jackson and Ragle. Holland was still alive but suffering terribly from his wound. He survived nearly a week. Ragle left a wife and two children.

During the same year, while Waford Johnson, his wife and three children were returning home from a neighbor's, they were fired upon by Indians lying in ambush near the road. Johnson, his wife and their eight year old daughter were killed instantly. The youngest child, an infant eighteen months old, was shot in the arm and thrown into a brush pile, where it lay until it was found next morning. The second child, a girl five years of age, made her escape, ran to the house and there met her aunt, who had just ridden up on horseback. She took the little girl up behind her, and fled to the house of Mr. Johnson's father. In 1864 a party of Indians came on Sam Binion, about five miles north of Burnet. While attempting to reach a neighboring thicket he was roped, killed and scalped. A short time after this, J. T. Hamlin was attacked near the same place. While being pursued he picked up a charred stick. When the Indians would charge up near him he would present the stick. This ruse proved effective; the Indians thought it was a gun, and finally abandoned the chase. Not long afterwards, while plowing in his field, Hamlin discovered an Indian near him. He broke across the field, the Indian in close pursuit. When he reached the fence he was so exhausted he could not climb over. Turning round, he met a Tonkawa Indian face to face, who exclaimed: "Me good Indian; me no hurt." Hamlin declared that, had he possessed the strength, he would have killed the young brave. During the summer of this year, —— Benson went into the woods for some timber, taking with him his little boy five years of age. While out in the woods they were surrounded by Indians. Benson ran from tree to tree, trying to defend himself with his axe and an iron wedge, but he was soon killed and scalped. His little boy was taken prisoner and kept for three years, but was finally ransomed by an agent of the United States at Fort Sill, and was returned to his mother in Burnet county, where he was still living a few years ago. In the month of February, 1868, R. Smith, while out hunting stock, was killed, scalped and his body fearfully mutilated. The Indians made frequent raids into Burnet county, and, as a natural result, the citizens often had skirmishes with them. Among those who rendered efficient service to that section was Captain James P. McGill. He was among the early settlers of the county, and in 1863 and 1864 commanded a ranging company. In 1864, while scouting the country, his scouts reported Indian signs. He sent them out to look for the enemy, and they had scarcely gotten out of sight when Captain McGill heard savage yells about a mile distant. Repairing to the spot, he found that Captain Allen, who also commanded a ranging company, had engaged the enemy. McGill joined in the fight. He was wounded in the engagement, and a man by the name of Murphy killed. In 1870 a party of eighteen Comanches came down into Burnet, stole about one hundred horses, and left for the mountains. They were pursued by fifteen hardy frontiersmen, under Andrew Field. The Texans overtook them, when a running fight ensued, in which one Indian was killed, five wounded and all the stolen horses recovered. This ends our list of incidents in Burnet county.

Murders and Battles in San Saba and Llano Counties.

CHANCY COUCH moved to San Saba county in about the year 1858 and resided there until his death. We think it was in the year 1860 that he left his house one morning to go into the woods for board timber. He requested his son to follow him in an hour or so, and by the time he arrived he would have the timber ready for sawing.

The son, in obedience to his father's instructions, had 1858 started out to join him, and when two or three miles from home he came across the wagon and oxen but his father was not with them. After searching well nigh all the day for his father he discovered late in the afternoon some buzzards collecting at a certain point. Cautiously approaching the spot where the ill omened birds were congregating, his worst fears were realized when he discovered his father's dead body pierced with arrows and so mutilated as to be almost beyond recognition. During the year 1862 the Indians killed Ben F. Linn. Linn was a young man who belonged to the ranging service. In 1862 he, with Tom Sloan, Ash Feazle, Bill York and two or three others, were out cow hunting on Deer creek, in San Saba county. They discovered a body of about ten Indians. The cow hunters immediately charged upon the Indians, who fled precipitately. A running fight was kept up for several miles, the cow boys firing into the Indians with their sixshooters and the savages shooting back with their bows and arrows. During the chase young Linn was shot in the lower part of the body and died a few hours afterward. During the same year a party of Indians surprised and killed Tom Cabinass, on Cherokee creek.

In the fall of 1862, Captain Williams, with a young man whose name was King, and two other young men, started from Bluffton with a drove of beeves to take them to Williams's ranch, in San Saba county. When not far from Baby

Head mountain, in the southern part of San Saba county, Captain Williams left the herd in charge of the three young men and rode off in the direction of a spring, saying that he would overtake them in a short time. After driving the beeves a few hundred yards the young men were startled by wild and savage yells and the clatter of horses' feet in their rear, and upon looking back they saw eight or ten Indians charging down upon them. King, who was riding a mule, was on the left of the herd, the other two young men were a little to the right, and ran off to the right of the cattle as fast as their horses could carry them. The last time they saw King he was vainly trying to get his mule to run. The next day his dead body was found a few hundred yards from where they last saw him. Nearly one half mile further on, the searching party found the body of Captain Williams. He had been shot with arrows, and after falling from his horse the savages had crushed his head with stones and scalped him. The tracks of Captain Williams's horse showed that he had got nearly to the spring and then turned and loped back in the direction of the cattle, and passed in a few feet of where King's mule was standing when last seen, and on for about a half mile where his body was found. It is supposed that Williams heard the yelling of the Indians and rushed back to see what was happening, and that seeing King in danger, he charged upon the Indians, thinking he might frighten them away, and depending upon the swiftness of his horse (which was a very fine one) for his safety. Captain Williams was a truly brave man, and had been of great service to the frontier in protecting it from the raids of the savage. When killed he was unarmed, and his death was due, no doubt, to that fact. The father of young King still lives in San Saba county. For several years after the close of the war the Indians continued their depredations in San Saba county. They killed Beardy Hall and Boze Woods in the western part of the county, and a man by the name of Merryman, on Jerry's Branch, about two miles north of the town of San Saba. The particulars are not at hand. C. C. Carter resided on the head waters of the Lampasas river, about sixteen miles north of Lampasas springs. Some time in 1865, he made an appointment to visit the house of his son-in-law, distant about four miles. When he had

HE KEEPS HIS APPOINTMENT BUT DROPS DEAD
AT THE GATE.

arrived within about a mile of his destination, he was fired upon by a party of Indians, who were in ambuscade, awaiting his approach. Although mortally wounded, he put spurs to his horse and fled as fast as possible. The Indians endeavored to intercept him, but failed. He succeeded in reaching his son-in-law's house, but dropped dead at the gate. The daughter ran to his assistance, but too late, as the Indians had accomplished their deadly mission, and Mr. Carter expired in a few moments afterwards.

In the spring of 1867 Miller and Morell loaded their wagon with corn and went to a mill about thirty miles distant to get it ground. On their way back, when crossing the valley of a small creek called Brady, they were attacked by a party of Indians on foot, who suddenly rushed out upon them from a dense thicket near the road side. The two men in the wagon, seeing the great odds against them, and having no arms but six shooters, put the lash to their horses and dashed down a steep, rocky hill. The jolting of the wagon caused Miller's six shooter to fall out of the scabbard, and one of the foremost Indians snatched it up and emptied its contents at him, but without effect. They then rushed furiously upon the wagon, using their bows, arrows and spears, as they had no fire arms. Miller and Morell used their pistol with deadly effect. Whilst some of the Indians were trying to spear them or shoot them with arrows, others endeavored to stop the wagon by throwing large stones in front of the wheels. In this manner the fight continued for some time, until Morell succeeded in killing another Indian with the last cartridge in his six shooter, which caused them to fall back temporarily once more. Seizing the opportunity, the men cut loose one of the best horses from the harness, mounted him and fled to a dense thicket near by. Finding it was impossible to enter it on horseback, they dismounted and went in on foot, and secreted themselves in the thickest brush they could find. The Indians came up, took the horse, but did not venture in the thicket. During the fight Miller received twenty-seven and Morell twenty-one wounds. That none of these wounds were fatal can only be accounted for by the fact that when the Indians attacked the wagon a drizzling rain was falling, which slackened their bow-strings, rendering it impossible to send the arrows with much force. The Indians returned to the wagon, emptied the corn meal in the road, took all the horses and left for parts unknown. The two wounded men suffered terribly for want of water, and as soon as they were satisfied the Indians had gone, Morell, who was not quite so badly hurt as his companion, crawled to a creek near by, and after he had slaked his own thirst, he pulled off one of his boots, filled it with water, and with great difficulty managed to carry it back to where he had left Miller, thereby, no doubt, saving his life. Miller and Morell not reaching home at the time they were expected, a party went out to look for them. When found they were in a terrible condition. They were unable to walk, and their clothes were stiffened with clotted blood. They were taken home, and both eventually recovered from their numerous wounds. These men lived in McCulloch county.

Reverend Jonas Dancer resided in Llano county, and so far as we know was the first man killed in that county by the Indians. The author first became acquainted with him in Travis county, where he lived in the year 1850. Some two years later, attracted by the mineral resources of Llano, he moved to that county. At the time Mr. Dancer moved into Llano there was but one other American settler in the county. After prospecting a couple of years, Mr. Dancer finally settled in a romantic little spot called "Honey Creek Cove." Llano county has long since been celebrated for its mineral resources, mountain scenery, fertile valleys, rippling streams and nutritious grasses. The spot selected by Mr. Dancer was one of the most picturesque in the county. Here game of all kinds and wild honey abounded in the greatest quantity. All of these combined attractions soon drew others to that section, and it was not long until the sound of the ax and hammer of the pioneer could be heard in many directions as the settlers began to construct their rude log cabins. Mr. Dancer was of the Methodist creed, and he soon succeeded in building up quite a large church. He was the first man to introduce the blessed gospel in that wilderness country. For several years these hardy pioneers lived in peace and happiness, pursuing their various avocations, but their dark day came at last. On the twenty-third day of May, 1859, if we have not been misinformed, Mr.

Dancer and others were to meet at a certain point to cut out a new road from Llano to the city of Austin. Always punctual in his appointments, Mr. Dancer, with tools in hand, repaired to the spot. From some cause the others failed to come. Dancer had a couple of horses which he hoppled, and thinking the balance of the party would soon arrive, began work by himself. Whilst thus engaged he was attacked by a party of five or six Indians. Being unarmed, Dancer fled to a deep ravine, closely pursued by the savages, who it seems attempted to rope him, but failed. Dancer, having reached the bed of the ravine, the Indians rushed up to the bluffs overlooking the same and poured a volley of arrows into the body of the unfortunate man. Finally overcome with loss of blood from his wounds, he walked around in front of a projecting rock in the bluff, deliberately sat down on a rock bench and there expired. The savages then came upon him, scalped him and otherwise mutilated his body. Such was the condition in which his body was found the following day by a searching party, who delivered it to his sorrowing widow and now fatherless children. The loss of this good man, who was looked upon as the father of the county, spread profound grief throughout that section. As a minister of the gospel, he was faithful to his charge; as a christian, he was faithful to duty, and as a neighbor, he was kind and obliging. The frontier suffered an irreparable loss in his death.

In May, 1862, Mr. Denyer went unarmed to look for stock. When half a mile from home, a party of Indians attacked him. He fled, the Indians pursuing and shooting at him. None of the arrows brought him down, and as he neared home he called to his family. Mrs. Denyer ran to him with his gun; as she did so the savages fled. Denyer was wounded fatally, and died the next day. A wife and several children mourned his loss.

In the fall of 1863, Harrison Miller, who had a sheep ranch on a small stream in Llano county, while eating dinner at his house, was suddenly surrounded by a party of Indians, and the first intimation he had of their presence was the whizzing of arrows through the door and windows. Springing up quickly, Miller seized his shot gun, which he presented, and in this way kept the Indians at bay. Watching his opportunity when all the Indians had congregated in front of the door, Miller sprang out of a back window, ran down the bluff into a little creek and made his escape. After plundering the house the Indians left, and within about one mile came upon Barzilla Payne, an old man, some sixty years of age, who also had a sheep ranch. Payne had gone out in search of his flock, which was being herded by a negro boy, and, after finding it, sent the boy to the house. The boy had scarcely gotten out of sight when he heard the firing of guns, and soon thereafter heard the old man cry out: "You can have me now." It was this same party, we believe, who killed Beardy Hall in San Saba county. These Indians, after killing Payne, were pursued, overtaken, and one Indian was killed and the balance dispersed. Soon afterwards the whites came across a lone Indian, by him himself, mounted upon a superb horse. The defiant rascal would canter along ahead of them, shaking his bow and lance, slapping his thighs and making all manner of contemptuous gestures. At first the Texans thought he was leading them into an ambuscade, but finally concluded to give him a chase. In going over rough ground the Indian's horse disabled himself in some way, whereupon the Texans rushed upon the Indian and slew him. Near the line of Gillespie and Llano counties, but in the latter, lived Mrs. Martha Youngblood, a widow with several children. In January, 1865, while two of her children, a boy about six years old, and a girl of four, were playing some distance from the house, a party of Indians crawled up near them, killed the boy and proceeded to the house. Mrs. Youngblood, seeing them coming, barred the doors. Denying the savages admittance, they tore off a plank from the walls of the room. The little girl, who had followed the Indians unobserved to the house, was standing near. The Indians attempted to rush in, but were met by the muzzle of a gun in the hands of Mrs. Youngblood. This caused them to fall back, and the little girl slipped in through the aperture made by the Indians. Thus, through the bravery of this lady was her own life and that of her children saved. A period of three years elapses, during which time, no doubt, many murders occurred, but we have no account of them.

The last we have to record, is the bloodiest tragedy ever enacted in Llano county. The name of Matilda S. Friend, even to this day, produces a thrill of horror in the breasts of those who are familiar with the history of the sad event which we are about to relate. The Rev. Jonas Dancer, whose cruel death has been recorded in the preceding pages, was the father of the illfated woman who, upon arriving at the age of womanhood, had married John S. Friend. The home of Mrs. Friend was situated in Legion Valley, some fifteen miles south of Llano, a small town containing at that time about one hundred inhabitants. Legion Valley is surrounded on all sides by mountains, with the beautiful Hond Creek meandering through it, finally emptying into the Sandy, a tributary of the Colorado river. On the fifth of February, 1868, while Mrs. Friend, in company with two or three ladies and a lot of children, were at the cow pen, situated about one hundred yards distant from her house, they were startled at the sight of some fifteen Indians passing by. The women, with the children, fled to the house and barred the door. The Indians, upon discovering that there was no man about the premises, turned their course towards the house also. At the time the attack was made upon the house, accounts vary as to the number of inmates, one placing it at six and two at eight. From them all we will try and give what seems to be the most reliable data. The names of the unfortunate inmates, as near as we can ascertain, are as ' follows: Mrs. Friend, Mrs. Samantha Johnson, Mrs. Rebecca Johnson, Miss Amanda Townsend (sister of one of the Mrs. Johnsons), a little girl named Malinda Cordle, Lee Temple Friend, stepson of Mrs. Friend, (a mere lad about eight years old), and two baby children, one being the child of Rebecca and the other of Samantha Johnson. The house was made of pickets, and when the Indians found that the door had been barred, they pulled out a couple of pickets. The only resistance made was by Mrs. Friend, who insisted upon the other ladies joining her in the defense, but they counseled conservatism, thinking probably the Indians would not harm them if they submitted quietly. There were two guns in the house, and Mrs. Friend, seeing an Indian about to enter through the aperture made by pulling out the pickets, seized one of the weapons and attempted to shoot, but the gun was wrested from her hands by an Indian buck, who doubtless would have shot her had not another Indian (possibly fearing an alarm being given from the report of the gun) snatched the gun from his hands. The Indian who had attempted to shoot was then struck by Mrs. Friend with a smoothing iron, which came near knocking him down. He recovered himself, drew an arrow from his quiver, and shot Mrs. Friend in the side. The arrow, striking a rib, glanced around the breast bone and came out on the opposite side. A second arrow passed through her arm, while the third struck her in the breast. After receiving the third wound, being unable to make further resistance, she calmly took her seat upon a bed, and leaned her head against a bed post. Thinking she was dead, one of the barbarous wretches commenced scalping her. This gave her so much pain she threw up her hand and caught hold of the knife. The Indian, in pulling the knife through her hand, cut it severely. In attempting to seize the knife the second time, the savage dealt her three blows, which completely disabled her. The brute then finished the operation of scalping at his leisure, and left the poor woman for dead. One of these devils incarnate, thinking there was possibly life remaining in his victim, returned, and gave the arrow sticking in her breast several severe jerks backward and forward, to see if she would flinch. Mrs. Friend, noticing the Indian returning, placed herself in exactly the same position she was while being scalped, and remained as if lifeless during all this painful torture. Satisfying himself that she was dead, the Indian left.

The ladies and children who were in the house when the attack was made, were all taken prisoners. Hearing their departing cries, Mrs. Friend arose and attempted to walk to the window, but was so weak from loss of blood was unable to stand. However, she managed to crawl to an opening in the side of the house, through which, with a sorrowful heart. she took the last look at her captured friends. When the India were out of sight, Mrs. Friend bound a cloth over her head, and, wounded as she was, went out and gathered up what few things the Indians had left and put them back in the house and shut the door. She then started on foot for a neighbor's house, a Mr. Bradford's, about a mile and a half distant. It was about sunset when she started, and she reached there about eight o'clock. On her way she slaked her thirst with snow, which had fallen that day sufficiently to cover the ground. As she approached the house, her presence was made known to the family by the fierce barking of the dogs. Bradford came out of the house and met her. A terrible sight she was, wounded, scalped and bleeding. Not knowing who it was in the dark, Bradford ran back into the house. She called to him, told him who she was, and he then came to her relief. He took her in, and at her request he proceeded to extract the arrows from her body. Bradford and all his family then fled from the house (fearing the Indians would attack it), and left Mrs. Friend all night alone, not even taking time to dress her wounds, or remove her bloody clothes. They merely made a little fire, set a bucket of water by her, and left the poor woman by herself, two miles from any other house.

About eight o'clock next morning two widow ladies came to her relief. The cloth on her head had dried and stuck so fast to the wound that it could only be removed by the use of hot water. Her whole body was so swollen from her wounds that it was with great difficulty her clothes were taken off. These benevolent ladies did all they could for her relief, but it was nearly eight o'clock in the evening before a physician arrived to dress her wounds. It was nearly a year before Mrs. Friend recovered, but she finally got well, and when heard from last, we have been informed, was living in the State of Kansas. Let us now return to the scene of the bloody massacre, and follow the unfortunate prisoners. During the night of the same day a runner arrived in the town of Llano announcing the sad tragedy. Early the next morning ten or twelve citizens were in the saddle, and off for Legion Valley. Arriving upon the ground, it was ascertained that the Indians had gone off in a southerly direction. "When about one mile and a half from the house (says Mr. Luce, now of Burnet county, but then a resident of Llano, and whose account of the pursuit we substantially adopt) we found on a large rock, six or eight feet high, Mrs. Johnson's babe, with its brains knocked out. Four miles further on the trail, on top of a mountain, we found

where they had stopped, built a fire, roasted their meat, and
from impress ons on the ground, we judged they had stopped
here for awhile.   At this place a trail or foot path was discovered leading out from the camp to a thicket about one
hundred yards distant.   Following the trail to this point,
we found the mangled body of Mrs. Johnson's eighteen
year old sister.   She had been tied down upon the cold
ground, which was covered with snow, and from all appearances, had been outraged in the most brutal manner.   She
was then killed, and her body mutilated almost beyond
recognition.   Continuing the pursuit some three miles further, off the mountains and down into the valley, not far
from the J. C. Talley place, we found the body of Mrs.
Johnson, stripped of nearly all her clothing, and the body
nearly eaten up by the hogs.   At this point our party divided,
a portion continuing the pursuit, while the balance remained
behind to bury the dead.   I, with six or seven others, pursued the trail.   Among those whose names I can now recall,
were George Miller, Orville Oatman and Frank Holden; the
names of the others I do not now remember.   The Indians,
after winding through the mountains, and collecting about
thirty head of horses, turned due west.   We followed them
five days, often traveling in the night when the trail could
be seen.   From the little tracks we had seen around the
water holes on the trail, we knew that the red devils had
the eight year old son of Mrs. Friend, and we continued the
pursuit to near Devil's River, and were but a short distance
behind them, when, for want of food, our horses gave out
and left us afoot."   In the account given us by Mr. Luce,
he says there were three women and three children in the
house when the attack was made.   We think it more than
likely there were seven or eight, as another account we
have states that the little girl, Malinda Cordle, was carried
off a captive with Mrs. Friend's little boy, remained a captive about eight months, when she was recovered by a body
of United States dragoons and sent to Fort Leavenworth,
Kansas; from there to Fort Arbuckle, and then returned
to her relatives in Texas.   The little boy remained a prisoner nearly five years, but was finally recovered by his
grandfather, Rev. Leonard S. Friend.   The little fellow, at
the time of his reclamation, could speak nothing but the

Indian dialect. It will be remembered that we mention two
ladies by the name of Johnson—each with a young babe.
The account which gives their names states that they
met a fate similar to the account Mr. Luce gives. In 1870
Mr. Whitlock was killed. He was a cabinet maker, but
this business not proving remunerative, he engaged in farming and stock raising. While at work on his farm, he
heard an unusual noise at his house, where he had left his
wife and two children, his little son being with him. Upon
looking up, he discovered a party of Indians surrounding his
house. Though unarmed, he rushed to the rescue of his wife
and children, but was killed in the attempt to reach them.
The wife and two children were then murdered and the little
boy taken prisoner. The following incident did not occur in
this section of the State, but Colonel Dalrymple being so well
known in Llano, we have concluded that this would be an
appropiate place for its insertion. In 1869 Colonel Dalrymple
went with Colonel Snively and a number of others from
Georgetown on a gold hunting expedition to the Wichita
mountains. After reaching that dangerous and unsettled
region of country they were attacked by a large party of
Indians, who fought them for some time at long taw, and
finding they could not effect much in that way, suddenly
charged upon the gold hunters, and a hand to hand conflict
ensued. Every one fought for his own life, and "upon his
own hook." One huge Indian rushed at Colonel Dalrymple
and endeavored to thrust his spear through him. But he
missed his aim, and only succeeded in sending it through
the Colonel's arm. Colonel Dalrymple, being a man of
great strength, seized the handle of the spear and broke it
in the middle. The order to retreat was given at that moment, and the Colonel rode off, carrying the spear and
broken handle in his arm until he reached a place of safety,
where it was extracted with great difficulty. He came
very near bleeding to death before his wound could be attended to properly. These Indians had good fire arms, and
they wounded a number of the gold hunters and killed
some of their horses in the fight. They paid pretty dearly,
however, for their victory, as they were seen carrying off
a number of their dead and wounded. Colonel Dalrymple
still resides at Georgetown.

Fight on Packsaddle Mountain.

THE following account of the fight on Packsaddle mountain, Llano county, between eight cowboys and twenty-one Apache Indians, was obtained from an old Texan and frontiersman who was in the vicinity at the time. About the first of August, 1873, I left Austin in company with two of my friends to search for a mythical silver mine said to exist somewhere on Packsaddle mountain in 1873 Llano county. On our arrival at the mountain we searched it thoroughly, as we supposed, for two days without finding so much as a "color," to say nothing of the camp of twenty-one Indians, who, at that very time, had established a rendezvous on the mountain. As we could find no trace of a mine on Packsaddle my two companions concluded they would go on and search for the silver mine said to have been worked by the old Spaniards near the old San Saba fort. I declined going any further with them for two reasons: In the first place I was mounted on a miserable little Spanish tacky that, when so disposed, would "buck" for half an hour under the shade of one tree without advancing a foot; and the second place, I and the ranging company to which I belonged, consisting of seventy-five or eighty men, had, in 1848, searched every nook and corner within five miles of the old fort without finding a vestige of the mine. I therefore told my two companions that if they still thought it worth while to go on to the old San Saba fort that I would wait for them at John Duncan's ranch, about two miles distant from Packsaddle mountain. Accordingly, we went to Duncan's ranch, and the next morning my friends left me there and started for the San Saba fort. There was a small stream near Duncan's, well stocked with perch, and by way of passing the time I concluded to go a fishing. I had gone, I suppose, about a mile down the creek, fishing as I went in various pools with more or less success, when I came to a deep one that was swarming with perch.

While fishing there and catching perch as fast as I could throw in my hook my attention was drawn to the rapid firing of guns in the direction of Packsaddle mountain, about a mile distant. At first I supposed that some cow boys were shooting their pistols at a mark, but I noticed that occasionally five or six guns would fire simultaneously, which satisfied me that a fight of some kind was going on. As I was at least a mile from Duncan's, and on foot, with no arms but a small pocket five shooter, and was not in very good health anyhow, I concluded to make my way back to the ranch as speedily as possible. So I gathered up my fish and started, keeping close to the timber bordering the creek, so that, as our generals used to say during the war, I might quickly change my base if it became necessary to do so. I had gone probably half a mile when I discovered two men galloping toward me. As they were too far off when I first saw them to tell whether they were white men or Indians, I partially changed my base to get under cover of the timber. As they came nearer I saw they were white men, and went out to meet them. They told me they had just had a hard fight with the Indians on Packsaddle mountain, that four of their men were wounded, and that they were on their way to Mr. Duncan's to ascertain if the people would give them permission to bring them there. I told them I was sure the people there would willingly do all in their power to aid their wounded men, and that I thought they had better return at once and bring them to the ranch. They concluded to do so and went off in the direction of Packsaddle, and I went on to the house. In about an hour the boys made their appearance at the ranch, all of them on horseback, although three of them were very severely wounded, one of them, the eldest of the Moss brothers, as I thought fatally. A messenger was immediately sent off to the nearest town for a physician, and everything was done that could be done for the wounded by Mr. Duncan and his family. From those who participated in this fight on Packsaddle mountain I obtained the following particulars relative to it:

A party of twenty-one Indians came into Llano county and had established a permanent camp on Packsaddle mountain, from whence they proceeded to reconnoitre the adjacent country to ascertain the best localities for plunder.

Late in the evening of the ninth of August, 1873, a cow came running up to Mr. Moss's ranch with an arrow sticking in her body, which was the first intimation the people had of the presence of Indians in the vicinity. It so happened there were eight cowboys at this ranch, and the next morning, each armed with a Spencer rifle and six shooter, started off with a determination of finding these Indians if they were still within the limits of the county. They had gone perhaps seven or eight miles when they came across a recent trail, made, as they supposed, by at least twenty Indians, who were riding shod horses. Nothing daunted by the prospect of coming into conflict with such a large force, the boys took the trail at once, which led off in the direction of Packsaddle mountain. They followed it until they came to the foot of the mountain, when it merged into an old Indian trail leading directly towards the summit. As the sign of recent travel over this trail was quite fresh, the boys were confident they would find the Indian camp somewhere on the mountain, and dismounting from their horses, they examined their arms to see that they were in order for the anticipated scrimmage. Remounting, they cautiously followed the old trail, which was very rough, until they had ascended perhaps half way to the summit, when they discovered an Indian sitting on a ledge of rocks, who had been stationed there, no doubt, to give warning of the approach of anyone from the valley below. When the boys first saw him he had a small looking glass in his hand, and was busily engaged in adorning his copper colored "phiz" with streaks of white and black paint. So engrossed was he with the labors of the toilet that he did not notice the approach of the boys until they were within a few yards of him, when he suddenly dropped his looking glass and paints, gave a keen yell and dashed off (as the boys supposed) for the neighboring camp. They followed him as rapidly as the nature of the ground would permit, and after going a short distance they came to a small plateau or mesa, at one end of which was the Indian camp, and at the other their horses were staked out to grass. Taking in the situation at once, the boys dashed in between the Indian encampment and their horses, and dismounting, made ready for battle. By this time the Indians had seized their guns, and after firing a volley at the boys, they rushed upon them in a body to drive them from their position and regain possession of their horses. At the first fire four of the boys were wounded, three of them so badly they were unable to fight, leaving only five to contend against twenty-one Indians. But as the Indians came to close quarters the boys poured such a continuous and deadly fire amongst them from their Spencer guns and six shooters that they faltered and finally fell back to their original position at the encampment. They quickly formed again, however, and again charged upon the boys, evidently with the determination of driving them from their position at all hazards; but the young Texans stood their ground firmly, and a desperate fight ensued, almost hand to hand, with six shooters, and again the Indians were repulsed and driven back to their encampment. Again and again they renewed their attack and endeavored to force the boys from the position they had taken between them and their horses, but each time with the same result. Finally they fell back into some thick underbrush in the rear of their encampment, which hid them entirely from view, and the boys, supposing they had abandoned the hopeless contest, laid down their guns and turned their attention to their wounded comrades.

While thus engaged the Indians, headed by their indomitable young chief who had made himself conspicuous in the fight by his daring, emerged from the thicket, apparently with the intention of making another charge upon the Texans. The latter quickly sprang to their guns and quietly awaited the onset. But when the Indians saw that the boys were ready to give them the same reception they had met with in their previous charges they advanced but a few paces beyond the thicket and came to a halt. Their young chief then turned to them and made them a harangue. The boys could hear every word he uttered, but although they could not understand what he said, they knew by his vehement gestures that he was urging his men to make one more effort to drive them from their position. But his harangue was of no avail. The sight of the cow boys and their deadly Spencer rifles leveled towards them was too much for them and they refused to advance. At length, finding he could not induce his men to make another charge upon the

Texans, he waived them back contemptuously with his hand, and, turning, he deliberately advanced solitary and alone towards them. He had his Winchester rifle in his hand, and every few paces he would stop and fire upon them. In this way he continued to advance until he was within a few yards of the place where the boys were stationed when he fell dead, pierced by half a dozen bullets. He evidently made up his mind to die rather than return in disgrace to his people. As soon as he fell his men retreated into the thicket, carrying with them in their blankets several of their dead and wounded. Their chief and two others were left dead on the ground. The boys, of course, did not attempt to follow them, as one-half their number was wounded, three of them very severely. The Indians lost everything they had except the arms the survivors carried off with them. The boys got all their horses, among them some very valuable ones; a large lot of robes, some fine Navajo blankets, silver mounted saddles and bridles, Winchester and Henry rifles and revolvers and all the camp equipments. Among the saddles was one marked with the name of the maker and "Tucson, Arizona." From this fact, as well as the fact that these Indians were much better armed and equipped than Comanches, it is supposed that they were Apaches from Arizona. This was the last raid the Indians ever made into Llano county. The following are the names of the boys who participated in the fight: W. B. Moss and his two brothers, S. R. and S. B.. Moss, Eli Lloyd, Archer Martin, Pinckney Ayres, Robert Brown and E. D. Harrington.

The author has been informed, whether truly or not he is unable to say, that the State of Texas had presented each of these boys with a fine Winchester rifle; but, if this is not so, all he has to say is that it ought to be.

Blanco, Mason, Kimble and Gillespie Counties.

IN December, 1865, Jackson, in company with his son-in-law, Mark Stewart, both of whom lived in Blanco county, were out in the woods hunting hogs. After hunting awhile without success, they separated. Soon after the separation Stewart heard Jackson call for him, apparently in great distress. Riding to the top of the hill, Stewart saw his father-in-law surrounded by Indians. Seeing that **1865** it would bé impossible to render him assistance, Stewart fled home, raised a party and returned, but too late. The old man had been stabbed and horribly butchered. On the twenty-third day of July, 1868, while Thomas Phelps and wife were fishing in Cypress creek, they were startled by the cries of a negro boy running toward them. The little fellow was being pursued by Indians, but dodged into a corn field and made his escape. The Indians then attacked Phelps and wife, killed them both, stripped them of their clothing, and, as they passed the house of the mother of Mrs. Phelps, hoisted upon their lances the bloody clothing of their victims to the view of the mother of the deceased lady. Mr. and Mrs. Phelps left two small children and a large relationship to mourn their loss. The Indians then went to the house of Benjamin Phelps, stole a lot of horses and passed on to the residence of a Mr. Johnson, where they murdered one of his sons, about twenty-one years of age, and took his twelve year old boy a prisoner, tied him on a horse and departed. The Indians, twenty-one in number, were overtaken by fifteen whites near Fort Mason, and being hotly pursued, they untied their little prisoner, set him down unhurt and then continued their flight. Having recaptured the boy, the Texans abandoned the chase and returned home, taking with them a lot of captured horses. During the year 1867, Allen Gentry, his fourteen year old brother and Felix Hall—all residents of Mason county—were out in the woods one day hunting hogs. After hunting

awhile the party separated, Allen Gentry going in one direction, his brother and Hall in another.   Soon after the separation, Allen Gentry was attacked by Indians.   In his flight
Gentry passed near his brother and Hall without seeing
them.   Instead of coming to his rescue, they took fright and
fled.   Gentry might possibly have escaped, but in trying to
ascend a steep mountain his horse failed, and this compelled
him to retrace his steps.   Failing to meet his brother and
Hall, and finding that the Indians were rapidly gaining
upon him, he dismounted, ran into a thicket, and from the
indications had made a gallant defense with his Henry rifle.
He was finally killed, however, scalped, and his body butchered in the usual manner.   Gentry left a wife and several
children.   His widow has since married, and lives in Mason
county.   In the fall of the same year Francis Johnson went
out early one morning afoot in search of his horse, found
him within about three miles of home, and while riding
along leisurely on his way back, was suddenly confronted
by a party of savages.   Being unarmed, Johnson sought
to escape by flight, and ran into a cluster of bushes.   The
Indians soon came upon him, killed and scalped him, placed
a couple of red painted arrows across his breast, took his
horse and left.   Mr. Johnson left a wife and ten children,
several of whom still reside in Mason.

John Williams and Nick Coulston were near neighbors
and lived on Bear creek, in Kimble county.   In the fall of
the year 1871 these two gentlemen went out to Fort Mc-
Kavett to purchase ammunition and supplies.   At the house
of either Williams or Coulston, we are not positive which,
there were several ladies and also a young man employed to
work on the farm.   At this time they had no apprehension
about Indians, as none had been seen for some time.   While
the young man was engaged at work on the farm some distance from the house the ladies discovered a party of Indians approaching, whereupon they immediately shut and
barred the doors.   The Indians at first were rather cautious
in approaching the house, but finding that no hostile demonstrations were made by the inmates they began to amuse
themselves by catching and riding the calves and sheep
around the yard and lots, varying the sport by shooting the
pigs, chickens and ducks with their arrows.   The Indians

THE FARCE BEFORE THE TRAGEDY.

were having a merry old time generally, not suspecting any resistance by the inmates. There were several loaded guns in the house, but the women did not intend to make use of them except as a last resort, hoping the Indians would leave. In this, however, they were mistaken, for after the red skins had tired of their amusements they turned their attention to business and began to batter down the doors. One of the ladies then fired a pistol to notify the young man in the field of their danger. This drew his attention and he foolishly ran towards the house without any arms. The Indians rushed on him as he came up, shot and scalped him in view of the women in the house. Seeing that the poor young fellow was being murdered Mrs. Coulston seized a shot gun, slipped it through an opening in the wall and poured a load of buckshot into the back of the Indian who was in the act of scalping him. The Indian dropped his knife and ran, the blood streaming from his back as he ran and soon fell dead. This made the Indians furious, as they had expected no resi tance from the white squaws. But fearing to force an entrance into the house they gathered some combustible materials with the intention of setting it on fire. As they were doing this Mrs. Coulston fired several times at them with some effect. It so happened that about this time Williams and Coulston were on their way home and were within a mile or so of the house. They discovered the trail the Indians had made, and alarmed for the safety of the family, they hurried on as fast as possible. The Indians had placed a spy on an eminence some distance off to watch if any one approached. He discovered the two men coming, ran in and gave the alarm. The Indians then withdrew from the house and concealed themselves in the brush. As the two men came galloping up the Indians rushed from their place of concealment and fired upon them, killing Williams's horse, which fell dead at the yard gate. But Williams was unhurt and nothing daunted he leveled his repeating rifle and he and his companion began pouring hot lead into their ranks. The Indians, discouraged by such determination and bravery, and the loss of one of their braves and the wounding of several others, gathered up their dead and wounded and left.

Mrs Coulston is said to have been a remarkably intelligent

lady, of fine physique, and possessed of rare personal beauty. Of her superior womanly courage, the above incident speaks in stronger terms than any language we might use. In the fall of 1872, a marauding party of Indians came down into Kimble county and stole a lot of horses. James Bradberry raised a party of his neighbors, and after pursuing the trail some distance, they came upon the Indians quite unexpectedly. Bradberry, who was in front some distance, discovered a single Indian by himself. He dismounted, cut down on him with his Henry rifle and brought the Indian to the ground. The Indians then appeared in force, when Bradberry slew another. The fight now became hot, during which four Indians were slain. They were too numerous, however, and Bradberry ordered a retreat. Just as he had mounted, and was in the act of turning his horse, he was shot in the back, the ball passing entirely through his body, and he fell dead. Before moving to Kimble, Bradberry lived in Williamson county, where the author formed his acquaintance. His sons, James and Theodore, now live in the Bradberry settlement, four miles west of Mason, on the road to Fort McKavett. During the year 1865, there lived at the head spring of the Perdinales, in Gillespie county, Mathew Taylor and family. With him also lived his son-in-law, Ely McDonald, and his family, composed of himself, wife and five children. About one or two o'clock on the eighth of August, 1865, during the absence of Mathew and his son J. J. Taylor, from the ranch, a band of twenty Kiowa Indians approached the house and secreted themselves in a thicket near the spring. Mrs. Gilead Taylor (another daughter-in-law of Mathew Taylor, who likewise lived with her father-in-law) went to the spring for some water. Just as she approached the spring she was shot in the breast with an arrow by an Indian lying in ambuscade. She turned and fled towards the house, but as she ran she was shot with an arrow in the back. She continued running until she reached the house, but in endeavoring to enter, she tripped and fell backwards, driving the arrow which was sticking in her back entirely through her body, killing her instantly. The Indians followed her and attacked the house, but Mr. McDonald, who was within, saw them approaching, and alone and unaided, he fought them for two hours, and prevented them from entering. At length, finding it would be a hard matter to take the house, the Indians resorted to strategy, They hoisted a white flag as an indication that they desired to make peace, and then retreated out of sight. When the Indians attacked the house Mrs. Hannah Taylor, McDonald's mother-in-law, ran out on the side opposite to that where the Indians made their appearance, and concealed herself in some bushes, and there she remained undiscovered until they went off, but they soon came back with reinforcements. McDonald, supposing they had abandoned the idea of making another attempt to take the house, was standing outside of his yard near the gate, when they suddenly showed themselves again. They rushed upon him, shot him several times, stabbed him repeatedly with their butcher knives, and then scalped him. They also scalped Mrs. Gilead Taylor, the lady they had shot at the spring, as previously mentioned. They then stripped her and McDonald of all their clothing, and entering the house they took all they wanted and destroyed what remained. They even ripped open the bed ticks and scattered their contents about the yard. One can readily imagine what must have been Mrs. McDonald's feelings whilst witnessing these scenes of carnage and rapine, and momentarily expecting that she and her helpless little children would be killed by these devils incarnate. Mahala McDonald, her eldest daughter, then a girl about ten years of age, was standing near the fire when the Indians entered the house, and one of them from "pure cussedness" pushed her into it, burning her hand so badly that her fingers were all drawn up, and out of shape, and they remain in that condition to this day.

After the Indians had plundered the house, they took Mrs. McDonald and her five children prisoners, tied them on horses, and carried them off. They subjected her and her children to the most brutal treatment. For the first six weeks of her captivity she was kept closely tied to prevent her from escaping. Her little children often suffered so much for the want of water that their tongues would protrude from their mouths, and when they cried for it, if a pond or creek was near by, the brutes would throw the little creatures into them, and amuse themselves by witnessing their struggles to regain the shore. Mrs. McDonald was a captive among the Indians for eight months, when she and her youngest child were ransomed in Kansas. The other four children were also shortly afterwards ransomed, and Mrs. McDonald returned with them to her father's house in Gillespie county.

Old Mother Taylor, who had concealed herself in the brush near by when the Indians made the attack, in attempting to return to the house after the Indians had left, got lost, wandered all the afternoon, all night, and the greater part of the next day. When found, she was wild, and in fact almost crazy. She now—1888—lives with her son-in-law, Monroe McDonald, on Little Devil's River, in Kimble county, at the advanced age of eighty-three years, but hale and hearty. She was known as the "Woman Preacher" of that section of country at an early day.

Let us now take up the thread of our narrative with Mrs. McDonald after her return from captivity. She remained a widow four years, and then married Peter Hazlewood, who originally came from Illinois, as did her first husband, Ely McDonald. Hazlewood lived for a while in Travis county, and then moved to Gillespie, destined to meet a similar fate to that of his wife's first husband.

In October, 1873, a party of Indians, fifteen or sixteen in number, passed down the west fork of Spring Creek and across and up the east fork, stealing all the horses they could find on their route—some twenty or thirty. As soon as it was known that Indians were in the settlement, all who could get horses gave immediate pursuit. The party consisted of L. M. McDonald, Peter Hazlewood, E. R. Jones, J. J. Taylor, T. T. Taylor, and Hudson Taylor. They soon found the trail, followed it as rapidly as possible, and overtook the Indians on the divide between Spring Creek and Threadgill Creek, about five miles from the place of starting. E. R. Jones, who was on a very fleet animal, rode ahead, and when within speaking distance of the Indians, he asked them, in Spanish, why they were driving off the settlers' horses. The Indians denied stealing the horses, and said they belonged to them. This reply was not satisfactory to the Texans, and the fight commenced. But the odds against them were too great, and after the fight had continued for about half an hour, the Texans were compelled to retreat,

.eaving one of their number, Peter Hazlewood, dead on the ground, killed by a bullet through his head. The cry was *sauve qui peut*, and the devil take the hindmost. The horses ridden by L. M. McDonald and H. Taylor finally gave out altogether, and the Indians rushed upon them. Taylor dismounted and took refuge in a dense thicket of shin oak bushes. Three Indians pursued McDonald, yelling and shooting at him as he ran. He ran into a thicket at the head of a ravine, jumped his horse down a six foot bluff, where he also abandoned him, and concealed himself in the brush near by, intending, as he said, "to sell his life at the very highest market price." Several of the Indians charged up to the edge of the thicket, yelling and shooting into it at random, but they did not venture in, whilst the others, McDonald thinks, from what he could hear, were holding a "pow wow" over the dead body of Peter Hazlewood.

In a little while the Indians who had followed him up to the thicket went back, and then all sounds ceased. McDonald pulled off his shoes and slipped out of his hiding place in his bare feet, taking his course homewards by a circuitous route of seven or eight miles, and when he got there his naked feet were wofully torn and bruised. It is more than probable the Indians would have succeeded eventually in killing H. Taylor and L. M. McDonald, but fortuately for them another party of Texans, some seven or eight in number, who had taken the Indian trail a half an hour or so behind them, made their appearance, and as soon as the Indians discovered their approach they hastily retreated. "I was with this party myself," says P. G. Temple, to whom we are indebted for the foregoing facts. "We passed near the dead body of Hazlewood, but did not see him, as the grass was very high; nor did we know that the party ahead of us had had a fight. Near there we collected eighteen head of horses abandoned by the Indians when they saw us coming up, lariats, moccasins and other traps they had thrown away. The Indians got H. Taylor's horse, saddle and hat, but failed to get McDonald's horse. When we returned for the dead body of Hazlewood, his horse was still standing under the bluff in the thicket where he had left him." Thus it will be seen Mrs. McDonald, now Mrs. Hazlewood, was left a widow the second time—the murderous

savages depriving her of her companion in each instance.
Two husbands murdered by the Indians, once herself a captive (together with her children) in their cruel hands, this
woman of iron nerve still clung to the frontier, and is now
living with her third husband, Mr. Pope, on the Guadalupe
river, in Kerr county. Her two sons by her second husband,
Hazlewood, are now about grown and living with her. Her
children by her first husband, who were captured with her,
are all married and reside in Gillespie and adjoining counties.

In the latter part of January or the first of February, of
the year 1865, Elizabeth and her daughter Alwilda McDonald were killed by the Indians about two miles below the
head of Perdinales river. They were on horseback, but
were overtaken and both killed, scalped and stripped of
their clothing. They were of the same family as Wiley
Joy, the old bear hunter from Arkansas.

Indian Outrages in Uvalde County.

FOR the following account of Indian outrages in Uvalde
county we are indebted chiefly to Mr. Ross Kennedy, a
well known citizen of that county: The first murder
committed by the Indians in Uvalde county of which
we have any account was Louis Thompson, who was killed
some time in September, 1859, while gathering pecans on
the Frio river. He was charged upon by a party of
1859 seven Indians, who evidently ran in between him and
his wagon, in which he had left his gun, and of course
he was killed without being able to make any resistance.
The same party of Indians, it is supposed, in October, killed
a Mr. White on Hondo creek, near where the main wagon
road crosses it. On the twenty-eighth of October, 1859, the
same band killed John M. Davenport on the main wagon
road, two miles east of the Sabinal river. Davenport was a
native of Tennessee and emigrated from Arkansas to

Uvalde in 1849. At one time he was captain of a minute company. He left a wife and five children. The day after he was killed about fifteen citizens collected together and took the Indian trail. Lieutenant Hazen, of the United States army, with fourteen men, also pursued the Indians, and on the second day out he overtook them on the west prong of the Nueces river. He charged upon them at once and the Indians retreated before him, occasionally making a stand at favorable localities. In this way a running fight was kept up for about nine miles, when the Indians went over a bluff almost perpendicular, thirty or forty feet in height, and the Texans abandoned the chase. Three Indians were left dead on the ground and Davenport's scalp, pistol, hat and clothing were recovered. Three of the citizens were wounded in this fight and Lieutenant Hazen also. The citizens gave great praise to Lieutenant Hazen and his men for their gallant conduct in this affair. These Indians were Lipans and Kickapoos from Mexico. John Bowls was a man about fifty years of age and came, we believe, to Uvalde from Greenville, Tennessee, some time in 1856. From his frequent use of the phrase, when excited, he was known as "Hog My Cats" Bowls. He lived on the Leona river. He was killed by Indians on the Sabinal while out in search of one of his horses. The horse was belled and it is supposed the Indians decoyed him into a thicket by rattling a bell, where he was killed without resistance, as he had no arms. When he failed to return, a party of citizens went out to search for him. They searched the country thoroughly for about a week but did not succeed in finding any trace of him. Finally, however, his remains were found by his son Greenville, partially devoured by wolves. About twelve months previous to his death Mr. Bowls had corraled a number of fine horses near his house. A party of Indians discovered the *caballada* and concluded to take possession of it. So one night when the moon was about full they cautiously crawled up to the corral and succeeded in driving the horses out; but just at this juncture the baying of their dogs alarmed the family, and Bowls and his sons ran out with their guns, drove the Indians off and rounded the horses back into the corral. But Bowls was not satisfied with merely regaining possession of his property. There was a ford on the river about half a mile from his house, where he supposed the Indians would cross, and he made for it with all the speed he could, so as to get there before the Indians arrived. As soon as he reached the crossing he concealed himself in some hackberry bushes a short distance above and patiently waited for Mr. Lo to put in an appearance. He was armed with a large double barrel gun, both barrels charged with about forty "blue whistlers" each, and powder in proportion. In a little while the Indians came up and halted within fair gun shot range on the bluff above him. The moon was shining brightly, and Bowls leveled the old blunderbuss upon them, took deliberate aim, pulled the trigger of the right hand barrel—and snapped. He instantly pulled the trigger of the left hand barrel, and it went off with the report of a small piece of ordnance, and at the same moment two Indians and one horse came tumbling over the bluff, and were as dead as hammers when they reached the bottom. A third Indian was also badly wounded by the old blunderbuss, and was subsequently trailed for several miles by his blood. Bowls's sons, hearing the report of his gun, hurried to his assistance, and when they came up they found the old man standing on the dead body of an Indian and exclaiming: "Hog my cats! you won't steal any more horses from me." The old man's sons, William and Greenville, are now living in the town of Uvalde. On or about the middle of March, 1860, an old gentleman by the name of Schroon, who lived at D'hanis, in Medina county, was killed by Indians. He was a native of Louisiana, was one of Castro's colonists, and immigrated to the colony about 1846. He was attacked by a party of twelve Indians whilst engaged in hauling fire wood, and as he had no arms with him, was quickly despatched. He left a wife and three children. "The same party of Indians the next morning" says Mr. Kennedy, "killed a Mexican boy about eighteen years old employed at my ranch, while he was out hunting stock. He was shot through the heart, and was dead before I came to his assistance, five minutes afterwards, but the Indians did not have time to scalp him.

"We always kept shod horses, dried beef and hard baked crackers for such emergencies, and in a very short time we started off, leaving my wife alone in the house with the dead body of the Mexican boy, who told us not to turn back until we had settled accounts with the Indians. About two hours after we started we were joined by General W. B. Knox with two men, who was under the impression that some mules stolen from his wagon train were in the possession of this party of Indians. Towards evening we lost the trail on the west branch of the Sabinal, six miles above the main wagon road. Near this place we found the dead bodies of two white men, —— Huffman and —— Wolf. Wolf's throat was cut from ear to ear, and the bodies were lying about twenty feet apart. We found there, also, the dead body of an Indian, killed as we supposed by Wolf. The Indians had placed it in the forks of a live oak tree, with his blanket rolled around him, and his shield, bow and arrows and other equipments were placed near it. We supposed, from the character of the "sign" on the ground, that Wolf and Huffman had made an attack on the Indians. I knew Huffman personally. He was a very daring and fearless man, and on several occasions, when riding express for the United States government, had been known to attack parties of Indians when alone. From this point, after some search, we found the trail again, going up the bed of Blanco creek to about twenty miles above the main crossing. The trailer, W. A. Crane, who was riding in front, suddenly halted, and looking back pointed to the Indian saddle horses grazing in a small glade about fifty yards distant on the right of the creek. I immediately motioned to the men to dismount, dismounted myself, had the horses tied securely and detailed two men to guard them, intending with the rest, under cover of a small ravine, to get in between the Indians and the cedar brakes, and thus cut off their retreat. General Knox was opposed to this movement—thought it best to make a direct charge upon the Indians; and contrary to my own judgment, this was done. The Indian horses were consequently stampeded by our approach, which gave the Indians timely notice of our presence, and they secreted themselves in the dense cedar brakes near their camp before we could get a shot at them. Everything they had, however, was captured—horses, shields, guns, bows and arrows, and all their camp equipage. The Indians had just barbecued a fat yearling, which was very acceptable to us. Before daylight we were back at Sabinal with the stolen *caballada.* Next day we went up and buried the bodies of Wolf and Huffman in the same grave." Henry Shane, a young man about eighteen years of age, was employed by Major Riordan to attend to his stock on Pinto creek, ten miles west of Fort Clark. Whilst out on the range, a party of sixteen Indians charged upon him, took him prisoner, whipped him severely with a rawhide strap and then tied him on the back of a mule. They then went off in a northwesterly direction and traveled until two or three o'clock the next morning, when they halted and encamped. They took young Shane from the mule, and after they had amused themselves by whipping him again severely with rawhide straps, they put him to bed with an old Indian who smelt worse, young Shane said, than a turkey buzzard's nest. The next morning they tied him on the mule and started off again. About nine o'clock they stopped for the purpose of getting some breakfast and untied young Shane. Just then it so happened that a party of United States soldiers from Fort Clark, guided by a Mexican by the name of Rookey, discovered the Indians and immediately charged upon them. Young Shane, taking advantage of the melee that ensued, fled for life and liberty, but not before one of his captors sent an arrow through his arm. Said he heard a good deal of shooting after he left, but does not know who whipped, the Indians or the United States soldiers. He said, however, that he had been badly "whipped" himself. He wandered about for four days in the woods without anything to eat except a small piece of dried meat, but eventually made his way back to Major Riordan's ranch, considerably worsted by his outing with the Indians. Major Riordan was very glad to see him again, bought him a new six shooter, with which he subsequently squared accounts with the Indians on several occasions for the whippings they had given him. Shane still lives in Uvalde county.

Henry M. Robinson and Henry Adams were killed by Indians at the Chalk bluff, on the Nueces river, about March 7, 1861, while on their way to Camp Wood. A. M. Robinson had been on the frontier for many years. He was a stockman and farmer and sometimes was employed at Fort

Inge to trail and fight Indians. He was married and left a wife and nine children, all now living in Uvalde county except one girl and a boy, hereafter mentioned. There were sixteen Indians in the party that murdered these men From the sign it was evident the two men had stopped to make coffee, and that the Indians crept upon them' under cover of some drift wood and killed them before they could use their guns. After killing Robinson and Adams the Indians went to Robinson's house, about seven miles from the Chalk bluff, and attacked it. Mrs. Robinson was on a visit to one of her neighbors at the time, and hearing some noise went to the door and saw the Indians chasing the children. A boy named George, about sixteen years old, who had a gun, fired upon the Indians and was immediately shot down himself. The balance of the children ran towards their mother. who soon afterwards joined them, and in her desperation she endeavored to drive the Indians back by throwing rocks at them, but such weapons were of little avail against guns and bows and arrows. They shot a girl about fourteen years old named Kilrey, who was visiting the Robinson family, but, strange to say, they made no attempt to shoot Mrs. Robinson and the other children and they all escaped. Courage is more highly esteemed among savages than anything else, and perhaps the Indians refrained from killing Mrs. Robinson and the rest in consideration of her heroic attempt to defend the children by throwing rocks. Although Miss Kilrey was shot with arrows, lanced, scalped and left for dead, she eventually recovered from her wounds and went to California. The Indians plundered Mrs Robinson's house, took everything they fancied, cut open the beds and scattered the feathers to the four winds of heaven, and appropriated all the provisions they could carry off. One of their acts was quite unaccountable. When they killed Robinson they took one of his socks. In his house they found his portrait hanging on the wall. This they took down, placed it on the floor and laid the sock they had stripped from the dead body across it. Henry Adams was unmarried and lived on Potranco creek, sixteen miles west of San Antonio. Says Kennedy: "I knew him to be a brave and determined man and I am satisfied he would have made a gallant fight if he had had any chance to use his arms." A. H. Robinson was a son of Henry M. Robinson, was about fourteen years of age and lived on Frio river with his mother and family, twenty-two miles north of the town of Uvalde. September 8, 1865, while out with his brother collecting fire wood a short distance from the house they were fired upon by a party of twelve Indians and A. H. Robinson was killed. His brother, however, was untouched, and running into some thick brush succeeded in making his escape. There was no man in the house at the time but the women hastily put on men's apparel, and taking guns in their hands, showed themselves to the Indians, and this warlike demonstration no doubt prevented them from making an attack upon it.

In October, 1866, a party of Indians came to the house of Robert Kinchelo, opened the gate and rushed into the yard. There were no men at the place at the time, but as soon as Mrs. Kinchelo discovered their approach she seized a Speucer rifle with the intention of defending herself and the other inmates of the house as best she could. Unfortunately, however, she did not know how to use it, and as the Indians ran to the door she leveled the gun on them, but it failed to go off, whereupon one of the Indians said to her in Spanish: "No bueno"—meaning that the gun was worthless. The two frightened women then hastily closed the door, placed a heavy table against it and seated themselves on top, hoping thereby to prevent the Indians from entering. Mrs. Kinchelo's son, a lad about ten years old, begged his mother to give him the gun, saying that he knew how to use it, but for some reason Mrs. Kinchelo refused to let him have it. The house was made of pickets, and in some places they were so far apart that the Indians could easily shoot between twem. Through these openings they shot Mrs. Kinchelo eleven times with arrows, when she grew so weak from the loss of blood that she fell to the floor. She then gave the gun to Mrs. Bolin, telling her that she was killed, and that she must defend herself and the children. Mrs. Bolin took the gun, but at the very moment she did so an Indian let drive an arrow through an opening between the pickets which penetrated her breast, and she fell dead. As there was no one left to guard the door, the Indians soon forced their way into the house. Before they did so, however, Mrs. Kinchelo crawled to the bed and

INDIAN SMOKE SIGNALS IN THE DISTANCE.

secreted herself under it, hoping the Indians might leave without observing her. But in this she was mistaken, for as soon as they entered the house they began to search for plunder, and whilst doing so one of them turned up the bed and, discovering her, thrust his lance repeatedly into her body. The poor woman fainted from pain and loss of blood, and supposing she was killed, the Indians left her where she was lying and began to plunder the premises of everything they could possibly carry off. The little boy, previously mentioned, as the Indians came through the front door, ran through the back one and hid himself near by, where he remained undiscovered until the Indians had taken all they wanted. From his place of concealment he watched the Indians as they went off, and saw them going towards a mountain near by. He then ran to the nearest house, about three miles distant, and told the people there what had happened. A Mr. Wiler Oburant, who was at this house, went around the settlement, collected all the men he could find and trailed the Indians to where they had crossed the mountain and repacked their animals, but they were unable to trail them any further. Mrs. Bolin's daughter, a girl seventeen years of age, was out from the house when the Indians attacked it. When she saw them approaching she climbed into a thick cedar tree and concealed herself until they left. She noticed that they came from and went back in the direction of the locality where Mr. Kinchelo's herder, a Mexican, was with his sheep. This, together with the fact that the Indians, the moment they entered the house, burst open a chest in which the Mexican knew Mr. Kinchelo kept his money and other valuables, induced the people to believe he had given them information, not only where they would find the money, but also that the men of the house were absent. The Mexican, no doubt being conscious of his guilt, and fearing that he would be put to death, attempted to escape from his guard, and was killed. Mrs. Kinchelo's infant was lying in its cradle when the Indians entered the house, but for some reason they left it unhurt. Notwithstanding the many lance and arrow wounds she had received, Mrs. Kinchelo finally recovered, and is now living in Sabinal with her children.

All's Well That Ends Well.

IN the year 1846 Colonel William S. Wallace, Pucket, Bud
Flint, Casner, James H. Henderson and one whose
name is not remembered, left Travis, county on a surveying expedition in the upper part of Comal county,
now in the county of Kendall. When in the midst of their
work, near the head of Simmons creek, some seventy-five
or eighty Comanche Indians were seen by two of
1846 the party, who hastened to find the others, and if possible, to secure a safe position from the inevitable
attack of the Indians. They succeeded in finding a deep
ravine, around the head of which the ground was smooth
and level. In this they took position, all except old Mr.
Pucket, who was out hunting that morning, and was cut
off from camp by the Indians. The ravine was deep enough
to hide the party securely from the sight of the Indians
till they would approach within a few rods of them. The
only point from which they could be seen any distance
was straight down the bed, and as there was in the bed of
the ravine a large amount of loose rocks, they soon succeeded in making a strong wall across that gave protection from that direction After rifling the camp and getting everything excepting the arms on the persons of the
surveyors, their guns and the two horses of those who
discovered the Indians, and securing the provisions and
what they could find in camp, the charge upon the ravine
was projected by the red skins. They formed some thirty
odd on horseback and about the same number of foot-
men, with a few guns, but mostly with spears, lances and
bows and arrows, and came in a body like a rushing tor-
nado which threatened to overwhelm the little party at a
single blow. But as they could not see the party, on arriving in about one hundred yards of the spot of concealment,
fearing a shot from the party or desiring to draw their
fire, made a circle, went back to a safe distance and formed

and came rushing, as before, to about the same point reached in the first charge. Failing to draw the fire of the party, they retired, as before, and at a safe distance stopped. They made a third and final charge, when Colonel Wallace, the commander of the squad, ordered the party to reserve their fire as before, but he would shoot. This he did, but saw no effect, unless it caused the enemy to circle as before, and retreated some two hundred yards, where they stopped and held a long parly and moved off in a body. After remaining for some time in their place of concealment, the party hastened across speedily to the head of Simmon's creek, thence down it to its mouth, in Curry's creek. Thence down it to the Guadalupe—being well protected by brush wood. Thence down the river to a convenient point, thence for New Braunfels, which they reached that night. They supposed all the time that poor old Pucket was killed by the Indians, so they sent a courier to Jack Hays, at San Antonio, for a party of rangers to search for and bury Pucket. Accordingly Major Chevalia and fifteen rangers were sent out for the purpose, but failed to find the lamented Pucket. The fact was, he was not chased by the Indians, but being on a fleet nag, he dodged the enemy in the cedar brake, and made his way safely to Austin. From the large number of Indians he had no hope for the safety of the little party, and supposed they were all killed. The United States dragoons had just been stationed at Austin, so the commander sent fifty dragoons with Pucket to bury the fated band of surveyors. After arranging for the burial of Pucket, the little band left New Braunfels for Austin. Now, let the reader imagine, if he can, the joyous feelings of the two doomed parties, when they met each other on the Rio Blanco, safe and sound, as when the expedition first started from Austin.

Jesse Lawhorn.

IN 1854 or 1855 Jesse Lawhorn, then in charge of Judge William E. Jones's place, who lived on Curry's creek, in the upper part of Comal, now Kendall county, took one of Jones's negro men and went in search of some oxen. When two or three miles from home seven Indians emerged from a thicket near by, mounted on fine horses stolen the night before from the adjoining neighborhood, Sisterdale, and gave chase to the two. The negro having but one idea, that was to move out as fast as he could in the direction of home, but Lawhorn seeing the Indians were mounted on horses fleeter than his, ran into a thicket, all the Indians after him but one. Here we leave him for the present and follow his brother in black. His bee line for home was hotly pursued by the remaining Indian. This line led him to a washout basin in Curry's creek, filled with mud and water, and being some fifty feet broad the horse could but jump into the midst of it. The horse mired and fell and the darkey abandoned him and crawled out on the opposite bank. At this time the Indian reached the other bank, and having a gun, fired at the negro but failed to hit him. The negro ran down the bed of the creek and reached home in safety, the Indian stopping to secure the horse. Poor Lawhorn was pressed into the thicket by one Indian, and being unarmed, as was also the negro, he was forced to save himself by flight if saved at all, and being on a spirited horse and having on keen spurs he literally plowed his way through vines and briars, hotly pursued by the Indian. When he would emerge from the thicket, the other Indians seeing his course, would meet and spear him as he came out Another chase would ensue, and as they were on faster horses, he would rush into another thicket, pursued as before and with the same result on coming out. This was repeated through a course of three miles, till he was surrounded by a bluff, almost perpendicular, but leading into a

1854

large thicket at its base, the height of the cliff not being less than forty feet. To plunge down this or be slain on the spot were the alternatives presented. He chose the first, and so fearful was the leap the Indians failed to follow him. From the sign the horse struck first on somewhat of a shelving rock, and reached the bottom the second leap without falling. The distance through the thicket the narrow way was about one hundred yards and thence to Anderson's house some six hundred. He could have thus secured his retreat, as the pursuers had to run some three hundred yards further around the bluff had not the Indian that pursued the negro, and who had the only gun among them, stationed himself where Lawhorn came out of the thicket and shot him dead. He had a wife and three or four children to mourn his sad fate. The stricken community assembled and with stricken hearts placed him in his last resting place.

George Durham on Guard.

IN 1842 the Comanche Indians gave to the colonists who had settled near Austin much trouble by their incursions. The most dangerous time was during that period in the month when the moon gave light at night The Indians would then venture down on foot from the upper Colorado, expecting to mount themselves on stolen horses with which to return. Woe then to the unfortunate settler who 1842 was caught by them alone. The habit of the early settler was never to enter the timber, after crossing a broad prairie, at the point where one observing him from a distance would expect him to enter it from his course, but after approaching nearly within gun shot, he would then gallop at his utmost speed for some distance parallel to the timber and then suddenly enter it. In this manner an ambuscade would often be avoided. For failing to observe this precaution, at an early day, ———, in 1842, lost his life about two miles from where Austin now stands. On a beautiful

morning in the spring of 1842 this young man crossed the
Colorado river mounted on a fine horse, rifle in hand to kill
deer.   He crossed at the ford just below where the Austin
city water works are now located.   He was cautioned to
be on his guard, for it was about the period of the full moon,
and it was known that Indian sign had been seen only a few
days before near town.   After hunting, as it was afterwards
discovered, out from the town and rather below, he crossed
the prairie near the heights some two miles south of Austin
and went straight to a grove of timber just west of the head
of Bouldin's branch.   There he was ambushed by foot Indians, who killed him with their arrows.   As he did not
return that night, George Durham and another friend crossed
the river the next morning to hunt for him.   After hunting
until late in the evening, they found his trail, and while
following it discovered the buzzards slowly wheeling in their
flight over the grove in which he was killed.   Knowing that
if he had been killed the Indians would not remain in the
vicinity, they entered the grove and soon found his body,
naked and horribly mutilated.   His hands had been cut off;
so had his nose and ears; his breast had been cut open, his
heart torn out and placed on his face.   No traces of a struggle were observed, and it was manifest that he had been
ambushed.

Durham and his companion placed two large logs about
five feet apart and then, with their tomahawks, cut some
poles and placed across them, on which they laid the mangled remains of their dead friend.   Durham agreed to remain
to keep the wolves away from the body while his friend returned to Austin for a gentle horse to convey the body to
town for burial.   Durham was a stalwart, bold Englishman
and took his position sitting down at the foot of a live oak
tree, some thirty or forty paces away from which he could
see the white body of the murdered man, on which the
moon light shone clear.   No sound disturbed the stillness except the hooting of the owls and barking of wolves.   He
was growing impatient for the return of his companion
when he heard a low, sepulchral grunt or groan, apparently
from the direction of the corpse.   In a little while it was repeated more distinctly.   Durham rose to his feet, and horror
stricken at the dreadful sound, cocked his gun.   The moon

shone full on the body of the dead man, on which he fixed his gaze, when, to his horror and amazement, he observed the arm of the corpse next to him move, and at the same time he was startled by a deep groan. A braver man never lived than Durham, but in relating the circumstances afterwards he stated that he felt his hair lifting his hat from his head and was impelled to walk with his gun presented directly up to where the dead man lay. When near the body a hog jumped from under the pole platform on which the corpse rested. It had approached unobserved to Durham from the brush, and the motion of the arm was caused by the hog seizing and attempting to eat it. When his companion returned with a gentle horse two long poles, were cut, the ends of which were fastened on each side of the horse's neck and the body tied up in a blanket was placed on a rude litter of sticks tied across the poles behind the horse. George Durham was for many years chief clerk in the Comptroller's office and was finally elected State Comptroller. Few men at our day have any idea of the perils that continually surrounded the early settlers of Austin from 1839 to 1846. Incessant watchfulness was required; the Indians often prowled at night through the streets of the village in search of horses or scalps, and the only security for their horses was in a barn or strong stockade constructed adjoining the cabins. Nearly all of the earliest settlers are gone and many thrilling incidents relating to Indian massacres and incursions can not now be described with that careful detail desired. From this cause the name even of the dead hunter watched over by Durham can not be given.

Big Foot Wallace Returns to his Old "Stamping Grounds."

A S THE last pages of our book were being published, Captain Wallace came to Austin, just to see, as he said, how his "old stamping ground" was getting along during his absence. He said he was under the impression that he would find it pretty much the same as

when he had last seen it; but, although the admission tended to lower him considerably in his own estimation, he was
bound to confess that the old place had advanced almost as
rapidly as it could have done if he had been present all the
time and supervised its progress in person. Although his
locks are whitened by the frosts of time, the old ranger and
hunter still bears himself as erect as an Indian, and his firm
and measured tread gives assurance that he would still
count for something, either in a bear fight or an Indian
"scrimmage."

In looking around the city, one thing particularly attracted his notice—the great number of meat markets and fruit
and vegetable stands. He said in his time there was only
one beef market in the place, run by old man Horst, who
ruled the citizens with a rod of iron. Whenever any "little
misunderstanding" occurred between old man Horst and
his patrons, he would refuse to supply them with beef, and
as it was beef or no dinner, of course they would soon be
starved into terms. On the suburbs of the city, he pointed
out to us the locality where he had lived for some months
(near the residence of the late George W. Sampson) in a
half faced camp. He identified the locality by a large live
oak, on the limbs of which, he said, he used to hang up his
deer hams, wild turkeys, etc.; and, he said, whenever he
had a good supply on hand, he was almost as important a
member of the community as old man Horst himself. After
he had looked at the new capitol building, we asked him
what he thought of it. "Well," said he, "it's a decided
improvement on the old log cabins that stood on the opposite hill, surrounded by a cedar stockade to keep the Indians
from scalping the members whilst they were making laws
for the country—but," he added, *sotto voce*, "I don't believe
there is any more talent among the solons gathered here to-
day in these granite halls than there was among those who
assembled in the old log cabins in the time of the republic—
but," said he, "don't mention it to any one, because, you
see, it might give a backset to that little relief bill of mine
now pending in the House."

"Wallace," said we, "didn't you tell us that you lived for
several months in a cave near Mount Bonnel?" "Yes," said
he, "I did." "For what reason," said we, "did you abandon

your comfortable 'half-faced camp' within the *city* of Austin, to take up your abode in a cave with the bats and cayotes?" "Well," said he, "the cave was right on the old Indian trail leading down to Austin, and I thought I would be able to keep my hand in by 'upping' one now and then; and besides, the cave was in the best hunting ground for bear in all this country, and bear meat, I can tell you, was a cash article then in Austin, where very frequently not a pound of 'old ned' was to be had for love or money. But," said he, "the main reason why I holed myself up in that cave was just this—and I'll tell you if you will promise not to peach on me." So we promised with a mental reservation. "Well, you see," said Wallace, "not long after I came to Austin, I made the acquaintance of a very pretty young lady (and young ladies then, in Texas, were not as plentiful as pig tracks round a barn yard.) I hadn't called to see her more than half a dozen times, when I came to the conclusion it was absolutely impossible for me to live without her any longer (even on bear meat and honey) and determined the very first chance that offered that I would 'pop the question' and 'snake her in' to my 'half-faced camp.' But, Sirs, this is a mighty uncertain world! I have always noticed whenever there was no meat in camp, and I got a good chance to shoot a deer, my gun was sure to snap or hang fire. The very day I intended to call on the young lady I was attacked with typhoid fever, and when I 'came to' some days afterwards my hair all fell out and my head was left as slick and bald as an El Paso onion. Well, Sirs, as you may suppose, this did not improve my looks much (and *there was room* for improvement) and I thought it would not be advisable to visit the young lady whilst I was in that fix, and as soon as I was able to get about, I went to that cave and staid there eating bear meat and greasing my head with the oil, to make my hair grow faster, for, of course, I was in a great hurry to get back to Austin. Now and then, by way of variety, I would go off with some of the boys upon a scout after Indians, and once, when we were badly used up by a large party of Comanches on the Llano, I congratulated myself on being bald headed, as there was no danger of my being scalped. The Indians might just as well have tried to scalp a Spanish gourd. After all, though,

I believe it would have been better for me to have pressed
my suit bald headed, than to have gone into that cave and
waited for my hair to grow out, for, as I have said, young
ladies, like bear meat, were cash articles then in Texas, and
in great demand, and it wouldn't do for a fellow to wait until
his bald head was covered with hair, before he 'staked out
his claim.' On my return to Austin, the first news I heard
was that the young lady had married another fellow a
month previously, who didn't have to wait for his hair to
grow before he 'popped the question.' When I heard this I
felt worse than I did when I had to ride twenty miles one
day with an Indian arrow sticking in the back of my neck,
before I could find anybody to cut it out. I really thought
I should be a 'cripple for life,' but I went right off and
joined the 'Mier expedition,' and after I had killed a Mexican or so at the battle of Mier—drawn a prize in the 'bean
lottery' that entitled me to march to the right, whilst those
who drew blacks were marched to the left and shot, I was
as well as ever."

Wallace gave us a description of several of his Indian
"scrimmages," but our book was so near completion that
we could insert only the following account of his fight with
Comanches in the Black hills, near the Nueces river: "In
1850 I was in command of some twenty rangers and was
attached temporarily to Colonel Hardee's force, at that time
operating on the Nueces river and between that stream and
the Rio Grande. Colonel Hardee had received orders from
General Brooks to make a thorough scout for Indians on
both sides of the Nueces. He therefore proceeded down the
east side of the river with his main force, whilst I and my
rangers were ordered to scout the country down the west
side. We left camp and went to Carrizo springs, where we
found some Indian sign, but none recently made. There
was an Indian trail, evidently several weeks old, leading
down the country from the springs, and we followed it for
about thirty miles to where it crossed the river to the east
side. My orders were to keep on the west side, and in consequence I did not cross but continued my route down the
river until I came to the coast near Corpus Christi without
seeing any more sign of Indians. There I received an express from Colonel Kinney, stating that Indians had been

seen very recently in the vicinity. I requested him to send
me a guide who could show me Indian sign; and I stated if
he failed to do so and carried us off on a wild goose chase
that I would hang him to a live oak limb and let the buzzards play seven-up for his carcass. The guide was sent,
and he conducted us to an Indian camp, where we found
they had killed a Mexican, had taken his *caballada* of mustang horses and gone up the river with them. We followed
their trail, but soon came to so many mustang trails leading
off in every direction that we could not follow the one
on which we had started. Where we lost the trail was
on the Agua Dulce creek, and we went from there to Fort
Merrill, at which place we were joined by Colonel Hardee
and his men. Soon afterwards Colonel Hardee ordered me
to go up the Nueces and to follow any fresh Indian trail I
might find. When I had gone about twenty miles above the
old Laredo road I found a fresh Indian trail, and followed it
across the river. There were but few Indians in the party,
and after crossing we came to where they had pitched camp
on the east side. We encamped at the same place, and
I went out to look for a deer, as we had no fresh meat. In
passing over a sandy locality on my way, I noticed a number of fresh mocasin tracks, and found a bunch of mesquite
beans hanging on a limb, which I knew had been placed
there as a signal to other Indians, and I therefore concluded
it would be prudent to return to camp. After dinner, we
saddled up, went to the mesquite tree where the bunch of
beans was placed, and near by we found the fresh trail of
three horses. We followed this trail until it crossed the
"Black Hills," which are seven or eight miles from the
river, where we struck a valley running east and west. We
went down this valley and came to an old Indian camp near
what had been a water hole, but it had dried up. There
we camped all night without water. At this camp we found
a United States infantry soldier's coat, a Mexican soldier's
coat and a bridle. We left this camp very early the next
morning, and after traveling three or four miles we came to
where there was a great deal of fresh "sign"—trails leading off in every direction. Following one of these, we
came to a place where the Indians had killed several mustangs. One of them was scalped but not otherwise muti-

lated. "What does that mean?" inquired one of my men. "It is intended," said I, "to let us know if we follow this trail any further that our scalps will be taken." However, this threat did not scare us "worth a cent," and we continued to follow the trail for about four miles beyond the locality where we had found the scalped horse. At that point, on the top of a ridge several hundred yards distant, we discovered an Indian sitting on his horse and holding a lance in his hand. He made signs to us and called out in Spanish: "If you want to fight, come over this way." He was riding a fine sorrel horse, and after he had shaken his lance at us several times he went off at a gallop. Some of the boys gave a yell and started in pursuit of him, and I had great difficulty in stopping them, but I finally succeeded and told them to go back to the pack mules and get all the ammunition we had as I was satisfied we would need it very shortly. In a few moments the Indian showed himself again on top of the ridge, and I ordered the men to stay where they were until I could go to a knoll near by and make a reconnoisance, for I was sure the lone Indian we saw had been stationed there to draw us into an ambuscade. When I reached the knoll I could see eleven other Indians below the point where the first one had made his appearance, and still further down their entire force of more than a hundred warriors. Just at this moment Sergeant Murphy came up, and asked me what I saw. "Indians," said I. "Where?" he asked. "Over yonder," I replied, pointing in the direction. "My God!" he exclaimed, as he turned to go back, "there's a thousand of them!" At that instant an Indian, whom I took to be the chief, sounded a whistle, and the eleven Indians we had first seen advanced and rode around us, but some distance away. I ordered my men not to fire upon them, as I understood very well the object of this maneuvre. After they had rode around us, finding we would not fire upon them, they galloped off toward the main body of the Indians lower down the valley. We followed them slowly, as I had no intention of being lured into a trap. The chief whistled again, and immediately twenty-five Indians left the main body and took their position in the rear, so as to act as a reserve force. There were about one hundred Indians in the main body, and the moment the chief sounded his whistle again, they charged upon us in double file, but when they reached a certain point within about one hundred yards, the files turned to right and left, circled around us, firing as they ran—but those who carried rifles dismounted, and taking their positions behind trees, began to pour hot shot upon us in a way that was anything but pleasant. We were not idle ourselves, and returned their fire so effectually that we killed several warriors, wounded a number, and killed and wounded many horses. Such a warm reception compelled them to draw off for a time, but they returned to their camp, mounted fresh horses, and charged upon us again more vigorously than before. My men, however, were all experienced frontiersmen and good shots, and we dropped them from their saddles so rapidly, and wounded so many others, that they hastily fell back again toward their camp. There they re-formed, and being joined by the reserve, which as yet had taken no part in the fight, they charged us for the third time in the most determined manner. But it was the same old thing—we pitched the rifle bullets into them so rapidly they couldn't stand the racket, and once more retreated toward their camp.

"In this charge upon us the great "medicine man" made himself very conspicuous—not by fighting, for he had no arms at all—but by circling round us in advance of the rest and waving a bunch of roots he held in his hands backwards and forwards. I saw he was doing us more harm by encouraging the others than if he had been armed, and I told several of the boys who were near me to stop his "conjuring." A number of guns were fired at him without effect, and it really seemed that his roots in some way protected him from our bullets. Finally, however, one took him squarely in the breast, and he pitched headforemost from his horse, roots and all—but he had hardly struck the ground when half a dozen Indians rushed forward and bore him off out of sight; consequently we did not know at the time whether he was killed or only wounded. Before the Indians made the fourth and final charge upon us the chief rode up and down the line, urging his men, as we plainly perceived, to come to close quarters and use the bow and arrow. "Now, said I to the boys, "prepare yourselves; for we are going to catch it hot and heavy." The next moment they charged upon us in a body, not dividing their force, as they had previously done. The chief was ahead, and I and several of the boys nearest to me leveled our guns upon him. "Shoot at his legs," said I, "and kill his horse, and I will kill him." He came straight for us, and when within about thirty yards three men fired at him. His horse turned a somersault, and the chief, who was some distance in advance of his men, jumped up and started back to them, when I fired and shot him in the right hip. He fell, yelling like a catamount, but rose up again on his left leg, when several Indians rushed up and bore him off the field, going back to their encampment near a water hole. We had been so long without water ourselves that we were suffering terribly for want of it. We therefore mounted our horses and made for their old camp, where we expected to find it. When we got within about one hundred and fifty yards of the camp I took ten men afoot, leaving the rest to bring on the horses and two of our men who had been wounded. I knew very well there were some Indians in the camp, but I determined to drive them from it at all hazards and get possession of the water hole. As I charged up I ordered my men not to run in a straight line, but zigzag fashion, to prevent the Indians hitting us. They did so, and although the Indians gave us a volley as we approached, no one was hurt. We returned their fire and Billy Johnson killed one dead, I shot another and Jim Brown a third. We would have killed them all, but a party from the main body of the Indians at that moment came to their rescue, and we were compelled to fall back towards the men we had left with our wounded and the horses. This ended the fight, which had lasted for several hours. When the rest of my men came up I went back to the water hole, but in the meantime the Indians had retreated out of sight and we saw nothing more of them. The Indian killed by Johnson had two plugs of tobacco in his shot pouch, which was a God send to us, as we had all been without a "chaw" for several days. We found plenty of water at the camp, but it was horrible stuff, for the Indians had been there for some time, and it was literally covered with filth of all kinds. We were so nearly famished, however, for water that we were not very squeamish as to quality, and bad as it was it quenched our terrible thirst. In this fight we killed twenty-two Indians, left dead on the ground, and wounded fifteen and killed many horses. Three of the men only were wounded. Rose, Louis Oget and Ruf. Hynyard. As some of our horses were badly wounded also we were unable to follow the Indians farther. Among those who were with me in this fight, and whose names have not been mentioned, were Jack Tannyhill, Edward Westfall, Sergeant Jim Brown, William Rice, Bib Miller, a German by the name of Frei and Thomas Rife, who is now, and has been for some time, custodian of the Alamo building in San Antonio. The names of the balance I can not now remember. In looking around the battle ground next morning we found a saddle hanging on a limb of a tree and beneath it a pile of brush. I knew that some "good Injun" was stowed away there and I told the boys to uncover him and see what he looked like. They did so and there lay the body of the great medicine man with his bunch of roots still in his hand, and one partially chewed, sticking in his mouth. I supposed, unlike the majority of medical men, he had great faith in his own remedies, and had tried to cure himself when wounded by chewing one of his roots, but it was no use, and in fact I don't believe the root has ever yet been found that will save a fellow when he has had a half ounce ball through his lights."

Such is the account just given by this veteran Indian fighter and scout regarding one of his Indian fights, and which was not referred to in the book published some years since, called "The Life and Adventures of Big Foot Wallace." The Legislature is now in session and a bill is pending to grant him a land certificate in lieu of one which was formerly granted for services to the State, but the benefit of which was lost to him on account of the want of familiarity with the requirements of law. He is one of the very few whose breasts were living bulwarks for the women and children against the scalping knife and tomahawk for more than twenty-five years. The lives of such men were spent in the camp, on the Indian trail and in savage warfare. He is now seventy-three years old—too old to work—but he looks around on a great State and on plenty and peace everywhere, secured by the struggles and privations of himself and his fellow rangers. Such men had no time to make money, and in the midst of plenty they alone are passing to the tomb with the fear of an old age of penury before them.

The State could well afford to pension them for their great services in the past and thus give that incentive to patriotic sacrifices which would result from a knowledge that the State would take care of the defenders when they shall become too old to take care of themselves. The speculator and money shark always followed close upon the heels of the pioneer and Indian fighter. One grew rich because the daring and watchfulness of the other enabled him to prosper. Our purpose has been to preserve to posterity some record of the dangers and bloodshed through which peace and security was obtained in Texas, but when we see how little regard is paid to the few surviving heroes of the frontier by the State, we fear that we are fast losing that sense of gratitude which a brave people should always feel for the defenders of a State, and without which there can not be virtue enough to preserve long the blessings which men like Captain Wallace purchased with their blood,

THE END.